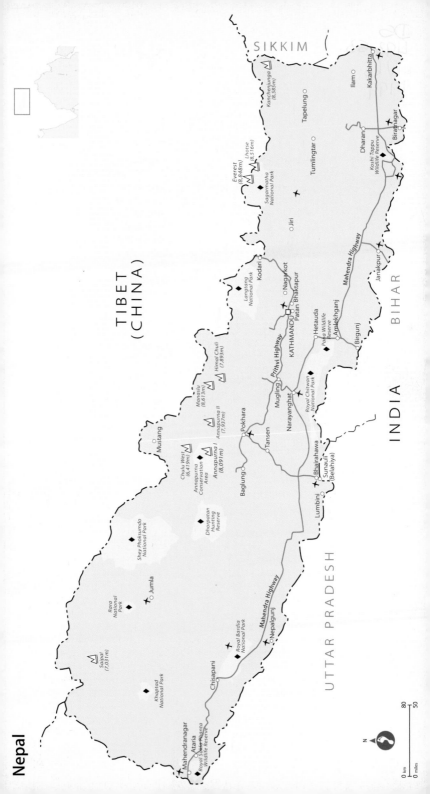

Nepal Handbook

Published by Footprint Handbooks
6 Riverside Court
Lower Bristol Road
Bath BA2 3DZ. England
T +44 (0)1225 469141
F +44 (0)1225 469461
Email discover@footprintbooks.com
Web www.footprintbooks.com

ISBN 1 900949 44 X
ISSN 1368-4299
CIP DATA: A catalogue record for this book
is available from the British Library

In USA, published by
Passport Books, a division of
NTC/Contemporary Publishing Group
4255 West Touhy Avenue, Lincolnwood
(Chicago), Illinois 60712-1975, USA
T 847 679 5500 F 847 679 2494
Email NTCPUB2@AOL.COM

ISBN 0-658-00016-0
Library of Congress Catalog Card Number
on file

© Footprint Books Ltd 1999
Second edition

Credits

Series editor
Patrick Dawson

Editorial
Senior editor: Sarah Thorowgood
Editor: Jo Williams
Maps: Sarah Sorensen

Production
Pre-press Manager: Jo Morgan
Typesetting: Emma Bryers
Maps: Richard Ponsford, Robert Lunn,
Claire Benison, Alasdair Dawson, Kevin
Feeney and Map Creator Ltd
Proof reading: John Work and Howard
David

Design
Mytton Williams

Photography & drawings
Front and back cover: Tony Stone Images
Inside colour section: James Davis Travel
Photography; Eye Ubiquitous; Pictures
Colour Library; Tony Stone Images;
Impact Photos; Art Directors and TRIP
Photo Library; Dave Saunders; Robert
Harding Picture Library
Illustrations by Della Denman and
Andrew Newton

Printed and bound
in Italy by LEGOPRINT

Nepal

Footprint Handbook

Tom Woodhatch

Each of us has to discover his own path – of that I am sure. Some paths will be spectacular and others peaceful and quiet – who is to say which is the most important?

Sir Edmund Hillary, in his autobiography, *Nothing Venture, Nothing Win*

Contents

1

7 A Foot in the Door
8 Highlights
13 Festivals
15 Spirit of adventure

2

17 Essentials

19 Planning your trip
19 Where to go
20 When to go
20 Special interest travel

21 Before you travel
21 Getting in
22 What to take

24 Money

27 Getting there
27 Air
29 Overland

31 Touching down
31 Tourist information
34 Rules customs & etiquette
36 Safety

38 Where to stay

40 Getting around
41 Air
42 Road
45 Other land transport
46 Travellers with special needs

47 Keeping in touch

50 Food & drink

53 Shopping

55 Holidays & festivals

58 Health
59 Before travelling
60 Further information
61 On the way
61 Staying Healthy
65 Other risks & more serious diseases
68 When you return home

68 Travelling with children

69 Further reading

72 Useful numbers

3

73 Trekking, mountaineering and rafting
77 Trekking seasons
78 Preparations
89 On the trek
90 Wildlife
91 Cultural & environmental sensivity
94 Safety & security
94 Health

96 Western Himalaya treks
96 Trek 1: Rara Lake
99 Trek 2: Jumla to Dunai

103 Annapurna Himal treks
103 Trek 3: Northern Circuit
108 Trek 4: Southern Circuit
114 Trek 5: Annapurna Base Camp
118 Trek 6: The Royal Trek
120 Trek 7: Tatopani & Baglung
123 Trek 8: Mustang

129 Langtang & Helambu treks
129 Trek 9: Gosainkund & Helambu
134 Trek 10: Syrabu to Tarke Ghayang

137 Everest Himal treks
140 Trek 11: Everest Base Camp
150 Trek 12: Gokyo Lakes
152 Trek 13: Lukla Escape

153 Eastern Himalaya treks
153 Trek 14: Makalu Base Camp
157 Trek 15: Kanchenjunga Base Camp

160 Mountaineering & mountain biking

161 Rafting

Left: colourful hats in traditional patterns and weaves, for sale in Bhaktapur.

6

4

169 **The Kathmandu Valley**
173 The land
176 People & culture

178 **Kathmandu**
181 Durbar Square Area
197 Pashupatinath
201 Swayambhunath
204 Bodhnath Stupa
211 Sleeping & eating
226 Entertainment
228 Festivals
230 Shopping
238 Local transport
239 Long distance
    connections
243 Directory
250 Short walks

260 **Patan**
261 Durbar Square
277 Sleeping & eating
278 Festivals
279 Shopping
281 Transport

282 **Bhaktapur**
283 Durbar Square
288 Taumadhi Square
290 Dattatraya Square
296 Sleeping & eating
297 Festivals
297 Shopping
298 Transport

5

299 **Beyond the three cities**
302 Budhanilikantha &
    Baghdwar
304 Sankhu, Vajra Jogini &
    Changu Narayan Mandir
307 Nagarkot
310 Kathmandu to Dhulikhel
311 Dhulikhel
316 Arniko Highway

319 Bishanku Narayan,
    Godavari & Phulchowki
320 Bungamati, Chapagaon
    & Lele
322 Chobhar, Pharping &
    Dakshinkali
326 Kirtipur
328 Ichangu Narayan Mandir,
    Nagarjun & Bani Bans
329 Kakani & the Trisuli Road

6

331 **Kathmandu to**
    Pokhara
335 Mugling
336 Gorkha
341 Pokhara

7

369 **The Terai**
374 The land
376 People
377 Economy

378 **West Terai**
378 Mahendranagar
381 Royal Sukla Phanta
    Wildlife Reserve
386 Royal Bardia National Park
394 Nepalgunj

398 **Central Terai**
398 Butwal
401 Bhairahawa & Sunauli
404 Lumbini
409 Tansen
414 Narayanghat
417 Royal Chitwan National
    Park
426 Sauraha
431 Tribhuvan Highway
432 Birgunj

436 **Eastern Terai**
436 Janakpur

442 Koshi Tappu Reserve
444 Biratnagar
447 Dharan
452 Ilam
450 Kakarbhitt

8

457 **Dolpa & Western Nepal**
460 Jumla
460 Khaptad National Park

9

463 **Road to Tibet**
466 Kathmandu to Lhasa
468 Lhasa

10

477 **Background**
479 History
488 Land
506 Religion
534 Culture
542 Modern Nepal

11

547 **Footnotes**
549 Useful words & phrases
553 Glossary
560 Shorts
561 Index
565 Maps
566 Coloured maps

Inside front cover
Hotel codes, map symbols,
telephone codes

Inside back cover
Basic vocabulary

Right: Kathmandu, musicians at funeral, Bodnath Stupa.

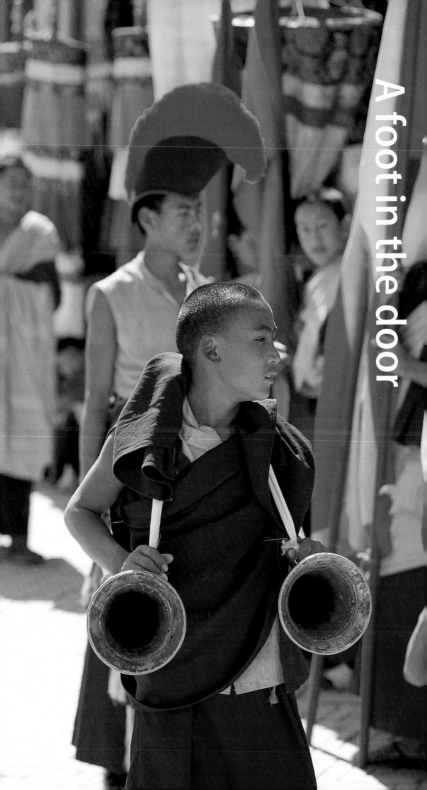

Highlights

Birthplace of the Buddha, home of the Gurkhas, roof of the world, land of legend and beauty: within its narrow confines Nepal contains an amazing range of cultural and physical environments and offers the visitor an abundance of contrasts and experiences. From the vast sweep of Himalayan peaks crowned by the highest point on Earth to the subtropical expanse of open countryside and wild jungle; from rivers racing powerfully through deep-cut gorges to weathered mountain deserts; and from city squares brimming with fairy tale temples to the timeless simplicity of remote villages untouched by the accoutrements of modern living, the country invites you to share in its vitality, to gain precious insight into a fast disappearing world and embark on truly life-enhancing journeys of discovery.

Namaste Nepal The Nepalis are a hugely friendly people. The traditional Nepali welcome - the Namaste ('I salute the divine in you') - is widely used and, for the most part, continues to be remarkably untainted by the modern cynicism so prevalent elsewhere. It is there in the simple lodges of a trekking route, in the local people encountered during a rafting trip or in one of the Terai's Tharu villages. It is there even in Nepal's towns and cities where time and again urban confusion is confounded by individual acts of kindness and generosity.

Kathmandu Valley With a wealth of stunning temples and monuments set against a backdrop of Himalayan peaks, the Kathmandu Valley is itself compelling enough reason to visit Nepal. Its liberal scattering of UNESCO World Heritage sites includes the famous 'monkey temple' of Swayambhunath. This marks the spot, according to Buddhist legend, of the Valley's 'self arising' with the giant lake being drained through the attractive Chobhar Gorge. On the other side of the city, the massive Bodhnath stupa is Nepal's largest and the focus of reverence for innumerable Tibetan Buddhist monks. In contrast, the mysterious Dakshinkhali Temple, where goats and chickens are sacrificed to its hungry goddess, is cloistered in forest south of the capital. Its intense, enigmatic atmosphere lingers in the memory long after you leave. Or there is the more munificent Pashupatinath Temple, a superb gold decked two roofed structure whose gentle deity draws visitors from throughout the Hindu world. It lies, as do so many of Hinduism's most sacred places, beside a river where the stepped banks are reserved for the pyres of the late great and good.

Patan & Bhaktapur For those who want to stay away from the hustle and bustle, but not too far away, there are the Valley's other two cities. Patan is Kathmandu's genteel southerly neighbour, a city also of history and fine monuments. Its location often affords better mountain views than the capital. Then there is rustic Bhaktapur, with its cobbled streets and temple squares and a sense of tradition and timelessness that belies the mere 10 kilometres separating it from Kathmandu.

Palaces & Pagodas The cities of Kathmandu, Patan and Bhaktapur each have their own Durbar ('Palace') Square crammed with ornate temples and pagodas, many of which have wood carvings astonishing as much for the scenes they depict as for the skill of their craftsmen. These remain as sublime legacies of the intense rivalry between ruling families in a Nepal that remained resolutely independent while India's mighty Moghuls were overrun by the British. Try visiting any Durbar Square early in the morning to see men start work and women arriving to make their floral offerings to the gods; or after dark, when candles, shadows, and wisps of incense give the temples a magical perspective.

Left: *The Buddha in the Bhumis-parshamudra at the Monkey Temple.*
Below: *the 'Annapurna Sanctuary', sacred to the Gurungs, encircled by stunning peaks*

Centre: *magnificent mountain views from Sarangkot near Pokhara.*
Left: *painted wooden images of Siva and Parvati look down from among the fine carvings on the Asta Yogini Mandir, Durbar Square, Kathmandu.*

10

Right: throwing a pot
in the Potters' Square
in Bhaktapur.
Below: drying chillies
in the sun in Patan.

Centre: worshippers
queue to enter a
temple at
Swayambhunath.
Right: women wade
through a Terai river
carrying reeds for
thatching.

Left: *a Buddha statue on the hill up to Swayambunath.*
Below: *Buddhist prayer wheels – each clockwise turn is a prayer said.*

Above: *monks gather at the Shechen Tenyi Dargyeling at Bodhnath.* **Left**: *Chandramahardoshan, at the National Art Gallery, Bhaktapur.*

Festivals

Whatever time of year you visit Nepal, or for whatever length of time, the chances are that you will encounter at least one of the many, many festivals that adorn the Nepali year. Indeed, Nepal has more days of festivals than there are days in the year, whichever of Nepal's several calendars you choose to use!

Ganesh & Dasain

The Ganesh festival, on the September full moon, ushers in the most spectacular festival season. The elephant-headed god, the bringer of success and remover of obstacles, is a particular favourite of the Kathmandu valley. It is closely followed by Dasain (or Durga Puja) which is the major festival of the year for Hindus everywhere. Each of its ten days has a special theme, marked by activities as varied as the planting and nurturing of seeds in sand and water from the holy rivers, to fasting and the sacrifice of animals to propitiate demanding deities. Go to Kathmandu's Durbar Square on the ninth day to witness elaborate sacrifices at the Taleju Mandir (the only day this magnificent temple is open to Hindus), followed by the ritual sprinkling of sacrificial blood on instruments, vehicles and even aircraft to ensure their safe and guarded future use. It all builds up to the climax on the tenth day of Vijaya Dashami which celebrates the ultimate victory of good over evil and when the devout will receive a tika of vermilion, curd and rice on the forehead.

Tihar

In complete contrast, this is followed by the gentle festival of Tihar (or Diwali), a five day long celebration of the harvest. It is marked by lights everywhere, and the sight of thousands of flickering candle flames on a dark city or village night is truly astonishing. Charity is shown even to dogs who, to their undoubted bewilderment, find themselves decorated with garlands and a tika on the forehead. The ubiquitous crow does not miss out on the festivities either, as a portion of the family meal is given to them on the first day of Tihar.

Holi

The most colourful, amusing, annoying, and riotous festival of all is Holi, celebrated in March. This is a day to wear old clothes and throw away inhibitions (or stay indoors!). Holi marks the beginning of Spring, with everyone throwing coloured powder and water at each other and everywhere spirits are high. It is hard not to laugh when an unsuspecting pedestrian gets splattered in colour from behind or above or from any other vantage point. But - yes, you've guessed it - the real test comes when it's your turn to be that unsuspecting pedestrian.

Buddhist festivals

Apart from the Hindu festivals, some of which are also shared by the Buddhists, the gompas or monasteries, often in remote sites, draw large gatherings of the hill people when they celebrate special days to mark the Buddha's life and those of the great masters. The lamas perform ritual dances, full of symbolic meaning, dressed in special masks and elaborate costumes, often to the accompaniment of rather strange music played out by authentic instruments of ancient design. It is a great opportunity for the community not only to renew their faith but also to dress up in their finery and enjoy themselves.

Don't lose the chance to attend at least some of the vast number and variety of the mountain kingdom's festivals. They will leave you with unforgettable memories.

Left: *Nepal, Marpha Gompha (Buddhist monastery). Masked Tibetan Buddhist Lama dancing at harvest festival.*

14

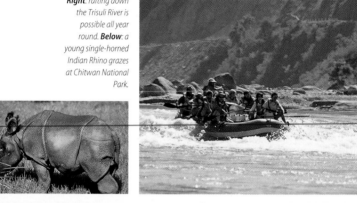

Right: rafting down the Trisuli River is possible all year round. *Below*: a young single-horned Indian Rhino grazes at Chitwan National Park.

Above: a trekker crosses the Tamur River in eastern Nepal on a rope suspension bridge. *Right*: a woolly yak, the great provider, poses in front of a farm house in the Khumbu Himal. *Next page*: prayer flags flutter over Bodhnath, the largest stupa in Nepal.

Spirit of adventure

It was not until 1951 that Nepal opened its doors to the outside world, but even then overseas visitors were restricted to certain destinations. During the 1990s areas previously off-limits have gradually been made accessible, areas which have remained unchanged for centuries and where it is conceivable that no Westerner has ever set foot. This is Nepal, where the age of exploration is alive and well.

Higher callings

Almost half of all visitors come to Nepal specifically for trekking. For many, their trek into the remote splendour of the highest region on the planet becomes one of those rare, life enhancing experiences. And there are hundreds of trekking routes to take, lasting anything from two days to more than three weeks. By far the two most popular areas are the Annapurnas and, following in the footsteps of Sir Edmund Hillary et al, the route to Everest Base Camp.

It is not only the mountains that contribute to the appeal of trekking. You will meet people from Nepal's many ethnic groups - those who continue the same nomadic pastoralism practiced by their family for generations, or the Bhotia, ethnic Tibetans whose communities are shaped by ancient Buddhist traditions, or the Sherpas ('eastern people') who have come to be almost synonymous with the great peak that dominates their region. Even if you miss the yeti, you will surely come across the yak. No animal better characterises the higher reaches of the Himalaya than this hairy 'grunting ox'. It is through such encounters that the trekker gains a privileged insight into ways of life usually seen only in the pages of a glossy geographical magazine.

Wet & Wild

It comes as no surprise that with the highest mountains in the world, Nepal also has some of the finest rafting rivers. Rafters can choose from any number of rivers and levels of difficulty. The Trisuli River, the country's most popular, is easy to reach from both Kathmandu and Pokhara. It is ideal for novices and passes through some gorgeous scenery. Many people combine a three day trip with a visit to Chitwan National Park, or even with a trek. The Kali Gandaki River, meanwhile, begins its long journey in the mountainous desert region of Mustang, near the Tibetan border. It flows through the Annapurna and Dhaulagiri mountains where it carves out the world's deepest river gorge and, at Rani Ghat, passes the ghostly ruins of a 19th century deserted palace.

Jungle Adventure

If getting close to wild animals appeals to your sense of adventure, then look no further than the Terai, Nepal's lowland belt. This northern section of the Ganges plains used to be completely wooded, but today only a fraction remains after years of deforestation. Happily, this seems to have been arrested. Conservation has made rapid progress, helped significantly by tourism. The Royal Chitwan National Park, a short flight or half day bus journey from Kathmandu, is the best known, while Bardia, in south west Nepal, is less commercialized and the Terai's largest park. Both are home to wild tiger, rhinoceros, elephant, deer, leopard, monkey, hyena, crocodile and a huge number of other animals. You can explore the jungle on foot, on elephant back or by jeep - whichever way you go, it's guaranteed a true adventure. Signs of life abound: broken branches and trampled trees, the urgent call of monkeys, or in the sudden bark of a frightened deer. And the incomparable thrill and sense of anticipation as you listen to twigs and leaves being trodden underfoot, or the heavy snorting of an unseen rhino in the trees ahead as experiences that stay with you for a long time afterwards.

In addition, the Sukla Phanta and Koshi Tappu Wildlife Reserves are a birdwatcher's idyll. Over 500 species live in the region, including birds of prey, water birds and highly colourful exotics. Look out for the squadrons of parakeets, for chirpy, bright bee-eaters scavenging the ground, and vultures and eagles soaring on the thermals.

Essentials

2

Essentials

19 **Planning your trip**

19 Where to go

20 When to go

20 Special interest travel

21 **Before you travel**

21 Getting in

22 What to take

24 **Money**

27 **Getting there**

27 Air

29 Overland

31 **Touching down**

31 Tourist information

34 Rules customs and etiquette

36 Safety

38 **Where to stay**

40 **Getting around**

41 Air

42 Road

45 Other land transport

46 Travellers with special needs

47 **Keeping in touch**

50 **Food and drink**

53 **Shopping**

55 **Holidays and festivals**

58 **Health**

59 Before travelling

60 Further information

61 On the way

61 Staying Healthy

65 Other risks and more serious diseases

68 When you return home

68 **Travelling with children**

69 **Further reading**

72 **Useful numbers**

Planning your trip

Where to go

Nepal opened its doors to the world for the first time in 150 years in 1951. In many respects it was still a medieval society. The people were charming and virtually untouched by the social, political and commercial changes taking place beyond its borders. Travellers were full of praise for this wonderful but economically backward land. Much has changed since 1951. Tourism has affected the outlook of many Nepalese. Yet Nepal retains its stunning natural beauty and much of its simple charm.

See also highlights, page 8

Essentials

The **Kathmandu Valley** is the cultural and political heart of the country. The **Durbar Square** in Kathmandu is the spiritual heart. The royal palace was at the centre of the city and was surrounded by temples and other important buildings. Many of the old buildings were re-built after the 1934 earthquake, not always to the original design. Visits to the **Pashupatinath**, Nepal's most important Hindu pilgrimage site and a World Heritage Site, can be combined with seeing the Buddhist Bodhnath. To the west of the city, **Swayambhunath**, high on a hill overlooking the city, is the oldest and most revered Buddhist site in Kathmandu. Away from the Square and temples, Freak Street was a mecca for hippies in the 1960s but is now just a tourist attraction. Today backpackers head for **Thamel** and **Chhetrapati** with their numerous restaurants and craft shops, which are particularly colourful during Dasain. There are also some lovely walks within and around the city.

Kathmandu Valley

Patan has been absorbed into Kathmandu but its Durbar Square is more densely packed with temples than either Kathmandu or Bharaktapur. It is the artistic and architectural centre of the valley.

Bharaktapur, the third city, preserved its medieval character better than the two other, more cosmopolitan, cities. It is known for its pottery, weaving and Nepali caps.

Beyond the three cities, the Arniko Highway heads for Tibet and the allure of Lhasa. Along the way, the hilltop retreats of Nagarkot, Dhulikhel and Kanai offer superb views of the high mountains.

The **Pokhara Valley** is situated in the centre of Nepal. Four hundred metres lower than Kathmandu, the valley is hemmed in far more closely by Himalayan giant peaks. Dominated by the Annapurna Massif to the north, the valley is dotted with lakes, of which **Phewa Tal** is the largest. Its beautiful setting has helped to make it Nepal's most popular tourist destination after Kathmandu.

Pokhara Valley

Consider spending time in the south of the country. The Terai, a narrow strip of land originally an area of mosquito infected jungle, is the point where the India land mass smashed into Central Asia resulting in the Himalaya. Here those areas not already cultivated have been turned into wildlife reserves. **Royal Chitwan National Park,** 120 kilometres south west of Kathmandu is the most visited. The **Royal Bardia Wildlife Reserve** is a possible alternative. From both tigers are best viewed from the back of an elephant. But there is more to the Terai than wildlife; **Lumbini** is the birthplace of the Buddha whereas **Janakpur** is the Terai's most important Hindu pilgrimage site. On its northern edge, the **Churia hills** are still growing. Here Ilam and Tansen are typical hill towns where traditional Nepali life endures.

The Terai

Beyond the Valley are the greatest mountains in the world. Some of the mountain regions, such as the **Solu Khumbu** (for Everest) and **Annapurna**, are immensely popular, while others such as West and East Nepal are barely known.

The mountains

When to go

The best time to visit Nepal depends largely on your tolerance and expectations, and on where you will be going. To varying degrees each season brings its own joys as well as trials. The peak tourist season extends from late September until the end of November when the post monsoonal air is clear and dry, when mountain views are at their best and when neither the Terai is too hot nor the trekking regions too cold. But it is also the time when queues for trekking permits are at their longest, hotels at their fullest, transport at its busiest and popular trekking routes at their most populated.

December, January and early February are the coldest months, especially at higher elevations and snow can limit trekking opportunities. Budget hotels without heating can be very chilly (see page 38), but there are fewer tourists and it's usually possible to negotiate substantial reductions in hotel rates.

From late February and into March and April, it gets warmer with almost all treks again fully accessible. This is the second peak tourist season with appeal both for trekkers and for travellers escaping the greater heat of the Indian plains, but rising dust and haze at lower elevations can make visibility variable at this time.

May and early June form the prelude to the coming monsoon. Increasing heat, occasional thunderstorms, humidity and haze in the lower regions combine to test the patience of permanent and temporary populace alike. The number of trekkers decreases, as views become obscured by haze and cloud and strenuous walking can get too warm for comfort at all but the higher elevations.

The monsoon arrives in Nepal in mid-June, pushing across most of the country from east to west and rinsing the air of its accumulated haze. Road travel can become difficult and hazardous at times, as some roads and trails are washed out or blocked by landslides, low cloud makes mountain visibility from lower lying areas very poor and leeches are at their most ubiquitous. Many trekking routes, especially those at lower elevations, become washed out or are at best slippery and deter all but the most determined trekkers. Trekking at elevations above the clouds, however, is possible, but of course these areas have to be accessed first. This is a good time to explore the Kathmandu Valley and Pokhara, with hotel rates at rock-bottom and many restaurants offering good discounts on their menus as well as generous happy hours. Travellers on very tight budgets will find this the cheapest time to visit Nepal. Putting aside the discomforts of heat, humidity and occasional heavy rainfall, the monsoon season offers a fascinating insight into the traditional life of rural Nepal. It is a time of hectic activity in the fields, of planting and harvesting rice and other crops. Any long distance bus journey will take you past villages where goats graze lazily and children play while all those old or young enough to work are planting, transplanting and harvesting rice from dawn to dusk, painstakingly drilling bunches of seedlings into prepared beds or cutting and threshing mature heavy-laden stalks. Many is the mountain road that offers spectacular views of terraced valleys where rice paddies in different stages of growth form a patchwork of shades of green: from the bright and shimmering lushness of young rice through deeper and darker greens to the golden hues of the mature crop awaiting harvest.

The monsoon begins to peter out from September, but even after the rainy season some routes may be blocked by flooding or landslides causing long delays.

Special interest travel

Trekking   For ease of organisation and the requirements of the different types of trek, Nepal is matchless. Nearly everyone will want to trek and we have a 96 page section starting on page 73 to help you get the best out of it.

In terms of regions, **Langtang, Gosainkund and Helambu**, all to the north of

Kathmandu, lack the 8,000 metre plus giants and are not quite as popular as Annapurna and Everest. The Langtang Valley is only 30 kilometres from Kathmandu.

Everest is the magnet of Nepal. Many are attracted by the mountain itself, others by the Solu Kumbu region, the home of the Sherpas, and some by both. The Everest Base Camp trek remains very popular.

Trekking from **Pokhara** tends to be towards the Annapurna Conversation Area. There are three classic treks: **Annapurna Circuit** (regarded by many as the 'classic'); **Annapurna Base Camp** and the **Jomsom Trek** (in reality the southern half of the Annapurna Circuit). The latter is ideal for those who want to travel light. Pokhara is also the gateway for treks into Mustang. Remote, cold and covered in snow through the winter, it is not particularly high but dust, cold and unrelenting winds make conditions harsh.

Eastern Nepal has a number of long treks up the Arun River towards Everest, to the Makalu Base Camp as well as to Kangchendzonga. Less developed than the classic treks, a high degree of self-sufficiency is required.

Western Nepal is the least developed trekking area. Treks from Jumla are isolated and tough and you need to be fully prepared before undertaking them. The trek to Rara Lake is a good option though.

A mountaineer's paradise, Nepal offers something for everyone. The major peaks are surrounded with rules and regulations and waiting lists can be long. It is worth bearing in mind that there are a number of Trekking Peaks which can be climbed. Permits are not required but, despite their name, mountaineering skills and equipment are prerequisites. There are a number of opportunities for biking: gently cycling around Kathmandu for example. For the more serious bikers, the Tribhuvan Highway has much to offer in terms of ascents and descents as well as fantastic scenery.

Mountaineering & mountain biking

Rapidly developing, the rivers of Nepal once more offer something for all both in terms of duration and difficulty. A trip is well worth considering.

Rafting

Before you travel

Getting in

Entry requirements Visas are required by all nationalities except Indians. They are available from Nepalese embassies and consulates abroad, at official border crossings with India (Mahendranagar, Nepalgunj, Sunauli [Belahiya], Birgunj and Kakarbhitta), Tibet (Kodari) and on arrival at Tribhuvan Airport, Kathmandu. Visa regulations can be rather complicated and are subject to change without notice, so it is advisable to check the current rules with a Nepalese embassy or consulate before travelling. The chief advantage in obtaining a visa in advance lies in the time and potential hassle saved on arrival. Each application should be accompanied by one passport size photograph. The following rules applied in 1999:

Visa fees must be paid for in US dollars. Carry US dollars of various denominations, as change is not always available. It is always better to obtain a visa in advance if you have time

Up to 15 days, single entry: US$15; **up to 30 days, single entry:** US$25; **up to 30 days, double entry:** US$40; **up to 60 days, multiple entry:** US$60.

Visa validity A maximum of 150 days may be spent in Nepal on a tourist visa in a year (January-December). Entry must be made within three months of the date of issue. A visa is officially only valid for the Terai region, the Kathmandu and Pokhara Valleys, and most of the towns linked by the country's main roads. It is not valid for any other areas, including trekking and rafting routes. If you are going on a rafting trip and the start point involves travel through an area not covered by the visa, you have to get the appropriate trekking permit from the Kathmandu or Pokhara Immigration Offices, along with any National Park entry fee receipt (also available at the park entrance).

Warning:
If you overstay your visa
you may be prevented
from boarding your
flight and will have to
apply for an extension,
as well as being liable
for a fine of twice the
extension fee

Visa extensions Tourist visas can be extended at the Kathmandu and Pokhara Immigration Offices and again require a passport photo. Beyond one month, extensions cost US$2 per day up to 90 days, then from 90 days to 150 days this increases to US$3 per day. Usually, visas cannot be extended further than three months after which at least one month must be spent outside Nepal before re-entry is permitted. Extending your visa beyond 120 days to 150 days continuous stay can only be done at the Kathmandu Immigration Office (not in Pokhara) and you have to show 'reasonable reasons' for wanting the extension. A former requirement to charge US$20 per day during the extension period no longer applies.

Customs

Prohibited and restricted items The import and export of narcotic drugs (processed or in their natural state), arms and ammunition is illegal. The export of antiques and artefacts over 100 years old is subject to tight control. Any item over 100 years old (or appearing so to a customs official), including precious and semi-precious stones, must be certified and a certificate obtained from the Department of Archaeology in Kathmandu (Ram Shah Path, T213701/2) before it may leave the country. Similar controls apply to gold, silver, wild animals and any part of their anatomy or any product made from them. These restrictions may be strictly enforced by thorough baggage checks at Kathmandu airport and other departure points.

Currency regulations There are no restrictions on the amount of foreign currency that can be brought into Nepal. Changing Nepalese Rupees back into foreign exchange requires certificates showing proof of exchange. You are supposed to change foreign currency at banks or authorized money changers only.

Duty free
restrictions

Tourists are permitted to bring in personal effects free of duty. Other duty free allowances include 200 cigarettes or 50 cigars, distilled liquor up to 1.15 litres or 12 cans of beer and 15 rolls of film.

The following items for personal use may be imported free of duty, but must be re-exported when you leave: one pair of binoculars, one movie camera with 12 rolls of film or one video camera with deck, one still camera, one music system with 15 tapes or one record player with 10 records, one perambulator, one children's tricycle, one sleeping bag and one walking stick.

Duty free shopping Kathmandu's Tribhuvan Airport has the country's only duty free shop. It has a small range of major international brands of tobacco and alcohol at competitive prices, a limited selection of perfumes (which you may be able to get for the same price in Kathmandu's New Road area), along with a small display of Nepalese handicrafts, most of which are more expensive even than in Thamel. At some destinations in South Asia, it may be possible to purchase duty free items on arrival. (**NB** Most duty free shops in European countries sell only to outbound passengers.) If your flight to or from Europe stops in Dubai and you are able to disembark, Dubai has one of the world's finest and best value duty free shopping complexes which is also available to transit passengers.

What to take

It is always best to keep luggage to a minimum. A sturdy rucksack or hybrid backpack/suitcase rather than a rigid suitcase covers most eventualities and survives bus boot, roof rack and plane/ship holds with ease. Serious trekkers will require a framed backpack (see Trekking section).

Light cotton clothes are best, supplemented by sweaters for evenings (September-April). Trekkers will need additional warm clothing and footwear. T-shirts and other clothing are widely available in Kathmandu and Pokhara often at very

Embassies and consulates

Australia *48 Mitchell St, McMahons Point, Sydney, NSW 2060, T02-9568815, F02-9568767; *Suite 23, 18-20 Bank Place, Melbourne, Vic 3000, T03-6021271, F03-6706480; *Suite 2, 16 Robinson St, Nedlands, WA 6009, T09-3862102, F09-3863087.

Bangladesh United Nations Rd, Rd R2, Baridhara Diplomatic Enclave, Dhaka, T601890, 601091.

Belgium *149 Lamorinier Straat, B-2018 Antwerp, T03-2308800.

Burma (Myanmar) 16 Natmauk Yeiktha, Yangon, T533168.

Canada *310 Duport St, Toronto M5R 1V9, T416-968 7252.

China 1 Sanlitun Xiliujie, Beijing, T5321795; Norbulingka Rd 13, Lhasa, Tibet Autonomous Region, T36890, 22881.

Denmark *2 Teglgaardstraede, 1452 Copenhagen K, T033-133165.

Finland *Erottaja 11A 14, 00130 Helsinki, T6802225.

France 45 bis rue des Acacias, Paris 75017, T46224867.

Germany Im Hag 15, 5300 Bonn, T0228-343097/8/9.

India 1 Barakhamba Rd, N Delhi 110 001, T (011) 332 9969/7361; 19 Woodlands, Sterndale Rd, Alipore, Calcutta 700 027, T033-711124/03.

Italy *Piazzale Medaglie d'Oro 20, Rome 00136, T348176.

Japan 14-9 Tokoroki 7-chome, Setagay-ku, Tokyo 158, T37055558.

Netherlands *Prinsengracht 687, Gelderland Building, 1017 JV Amsterdam, T020-250338.

Pakistan House No 506, Street No 84, Attaturk Ave, Ramna G-6/4, Islamabad, T210642, 212754.

Philippines *1136-38 United Nations Ave, Paco 2803, Manila, T598393.

Spain *Mallorca 194, Pral 2A, 08036 Barcelona, T03-3231323.

Sweden *Eriksbergsgatan 1A, S-114 30 Stockholm, T08-6798039.

Switzerland 1 rue Frederic Amiel, 1203 Geneva, T022-3444441; *Asylstrasse 81, 8030 Zurich, T01-475993.

Thailand 189 Soi 71 Sukhumvit, Bangkok, T3917240, 3902280.

UK 12A Kensington Palace Gardens, London W8, T0171-2296231/1594.

USA 2131 Leroy Place NW, Washington DC 20008, T202-6671551); 820 Second Ave, Suite 202, New York 10017, T212-3704188); *1500 Lake Shore Drive, Chicago, IL 60610, T312-7879199); *Heideberg College, Tiffin, OH 44883, T419-4482202); *Suite 400, 909 Montgomery St, San Francisco, CA 94133, T415-4341111); *16250 Dallas Parkway, Suite 110, Dallas, Tx75248, T214-9311212; *212 15th St NE, Atlanta, GA 30309, T404-8928152.

* indicates honorary consuls where an additional service charge may be made.

Essentials

reasonable rates. Some find open shoes or sandals best in hot weather, with or without light cotton socks, but it is also important to guard against blisters, cuts and bruises which are common problems with unprotected feet. Comfortable shoes or trainers are good options, particularly if walking in one of the national parks. A pair of Teva type sandals are comfortable and practical and these are also available in Nepal very much more cheaply than in Europe or America. Laundry services are usually speedy, but also rather more expensive than in India, a fact that has led to the establishment of several private laundry services in Kathmandu and Pokhara. Dress is rarely formal. For travelling, loose clothes are most comfortable. Modest dress for women is advisable; also take a sunhat and headscarf.

Everybody has their own list. Obviously what you take depends on where you are intending to travel and also what your budget is. The following can make travelling in Nepal easier and more comfortable. It is not exhaustive. For trekkers, see also the Trekking section, page 82. **Air cushions** for hard seating; **Bumbag**; **Contact lens**

Checklist
See page 59 for a suggested health kit

cleaning equipment – not readily available in South Asia; **Earplugs**; **Eye mask** to help you sleep in noisy and poorly curtained hotel rooms; **Insect repellant** and/or mosquito net, electric mosquito mats, coils (also available locally); **travel pillow** for neck support; International driving licence; Photocopies of **essential documents** (with spare passport photos); **Short wave radio**; **Sun hat**; **Sun protection cream** – factor 10 plus; **Sunglasses**; **Swiss Army knife** (with tin and bottle openers); **Tissues/toilet paper**; **Torch** and spare batteries; Compact **umbrella** (excellent protection from sun, rain and unfriendly dogs); **Wipes** (Wet Ones or equivalent); **Zip-lock bags**.

If you are intending to stay in **budget** accommodation, you might also include: Cotton sheet sleeping bag; Money belt; Padlock/s with chain (for hotel room and backpack); Plastic sheet to protect against bedbugs on mattresses; Soap; Towel; Universal sink plug.

Money

Cost of living The cost of living is low by western standards. The top of the range hotels and the best restaurants can be cheaper than their equivalent in the West. Budget accommodation in Kathmandu and Pokhara is plentiful. These are often excellent value and are invariably negotiable, especially during off-peak season. The quality of food in these two cities is infinitely better than what is usually served up as tourist fare in India, but then prices are also rather higher. A main course in one of central Kathmandu's tourist restaurants would cost in the region of US$1.80-2, with a bottle of beer about the same. Outside the Kathmandu Valley and Pokhara, the price of food reduces dramatically, but with it the choice which is usually limited to *dal-bhad-tarkari* or a variation thereon, and a typical Nepali meal here might cost US$0.50-US$0.90. Road transport is the most popular (if not always the most convenient or comfortable) way of travelling through Nepal and is very cheap. The 18-hour bus journey from Kathmandu to Kakarbhitta in the far east of Nepal, for example, costs about US$6, while the attractive and much travelled 8-hour ride from Kathmandu to Pokhara is no more than US$5.

Price fixing There is a distinctly multi-tiered pricing system that operates in Nepal. The bottom tier of the scale would be the price charged to a Nepali for a particular item and represents its realistic market value. At the top end, meanwhile, is the price that would be expected from a Westerner for the same item and this is often hyper-inflated. A middle tier, bridging the gap between the above, is sometimes seen to apply to Indians, but this is generally less fixed and sometimes surrounded by a sense of ambiguity in the seller's mind as to whether or not Indians are in fact 'foreigners'. In general, though, sellers are often more willing to accept a lower price from Indians than from those from outside South Asia.

With the steady increase in the number of foreign tourists visiting Nepal, distinctions are slowly emerging in the perceptions of shopkeepers, particularly in Kathmandu, between different nationalities of tourists. One hotel owner in Kathmandu considered Americans the most likely to pay the highest prices, while a French visitor claimed to have made significant savings in shops by saying he was Russian!

Exchange If you are trekking individually you will need cash, as it is virtually impossible to exchange foreign currency or Travellers' cheques in more remote areas. (**NB** Beware of pickpockets at the start of any trek.) Most Travellers' cheques are accepted at banks and major hotels. Be sure to keep encashment certificates, as these are required to re-convert your Nepalese rupees when you leave the country. There is a bank at Kathmandu Airport, both before passport control and after. The fact that Indian

Essentials

Approximate Exchange Rates (November 1999)

US $1	Rs 68	Canadian $1	Rs 47
UK £1	Rs 110	Dutch G1	Rs 32
Euro 1	Rs 71	French Fr1	Rs 11
IN Rs 1	Rs 1.58	German DM1	Rs 36
Aus $1	Rs 43	Swedish Kr1	Rs 8.26
Belgian Fr1	Rs 1.77	Swiss Fr1	Rs 45

Rupees are widely accepted means that you can often get away with changing only a minimal amount and pay hotel bills etc, in Indian Rupees, thereby reducing losses incurred in constant exchange transactions.

Credit cards

Major credit cards are increasingly accepted in the main tourist centres, though in smaller towns it is still rare to be able to pay by credit card. Payment by credit card can sometimes be more expensive than payment by cash, especially in respect of flight tickets and telecommunications, because an additional commission is charged – often around 3% but sometimes up to 6%. However, shopping by credit card for items such as handicrafts, clothing and carpets from larger dealers does not mean that you have to accept the first price asked. Bargaining is still expected and essential. Visa, Mastercard and American Express cardholders can use their cards to obtain either cash or Travellers' cheques in Kathmandu and Pokhara.

Currency

The **rupee** (abbreviated to **Rs**, or **Re** in the singular) is divided into 100 **paisa**. Notes come in denominations of Rs 1,000, 500, 100, 50, 20, 10, 5, 2, and 1. Coins exist in denominations of Re 1, and 50, 25, 10, and 5 paisa, although most tourists will not usually encounter the lower value coins. Notes of higher denomination are extremely difficult to change outside the main towns and on trekking routes. Major international currencies are readily accepted and many hotels and travel agents expressly ask to be paid in US$. The Indian Rupee is also widely accepted at the recognized market rate (fixed rate IN Re1 = N Rs1.60 in 1999), but this can also lead to confusion when paying by a combination of Nepalese and Indian currencies. When negotiating the price of an item (especially near the border), be sure that both yourself and the trader are talking the same currency. This applies particularly in the border towns. In Kathmandu, Pokhara and most Terai towns, the Indian Rupee is accepted almost as a parallel currency and is commonly referred to as 'IC', with the Nepali currency called 'NC'.

Travellers' cheques (TCs)

Most TCs are accepted without difficulty, but some companies only accept TCs from the biggest companies. TCs nearly always have to be exchanged in banks or hotels, and can only very rarely be used directly for payment. You have to show your passport when changing TCs. There can be a wide variation in the exchange rates offered by different hotels, so it is worth taking time to compare rates and commissions, especially if you are changing a large amount. Best rates are usually offered by the private banks and money changers. Almost all banks dealing with foreign exchange will accept US$ and £ Sterling. Other major currency TCs are also accepted in the main tourist centres. **Warning** If you cash sterling, always make sure that you have been given Rupees at the sterling and not at the dollar rate.

Black market
These transactions are, of course, illegal and penalties may be enforced

The black market for hard currency exchange is most active in the tourist areas of Kathmandu, but exists (although pursued much less vigorously), in Pokhara and some other towns. It is almost impossible to walk through Central Thamel without hearing the whispered questions, "Hello, change money? Buy carpet?" The most popular currency is the US$, followed by the £ Sterling and then by other major currencies.

Wealth, charity and perceptions of tourists

Nepal is one of the poorest countries in the world in terms of GDP per capita, so it is not surprising that many Nepalis consider even the backpacker on the tightest budget as immensely wealthy, especially given that their flight to Nepal may well have cost more than the average person's annual income. Attempts at explaining student or other relative poverty at home are unlikely to be understood. Foreigners are thus regarded as legitimate participants in a system of inflated pricing according to an unbridled law of supply and demand; an informal variation on, for example, the structure of domestic airfares. Is this to be decried as exploitation or to be condoned as a justifiable fall-out of global economic disparities?

It is often argued that the relative affluence of tourists visiting a country where a majority of people face continuous and unending battles to provide themselves and their families with the basic essentials of a subsistence existence imposes a moral obligation on the more fortunate to help alleviate this burden. If you accept that assumption, there follow questions on how the obligation can most effectively be met: in other words, I want to help, but how? There is no single satisfactory answer; indeed, the more you think about it, the more questions arise.

On a national scale there are numerous charities working towards the alleviation of poverty in Nepal while multilateral government aid contributes to the development of the country's infrastructure through the construction of roads, buildings, power supplies and so on. But what do you do when faced with the choice of paying the exhorbitant asking price for an item or bargaining for a realistic, market-rate price? If you pay the higher price, you ensure a good profit for the trader which will contribute to an improvement in his standard of living. But it will also help in creating or maintaining a false economy which will be applied also to future visitors, including those on a shoe-string budget. Then what of the trickle-down effect which ultimately benefits more people? It is difficult to guage the validity of this argument. On the one hand, the more money that comes into Nepal, the greater the likelihood that those who are really poor will eventually come to benefit in some way; but on the other, how much of the money that you give to a shopkeeper will eventually reach the people most in need (who are they? where are they?), or will it only further line the pockets of those who already have?

Ultimately, it is for individual visitors to decide for themselves whether they are prepared to pay substantially over the odds, though part of the decision will already have been taken for them by previous visitors. Alternatively, there is the option of making a donation to an organization involved in aid or development work (especially in rural areas), which is probably the most effective way of helping in the longer term.

....

Large denomination notes are preferred and dealers will usually pay marginally better rates for a US$100 dollar bill, for example, than for a bulky bundle of US$1 bills. Exchange rates on the black market are normally a few per cent higher than the official bank rate, but are influenced by the amount to be exchanged, by the denomination of notes and by how well you can bargain. It is also worth checking the trend over a few days of the currency to be exchanged: if it is gaining strength against the rupee the chances are that you will be able to negotiate a very good rate, but if it has been losing dealers are generally more cautious in what they will accept.

Transferring money You can do this through *Grindlays Bank* and *American Express* in Kathmandu. Also through Grindlays branches in other major towns, though this will take longer as all international transfers go through the capital and local offices are not accustomed to dealing with such transactions. This is a very expensive way to get money, because of the high charges that are levied. If you have a credit card (*American Express, Mastercard, Visa*), you would be better off getting an advance. Compare rates and commission offered by the different banks and money changers.

Getting there

Air

Kathmandu's Tribhuvan Airport (the only international airport in Nepal) is served by several international airlines and has direct scheduled flights to and from South Asia, Southeast Asia, Tibet, the Middle East and Europe. Flights to/from North America, Australia, South Africa and East Asia involve an *en route* change of aircraft or airline. There are also a number of charter flights catering for inclusive tour packages from Europe.

Scheduled flights to **Europe** are operated by Aeroflot (change in **Moscow**), Qatar Airways (change in **Qatar**), Austrian Airlines to Vienna, Transavia Airlines to Amsterdam and Royal Nepal Airlines Corporation [RNAC] to **London, Frankfurt** and **Paris**. Flights to **India** by RNAC (Delhi, Bombay and Calcutta) and Indian Airlines (Delhi, Bombay, Varanasi and Calcutta); to **Tibet** (Lhasa) with China South West Airlines; to **Bhutan** (Paro) with Druk Air; to **Bangladesh** (Dhaka) with Biman Bangladesh Airlines (with onward connections to **Europe, North America** and **Southeast Asia**); to **Pakistan** (Karachi) with PIA; to **Bangkok** with Thai Airways and RNAC; to **Hong Kong** with RNAC; to **Singapore** with Singapore Airlines and RNAC; to **Japan** (Osaka) with RNAC; to **Shanghai** with RNAC; and to **Dubai** with RNAC.

Budget flights If both your time and budget are limited and you are visiting Nepal only, Bangladesh Biman, Aeroflot and Qatar Airways usually offer the cheapest flights from Europe. But if you are spending more time in the region, it can work out cheaper to fly to Delhi and continue to Nepal with Indian Airlines or RNAC, or overland. One of the ironies in the structure of international air fares is that it is usually cheaper to fly an indirect route, changing aircraft in a third country. This, of course, costs airlines considerably more in operating costs than flying non-stop! It is always advisable to book through a bonded travel agent which can guarantee your return/onward flight if your airline cannot.

London has some of the most competitive fares on flights from **Europe**. Fares vary according to season, but if you hunt around you can probably get a flight for around £440 return from London. The cheapest flights from London to Delhi start at around £300 return (but note that these airlines are not necessarily those you would always choose to fly with!) and rise to about £550 return on the major airlines. Check the classified travel advertisements in national and local papers (London's Evening Standard is good), along with the free travel magazines around major railway stations for 'bucket shop' fares. (**NB** An additional fee may be charged by some agents if you are paying by credit card.) The Air Travel Advisory Bureau (T0171-6365000) is an advertising service for low cost flights, though it does not vouch for the reliability of its advertisers. Travel agents specializing in flights for students or young people do not always offer the cheapest fares and may not offer you flights on certain airlines.

Fares from **North America** are relatively expensive if you book your entire trip from there. You may be able to reduce them by getting a cheap flight to either London (from the east coast) or Bangkok (from the west coast) and booking your onward flights from there. Again, check the classified travel ads in the national and local press.

Fares from **India** are set by the two governments and are not discounted. The only exception applies if you are under 30 years of age when you are eligible for a 25% discount.

Bangkok is the London of **Southeast Asia** for budget flights. There are also some good deals on flights from Bangkok, Hong Kong, Singapore and Tokyo with Biman Bangladesh Airlines, changing in Dhaka; additionally (though more expensive), on Thai Airways from many Southeast and East Asian destinations, changing in Bangkok.

Overland

It is still possible to travel overland to Nepal from Europe by car, motorbike or bus, or even by bicycle. The re-opening of Iran to travellers of most nationalities (except Americans) has reinstated the Istanbul-Tehran-Quetta route which was very popular in the 1970s. It is still necessary to take advice on travelling through Eastern Turkey, although the route through Dogubayazit to the Iranian border is usually open. The road through Iran is now generally excellent, and there is also a good road to Nok Kundi, though there are speed breakers and road block chains (without warning) which are particularly dangerous for motorbikers. It is possible to go through Pakistan and India quite quickly if time is short, but there is also a great deal to see. Both the *Footprint Pakistan Handbook* and the *Footprint India Handbook* are excellent travelling companions.

One recent biker has written to recommend reasonably priced **accommodation** in major centres in Iran. In **Zenjan**: *Hotel Sepid*. In **Isfahan**: *Nazhk Jahan*, Main Blvd; *Bam Inn* with rooms and a very pleasant camping site. The Iran-Pakistan border at **Taftan** is open from 0800-1200 and 1600-1800. **Sleeping** *Camping*, Customs Ground; also new *Tourist Motel*.

After Taftan the main major town is Quetta, 600 km. Buses take approximately 13-14 hours. **Sleeping** Good *Rest Houses* at **Yakmach** and **Padag**; avoid Dalbandin if at all possible, where the rest house is really bad. In **Quetta**: **D** *Bloom Star*, Stewart Rd, T833350, some a/c rooms, pleasant gardens; **E** *Hotel de Luxe*, Jinnah Rd, good value; *Muslim Hotel*, Jinnah Rd, T71857, room with bath, hot water, fan, 1st floor lighter and marginally cheaper.

There are five official border crossing points between India and Nepal. All are in the southern Terai region, either directly on or near the Mahendra Highway, the main east-west road through Nepal. All have bus and/or air connections with Kathmandu. Theoretically, you can cross the border at any time of day or night, though you will probably have to wake the officials if you arrive very late. **NB** Travelling by bus after dark through the Indian state of Bihar is not recommended, as there have been numerous reports of buses ambushed by gangs of armed robbers. **Warning** At Immigration, clerks may demand an unauthorized 'fee' – do not pay unless a receipt is given.

Mahendranagar, in the far southwest of the country, has road connections with Delhi. The stretch of the Mahendra Highway from Mahendranagar to Nepalgunj is in appalling condition and is an extremely bumpy ride. Heading east from Mahendranagar, you can break the long journey to Kathmandu with a stay at Royal Bardia National Park, some five hours by bus from the border. Alternatively, the fine Sukla Phanta Wildlife Reserve is minutes from Mahendranagar. The town has a grass strip airport, although there were no flights operating in or out in 1999.

Nepalgunj is effectively a regional capital for southwest and West Nepal and lies a few km south of the Mahendra Highway. There is an airport with frequent flights to Kathmandu and it is the hub of RNAC's operations in West Nepal with flights to many of the more remote and mountainous destinations, including Jumla. It is an easy 3-hour bus journey to the Royal Bardia National Park, while buses to both Kathmandu and Pokhara take around 14 hours. South of the border, there are road and rail links with Delhi as well as Lucknow, Kanpur, Faizabad (for Ayodhya) and Gorakhpur.

Overland from Europe

To/from India

Essentials

Sunauli (Belahiya) lies at the southern end of the Siddhartha Highway which runs from here to Pokhara, via Butwal and Tansen. Nearby is Lumbini, the birthplace of the Buddha and an important Buddhist pilgrimage site with archaeological ruins. Sunauli (Belahiya) is an unattractive place and it is better to stay in either Bhairahawa (4 km to the north) or in Butwal (40 minutes by bus), both of which have a range of better accommodation. There are frequent buses from the border to Pokhara (8 hours), Royal Chitwan National Park (4 hours) and Kathmandu (8 hours). The nearest airport is north of Bhairahawa which has flights to Kathmandu. Gorakhpur is the nearest Indian city and there are several buses throughout the day. Varanasi is a bus journey of about nine hours.

Birgunj is at the southern end of the Tribhuvan Highway, the first major road to be constructed in Nepal. It's a convenient crossing point for the Royal Chitwan National Park, a 4-hour bus journey away. The majority of buses to Kathmandu take the longer route via Narayanghat and Mugling, because of the poor condition of the Tribhuvan Highway. The journey time to both Kathmandu and Pokhara is around eight hours. Across the border is Raxaul Bazaar which is the terminus of a narrow gauge railway line. It's difficult to get a reservation on trains from Raxaul. Patna is a 6-hour bus journey away and is a busy railway junction with frequent connections to Delhi and Calcutta. It also has a foreign tourist ticket quota where you can usually get a reservation to most destinations quite quickly.

Kakarbhitta is in the far southeast of Nepal. It is a long bus journey to Kathmandu (18-20 hours), so you might think about stopping overnight *en route*. You can get to the attractive hill station of Ilam, the centre of Nepal's tea growing region, in around five hours. Alternatively, break the journey at Janakpur, the Terai's most important Hindu town. The nearest major airport is at Biratnagar (3-6 hours by bus), which has frequent flights to Kathmandu and also to the mountain villages of Tumlingtar and Taplejung. On the Indian side, Siliguri is a short bus or auto-rickshaw ride away, from where buses and jeeps head up to Darjeeling and buses go to Calcutta (12 uncomfortable hours). Trains to Calcutta (14 hours) leave from the neighbouring town of New Jalpaiguri. The nearest airport is at Bagdogra, between Siliguri and the border, which has regular flights to Calcutta and Delhi.

Warning Many travel agencies in Kathmandu, Pokhara and Nepal's border towns offer inclusive through ticketing to destinations in India. While some of these deals are genuine and trouble-free, others require you to collect the ticket for your journey from another travel agency in one of the border towns or/and again at an intermediate town in India. There are two main drawbacks to this system. First, the more people are involved in such a transaction, the greater is the potential for 'mistakes' to occur; and, second, you may not actually end up with the routing, time or class of travel that you thought you had paid for. The best way to avoid hassle is by booking through a good and reliable travel agent.

Travelling to Tibet Officially you can visit Tibet only as part of an organized group tour (minimum five people) with a recognized tour operators, and not independently. The tour operator will make all visa and travel arrangements. Prices vary seasonally and according to what is included, eg flying to Lhasa or travelling overland. Tibet lies in the rainshadow of the Himalaya, and most of the country is unaffected by the monsoon. The tourist season lasts from April to November. The **best time to go** is from September-October, with May and June the best months for trekking. During the monsoon, however, the overland trip is subject to delays, because frequent landslides can make sections of the Arniko Highway (especially between Barabise and Kodari), impassable.

For a four to eight day trip, expect to pay from US$365 including 1-way flight, on the basis of sharing a twin room and including breakfast. Visa fees are extra. Prices rise to over US$2,000 for a 14-day tour with single room. China South West Airlines operates two flights a week (Tuesday and Saturday) in season between Kathmandu and Lhasa. **NB** Tickets are usually non changeable, non endorsable and non refundable.

Visas are valid for the length of your tour. Fees are set reciprocally and vary dramatically according to nationality. In 1999, they were: Australia US$15; Austria US$8; Belgium US$22; Brazil US$60; Canada US$38; Denmark (free); France US$24; Germany US$20; Holland US$22; Italy US$11; New Zealand US$38; Norway (free); Russia US$72; Spain US$21; Switzerland US$12; UK US$39; USA US$10. Visas for Tibet must be issued by the Chinese Embassy in Kathmandu (Chinese visas issued elsewhere are not valid for travel from Nepal). The Embassy is open Monday, Wednesday and Friday from 1030-1130. Visas usually take about a week to process, although there is said to be an 'express' service available – details from your tour operator. It may be possible to extend your visa in Lhasa at a fee of around US$40 per week.

Tour Operators Kathmandu has several tour operators arranging trips to Tibet. At the top end is *Tibet Travels and Tours* (T231130, F228986) on Tridevi Marg, diagonally opposite the Immigration Office. This professional and reliable company offers a number of tour itineraries, including an 8-day trip to Lhasa, cycling tours, and pilgrimages to Mt Kailash and Lake Manasarovar. Slightly cheaper are the popular *Green Hill Tours* (T414803, F419237) and *Ying Yang Travels* in Central Thamel. All have slide shows which are widely advertised and before you leave there is a briefing on the country along with advice as to what to expect and what to take.

Touching down

A departure tax of Rs 50 is levied for domestic flights, though this is included in the price of dollar fare tickets. Rs 600 is payable for departures to other SAARC countries (India, Pakistan, Bangladesh, Bhutan, Sri Lanka and the Maldives) and Rs 700 for all other international destinations. Departure tax can only be paid in Nepalese Rupees: it is worth setting the amount aside for when you leave. **Airport tax**

Whether entering Nepal by air or overland, a valid passport and visa is required. Disembarkation cards with an attached customs declaration form will be handed out during the flight to Kathmandu; the same forms are used also at land borders. The customs declaration should be handed to customs officials after you have collected your luggage. **Documentation**

Tourist information

There are no official government tourist offices overseas which, on the face of it, seems rather curious given both the increasing importance of tourism in Nepal's economy and its further potential. Some embassies and consulates abroad, though, do have a few tourist handouts including a free 70 page Visitors' Guide with a range of introductory information on Nepal such as useful addresses, dates and formalities. (It can also advise on the best veterinary hospitals to which you can take your household pets for treatment.) While Kathmandu airport has a tourist counter, the central tourist office on Kathmandu's Ganga Path (T211203) is better equipped. The Department of Tourism is situated behind the National Stadium at Tripureshwar. There is also a number of free monthly publications, including *Traveller's Nepal*, available at Kathmandu airport, larger travel agencies and upmarket hotels, which carries features on various aspects of tourism in Nepal. You will usually get the most up-to-date information on trekking, food, hotels, other essentials and matters of interest by talking to other travellers. The small tourist office in Pokhara, located opposite the **Tourist offices** airport terminal, has yet to achieve excellence in customer service, but (with friendly encouragement) can provide basic tourist information relating to Pokhara and the surrounding areas. Open Sunday-Friday from 1000, closing time varies according to season, early closure Friday 1500.

There are other official tourist information centres at Bhairahawa, Birgunj, Janakpur and Kakarbhitta, but don't expect too much.

Specialist tour operators
Telephone numbers are listed under Useful numbers, page 72

There are a number of tour operators in Europe, the USA, Australia and New Zealand offering package holidays to Nepal. Increasingly, packages are also being offered by travel agents in India. Check with your local travel agent as to which company is offering what and when. Note that all-inclusive packages usually work out much more expensive than if you were to make your own arrangements, especially if the holiday includes a trekking or rafting trip. The only major advantage of going with an organized tour is peace of mind together with the time saved in making arrangements when you arrive.

Trekking permits
See also the Trekking section, page 80

These are required for all areas not covered by the visa, and state the trek's duration and route. Even if you are not going on an organized trek you must get a trekking permit if venturing further than a day's walk from a main road north of the Terai. These are available only from the Immigration Offices in Kathmandu and Pokhara. A separate permit is required for each trekking area you intend to visit and each application should be accompanied by two passport photos. Fees start from US$5 per week for the more popular trekking regions (Annapurna, Langtang, and Everest for example), but can be as high as US$700 for a 10 day trekking permit for Mustang. Numerous permit inspection posts are located strategically along trekking routes and will turn back trekkers without the necessary permit; in some restricted areas of western and northern Nepal, this can also lead to deportation.

An International Student Identity Card (ISIC) may be of help in negotiating certain travel and other discounts, but on the whole their use is limited in Nepal. If you have one, however, take it: you never know when or where it may come in handy, especially if you are also travelling beyond Nepal.

Student cards

Aside from aid agencies and the hotel and catering trade, there are few foreigners in formal employment in Nepal. Work permits are required which should normally be obtained before entering the country. Your employer applies for the permit, a process which can take months. If you arrange to work after arriving in Nepal, you should leave the country while the paperwork is negotiated. It is almost impossible to change a tourist visa into a work permit. However, you may be able to find informal temporary work teaching English at a private language school in Kathmandu, but the pay is very low and would not usually be sufficient to support yourself. Other job opportunities may be available from time to time for experienced, qualified and connected trekking or rafting guides. Also, meditation instructors may find short term placements in one of Kathmandu's yogic establishments, while professional masseurs have been known to enlist the help of qualified assistants at peak times.

Working in Nepal

    A number of international aid agencies work in Nepal and employ health and nutrition professionals as well as specialists to work on education, agriculture, forestry, water, engineering and other social and environmental projects. These positions often require a commitment of at least two years and recruitment is generally handled by the head office or a regional centre of the co-ordinating agency. If you are looking for an insight into aid and development work, you might try approaching an organization to see if they could benefit from a few days of your voluntary help. For addresses, see under Kathmandu page 248 and Patan page 249

There are several good topographical maps of Nepal which are available in good bookshops abroad. There is probably no map which is completely accurate, but the German *Nelles* map (**Nepal**) is good, with a 1:1,500,000 map of the entire country on one side, and a 1:500,000 map of the central and most visited section of the country (from Butwal to Biratnagar in the south, from Jomsom to Kanchenjunga in the north, including both the Indian and Tibetan borders), on the other. It also has inset maps of Kathmandu city (1:15,000) and the Kathmandu Valley (1:75,000). The Nepali *Mandala* map series has a 1:800,000 country map (**Nepal**). Other maps include the *Asian Highway Route Map* (**India-Nepal-Bangladesh**). Scale 1:1,250,000. Includes information on these areas as well as geography, places of interest, advice to motorists, road conditions and traffic regulations.

Maps

(side margin, vertical) Essentials

Essentials

Touching down

Hours of business Government offices are open 1000-1700 Sunday-Thursday, 1000-1500 Friday, closed Saturday. Don't leave things until the last minute, especially on Friday when work begins to wind down from lunchtime. Some government offices close an hour earlier in winter. Banking hours are 1000-1400 Sunday-Thursday, 1000-1200 Friday, closed Saturday. In the main tourist areas, shops are open on Saturday, but tend to start business later than on other days.

IDD: 977 Long tones with long pauses means it is ringing. Equal tones with long pauses indicate engaged.

Official time Nepal is 5¾ hours ahead of GMT, and 15 minutes ahead of Indian Standard Time. In a region dominated politically and economically by India, this 15 minute difference is one way by which Nepal is seen to assert its independent identity. As elsewhere in South Asia, punctuality is perceived approximately and is often the exception to the rule. Patience is therefore required.

Electricity Major towns have electricity; 220 volts, 50 cycles. The existence of electricity in many parts of Nepal is a fairly recent phenomenon, although it is still rare to find more than a limited supply in

many smaller towns and rural areas. Many remote mountain villages have no electricity. Gradually, this is changing. Sauraha, the Chitwan village where most visitors stay, introduced electricity in 1995 and by 1997 almost all its tourist accommodation and restaurants were connected; the lodges inside the park, however, have no electrical supply and rely on generators and paraffin lamps. Even in Kathmandu and Pokhara, temporary power cuts (known as 'load-shedding') are common. These rarely last longer than an hour or two, but during and before the monsoon heavy storms occasionally affect power lines which can result in power cuts of a day or more.

Much of the country's electricity is generated by hydro-electric units, so supply is largely dependent on river levels and is most variable in the period leading up to the monsoon when water levels are low.

Power surges and troughs are common and can affect your equipment. Some people use stabilizers to protect personal computers or other expensive equipment.

Sockets are usually three pin (round), but can take two pin plugs. Adaptors from three to two pin are readily and cheaply available in European electrical and hardware shops and at main airports. They are less common in Nepal, so it is advisable to bring one with you from home.

A range of **trekking** maps are available overseas as well as in Kathmandu and Pokhara. These are of variable reliability, though the two most trekked regions (Annapurnas and Everest region) are well covered. Northwest Nepal has very poor cartographic coverage. Names of villages and landmarks vary considerably between different maps which can lead to confusion. (See the **Trekking** section.)

Rules, customs and etiquette

Cleanliness and modesty are appreciated even in informal situations. Nudity is not appreciated and causes widespread offence. Displays of intimacy between a man and a woman are not considered suitable in public. Though Nepali men and women never hold hands in public, you will often see men holding hands. This is an accepted expression of friendship without other significance. Nepal is one of the safest countries in the world for unaccompanied women and the harrassment that is common in many other South Asian towns and cities is almost absent here. Crime rates, however, although low by international standards, are increasing in some areas, so it is always better to be both courteous and wise and not to invite unwanted attention by wearing revealing or tight fitting clothes. It is not advisable for women to trek alone, especially along less popular routes.

Great warmth and hospitality will be experienced by most travellers, but with it comes an open curiosity about personal matters. Don't be surprised if total strangers on a bus or elsewhere ask details about your job, income and family circumstances. Socially, Nepali women can be shy and may appear to be ignored, although they perform a vital social and economic role in many areas. The role of women also differs among different communities and ethnic groups. Some hill communities, for example, have a matriarchal society in complete contrast to male dominated societies of the Terai.

Local customs & social behaviour

Use your right hand for giving, taking, eating or shaking hands, as the left hand is considered to be unclean. Women do not shake hands with men, as this form of contact is not traditionally acceptable between acquaintances. Do not photograph women without permission. The feet are also considered unclean. It is considered rude and disrespectful for someone to put their feet up on a chair or table, for example, or to kick someone else even in jest. It is not considered proper to step over someone else. Shoes are customarily removed before entering a room or someone's house.

The greeting when meeting or departing used universally by Hindus throughout South Asia is the palms joined together as in prayer usually accompanied by the word *Namaste*, which translates as "I salute all the divine qualities in you". 'Thank you' (*dhanyabad*) is often expressed by a smile and a slight sideways-and-upwards movement of the head. Generally, verbal expressions of thanks are neither expected nor proffered. A formal greeting to one's elders or superiors (the two are sometimes considered inseparable) is to bend down and touch the feet. This is not done at every meeting, but in traditional households a wife may touch her husband's feet first thing each morning. This greeting is not expected of foreigners.

To give something respectfully, the item is usually offered with the right hand while the left hand touches the forearm or elbow, and the head is slightly bowed. You may see this, for example, when a waiter hands you your restaurant bill.

Nepali culture has many other do's and don'ts, some of which are specific to a certain caste, community or religion. In the main tourist centres, people have become accustomed to the different habits of Westerners, but any demonstration of Nepali customs by visitors is invariably appreciated. Kesar Lall's interesting and entertaining booklet, *Nepalese Customs and Manners*, is available inexpensively in Kathmandu and is full of local proverbs, superstitions and social observations.

Visiting religious sites

Visitors to Hindu temples should observe customary courtesy, especially in clothing. Although non-leather footware may be permitted in some temples, it will be appreciated if shoes are removed as a matter of course before entering a temple. Other leather items of clothing (for example watch straps, handbags and belts), should also be removed. Some people (including Nepali and Indian Hindus) keep their watch in a pocket while inside the temple, though this should be done discreetly.

Non-Hindus are sometimes not permitted into the inner sanctum of Hindu temples and occasionally not even into the temple itself. Look for signs or ask. Offering boxes are provided for those who wish to make donations which should not normally be handed to priests or monks since they may be forbidden to touch money. It is also not customary to shake hands with a priest or monk – a Namaste will suffice as a greeting.

Special rules apply to visiting **Buddhist** shrines which are sometimes seen to be used also in Hindu temples. Walk clockwise around the stupa (or deity) and on the left hand side in monasteries. Many Buddhist monasteries are open to all; you may even visit the resident lama (priest). If you wish to make a contribution, put money in the donations box. It will be used for the upkeep of the temple or monastery.

You must not touch somebody else's food. You will notice that the Nepalis, when drinking water from a bottle or glass, may pour the liquid without their mouth

Essentials

touching the container. In this way they avoid ritual (as well as actual) pollution. The kitchen in a Hindu home is sacred, so non-Hindus should ask before entering.

If visiting one of Nepal's few **Mosques**, women should be covered from head to ankle. Mosques may be closed to non-Muslims shortly before prayers.

Photography | There are abundant photographic opportunities throughout Nepal and a camera is a must. Many Nepalis like being photographed, particularly if you have a polaroid and can give them a copy. If in any doubt, ask, but you are encouraged not to pay. Most festivals allow photography. Participants sometimes go into a trance and may act unpredictably. It is safest to avoid taking photographs under such circumstances. Sensitivity in what, where and when you photograph is recommended. Great discretion is required at funerals in particular. Although held in the open, a funeral is a private and intensely emotional occasion (as in the West), so if you really do want to take a photograph, don't intrude, be sensitive and discreet about it. The photography of other outdoor activities, such as washing, (women) bathing and (men) urinating, also require sensitivity unless you want to be chased away by the disgruntled subject of your snap.

Tipping | Tipping has only very recently become common practice in Nepal and even now it is expected only in the major tourist centres. In expensive establishments, tip up to 10%; in smaller places, the loose change of Rs 10 will be appreciated. Check whether the bill already includes a service charge. **NB** Taxi drivers do not expect a tip, as the fare you are paying is probably more than enough. The tipping of porters on treks is now expected and can be a problem especially if you are part of a group. See page 36: for further suggestions about this.

Safety

Probably the greatest risk to your safety comes from the hazards inherent in adventure activities, such as rafting and trekking. See those sections of this handbook for further information. Violent crime against foreigners is extremely rare. Bus travel has its joys (for example when you arrive) as well as perils (for example en route). Travelling on the roof can be fun for a while, but is definitely not advised along unmade stretches of road or on mountain roads. Be aware that once you are on the roof, it can be difficult to exchange that berth for a seat below.

Begging | There are relatively far fewer beggars in Nepal than in India. Most congregate in and around major religious pilgrimage sites, with some in the Thamel area of Kathmandu and, occasionally, in Pokhara. Begging is rarely aggressive in Nepal. Whether or not to give is a real dilemma that confronts most visitors. If you do give, you will be helping that person for a short time, but this encourages dependency and will almost certainly prompt more people to come begging in Kathmandu. Most trekkers come across children in the mountains asking for pens or Re 1 or Rs 5 or, if they're really bold, Rs 10 and more. Some people find it appropriate to give food rather than money. Alternatively, you might think about making a donation to a charitable aid or development organization which works to combat poverty (especially in rural areas), the root cause of begging.

Confidence tricksters | Although Nepal suffers far less from confidence tricksters than some other countries, take care in the main tourist centres where pickpocketing is not unheard of. Be careful with any major purchases, expensive 'silk' carpets, gold and precious stones being some of the main ways in which travellers have been conned into parting with huge sums for something of little value. It is advisable to make all your travel arrangements (particularly for combination bus/train journeys to India), with a good and reputable agency, or in the case of rafting or trekking trips, book directly with the operator instead of an agent wherever possible.

Narcotic drugs are illegal in Nepal. Some drugs, especially cannabis and its derivatives, **Drugs** are widely and openly available, however, and the musty stench of a burning joint is seldom far from innocent nostrils in the main tourist areas. It is as revealing as it is incongruous that the high moral tone occasionally adopted by official sources in attacking the evils of drugs can co-exist with little or no apparent attempt made to eradicate the many cannabis plants (*Cannabis sativa*) that grow wild in fields, gardens (including those of government buildings), along the roadside and elsewhere in several parts of the country.

Although drug laws have been tightened in recent years under pressure from the international community, enforcement remains somewhat random. When they are enforced, though, Westerners can expect harsh penalties, including lengthy imprisonment. Some people cite scientific 'evidence' in asserting cannabis to be a relatively innocuous substance, but even if this is so, the fact that it is illegal should be respected. Never be lulled into attempting to take drugs across an international border. Awareness of the conditions prevailing in Nepal's jails should act as a strong deterrent. It is worth remembering, moreover, that diplomatic assistance in drug related cases may be provided with less than whole-hearted enthusiasm and that many travel insurance policies specifically exclude loss, damage, injury or other occurrences attributable to the effects of alcohol or drugs.

There are innumerable police checkpoints dotted throughout the length and breadth **Police** of the country. You will certainly encounter some if you go trekking, when you may be asked to show your passport, trekking permit and park entry receipt where applicable. Outside the trekking regions, however, most visitors will have little if any contact with the police. You will be lucky if you meet a policeman with a good conversational command of English. Most insurance policies require you to report a theft or other incident related to a future claim to the police and to get a written report. If the police attend an incident involving you or your group, it **always** pays to be courteous and patient as well as firm, even if you don't understand what is being said. In the event of any serious trouble, insist that you are able to contact your embassy.

Take good care of your personal valuables, both when you are carrying them and **Theft** when you have to leave them in hotels or other places. You cannot regard hotel rooms as automatically safe. It is wise to use hotel safes for valuable items, though even they cannot guarantee security. It is best to keep travellers' cheques and passports with you at all times. Money belts worn under clothing is one of the safest options.

Travelling bags and cases should be made of tough material, if possible not easily cut and external pockets (both on bags and on clothing), should never be used for carrying money or important documents. Strong locks for travel bags and cheaper hotel rooms are invaluable.

In general, Nepal is remarkably safe for women travelling alone, particularly in the **Women** main tourist areas of the Kathmandu Valley, Pokhara and the Royal Chitwan National **travellers** Park. It is not advisable, however, for women to trek alone (see also the **Trekking** section). Travel in some of the Terai towns, where attitudes towards Western women are more in keeping with those of India and may be influenced by the portrayal of women in Hollywood and other varieties of film, can pose potential problems of harrassment for unaccompanied women. Women can reduce any risks by avoiding revealing or tight fitting clothing and by staying in better hotels or those popular with other Western tourists.

Where to stay

*Most cheaper guest houses do not have heating systems in the room, so it can get very cold in winter particularly in the trekking regions. Some may provide a portable coal fire to heat the room. These should be used with extreme caution, as they give off carbon monoxide, a highly toxic gas that can be fatal within minutes. **Always** open the window if you are using one, and **never** go to sleep without ensuring proper and continued ventilation. Ask for more blankets.*

Both **Kathmandu** and **Pokhara** have a very wide range of accommodation, from international standard luxury hotels to bottom of the range budget guest houses. You can stay cheaply by Western standards and most hotels in these cities are clean and comfortable. During the peak seasons (March-April and October-November), rooms are often heavily booked. Although you may not be able to get a room in your first choice hotel, both cities have an invariable surplus of accommodation so it is never usually a problem to find a decent room close by.

Most of the accommodation available in the Royal **Chitwan** and **Bardia** National Parks consists of 'Tharu-style' lodges. Tharus are one of the Terai's dominant ethnic groups and 'Tharu-style' translates as small mud-walled and floored huts/cottages with thatched brushwood roofs. Each cottage consists of one or more bedrooms, with attached or separate bathroom. Sauraha, the village beside Chitwan which has all the park's budget accommodation, now has electricity. Thus, many rooms have been equipped with fans and electric light, which presumably also makes them less Tharu-like. Thakurdwara, Bardia's budget accommodation village, has no electricity. Both parks also have a smaller range of luxury accommodation.

Accommodation along **trekking** routes varies. In the popular Annapurna and Everest regions, there are now a number of good hotels with hot water and sometimes Western-style menus. Some also have a generator to supply electricity. The accommodation in other trekking regions, though, remains traditional and consists mainly of dormitory sleeping arrangements with or without a bed. Prices are usually extremely low (less than Rs 100 per night, occasionally free if you pay for the food).

Most of the hotels in the **Terai** towns and cities will be familiar if you have just arrived from India. Surprisingly, budget accommodation is often comparatively more expensive for the standard offered than in Kathmandu. All Terai towns have a number of budget establishments, while mid-range accommodation is more scarce and there are virtually no luxury hotels.

Air conditioning Only the larger hotels have central air conditioning. Elsewhere a/c rooms are cooled by individual units and occasionally large 'air-coolers'. These can be noisy and unreliable. When they fail to operate, tell the management as it is often possible to get a rapid repair or to transfer to another room where the unit is working. Air conditioners use a lot of electricity so a/c rooms are usually considerably more expensive than those without.

Bathroom & toilet facilities All **AL** and **A** category hotels have bathtubs. Increasingly, hotels in the **B** and **C** (and sometimes even **D**) categories are also installing tubs, a fact that is often advertised with pride. Many hotels now use solar panels for heating water. Despite claims of '24-hour hot water', it is often better to take your shower before supplies run out, that is, early in the morning or evening. On trekking routes, cheaper lodges may have limited water supplies but will usually provide buckets of hot water with which to wash. It is advisable to wear flip-flops in the bathroom to guard against worms, fungi and other infections.

Most tourist hotels (even some of the budget ones) have at least some bathrooms with Western style WC toilets. Squat toilets are the norm throughout South Asia which perhaps explains the curious angle at which WCs are placed in many cheaper hotel bathrooms, where the user either sits within intimate distance of the wall or must rotate by 90° for comfort. Traditionally, the left hand in combination with a jug of water is used in South Asia instead of toilet paper. For this reason the left hand is considered unclean and is not used for eating or handling food. Some people develop an appreciation for this method as environmentally sound, but it is also a principal means by which disease is transmitted if hands and fingernails are not properly cleaned.

Hotel classifications

The following classifications are **not** *star ratings, and individual facilities may vary. Given that hotel rates fluctuate enormously according to season and visitors' bargaining abilities, these categories are not fixed, but instead reflect the published tariff of the best double room in peak season. Even in peak season, however, it may be possible to get reductions – always ask if any is available. Many C and D hotels also have 'suites' for which a substantial premium may be charged, while others may have a range of rooms extending across two or three price categories.*

AL *Rs 7,500+ (about US$110+) – International class luxury hotels, found mostly in Kathmandu. All facilities for business and leisure travellers to the highest international standard.*

A *Rs 4,500-7,500 (about US$70-110) – International class. Central a/c, rooms with attached bathrooms, telephone and TV with video channel, a business centre, multi-cuisine restaurants, bar and all the usual facilities including 24-hour room service, shopping arcade, currency exchange, laundry, travel counter, swimming pool and sometimes other sports such as tennis. They often have a hairdresser, beauty parlour and a health club, and accept credit cards.*

B *Rs 3,250-4,500 (about US$50-70) – Many of the facilities of* **A**, *but often smaller and without business centre, swimming pool and sports facilities and lacking the feeling of international luxury. Usually centrally a/c and bathtubs in bathrooms.*

C *Rs 1,300-3,250 (about US$20-50) – Often the best hotels available in medium and small towns, but not always the best value. Many are new hotels designed to appeal particularly to Indian families and businessmen, as well as to Western visitors. Some bathrooms will have bathtubs, a facility that usually*

commands a small premium; toilets may be of the 'squat' or 'sit down' variety. The entrance and reception areas are usually more 'grand' than D and E price hotels, but the quality of the rooms is often no better despite the higher price. The quality of food can be variable and laundry charges exhorbitant. Comfortable, many individually a/c rooms or air-cooler, sometimes central a/c, restaurant, exchange facilities, travel agent, and accept credit cards.

D *Rs 325-1,300 (about US$5-20) – Many in this category will have a range of rooms, some at the bottom end of the price range, others at the top. Sometimes a/c rooms (or air-cooler) with attached (shower) bathroom, intermittent hot water and usually an overhead fan. Some rooms have TV perhaps often with satellite channels, while most hotels in this category have a TV lounge usually located in or near the reception area. Restaurant, bar facilities and room service normally available. This is the most popular category of accommodation among tourists and most of the established hotels will be familiar with the demands of Western tourists.*

E *Up to Rs 325 (about US$5) – Simple, basic rooms with common bathrooms or attached with 'squat' toilet and metal pipe shower. Hot water, if available, may be restricted to winter. Usually no room fan, although one may be provided on request. Normally family-run with no restaurant, but meals may be served in the room if notice is given. Many do not provide top sheets, pillow cases or towels. Overall hygiene is usually at the lower end of tolerable.*

NB *The following abbreviations are used in descriptions of hotel facilities:* **rm** *= room;* **bath** *= attached bathroom and toilet;* **tub** *= bathtub;* **a/c** *= air conditioning;* **T** *= telephone;* **F** *= fax;* **nr** *= near;* **incl** *= including.*

Essentials

Toilet paper is available in the main tourist centres: most of it is made in China, is expensive, luminously pink and rather coarse. If you are travelling directly to Nepal, you might want to bring a supply with you from home – this will also leave more room in your luggage for souvenirs when you leave. Alternatively, stock up with some better quality varieties in India. Occasionally, a few of the 'supermarkets' in Kathmandu and Pokhara sell toilet paper imported from Europe, but at very inflated prices.

Insects   Mosquitoes can penetrate even the best hotels. In cheaper hotels, you have to be prepared for a wider range of insect life, including flies, cockroaches, spiders, ants and gekhos. The gekho is a pale green and very shy lizard whose suction feet allow it to attach itself to the wall and ceiling. It is found and generally welcomed in most homes, as it feeds on mosquitoes, flies and other small insects. It is capable of remaining quite motionless but ever watchful for minutes at a time before moving cautiously towards its prey in short bursts before capturing it with a darting tongue. It is harmless to humans. Poisonous insects, including scorpions, are extremely rare in towns, but are present in rural areas and have been seen in the Royal Chitwan National Park and Sauraha. Hotel managements are nearly always prepared with insecticide sprays, and will come and spray rooms if asked. It is worth taking your own insect repellent if you are travelling through the Terai especially and to places off the main hotel routes. Remember to shut windows and doors after dusk. Plug-in electrical devices, used with insecticide 'mats', are now widely available (ask for one at the hotel reception), as are mosquito coils which burn slowly to emit a scented smoke. **NB** one coil will usually last for up to six hours, but can be extinguished when placed directly in a breeze (for example from a fan), so it may be best to put it under the bed but away from flammable materials. Many small hotels in the Terai, Kathmandu, Pokhara and Sauraha provide mosquito nets. Dusk and early evening are the worst times for mosquitoes: socks, trousers and long-sleeved shirts are recommended, especially out of doors. At night, fans can be effective in keeping mosquitoes off.

Laundry   Most hotels offer a laundry service which will be done by the dhobi wallah ('laundry man'). Laundry charges are often inexplicably expensive. Many hotel rooms have notices discouraging you from doing your own clothes washing and warning of fines if you do, though these are rarely (if ever) followed up. A popular reason given for this approach is scarcity of water, although concerns for local water supplies are not widely evident in other activities. You can usually get your clothes washed more cheaply by going directly to the laundry man and negotiating the rate with him. There are a few places in Kathmandu and Pokhara which offer a laundry service; again, rates are negotiable.

Room prices   These are extremely flexible. Published tarriffs are rarely adhered to in **C**, **D** and **E** category accommodation. Negotiating the price of your room **before** you check in is expected. Discounts vary according to general demand. When you reach an agreement, make sure that there is a clear understanding as to whether the price includes or excludes tax, and (especially in the Terai) that the price is in Nepali and not Indian rupees.

Getting around

Unless you fly, bus is the only real way to get around Nepal and most visitors to the country will sample at least one bus journey. **Kathmandu** is the largest city and has taxis, buses and auto- and cycle-rickshaws for local transport, although most parts of the city are accessible on foot. Although it is relatively small, **Pokhara** also has taxis and a few buses that link the main tourist areas around the Phewa Tal with the older bazaar area to the north. The principal means of local transport in the **Terai** towns and cities is the cycle rickshaw. Some do have taxis, but these are used mainly for longer distances. Again, most are small enough for all areas to be accessible by foot. In the **mountainous** regions, the traditional and still dominant means of getting around is walking, that is, trekking.

Air

Kathmandu is the hub for most of Nepal's domestic aviation, though there are regional hubs at Nepalgunj (serving the more remote destinations in West Nepal), and Biratnagar (likewise for East Nepal). Royal Nepal Airlines Corporation (RNAC), the national carrier, has a major domestic operation which carried almost 700,000 passengers in 1994. Private carriers operate on important routes and include: Necon Air, Lumbini Airways, Buddha Air and Yeti Airways. The 44 seater 'Avro' is the largest aircraft used on domestic routes. The smallest aircraft in regular operation are the Dornier 228 (18 seats) and the Twin Otter (17 seats). RNAC also has a five seater Pilatus Porter. On some of its longer Avro flights, Necon organizes a raffle in which all passengers participate for a free flight ticket. Newspapers are available on most flights, but curiously they are collected from you when you land.

Officially, you have to check in for domestic flights one hour before departure. Longer is recommended on flights which may be drastically overbooked (for example Lukla and Jumla) and where there is a chance that your reservation will not be honoured. On other routes, you will find people arriving just a few minutes before departure. Security checks involve physical checks of each passenger and their luggage. Regulations are known to be interpreted to the letter at times: on one occasion a cigarette lighter was removed from the passenger's pocket and actually checked in as a separate piece of luggage! Carry any knives or other potential weapons only in your checked baggage. At less busy airports, a claxon is sounded a few minutes before arrival of the inbound aircraft. This is to advise people of the imminent arrival so that goats, buffaloes and other grazing livestock may be removed from the runway in time.

The smaller planes offer probably the most exciting way of flying in Nepal. Navigation along some routes is largely visual, and the approach to many small airstrips is entirely visual: if the pilots can't see the runway, your flight diverts. There are some truly spectacular routings with stunning views of the Himalaya below you, around you and above you. Pilots have been trained in the USA to CPL level and are, of course, familiar with the Himalayan terrain and weather. It is worth considering from

Principal domestic air routes

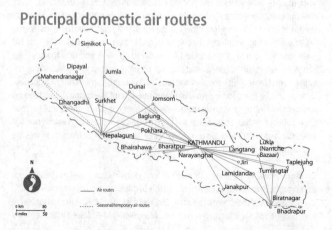

which side of the aircraft you are likely to get the best views and ask for that side on check-in or, (if there is no seat allocation), try to be among the first to board. This applies also to flights to/from the Terai.

For flying buffs, the key is as follows: H = tarmac runway; G = grass runway; Town Name; runway length in feet; runway direction in degrees; elevation above sea level in feet

Many domestic airports have grass runways, sometimes very short and memorable. (STOL = 'Short Take-Off and Landing'). The following is a list of selected airports: (H) **Kathmandu**: 10,000; 200-020; 8,500; (H) **Bhairahawa**: 5,000; 100-280; 358; (G) **Bharatpur**: 3,800; 320-140; 600; (H) **Biratnagar**: 5,000; 090-270; (G) **Jiri**: 1,200; 320-140; 6,000; (G) **Jomsom**: 2,000; 060-240; 8,800; (G) **Jumla**: 1,600; – ; 8,500; (G) **Lukla**: 1,600; 070-250; (G) **Mahendranagar**: 2,900; 170-350; (H) **Nepalgunj**: 5,000; 260-080; 540; (G) **Phaplu**: 2,230; 020-200; 7,910; (H) **Pokhara**: 4,700; 030-210; 8,000; (G) **Simikot**: 1,800; 100-280; 9,246; (G) **Syangboche**: 1,330; 130-310; 12,297; (G) **Taplejung**: 1,950; 070-250; 7,800.

Helicopters Helicopters are adaptable and can fly to many places unreachable by fixed wing aircraft. They are used for mountain rescue as well as for cargo and passenger flights. In addition to RNAC, there are a number of private helicopter operators including Asian Airlines, Dynasty Aviation, and Himalayan Helicopters. Most use the large Russian MI-17, though you will also find smaller American made Bell and the French Ecureil helicopters. Some operate 'mountain flights' from Kathmandu and Pokhara and others offer a morning visit to Everest Base Camp and elsewhere. Most work mainly on a charter basis. Private charters can be arranged quite rapidly. Reckon on no less than US$1,000 per block hour for the MI-17. Ask around at **good** travel agents, for example on Durbar Marg in Kathmandu, or contact the company directly (see the Kathmandu Transport section).

Road

Bus Bus travel is extremely cheap by Western standards, and buses link Kathmandu with most parts of the country. As with domestic aviation, Kathmandu is the main centre of operations while Nepalgunj and Biratnagar serve as important regional hubs. A long bus journey invariably demands considerable physical and mental **endurance** especially if you are tall, as all buses are built for a smaller physique than that of the typical European or North American. There is compensation, however, in the many areas of stupendous natural beauty through which you travel.

Officially, **tourist buses** serve only three destinations from Kathmandu: Pokhara, Chitwan and Nagarkot. Departures are at around 0700 for Pokhara and Chitwan. (Many private buses also proclaim themselves as 'tourist bus', a claim often further embellished with the words 'Deluxe' or 'Luxury' which may seem entirely inappropriate until you see the non-deluxe alternative.) Official 'tourist buses' are government operated, are generally in relatively roadworthy condition and are supposed to limit passenger numbers to the number of seats. **Private buses** may be full to overflowing, with room for baggage (and more passengers) on the roof. **NB** Make sure that your luggage is locked. They will usually not depart until the bus is full and will make regular stops en route to pick up more passengers. Government run **Sajha** buses (sometimes known as 'the blue bus') use fairly comfortable old Japanese vehicles and have a good network of routes throughout the country. They have no roof racks for luggage and, again, the number of passengers is not supposed to exceed the number of seats. In peak season, it is best to **book** a couple of days in advance, but when demand is slack, you can usually wait until the previous day. Many bus **fares** are negotiable when booking through a travel agent or your hotel.

Don't sit on the metal casing beside the gear stick, as it gets very hot

Comfort However positive your outlook, long distance bus travel in Nepal is not comfortable. Seats often recline and are usually padded, but a couple of hours into the journey will reveal the extent of padding. Leg-room is limited by the (reclining) seat in front and the invariable baggage in the aisle. Many Nepalis are blessed with the ability to fall asleep in the most awkward positions, so you may end up with an additional head on your shoulder or leg on your knee. The poor condition of many roads, combined with the brinkmanship of many drivers, can make for an unpredictable journey. Remember, though, that Nepali bus drivers have an excellent knowledge of the roads and are highly experienced in driving in those conditions. Bring an inflatable sitting or head **cushion**.

Seating arrangements are 2x2 (that is, 2 seats either side of the aisle), 2x3 or 3x3. If there is a choice, ask for a 2x2 bus. You can request your seat at the time of booking. On many buses, those with the most legroom are in the front row behind the driver and immediately behind the door. Those best avoided include the back row which often does not recline, those above wheels and those in the very front next to the driver.

Most buses have audio systems which, when operational, are wont to play Hindi film **music** very loudly. A few also have videos, so you get to see the film as well. You may think about bringing some ear plugs for when you want to rest.

Day bus vs night bus Most medium to long journeys (that is from around six hours to 15 hours), offer the choice of travelling by day or night. The advantages of going by day are that you can see the often spectacular countryside through which you are travelling and that you won't suffer from a terrestrial version of jet-lag. Journey times are often longer by day, however, as there is more traffic on the road and buses stop frequently to pick up more passengers and their cargo (which may include livestock). There are fewer such stops on a night bus and, even if you can't sleep, you will probably be able to doze. If you wonder why music suddenly blasts through your darkened cabin, it is probably to help the driver stay awake. Some of the more precipitous routes also become more adventurous by night. Most journeys over 15 hours leave from early afternoon to late evening.

Nepal has a poor surface transport infrastructure. There are a handful of **highways** with a combined length of 2,032 km linking the main towns and cities. These are not highways in the Western sense, but are mainly single lane in each direction, occasionally just single lane and, along certain stretches of the Mahendra Highway in the far southwest, no discernible lane at all.

The Arniko Highway This follows an ancient trade route and runs from Kathmandu leaving the Valley through Dhulikhel before veering north to **Kodari** and the Tibetan border. This is the only official land crossing point for foreigners between Nepal and Tibet. Beyond Bansbari, regular landslides cause major delays during the monsoon.

Highways

Nepal's Highways

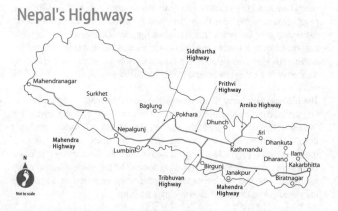

Essentials

The Mahendra Highway This is Nepal's most important road and runs the length of the Terai from Mahendranagar in the west to Kakarbhitta in the east. A number of major junction towns have developed out of erstwhile villages along the highway: Butwal (at the junction of the Siddhartha Highway, with Sunauli and Lumbini to the south and Tansen and Pokhara to the north), Narayanghat (with a direct and much used link to Mugling on the Prithvi Highway), Hetauda (at the junction with the Tribhuvan Highway, with Birgunj to the south and the Prithvi Highway and nearby Kathmandu to the north), and Itahari (with Biratnagar to the south and Dharan and Dhankuta to the north).

Most of the Mahendra Highway is in reasonable condition, although a fairly long stretch between Chisapani and Mahendranagar follows an unmade zigzagging route through intermittent forest. In complete contrast, perhaps its most attractive stretch is immediately east of Chisapani, as it follows a smooth, well surfaced section through the Royal Bardia National Park where you can see deer, wild peacocks and other animals foraging along the roadside and in the forest margins. For much of its long course, the highway runs through or beside the Terai's ever diminishing forested belt, which consists largely of sal (*Shorea robusta*) trees. Now and then, monkeys make an appearance from the forest. The highway runs north of the Chitwan National Park, through Narayanghat to Hetauda where it joins the Tribhuvan Highway. The two roads combine briefly before the Mahendra Highway continues its eastward course from Amlekhgunj, by the entrance to the Parsa Wildlife Reserve. It crosses the mighty Sapt Kosi River west of Biratnagar before heading to Kakarbhitta and leaving Nepal for Siliguri.

The Prithvi Highway Probably the road most travelled by visitors to Nepal, the Prithvi Highway links Kathmandu with Pokhara. It is in fair condition for most of the way, though a stretch east of Pokhara is in poor condition. Soon after leaving the Kathmandu Valley, the road meets the Tribhuvan Highway at Naubise. It follows the Trisuli River as far as the unattractive junction town of Mugling, midway between Kathmandu and Pokhara. Thereafter, it continues along the Marshyangdi River before that river turns north to its source high in the Annapurnas. The scenery along most of the Prithvi Highway is quite superb, with picturesque river valleys and hillsides, and snow capped mountains forming a spectacular horizon.

The Siddhartha Highway This road links Pokhara with Sunauli (Belahiya) on the Indian border, and is a highway in both senses of the word. But for the short stretch between Sunauli (Belahiya) and Butwal, the road is in dreadful condition. It snakes its way, often precariously, through the Mahabharat and Churia Hills. At times the road is no more than a single lane carved into the hillside, with numerous blind corners. Overtaking along these stretches should be impossible, but is somehow accomplished by some impatient drivers. Others have found, to their ultimate cost, that they shouldn't really have tried. There are, nevertheless, some fine views. The highway passes Tansen, an attractive hill town, before descending to the Terai which it meets at Butwal. From here, it is an easy 40-minute ride to the border. Nearby is Lumbini, the birthplace of the Buddha. Most buses between the border and Pokhara take the much longer (and safer) route via Narayanghat and Mugling; the journey time is the same as along the Siddhartha Highway.

The Tribhuvan Highway This was the first highway to be constructed in Nepal, and was the first direct motorable route from India to Kathmandu. It is also known as the Tribhuvan Rajmarg, or simply as the Rajmarg ('Royal Way'). It is narrow, constantly undulating and shows its age. Because there are few buses that take this route (prefering instead to go via Mugling and Narayanghat), it is the highway that fewest Western visitors will experience. It is known, however, for the village of Daman which has probably the finest panoramic view of the Himalaya extending (on a good day) from Dhaulagiri in the west to Everest in the east.

Car rental usually comes with a driver and is widely available in Kathmandu and, not so widely, in Pokhara and most Terai towns. You can hire anything from the good Indian made Maruti cars and vans to Japanese cars, Land Rovers and four wheel drive jeeps. Hire can be done through your hotel or a good travel agent; car rental companies are fairly well advertised in Kathmandu.

Note that formally renting a vehicle can be relatively expensive, though rates are usually quite negotiable. It often works out significantly cheaper to 'charter' a taxi for the day. You should agree on the route and the length of time you want it for at the time of negotiating the price. Check also whether the taxi is permitted to go where you want to: some are restricted to certain parts of the Kathmandu Valley, for example, and are liable for fines/bribes at any of the police checkpoints beyond their permitted area.

Other land transport

There are many **cycle** hire places in Kathmandu and Pokhara where you can hire anything from a good mountain bike to heavy, old, rusty specimens. Cycling is undoubtedly one of the best ways of exploring the city and countryside. Most places within the **Kathmandu Valley** are accessible by bike (though there are a few steep climbs and descents) and a day trip allows you to build up a healthy appetite for dinner in one of the capital's many excellent restaurants. From **Pokhara**, there are some good routes into the surrounding village areas and to the valley's other lakes.

Cycle hire is less available in the **Terai**, though you will often be able to find a basic bike to hire privately through your hotel. The Terai countryside is mainly a combination of forest and wide open farmland scattered liberally with traditional villages. There is a wide range of exotic birdlife. The land is largely flat, so cycling is easy and is by far the best way to get an insight into the traditional life which characterizes the important rural areas of the Gangetic Plains. **NB** Check the condition of the bike (for example gears, brakes, tyres, pump) before you take it. Lock the bike securely when you leave it anywhere.

Kathmandu and Pokhara are the only places where you can find a selection of **motorcycle** hire places. Elsewhere, you may be able to hire a motorbike privately. You will have to show, and carry with you, your international driving licence. You will probably also have to leave a substantial deposit (get a receipt). Make sure that your travel **insurance** covers you for motorcycling; it may be listed under 'dangerous activities' and therefore excluded.

There are two types of rickshaw: the 3-wheeler 'auto-rickshaw' (like the Thai tuktuk), and the cycle rickshaw. The **auto-rickshaw** is found in Kathmandu, Pokhara and all the major Terai towns. These seat up to five passengers (or more). You can hire them as you would a taxi. Although most have meters, the drivers are often unwilling to use them and you usually have to bargain the price **before** setting off. Fares are around half those of a taxi and they are a good (though very polluting) way of getting around town, often squeezing through impossibly narrow gaps in the traffic. Some auto-rickshaws run on specific routes like a local bus. They usually won't leave before the vehicle is at least full and fares are fixed at just a few rupees.

The **cycle-rickshaw** is a curious though useful contraption for travelling short distances. The tricycle seats two (small to medium sized) people. Although not especially comfortable, they are a good way to tour a town or city. A 2-hour sightseeing ride should cost around Rs 100, while local rates are about Rs 4 per km.

Taxis are widely available in Kathmandu and Pokhara, less so elsewhere. Most are comfortable Indian Maruti or Japanese cars. Narayanghat has Nepal's only fleet of Indian Ambassador cars (similar to the old Morris Oxford). All licensed taxis should use their meter (always set in Nepali, not Indian, rupees), though you will often be faced

Vehicle hire

Cycles & motorcycles

When embarking on a long bike trip, make sure that you have enough water with you, as safe drinking water is not widely available. Water from deep tube wells should be reasonably safe to drink, though there is a risk of contamination from dirty pipes

Rickshaws

Taxis

Essentials

with having to negotiate a rate: always do this **before** departure. If you have a rough idea of what the fare should be, but less of an idea of the exact route, it may be better to settle the price before leaving so that you don't end up on an unscheduled sightseeing tour and an excessively high meter fare. Sometimes, meter calibration lags behind the officially set tariff in which case a percentage surcharge will be payable – check. If you begin or end your journey in one of the major tourist parts of town (for example Kathmandu's Thamel and Pokhara's Lakeside), some drivers may demand an additional surcharge: don't pay.

Tongas   Only **Nepalgunj**, in Southwest Nepal, has tongas. These are horse-drawn carts and they run on fixed routes, including to and from the border. Sadly, tonga travel is not quite as romantic as it sounds: it is slow and, because of the number of people crammed onto the platform, really quite uncomfortable.

Travellers with special needs

Disabled   Nepal is a difficult, though certainly not impossible, country for disabled travellers.
travellers   Travelling alone is not recommended if you have walking difficulties, as there are probably just too many uneven surfaces and slopes to climb and descend. With an able-bodied companion, however, there is much that Nepal has to offer and, depending on the disability, there is no reason why you can't enjoy several activities such as elephant rides through the jungle or sightseeing trips by bus or car. Daily 'mountain flights' from both Kathmandu and Pokhara offer superb aerial tours of the Himalaya.

Basic wheelchairs are available on arrival at Kathmandu airport, which also has a lift. The airports at Pokhara, Bharatpur (for Chitwan) and Nepalgunj (for Bardia) are all ground level. Boarding any of the smaller aircraft may pose a few problems, but there will always be people willing to help. In Nepal, you will sometimes see disabled people being carried, perhaps on someone else's back. Although this may seem somewhat elementary, it is actually quite practical in many instances and can help overcome several potential difficulties. When flying, request the pilot to radio ahead so that a wheelchair or other assistance will be ready on arrival. You can also ask your hotel to send a vehicle to meet you: most will readily do so.

Generally, facilities for the disabled are few and far between, so bring your own wheelchair and other walking aids and equipment. Also bring any medication you require. Hotels are not particularly well geared up for disabled guests, though many of Kathmandu's better hotels have lifts and ramps. This is less so in Pokhara, but there are plenty of decent hotels with accessible ground floor rooms. At Chitwan, only the Royal Hotel (in Sauraha) has ramps, together with experience of the needs of disabled visitors. At Bardia, the helpful and professionally run Tiger Tops has all ground level accommodation in comfortable rooms with attached bathroom and a ground level restaurant and bar. They also have jeep tours through the jungle. To visit Lumbini, two possible bases are the Lumbini Hokke Hotel at Lumbini itself and the Nirvana Hotel at nearby Bhairahawa. It is always advisable to book your hotel in advance and ask specifically about access to the room, the bathroom, the restaurant and all other parts.

Keeping in touch

Nepali is the official national language of Nepal. In addition, there are over 30 other languages spoken as mother-tongue in different parts of the country and many more regional dialects. English is spoken in Kathmandu, Pokhara and Chitwan but is little used or understood elsewhere. In the Terai's main towns and cities and also along the major trekking routes, you will find people with a competent command of tourist English.

According to the 1991 census, Nepali is spoken as a mother tongue by more than nine million people and is followed in importance by Maithili (over 2 million), Bhojpuri (1.4 million) and Tharu (1 million). Other important regional languages include Abadhi (375,000), Gurung (230,000), Hindi (170,000), Limbu (250,000), Magar (430,000), Newari (700,000), Rai/Kiranti (440,000), Sherpa (120,000), Tamang (900,000) and Urdu (200,000). Minor languages recorded in the census include Byanshi (1,300) and Kumhale (1,400).

Origins of the Nepali Language Like the other languages of the northern regions of the Indian subcontinent, Nepali is one of the **Indo-Aryan** family of languages brought from Central Asia by the Aryans from around 1500 BC. In 1787, Sir William **Jones** (1746-94), a judge in Calcutta's Supreme Court as well as an eminent Orientalist and founder of India's Asiatic Society, discovered that these languages were etymologically related to European languages of Latin and Greek descent.

The original Old Indo-Aryan language gave rise to **Sanskrit**, one of the great languages of classical civilization from which Nepali derives and which remained dominant in the region, as a written if not a spoken medium, until the end of the 1st millennium AD. Sanskrit was first codified by the scholar **Panini** (c 7th to 5th century BC) in his modestly named opus *Astadhyayi* ('Eight Lectures'), the first major grammar of Sanskrit. Although it consists of a highly concentrated collection of 4,000 aphoristic observations, it is still considered by many scholars to be the finest grammar ever produced. The early dominance of Sanskrit, however, served to veil the development of both Nepali and other regional languages, so records are indistinct.

New forms of Indo-Aryan began to emerge from the 11th century, the most direct ancestors of today's languages. Modern Nepali is greatly influenced by Hindi. In common with Hindi (and Marathi), Nepali uses the **Devanagari script** ('the script of the city of the gods', sometimes just known as 'Nagari') which derived from the Brahmi script of ancient India. The Prakrit used by Emperor Ashoka in his Lumbini inscriptions is in the Brahmi script.

Nepal's postal system is slow, particularly if you are posting or receiving air mail outside Kathmandu. To Europe, North America, Australia and New Zealand, air mail letters take often around two weeks to arrive, while those to or from India can take even longer.

Post Offices (open daily except Saturday) sell stamps. When you post your letter, ask to see it being franked; this avoids any later temptation to remove and re-sell the stamp. In Kathmandu and Pokhara you will find it considerably easier to use one of the many private posting agencies which also sell stamps. This service is frequently offered by phone/fax booths. A nominal fee is charged, or none at all if you've just made a long phone call abroad.

There are two main ways to send **parcels**. You can post them at the **Foreign Post Office** (in GPOs; next to the GPO in Kathmandu). This can be a tiresome chore, as you have to leave the parcel open for inspection, fill out a customs declaration form, pay tax where applicable, have the parcel stitched up and sealed with wax, then weighed before you pay. By international standards, rates are extremely reasonable whether you send it by air or sea. Alternatively, you can spend more and send it through a reputable **private** freight company or **courier**. There are plenty of these in Kathmandu and a couple in Pokhara.

Language

See under Footnotes, page 549 for pronounciation guide, words and phrases and a basic dictionary

A basic vocabulary appears on the inside back cover (under the flap)

Essentials

Postal services

You can receive mail at the **poste restante** in Kathmandu and Pokhara GPOs. Letters should be addressed (with your surname in **capital letters** and **underlined**) to the Poste Restante, GPO, Kathmandu/Pokhara. You must show your passport for identification when collecting mail. Aerogrammes can arrive more quickly than envelopes. It is a good idea for envelopes to be additionally sealed with sellotape.

If you are an **American Express** cardholder, or have their travellers' cheques, you can make use of their private poste restante service. The office is just off Durbar Marg (American Express (Poste Restante), Jamal, Kathmandu).

Telephone, Fax & Email

See inside front cover (under flap) for telephone dialling codes

Phoning or faxing from Nepal is very expensive. Calls are charged by the **minute**, not second, so you must be careful when dialling. A wrong number or answerphone is charged at one minute. In 1999, the rate for a call to Europe and North America was around Rs 180 per minute; and Rs 40 per minute to India. It is a little cheaper if you phone from the GPO in Kathmandu, but you will be charged a minimum of three minutes. Rates are generally more expensive outside Kathmandu. Hotel rates are often astronomical.

Calling **India** can be difficult, especially from remote areas or indeed from anywhere that is far from Kathmandu. It often takes a long time to get a line which may then be very poor. If you have to get an urgent message to India from outside the Kathmandu Valley or Pokhara, it is usually quicker to phone someone in Europe/America and ask them to relay the message for you.

Most ISD/IDD/STD (International Standard Dialling/International Direct Dialling/Standard Trunk Dialling) booths will allow you to receive calls ('**call-back**') at around Rs 5-10 per minute.

There are numerous **fax** bureaux in major towns throughout Nepal. Charges are the same as phoning. Receiving a fax generally costs between Rs 10-20.

There is an ever increasing number of **Email** operators in Kathmandu and Pokhara. In 1999, the cost of internet/email time was around Rs 5 per minute.

Internet websites: Kathmandu and Pokhara both now have a good range of 'cyber cafés' where you can surf the net at around Rs5 per minute. There are an increasing number of websites which have information about Nepal, including Nepali newspapers and travel information. The following offers a brief selection. Try also searching for key words.

www.info-nepal.com; www.south-asia.com/nepal; www.catmando.com; www.himkooh.com; www.nepalnews.com

Media   **Cinemas** Every town has its cinema and every cinema shows Bombay produced Hindi films. Commonly known as 'Bollywood movies', these constitute the mainstay of celluloid entertainment throughout South Asia. You can often follow the action and the story without knowledge of Hindi. Hollywood and other Western films are rarely shown in cinemas, but several Kathmandu restaurants show videos.

Newspapers and magazines Nepal has a large number of national, regional and local Nepali language **newspapers** and three national English language dailies: *The Rising Nepal* (government run), *The Kathmandu Post* and *The Everest Herald*. All are published in Kathmandu and are available in Pokhara and other towns near Kathmandu later the same day. In the major Terai towns, they arrive the following day, and two or more days later elsewhere. All run to around eight pages, including local, national and international news as well as sport. *The Kathmandu Post* carries a daily cartoon (*O Tempora! O Mores!*) with witty and perceptive portrayals of Nepali political life. The weekly Independent offers analysis of political and other current affairs.

Formerly concerned only with Nepal, the excellent *Himal* **magazine** now covers the entire South Asian region. It carries thoughtful articles on various aspects of life

Missed Nomers

Problems with spelling are something that most people are familiar with at some time or another. Generations of travellers to the countries of S Asia, however, will have encountered valiant attempts at writing something in English, perhaps the author's second or even third language, where phonetic spelling, idiomatic idiosyncrasies or other innocent errors have resulted in a complete change of intended meaning. The following is a brief selection of some of Nepal's finest and is included in full appreciation of this observer's own linguistic inadequacies.

Hotels
A Terai town: Luxury Felicity Available To All Guests
Paknajol, Kathmandu: Baby sitars on request
Lakeside, Pokhara: Children stay free if they have parents
Lakeside, Pokhara; Homely Atmosphere and Quit
Sauraha: A fiendly place to stay
Nepalgunj: Bar and room shervish
Bhairahawa: Check Up Time: 12 noon
Lumbini: All praying facilities for interested Buddhists

Restaurants
Lakeside, Pokhara: We take care of your portion
Breakfast
Lakeside, Pokhara: Bold Egg
Thamel, Kathmandu: Swish Breakfast
Entrées
Thamel, Kathmandu: Boiled Children
Bhagawan Bahal, Kathmandu: Pork: Roast Lion
Thamel, Kathmandu: Chicken stuffed with rice, plum, garlic and medicine

Janakpur, and elsewhere: Chicken Lollipop
Chhetrapati, Kathmandu: Vegetable Pagoda
Desserts
Thamel, Kathmandu: Banana c/turd (and Other Tempting Desserts)
Drinks
Chhetrapati, Kathmandu: Milk, every temperature
Thamel, Kathmandu: Bloody Merry
Thamel, Kathmandu: We serve the finest Tibetan cousin

Advertisements
Lainch: Amulya – for testier tea
A free travel magazine: Deutsch sprechen? Kein not problem Italiano? Firest try, then speak to ***** Trekking Ltd
A Terai town: Doctor's Chambers: Specialist in sexual diseases. (ISD/STD facilities available)
A tour brochure: Departure for Kathmandu by helicopter and drop at hotel

---

across the subcontinent, including topics on aid and development, the environment, current affairs, political analysis, art and culture, and book reviews. It is published every two months and is highly recommended. *Everest Voice* is the quarterly publication of Everest Peace Corps International. Its focus is very much on matters relating to conservation of the Himalayan ecology and environment. There are several free magazines aimed at tourists which carry interesting features related to travel in Nepal as well as lists of important phone numbers and up-to-date flight schedules. One of the best of these is *Travellers' Nepal* which is available in good travel agents and hotels; you may be handed a copy as you emerge from customs at Kathmandu airport.

Foreign newspapers include the *International Herald Tribune*, widely available in Kathmandu and also from a couple of shops along Lakeside, Pokhara. It is published in Singapore, arriving in Kathmandu the next day. *The Times of India* is the most obtainable Indian paper, but can normally be found in Kathmandu only.

Radio Radio Nepal is the government-run national radio station, but because of the mountainous terrain it can reach less than two thirds of the population. Interestingly, a report published by the Namedia Foundation Research and Publication Centre in Delhi in 1986 showed that, on available figures, Nepal had the lowest ratio of people per radio set in South Asia and the highest for TV sets.

Travellers in Nepal can receive the BBC World Service and other international broadcasting services with which to keep updated on international developments. Most frequencies are on short wave and the quality of reception is variable. You can often get the same transmission on different frequencies. If you are experiencing difficulty in reception, try making an extended aerial of copper wire or positioning your radio differently. Short wave reception is often better on higher frequencies (lower metre bands) during the day and on lower frequencies (higher metre bands) after dark.

Short wave radio BBC World Service The BBC broadcasts World News at 45 minutes past every hour (Nepal time) and sports news at 30 minutes past the hour occasionally through the day. Try one or more of the following frequencies between 0545 and 0015 (Nepal time): 5965 kHz (49m), 5975 kHz (49m), 9510 kHz (31m), 9740 kHz (31m), **11750 kHz (25m)**, 11955 kHz (25m), **15310 kHz (19m)**, 17785 kHz (16m) and 17790 kHz (16m).

If you are in North Nepal, additional frequencies for China include: 15280 kHz (19m), 15360 kHz (19m), 17760 kHz (16m) and 21660 kHz (13m).

If you are in West Nepal, additional frequencies for West India and Pakistan include: 9410 kHz (31m) and 9605 kHz (31m).

If you are in Southeast Nepal, additional frequencies for Southeast Asia include: 6195 kHz (49m), 7110 kHz (41m), 11765 kHz (25m) and 15360 kHz (19m).

Deutsche Welle The German Deutsche Welle broadcasts to South Asia in German at various times of the day. Try any of the following frequencies (KHz): 7315 9655, 9835, 11795, 12055, 13780, 15725, 17845 and 21560.

Voice of America Transmits to South Asia from 0645 to 0845, and from 1945 to 2345 daily (Nepal time) on the following frequencies (KHz): 6110, 6160, 7115, 7205, 7215, 9635, 9645, 9700, 9760, 9770, 11705, 11725, 11820, 15170, 15205, 15250, 15255, 15395, 15425, 17740, and 17820.

Television Nepal has one national TV station, **Nepal Television**, which began broadcasting only in 1985 and has the News in English at 2215 daily. In many areas as far north as Kathmandu and Pokhara, you can usually receive the Indian national **Doordashan** channels. Satellite TV has made a big impact in Kathmandu, Pokhara and Terai towns. There are many channels showing **Hindi movies**. Other international channels widely available include those of the **Star TV** network (the Asian arm of Europe's Sky TV), for example Star Plus, Star Movies and Star Sports, along with the American **ESPN** sports channel and the **CNN** news channel. You can also get **BBC World**, the 24-hour TV version of radio's World Service, with regular quality and in-depth news coverage and occasional documentaries and lifestyle programmes. Both ESPN and Star Sports have good coverage of international **cricket**, while ESPN broadcasts English Premiership **football**. You can find listings in the English language daily newspapers.

Food and drink

Food
A food glossary appears on page 552

There are several regional variations in Nepali food, but one dish more than any other has come to characterize the country's cuisine: **dal-bhad-tarkari**. *Dal* is a lentil sauce that is eaten with the *bhad* (rice). *Tarkari* is a generic name for (vegetable) curry and can be prepared in different ways according to seasonal availability of vegetables and local preferences. It is often served with *achar* (pickles) which do much to enhance its

Recipe: Dal-Bhad-Tarkari

Ingredients
Rice, cauliflower*
Cabbage*
Tomatoes
Onions
Potatoes
Beans*
Chilli
Garlic
Ginger
Garam Masala (Curry powder)
Salt
Black Pepper
Dal (Lentils)
(*or other seasonal vegetables)

Method
1 Start cooking the rice. Remove when cooked.
Tarkari
2 Cut the potatoes into small pieces and fry in a little oil for a few minutes.
3 Chop the cauliflower, cabbage, tomatoes, onions, beans, garlic, chilli and ginger and add to the potatoes along with the garam masala and salt and pepper to taste.
4 Fry for 10 minutes, then add some hot water and simmer for a further 20-25 minutes.
Dal
5 Bring water to the boil and add the lentils together with a little garlic, ginger, chilli, salt and black pepper according to taste.
6 Simmer for 30 minutes, stirring occasionally.

In theory, the rice, dal and tarkari should be ready at about the same time.

Serving
To serve, either pour the dal over the rice and place the tarkari at its side, or serve thali style. Alternatively, erect a sign advertising Typical Nepali Food.

overall appeal. Meat curry is also popular, but as meat is expensive many households only have it on special occasions. Tibetan influences increase the further north you go, although perennial favourites, such as the momo (a stuffed dumpling, fried or steamed), are widely available in the lower regions too. In the trekking regions, you are likely to encounter little other than Nepali food, which some people may find slightly monotonous. The choice is greater in the Terai where you will also find many excellent Indian dishes.

Nepalis traditionally eat with the (right) hand only. Cutlery is not used, though it is usually found in hotels and restaurants that cater to Western tourists – ask whether it is available. Typically, you will often be given a plate of dal-bhad-tarkari (along with pickles), with refills periodically served (perhaps from a bucket with a ladle), until you have eaten enough. There are several restaurants in Kathmandu and Pokhara serving 'Typical Nepali Food'. This generally consists of rice, dal and two or more types of tarkari (with or without meat), sometimes accompanied by *rakshi* (local alcoholic brew), and followed by a Nepali sweet and tea. Be aware that most of these places cater specifically to tourists. Kathmandu has two exceptional Nepali restaurants (*Thamel House* in Thamel and *Bhanccha Ghar* in Kamaladi), that stand head and shoulders above most others and where it is well worth spending a little more to savour the best in Nepali cooking.

Kathmandu is an eater's paradise with restaurants offering generally excellent interpretations of Western, along with Indian and Tibetan, dishes at reasonable prices. If you have been travelling for any length of time through the Terai, this will come as a pleasant change, though restaurants are often more expensive than in Indian towns and cities. Inevitably, interpretations do occasionally misfire, as one visitor discovered when his 'potato salad' turned out to be a cold sliced boiled potato!

The city has acquired a justifiable reputation for its steaks: served with garlic sauce, with cheese, with rum, brandy, mushroom, pepper, onion or any other variety of sauce, or the plain fillet steak, sometimes called *mignon*, *classic* or *a la francaise*. Steaks are sometimes buffalo meat (*buff*), because of the sacredness of the cow to Hindus. Often in Kathmandu, however, it will be genuine beef that is served, specially imported from India. One steak restaurant is said to import up to 40,000 kg of beef per year from Calcutta for its two branches. A luxury hotel in Kathmandu, meanwhile, goes as far as importing its sirloin from the USA, lamb from New Zealand and salmon from Norway, while a Korean restaurant brings ginseng from Seoul to impart genuine flavour to its stuffed chicken.

| Nepali eating customs | A cup of tea usually starts the morning, followed by a substantial brunch late in the morning. If you are invited to a meal, socializing takes place before dinner (which may be served late by Western standards), and guests often leave soon after finishing the meal. Remember that only the right hand should be used for eating, handling and passing food or drink. You may be offered paan, a typically South Asian mixture of chopped betel nuts and sweet masalas wrapped in a betel leaf, after the meal. This is often taken as an aid to digestion. It is customary in many households for women to remain in the background during the meal and to eat only after the men have finished their food. The kitchen in a Hindu home is sacred, so non-Hindus should ask before entering. |

Drink   **Alcoholic drinks**   International brands of **beer** made in Nepal include San Miguel, Guinness, Carlsberg and Tuborg. Nepali beers include Star, Tiger and Iceberg. If you have just arrived from India, you will notice the contrast in attitudes towards consumption of alcohol: while there is very little advertising of brands of beer in India, you can turn few corners in Nepal's towns and cities without being confronted with at least one huge hoarding or painted wall.

Nepal also produces **spirits**, including rum, whiskey, vodka and gin. They are inexpensive, but most are really awful and are best consumed with a (large quantity of) mixer. You can also get Indian spirits, some of which have improved greatly in recent years.

Himalayan country liquor includes **chang**, a type of beer usually made of barley or millet. In the middle and lower reaches of the country, **rakshi** is more common. This rice-based concoction can be highly intoxicating, though there are many varieties. It is often served at wedding receptions or other special occasions in some communities. **Arak** is produced from potatoes and **tongba** is the Tibetan drink. Though they are interesting to sample, the taste can leave much to be acquired.

The role of alcoholic drinks varies between different communities. In the higher, colder regions of the Himalaya, it is often as normal for women to drink as it is for men, while in some Terai communities alcohol is rarely consumed by men and never by women. The ill-effects of alcohol are widely recognized by women in particular throughout Nepal and experience has led some to regard it as the 'demon drink'. A women's pressure group has succeeded in prohibiting the sale of alcohol in the Kanchanpur district of Southwest Nepal (the Mahendranagar area), though this has led to an increase in the clandestine production of rakshi and to the 'smuggling' of alcohol from neighbouring districts.

Soft drinks   There are several international brands of soft drink available in Nepal, usually in 250 millilitre and one litre bottles. Canned drinks are making a gradual entrance, but are more expensive than the bottles. Drinking straws are rarely available from shops and stalls. It is advisable to clean the rim of the bottle before drinking.

You may see green coconuts being sold on the street. The **coconut water** is tasty and refreshing and is said to be good if you have a stomach upset. **Lassi** is another popular and refreshing drink made of yoghurt (curd) with crushed ice and sugar. You can also get fruit lassis, salt lassi and, in some places, *bhang lassi*.

Tap water is not filtered, so should not be used as drinking water. In the cities it may have been treated, but this does not necessarily eliminate harmful bacteria. People generally experience few ill effects from using tap water for brushing teeth. In most restaurants, you will automatically be given a glass of water. Ask whether it has been filtered and/or boiled. In larger hotels and restaurants, the drinking water you are served will usually have been safely purified, but in smaller places you should be more wary and perhaps avoid the water until you are sure that it is safe to drink. Similarly, ask whether the ice has been made of boiled or safely filtered water. Bottled mineral water is widely available in the main tourist areas and elsewhere. Generally, this is perfectly safe to drink, but it has been known to contain more than just minerals. **Water & ice**

If you're trekking or heading off the beaten trail, bring some iodine or other water purifying tablets with you. Restaurants in Kathmandu and Pokhara increasingly advertise that their vegetables have been soaked in iodine water. The worst that most people suffer in Nepal is a minor stomach upset, so be cautious but don't let it stop you from enjoying your food and drink.

Shopping

Nepal is a shoppers' paradise. Remember to bargain for everything (see below). Increasingly, shops in the main tourist areas are accepting credit cards, though it's always better to carry cash as well. Kathmandu's **New Road** area has a number of Western style stores specializing in cosmetics, electronic goods and clothing at prices that compare favourably with Europe. This area is particularly popular with Indian visitors. **Books** are generally cheaper than in the West, but significantly more expensive than in India. Kathmandu and, to a lesser extent, Pokhara are the only places with a good range of bookshops. Most bookshops will buy back books at up to half their previous sale price. There is also a wide selection of **handicrafts** which make attractive souvenirs. **NB**: The bronze and metal statues sold as antiques are mostly mass produced and artificially 'aged'. This will be obvious from the price. Antiques can not be taken out of the country and Nepali **Customs are strict on departure**. You need a **permit** from the Department of Archaeology if you want to take out any article which appears to be over 100 years old.

Bargaining is the norm and is expected during the course of most purchases. There are 'fixed price' shops in Kathmandu, Pokhara and elsewhere (for example supermarkets and the more expensive stores on and around Kathmandu's New Road). Some other establishments have signs indicating 'fixed price', which often means that the prices are in fact ripe for negotiation. In most cases, the bottom price that will be accepted from Westerners for a particular item is significantly higher than that for Nepalis, while there is no upper limit to what will be accepted. **Bargaining**

Before making a purchase – especially an expensive one – it is worth doing a little research on approximately what you should be paying. Also shop around, as similar items may be sold in other shops and locations at vastly differing prices.

You can get good cotton clothing (ready-made or tailored) in Kathmandu, Pokhara and elsewhere, often at very reasonable prices. Sweaters, other warm clothing and trekking attire are also popular and easily available. **Clothing** *Check the stitching before you buy*

These are produced by wooden blocks on locally produced paper. The subjects are usually Nepali, Tibetan or Chinese deities. **Rice paper prints**

(*Paubha* in Newari) This is the traditional Tibetan painting of religious and ceremonial subjects, often of gods, deities, mandalas and the wheel of life. The central **Thangka**

Essentials

Shopping – Nepalese style

It is always worthwhile establishing a good rapport with the shopkeeper. If you have your eye on an item in a shop, you might start by wandering in somewhat disinterestedly. Don't touch the item and avoid looking at it directly, as over-enthusiasm can lead to increased resistance when it comes to discussing the price. Look around and perhaps ask the price of some other items before turning your attention to what you really want. Don't rush. Let things proceed at their own pace, keep the discussion going and remember that it is in the shopkeeper's

interest to secure a sale. Don't offer too much less than the item is worth (or than you are prepared to pay), or the shopkeeper will assume that you're not genuinely interested or guess that you've no idea of its value which will further inflate the final price. Let him drop the price instead: he will. It is incorrect to assume that the right price to pay is half way between his first offer and yours. On completion of negotiations, a peeved expression on the face of some shopkeepers is as routine as the speed with which it evaporates.

figure of a deity is usually surrounded by images of lesser gods. The paintings are on cloth (often silk) and were a convenient way of carrying and storing a religious icon. They are believed to have been originated by Nepali artists who took them to Tibet along with illuminated manuscripts and metal sculptures, as early as the 10th century. Bhaktapur is the home of many professional thangka painters.

Tibetan Carpets   There is considerable variation in the manufacturing process and quality of Tibetan carpets. Tibetan usually means that the carpet has been made by Tibetans in Nepal (many in Patan's southern district of Jawalakhel, and at Bodhnath). Traditional designs include dragons, geometric and floral patterns. You can get one small enough to pack into a suitcase. **NB** Take extra care when shopping for carpets, as there is a good trade in full- and partly-fake silk being sold as pure silk. Kashmiri silk carpets are often higher quality than the Tibetan ones and thus command higher prices.

Sending purchases home   If you cannot carry your goods with you, you can ship them, though this can be risky and expensive. The Foreign Post Office requires inspection by officials before you can wrap your purchases for mailing.

Other Nepali crafts include the **khukuri**, the traditional Gurkha knife. The genuine ones come with two extra smaller knives for skinning and the main blade has a notch to stop blood reaching the handle. The **woodcarving** craftsmen are concentrated in Bhaktapur. **Tibetan** crafts include prayerwheels and other religious items. Check inside the wheel for the *Om mani padme hum* mantra printed on a paper roll. Crafts sold around Bodhnath and Swayambhunath are often highly priced. Jewellery trinkets with turquoise setting are good value, while stamps and coins attract collectors. Gold and silver jewellery should only be bought from reputable shops.

Film   Film and photographic accessories are readily available in Kathmandu, Pokhara and some major towns. Check expiry dates of film. It is better to bring plenty of film with you if you are entering Nepal through one of the land border crossings, as it may be unavailable locally. Also stock up in Kathmandu before trekking or heading off into any of the more remote areas. Some shops in Sauraha (Chitwan) may have film, but it can be old and the supply is unreliable. Processing can be done reliably in Kathmandu, using Western equipment. Rates are generally quite reasonable but do vary, so shop around. Some processing shops will give a substantial discount for bulk processing, and in any case it is always worth bargaining before you hand your film in. Disposable cameras (and their processing) are now available in Kathmandu.

Several monuments, parks, etc charge an additional 'camera fee' which can be more expensive than your own admission fee. There is no restriction on bringing movie cameras into Nepal, though the fee for using one may be astronomical

Holidays and festivals

Nepal has a range of calendars, including two solar calendars (the Nepali and Gregorian are in common use) and three lunar calendars: the Nepali, Newari and Tibetan! The latter affects the Buddhist festival dates, the full moon being especially auspicious. Eclipses are often thought to be a bad omen.

The Nepali Calendar Also known as **Bikram Samvat (BS, or BE for Bikram Era)**, this is the official calendar and is followed by the government in its administration. Your official travel documents will also be dated according to this calendar. It is 57 years ahead of the Western (Gregorian) calendar, with new year beginning in mid-April (the month of Baisakh). Thus, from mid-April **1999** it is the year 2056 BS/BE; **2000** is 2057 BS/BE; **2001** is 2058 BS/BE; and **2002** is 2059 BS/BE.

Both Nepali and Gregorian years have 365 days, but the former has 12 months lasting from 29 to 32 days. The Nepali **financial year** begins in mid-July. This calendar is named after King Bikram Aditya, who reigned in Ujjain (modern day Madhya Pradesh) in India. It was first followed by the Licchavis, becoming fully established during the Malla era.

The Newari Calendar This regional calendar is called Newari Samvat (abbreviated to **NS**) and is used only by the Newars of the Kathmandu Valley. It is 879 years behind the Gregorian calendar. It was introduced by the Mallas with new year falling in mid-November. Thus, from mid-November **1999**, it is 1120 NS; **2000** is 1121 NS; **2001** is 1122 NS; and **2002** is 1123 NS.

The Tibetan Calendar This is a lunar calendar which is calculated each year by astrologers. It is based on a cycle of 60 years, each of which is named after 1 of 12 animals and 1 of 5 elements in combination. A calendar year normally contains 12 months, but the addition of an extra intercalary month for astrologers is not uncommon. In general, the Tibetan lunar month is about two months behind the Western calendar. In order to work out how major events in the Tibetan calendar correspond to dates in the Western calendar, it is necessary to wait until late autumn or winter when the following year's calendar is prepared. The **10th** day of every month is dedicated to Padmasambhava who introduced the highest Buddhist teachings from India in the 8th century. The **25th** day of each month is a Dakini Day, associated with the female deities who are agents of Buddha-activity. The **29th** day of every month is dedicated to the wrathful doctrinal protector deities, while the **15th** and **30th** are associated with the Buddha, and the **8th** day with the Medicine Buddha.

The Kali Era This calendar is largely associated with religious observances and festivals and is not generally used for administrative purposes. It is based on lunar and solar criteria and is rather complicated, but runs roughly as follows: lunar months are divided into two fortnights (*paksha*), comprising the bright half (*shukla paksha*) and the dark half (*krishan paksha*). Several Hindu festivals take their name from 1 of the 14 days of the paksha, which are: Pratipada (1), Dwitya (2), Tritya (3), Chaturthi (4), Panchami (5), Shasthi (6), Saptami (7), Astami (8), Nabami (9), Dashami (10), Ekadashi (11), Dwadashi (12), Trayodashi (13) and Chaturdahi (14). The lunar months are: Magh (January-February), Phalgun (February-March), Chaitra (March-April), Baisakh (April-May), Jyestha (May-June), Asadh (June-July), Shravan (July-August), Bhadra (August-September), Ashwin (September-October), Kartik (October-November), Marga (November-December) and Paush (December-January).

Eternity is divided into three units, the smallest being an 'age' (*yuga*), of which there are 4: Krita, Treta, Dwarpar and Kali (the present yuga which began in February 3102 BC, and lasts around 432,000 solar years). Together, these form one 'great age' (*maha*

Calendars

Essentials

yuga). Finally, 1,000 *maha yuga* make 1 *kalpa* which lasts some 4,320,000,000 solar years. 1 *kalpa* is considered to be 1 day in the life of Brahma. Brahma is the creator, one of the supreme trinity of Hindu gods.

Festivals Exact dates of festivals change annually according to astrological calculations. The Dept of Tourism in Kathmandu publishes an annual brochure, so check. The Nepali New Year is in mid-April and the two most important festivals are Dasain and Tihar in September/October. (Nepali months are in brackets.)

January-February (*Magha*) **Magha Sankranti** marks the transition from winter to spring. **Tribeni Mela**, on the new moon, is held on the banks of the Narayani River. **Basanta Panchami** celebrates the start of the spring season. Ceremonies at Kathmandu's Hanuman Dhoka Palace, street parades by children and dedications at temples characterize this festival. **Magha Purnima** is celebrated on the last day of Magha, when bathers walk from the Bagmati River ghats to various temples and take a ritual bath in the Salindi River.

February-March (*Phalgun*) **Rashtriya Prajatantra Divas** (or **Democracy Day**) includes parades and processions to celebrate the 1951 overthrow of the autocratic Rana régime. **Holi** is a colourful festival to mark the beginning of spring. People put on new clothes which get ruined when they go round throwing coloured powder, coloured water and just plain water (often in small balloons and the like), at each other. Also celebrated throughout India. The **Tibetan New Year** is marked by colourful processions and vigils, especially at Swayambhunath and Bodhnath. **Maha Shiva Ratri** ('Great Shiva's Night') is marked with special celebrations at Pashupatinath which hosts a giant mela (fair). There are all night vigils and music, while many pilgrims take a holy bath every three hours. There is also a gun salute at Kathmandu's Tundikhel and thousands of oil lamps and bonfires at night brighten the festivities.

March-April (*Chaitra*) **Ghorajatra** is celebrated especially in Patan with horse races and displays of gymnastics and horsemanship. Animal sacrifices are offered in the temples of the Ashta Matrikas ('8 mother goddesses'). **Pasa Chare** is a Newar festival, a time of hospitality among Newari people. On the same day as the horse show of the Ghorajatra festival, the demon Gurumpa is carried to the Tundikhel in a midnight procession. **Chaitra Dasain** and the festival of the **Seto Macchendranath** occur simultaneously in Kathmandu. **Ram Navami**, at the magnificent Janaki Mandir in Janakpur, celebrates the birthday of Rama.

April-May (*Baisakh*) **Nepali New Year** celebrations of **Bisket** in Bhaktapur. **Balkumari Jatra** in Thimi, and **Rato Macchendranath Jatra** in Patan. **Matatirtha Snan** in late April is highlighted by ritual baths at Matatirtha, near Thankot, for people whose mothers have died in the past year. **Astami** is highlighted in Naxal by ritual sacrifices to ensure a prosperous summer. **Buddha Jayanta** is celebrated throughout Nepal to mark the birthday of the Buddha. There are many pilgrimages to Buddhist shrines, especially to the Swayambhunath and Bodhnath stupas.

May-June (*Jyestha*) **Sithinakha**, throughout the Kathmandu Valley, celebrates the 'divine warrior' by giving domestic offerings. **Mani Rimdu** is a 3-day Sherpa religious festival at Namche Bazaar's Thame Monastery. Monks seek to gain merit by performing masked dramas and dances. The festival is repeated six months later at the Thyangboche Monastery.

June-July (*Asadh*) **Tribhuvan Jayanta** is a national holiday held in honour of the late King Tribhuvan. A ceremony is held at Tripureshwar, at the statue of the late king.

July-August (*Shrawan*) **Ghanta Karna** is held in all Newar settlements and marks the completion of the paddy planting season in the Kathmandu Valley. The festival is a remnant of demon worship and the decorations are intended to ward off evil spirits. **Naga Panchami**, in the Kathmandu Valley, honours the nagas, the divine serpents with control over rain. Celebrations include pinning paintings depicting nagas to doors and being blessed by priests. Lakhe, mask dancing, also starts in Kathmandu. **Janai Purnima**, or **Rakshya Vandhana**, is celebrated in honour of Shiva Mahadev ('Shiva Great God') with special festivities held at the Kumbeshwar Mandir in Patan and at Gosainkund Lake in the mountains north of the Valley. Brahmins and Chhetris renew their munja (sacred thread) on this day, while priests distribute yellow threads (*rikhi doro*) to other castes.

August-September (*Bhadra*) **Gaijatra**, **Indrajatra** and **Dasain** fall within 30 days of each other. Indrajatra starts in Bhaktapur with the erection of a tall wooden pole to honour the God of Rain. **Krishnastami** is celebrated in 11 sanctuaries and temples dedicated to Krishna, especially the Krishna Mandir in Patan's Durbar Square which commemorates Krishna's birth with offerings of tulsi plants. **Pancha Dan** (or **Banda Jatra**), the festival of the five summer gifts, is celebrated at the Swayambhunath stupa and throughout the Kathmandu Valley. Women give rice and grains to priests who march through the streets chanting hymns. **Gokarna Aunshi**, Fathers' Day, is highlighted by ritual bathing in the Bagmati River at Gokarna commemorating fathers who have died during the year. **Teej Brata** is marked throughout the Kathmandu Valley with prayers to Shiva and Parvati for a happy married life. Married women traditionally wear their scarlet and gold wedding saris and ceremonial baths in the Bagmati honour husbands.

September-October (*Ashwin*) The **Ganesh Festival**, on the September full moon, honours Ganesh without whose blessing no religious ceremony or major undertaking begins. **Dasain** (or **Durga Puja**) is the major annual festival. On the 1st of the 10-day festival, puja is marked in homes by planting and nurturing barley seeds in sand and water from the holy river. The devout bathe in holy places over the next nine days. On Phulpati, the 7th day, sacred flowers and leaves from the Gorkha palace reach Kathmandu where they are received by crowds accompanied by brass bands at the Hanuman Dhoka gate and the firing of guns in the Tundikhel. On the 8th day, Mahasthami, the devout fast and sacrifice animals including buffaloes, sheep and goats on *Kalratri* ('black night'). This is followed on the 9th day with elaborate mass sacrifices at the magnificent Taleju Mandir in Kathmandu's Durbar Square (open to Hindus on this single day alone) and the sprinkling of the blood blessed by the temple's eponymous goddess on all vehicles and instruments in the hope of preventing accidents. The climax is on the 10th day, Vijaya Dashami (the Day of Victory), which marks the triumph of Rama and Durga over evil. Hindus receive a tikka of vermillion, curd and rice on the forehead from elders to ensure health and happiness. The fortnight ends with the full moon night when many women start a month-long fast. Dasain has eight days of masked dances in Patan's Durbar Square with kite flying and erection of bamboo swings.

October-November (*Kartik*) **Tihar** (or **Diwali**) is the 5-day festival of lights. On the 1st day, small lamps are lit and the first portion of the family meal is given to crows. On the second day, dogs are decorated with garlands and a tikka on the forehead. The crow and the dog are associated with Yama, the god of death, who is propitiated with offerings and thanks. The 3rd day is marked with worshipping and garlanding cows. It is also Lakshmi Puja when thousands of tiny wick lamps and candles are lit on windowsills and in homes throughout the country, a truly wonderful sight, to invite the goddess of fortune to enter the home, and fireworks are set off. The 4th day is

Essentials

Newari New Year when people worship the divine in one's self (Ma Puja – 'me worship') and families get together. The 5th and final day is Bhai Tika, when sisters place multicoloured tikas on their brothers' foreheads to protect them from evil, and brothers make generous gifts in return. Tihar marks the end of the harvest, the beginning of the year and the worship of animals. **Haribodhani Ekadasi** is a pilgrimage in honour of Vishnu to Budhanilikantha.

November-December (*Marga*) **Bala Chaturdasi** is celebrated with a pilgrimage to Pashupati and offerings to the deity, Pashupatinath. Lighting of oil lamps on the 1st night of celebrations is followed by a morning bath in the Bagmati River. Pilgrims follow the traditional route through the Mrigasthali Forest offering seeds and sweets so that dead relations can benefit in the next world. **Vivaha Panchami** in Janakpur recalls Rama's marriage to Sita with drama, dance and music.

December-January (*Paush*) **Constitution Day** is celebrated in every town and commemorates the 1962 Constitution Act in tribute to the late King Mahendra. The **Birthday of His Majesty the King** is celebrated throughout Nepal with ceremonies, processions and military parades. King Birendra Bikram Shah Dev was born on 28 December 1945.

Health

To get the most out of your time in Nepal, it is important to take good care of your health. This can and should begin before leaving home. Although no certificates of vaccination are required to enter the country, it is wise to check the current recommendations for inoculations with your GP long enough in advance to ensure that you do get a complete course of jabs. It can take several weeks to complete a course of vaccinations and inoculations. In the UK, there are several travellers' health centres which will do your vaccinations and are well qualified to advise on up-to-date health matters. These include centres at London's Heathrow and Gatwick airports, as well as the excellent British Airways shop/health centre on Regent St. However, these are considerably more expensive than going along to your own GP.

A sense of what and what not to eat and drink is usually acquired fairly quickly by trial and error, by observing the eating habits of other travellers, or by the monotony of being over-cautious during the first few days which can lead to reckless indulgence in a range of delicacies that had previously remained off-limits. With most people suffering no more than a stomach upset during their travels in Nepal, a sensible balance of caution and pragmatism should overcome any inclination towards dietary paranoia – a condition which itself can be as debilitating as the occasional bout of diarrhoea.

Medical facilities

If you do get concerned about an illness, however, medicines are available from pharmacies located in most towns and do not require prescriptions. The majority of doctors are based in Kathmandu and your embassy may be able to provide a list of recommended medical and dental practitioners. There are a handful of private clinics in Kathmandu aiming to provide Western standards of health care. Nepal has few hospitals and those that do exist have very limited resources, so it becomes especially important that your travel insurance covers emergency medical repatriation. If you wear glasses or contact lenses, bring your prescription with you to Nepal. Optical costs are considerably lower in South Asia than in the West, and some people have been known to have had a second pair made up for their future use.

Before travelling

Take out medical insurance. Make sure it covers all eventualities especially evacuation to your home country by a medically equipped plane, if necessary. You should have a dental check up, obtain a spare glasses prescription, a spare oral contraceptive prescription (or enough pills to last) and, if you suffer from a chronic illness (such as diabetes, high blood pressure, ear or sinus troubles, cardio-pulmonary disease or nervous disorder), arrange for a checkup with your doctor, who can at the same time provide you with a letter explaining the details of your disability. Check the current practice in Nepal for malaria prophylaxis (prevention). If you are on regular medication, make sure you have enough to cover the period of your travel.

More preparation is probably necessary for babies and children than for an adult and **Children** perhaps a little more care should be taken when travelling to remote areas where health services are primitive. This is because children can be become more rapidly ill than adults (on the other hand they often recover more quickly). Diarrhoea and vomiting are the most common problems, so take the usual precautions, but more intensively. Breastfeeding is best and most convenient for babies, but powdered milk is generally available and so are baby foods in most countries. Papaya, bananas and avocados are all nutritious and can be cleanly prepared. The treatment of diarrhoea is the same as for adults, except that it should start earlier and be continued with more persistence. Children get dehydrated very quickly in hot countries and can become drowsy and uncooperative unless cajoled to drink water or juice plus salts. Upper respiratory infections, such as colds, catarrh and middle ear infections are also common and if your child suffers from these normally take some antibiotics against the possibility. Outer ear infections after swimming are also common and antibiotic eardrops will help. Wet wipes are always useful and sometimes difficult to find in Nepal, as, in some places, are disposable nappies.

There is very little control on the sale of drugs and medicines in Nepal. You can buy any **Medicines &** and every drug in pharmacies without a prescription. Be wary of this because **what to take** pharmacists can be poorly trained and might sell you drugs that are unsuitable, dangerous or old. Many drugs and medicines are manufactured under licence from American or European companies, so the trade names may be familiar to you. This means you do not have to carry a whole chest of medicines with you, but remember that the shelf life of some items, especially vaccines and antibiotics, is markedly reduced in hot conditions. Buy your supplies at the better outlets where there are refrigerators, even though they are more expensive and check the expiry date of all preparations you buy. Immigration officials occasionally confiscate scheduled drugs (Lomotil is an example) if they are not accompanied by a doctor's prescription.

Self-medication may be forced on you by circumstances so the following text contains the names of drugs and medicines which you may find useful in an emergency or in out-of-the-way places. You may like to take some of the following items with you from home: **Sunglasses** ones designed for intense sunlight; **Earplugs** for sleeping on aeroplanes and in noisy hotels; **Suntan cream** with a high protection factor; **Insect repellent** containing DET for preference; **Mosquito net** lightweight, permethrin-impregnated for choice; **Tablets** for travel sickness. **Tampons** can be expensive in some countries in Nepal; **Condoms; Contraceptives; Water sterilizing tablets; Antimalarial tablets; Anti-infective ointment** eg Cetrimide; **Dusting powder** for feet etc containing fungicide; **Antacid tablets** for indigestion; **Sachets of rehydration salts** plus anti-diarrhoea preparations; **Painkillers** such as Paracetamol or Aspirin; **Antibiotics** for diarrhoea etc; **First Aid kit** Small pack containing a few sterile syringes and needles and disposable

Essentials

Essentials

gloves. The risk of catching hepatitis etc from a dirty needle used for injection is now negligible in Nepal, but some may be reassured by carrying their own supplies – available from camping shops and airport shops.

Vaccination & immunization   **Smallpox** vaccination is no longer required anywhere in the world. Neither is **cholera** vaccination recognized as necessary for international travel by the World Health Organization – it is not very effective either. You may be asked for a Yellow Fever certificate if you have been travelling in a country affected by the disease immediately before travelling to Nepal. The vaccination is practically without side effects and almost totally protective.

Although no certificates of vaccination are required to enter Nepal, it is wise to check the current recommendations for inoculations with your GP. Vaccination against the following diseases are recommended:
Typhoid   A disease spread by the insanitary preparation of food. A number of new vaccines against this condition are now available; the older TAB and monovalent typhoid vaccines are being phased out. The newer, eg Typhim Vi, cause less side effects, but are more expensive. For those who do not like injections, there are now oral vaccines.

Poliomyelitis   Despite its decline in the world this remains a serious disease if caught and is easy to protect against. There are live oral vaccines and in some countries injected vaccines. Whichever one you choose it is a good idea to have a booster every 3-5 years if visiting developing countries regularly.

Tetanus   One dose should be given with a booster at six weeks and another at six months and 10-yearly boosters thereafter are recommended. Children should already be properly protected against diphtheria, poliomyelitis, pertussis (whooping cough) and measles, all of which can be more serious infections in Nepal than at home. Measles, mumps and rubella vaccine is also given to children throughout the world, but those teenage girls who have not had rubella (German measles) should be tested and vaccinated. Hepatitis B vaccination for babies is now routine in some countries. Consult your doctor for advice on tuberculosis inoculation: the disease is still widespread in the region.

Infectious Hepatitis   Is less of a problem for travellers than it used to be because of the development of two extremely effective vaccines against the A and B form of the disease. It remains common, however, in Nepal and protection is strongly recommended. A combined hepatitis A & B vaccine is now licensed and will be available in 1997 – one jab covers both diseases. Use condoms against Hepatitis B.

Other vaccinations   Might be considered in the case of epidemics eg meningitis. There is an effective vaccination against rabies which should be considered by all travellers, especially those going through remote areas or if there is a particular occupational risk, eg for zoologists or veterinarians.

Further information

Further information on health risks abroad, vaccinations etc may be available from a local travel clinic. If you wish to take specific drugs with you such as antibiotics these are best prescribed by your own doctor. Beware, however, that not all doctors can be experts on the health problems of remote countries. More detailed or more up-to-date information than local doctors can provide are available from various sources. In the UK there are hospital departments specializing in tropical diseases in

London, Liverpool, Birmingham and Glasgow and the Malaria Reference Laboratory at the London School of Hygiene and Tropical Medicine provides free advice about malaria, T0891-600350. In the USA the local Public Health Services can give such information and information is available centrally from the Centre for Disease Control (CDC) in Atlanta, T404-3324559.

There are other computerized databases which can be assessed for up-to-the-minute, destination-specific information. In the UK there is MASTA (Medical Advisory Service to Travellers Abroad), T0171-6314408, F0171-4365389, Tx8953473 and Travax (Glasgow, T0141-9467120, ext 247). Other information on medical problems overseas can be obtained from the book by Dawood, Richard (Editor) (1992) *Travellers' Health: How to stay healthy abroad*, Oxford University Press 1992, £7.99. We strongly recommend this revised and updated edition, especially to the intrepid traveller heading for the more out of the way places. General advice is also available in the UK in *Health Information for Overseas Travel* published by the Department of Health and available from HMSO and *International Travel and Health* published by WHO, Geneva.

On the way

For most travellers a trip to Nepal means a long air flight. If this crosses time zones then jetlag can be a problem. The main symptoms are tiredness and sleepiness at inconvenient times and, conversely, a tendency to wake up in the middle of the night feeling like you want your breakfast. Most find that the problem is worse when flying in an easterly direction. The best way to get over jetlag is to try to force yourself into the new time zone as strictly as possible. This may involve, on a westward flight, trying to stay awake until your normal bedtime and on an eastward flight, forgetting that you have lost some sleep on the way out and going to bed relatively early but near your normal time on the evening after you arrive. The symptoms of jetlag may be helped by keeping up your fluid intake on the journey, but not with alcohol. The hormone melatonin seems to reduce the symptoms of jetlag but is not presently licensed in most of Europe although it can be obtained from health food stores in the USA.

On long-haul flights it is also important to stretch your legs at least every hour to prevent slowing of the circulation and the possible development of blood clots. Drinking plenty of non-alcoholic fluids also helps.

If travelling by boat then sea sickness can be a problem – this is dealt with in the usual way by taking anti motion-sickness pills.

Staying healthy

The thought of catching a stomach bug worries visitors to Nepal but there have been great improvements in food hygiene and most such infections are preventable. Travellers' diarrhoea and vomiting is due, most of the time, to food poisoning, usually passed on by the insanitary habits of food handlers. As a general rule the cleaner your surroundings and the smarter the restaurant, the less likely you are to suffer.

Intestinal upsets

Foods to avoid: uncooked, undercooked, partially cooked or reheated meat, fish, eggs, raw vegetables and salads, especially when they have been left out exposed to flies. Stick to fresh food that has been cooked from raw just before eating and make sure you peel fruit yourself. Wash and dry your hands before eating – disposable wet-wipe tissues are useful for this.

Shellfish eaten raw are risky and at certain times of the year some fish and shellfish concentrate toxins from their environment and cause various kinds of food poisoning. Pasteurized milk is now widely available in Nepal as is pasteurized **cheese, ice cream**

and **yoghurt**. On the whole matured or processed cheeses are safer than the fresh varieties and fresh unpasteurized milk from whatever animal can be a source of food poisoning germs, tuberculosis and brucellosis. This applies equally to ice cream, yoghurt and cheese made from unpasteurized milk, so avoid these homemade products – the factory made ones are probably safer.

Tap water is rarely safe outside the major cities, especially in the rainy season. Stream water, if you are in the countryside, is often contaminated by communities living surprisingly high in the mountains. Filtered or bottled water is usually available and safe, although you must make sure that somebody is not filling bottles from the tap and resealing it. Ice for drinks should be made from boiled water, but rarely is, so stand your glass on the ice cubes, rather than putting them in the drink.

Travellers' diarrhoea
: This is usually caused by eating food which has been contaminated by food poisoning germs. Drinking water is rarely the culprit. Sea water or river water is more likely to be contaminated by sewage and so swimming in such dilute effluent can also be a cause.

Infection with various organisms can give rise to travellers' diarrhoea. They may be viruses, bacteria, eg Escherichia coli (probably the most common cause worldwide), protozoal (such as amoebas and giardia), salmonella and cholera. The diarrhoea may come on suddenly or rather slowly. It may or may not be accompanied by vomiting or by severe abdominal pain and the passage of blood or mucus when it is called dysentery.

How do you know which type you have caught and how to treat it?

If you can time the onset of the diarrhoea to the minute ('acute') then it is probably due to a virus or a bacterium and/or the onset of dysentery. The treatment in addition to rehydration is Ciprofloxacin 500 mg every 12 hours; the drug is now widely available and there are many similar ones.

If the diarrhoea comes on slowly or intermittently ('sub-acute') then it is more likely to be protozoal, ie caused by an amoeba or giardia. Antibiotics such a Ciprofloxacin will have little effect. These cases are best treated by a doctor as is any outbreak of diarrhoea continuing for more than three days. Sometimes blood is passed in amoebic dysentery and for this you should certainly seek medical help. If this is not available then the best treatment is probably Tinidazole (Fasigyn) one tablet four times a day for three days. If there are severe stomach cramps, the following drugs may help but are not very useful in the management of acute diarrhoea: Loperamide (Imodium) and Diphenoxylate with Atropine (Lomotil) They should not be given to children.

Read the leaflet carefully as the amount of fluid intake is quite high: the odd glass will not have much effect
: Any kind of diarrhoea, whether or not accompanied by vomiting, responds well to the replacement of water and salts, taken as frequent small sips, of some kind of rehydration solution. There are proprietary preparations consisting of sachets of powder which you dissolve in boiled water or you can make your own by adding half a teaspoonful of salt (3.5 gms) and four tablespoonsful of sugar (40 gms) to a litre of boiled water.

Thus the linch pins of treatment for diarrhoea are rest, fluid and salt replacement, antibiotics such as Ciprofloxacin for the bacterial types and special diagnostic tests and medical treatment for the amoeba and giardia infections. Salmonella infections and cholera, although rare, can be devastating diseases and it would be wise to get to a hospital as soon as possible if these were suspected.

Fasting, peculiar diets and the consumption of large quantities of yoghurt have not been found useful in calming travellers' diarrhoea or in rehabilitating inflamed bowels. Oral rehydration has on the other hand, especially in children, been a life saving technique and should always be practised, whatever other treatment you use. As there is some evidence that alcohol and milk might prolong diarrhoea they should be avoided during and immediately after an attack.

Diarrhoea occurring day after day for long periods of time (chronic diarrhoea) is notoriously resistent to amateur attempts at treatment and again warrants proper diagnostic tests (most towns with reasonable sized hospitals have laboratories for stool samples). There are ways of preventing travellers' diarrhoea for short periods of time by taking antibiotics, but this is not a foolproof technique and should not be used other than in exceptional circumstances. Doxycycline is possibly the best drug. Some preventatives such as Enterovioform can have serious side effects if taken for long periods.

Paradoxically **constipation** is also common, probably induced by dietary change, inadequate fluid intake in hot places and long bus journeys. Simple laxatives are useful in the short term and bulky foods and plenty of fruit are also useful.

Spending time at high altitude in Nepal is almost inevitable, but can cause medical problems, all of which can be prevented if care is taken. Before leaving you should ask your doctor for advice on treatment/prevention of altitude sickness.

High altitude

On reaching heights above about 3,000m, heart pounding and shortness of breath, especially on exertion are a normal response to the lack of oxygen in the air. A condition called acute mountain sickness can also affect visitors. It is more likely to affect those who ascend rapidly, eg by plane and those who over-exert themselves. Acute mountain sickness takes a few hours or days to come on and presents with a bad headache, extreme tiredness, sometimes dizziness, loss of appetite and frequently nausea and vomiting. Insomnia is common and is often associated with a suffocating feeling when lying in bed. Keen observers may note their breathing tends to wax and wane at night and their face tends to be puffy in the mornings – this is all part of the syndrome. Anyone can get this condition and past experience is not always a good guide: the author, having spent years in Peru travelling constantly between sea level and very high altitude never suffered symptoms, then was severely affected whilst climbing Kilimanjaro in Tanzania.

The treatment of acute mountain sickness is simple – rest, painkillers, (preferably not aspirin based) for the headache and anti sickness pills for vomiting. Oxygen is actually not much help, except at very high altitude. Drinking large quantities of non-alcoholic fluids always helps to counter some of these effects.

To **prevent** the condition: on arrival at places over 3,000 metres have a few hours rest in a chair and avoid alcohol, cigarettes and heavy food. If the symptoms are severe and prolonged, it is best to descend to a lower altitude and to reascend slowly or in stages. If this is impossible because of shortage of time or if you are going so high that acute mountain sickness is very likely, then the drug Acetazolamide (Diamox) can be used as a preventative and continued during the ascent. There is good evidence of the value of this drug in the prevention of acute mountain sickness, but some people do experience peculiar side effects. The usual dose is 500 mg of the slow release preparation each night, starting the night before ascending above 3,000 metres. The *Himalayan Rescue Association* has a good pamphlet on Mountain Sickness (try the Alpine Club or British Mountaineering Association).

Watch out for **sunburn** at high altitude. The ultraviolet rays are extremely powerful. The air is also excessively dry at high altitude and you might find that your skin dries out and the inside of your nose becomes crusted. Use a moisturiser for the skin and some vaseline wiped into the nostrils. Some people find contact lenses irritate because of the dry air. It is unwise to ascend to high altitude if you are pregnant,

Essentials

Essentials

especially in the first three months, or if you have a history of heart, lung or blood disease, including sickle cell.

A more unusual condition can affect mountaineers who ascend rapidly to high altitude – **acute pulmonary oedema**. Residents at altitude sometimes experience this when returning to the mountains from time spent at the coast. This condition is often preceded by acute mountain sickness and comes on quite rapidly with severe breathlessness, noisy breathing, cough, blueness of the lips and frothing at the mouth. Anybody who develops this must be brought down as soon as possible, given oxygen and taken to hospital.

A rapid descent from high places will make sinus problems and middle ear infections worse and might make your teeth ache. Remember that the Himalaya and other mountain ranges are very high, very cold, very remote and potentially very dangerous. Do not travel alone, when you are ill or if you are poorly equipped. Mountain rescue is extremely difficult and medical services may be poor. Lastly, don't fly to altitude within 24 hours of SCUBA diving. You might suffer from 'the bends'.

Heat & cold Full acclimatization to high temperatures takes about two weeks. During this period it is normal to feel a bit apathetic, especially if the relative humidity is high. Drink plenty of water (up to 15 litres a day are required when working physically hard in the tropics), use salt on your food and avoid extreme exertion. Tepid showers are more cooling than hot or cold ones. Large hats do not cool you down, but do prevent sunburn. Remember that, especially in the highlands, there can be a large and sudden drop in temperature between sun and shade and between night and day, so dress accordingly. Warm jackets or woollens are essential after dark at high altitude. Loose cotton is still the best material when the weather is hot.

Insects These are mostly more of a nuisance than a serious hazard and if you try, you can prevent yourself entirely from being bitten. Some, such as mosquitos are, of course, carriers of potentially serious diseases, so it is sensible to avoid being bitten as much as possible. Sleep off the ground and use a mosquito net or some kind of insecticide. Preparations containing Pyrethrum or synthetic pyrethroids are safe. They are available as aerosols or pumps and the best way to use these is to spray the room thoroughly in all areas (follow the instructions rather than the insects) and then shut the door for a while, re-entering when the smell has dispersed. Mosquito coils release insecticide as they burn slowly. They are widely available and useful out of doors. Tablets of insecticide which are placed on a heated mat plugged into a wall socket are probably the most effective. They fill the room with insecticidal fumes in the same way as aerosols or coils.

You can also use insect repellents, most of which are effective against a wide range of pests. The most common and effective is diethyl metatoluamide (DEET). DEET liquid is best for arms and face (care around eyes and with spectacles – DEET dissolves plastic). Aerosol spray is good for clothes and ankles and liquid DEET can be dissolved in water and used to impregnate cotton clothes and mosquito nets. Some repellents now contain DEET and Permethrin, insecticide. Impregnated wrist and ankle bands can also be useful.

If you are bitten or stung, itching may be relieved by cool baths, antihistamine tablets (care with alcohol or driving) or mild corticosteroid creams, eg. hydrocortisone (great care: never use if any hint of infection). Careful scratching of all your bites once a day can be surprisingly effective. Calamine lotion and cream have limited effectiveness and antihistamine creams are not recommended – they can cause allergies themselves.

Bites which become infected should be treated with a local antiseptic or antibiotic cream such as Cetrimide, as should any infected sores or scratches.

When living rough, skin infestations with body lice (crabs) and scabies are easy to pick up. Use whatever local commercial preparation is recommended for lice and scabies.

Crotamiton cream (Eurax) alleviates itching and also kills a number of skin parasites. Malathion lotion 5% (Prioderm) kills lice effectively, but avoid the use of the toxic agricultural preparation of Malathion, more often used to commit suicide.

Ticks They attach themselves usually to the lower parts of the body often after walking in areas where cattle have grazed. They take a while to attach themselves strongly, but swell up as they start to suck blood. The important thing is to remove them gently, so that they do not leave their head parts in your skin because this can cause a nasty allergic reaction some days later. Do not use petrol, vaseline, lighted cigarettes etc to remove the tick, but, with a pair of tweezers remove the beast gently by gripping it at the attached (head) end and rock it out in very much the same way that a tooth is extracted. Certain tropical flies which lay their eggs under the skin of sheep and cattle also occasionally do the same thing to humans with the unpleasant result that a maggot grows under the skin and pops up as a boil or pimple. The best way to remove these is to cover the boil with oil, vaseline or nail varnish so as to stop the maggot breathing, then to squeeze it out gently the next day.

Sunburn The burning power of the tropical sun, especially at high altitude, is phenomenal.

Always wear a wide brimmed hat and use some form of suncream lotion on untanned skin. Normal temperate zone suntan lotions (protection factor up to 7) are not much good; you need to use the types designed specifically for the tropics or for mountaineers or skiers with protection factors up to 15 or above. These are often not available in Nepal. Glare from the sun can cause conjunctivitis, so wear sunglasses especially on tropical beaches, where high protection factor sunscreen should also be used.

Prickly heat A very common intensely itchy rash is avoided by frequent washing and by wearing loose clothing. Cured by allowing skin to dry off through use of powder and spending two nights in an a/c hotel!

Athletes foot This and other fungal skin infections are best treated with Tolnaftate or Clotrimazole.

Other risks and more serious diseases

Remember that rabies is endemic throughout Nepal, so avoid dogs that are behaving strangely. If you are bitten by a domestic or wild animal, do not leave things to chance: scrub the wound with soap and water and/or disinfectant, try to have the animal captured (within limits) or at least determine its ownership, where possible, and seek medical assistance at once. The course of treatment depends on whether you have already been satisfactorily vaccinated against rabies. If you have (this is worthwhile if you are spending lengths of time in developing countries) then some further doses of vaccine are all that is required. Human diploid vaccine is the best, but expensive: other, older kinds of vaccine, such as that derived from duck embryos may be the only types available. These are effective, much cheaper and interchangeable generally with the human derived types. If not already vaccinated then anti rabies serum (immunoglobulin) may be required in addition. It is important to finish the course of treatment whether the animal survives or not.

Essentials

AIShemasc In Nepal AIDS is increasing but is not wholly confined to the well known high risk sections of the population, ie homosexual men, intravenous drug abusers and children of infected mothers. Heterosexual transmission is now the dominant mode and so the main risk to travellers is from casual sex. The same precautions should be taken as with any sexually transmitted disease. The Aids virus (HIV) can be passed by unsterilized needles which have been previously used to inject an HIV positive patient. Check that needles have been properly sterilized or disposable needles have been used. If you wish to take your own disposable needles, be prepared to explain what they are for. The risk of receiving a blood transfusion with blood infected with the HIV virus is greater than from dirty needles because of the amount of fluid exchanged. Supplies of blood for transfusion should now be screened for HIV in all reputable hospitals. Catching the AIDS virus does not always produce an illness in itself (although it may do). The only way to be sure if you feel you have been put at risk is to have a blood test for HIV antibodies on your return to a place where there are reliable laboratory facilities. The test does not become positive for some weeks.

Malaria In Nepal malaria is theoretically confined to coastal and jungle zones, but is now on the increase again. Certain areas are badly affected particularly by the highly dangerous falciparum strain. Mosquitos do not thrive above 2,500 metres, so you are safe at altitude. There are different varieties of malaria, some resistant to the normal drugs. Make local enquiries if you intend to visit possibly infected zones and use a prophylactic régime. Start taking the tablets a few days before exposure and continue to take them for six weeks after leaving the malarial zone. Remember to give the drugs to babies and children also. Opinion varies on the precise drugs and dosage to be used for protection. All the drugs may have some side effects and it is important to balance the risk of catching the disease against the albeit rare side effects. The increasing complexity of the subject is such that as the malarial parasite becomes immune to the new generation of drugs it has made concentration on the physical prevention from being bitten by mosquitos more important. This involves the use of long sleeved shirts or blouses and long trousers, repellants and nets. Clothes are now available impregnated with the insecticide Permethrin or Deltamethrin or it is possible to impregnate the clothes yourself. Wide meshed nets impregnated with Permethrin are also available, are lighter to carry and less claustrophobic to sleep in.

Prophylaxis & treatment If your itinerary takes you into a malarial area, seek expert advice before you go on a suitable prophylactic régime. This is especially true for pregnant women who are particularly prone to catch malaria. You can still catch the disease even when sticking to a proper régime, although it is unlikely. If you do develop symptoms (high fever, shivering, headache, sometimes diarrhoea), seek medical advice immediately. If this is not possible and there is a great likelihood of malaria, the treatment is:

Chloroquine, a single dose of four tablets (600 mg) followed by two tablets (300 mg) in six hours and 300 mg each day following.

Falciparum type of malaria or type in doubt: take local advice. Various combinations of drugs are being used such as Quinine, Tetracycline or Halofantrine. If falciparum type malaria is definitely diagnosed, it is wise to get to a good hospital immediately as treatment can be complex and the illness very serious.

Infectious hepatitis (Jaundice) The main symptoms are pains in the stomach, lack of appetite, lassitude and yellowness of the eyes and skin. Medically speaking there are two main types. The less serious, but more common is Hepatitis A for which the best protection is the careful preparation of food, the avoidance of contaminated drinking water and scrupulous attention to toilet hygiene. The other, more serious, version is Hepatitis B which is acquired usually as a sexually transmitted disease or by blood transfusions. It can less commonly be transmitted by injections with unclean needles and possibly by insect bites. The symptoms are the same as for Hepatitis A. The incubation period is much longer (up to six months compared with six weeks) and there are more likely to be complications.

Hepatitis A can be protected against with gamma globulin. It should be obtained from a reputable source and is certainly useful for travellers who intend to live rough. You should have a shot before leaving and have it repeated every six months. The dose of gamma globulin depends on the concentration of the particular preparation used, so the manufacturer's advice should be taken. The injection should be given as close as possible to your departure and as the dose depends on the likely time you are to spend in potentially affected areas, the manufacturer's instructions should be followed. Gamma globulin has really been superceded now by a proper vaccination against Hepatitis A (Havrix) which gives immunity lasting up to 10 years. After that boosters are required. Havrix monodose is now widely available as is Junior Havrix. The vaccination has negligible side effects and is extremely effective. Gamma globulin injections can be a bit painful, but it is much cheaper than Havrix and may be more available in some places.

Hepatitis B can be effectively prevented by a specific vaccine (Engerix) – three shots over six months before travelling. If you have had jaundice in the past it would be worthwhile having a blood test to see if you are immune to either of these two types, because this might avoid the necessity and costs of vaccination or gamma globulin. There are other kinds of viral hepatitis (C, E etc) which are fairly similar to A and B, but vaccines are not available as yet.

Can still occur carried by ticks. There is usually a reaction at the site of the bite and a **Typhus** fever. Seek medical advice.

These are common and the more serious ones such as hookworm can be contracted **Intestinal** from walking barefoot on infested earth or beaches. **worms**

Various other tropical diseases can be caught in jungle areas, usually transmitted by biting insects. Leishmaniasis (Espundia) is carried by sandflies and causes a sore that will not heal or a severe nasal infection. Wearing long trousers and a long sleeved shirt in infected areas protects against these flies. DEET is also effective. Epidemics of meningitis occur from time-to-time.

This is a very rare event indeed for travellers. If you are unlucky (or careless) enough to **Snake bite** be bitten by a venomous snake, spider, scorpion or sea creature, try to identify the creature, but do not put yourself in further danger. Snake bites in particular are very frightening, but in fact rarely poisonous – even venomous snakes bite without injecting venom. What you might expect if bitten are: fright, swelling, pain and bruising around the bite and soreness of the regional lymph glands, perhaps nausea, vomiting and a fever. Signs of serious poisoning would be the following symptoms: numbness and tingling of the face, muscular spasms, convulsions, shortness of breath and bleeding. Victims should be got to a hospital or a doctor without delay. Commercial snake bite and scorpion kits are available, but usually only useful for the specific type of snake or scorpion for which they are designed. Most serum has to be given intravenously so it is not much good equipping yourself with it unless you are used to making injections into veins. It is best to rely on local practice in these cases, because the particular creatures will be known about locally and appropriate treatment can be given.

Essentials

Essentials

Treatment of snake bite Reassure and comfort the victim frequently. Immobilize the limb by a bandage or a splint or by getting the person to lie still. Do not slash the bite area and try to suck out the poison because this sort of heroism does more harm than good. If you know how to use a tourniquet in these circumstances, you will not need this advice. If you are not experienced do not apply a tourniquet.

Precautions Avoid walking in snake territory in bare feet or sandals – wear proper shoes or boots. If you encounter a snake stay put until it slithers away and do not investigate a wounded snake. Spiders and scorpions may be found in the more basic hotels. If stung, rest and take plenty of fluids and call a doctor. The best precaution is to keep beds away from the walls and look inside your shoes and under the toilet seat every morning. Certain tropical sea fish when trodden upon inject venom into bathers' feet. This can be exceptionally painful. Wear plastic shoes when you go bathing if such creatures are reported. The pain can be relieved by immersing the foot in extremely hot water for as long as the pain persists.

Dengue fever This is increasing worldwide. It can be completely prevented by avoiding mosquito bites in the same way as malaria. No vaccine is available. Dengue is an unpleasant and painful disease, presenting with a high temperature and body pains, but at least visitors are spared the more serious forms (haemorrhagic types) which are more of a problem for local people who have been exposed to the disease more than once. There is no specific treatment for dengue – just pain killers and rest.

Dangerous Apart from mosquitos the most dangerous animals are men, be they bandits or
animals behind steering wheels. Think carefully about violent confrontations and wear a seat belt if you are lucky enough to have one available to you.

When you return home

Remember to take your antimalarial tablets for six weeks after leaving the malarial area. If you have had attacks of diarrhoea it is worth having a stool specimen tested in case you have picked up amoebas. If you have been living rough, blood tests may be worthwhile to detect worms and other parasites. If you have been exposed to bilharzia (schistosomiasis) by swimming in lakes etc, check by means of a blood test when you get home, but leave it for six weeks because the test is slow to become positive. Report any untowards symptoms to your doctor and tell the doctor exactly where you have been and, if you know, what the likelihood of disease is to which you were exposed.

The above information has been compiled from information supplied and received from Dr David Snashall, who is presently Senior Lecturer in Occupational Health at the United Medical Schools of Guy's and St Thomas' Hospitals in London and Chief Medical Adviser to the British Foreign and Commonwealth Office. He has travelled extensively and keeps in close touch with developments in preventative and tropical medicine.

Travelling with children

Children of all ages are widely welcomed, being greeted with a warmth in their own right which is often then extended to those accompanying them. In the big hotels, there is no difficulty in obtaining safe baby **foods**. Western varieties of baby food are also available in Kathmandu's supermarkets and, occasionally, in Pokhara, but not elsewhere. You can also buy Western disposable **nappies** here, though they are expensive. If you have the space in your luggage, bring these along with packets and jars of food with you. Both Kathmandu and Pokhara have a wide range of excellent restaurants of all types where it will normally be perfectly safe for a child to eat. Elsewhere, it doesn't harm a child to eat an unvaried and limited diet of familiar, packaged food for a few weeks if the local dishes are not acceptable, but it may be an idea to get vitamin and mineral supplements. To help young children take anti-malarial **tablets**, one suggestion is to crush them between spoons and mix with a teaspoon of dessert chocolate (for cake making) bought in a tube.

Extra care must be taken to protect children from the **sun** and **heat**. Use creams, hats, umbrellas, etc, and avoid being out in the middle of the day when it is hot. Cool showers or baths help if the children get too hot. **Dehydration** can be counteracted with plenty of drinking water – bottled, **boiled** (furiously for five minutes) or purified with tablets. Preparations such as 'Dioralyte' may be given if the child suffers from diarrhoea. Moisturizer, zinc and castor oil (for **sore bottoms** due to change of diet) are worth taking. Mosquito nets or electric **insect repellents** at night are usually provided in non-a/c hotel rooms (ask for them if they're not), but insect repellent preparations are a must. The biggest hotels provide **baby sitters**.

Take extra care on hotel **rooftop** gardens, where walls may be low or unsafe. A **pram** is definitely a good idea for younger children who can soon get worn out by constant uphill and downhill walking. With proper preparation, there is no impediment to **trekking** with young children, though it is better to choose a popular route (eg in the Annapurnas) where there are decent facilities and to go with an organized, escorted trek. Many Nepali women carry their children in a type of backpack which you can buy locally. Make sure that there are enough porters to enable you to look after the children.

Further reading

While there are nowhere near as many titles on Nepal as on India or China, there is nevertheless a reasonable choice of publications covering a wide range of topics.

Amatya, S (1991) *Art and Culture of Nepal* Jaipur. A unique survey of aspects of Nepal's cultural heritage, though hard to follow at times. Gajurel, C and Vaidya, K (1984) *Traditional Arts and Crafts of Nepal* New Delhi. Harle, JC (1986) *The Art and Architecture of the Indian Subcontinent*, London. Hutt, M (1994) *Nepal: A Guide to the Art and Architecture of the Kathmandu Valley* London. An interesting and accomplished work accessible to all levels of reader, available in Kathmandu and overseas. Singh, M (1968) *Himalayan Arts* London.

Art & architecture

Essentials

Buddhism   Chen, KS (1968) *Buddhism: The Light of Asia* New York. Conze, E (trans) (1959) *Buddhist Scriptures* Penguin: London. With good introductory notes to all 10 chapters. Conze, E (1980) *A Short History of Buddhism* George Allen & Unwin: London. Dowman, K (1981) *A Buddhist Guide to the Power Places of the Kathmandu Valley* Kailash, Vol VIII, No 3-4. Snellgrove, DL (1957) *Buddhist Himalaya* Bruno Cassirer: Oxford.

Development &   Bista, DB *Fatalism and Development* New Delhi. Ives, JD and Messerli, B (1989)
aid   *Himalayan Crisis: Reconciling Development and Conservation* Routledge and Keegan Paul: London. An excellent review of the debate over environmental change in the Himalaya, recommended. O'Dea, P (1993) *Gender Exploitation and Violence: The Market in Women, Girls and Sex in Nepal* UNICEF: Kathmandu. A disturbing report on the trade in Nepali women as prostitutes and the role of development agencies in combating the same. Seddon, D *Nepal: A State of Poverty,* Routledge: London.

Geography &   Bradnock, RW (1983) *Agricultural Change in South Asia,* New York. Gansser, A (1964) *The*
geology   *Geology of the Himalaya,* London. Hagen, T (1980) *Nepal: The Kingdom in the Himalaya,* Berne. An excellent, though now rather dated, book, well illustrated throughout. Jest, C (1981) *Monuments of Northern Nepal* UNESCO: Paris. Nieuwolt, S (1977) *Tropical Climatology: An Introduction to the Climates of Low Altitudes* London.

Hinduism   O'Flaherty, W (1974) *Hindu Myths* Penguin: London. A sourcebook translated from the Sanskrit. Majumdar, RC (ed) (1957) *The Vedic Age,* London. Mascaro, J (trans) (1965) *The Upanishads* Penguin: London. With a sensitive and inspired introduction, highly recommended for even the casual Western reader. Rajagopalacharya, C (1979) *The Mahabharata* Bharatiya Vidya Bhavan: Bombay. Stutley, MJ *Dictionary of Hinduism.* Walker, B (1968) *Hindu World: An Encyclopedic Survey of Hinduism,* George Allen & Unwin: London. More than 700 articles in 2 volumes.

History   Bahadur, Pudma J *Life of Maharaja Sir Jung Bahadur of Nepal* Pioneer Press: Allahabad. Kirkpatrick, F *An Account of the Kingdom of Nepal* London, 1800; New Delhi, 1969. Landon, P (1928) *Nepal* London. 2 volumes, reprinted. One of the best early views of Nepal by a foreigner. Oldfield, HA (1975) *Views of Nepal, 1851-1864,* (reprint) Kathmandu. Regmi, DR (1969) *Ancient Nepal,* Calcutta; *Medieval Nepal,* Calcutta (1965). Schwartzberg, JE (1978) *A Historical Atlas of South Asia,* Chicago. A spectacular (and spectacularly expensive) survey, highly recommended. Shaha, R (1970) *Heroes and Builders of Nepal* Calcutta, (5th ed). Stiller, LF (1993) *Nepal: Growth of a Nation* Kathmandu. A very good and eminently readable account from the earliest times to the present, recommended. Stiller, LF (1973) *The Rise of the House of Gorka,* New Delhi. Prithvi Narayan Shah's conquest and the process of Nepal's unification. Whelpton, J (1983) *Jang Bahadur in Europe,* Kathmandu. Wright, D (1958) *History of Nepal,* (reprint) Calcutta, Shushil Gupta. A good early history.

India   Allchin, B & R (1982) *The Rise of Civilisation in India and Pakistan* CUP: Cambridge. The most authoritative survey of the origins of Indian civilisation. Basham, AL (ed) (1975) *A Cultural History of India* OUP: Oxford. A collection of excellent academic essays, which wear their learning lightly; *The Wonder That Was India,* London, Sidgwick & Jackson (1985). Still one of the most comprehensive and readable accounts of the development of India's culture. Bradnock, RW (1999) *India Handbook* Footprint Handbooks: Bath. One of the present series, full of up to date information with over 300 maps, by an international authority on India. Tully, M (1991) *No Full Stops in India* London, Viking: London. An often superbly observed (but controversially interpreted) view of contemporary India.

Gonda, J (1975) *Vedic Literature*, Wiesbaden. *Journal of South Asian Literature*. Keith, AB (1920) *A History of Sanskrit Literature*, Oxford. Lambert, HM (1953) *Introduction to the Devanagari Script*, London. Lonely Planet, *Nepali Phrasebook*, a pocket book with useful phrases and words. Riccardi, T Jr (1971) *A Nepali Version of the Vetalapanchavimsati*, New Haven. Rubin, D (1980) *Nepali Visions, Nepali Dreams*, New York. Shackle, C (1985) *South Asian Languages* SOAS: London. Shapiro, MC and Schiffman, HF (1981) *Language and Society in South Asia* Delhi. Shrestha, CK and Karki, TB *A Beginner's Course in Spoken Nepali* Kathmandu. A glossy booklet with useful phrases and vocabulary.

Anderson, Mary M (1971) *Festivals of Nepal* Allen & Unwin: London. Bista, Dor, *People of Nepal*, Kathmandu, HMG of Nepal. Dumont, L (1980) *Homo Hierachicus: The Caste System and its Implications* Chicago. Furer-Haimendorf, C von (1964) *The Sherpas of Nepal*, Berkeley, University of California and *The Naked Nagas*. Both are sensitively written anthropologies by a world authority on tribal people of South Asia. Gurung, H *Vignettes of Nepal*, Kathmandu. Gurung, H (1994) *Nepal Main Ethnic Caste Groups by District*, Kathmandu. Pamphlet interpreting results of the 1991 census. Lall, K (1993) *Folk Tales from the Himalayan Kingdom of Nepal* Kathmandu. One of a series of small folklore books widely available in Kathmandu. Lall, K (1990) *Nepalese Customs and Manners*, Kathmandu. Delightful booklet detailing if not explaining local conventions and superstitions. Maloney, C (1974) *Peoples of South Asia* Rheinhart & Winston: New York. A wide ranging and authoritative review. Messerschmidt, DA (1976) *The Gurungs of Nepal*, Warminster. Nepali, GS *The Newars*, United Asia Publications: Bombay.

Banskota, NP (1981) *Indo-Nepal Trade and Economic Relations* New Delhi. Economist Intelligence Unit *Nepal Profile* London. Published annually, probably the most comprehensive and reliable source of information on events and developments; *Nepal Report*, London. Published quarterly. Lama, MP (1985) *The Economics of Indo-Nepalese Co-operation* New Delhi. Mishra, PK (1979) *India, Pakistan, Nepal and Bangladesh* New Delhi. Ramakant (1986) *Nepal, China and India* New Delhi. Shaha, R (1995) *New Directions in Nepal-India Relations* Delhi.

Hinnells, JR (ed) (1985) *A Handbook of Living Religions* London. Johnston, W *Being In Love; Letters to Contemplatives; Lord, Teach Us To Pray; Silent Music*, Harper Collins: London. All are profound books, though written in clear and sparkling prose by an Irish Jesuit priest who has spent much of his life in Japan and considers the approach of Buddhist mysticism to be eminently suited to the practice of Christianity, recommended. Smart, N (1969) *The Religious Experience of Mankind* New York. An enduring classic. Zaehner, RC (ed) (1993) *The Hutchinson Encyclopaedia of Living Faiths* Oxford.

Farmer, BH (1991, 2nd ed.) *An Introduction to South Asia* Methuen. Perhaps the best and most balanced short introduction to modern South Asia. Robinson, F (ed) (1989) *The Cambridge Encyclopedia of India* CUP: Cambridge. Excellent and readable introduction to many aspects of South Asian life. Beginning to show its age in the absence of a much needed revised edition.

Batchelor, S (1987) *The Tibet Guide* Wisdom Publications. Information on the Buddhist sites of Central and W Tibet. Chen, V (1994) *Tibet Handbook*, Moon Publications. Good trekking information. Craig, M (1992) *Tears of Blood*, Harper Collins. Recent history. Dalai Lama *Freedom in Exile* and *My Land and My People*. Autobiographical works. Dorje, Gyurme (1999) *Tibet Handbook* Footprint Handbooks: Bath. One of the present series and the only comprehensive guide to the Tibetan Plateau by one of the world's leading scholars of the region. Foreword by the Dalai Lama. McCue, G (1991) *Trekking in Tibet* Leicester. Richardson, H (1984) *Tibet and Its History* Shambhala.

Essentials

Travel Guides
see also the Trekking section

Allardice, D. and Knowles, P (1993) *White Water Nepal*, London. The definitive, though expensive, rafting guide. Dowman, K (1993) *The Great Stupa of Boudhnath* Kathmandu. A good brief guide to the myths, history and relevance of the stupa. Hatt, J (1999) *The Tropical Traveller: the Essential Guide to Travel in Hot Countries*. Excellent, wide ranging and clearly written common sense, based on extensive experience and research. Hoefer, H (1990) *Kathmandu* Singapore. An Insight guide notable for its many superb photographs which capture the essence of life in the Valley.

Travelogues

In addition to the following, there are many superb coffee-table photographic books. Beal, S (1906) *Buddhist Records of the Western World*, London. Beal, S (1911) *Life of Hiuen Tsang*, London. An account of one of the earliest foreign (Chinese) visitors to Nepal. Greenwald, J, *Shopping for Buddhas* and *Mister Raja's Neighbourhood*. Entertaining accounts of travel through Nepal. Legge, J (1886) *Travels of Fa Hien* Oxford. Matthieson, P (1979) *The Snow Leopard* London. This account of travelling through NW Nepal in search of the elusive feline has become a classic of travel writing. Murphy, D *The Waiting Land*. Peissel, M (1966) *Mustang: A Lost Tibetan Kingdom*. A brilliant description of the author's travels through the mountain desert, with some superb photographs; *Tiger for Breakfast*, London. Pye-Smith, C *Travels in Nepal*, London. One of the most popular and insightful travelogues. Somerville-Large, P *To the Navel of the World*.

Mountaineering
see also the Trekking section

Bonnington, C (1971) *Annapurna South Face* London, Cassell: London; and *Everest the Hard Way* Hodder & Stoughton: London (1979). Herzog, M, *Annapurna*. Describes the first successful ascent. Hillary, E (1955) *High Adventure* Dutton: New York. Messner, R *All 14 Eight-Thousanders* Crowood. Tilman, HM (1948) *Two Mountains and a River*, Cambridge University Press: Pakistan.

Wildlife

Ali, SA and Ripley, SD (1968-74) *Handbook of the Birds of India and Pakistan Together with those of Nepal, Sikkim, Bhutan and Ceylon* Bombay. 10 volumes. Fleming, RL Sr and RL Jr (1979) *Birds of Nepal* Kathmandu. Definitive work, now out of print and commanding prices of up to $200 in Kathmandu's second hand bookshops. Gurung, KK (1983) *Heart of the Jungle*, London. Good survey of the wildlife of Chitwan National Park, out of print. Stainton, JDA (1972) *The Forests of Nepal* Murray: London.

Useful numbers

Tours & tour operators

UK: *Exodus*, T0181-6755550. *Explorasia*, T0171-6307102. *Gateway to Asia*, T01283-821096, F01283-820467, www.gateway-to-asia.com. *Himalayan Kingdoms*, T0117-9237163. *Promotion Nepal (Europe) Ltd*, T0171-2293528. *STA Travel*, T0171-3616161. *Trans Himalaya*, T01373-455518.

USA: *Abercrombie & Kent*, T312-9542944. *Archaeological Tours*, T212-9863054. *Distant Horizons*, T617-2675343. *Erickson Travel, Inc.*, T800-208-8129, F206-285-9252, info@ericksontravel.com. *Mountain Travel*, T415-5278100. *Myths and Mountains*, T800-670-6984, www.mythsandmountains.com. *Tiger Tops International*, T415-3463402.

Trekking

3

Trekking

77 Trekking seasons

78 Preparations

89 On the trek

90 Wildlife

91 Cultural & environmental sensivity

94 Safety and security

94 Health

Western Himalaya treks

96 Trek 1: Rara Lake

99 Trek 2: Jumla to Dunai

Annapurna Himal treks

103 Trek 3: Northern Circuit

108 Trek 4: Southern Circuit

114 Trek 5: Annapurna Base Camp

118 Trek 6: The Royal Trek

120 Trek 7: Tatopani & Baglung

123 Trek 8: Mustang

Langtang & Helambu treks

129 Trek 9: Gosainkund & Helambu

134 Trek 10: Syrabu to Tarke Ghayang

Everest Himal treks

140 Trek 11: Everest Base Camp

150 Trek 12: Gokyo Lakes

152 Trek 13: Lukla Escape

Eastern Himalaya treks

153 Trek 14: Makalu Base Camp

157 Trek 15: Kanchenjunga Base Camp

160 **Mountaineering & mountain biking**

161 **Rafting**

Fortunately, Nepal offers probably the finest and the greatest diversity of trekking opportunities in the world. There are routes and choices of terrain to suit most people. It's important to remember that the more difficult treks are not necessarily the best: what one person gains by walking from Jiri to Everest Base Camp, another will get from a short trek north of Pokhara or by strolling through the hills of the Kathmandu Valley. Other than proper planning and taking informed, sensible care of yourself, your fellow trekkers and surroundings whilst en route, there is no definitive 'way' of trekking nor any speed at which you have to walk: the main thing is to enjoy the experience.

***NB** This section gives an idea of the trekking opportunities in Nepal and will help in planning and organizing your trek. It is intended only for guidance and is not a substitute for the detailed route descriptions and good maps that a specialist publication will provide. Consult the book and map lists on pages 87-89 for our recommendations and always obtain local advice.*

Origins of trekking

The word *trek* came into the English language from the Afrikaans. It was first widely used in the early 19th century by the *vortrekkers*, the early Dutch colonizers of South Africa. The verb *trekken* meant 'to draw a vehicle or load' or 'to migrate', and carries connotations of hardship and physical endurance. Trekking through the Himalaya has only come to be a leisure activity or sport since the mid-20th century; before then (as, indeed, is often the case still today), the only way to get from one point to another was to walk. The earliest long distance Himalayan trekkers would have been traders carrying goods, typically along one of the trade routes between India and Tibet.

Modern day trekkers will be following in the footprints of Bill Tilman (see box), one of the most intrepid of 20th century British explorers and the first Westerner to be granted permission to trek for pleasure in 1949 – a full two years before Nepal was opened to tourists. It was not until 1965, though, that the first organized trekking trip for amateurs was arranged in Nepal, doubtless influenced by the increased popularity and high profile coverage of expeditions led by Chris Bonnington et al. Since then, trekking has grown into one of the country's more important economic activities; indeed, more people visit Nepal annually for trekking than on business! In 1991, 42,308 trekking permits were issued; just three years later, this figure had risen to 76,865 permits issued.

Prominent peaks

The sheer scale of such a concentration of rocky might as in the Nepal Himalaya is hard to comprehend, though may be illustrated by the hypothetical calculation that if you were to put the highest mountains of Britain (Ben Nevis), France (Mont Blanc) and Australia (Kosciusko) on top of each other, their combined height would be less than any of the individual heights of Makalu, Lhotse, Kanchenjunga and Everest in Nepal! Of the world's 14 peaks higher than 8,000 metres, eight out of the highest 10 are in Nepal. They are: Everest (8,848 metres), Kanchenjunga (8,598 metres), Lhotse (8,511 metres), Makalu (8,475 metres), Dhaulagiri (8,167 metres), Manaslu (8,162 metres), Cho Oyu (8,153 metres) and Annapurna I (8,091 metres).

Of course, climbing expeditions for all the above require experience, detailed planning and mountaineering permits. There are, however, 18 lesser peaks euphemistically designated as '**trekking peaks**' which are open to trekkers. The somewhat arbitary distinction effectively means that climbers can bypass the ponderous and costly process of applying for a mountaineering permit. Many of these peaks nevertheless require high standards of climbing skills and should not be attempted lightly. They are:

Mera Peak 6,654 metres; Chulu Peak 6,584 metres; Singu Chuli (Flute Peak) 6,501 metres; Hiunchuli 6,441 metres; Chulu West 6,419 metres; Kusum Kanguru 6,367 metres; Parchemuche 6,187 metres; Imja Tse (Island Peak) 6,183 metres; Lobuche 6,119 metres; Pisang 6,091 metres; Kawande 6,011 metres; Ramdung 5,925 metres; Paldor Peak 5,896 metres; Khongma Tse (Mehra) 5,849 metres; Kangja Chuli 5,844 metres; Pokalde 5,806 metres; Tharpu Chuli (Tent Peak) 5,663 metres; Mardi Himal 5,587 metres.

Trekking seasons

October and **November** are the best months. The air is clear and the vegetation still lush after the monsoon. Both day and night temperatures are pleasant at lower elevations, ranging from around 25°C to 3°C. Above 3,000 metres, meanwhile, temperatures may drop to well below zero at night. But these are also the months when the major trails are at their busiest and when flights and guest houses are often fully booked.

December and **January** are colder, especially at higher altitudes, and generally dustier. This is probably the best time of year for completely unobstructed views. High passes, such as Thorung La on the Annapurna Circuit, can be closed, so you will have to take more equipment. Everest looks bare with little snow cover.

From **late February** temperatures begin to rise with the steady heating of the Tibetan High Plateau. **March** and **April** are hazy with views becoming obscured. However, this is the best time of year for seeing both wildlife and the blossoming of the Himalayan flora, notably the rhododendron. **May** is very hot and quite dusty. Streams are nearly dry and there are regular thunderstorms.

Trekking during the **monsoon** can be recommended only for the most ardent and experienced. The climate is hot, humid and uncomfortable at lower elevations. Rivers also rise dramatically and often become unfordable, while many trails become treacherously slippery and cloud obscures mountain views for much of the time. Equipment gets damp and heavier and you will be able to cover shorter distances. It is, however, the time when the vegetation is at its most luxuriant. Weather in late **September** is unpredictable, but the trails are much less crowded and hence more pleasant.

NB Beware of **leeches** during the monsoon. They sway on the ground and on twigs and bushes waiting for a passer-by and get in boots when you are walking. They feed on blood, but their bite contains an anaesthetic so you may not feel them. They drop off when they are full leaving you with blood soaked boots and legs. Don't try pulling one off, as the head will get left behind and cause infection. Pour some salt, or hold a lighted cigarette to it, which will encourage its rapid departure. Before starting off in the morning it may help to spray socks and bootlaces with an insect repellent.

Himalayan trekking regions

▲ **Trekking regions**
1 Western Nepal
2 Annapurnas
3 Mustang
4 Langtang, Helambu & Gosainkund
5 The Everest Region (Also known as Solu Khumbu)
6 Eastern Nepal

Bill Tilman: mountaineer, explorer and travelling sail's man

Even today, with established routes, plentiful accommodation and other facilities, a trek through the Himalaya is not everybody's idea of a relaxing holiday. But it would have taken an unusual spirit to pioneer the sport in challenging and remote areas where Westerners had scarcely been heard of before. Harold William Tilman was such a man.

Born in Cheshire, in the north of England, in 1898, he served with the Royal Artillery on the Western Front during WW1. His first mountaineering exploits came during his time as a planter in Kenya when he climbed several east African peaks with compatriot Eric Shipton, including the first successful ascent of Midget Peak, Mt Kenya in 1930. Together with Shipton, he next turned his attention to the Himalaya, participating in the attempt to climb Everest in 1935 and then leading the expedition of 1938. These and similar expeditions of the time are widely considered to have paved the way for Hillary's first ascent of Everest in 1953. They also prompted his interest in trekking

in Nepal and in 1949 he obtained permission to trek in the Helambu and Kali Gandaki regions. In between, he made another first ascent – of Nanda Devi in 1936. His climbing activities were interrupted by the outbreak of WW2, during which he served in the Western Desert, in France and with the Italian resistance behind enemy lines in Albania.

Following their fruitful travels from China through Central Asia in 1948, he and Shipton made an unsuccessful attempt to climb Annapurna IV. This effectively marked the end of Tilman's mountaineering career but, after a brief period as consul in Burma, he began long distance sailing. In the course of the next 20 years, he circumnavigated both South America and Africa, and sailed through the waters of the Arctic and Antarctic, journeys which included two shipwrecks. His final voyage began in Southampton in 1977, bound for the South Shetland Islands. He left Rio on 1 November of that year, but never reached his destination.

Preparations

Good preparation, especially if you are trekking independently, goes a long way to ensuring that yours is a trek that is safe and enjoyable. The following is a general introduction of things to do and to think about before setting off and will suffice for most people. For more detailed discussions, consult a specialist trekking manual.

Ways of trekking

This is the first choice you will have to make and there are essentially four options: the escorted trek organized overseas, the locally organized trek with guides and/or porters, the independent *bhatti* ('teahouse') trek, and the backpacking camping trek.

Escorted Treks Organized Overseas A company or individual with local knowledge and expertise organizes a trip and sells it. Some or all camp equipment, food, cooking, planning the stages, decision making based on progress and weather conditions, liaison with porters, shopkeepers, et cetera are all taken care of.

This has the advantage of being a good, safe introduction to the country. You will be able to travel with limited knowledge of the region and its culture and get to places more easily which as an individual you might not reach, without the expense of completely kitting yourself out. You should read and follow any advice in the preparatory material you are sent, as your enjoyment greatly

Trekking for all?

Almost half of all overseas visitors to Nepal spend a part of their travels on a trek. While most return enthused, for some the levels of hygiene and relative lack of amenities are just too much. Especially in some of the higher regions, trekking is unquestionably hard work. A bout of illness, for example, or an ill fitting pair of boots can ruin a trip. Occasionally you will hear comments such as 'I've never had so many blisters – it was agony!', and/or 'It's beautiful all right, but I really don't see what all the fuss is about', but these are seldom and show that we live in a world of diversity. To get the most out of your trek, think about how you will approach it – will you go independently, taking all supplies with you and camping out at night, or will it be in a group on a pre-arranged trek with an established company? It is important to choose a style and route that fits your experience and degree of fitness.

depends on it. This applies particularly to recommendations concerning physical fitness.

An escorted trek involves going with a group. If you are willing to trade some of your independence for careful, efficient organisation and make the effort to ensure the group works well together, the experience can be very rewarding.

Ideally, there should be no more than 20 trekkers in a group, and preferably less. Before booking check the itinerary (is it too demanding, or not adventurous enough?) and what exactly is provided by way of equipment.

Locally Organized Treks

Trekking companies in Kathmandu and Pokhara will organize treks for a fee and provide all Sherpas, porters, cooks, food and equipment, but it also requires effort and careful thought on your part. This method is recommended for groups that want to follow a specific itinerary and demands greater control than would be offered on escorted group treks. You can make arrangements before arriving in Nepal, but it may be advisable to wait until you are in the country though you should allow at least a week to make arrangments.

NB You have to follow a pre-arranged itinerary, as porters expect to arrive at certain points on schedule. Although many Sherpas speak some English, there may be communication problems and misunderstandings. Reputable agencies offer an excellent service, and the Sherpas, often highly skilled, will make every reasonable effort to accommodate you. The agency will probably insist that you take one with you as leader who will act in your interest and on your instructions.

Independent *Bhatti* Trek

Also known as 'teahouse trekking'. Comparitively cheap, it requires little equipment, but facilities are basic. This is probably most suited to those who have trekked in Nepal before. You carry clothes and bedding, as with youth hostelling, and for food and shelter you rely on bhattis. These are inns or teahouses (often run by Thakalis), homes along the trekking route where, for a few rupees a night, you get a space on the floor, a wooden pallet or a camp bed, or in the more luxurious inns, a room and a shower. The food is simple – usually dal-bhad-tarkari which, although repetitive, is healthy and can be tasty. On the popular treks to Everest and in the Annapurna region, such delicacies as apple pie, carrot cake and pancakes may be available, and can be washed down with soft drinks or beer (at a premium).

This approach brings you into closer contact with local people, the limiting factor being the routes where accommodation is available.

NB Bed bugs are common (carry a thin plastic sheet) and kitchen hygiene may be poor. With an organized group, companies have reputations to maintain and try to comply with Western concepts of hygiene.

Independent Backpacking Trek Hundreds of people arrive in Nepal each year with a pack and some personal equipment, buy some food and set off trekking, carrying their own gear and choosing their own campsites or places to stay. Of all the regions in the Himalaya, Nepal caters for this group best. There are some outstandingly beautiful treks, though they are often not the 'wilderness' sometimes conjured up.

NB Many areas outside the Kathmandu Valley are quite densely populated. Supplies of fuel are scarce and flat ground for camping rare. It is not always easy to find isolated and 'private' campsites.

Insurance

This is really important. Travel insurance is not available in Nepal, so get a policy before leaving home. Make sure that it includes trekking – some policies explicitly exclude Himalayan trekking, but you can usually have it included on payment of an additional premium. It should also cover air evacuation, repatriation by air ambulance and medical expenses. Make sure that you know what is included and what is not. Leave a copy of the policy and any important telephone numbers with a family member at home and make sure that they know what to do with it in case of emergency. The price of insurance can vary dramatically, even for similar levels of cover and some are quite extortionately priced. It is well worth shopping around and comparing policies and prices well in advance. Policies directed at young people and students do not necessarily offer the best value. Check the classified travel advertisements in a newspaper.

Trekking permits

Your visa to enter Nepal effectively allows you to travel throughout the Terai and the Kathmandu and Pokhara Valleys. A trekking permit is required for all Himalayan destinations. Trekking permits can only be obtained in Nepal, at the **Immigration Offices** in Kathmandu (Baneshwar) and Pokhara (between the airport and Phewa Tal). The Kathmandu office deals with applications for all areas, while the Pokhara office has been known to issue permits for the Annapurna region only. In theory, you can also get a trekking permit for the Kanchenjunga region (groups only) on arrival at the immigration office in Kakarbhitta. However, immigration officials are known to be reluctant to issue these and instead direct trekkers to Kathmandu, a mere 20 hour bus journey away.

Immigration Office Open for depositing applications 1000-1300 Monday-Thursday, 1000-1200 Friday. Your permit will normally be ready for collection the same day, 1400-1700 Monday-Friday. The office is closed on Saturday. The Immigration Office, in Baneshwar, is a Rs 60 taxi or auto-rickshaw ride from Thamel. A *Hot Breads* shop opposite has a range of snacks and soft drinks. Arrive early, especially in the peak trekking season when queues are very long. If you are going as part of an organized trek, your trekking company will arrange the permit for you. If you are trekking independently, a reputable company may agree to get the permit for you on payment of a service charge. Application forms are colour coded according to different trekking regions – make sure that you are given the right form. Two passport photos are required and you have to specify the route, including any side trips or likely variations. The office also handles

Trekking agencies and services

Both Kathmandu and Pokhara have a huge number of places offering organized treks. It is better to book through a trekking **operator** as distinct from any of the more numerous trekking agents. The agents simply sell the trek on commission, much as a travel agent sells holidays and may thus not be fully informed of the trek's particulars and may not take responsibility for any problems encountered on the trek.

The following companies, based in Kathmandu, make arrangements for many foreign companies and also offer the 'instant trek' service. They offer relatively expensive trips to include mess tents, dining tables, chairs, food, porters, cooks, sirdar (guide/head Sherpa), and toilet tent.

Ama Dablam Trekking (T 410219), Lazimpath. **Himalayan Encounters** Kathmandu Guest House, Thamel. **Malla Treks** (T 418389), Malla Hotel, Lekhnath Marg. **Mountain Travel** (T 414508), Naxal. **President Treks and Expeditions** (T 228873), Durbar Marg. **Sherpa Co-operative Trekking** (T 224068), Durbar Marg. **Tiger Mountain** (T 414508), Hattisar.

In addition, there are smaller companies organising cheaper and less lavish treks. Camping equipment may be taken or accommodation may be arranged in bhattis.

Above The Clouds Trekking (T 416909), Thamel. **Asian Trekking** (T 412821), Tridevi Marg. **Cho-Oyu Trekking** (T 418890), Lazimpath. **Glacier Safari Treks** (T 412116), Thamel. **Himalayan Expeditions** (T 522770), Thamel. **Himalayan Journeys** (T 226139), Kantipath. **Last Frontiers Trekking** (T 416146), Lainchaur. **Macchapuchare Trekking** (T 227207), **Thamel. Mandala Trekking** (T 228600), Kantipath. **Snow Leopard Trekking** (T 414719), Naxal. **Summit Nepal Treks** (T 525408), Summit Hotel, Patan. **Wilderness Experience** (T 220534), Kantipath.

There are many other small companies in Kathmandu, especially in Thamel and Durbar Marg, but take care to find out exactly what is being offered.

NB Make sure that both you and the trekking company understand exactly who is to provide what equipment. For high altitude treks, porters will expect warm clothing. A Sherpa guide will cost more and although he may be prepared to carry a load, his principal function will be as a guide and overseer for the porters.

visa extensions, though a trekking permit automatically extends your visa.

Fees are payable at the time of application, either in US$ or at the convertible Nepali Rs rate and were as follows in 1999: **Permit fees**

Dolpo: US$10 per week for the first four weeks, then US$20 per week

Upper Dolpo: US$700 per week, then US$70 per day

Humla: US$90 for the first week, then US$15 per day

Kanchenjunga: US$10 per week for the first four weeks, then US$20 per week

Manaslu: US$90 per week September-November, US$75 per week December-August

Mustang: US$700 per week for the first four weeks, then US$70 per day

All other areas: US$5 per week for the first four weeks, then US$10 per week.

Trekking

'Eco-Treks'

The quest for a distinctive image combined with growing global concern for the environment have resulted in several companies offering so called 'eco-treks'. The impression is of minimal impact trekking, ie 'take only photos, leave only footprints'. A number of trekking companies do indeed try to take such an approach for which they should be lauded and which, ideally, would be routine for all operators. Others, meanwhile, have made claims of environmental sensitivity which are subsequently shown to have been at variance with actual practices.

Interpretations of eco-trekking (or 'eco-tourism') vary. In the course of research for this handbook, two trekking companies offering ecological-environmental sounding treks could give only the vaguest idea of issues relating to conservation of the environment. Asked as to the reason for the name, one replied that it sounded good and would appeal to trekkers, while the other said that on the trek you could see the beautiful environment and ecology of the Himalaya. Both, of course, are right. But if you want to go on an organized trek with a company that is serious about minimizing their impact on the environment, talk to people who have just returned from a trek and be prepared to shop around and ask plenty of questions before you book.

Restricted areas   Several areas previously off-limits for reasons of national security and cultural and environmental conservation began to be opened to trekkers in the early 1990s. In a deliberate attempt to continue to protect their environment and culture and also because of the revenue they generate, regions such as Mustang remain effectively restricted for many by the prohibitive cost of the trekking permit. Other conditions may also apply to treks in these areas. These include permits being issued to groups only, the employment of a liaison officer (see below), the carrying out of all garbage, prohibition of the use of wood for fuel, and compulsory insurance for all members of the group.

The role of the **liaison officer,** who is seconded from the army, the police or the civil service, has been defined to include acting as interpreter, responsibility for ensuring that there is no deviation from the specified route or from ecological guidelines, to settle disputes, liaise with police and take responsibility for the discipline of the group.

Equipment and clothing

Some hire shops may demand a passport or travellers' cheques as deposit: don't give

If you have good equipment, it is worth taking it even though good quality equipment can be bought or **hired** from a variety of trekking shops in Kathmandu and, to a lesser extent, in Pokhara. On the Everest trek, Namche Bazaar also has shops selling clothing and equipment. The daily hire charges are usually quite small, but a large deposit may be required, for example US$100.

Backpacks   It is worth spending money on a good, ergonomically designed **rucksack**, preferably one that has padded contours, a light (for example aluminium) internal frame and comfortable **waist bands** that allow the weight of the load to be shifted from the shoulders. Several models have small detachable packs which can be used as day packs if you are trekking with porters. In any event, a separate **day pack** is essential. **Women** should consider taking a pack specially designed for wider hips. Other things to consider include: is the backpack **lockable**? Is it **waterproof**? Is it sufficiently **hardy** for your trek? Or, if you are going on a fully organized escorted trek, do you really need that up-to-the-minute super expensive backpack?

What you take depends on where and when you will be trekking. Loose, light **cotton** trousers or long shorts for men are good for low altitude treks, and skirts for women (see also below). In colder, higher altitude treks, take a combination of **thermal** underwear, warm **woollen** sweaters and a woollen or synthetic pile **jacket**. **Water** and **windproof** jacket and trousers to go over are also good in extreme conditions. Because much body heat is lost through the extremities, it is important to take good **socks**, **gloves**, a woolly **hat** or balaclava, and perhaps a shawl. Daytime temperatures can get quite warm, so bring light, loose fitting cotton clothing. A wide brimmed hat is also useful.

Clothing & footwear

NB Nepali society generally considers it improper for men to wear shorts or not to wear a top.

Should be comfortable as well as providing adequate ankle support. Again, what you take will depend on where you are trekking. Good quality **trainers** are quite adequate for many of the lower level treks. Make sure they provide suitable shock absorption and that the soles have good grip. If you are wearing boots, you could take a spare pair of trainers: they are good for fording streams and for changing into after several days hard walking. **Boots** are a must on the higher and more challenging treks. It is essential that they are **worn in** before you set off, otherwise you are in for a very uncomfortable trek. They should come over the ankle (particularly important on a downhill walk), provide good grip and shock absorption, and be waterproof. Those with a metal shank in the sole are the most robust and supportive.

Footwear

There are two main criteria which women should consider in choosing what clothing to take. Nepalis attach considerable importance to **modesty** of dress. In practice, this means that women should not wear revealing low-cut tops, skirts above the knee, or shorts. Although Nepal is as safe for women as anywhere, if you ignore this basic dress code you are liable to invite unwelcome and potentially troublesome attention from men, as well as not being accepted by local people. The second consideration is **practical**. A full length skirt, for example, is culturally appropriate and also makes toilet trips a lot easier than shorts.

Women's wear

There are numerous shops in Kathmandu and Pokhara selling a range of packed and tinned **foods** suitable for taking on a trek. In Kathmandu, supermarkets along Lazimpath, in the New Road area and increasingly around Thamel carry large stocks of imported foods, including pasta, tea, coffee, biscuits, muesli, chocolate and sachets of vitamin-enriched powdered drinks. (**NB** Check expiry dates.) Similarly along the main Lakeside road in Pokhara, though prices here can be higher than in Kathmandu. Some varieties of **bread** available in the Thamel bakeries can last for days. You can buy Nepali yak **cheese** from several cold stores around the city or from the dairy shop on Lekhnath Marg (diagonally opposite the Malla Hotel towards the Royal Palace). Imported cheeses are sold in the *Old Vienna Delicatessen* shops/restaurants in Thamel and on Kantipath and at supermarkets.

Food & cooking equipment

The use of **firewood** is banned in the national parks, so you have to carry kerosene **stoves** with you. National park officials may check to see that you have your own cooking equipment with you when you enter. In the event of getting lost or stranded, it may be wise to take a stove in case, even if you are eating at lodges. Kerosene is sporadically available in the mountains, but may be impure so take sufficient supplies with you. You can hire jerry cans from shops in Kathmandu and Pokhara. You could also take a strainer (for example of fine

The mountain people of Nepal

In addition to the Paharis, 'people of the hills' who inhabit the lower margins of the Himalaya, there are two broad classifications of peoples living in the mountains: the Bhotias who live in the northern border areas, and the other ethnic groups.

Magars

The Magars originate in the western and central areas of Nepal, though are found in scattered communities throughout the country. They may be of either Hindu or Buddhist faith. Traditionally hill farmers inhabiting the lower slopes, they are also known for their fighting abilities and many have been recruited into Gurkha regiments of the British and Indian armies. There is thought to be a strong cultural bond between Magars and Gurungs.

Gurungs

The Gurungs also originate in the central and western parts of Nepal, though have tended to inhabit higher areas adopting a lifestyle of sedentary agriculture and nomadic pastoralism. Like the Magars, Gurungs have also been well represented in Gurkha units. They are predominantly Buddhist, though small Hindu and Shamanist communities exist. In recent years, many Magars have become involved in the hotel business, especially in the Pokhara region.

Thakalis

The Thakalis originate from the Kali Gandaki Gorge and, like many Nepali groups, have been subject to both Hindu and Buddhist influences. Adept entrepreneurs, they have cashed in on the trekking boom and have established little hotels all along the Annapurna Circuit and have also extended their influence to other parts of the country. They are only about 10,000 in number. Before Nepal was opened up to tourism, their economy was dominated by subsistence farming and, in the Kali Gandaki area, by salt trading.

Tamang

The Tamang are found around the Kathmandu Valley and in central and eastern Nepal. Mainly Buddhist, they form a significant proportion of the porters in these regions, but many are also engaged in agriculture as smallholders and day labour. The Tamang language originates from the Tibeto-Burmese family.

Newars

The Newars are of Mongolian origin and are the dominant ethnic group of the Kathmandu Valley and surrounding central areas of Nepal. Their numbers total around 700,000. Despite their geographical origins, the majority are now Shaivite Hindus following received Hindu

Ghandrung Village, the home to many Gurung

customs, although communities of Newari Buddhists do remain. They represent perhaps the greatest synchronism of the Tibetan and Indian traditions of any of Nepal's ethnic groups and also incorporate aspects of animism. The Newari language has been influenced by both the Tibeto-Burmese and Indo-European families. Traditionally Nepal's leading traders, Newars once organized trains of basket carrying porters over the trans-Himalayan passes to Tibet. They are also remarkable craftsmen and developed the unique building style that successfully blends influences from India, China and Tibet, with carved wood beams and pagoda-like temple roofs.

Kirantis

The Kirantis are comprised of Rai and Limbus and are the oldest known peoples of Nepal. They live in the eastern hills of Nepal, the Rais being concentrated in the Solu Khumbu, Dudh Kosi and Arun Valley regions, while the Limbus are east of Arun Valley, in the Kanchenjunga region and also extend into northern parts of West Bengal in India. Both groups have supplied recruits to Gurkha regiments and reference is made to their fighting spirit in the Hindu epic Mahabharata. Of Mongoloid features, both have Tibeto-Burmese languages. The religion of the Limbus incorporates elements of Buddhism and Shamanism, while that of the Rais is more influenced by Hinduism.

Sunwars and Jirels

These related groups are small in number and are found in the area around and to the east of Jiri, the place that gives the Jirels their name. Their religion is significantly influenced by Hinduism, but has distinct practices and deities.

Bhotia

The Bhotia live in the northern parts of Bhutan, Sikkim, Nepal and along the Indo-Tibetan border in Garhwal, Kumaon and Himachal Pradesh. They are a Mongoloid people who gradually moved off the Tibetan Plateau. Tibetan Buddhism plays an important part in shaping Bhotia society. The monastery is at the centre of the social environment, and the prayer flags, prayer wheels and chortens are a vital part of daily life.

The Bhotia Economy   Other Bhotia groups combine the same activity as the Sherpas:subsistence agriculture, animal husbandry and trade, the last two complementing the first because the altitude at which they live only permits one cropping season per year. The crops grown are hardy: wheat, barley, buckwheat and potatoes. The livestock includes sheep, goats and yaks (Bos grummans). Yaks provide many essentials of daily life, the cows producing one litre of rich milk daily. Reflecting how little most ethnic groups moved from their native soil, the suffix pa, as in Lopa, means 'people of'.

Ethnic Tibetans

Many thousands of Tibetans fled their homeland as a result of the Chinese takeover. Most are now resident in and around the Kathmandu and Pokhara Valleys, but some have remained in Bhotia country where they have been highly successful in integrating with local populations, especially through intermarriage.

Baragaunle

The name means '12 village people'. The Baragaunle are also ethnically Tibetan and live in the Muktinath Valley and follow a form of Lamaistic Buddhism that also incorporates elements of animism.

Dolpopas

With a population of no more than a couple of thousand, Dolpopas live in remote areas north of Jomsom and Muktinath. A hard working people, they

Trekking

Trekking

are nomadic pastoralists, traders and weavers.

Limipas

The Limipas are a small group living in the Limi Valley in the northwest of Nepal.

Lopas

Lopas live in Lo Manthang, the capital of the high and arid region of Mustang, once an independent state. Of Tibetan ethnicity, they follow Tibetan Buddhism and number about 6,000.

Manangis

Known also as Manangpa or Nyeshang, this group live in the Manang region and along the northern stretches of the Marshyangdi River. They are perhaps the wealthiest of any Bhotia groups thanks to a still extant 18th century decree by Rana Bahadur Shah which gave them trading priviliges with Tibet and which has today been adapted to the trade of luxury items, some of which find their way to Kathmandu.

Sherpas

Sherpas live in the Solu Khumbu region of glacial valleys at the southern approaches to Everest. Their name tells of their origin (Sha – east, pa – people) and has come to be almost synonymous with the great peak that dominates their country. They immigrated from Tibet around 600 years ago. Earlier they were traders and porters, carrying butter, meat, rice, sugar, paper and dye from India, and salt, wool, jewellery, Chinese silk and porcelain from Tibet and beyond. The closure of the border following the 1962 border war between India and China undermined their economy. Fortunately, with the arrival of mountaineering expeditions and trekkers, the Sherpas found their load carrying skills, both on normal treks and in high altitudes, in great demand. The Khumbu region has provided a valuable contigent of able bodied, hardy and seemingly fearless Sherpa porters and guides. Over 80 years they have built up a mountaineering reputation as the élite of Himalayan porters. Early expeditions took Sherpas from Darjeeling to climb in far flung places in the Himalaya. They were often referred to as 'Tigers', but they were rarely accorded the recognition of their full worth. Sherpa Tenzing, the best known Sherpa guide for his involvement with the first Western expedition to reach the summit of Everest, received the British civilian award for bravery, while John Hunt, the expedition leader, was elevated to the peerage and Edmund Hillary was knighted.

gauze mesh) for sifting out impurities. The **MSR stove** is lightweight and has been recommended for its efficiency. Make sure that you also take spare parts for the stove. If problems occur, start by ensuring that the pump is always properly oiled and that the vaporizing jet holes are clear. A **pressure cooker** reduces cooking times thereby saving fuel.

Tents & sleeping bags
A good quality **tent** able to provide high levels of insulation as well as protection from high winds (for example domed or tunnel) is crucial if you are camping out in low temperatures. A good **sleeping bag** is also vital. A sheet sleeping bag can be used inside the main sleeping bag for warmth and comfort, and may also suffice for sleeping at lower, warmer alititudes. A thick foam or inflatable undermat is lightweight; it helps considerably with insulation and is a lot more comfortable than the hard ground.

Medical Kit
(See also **Health Information** section) Take a small medical kit which might include water purification tablets or solution, oral rehydration salts/solution, plasters, bandages, antiseptic cream, anti-diarrhoea medicine (for example imodium), and pain killers (for example aspirin, paracetamol).

Vitamins and minerals are useful to have as a dietary supplement, particularly on longer treks.

Before you leave for Nepal, you might think about asking your doctor for advice on treatment/prevention of altitude sickness. Some, though not all, GPs may also be willing to prescribe antibiotics in advance for treatment of common infections likely to be encountered on the trek.

Sunglasses are an essential item, especially if you are trekking above the snow-line. Make sure that they are of the type to absorb both ultraviolet and visible light. Cheaper varieties do not filter out harmful rays and can seriously damage your eyes. If you wear **contact lenses** bring a spare pair. Disposable lenses have been recommended.

Women should carry extra tampons or sanitary towels. Imported brands are increasingly available in Kathmandu's supermarkets, but are not available along the trekking routes. High altitude can affect the menstrual cycle and cause irregular periods.

Contraception It is advisable not to take oral contraceptives if you are spending any time above 4,000 metres (13,000 feet). Because of potential blood clotting problems associated with the pill, it is best to discontinue it several weeks before going to altitude. Indian-made condoms are available in Nepal's towns and cities, but are said to be less reliable and smaller than Western varieties.

Money

Your expenses while are on the trek are likely to be relatively low. Indeed, there is little to spend your money on other than food and accommodation. Neither credit cards nor travellers' cheques are accepted along any treks, so you have to take cash. You should carry a supply of **low denomination notes**, as it is virtally impossible to change higher denominations anywhere in the mountains or in remote rural areas.

Books

There is no shortage of trekking guides and travelogues, available both in Nepal and in Europe and the USA. The main problem with all trekking guidebooks is that they are soon out of date. Route descriptions may have been accurate at the time the trek was researched, but topography changes with season (is the river a raging torrent or a mere trickle of water?) and routes change through, for example, access to a new and better trailhead, established paths being washed away, the construction or destruction of bridges and so on. The following is a small selection of available titles.

Armington, Stan (1994): *Trekking in the Nepal Himalaya* (Hawthorn, Australia. Lonely Planet Publications, various editions). A popular guide from a knowledgeable and experienced trekker. Covers all the main treks and others with detailed and easy to follow route descriptions.

Bezruchka, Stephen (1997): *Trekking in Nepal: A Traveller's Guide* (Leicester, Cordee; Seattle, The Mountaineers, seventh edition). An excellent and comprehensive guide to all aspects of trekking in Nepal. Route descriptions, advice on preparing a trek and a good health care section. Informative, perceptive and resounding with palpable affection for the country.

Brewer Lama, Wendy (1992): *Trekking Gently in the Himalaya*

(Kathmandu, Sagarmatha Pollution Control Project). Booklet with useful tips for trekkers.

Byers III, Alton C (1987): *Treks on the Kathmandu Valley Rim* (Kathmandu, Sahayogi Press, various editions). Descriptions of shorter treks.

HMG of Nepal (1995): *Trekking in Nepal* (Kathmandu, Dept of Tourism). Free booklet covering the major treks.

O'Connor, Bill (1990): *Adventure Treks Nepal* (Wiltshire, Crowood; Seattle, Cloudcap). Personal accounts of trekking and climbing trips.

O'Connor, Bill (1989): *Trekking Peaks of Nepal* (Wiltshire, Crowood; Seattle, Cloudcap). A guide to trekking/climbing the defined peaks.

Rowell, Galen (1980): *Many People Come, Looking, Looking* (Seattle, The mountaineers). Personal travelogue with stunning photographs.

Swift, Hugh (1993): *Trekking in Nepal, West Tibet and Bhutan* (San Francisco, Sierra Club). An overview of various routes and the region.

Tucci, Guiseppe (1982): *Journey to Mustang* (Kathmandu, Ratna Pustak Bhandar). A fascinating account from a 1950s trip.

Maps

There is a fairly wide range of trekking maps available in Kathmandu. *Pilgrims Bookshop* in Thamel has a good stock but can be expensive. Because of their popularity, the Annapurna and Everest regions have the best cartographic coverage. Maps of northwest Nepal in particular are often hard to come by and are generally less accurate than others.

The Austrian *Schneider* (or *Research Scheme Nepal Himalaya*) series are printed in colour and are widely considered to be the best, but they are also the most expensive. There are *Schneider* titles (1:50,000) covering the region from Kathmandu to far eastern Nepal, including Everest and Kanchenjunga. There is also a 1:100,000 map of Helambu and Langtang, but this is not as accurate as those of the eastern regions.

The Nepali produced *Mandala* (or *Latest Trekking Map*) series of maps are much cheaper and the most popular with trekkers. Some are full colour, others are blue dyeline. This series is widely acknowledged to be of variable accuracy, though is usually sufficient for most trekkers. Most trekking regions are covered, scales from 1:50,000 to 1:200,000. Other locally produced maps include the colour *Nepa* series.

Cartography surreptitiously carried out for the Survey of India in the 1920s (in true Kiplingesque 'Great Game' style) resulted in the mapping of Nepal as never before and forms the base for several maps still in use today. These include the following sheets, by the German *Arbeitsgemeinschaft für vergleichende Hochgebirgsforschung* (commissioned by *Nelles*): Khumbu Himal (Nr 2), Lapchi Kang (Nr 3), Rolwaling Himal (Nr 4), Shorung/Hinku (Nr 5), Tamba Kosi (Nr 6), Dudh Kosi (Nr 7), all at scales of 1:50,000. They also publish two further maps, of 1:100,000 scale: Helambu-Langtang (Nr 8), and Annapurna (Nr 9).

A 1960s series of *US Army Map Service* maps (U502 series, 1:250,000) was also based on the Survey of India maps and covers much of the Himalayan region. These are rarely available in Nepal. While the topography is fairly accurate, elevations are not and many villages do not appear.

The *KMTNC* publishes one of the best maps (1:125,000) of the Annapurna region, while the Everest region is well covered by *Royal Geographical Society* and *National Geographic* maps.

New are the *Finnmap* series (1:50,000) which cover all of Northeast Nepal. 37 sheets cover Langtang, Khumbu and Kanchenjunga.

The following outlets all stock a wide range of maps.
Germany: *ILH Geo Buch Verlag*, Honigwiesen Str 25, Postfach 80 08 30, D-700 Stuttgart 80. *Geo Buch Verlag*, Rosental 6, D-8000 München 2.
Italy: *Libreria Alpina*, Via C Coronedi-Berti 4, 40137 Bologna, Zona 3705.
Switzerland: *Travel Bookshop*, Rindermarkt 20, 8001 Zurich.
UK: *Cordee Books*, 3A De Montfort Street, Leicester LE1 7HD (T0116-2543579; F0116-2471176). *Stanfords*, 12-14 Long Acre, London WC2E 9LP (T0171-8361321; F0171-8360189).
USA: *Maplink*, 25 East Mason Street, Santa Barbara, CA 93101. *Michael Chessler Books*, PO Box 2436, Evergreen, CO 80439. *US Library of Congress, Geography and Map Division*, 101 Independence Avenue, Washington DC 20540.

On the trek

Nepalis eat very little breakfast, but have a large early lunch at around 1000, then a second meal later in the day around sundown. On an organized trek, you will probably be woken at around 0600, have a light breakfast, start walking at around 0730, stop for a cooked midday meal at around 1100, start again a couple of hours later and arrive in camp at around 1500-1600. This routine differs from other regions of the Himalaya, so don't be surprised when the porters stop mid-morning for their main meal. *— Daily Routine*

The footpath is the principal line of communication between villages. Especially in the main trekking regions, paths tend to be very good, well graded and in good condition, but without many flat stretches. *— Terrain*

The popular treks such as the Annapurna circuit and Everest Base Camp have quite good hotels with private rooms, occasionally showers and reasonable menus. On less popular routes there are *bhattis*. *— Accommodation*

It is important to maintain a balanced diet and to keep properly hydrated. If you are self catering, a large collapsable plastic water container is very useful and will save numerous trips to the water source. *Bhatti* food consists largely of dal-bhad-tarkari, although on the popular treks you might also find Western items on the menu. You can significantly reduce both waiting time and cooking fuel if you order your food as a group. Eating utensils may be provided, but is customary to eat with your right hand. Never use your left hand for eating or handling food, as it takes the place of toilet paper in Nepal and throughout South Asia. *— Food & water*

These are dotted along all trekking routes and elsewhere. Your trekking permit, passport, park entrance receipt, et cetera may be checked, and you will probably be asked to enter your name in a register. It can take up to an hour for a large group to go through the formalities. If you are with a liaison/environment officer, he will usually deal with everything. Don't avoid them, as this may raise suspicion. In emergencies, messages may be relayed to you through police checkpoints. *— Police Checkpoints*

Guides and porters can be hired in Kathmandu through trekking companies, equipment shops, hotels, restaurants and elsewhere. It is best to talk to recently returned trekkers who can make recommendations (or give warning!). Also check the noticeboards, including those at the HRA and KEEP offices, around Thamel for referrals and suggestions. On the main routes you may not need a *— Guides & Porters*

Trekking

guide, especially if you have the confidence of having trekked before, but having one can make things a lot smoother *en route*, for example by reducing instances of being ripped off, helping in emergencies and so on. The ability to communicate easily is also an important consideration, so try to find a guide with a reasonable knowledge of English.

The majority of guides and porters are decent and reliable, but those who are not make it important to 'shop around' and not necessarily hire the first person to offer his services. You will invariably be shown a note book or a stack of letters from satisfied trekkers, though you might want to ask for other references which can more easily be substantiated. During the peak trekking seasons (October-November and March-April) the demand for trekking personnel is at its highest, so it pays to begin making enquiries as early as possible if you want the best crew. Some people have found those guides and porters from the mountainous ethnic groups to be more reliable than those originating in Kathmandu, Pokhara and other lower regions, but this is not a general rule. **Sherpas** are an ethnic group from the Everest and Solu Khumbu region and have long been regarded as the quintessential Himalayan guides. The **Sirdar** is the guide, or head guide and generally does no carrying. There are a small number of places in both Kathmandu and Pokhara where **women** can hire female guides – ask around.

The guide will contribute to many of the decisions to be taken during a trek, such as where to camp and which route to follow. It is not unknown for these judgements to be influenced by considerations extraneous to the requirements of your trekking party. It is worthwhile, therefore, to agree on routes and the location of overnight stops before you start.

You will have to provide your porters with **clothing** and **equipment** for snow and cold weather, as well as **insurance**. This includes footwear, warm clothes and protective glasses or goggles. If you are camping out, remember to provide shelter, food and cooking equipment for all personnel. You are also responsible for the costs of porters' and guides' transport throughout the trek as well as on the return. The individual duties and system of **wages** for porters and guides can seem rather complicated and reflect the hierachical structure of Nepali society. Ask trekking agencies, recently returned trekkers, or at the KEEP/HRA office in Thamel, to get an idea of what to pay. Rates will vary according to their experience and linguistic abilities, the law of supply and demand (that is where and when you hire) and what else is included, for example food, clothing, et cetera. They should be neither miserly nor inflated but reasonable: paying too little is irresponsible and if you pay too much you will set a precedent that future trekkers with fewer resources may be unable to follow.

Tipping has become routine and is expected if you are trekking with porters and other Nepali personnel. Speak to recently returned trekkers or to KEEP/HRA for current rates. It is advisable to decide on the approximate amount your group will tip before leaving, remembering that there is a hierachy among porters, cooks, Sherpas, guides, et cetera and making allowance for performance. Set aside in advance your own share of the overall tip according to how much each person will receive.

Wildlife

The Himalayan region encompasses a range of flora and fauna, though vegetation and the animal life it supports grows more luxuriant with the drop in altitude. Widespread deforestation both in the Himalaya and elsewhere has removed the natural habitat of a large number of mammals and has increased the significance of the Himalaya as a home for many remaining species.

The dominant oaks and conifers of the moist lower regions give way to dense and often extensive stands of rhododendron and pine from about 2,500 metres. The Himalayan cypress and cedar are found in west Nepal and in the Karnali area. Various species of bamboo are common especially in the Annapurnas. They require a very moist climate to thrive and in these areas you will often see numerous types of orchid and other wild flowers. Broad stands of fir are found up to about 3,500 metres, above which the more resilient birch extends in forests to the tree line, that is the maximum altitude for tree growth, just below 5,000 metres. Above this point, snow inhibits much plant growth, though grassland, shrubs and sporadic flowering plants may grow for a further 1,000 metres.

Flora

The best time to see Himalayan flowers in bloom is from March-May, when rhododendrons, the national flower, blossom in a startlingly attractive deep red, along with numerous other plants.

Deer, including the muntjak and the rare musk deer, are amongst the most common **mammals** and are found in the lower regions, especially in forest margins and near water sources. Black bears are common, though infrequently seen, at altitudes of up to 3,700 metres, while primates, including the red panda and grey langur, also inhabit lower level forests. The common leopard is the only large feline to inhabit these regions and does so in significant numbers, although it too is rarely sighted. The arboreal clouded leopard and the fabled snow leopard live respectively in the higher altitude birch forests and above the treeline, but are among the most elusive of all Nepal's mammals. Wild goats and sheep include the Ibex and Markhor of the western Himalaya; the tahr, inhabiting forests and steep and scraggy slopes up to 3,500 metres; and the blue sheep feeding on grassy slopes above 3,500 metres.

Fauna

The Himalaya are home to several species of **bird** at elevations up to 4,000 metres and higher, including many migrating varieties. Birds of prey are common and include several species of vulture. Brightly coloured flycatchers and sunbirds are frequently seen, the latter being particularly prominent in rhododendron forests. The bird life changes abruptly beyond 4,000 metres, where snow pigeons, choughs and snow cocks are among species adapted to the colder, rarer environment.

NB It is against the law to take away most species of flora and fauna from the Himalaya. In 1996, Kathmandu airport officials arrested a traveller about to leave the country with 200 species of butterfly for his collection.

Cultural and environmental sensitivity

There are many publications devoted to this subject. Some approach the issue with an almost evangelistic zeal which, whilst their sincerity is not in doubt, inadvertently results in a kind of manifesto of ecological correctness that can intimidate the reader. The question of how to act, of what to do and what not to do, is ultimately up to the individual trekker. But by finding out about some of the customs of Nepali society and about the pressures placed upon the environment by trekkers, not only will you be able to interact better with local cultures and thereby get more out of the trek yourself, but you will also be able to make a positive contribution to protecting the fantastic though delicate beauty

Trekking

of the Himalaya which probably drew you there in the first place. It may also prompt a deeper interest in the region and in the complex relationships between man and the environment.

The logic behind some customs and manners is straightforward, while others seem at best obscure. By understanding the reasons for doing things (or by accepting them when they are incomprehensible), you will find them a lot easier to observe. They can vary considerably between different communities and from place to place.

Customs   Many are concerned with cleanliness and appearance. When **eating** or handling food, Nepalis use only their right hand. The left hand is used in conjunction with a jug of water in place of toilet paper, a practice some consider to be ecologically correct but which also contributes to the transmission of disease if hands and fingernails are not cleaned properly afterwards. Slurping hot drinks and eating noisily is an accepted expression of enjoyment of the food. Similarly, burping after a meal is also understood as a mark of appreciation (but note that a loud, exaggerated belch will certainly be recognized for what it is). In some households, only the cook is permitted to enter the kitchen. Food is considered by some castes to have been ritually 'contaminated' upon contact with a person of a lower caste, which includes Westerners who are outside the caste system. Some castes will also not eat in the presence of lower castes: this is a social norm and is not meant to be offensive. Beef is generally not eaten by Nepalis and the slaughter of cattle is illegal. When **drinking**, many Nepalis will not allow the rim of the glass or bottle to touch their lips. The impressive pouring of water into the mouth, down the throat and into the stomach in a single action without appearing to swallow does not come naturally to most Westerners. To try, start by pouring a small amount and gradually increase. If you pour too much you can end up spluttering, soaked and with a rapid build up of gas. During menstruation, a woman is considered ritually 'unclean' and, strictly speaking, should neither cook for the family nor enter a temple.

It is worth underlining the importance of proper **dress**, especially when trekking outside the more popular routes. Nepalis do not consider it decent for men to walk baretop, and shorts are often frowned upon. Women are not thought to be properly dressed if they wear skirts above the knee, low cut or revealing tops, or tight fitting clothes. Take care also when you are washing and bathing. If you are in the vicinity of local people, don't bathe topless or in the nude. At best, people will be highly shocked.

Many Nepalis are highly **superstitious** and hold a firm belief in astrology, in omens and spirits. These are deeply held beliefs which it is both impolite and unwise to ridicule. Numbers are often considered auspicious. The number three, for example, is thought to be unlucky. When a payment is made, or money given as a wedding present, the amount will often end in one and will never be an even number. Handing someone a red chilli or putting it on another's plate is believed to result in an argument. The crow is considered a bad omen – you will occasionally see dead crows hung outside a house to ward off misfortune. The spirits of the dead are believed to play an active role in the world. The souls of one's ancestors may be honoured in rituals and food prepared and left out for them.

Environment   The main problem posed to the environment by trekking is the belief of individual trekkers that their impact makes little or no difference. This is quite likely true, but it makes a big difference when there are many thousands of individual trekkers each leaving their own small amount of rubbish here and uncovered toilet offerings there. What can I do about it?

When going to the **toilet**, find a suitably discreet spot a good distance from a river or water source (at least 30 metres). This will avoid the gradual seepage of excrement into other people's supply of drinking water. Dig a hole in which to bury the waste matter (bring a small plastic trowel) and cover it up. Alternatively, burn the toilet paper or, when the ground is hard, cover everything with rocks. Some groups use one large plastic bag in which to collect all toilet paper, packed individually, for burning later: it's only embarrassing to start with.

Garbage is an eyesore as well as a pollutant and there is nobody who comes and clears up afterwards. Increasingly, groups are employing an extra porter to carry out all the rubbish generated on the trek. Alternatively, you can separate the biodegradable waste and burn and bury it. The rest can be carried out. Remember that those things that are biodegradable may take many years to degrade, and that the colder it is the longer it takes.

Garbage

Trekking is just one of the factors contributing to **deforestation** in the Himalaya, but it is significant. It's difficult to measure exactly either the rate at which forests are being denuded or how quickly they are regenerating. It is certain, though, that the former is happening on a disturbingly large scale whereas the latter takes generations. Much deforestation, moreover, is concentrated in areas which include several trekking routes. The use of **firewood** is banned in all national parks and trekkers have to use liquid fuel stoves. The same is encouraged elsewhere, but when you do have to use wood there are things you can do to keep it to a minimum. For example, cook at the same time for all members of the group, using a pressure cooker if you have one. Restrict the amount of hot water for washing and cleaning. Use chemicals to purify drinking water instead of boiling it. If you have a choice, stay at a *bhatti* with solar energy or one that uses kerosene for cooking, and order your food at the same time. Remember to include your group's Nepali crew in cooking and accommodation arrangements. Generally encourage the use of non-timber fuels (see also the **Deforestation, Degradation and Conservation** section).

Energy

The motto of the Sierra Club is worth remembering: 'Leave only footprints, take only photographs'.

The economy of the Himalaya is overwhelmingly **agricultural**. The fertility of the land in the High Himalaya, however, is poor, yields are low and agriculture is areally demanding and subsistence oriented. Covering one third of Nepal's land, this region has only eight percent of its people. Nomadic pastoralism complements agriculture. Livestock are particularly important for their provision of manure and draught labour. The Middle Ranges, meanwhile, of which the Kathmandu and Pokhara Valleys form part, include some areas of high fertility where agriculture is intensive. Elsewhere, elaborate terracing, the careful collection and application of animal manure as fertilizer and a cropping pattern designed not to overtax the land can not disguise the fact that soils are low in productivity, the opportunities for irrigation limited and crop yields stagnant. **Tourism** is important to the local economies of isolated areas, while the known deposits of **minerals** such as coal, iron ore, pyrites, limestone and mica are generally too small to be mined commercially. The river systems suggest tremendous potential for **hydroelectric** development, but the Himalayan Valleys offer a costly and dangerous environment for large scale development.

Economy

Safety and security

Trekking in Nepal is generally as safe as you want it to be. Of course, there are occasional natural occurences which do present significant dangers, but these are a function of the environment through which you are travelling. Good preparation and equipment and the avoidance of unnecessary risks can go a long way towards minimizing the chance of any serious mishaps happening to yourself, your fellow trekkers and Nepali crew. The flyers' adage that "There are bold pilots and there are old pilots" can apply just as well to trekkers.

Crime was formerly extremely rare in Nepal. It is still low by international standards, but is on the increase. You can reduce criminal opportunism by hiring porters and guides by recommendation through reliable intermediaries, by keeping all valuables and other items not available locally out of sight and your luggage locked and, especially for women, by not trekking alone and by dressing modestly in accordance with Nepali norms. Most embassies are happy to encourage trekkers to register themselves, the dates and exact routes of their trek. You can also register at the KEEP/HRA office in Thamel.

All **insurance** policies require you to report a theft or any other occurence relating to a claim (including receipts) to the nearest police station and to get a written report on official headed paper.

Health

Acclimatisation and Acute Mountain Sickness (AMS) You may experience AMS in its mildest form. It occurs when an ascent above 3,300 metres (10,000 feet) is attempted too quickly. The body tries to adapt to the considerably reduced concentration of oxygen in the atmosphere of higher altitudes. Mild symptoms include a slight shortness of breath, a mild headache, nausea and dizziness, loss of appetite and increased urine output. If the trekker remains at the altitude where these symptoms first appeared, they will gradually disappear as the body becomes acclimatized. These mild symptoms are nothing to worry about. Most people are affected, regardless of age, sex or physical fitness. If symptoms are severe, however, you should descend **without delay**. If possible the descent should be assisted, for example be carried by fellow trekkers, porters, or animals. It is often easier to detect symptoms in others than in yourself, so keep an eye on the other members of your party if you are climbing above 3,000 metres.

The maxim 'walking high, sleeping low' is worth remembering. You can go quite high and manage for short periods and all will be well if you camp much lower. The *Himalayan Rescue Association* has a good pamhlet on Acute Mountain Sickness. **Warning** A continued ascent beyond the body's ability to adjust may ultimately induce a total breakdown in the acclimatisation process. This condition is potentially fatal. It can be prevented by understanding the causes and taking the necessary precautions. It is **essential** to read '**Acute Mountain Sickness**' in the Health Section in this Handbook.

Other health hints Take extra care to avoid **sun burn** and **snow blindness**. Take great care of your **feet**. **Dehydration** is a constant threat at altitude due to the cold dry air: thirst is not a reliable indicator of your body's needs. Drink as much as possible throughout the day, preferably 3-4 litres.

Himalayan Trust code of practice

By following these simple guidelines, you can help preserve the unique environment and ancient cultures of the Himalaya.

Limit deforestation – make no open fires and discourage others from doing so on your behalf. Where water is heated by scarce firewood, use as little as possible. When possible, choose accommodation that uses kerosene or fuel efficient wood stoves.

Remove litter, burn or bury paper and carry out all non-degradable litter. Graffiti are permanent examples of environmental pollution.

Keep local water clean and avoid using pollutants such as detergents in streams or springs. If no toilet facilities are available, make sure you are at least 30m away from water sources, and bury or cover waste.

Plants should be left to flourish in their natural environment – taking cuttings, seeds and roots is illegal in many parts of the Himalaya.

Help your guides and porters to follow conservation measures.

As a guest, respect local traditions, protect local cultures, maintain local pride.

When taking photographs, respect privacy – ask permission and use restraint.

Respect holy places – preserve what you have come to see, never touch or remove religious objects. Shoes should be removed when visiting temples.

Giving to children encourages begging. A donation to a project, health centre or school is a more constructive way to help.

You will be accepted and welcomed if you follow local customs. Use only your right hand for eating and greeting. Do not share cutlery or cups, etc. It is polite to use both hands when when giving or receiving gifts.

Respect for local etiquette. Loose, light weight clothes are preferable to revealing shorts, skimpy tops and tight fitting action wear. Hand holding or kissing in public are disliked by local people.

Observe standard food and bed charges, but do not condone overcharging. Remember when you're shopping that the bargains you buy may only be possible because of the low income of others.

Visitors who value local traditions encourage local pride and maintain local cultures. Please help local people gain a realistic view of life in Western countries.

The Himalaya may change you – please do not change them.

Make sure that you have travel **insurance** that covers you for trekking in the Himalaya, air evacuation, medical treatment and repatriation by air ambulance. Emergency rescue, as Wendy Brewer Lama stresses in *Trekking Gently in the Himalaya*, is 'never a right, always a privilege and is extremely costly'.

Emergencies

Trek 1
Rara Lake

Set in one of the most isolated regions of Western Nepal the trailhead is Jumla at 2,240 metres above sea level. Whilst the trek route rarely rises above 3,450 metres there are views of nearby peaks Patrasi Himal (6,860 metres) and Jagdula Himal (5,785 metres). The trek runs from the historic centre of Western Nepal Jumla to the Rara National Park which protects Nepal's largest lake and a variety of wild-life. From the Ghurchi Lagna Pass there are good views of the Mugu Karnali River. The trek returns to Jumla through the villages of Botan and Sinja.

Briefing

Access: Flying is the easiest and safest way to get into Jumla. There are flights from Kathmandu (US$143) and Nepalgunj (US$44), and at certain times of the year also from Pokhara. Reservations are not easy to get and there are weight restrictions.

Trailhead: Jumla

Duration: 9 days

Best trekking season: April-September

Altitude: The majority of the trek is between 2,500 and 3,500 metres.

Equipment: There are tea shops along the route, but you will need to take your own

provisions and ensure that you take enough water for the first and the last six hours.

Organization: Guides are essential.

Permit cost: US$5 per week for the first 4 weeks, then US$10 per week. Permit fees are payable either in US$ or at the convertible Nepali Rs rate. Permits are available at the Kathmandu or Pokhara Immigration offices. Rs 650 entrance fee is payable for entry into Rara National Park.

Maps: Mandala Latest Trekking Map Jumla To Api and Saipal Himal (1:250,000). Part of the trek is included in Mandala's Dolpa:Julma to Jomsom (1:20,000). Also US Army Map Service sheet NH44-11.

Day 1   **Jumla to Uthagaon**   From Jumla, walk west along the north bank of the **Tila River** down an old trade route. It is not uncommon to see baggage trains of goats and horses plying the route. After some distance, the trail turns north up the **Chaudhaise River**. **Uthagaon** (2,530 metres) is the first village you come to and you can camp here.

Day 2   **Uthagaon to Bumra**   From Uthagaon climb through the gorge of the **Ghurseni Khola** through pine forest to the small town of **Patmara**. Beyond here water can be a problem and the limiting factor in deciding where to camp. There is a climb through rhododendron and birch forest to the 3,400 metres pass leading to the **Sinj Khola valley**. From here there are views east towards

Patrasi Himal (6,860 metres) and Jagdula Himal (5,785 metres). There is a shepherd's hut near the pass close to a small waterfall. From the pass you descend to the **Sinj Khola** and along the populated valley. The village of **Bumra** (2,580 metres) is on the north side of the valley.

Bumra to Chautha   From Bumra, you climb quite steeply to the tributary   Day 3
valley of the **Chautha Khola** and the village of Chautha which has a small hotel. You can stay here or push on for a further one hour or so to make the fourth day's walk easier.

Chautha to Lake Rara   The upper Chautha Khola Valley is also well wooded.   Day 4
The **Ghurchi Lagna Pass** (3,450 metres) offers good views of the **Mugu Karnali River** which feeds into the Karnali to the west, and of the peaks on the Tibetan border. From the pass you have a choice. You can either go left and follow the ridge and descend to **Lake Rara** from the south, or descend to the village of **Pina** (2,400 metres) in the **Mandu Khola valley**, then turn north-west, cross the intervening 3,000 metres ridge and approach the lake from the southeast. The latter is the easier even though you have first to descend then ascend to reach the lake. You can break the journey at Pina. The former ridge walk is steeper, reaches 4,000 metres and offers magnificent views, though it is not easy to pick up without a local guide.

Lake Rara   The lake is 10 square-kilometres in area and has a circumference   Days 5 & 6
of around 13 kilometres. There are numerous places to camp around the lake. In spring the area is carpeted with flowers. The **park entrance** is on the north

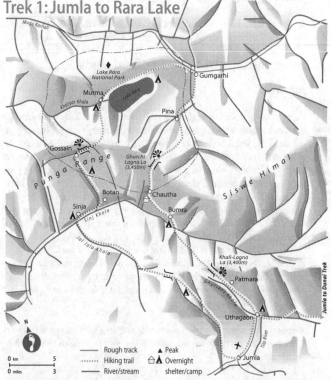

Trekking

Trek 1: Jumla to Rara Lake

side of the lake. To return to Jumla you can go by the same route or take the route which leaves the lake to the west. **Rara National Park** At 106 square-kilometres Rara is the smallest of Nepal's national parks. It was established in 1976 to protect Lake Rara, Nepal's largest lake and to conserve the area's ecology. There are commanding views of the lake and surrounding forests and countryside from the park's highest point, **Chuchemara Danda** (4,087 metres). On the northern side of the lake are **Ruma Kand** (3,731 metres) and **Malika Kand** (3,444 metres). The river flowing from the lake to the west feeds into the mighty **Karnali River** some 30 kilometres away. The area also supports a range of **wildlife**, including the rare Red Panda, musk deer, bears, wolves, leopards and a variety of birds. The lake itself shelves steeply to a depth of 127 metres at its deepest. Surrounded by coniferous forest, it is very cold and clear blue, and you can see fish which form an important part of the local diet. To the north is the army camp. See the lake first thing in the morning when it is absolutely still and reflects the mountains to the east and south.

Day 7 **Lake Rara to Gossain** Follow the **Khatyar Khola** a couple of kilometres to the village of **Murma**. Cross the river and walk south, climbing a 3,300 metres pass. Views from here are good. You cross into the **Ghatta Khola valley**, descending to **Gossain** (3,100 metres). There are several good camping sites here.

Day 8 **Gossain to Sinja** A short and easy walk. Follow the Ghatta Khola down to its confluence with the **Sinja Khola** (which you crossed upstream on the third day). The village of **Botan** is near the confluence. Turn right and go along the north bank of the Sinja (2,400 metres). There is a 14th century ruined Malla palace across the river.

Day 9 **Sinja to Jumla** From Sinja, the trail follows the **Jal Jala Khola** to its source below a 3,500 metres pass. A meadow just below the pass makes a good campsite if you wish to break this long march into two more relaxing days. From this pass you descend through birch and pine forest to **Jumla**.

Jumla

Because foodstuffs are flown into Jumla from Nepalgunj, it is usually much easier to get reservations on flights from Jumla to Nepalgunj than the other way round.

Lying 2,240 metres above sea level, 360 kilometres west of Kathmandu and 150 kilometres north of Nepalgunj, Jumla boasts a rich past. It was the 14th century capital of the Khasa Mallas whose kingdom extended from the Kali Gandaki near Pokhara to the Kumaon region of India in the west and from Taklakhar in West Tibet to the Terai. There are several finely carved **temples** in the town which attest to its period of greatness. The local population is Hindu **Thakuri**.

Jumla is the focal centre of northwest Nepal and an important market town. The region is not self sufficient in food, however, and therefore depends on imports of basic foodstuffs from Nepalgunj. Porters are difficult to find and often do not speak English.

The main **bazaar** area is 15-20 minutes walk from the airport. It has 24 hour electricity. There are several *bhatti* lodges and dal-bhad-tarkari stalls and restaurants, but no Western food. There are also a number of small and fairly basic provisions shops (some even sell chocolate), though it can be very difficult to get provisions beyond Jumla.

Airport The grass strip airport is served mainly by Twin Otters and Dorniers. It is an interesting approach through a valley with mountains sloping above you on either side.

Trek 2
Jumla to Dunai

Set in the Dolpa region of Nepal this trek passes through Thakuri settlements in its initial stages. From the Mauri Lagna Pass it is possible to get views of the nearby peaks of Gu Tumpa (5,806 metres) and Mata Tumpa (5,767 metres). The highest point of the trek is the pass near Balang Bhanjyan (3,840 metres). There is a choice of trails once you reach Tibrikot; both the routes north and south of the river lead to Dunai. From Dunai there is a possible option of a trek to the Dhorpatan Hunting Reserve which leads back to Pokhara.

....

Briefing

Access: Flying is the easiest and safest way to get into Jumla. There are flights from Kathmandu (US$143), Nepalgunj (US$44), and at certain times of the year from Pokhara. Reservations are not easy to get and there are weight restrictions.

Trailhead: Jumla.

Duration: 6 days.

Best trekking season: April-September.

Altitude: Much of the trek is over 3,000m, reaching 3,840m at the pass near Balang Bhanjyan.

Equipment: Take all equipment, food

and provisions: little can be bought along the route.

Organization: Best to go with an organized self sufficient group.

Permit cost: US$10 per week for the first 4 weeks, then US$20 per week. Permit fees are payable either in US$ or at the convertible Nepali Rs rate. Permits are available at the Kathmandu or Pokhara Immigration offices.

Maps: Dolpa (by Paolo Gondini). Mandala Latest Trekking Map Dolpa: Jumla to Jomsom (1:200,000). US Army Map Service sheets NH44-11&12 are not recommended.

....

Jumla to Gothichaur Start early. Head past the airport and continue down to cross the bridges that span the confluence of the **Chaudhabise** and **Tila Kholas**. You follow the path south of the Tila Khola through the farming villages of **Devalgauri** and **Garjyakot** before climbing steadily up through meadows of flowering plants to camp at **Gothichaur**. Day 1

Gothichaur to Churta You descend from Gothichaur, crossing the Gothichaur Khola and then walk for a while south of the **Bapila Khola** (an extension of the Tila Khola). Before the village of Gorhigaon take the left hand trail and cross the Bapila Khola, following along the northern bank of the **Churta Khola** to the small village of **Churta**. Day 2

Day 3 Churta to Rimi From Churta continue as yesterday along the northern bank of the Churta Khola before crossing it to the south. There begins a steep climb through forest towards and across the Mauri Lagna Pass. Though hard work, this is a particularly beautiful part of the trek with many flowers and patches of rhododendron forest which bloom in April. From the pass you have stunning views to the northeast of Gu Tumpa (5,806 metres) and Mata Tumpa (5,767 metres). The trail undulates as you walk through tracts of oak and pine forest towards the village of **Chaurikot**. Crossing the ridge you enter the **Bheri Khola** valley and continue on to find a campsite at **Rimi**.

Day 4 Rimi to beyond Balangchaur A hard day's walk ahead which begins with a descent down into the valley and crosses the Bheri Khola to the village of **Kaigaon**. The village has a small shop and a *bhatti*. From Kaigaon, the ascent is fairly gentle at first before becoming very steep and challenging. You eventually reach the **pass** near **Balang Bhanjyan** (3,840 metres), where the forest is dominated by oak and rhododendron trees. The trail undulates from here to the village of **Balangchaur** after which it begins a descent towards a river valley.

Day 5 To Tibrikot (Tripurakot) Another challenging day, but with nothing as steep as yesterday. Pass through the villages of Pahada and Likhu, following the river valley to **Tibrikot**. The attractive village lies above the **Thuli Bheri Khola** and has good views of the valley.

Day 6 Tibrikot to Dunai The trail follows the Thuli Bheri Khola all the way to Dunai, but you have a choice of taking the route north or south of the river. The one south of the river also leads to the main Dolpa **airport** at **Juphal** village. It has regular flights to Nepalgunj – early morning arrivals and departures only because of the high winds that begin from mid-morning. The **Shey-Phoksumdo National Park** office is located by the army camp on the northern bank of the Thuli Bheri Khola where it meets the **Shey-Phoksundo Khola** (or Suli Gad). **Dunai** has a few simple lodges.

From Dunai There are routes to **Dhorpatan Hunting Reserve** and on towards **Pokhara** and **Tansen**. It is possible to do the difficult circular trek to **Lake Phoksumdo** which brings you back on to the Jumla-Dunai route. **NB** This is a very hard trek involving several steep and potentially hazardous sections. Much of the time is spent above 3,000 metres (10,000 feet). There are no shops or accommodation along the route. Shey-Phoksumdo National Park entrance fee Rs650. The following is a brief outline of the route.

Day 7 Dunai to Roha Walk back alongside the Thuli Bheri Khola then follow the **Shey-Phoksumdo Khola** to the north. The trail leads along the east bank, and continues its climb to **Roha**.

Day 8 Roha to Reji The trail leads through the rocky countryside and forest to Hanke, the official entrance to the national park where you pay the entrance fee. It is a series of ups and downs as you continue to the small settlement of **Sepka** (Chepka). After some distance there is a steep climb through patchy forest, then a very steep and potential dangerous descent into the river valley. Further on, the small village of **Reji** is reached by crossing the river by a make-shift rocky walkway.

Day 9 Reji to Lake Phoksumdo Return to the main trail on the eastern side of the river and follow it until you reach the confluence of the Shey-Phoksumdo and

Pungmi Kholas. Just beyond the confluence, the main trail crosses the river and climbs towards **Ringmo** village, passing nearby a 330 metres high waterfall, said to be the largest in Nepal. You descend to Ringmo and the official campsite is on the southeast side of Lake Phoksumdo.

Rest Day at Lake Phoksumdo

Day 10

Shey-Phoksumdo National Park Established in 1981, this is the largest national park in Nepal, covering an area of 3,555 square-kilometres which straddles Dolpa and Mugu districts and extends across the Kanjiroba Himal to the Tibetan border. It contains many peaks of over 6,000 metres and also encompasses a range of environments, from the lower Himalaya to the arid vastness of the southern Tibetan Plateau. With the exception of a few shrubs and isolated areas of low fertility, the latter is almost devoid of vegetation, while the lower elevations have intermittent temperate forests of, for example pine, oak, willow, poplar and walnut. The park's wildlife is a combination of species adapted to the high cold climate, including those endemic to the Tibetan Plateau such as gazelle and wild yak and those of lower elevations including deer, blue sheep, wolves, leopards and monkeys. But the most famous, and elusive, resident is the **snow leopard** (*Panthera uncia*), found at higher altitudes. This endangered species is indigenous to the mountain ranges of Central Asia. About 1.2 metres long with a 90 centimetre tail, it has a relatively small head and a thick milk-grey coat and rosette spots.

The park's two main attractions are the **Phoksumdo Lake** and the **Shey Gompa**. Its principal festival takes place on the August full moon day, when villagers from throughout the Dolpa district make a pilgrimage to Shey Mountain, then trek around its base on each of three consecutive days. Trekking in the region, however, is notoriously difficult. There are no facilities, you have to carry in all your equipment (including kerosene and stoves) and the terrain is steep and dangerous. The only practical time to visit is from March-November.

Lake Phoksumdo to Pungmi Return through Ringmo along the route you Day 11 took on Day 9 as far as the confluence of the Shey-Phoksumdo and Pungmi

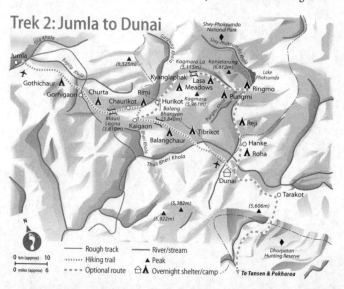

Trek 2: Jumla to Dunai

Kholas, then head west along the North bank of the **Pungmi Khola** to the village of **Pungmi**.

Day 12 Pungmi to Lasa Meadows The trail continues to follow the Pungmi Khola and crosses it as the trail veers to the left. The walk is effectively a northerly route around the spectacular Kagmara peaks, the highest being 5,961 metres.

Day 13 Lasa Meadows to Kagmara Phedi After crossing a stream there is a climb up to the Kagmara Pass (5,115 metres) before descending towards the **Garpung Khola** valley and camp.

Day 14 Kagmara Phedi to Kyanglaphak The trail follows the southern bank of the Garpung Khola and gradually descends towards the village of Kyanglaphak.

Day 15 Kyanglaphak to Kaigaon The descent continues and the Garpung Khola joins the Jagdula Khola. A short distance beyond the confluence, the trail crosses the Jagdula, continuing past the village of **Hurikot** to **Kaigaon**, where it joins the route to **Jumla** (Day 3).

The Annapurna Circuit

*The **Annapurna Circuit** is considered by many to be the best trek in Nepal, surpassing the Everest trek in terms of scenic and cultural variety, and it is the country's most popular trek, although it is also quite arduous. However the recent introduction of tourism means that many people now speak English, but traditional cultural values are rapidly being discarded.*

The best mountain views are during October and November. The circuit is best done anti-clockwise so as to be in a good position for the crossing of the Thorung La Pass (5,410 metres), which is snowbound from mid-December to mid-April. You do have to be fit for this trek.

Trek 3 Northern Circuit: Dumre to Muktinath

Set in the Northern section of the Annapurna Circuit this trek offers stunning views of the Annapurna mountain range. During the initial stages of the trek you are led through several traditionally Tibetan villages and past the ruined Gaonsahar fortress. You have to be very fit for this trek, as the altitude varies dramatically between 790 metres and 3,360 metres.

Most treks start from the village of Dumre, 70 kilometres east of Pokhara on the Prithvi Highway. It can be reached quite easily and has a few basic hotels, though it is better to make an early start from Pokhara than spend the night at Dumre. Dumre has a few shops for last minute provisions shopping. There is a road to **Bhote Odar**, a three hour walk south of Besi Sahar, which has a police checkpoint, shops and trekkers' lodges. Above the village to the west is the ruined fortress of **Gaonsahar** (1,370 metres). *Days 1-2*

Besi Sahar to Bahundanda The first half of the trek follows the Marshyangdi River which divides the Annapurna and Manaslu massifs. Keep on the west *Day 3*

Briefing

Access: Some trekkers start from Pokhara by walking to **Begnas Tal** and **Rupa Tal**, the Pokhara Valley's other two lakes, then through **Karputar** to **Besi Sahar** (790 metres), 41 kilometres from Dumre.

Trailhead: Pokhara or Dumre.

Duration: 10 days.

Best trekking season: April-May and October-November.

Altitude: This is a serious problem. The highest point is the Thorung La pass at 5,410m, best approached from the Manang Valley. From the Muktinath side you have to make a 1,300m ascent and a 900m descent during one day.

Equipment: Some provisions are available along the route. Warm clothing and protective sunglasses are essential.

Organization: Can be done individually or as part of a group.

Permit cost: US$5 per week.

Maps: Arbeitsgemeinschaft für vergleichende Hochgebirgsforschung Annapurna (1:100,000) expensive but good. King Mahendra Trust for Nature Conservation/ACAP Annapurna Conservation Area (1:125,000). Mandala Latest Trekking Map Pokhara to Jomsom & Manang (Round Annapurna Himal). US Army Map Service sheet NH44-16.

....

bank of the river and cross the 150 metre gorge. You then walk through terraced fields and forest to reach **Khudi**, the first Gurung village of the trek. You continue to **Bhulbule** (825 metres) where you cross the river to the east bank. Further on you cross the **Nagdi Khola**, just beyond the village of Nagdi at its mouth.

The trail up the Marshyangdi Valley gives excellent views of the Himalayan peaks. Dominating the eastern skyline is Manaslu (8,156 metres), **Himalchuli** (7,893 metres), **Peak 29/Manaslu II/Ngadi Chuli** (7,835 metres) and **Baudha Himal** (6,672 metres).

Above Ngadi is Usta and then a steady climb to **Lampata** (1,135 metres) and **Bahundanda** (1,310 metres) is one kilometre further on. Both are Manangi villages. Lampata has better accommodation. Bahundanda is the most northerly Brahmin village and has reasonable camping sites.

Day 4 **Bahundanda to Chyamje** From Bahundanda the path drops steeply to Syange (1,100 metres). Cross the Marshyangdi by a suspension bridge. Syange has a number of places to stay. The trail then climbs high above the river along steep hillsides of rhododendron and pine forest to **Jagat** (1,070 metres). **Chyamje** (1,300 metres) after one kilometre has accommodation and shops.

Day 5 **Chyamje to Bagarchap** This walk is to Bagarchap where the Marshyangdi curves west and enters the Manang Valley. The climate and cultural landscape both change. A long uphill climb brings you to **Tal** (1,675 metres), a pretty village at the foot of a picturesque waterfall, the southernmost village of Manang district.

Cross the broad flat valley, once a lake bed, through fields of corn, barley and potatoes, then climb steeply up a stone stairway to 1,860 metres. The stairway then descends to Orad where the vegetation consists of blue pine and fir. Drop down to **Dharapani** (1,890 metres), a Tibetan Buddhist village with chorten entrances at each end.

Over a spur is Bagarchap (2,160 metres), a small bazaar town of closely packed, wooden roofed Tibetan style houses. Timber for building is comparatively abundant in this region which marks the transition between the monsoonal region south of the main Himalayan axis and the more arid rainshadow area to the north. Further on, wood is replaced by slate as a roofing material.

Bagarchap to Chame Walk a rough and rocky trail through forest to Danejung (2,290 metres) and **Tyanja** (2,360 metres). **Kopar** (2,590 metres) lies in a meadow between **Tyanja** and **Chame** (2,685 metres) which has a post office, accommodation and a bank. There are fine views of **Annapurna II** (7,937 metres) as you approach Chame, the district headquarters. _Day 6_

Chame to Pisang Between Chame and Pisang the rainshadow effect can be seen as the forests become sparser and the density of juniper increases. The valley is steep and narrow and the path crosses the river twice. By the second bridge at 3,040 metres is the Paungda Danda rock face that arches upwards for more than 1,500 metres. The trail climbs further into the upper Marshyangdi Valley and to **Pisang** (3,200 metres), a large sprawling village with plentiful accommodation, good camping grounds and a _mani_ wall. _Day 7_

Pisang to Manang The Manang region was only opened for trekking in 1977, so the facilities are not as developed as on the Pokhara to Jomsom sector. The inhabitants of Manang village, though, are among the most sophisticated in Nepal. The region receives relatively sparse rainfall, reflected in the crops – barley, buckwheat and potatoes. The semi-arid conditions and altitude allows only one cropping season per year. _Day 8_

By Himalayan standards, this should be a poor village. However, in 1784 King Rana Bahadur Shah granted the Manangi people special trading rights which they have enjoyed ever since. Today, they trade local gold, silver,

Trek 3: Annapurna Circuit North

Trekking

turquoise and other gems for cameras, watches and other electronic goods from other parts of Asia. Affluent, westernized in dress and with many speaking English, they have also been quick to seize the opportunities presented by mass trekking. The village has a number of popular hotels and also sells Tibetan sweaters, hats and gloves – but prices are high.

After leaving Pisang, you climb up a ridge that cuts across the valley and has a good view of the valley and the Tilicho Peak (7,132 metres). Descending into the upper valley, the trail divides into two, the northerly one taking a route via **Ghyaru**. It rejoins the southern trail at **Mungji** (3,360 metres). This route involves less climbing. It runs past **Ongre** (3,325 metres), with an airstrip that caters exclusively to the Manang trading community. The village has a police checkpoint and a number of lodges. A 30 minutes walk beyond Ongre on the left is the valley leading up to **Annapurna III** (7,555 metres) and **Annapurna IV** (7,525 metres). Close by is the Nepal Mountaineering Association mountaineering school. The Himalayan Rescue Association has a clinic here.

At **Mungji** the path crosses the Marshyangdi again to reach **Braga** (3,475 metres) which has accommodation and a camping ground below. The gompa here is believed to be around 500 years old and belongs to the Kagyu-pa Tibetan Lamaist Buddhist sect. A climb up **Braga Hill** offers a stunning panorama of the Annapurna group. **Manang** (3,535 metres) is 30 minutes further on.

Day 9   Manang to Phedi   You have now travelled from an altitude of 440 metres at Dumre to 3,585 metres at Manang, a gain of over 3,000 metres although in real terms you have climbed double that. However, because of the gradual ascent, you should be well acclimatized having made a daily height gain of around 500 metres. NB This is the altitude to which people can travel fairly rapidly and feel little or no ill effect from it. But from now on you have to be much more careful. It is a two day walk to Muktinath with a crossing of the **Thorung La** pass (5,416 metres) *en route*. This means that you will be gaining nearly 2,000 metres in less than two days.

Warning This can and often does induce mountain sickness. You can choose to spend this day in and around Manang, becoming acclimatized and relaxing rather than charging on. There is a comfortable side trip to the glacial lake fed by the ice fall on **Gangapurna** (c 4,000 metres).

The next village after Manang is Tengbi (3,805 metres). Just beyond it the path veers right. To the left is a track leading up a side valley to **Tilicho Lake**. Above **Gunsang** village (3,960 metres) there is a juniper forest, the source of firewood for the nearby villages. Further on is **Ledar** which has shops. You are now in the **Jarsang Khola** valley, one of the source streams of the Marshyangdi. The track continues upwards along the east bank of the stream, crosses it at 4,310 metres, traverses a scree slope, then descends to **Phedi** (4,420 metres) which has accommodation and a campsite below. There are other lodges within 10 minutes' walk.

Snow and blocked passes can mean overcrowded lodges and campsites leading to unsanitary toilet facilities

Day 10   Phedi, across the Thorung La pass to Muktinath   It is not necessary to start for the pass too early (for example 0300 as some do), as it can be extremely cold. A 0500-0600 start gives you only an hour at most in the bitter cold before it is light. The trail is well defined and it has been used for centuries by traders though it seems to go on for ever and has a number of dispiriting false summits. It takes around four hours from Phedi. In December and January a crossing of the pass is well nigh impossible and at all times care is needed. There is a chorten and prayer flags to mark the pass and views are magnificent. You can see the north faces of the Annapurnas, the Kali Gandaki Valley and **Thorungtse** (6,482 metres). Some well-equipped parties camp on the pass

The first ascent of Annapurna

Annapurna was the first peak over 8,000m to be climbed. The successful assault is a reminder that the mountains are both awe-inspiring and dangerous. The French expedition, led by **Maurice Herzog**, arrived in Nepal in April 1950. Europeans knew nothing of either Dhaulagiri or Annapurna. The French spent the better part of a month reconnoittering the Dhaulagiri massif before giving up. "Dhaulagiri isn't just difficult, it's impassible. I never want to set foot on that mountain again," one of the team wrote later. Although Herzog and his companion Lachenal suffered appalling frostbite injuries on their attempt to climb Annapurna and had a succession of miraculous escapes, they reached the summit and, with the help of their Sherpa porters and team, returned. Both lost fingers and toes and took nearly a year to regain their health. It was just one of the tales of heroism and endurance which the mountains have continued to witness.

Trekking

and climb higher on the peaks around it.

Warning Great care is needed for the descent (1,600 metres), which is far more tiring than the ascent. As the trail descends through snow, moraines and grassy slopes into Muktinath, the symmetrical summit of **Dhaulagiri** (8,167 metres) appears on the southern horizon. The final part of the day's walk is along the upper part of the **Jhong Khola** valley, past a few *bhattis* which sell drinks and have beds, to **Muktinath** (3,800 metres). Most of the accommodation is in **Ranipowa**, about 10 minutes from the temple.

This completes the northern half of the Annapurna Circuit. The remaining part of the journey to Pokhara is along the Pokhara-Jomsom trail, described next on pages 108-113.

Trek 4
Southern circuit:
Pokhara to Jomsom

In the south of the Annapurna region, this trek contains incredible altitude, climate and cultural contrasts. The gorge in-between the Annapurna and Dhaulagiri mountains leads the trekker from the rain-sodden (in summer), well vegetated and lush southern slopes of the Himalaya, to the arid zone where only the hardiest crops survive. You also move from a predominantly Hindu area to one steeped in the culture of Tibetan Buddhism.

In the first few days' trek out of Pokhara, there are a couple of possible variations. From Deorali, just beyond Poon Hill there is a single trail. There are some interesting side trips so allow a few extra days for flexibility.

Briefing

Access: Pokhara is very accessible either by air or by road. The main road through the region leads to Pokhara.

Trailhead: Pokhara.

Duration: 7 days

Best trekking season: October-December

Altitude: The route passes through the deepest gorge in the world, between the mountains Annapurna and Dhaulagiri. However the trek does go as high as 3,710m at Muktinath.

Equipment: It is possible to get provisions along the trek, but all equipment should be taken.

Organization: Either individually or as part of a group.

Permit Cost: US$5 per week.

Maps: Arbeitsgemeinschaft für vergleichende Hochgebirgsforschung Annapurna (1:100,000) is expensive but good. King Mahendra Trust for Nature Conservation/ACAP Annapurna Conservation Area (1:125,000). Mandala Latest Trekking Map Pokhara to Jomsom & Manang (Round Annapurna Himal). US Army Map Service sheet NH44-16.

Day 1 **Pokhara to Naudanda** From the Shining Hospital a jeep track follows the Seti River to its confluence with the **Yamdi Khola**. The road then climbs up to the Tibetan Camp and the large village of **Hyangja** (1,070 metres). Beyond these, the road leaves the Seti River and ascends the spur that separates the two rivers. The wide grassy track then follows an irrigation ditch to **Suikhet** (1,125 metres). Alternative trails make short cuts across the terraced fields during the dry season. Suikhet has a number of bhattis on the far side of the village.

Continue along the river for 30 minutes, then cross to the southern side of the valley and climb the ridge between the Yangdo Khola and the **Harpan Khola**. The 370 metre climb gives views of the Pokhara Valley and Phewa Tal. **Naudanda** (1,430 metres) lies along this ridge and has a police checkpoint and accommodation ranging from simple *bhattis* to reasonably good Western style hotels. Allow about five hours for the journey. Make sure that you have your trekking permit, as the police are conscientious. You may notice the noise of barking dogs, particularly on the first night of the trek, if you are sleeping near or in a village.

Naudanda to Birethanti/Tirkedhunga/Hille At the far end of Naudanda you have a choice of trails. Both converge but the right hand track is shorter. The trail climbs to **Khare** (1,710 metres), a dispersed village at the head of the **Yamdi Khola** valley. Proceed down the stone steps below the British Agricultural Research station and rehabilitation centre for retiring Gurkha soldiers. After about one hour, you reach **Lumle** (1,585 metres). Keep to the main paved street and continue along the side of the ridge. The track then descends to **Chandrakot** (1,550 metres) with excellent views of Annapurna and Macchapuchare. Descend to and cross the **Modi Khola** to reach **Birethanti**

Day 2

Birethanti is a good stopping point if you are coming the other way on the Annapurna Circuit

Trekking

Trek 4: Annapurna Circuit South

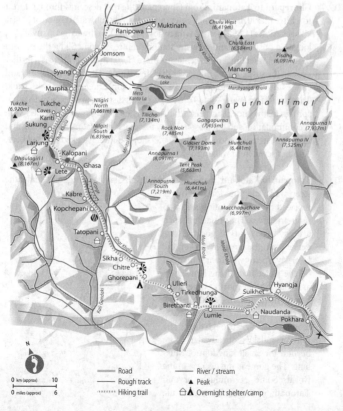

which has some good accommodation. The trail follows the bank of the **Bhurungdi Khola** past some delightful waterfalls (especially in Autumn). Cross the suspension bridge, which climbs steadily up the side of the valley to **Hille** (1,495 metres) and **Tirkedhunga** (1,525 metres). Both villages have accommodation and are good halting places after over six hours' walk.

You can also cover this rather unexciting section by taking a bus to Lumle before starting the walk. There are numerous buses that go along the newly built **Baglung** road from north of the bazaar area in Pokhara.

Day 3 **Birethanti/Tirkedhunga/Hille to Ghorepani** The path descends from Tirkedhunga to cross the river, then steeply ascends some stone steps for 600 metres to Ulleri (2,070 metres), a large Magar village. Continuing above the village, you pass through cultivated area and some pastures to a dense forest of rhododendron, daphne and azalea mixed with giant conifers. Some three hours beyond Ulleri and after crossing three streams by bridge, you reach **Thante** (2,460 metres) in a small clearing. The track gets muddy after snow melt and during the monsoon, necessitating detours. There is a good campsite on the hill behind the first group of huts. **Ghorepani** ('Horse Water' in Nepali and Hindi) is an hour's walk further on, and 15 minutes beyond is the pass at **Deorali** (2,834 metres) where you can stay. An hour's climb from **Ghorepani** is **Poon Hill** (3,030 metres) where a wooden tower offers a spectacular panorama of Dhaulagiri, Tukche, Nilgiri, Annapurna I and Annapurna South. Best at dawn. This has been a day of some seven hours' walking.

Day 4 **Ghorepani to Tatopani** From Ghorepani, the trail descends through forest to **Chitre** (2,390 metres), then enters an extensively cultivated region of Magar villages. **Sikha** (1,890 metres) is three hours from Deorali and has many shops, lodges, a post office and an army training centre. Beyond Sikha the descent becomes stonier but it quite gentle to **Ghare** (1,705 metres). There is a further drop to the suspension bridge over the **Ghar Khola**. The trail turns north and crosses the **Kali Gandaki** on a steel suspension bridge to the west bank. **Tatopani** ('Hot Water', 1,189 metres) is a short distance upstream and has hot springs below the village near the river. The village is well provided with accommodation and good food. Many places use generators for cooking and lighting. There is a municipal bath and shops are well stocked and sell beer. Another seven hour walking day.

Day 5 **Tatopani to Kalopani** You are now in the Kali Gandaki Gorge and, under the steep walls, the pine forest above is replaced by low vegetation suited to semi-arid areas. The presence of such a deep, boldly carved gorge is evidence that the great rivers of the Himalaya, many with their source not on the watershed of the Himalayan axis but further north, were there before the mountains. As these rose, the rivers maintained their courses by eroding a passage through them. The Kali Gandaki's headwaters are beyond the small kingdom of Mustang. The gorge is the deepest in the world. Some 30 minutes beyond **Tatopani** is the confluence of the

Della Dennian

The Thakalis

Traditionally subsistence farmers, the Thakalis have cashed in on the trekking boom since the 1960s by establishing many small hotels along the main routes of the Annapurna region. They have had a virtual monopoly on the lucrative trade and have developed a keen business sense. The secret of their success lies in a system of communal investment (dighur) where family members or friends pool a fixed amount of money per person and give the total to one among them. The recipient can use it at his own discretion and his only obligation is to contribute to the dighur. When everyone has received their lump sum, the group is dissolved. The system is based on trust and encourages individualism.

Thakalis are related to the Magars, Tamangs and Gurungs, and their religion is a mixture of Hinduism, Buddhism, shamanism and animism. In this they differ from their Tibetan related neighbours in Mustang. Their sturdy houses are built with flat stones cemented together with clay. They cultivate barley and potatoes, an indication of the severity of the climate and their flat roofs are used for drying grain and hay. Yaks are good grazing livestock and the milk is drunk and made into cheese, while Yak hides and coarse wool are also used for clothing. Juniper is often used for tea.

Kali Gandaki and the **Miritsi Khola**. Herzog's French expedition base camp was located at its source.

The next small hamlet is Rukse Chhara (1,550 metres), with a spectacular waterfall just beyond. You cross this on a wooden bridge to the east bank and continue to **Kopchepani** where there is a 'Welcome to Mustang' signboard. This is in the southernmost part of the district of Mustang and the old kingdom is still a long distance off. The trail forks: both routes take you to **Ghasa** after about a three hour walk.

The older left hand trail carved out of the overhanging rock climbs abruptly, then continues north along the western wall of the canyon. Several precarious looking, rickety but safe bridges span gaps between ledges. It is best avoided during the rainy season as you may be hit by falling debris. First you climb steeply up the hillside and remain high, passing the village of Kabre after about 30 minutes. This is below the steepest part of the gorge but roaring winds can make it tiring. After two hours, the gorge widens and the trail descends to a gravel bar and a bridge to the other side. **Ghasa** is 30 minutes further on.

Ghasa (2,000 metres) is a long strung out Thakali village and marks the southern limit of Lamaist Buddhism: the Kali Gandaki gorge is effectively a tunnel through to another world. On the northern side not only does the vegetation and the culture change, but also the name of the river – it becomes the Thak Khola. The middle of Ghasa has the best accommodation, while Upper Ghasa has fine chortens.

The trail ascends steadily but not too steeply through forests to the Lete Khola. After about an hour, the canyon widens further and the trail turns a corner to reveal a magnificent view of **Dhaulagiri** and its ice fall. Across the river is an impressive cliff. This can be quite a noisy place as dislodged rocks from the cliff crash down into the canyon and the ice fall shifts.

You then descend into the ravine which enters the Kali Gandaki about one kilometre to the right. You cross the stream on a wooden bridge or a log laid across it. The trail then climbs up to Lete (2,470 metres), another village along a river terrace which joins **Kalopani** ('Black Water') about 20 minutes further on. Encircled by peaks, Kalopani has an air of prosperity, with guesthouses, restaurants and a camping ground. Allow nine hours for the walk; a full but varied and enjoyable day.

Day 6 **Kalopani to Jomsom** There are two trails to Tukche which is three hours away. On the east bank of the river, the trail rises above the gravel bar that stretches up to Jomsom. You pass through **Dhumpu** after 15-20 minutes and another settlement after another 45 minutes. The trail then leaves the valley floor to cross a wooded ridge above some cliffs, before descending to the gravel bar once more. You can either remain on the bank or walk up the riverbed. In dry weather, the latter is more direct. The views of Dhaulagiri and Annapurna are wonderful. After 30 minutes you reach a bridge. On the west bank is the village of **Larjung** (2,560 metres) which has accommodation. If you stay on the east bank you have to cross the river on a series of temporary bridges just before Tukche.

The west bank trail climbs to Sukung then descends through forest to Larjung. A little further on is **Kanti** (also known as **Khopang**) (2,560 metres) and between are some of the best views of the mountains of this stretch of the Thak Khola. You also pass the old monastery of **Rani Gompa**. Above **Kanti** is a row of caves housing Buddhist shrines and relics.

Tukche (2,590 metres) was an important place on the old trade route. Caravans from Tibet bartered their goods of salt and wool for grain and other goods carried up from the south. It was once the most important Thakali village, but with the loss of trade many families moved out. Tourism has been a welcome substitute.

Della Denman

Beyond Tukche the going is made difficult by the wind which is funnelled down between the mountains. Junipers and small pines begin to dominate the increasingly arid land. An hour further on is the government experimental farm at Marpha (2,665 metres) which also has an important monastery at the southern end. There are some excellent guest houses with private rooms, menus, indoor toilets and often room service. Across the river is a Tibetan carpet factory. From **Marpha** there is a difficult but immensely rewarding side trip to the **Tilicho Lake** at the foot of **Tilicho Peak**.

North of Marpha the trail is wide and easy to follow. The Longpoghyun Khola flows down from the **Meso Kanto** pass (5,099 metres) to the east. The village of **Syang** is just beyond and then you pass the Jomsom airstrip. Allow eight hours from Lete/Kalopani to Jomsom.

Jomsom (from *Dzongsam*, 'New Fort', 2,713 metres), is the major centre of the region now and has airlinks with both Kathmandu and Pokhara and there are hot springs in the hillside to the west. On the river valley floor there are large *shaligrams* (ammonite fossils) to be found. Jomsom also has a small hospital and a police checkpoint. Trekkers on the Annapurna Circuit and coming from the Manang Valley must have their passes stamped here.

NB Flights are often delayed in winter because of a combination of fog in the Kathmandu Valley, which usually doesn't lift until mid-morning and high winds around Jomsom which usually start at around the same time. When a number of flights have been delayed, there is a serious backlog of anxious, often frenzied travellers. Allow sufficient time so that, if necessary, you can trek back to Pokhara in four days. Flights from Pokhara tend to be more reliable as the Pokhara area is less prone to fog and flights arrive earlier. Nevertheless, fog in Kathmandu can still cause system-wide havoc.

Jomsom to Muktinath The trail follows the river then crosses it and contin- Day 7
ues up the valley to Chhancha Lhumba (2,370 metres). From here the direct route to Muktinath climbs a plateau above the village, then turns east up the **Jhong Khola** valley. The landscape is quite arid and bare here, but the views are excellent. From **Khingar** (3,200 metres) the walk is across meadows and poplar groves and orchards. The trail climbs above the river to **Jharkot** (3,500 metres), a Tibetan style village with some accommodation. From here, the trail climbs further to **Muktinath** (3,710 metres), the end of this southern section of the **Annapurna Circuit**.

The first part of Muktinath is called Ranipowa. Most of the accommodation is here and it is busy with trekkers and pilgrims to the Hindu Vaishnavite **Jiwali Mayi Mandir** and the Buddhist gompa. Inside the temple is a spring and an eternal flame from gas emanating from the ammonite slate. This combination of earth, water and fire is considered particularly holy and attracts devotees of both faiths. The main religious **festival** takes place during full moon in August/September and attracts thousands of pilgrims. Tibetan traders can spoil the atmosphere with their persistence.

From Muktinath There is an interesting detour to **Kagbeni**. From **Chhancha Lumbha**, a trail follows the river to **Kagbeni** (2,810 metres), the furthest north that tourists can travel before Mustang. The village has dormitory accommodation and gives a taste of what Mustang is like although contact with visitors has already had some impact. The houses are of mud and stone and are tightly packed. There are striking chortens and a large gompa. From Kagbeni the trail makes a steep ascent up the Jhong Khola valley and joins the Muktinath route below Khingar.

Trek 5 Annapurna Base Camp

Based in the southern part of the Annapura region, this trek enables you to get right into the massif and you are surrounded by peaks. All along the trek there are views of the nearby mountains, especially at Chomrong, a Gurung village with superb views of Annapurna South and Macchapuchare. The latter end of the trek is relatively steep.

....

 Briefing

Access: The Annapurna region is accesssible through Pokhara, which has both air and road access.

Trailhead: Pokhara.

Duration: 9 days.

Best trekking season: April-May, and October-November.

Altitude: The early stages of the trek remain under 2,000 m, but after reaching Chomrong the trek climbs rapidly to the base camp at 4,095m.

Equipment: It is possible to get

provisions along the route but all equipment should be taken.

Organization: Permit Cost: US$5 per week. Annapurna Conservation Area entrance fee Rs 650.

Maps: Arbeitsgemeinschaft für vergleichende Hochgebirgsforschung Annapurna (1:100,000) is expensive but good. King Mahendra Trust for Nature Conservation/ACAP Annapurna Conservation Area (1:125,000). Mandala Latest Trekking Map Pokhara to Jomsom & Manang (Round Annapurna Himal). US Army Map Service sheet NH44-16.

....

Day 1 **Pokhara to Tolka** Take a bus or taxi to just beyond Suikhet on the new Baglung road. The walking trail heads off in a northwest direction soon after the road turns to the left. Continue along here to **Dhampus** (1,600 metres), a ridge village with the first good views of the mountains to the north. With several lodges this is a possible night stop, but the village has a bad reputation for crime, so take extra care of your belongings if you do stop here. Continue the gentle climb along the ridge as the trail turns northwest a short distance from Dhampus. The stony path is easy to follow as it goes through forest and crosses a couple of streams on its way to **Pothana** (1,900 metres), another possible night stop with a few lodges. Soon after leaving Pothana, the trail divides.

Follow the right hand path in a northward direction as it ascends through forest to another good viewpoint at 2,149 metres. Thereafter, it is a fairly steep descent into the **Modi Khola** valley and through the village of **Bhichok**, continue along the northern side of a rocky ridge before again veering north to **Tolka** (1,710 metres) where there are several *bhattis*.

Tolka to Chomrong Today's walk follows the course of the Modi Khola. The trail leaves Tolka following the countours about 600 metres above the river. The first village you come to is **Landrung** (1,550 metres), a traditional Gurung settlement. High on the opposite side of the river, you can see the village of **Ghandrung**. From here, the path descends along terraced slopes and forest down to the river. You cross the river at **New Bridge** (or Shiuli, or Naya Pul). It is a gentle climb for the first one kilometre or so after crossing the bridge, but immediately after crossing a small stream there is a steep ascent of some 500 metres to the point where your trail joins that from Ghandrung. From here it is

Day 2

Trekking

Trek 5: Annapurna Base Camp

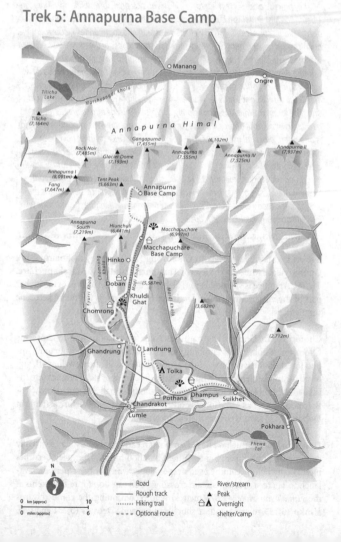

The Gurungs

As a dominant ethnic group of the Annapurna region, the Gurungs are traditionally agricultural communities but are known also for their loyal service in Gurkha regiments of the British and Indian armies. Little is known of their origins and their history and traditions have largely been transmitted orally. It is believed that the first Gurungs migrated south from Tibet and established themselves in the villages of Kaski, Ghandrung and elsewhere north of Pokhara.

They practise a religion similar to Tibetan Lamaist Buddhism but influenced also by Brahmanical Hinduism as well as animism and their language, Gurungkura, is of the Tibeto-Burmese family. All Gurungs wear the rup around their neck, a yellow string consisting of seven individual threads and knots for women and nine for men. While this is principally a religious or cultural adornment, the rup is also put to practical use with keys, coins, cigarettes and other small items often tied into it.

Gurung society is characterized by a hierachical structure of jats, in many ways similar to the Hindu caste system. It is an intricate and complicated system, but there are two broad divisions. The Char Jat, or 'four clans', are considered socially above the Sola Jat, or '16 clans'. Each jat has further subdivisions. Strict marriage customs have helped to preserve Gurung 'purity'. Although marriage is permissible between the various clans of the Sola Jat or between those of the Char Jat, intermarriage of Sola and Char Jat is not allowed. There are differences, however, between Gurungs of different regions. Among lowland Gurungs, for example, polygamy (one husband, multiple wives) is an accepted norm, while polyandry (one wife, multiple husbands) is characteristic of highland communites. Before marriage, the horoscopes of the prospective couple are consulted for compatibility. Representatives from the groom's side will then go to the bride's home for marriage 'negotiations', discussions which would typically include arrangements for the ceremony and, just as important, those for the dowry. Once all these have been satisfactorily completed, the groom will send offerings to the bride's family which must include a goat and a pot of curd (yoghurt). Acceptance of the curd is the final confirmation that the marriage will take place.

a short and fairly level walk to **Chomrong** (2,000 metres). Chomrong is a Gurung village with superb views of **Annapurna South** and **Macchapuchare**. The ACAP office is situated here. The better accommodation is in the higher part of the village, while the older, lower part has shops including kerosene suppliers.

Day 3   **Chomrong to Doban**   The path descends from Chomrong to cross the Chomrong Khola before climbing steeply through rhododendron and bamboo forest up the west bank of the **Modi Khola**. Soon after levelling off, you reach the tiny settlement of **Khuldi Ghat** before another steep descent into the valley. The trail follows the river through another small settlement known as **Bamboo** which has some lodges and crosses three streams before arriving at **Doban** (2,430 metres) where there is accommodation.

Day 4   **Doban to Macchapuchare Base Camp**   Start early and begin today's virtually continuous climb through intermittent bamboo forest. The valley becomes increasingly hemmed in by ever steeper slopes which witness periodic avalanches. There are regular stream crossings. You can stop for refreshments at the *Himalayan Hotel* (2,873 metres) before continuing the climb towards **Hinko** (3,139 metres) and, a short way beyond, **Deorali** (3,231 metres).

Accommodation is available at both. The next settlement you come to is **Bagar** (3,300 metres) which also has a couple of lodges. The final stretch of today's long walk passes a German meteorological station before you eventually reach **Macchapuchare Base Camp** (3,500 metres) where there are lodges (open in peak season only) and magnificent views of the surrounding mountains including, of course, a close up of **Macchapuchare** (6,997 metres).

Macchapuchare Base Camp to Annapurna Base Camp It's a hike of around two hours to Annapurna Base Camp (4,095 metres). The route follows the left hand tributary of the Modi Khola which divides just before Macchapuchare Base Camp. There are a couple of lodges along here.

Day 5

Annapurna Base Camp to Pokhara The way back is mostly downhill and is a lot easier. The following variation can be done on Days 7-9 on the return to Pokhara.

Days 6-9

Take a bus or taxi from Pokhara as far as **Lumle** on the new Baglung road. The trail passes through Lumle village and climbs gently to the next village, **Chandrakot** (1,600 metres). Here the trail divides. Instead of continuing down to the Modi Khola, bear northeast along the terraced slopes then through oak forest to **Tanchauk**. Continue along the contour past the small hamlet of **Huwanri**. A few minutes beyond Huwanri, the path descends into the river valley and crosses the **Modi Khola** by a suspension bridge. From here there is a fairly steep climb, but the trail levels off soon after **Kimche** (1,600 metres). The route then undulates fairly easily until you reach the large village of **Ghandrung** (or Ghandruk, 2,012 metres), which is last place for making phone calls on this trek.

From Ghandrung, you have a choice. You can either bear east towards Landrung and join the trail described above on Day 2. Alternatively, leave Ghandrung to the northwest and cross the **Kyurri Khola**. There is a climb from the river to the small settlement of **Kumron** (2,230 metres), followed by a steeper climb to **Kyumnu** where you cross a river. It is steeper still from Kyumnu to join the trail from Tarapani to Chomrong: a short stretch during which you ascend over 600 metres. Bear east and descend to join the Landrung to Chomrong trail a short way from Chomrong.

Trekking

Trek 6
The Royal Trek

*This trek is a good option if you don't have the time or energy for a longer trek. It takes in the area to the northeast of the Valley's other two lakes, **Begnas Tal** and **Rupa Tal**. There is no really demanding terrain to be covered and the walk has some excellent views of the **Annapurna** and the **Manaslu** ranges. It has become known as the **Royal Trek** after Prince Charles walked this route.*

 Briefing

Access: It is possible to reach Pokhara relatively easily by either road or air.

Trailhead: Pokhara

Duration: 4 days

Best trekking season: April-May, and October-November

Altitude: Under 1,500m

Equipment: All equipment and provisions should be taken.

Organization: Trek can be done independently or in an escorted group.

Permit cost: US$5 per week.

Maps: Any decent map of the area betwen Pokhara, the Madi Khola and the Prithvi Highway.

Day 1 **Pokhara to Kalikathan** Take a taxi to the trailhead by the army camp at Bijayapur, just off the Prithvi Highway and some seven kilometres from Lakeside. From here it is a gentle climb through several small settlements and up the **Rakhi Danda** hill to **Kalikathan**. There are fine views from here across the **Bijayapur Khola**, a tributary of the **Seti Khola** and a panorama of Himalayan peaks dominated by **Macchapuchare** in the foreground.

Day 2 **Kalikathan to Syaglung** Most of today's walk follows the ridge with a few ups and downs. You first pass through Thulakot (1,419 metres) then **Maji Thana**, both of which have tea shops. To your left, some 500 metres below, is the **Madi Khola** which has its source in the **Lamjung Himal**, about 35 kilometres to the north. There is a short climb as the trail veers to the south through **Jintithar** (1,210 metres) before changing to a southeast course to the Gurung village **Syaglung** which has some excellent mountain views.

Day 3 **Syaglung to Chisapani** After contouring the Syaglung Danda, there is a sharp descent as you head south. You cross the trail of the anti-clockwise Annapurna Circuit trek which continues east to join the Marshyangdi River, then climb to Chisapani. There are numerous *Chisapanis* throughout Nepal – the name means 'Cold Water'.

Deforestation, degradation and conservation

The Himalaya represent an extremely fragile environment which faces grave long term problems of degradation. Although the region is on one of the Earth's major earthquake belts, the greatest threat is posed by continued human interference. Rapid population growth, especially over the last 50 years, has resulted in increased pressure on land which in turn has led to deforestation in the Himalaya on a massive and unprecedented scale. The effects are far from restricted to the loss of precious animal habitats or to aesthetic denudation although, of course, these also form the bases for strong arguments in their own right. Serious consequences of deforestation include potentially catastrophic erosion particularly during the monsoon and in periods of abnormally high rainfall when landslides result in loss of life as well as causing immense damage to the agricultural land and houses.

Although the scale of the problem makes it extremely difficult to prove a link with a high degree of scientific certainty, further consequences may be experienced in other parts of the country, in India and as far away as Bangladesh. The argument is as follows: deforestation results in increased erosion leading to both higher river flows and silt levels. The former may exacerbate the devastation caused by floods during the monsoon and in times of abnormal rainfall, while the latter can severely obstruct the flow of water in the dry season leading to damaging shortages of irrigation water further downstream. Since most of Nepal's rivers eventually feed to and through the Ganges delta, the direct consequences of local deforestation in even any of the more remote areas of the Himalaya may not be confined to Nepal alone. Half a million people were made homeless and 20,000 hectares of crops were lost when the Sun Kosi River system breached its banks in the northern Indian state of Bihar in September 1984. Bangladesh, meanwhile, is especially sensitive to changes in water levels, with both its population and economy highly susceptible to the interaction of regular inundation (monsoonal or cyclonic) with human interference as far away as in Nepal. The country has been only partially successful in placing these concerns on the international agenda.

A substantial proportion of the 300,000 tourists visiting Nepal annually spend some time trekking. While the country has benefited economically, it has also faced increasing pressure on the environment. The two most serious problems caused by the trekking industry are in the demand for firewood and in the garbage left along trekking routes. There is an estimated 16,500 kg of rubbish left behind by trekkers and mountaineering expeditions on Mt Everest over the last 40 years.

But it is the predicament of cutting down trees for fuel and building which is ultimately the more damaging. The reasons are threefold. First there is the high demand for food and hot water by trekkers. Second, sources of alternative heating and cooking fuels are scarce and costly in relation to the 'free' supplies amply provided by the forest. The third reason is to do with culture and poverty. When faced with the choice of 'cutting down a few trees' or paying relatively large sums of scarce money for kerosene, the quest for economic survival is compelling and invariably prevails over conservation arguments. The notion of environmental conservation, moreover, is seen, if at all, as an ideal that is able to be espoused only by those societies or socio-economic classes in which there is sufficient wealth for alternative fuel sources and building materials to be routinely employed. It is, in short, a luxury that the majority of traditional Himalayan communities are ill able to afford.

Trekking

Chisapani to Pokhara The trail descends from the ridge-top camp towards   Day 4
Rupa Tal. There are some delightful short walks around this lake and the larger
Begnas Tal just to the northwest. From here, you rejoin the Prithvi Highway
for the short drive back to Pokhara.

Trek 7 Tatopani and Baglung

Pokhara
KATHMANDU

Based in the south of the Annapurna region, this route leads through Tatopani in its early stages. Throughout the trek the altitude varies. The Baglung road is relatively good.

Briefing

Access: *Pokhara is very accessible either by air or by road. The main road through the region leads to Pokhara.*

Trailhead: *Pokhara*

Duration: *6 days*

Best trekking season: *Late Autumn*

Altitude: *Initial stages of the trek are under 3,000m.*

Equipment: *It is possible to get food and accommodation along the trail.*

Organization: *Possible to trek individually or in groups.*

Permit cost: *US$5 per week*

Maps: *Arbeitsgemeinschaft für vergleichende Hochgebirgsforschung Annapurna (1:100,000) is expensive but good. King Mahendra Trust for Nature Conservation/ACAP Annapurna Conservation Area (1:125,000). Mandala Latest Trekking Map Pokhara to Jomsom & Manang (Round Annapurna Himal). US Army Map Service sheet NH44-16.*

Day 1   **Pokhara to Naudanda** From the Shining Hospital a jeep track follows the Seti River to its confluence with the **Yamdi Khola**. The road then climbs up to the Tibetan Camp and the large village of **Hyangja** (1,070 metres). Beyond these, the road leaves the Seti River and ascends the spur that separates the two rivers. The wide grassy track then follows an irrigation ditch to **Suikhet** (1,125 metres). Alternative trails make short cuts across the terraced fields during the dry season. Suikhet has a number of *bhattis* on the far side of the village.

Continue along the river for 30 minutes, then cross to the southern side of the valley and climb the ridge between the Yangdo Khola and the **Harpan Khola**. The 370 metres climb gives views of the Pokhara Valley and Phewa Tal. **Naudanda** (1,430 metres) lies along this ridge and has a police checkpoint and accommodation ranging from simple *bhattis* to reasonably good Western style hotels. Allow about five hours for the journey. Make sure that you have your trekking permit, as the police are conscientious. You may notice the noise of barking dogs, particularly on the first night of the trek, if you are sleeping near or in a village.

Naudanda to Birethanti/Tirkedhunga/Hille At the far end of Naudanda Day 2 you have a choice of trails. Both converge but the right hand track is shorter. The trail climbs to Khare (1,710 metres), a dispersed village at the head of the **Yamdi Khola** valley. Proceed down the stone steps below the British Agricultural Research station and rehabilitation centre for retiring Gurkha soldiers. After about one hour, you reach **Lumle** (1,585 metres). Keep to the main paved street and continue along the side of the ridge. The track then descends to **Chandrakot** (1,550 metres) where you get excellent views of Annapurna and Macchapuchare. You then descend to and cross the **Modi Khola** to reach **Birethanti** which has some good accommodation. (This is also a good stopping point if you are coming the other way on the Annapurna Circuit.) The trail follows the bank of the **Bhurungdi Khola** past some delightful waterfalls (especially in Autumn). Cross the suspension bridge, which climbs steadily up the side of the valley to **Hille** (1,495 metres) and **Tirkedhunga** (1,525 metres). Both villages have accommodation and are good halting places after over six hours' walk.

You can also cover this rather unexciting section by taking a bus to Lumle

Trek 7: Tatopani & Baglung

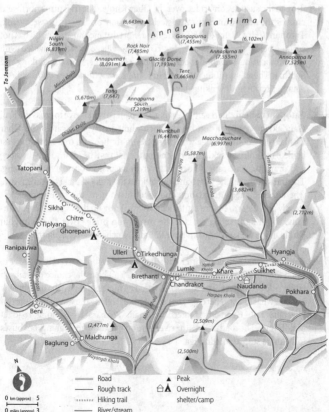

═══ Road	▲ Peak
— Rough track	⌂▲ Overnight
⋯⋯ Hiking trail	shelter/camp
— River/stream	

0 km (approx) 5
0 miles (approx) 3

Trekking

before starting the walk. There are numerous buses that go along the newly built **Baglung** road from north of the bazaar area in Pokhara.

Day 3 **Birethanti/Tirkedhunga/Hille to Ghorepani** The path descends from Tirkedhunga to cross the river, then steeply ascends some stone steps for 600 metres to Ulleri (2,070 metres), a large Magar village. Continuing above the village, you pass through cultivated area and some pastures to a dense forest of rhododendron, daphne and azalea mixed with giant conifers. Some three hours beyond Ulleri and after crossing three streams by bridge, you reach **Thante** (2,460 metres) in a small clearing. The track gets muddy after snow melt and during the monsoon, necessitating detours. There is a good campsite on the hill behind the first group of huts. **Ghorepani** ('Horse Water' in Nepali and Hindi) is an hour's walk further on, and 15 minutes beyond is the pass at **Deorali** (2,834 metres) where you can stay. An hour's climb from **Ghorepani** is **Poon Hill** (3,030 metres) where a wooden tower offers a spectacular panorama of Dhaulagiri, Tukche, Nilgiri, Annapurna I and Annapurna South. Best at dawn. This has been a day of some seven hours' walking.

Day 4 **Ghorepani to Tatopani** From Ghorepani, the trail descends through forest to **Chitre** (2,390 metres), then enters an extensively cultivated region of Magar villages. **Sikha** (1,890 metres) is three hours from Deorali and has many shops, lodges, a post office and an army training centre. Beyond Sikha the descent becomes stonier but it quite gentle to **Ghare** (1,705 metres). There is a further drop to the suspension bridge over the **Ghar Khola**. The trail turns north and crosses the **Kali Gandaki** on a steel suspension bridge to the west bank. **Tatopani** ('Hot Water', 1,189 metres) is a short distance upstream and has hot springs below the village near the river. The village is well provided with accommodation and good food. Many places use generators for cooking and lighting. There is a municipal bath and shops are well stocked and sell beer. Another seven hour walking day.

Day 5 **Tatopani to Beni** Start early. Leaving Tatopani you first have to cross the **Kali Gandaki** by a suspension bridge, then immediately afterwards, the **Ghar Khola** by a wooden bridge which brings you to the main trail along the east bank of the Kali Gandaki. Continue along the path as it heads through the steep and dramatic landscape. Cross the river by suspension bridge at **Tiplyang**. The trail climbs up the west bank and follows the Kali Gandaki to **Ranipauwa** where there is accommodation and food. From here, the valley slopes less steeply and there are more settlements, particularly on the western side. Continue south and having crossed the suspension bridge over the **Rahughat Khola**, it is a walk of about an hour to **Beni**, which has several *bhattis*.

Day 6 **Beni to Pokhara** It is a shorter walk than yesterday, but start early in order to catch the bus from near Baglung to Pokhara. You have the choice of trails on either side of the river. The east bank is used by mule trains and the terrain may be somewhat easier. There are a couple of bridges along the way. The route follows the Kali Gandaki to meet the main Pokhara to Baglung road at Maldhunga. The road crosses the river here on its way up to Baglung, but buses to Pokhara stop at Maldhunga.

Trek 8 Mustang: Jomsom to Lomanthang

Jomsom

KATHMANDU

Trekking

The Mustang (pronounced Moo-stang) region was only opened to trekkers in 1992 and the number of trekking permits issued each year is still restricted. Remote, cold and covered in snow through the winter, the trek is also effectively closed to trekkers from the end of October until late March. It is not a particularly high trek, but even in summer the cold, dust and unrelenting afternoon winds can make the trek harsher than other treks in Nepal. The fine dust invades everything, especially cameras. The region is sparsely populated and the villages are scattered unevenly along the route, making some trekking days very long while others seem too short. Unlike many other treks, there is little opportunity to vary the itinerary.

Geography

The small and isolated kingdom of Mustang occupies just over 3,000 square-kilometres with an average altitude of 4,000 metres, just below the Photu La pass (4,600 metres), which is itself only 75 metres above the Tsangpo plain of Tibet. In all respects, geographically, climatically and culturally, it belongs to Tibet. Today it is a Nepalese district with a certain degree of autonomy. The Thak Khola/Kali Gandaki originates here and flows out of the Mustang valley in a series of deep gorges. It has been vividly described by the French anthropologist Michel Peissel in his book *Mustang: The Lost Kingdom*.

History

Also known as the Kingdom of Lo, Mustang is said to have existed as an independent state as early as the fifth century AD, but was absorbed into Tibet under Songtsenampo in the seventh century. Later it achieved a degree of independence, becoming an important centre of the Lamaistic Sakyapa sect. After the disintegration of Gumthang in the early 15th century, Gayalpo Ame Pal (1380-1450) founded a dynasty that has survived until the present day. The present king, Jigme Palbar Bista, the 25th after Gayalpo Ame Pal, was born in 1930. The population is about 6,000.

The Mongols overran it in the 17th century and in 1760 the Raja of Jumla conquered it. It passed to the Gurkhas 30 years later who also appreciated its strategic and commercial significance on the Salt Straight from the middle hills to Tibet. The Thakalis gradually wrested control of the salt-grain trade from Mustang and when Indian salt replaced Tibetan salt in Nepalese markets, its fortunes declined further. The drying up of most of the trade saw Mustang retreat into its own remote shell. Now, the principal economic activity is subsistence barley farming in small irrigated tracts near the rivers. This is complemented by yak, horse, mule and goat breeding and rearing, the yaks being used in the fields. There is a significant nomadic pastoralist element in the lifestyle which has been dictated by the climate and the arid environment.

Briefing

Access: It is possible to get to Jomsom by air, or by trekking from Pokhara (see trek 9).

The Mustang trek is also very expensive. The trekking permit in 1999 cost US$700 for the first 10 days and US$70 per person a day thereafter. A one week permit is defined as seven days, not nights, starting and ending at Kagbeni. Although it is possible to trek to and from Lomanthang in seven days it would be a marathon trek and would not allow for any sightseeing in Lomanthang. Any reasonable trek in Mustang should therefore allow between 10 days and two weeks.

On top of the royalty, other necessary costs would be paid separately. These, too, are high. Kagbeni, at the start of the trek, is three hours' walk north of Jomsom. There are daily flights every morning to Jomsom from Pokhara, so you must spend a night in Pokhara en route to Jomsom. Flying in either direction is not cheap, but saves five days of walking. However, the five or six days' porterage to take in food, stoves, tents and kerosene, which are required to be taken in by law, plus the salary of camp staff to and from Jomsom, have to be added, significantly increasing the total cost.

If you have the time, it is well worthwhile to walk from Pokhara, visit Lomanthang, then trek back to Jomsom and fly or walk back to Pokhara. **NB** Jomsom can suffer from serious flight delays and cancellations.

Trailhead: Jomsom

Duration: 12 days

Best trekking season: April-October

Altitude: Rises almost 5,000m, can be a problem at the end of the trek when descent on return to Jomsom is rapid.

Equipment: Trekkers must be fully equipped and groups must include tents, cooks and porters.

Organization: Organized, escorted groups only. Recommended maximum of group size – 10.

Permit cost: US$700 for 10 days, US$70 per day thereafter. If trekking from Pokhara to Kagbeni you must pay the extra Annapurna fee of US$5 per week. Your registered trekking agent should be able to inform you about detailed arrangements. Also note the terms and conditions under which permits operate in Mustang.

Maps: Nepa Maps Mustang (by Paolo Gondini) covers the route from Jomsom to Lomanthang and N to the border and is widely available in Kathmandu, scale 1:125,000. Also US Army Map Service sheets NH44-12, NH44-16, NH45-9 and NH45-13.

People
: The inhabitants of Mustang are Bhotias and pure Tibetans, and both follow Lamaistic Buddhism. In the south of what is now Mustang district are the **Thakalis** who are related to the middle hill group of Gurungs, Magars and Tamangs and who provide a bridge between the two largely geographically determined cultures.

Day 1
: **Jomsom to Kagbeni** Walk due north from Jomsom. The route crosses a short hanging bridge just out of Jomsom, then follows the Kali Gandaki River. The route is barren, with rocks and sand, though the surrounding peaks – Dhaulagiri (8167 metres) and **Tukuche** (6920 metres) in the western Nilgiri – and the whole Annapurna massif to the south and southwest surround it.

Day 2
: **Kagbeni to Chhuksang** Kagbeni is a pretty village with about 90 families, and electricity supplied by erratically functioning wind energy. Most are traders who have been a link in the supply of food and essentials between Mustang and

the land of Lo and the rest of Nepal. There are a few lodges at the centre of the village. The *Nilgiri View* is the first you will encounter as you arrive in Kagbeni from the south. Permit formalities, which can take up to one hour or more, will be dealt with by your trekking group's environmental officer at the police

Trek 8: Jomsom to Lomanthang

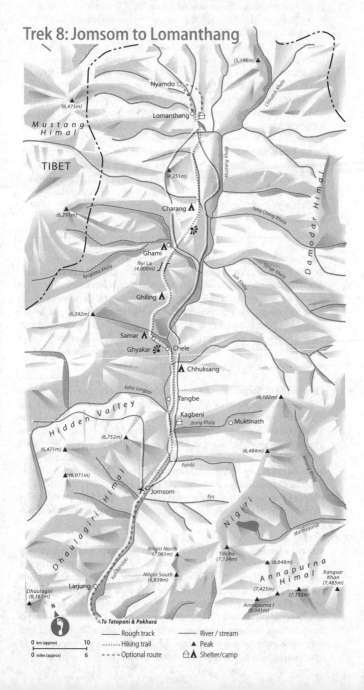

—— Rough track	—— River / stream
········ Hiking trail	▲ Peak
▬ ▬ ▬ Optional route	⌂▲ Shelter/camp

0 km (approx) 10
0 miles (approx) 6

Mustang's mountain monarch

Logyalpo Jigme Palbar, the Rajah of Mustang, is far removed from most people's image of royalty. Born in 1932, he is the 25th in a line of kings of the Palbar dynasty which has ruled Mustang since the 14th century. Although his duties are now predominantly ceremonial, he remains the highest authority in this remote region and is regularly called upon by Lopas, the name given to the people of Mustang, to dispense royal counsel or arbitrate in disputes.

Mustang's historical isolation has given the tiny kingdom a unique character, one in which the monarch is strongly identified with his people. He reigns from the four-storeyed palace dominating Lomanthang, but performs 15 daily processions, or chakras, around the town

walls accompanied by as many fellow Lopas as are awake at dawn. Following a breakfast of Tibetan bread and sojapurja, tea churned with butter and salt (some travellers find this easiest to drink when they think of it as soup rather than tea), the king busies himself with daily administrative tasks until lunch at noon which usually consists of dal-bhad-tarkari, eaten from low, ornately carved tables brought by his ancestors from Tibet. King Jigme is said to be a deeply religious man, reading from the Buddhist scriptures every afternoon, performing prayers morning, noon and night and taking comfort from the sound of prayer flags rustling in the night air which, he says, reminds him of 'the impermanence of this life'.

checkpoint, where the trail leads north out of Kagbeni. From the village, follow the widening trail due north, crossing endless stretches of sand, pebbles and boulders. Mule trains on long distance routes pass frequently. Much of the first half of the day is uphill, sometimes quite steep and, depending on the season, you can either walk along the dry river valley occasionally traversing tributaries of the Kali Gandaki, or there is a path alongside the flowing river. From the lunch stop at **Tangbe** village, the path flattens out for the two hour walk to **Chhuksang**, a large settlement populated by a mixture of Gurung, Thakalis and some families from the land of Lo. There is a small stone and mud Buddhist Gompa.

Day 3 **Chhuksang to Samar** This long and secluded valley offers a sharp change, both in topography and in culture, lifestyle and landscape. Settlements are more scattered, smaller and more basic. The valley is very dry and much of the soil is poor, so agriculture is restricted to isolated patches creating a brown and intermittently green landscape. A little ahead of Chhuksang the trek crosses a small bridge spanning the Mustang Khola River. Look out for attractive caves hollowed in the magnificent red cliffs along the river. The trail veers northwest climbing steeply. Just north of **Chele** is a spectacular view of the earth-walled village of **Ghyakar** over a wide canyon and is followed a little further on by another deep and sheer canyon. The day is a hard five hours' walk to the campsite at the village of **Samar**.

Day 4 **Samar to Ghiling** The trail is uphill for an hour then undulates, passing through some relatively fertile valleys and climbing over ridges before descending to the village of Shyangmochen where Nepali refreshments are available. The environment is largely arid with occasional oasis-like villages typical of Mustang. From here, a climb over a further ridge leads to a temporary separating of the trail: the left fork is the more direct route to the north via the tiny village of **Tama Gaon** towards the **Nyi La** pass, while the right fork leads to the overnight stopping point of **Ghiling**. Ghiling is a one hour descent from this junction, nestled in a valley between two hills.

Ghiling to Ghami Ghiling may be visited during a morning break. The trail is Day 5
a steep climb up to a ridge (the Nyi La pass) at almost 4,000 metres, about two
hours' walk. After this pass you enter Mustang (or Lo) proper. An easy 30 minutes' descent from here and you reach another junction from where a short
walk to the west brings you to Ghami, the night stop. Ghami is a small village
sheltered by overhanging mountain cliffs and beside a clear stream. The trail
passes many small Buddhist monuments (*chortens*).

Ghami to Charang This day's trek passes through perhaps the driest region Day 6
of Mustang. After the bridge crossing the Tangmar Chu River, the trail crosses
soft dry soil which is particularly trying when going uphill. The difficulty is
compensated by magnificent views, with gentle slopes to the north contrasting
with rugged mountains to the east and west. The climb from the Tangmar Chu
River passes one of Nepal's longest *maani* walls, built of stone and inscribed
with the Buddhist *Om maani padme hum* mantra. The total walk to **Charang** is
at least five hours. It is a large spread-out village, inhabited totally by the people
of Lo. Charang is perched on a cliff overlooking a canyon. It has some gompas,
a camping ground and a small lodge, while a hydro-electric plant provides the
village with electricity.

Charang to Lomanthang There is an opportunity to explore Charang village Day 7
and its large old monastery. It is also possible to see the nearby secluded village
of Dhakmar. Although today is only a four hour walk, it is mainly uphill. As the
trail widens, it passes through a barren wilderness of pale pastel rock and earth
where even occasional shrubs dotted along valleys and on slopes carved like
organ-pipes struggle to survive. The first sight of **Lomanthang**, the capital of
Mustang, is from a ridge about 30 minutes' walk from the walled town, with
the 'plain of prayerful aspiration' in the foreground. Lomanthang consists of
about 100 houses.

Lomanthang To enter Lomanthang, walk in an anti-clockwise direction Day 8
until you reach the main entrance on your left. The town is arranged around
the palace, built of stone like the other houses, next to the main street just east
of the centre and the monastery and religious buildings which occupy much of
the northern and western quarters, while Lomanthang's residential area of
some 160 households is concentrated to the south. A school and police office is
located outside the wall opposite the entrance and there is a small and very
basic clinic north of the wall. It is an interesting place to spend a rest day, but
basic accommodation is also available in a part-time guest house above the
post office, not far from the palace.

The four storeyed palace dominates the central area of the town and is home
to Lo's Raja and Rani. There are also four gompas, but access to these is highly
discretionary. Historically, Lomanthang prospered as a staging post in the
trade of wool and salt along the Kali Gandaki to Tibet, but today many of its
people (called Lo-pas) migrate seasonally as far south as India for work. One
or two excursions from Lomanthang are possible, but travelling north is especially subject to restrictions which are enforced by the police.

Excursions from Lomanthang There is a possible short excursion from
Lomanthang which can be taken over two days. The first day goes to **Nhejung**,
while the second day returns to Lomanthang via **Nyamdo** and **Thinkar**.

Lanthang to Ghami The route described above follows the eastern trail
between Ghami and Lomanthang, but another possible route exists heading in

Trekking

a southwest direction from Lomanthang. This is a longer walking day and at times the trail is much less clear than the eastern route, so taking a local guide is recommended. After two ridges you come to the **Ghar Gompa** and the nearby **Logekar** village beside the Charang Khola River. Further south and situated in a small but relatively fertile valley is the attractive village of **Dhakmar** from where it is a short walk to Ghami.

Day 9 **Lomanthang to Ghami** A brisk downhill or flat walk by the same route takes about seven hours. (See also Options below.)

Day 10 **Ghami to Ghiling** A further gentle descent crossing the Nyi La pass, then along mostly flat trails for five hours.

Day 11 **Ghiling to Kagbeni** A long day's walk of about eight hours, stopping at Chhuksang for lunch before continuing south along the Kali Gandaki to reach Kagbeni by nightfall.

Day 12 **Kagbeni to Jomsom** The descent to Jomsom (on the valley floor, about 5,000 metres below), is rapid, through dramatic arid lands. Following the previous few days, Jomsom can seem almost bustling. It is a 'major' village on the Kali Gandaki trading route.

Trek 9
Helambu

KATHMANDU

Based around the Langtang Valley region this trek is not as popular as the Everest and Annapurna regions because it lacks the 8,000 metre giants. However this trek does contain its own rewards and is convenient for travellers on their way to Kathmandu or Tibet. The trek also leads you through the Langtang National Park which is the largest park in the Himalyan region, containing 45 villages and a variety of wildlife.

From Syabru, there is the more difficult option of continuing further east to Langtang Village and Kyanching Ghyang, then trekking south across the Ganja La Pass (5,122 metres) to Tarke Ghayang before joining the previous route back to Kathmandu.

Briefing

Access: This area is relatively accessible, especially from Kathmandu. The **Helambu** area is about 60 kilometres north of Kathmandu. It consists of a number of valleys of which the **Malemchi** is the most important. The people are **Sherpas**, but are distinct from those in the Solu Khumbu and Everest regions. There are various options for trekking in Helambu, including routes to/from Langtang via Gosainkund as well as a popular one week circuitous route via Panchkhal (52 kilometres north of Kathmandu) and Mahakhal. The entrance to the **Langtang Valley** is only 30 kilometres from the capital. The modern route through the **Trisuli River Gorge** follows an ancient trade route to Tibet.

Trailhead: Kathmandu

Duration: 9 days

Best trekking season: Possible all year

as long as you do not make crossings out of the Langtang valley

Altitude: A rapid climb from under 2,000m to 4,610m at the Lauribina Pass.

Equipment: Take all equipment, although it is possible to get provisions along the trail and at the trailhead.

Organization: Parts of the trek should not be attempted without a guide.

Permit Cost: US$5 per week. Langtang National Park entrance fee Rs 650.

Maps: Mandala's Helambu-Langtang-Gosainkund (1:100,000) is in colour and covers the whole region as far N as Langtang Lirung and from the Trisuli River in the W to the Bolephi Khola in the E. Schneider Helambu-Langtang (1:100,000). US Army Map Service sheets NH45-13 ('Jongkha Dzong') and NG45-1 ('Kathmandu').

Kathmandu to Dhunche Dhunche (1,966 metres) is the trailhead, about four hours' drive from Kathmandu. From near Rani Pauwa (29 kilometres) there are good views of Annapurna II, Ganesh Himal and Manaslu. Up to Day 1

about 1,500 metres, the valley is inhabited by Brahmins and Chhetris; the houses have shingle roofs weighted down with stones. Tamangs live in the higher altitudes. Barley is cultivated on terraces. Dhunche is a compact village with a few hotels, a police checkpoint where you have to show your trekking permit and a park office where you pay the entrance fee of Rs 650 and where you can get an insight into the park's ecology. Keep your ticket, as you will probably have to show it again later.

Day 2 **Dhunche to Syabru** A short distance from Dhunche, the trail crosses the Trisuli River. This is followed by a short stiff climb to the intersection of the Langtang Valley and Gosainkund trails. Take the left hand trail which leads to **Bharku** (1,860 metres). From here, there is a fairly new trail which climbs over the ridge to **Syabru** (2,130 metres), situated on a spur a few 100 metres below the pass. Many of the village houses offer basic accommodation. The other trail is longer and heads north alongside the Trisuli River to **Syabru Bensi** (1,462 metres), situated at the confluence of the **Trisuli, Bhote Kosi** and **Langtang** Rivers and continues through **Syarpa Gaon** (2,581 metres). The former route saves a day and climbs steeply above Bharku to a 2,300 metres

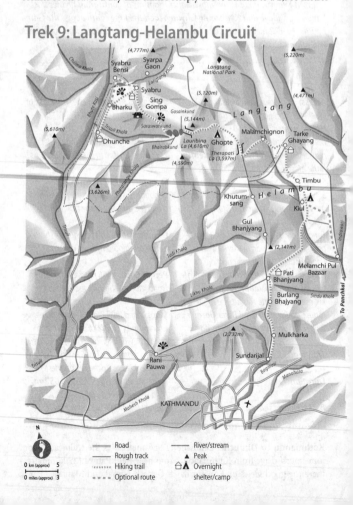

Trek 9: Langtang-Helambu Circuit

The Holy Waters of Gosainkund

Hindu myth tells how Shiva came down from his sacred home on Mt Kailash to meditate while other gods were churning the world's oceans for amrit, the legendary elixir of immortality. When, however, their churning produced burning poison instead of amrit, they turned to Shiva for protection. Shiva swallowed the poison and thereby saved the world. But the poison so burned his throat that Shiva ran to the Himalaya, flinging his trishul, or trident, into the mountains. Water began to flow from three springs and created lakes. Shiva threw himself into the largest of these, Gosainkund, and cooled his throat in its icy waters.

Shaivite pilgrims come from far and wide to worship here and some even say that they can see Shiva in the form of a rock at the bottom of the lake. Some believe that Gosainkund is linked by underground channels to the Kumbeshwar Mahadev Mandir in Patan, where those that can not make the journey to the lake worship during the August full moon festival.

pass from which you can see Langtang Lirung, Ganesh Himal and into the Tibetan mountains.

Syabru to Sing Gompa From Syabru there is a confusing trail that involves a lot of climbing. You have to stay to the right of the spur and travel in a southerly direction. Stay high and cross the ridge into the Trisuli Khola Valley. About one hour's walk from the ridge, you reach **Sing Gompa** and **Chandan Bari** (3,350 metres) where there is a small cheese factory. A local guide is recommended for the next few days' walk.   Day 3

Sing Gompa to Gosainkund The trail continues upwards through forest. There are no villages, only a few shepherds' huts. There are magnificent views of **Himal Chuli** (6,893 metres) and **Manaslu** (8,156 metres) to the west and **Langtang Lirung** to the north. The trail tends to follow the ridge and descends to the first lake, the small **Saraswatikund** at 4,100 metres. A few stone shelters are situated around the lake. A little way after Saraswati Kund is **Bhairabkund** with **Gosainkund** (4,380 metres) just beyond. Gosainkund was formed, according to legend, by Shiva thrusting his *trishul* (trident) into the mountain to create the three springs. It attracts numerous Shaivite pilgrims to *Janai Purnima*, the full moon festival in July/August, who come to bathe in the lakes' holy waters.   Day 4

Gosainkund to Ghopte Either return down the valley to Dhunche or cross over into the Helambu region. The latter climbs through rugged country, passing a few more small lakes before ascending quite steeply to cross the **Lauribina Pass** (4,610 metres). There are good views from here. You then descend along a stream and ascend a forested ridge. **Ghopte** (3,566 metres) has a cave shelter.   Day 5

Ghopte to Tharepati and Tarke Ghayang From the ridge you descend towards the valley, mostly through forest and passing the occasional shepherd's hut. After crossing a stream at 3,310 metres, you climb to the **Tharepati Pass** (3,597 metres). You can continue along the ridge through Khutumsang, Gul Bhanjyang and Pati Bhanjyang to Burlang Bhajyang and Sundarijal where you can catch a bus back to Kathmandu. Alternatively, go down into the valley to **Tarke Ghayang** and walk out by the easier valley route. The ridge walk is tiring, as there are constant ups and downs and the path is indistinct in places. To reach Tarke Ghayang, you drop down to cross the **Malamchi Khola** just beyond the village of **Malamchigaon**   Day 6

(2,560 metres) and then climb steadily. Tarke Ghayang is the main village in Helambu and has a choice of accommodation. The renovated gompa is quite impressive. The Helambu Sherpas are a trading community. **Warning** The 'antique' items sold here are more likely to be new manufactures brought from Kathmandu and Patan and then artificially 'aged'.

Day 7 **Tarke Ghayang to Kiul** The easiest way is to take the path to Timbu and then follow the Melamchi Khola down to Kiul. Descend through rhododendron forest passing several chortens and *mani* walls to **Kakani** (2,058 metres) and **Timbu** where the countryside is more extensively cultivated. This also marks the boundary between Helambu Sherpa country to the north and the Newar and Chhetri Hindu dominated areas to the south. The trail now descends steeply past the village of **Karkadanda** to **Kiul** (1,280 metres). A longer walk follows the ridge running down the east side of the valley to Melamchi Pul Bazaar before continuing along the Indrawati River to Panchkhal on the Kathmandu to Kodari road.

Day 8 **Kiul to Pati Bhanjyang** The area becomes ever more populated as the route goes through villages and settlements in rapid succession. Follow the river downstream and cross by the suspension bridge towards **Mahankal** (1,219 metres) which marks the end of a minor road that joins the Arniko Highway some 30 kilometres to the south. Continue south along this track which crosses the **Ghyalthum Khola** and descends into **Talamarang** (940 metres). Cross the **Talamarang Khola** then follow it up towards its source, first walking through terraced fields and then into the boulder strewn valley. Above and to the south is **Batase** village, below the 1,900 metres ridge. Go over the ridge, then veer to the west and descend gently towards **Pati Bhajyang** (1,768 metres), a large Tamang village with accommodation, shops and a police checkpoint.

Day 9 **Pati Bhanjyang to Sundarijal and Kathmandu** Follow the ridge as it climbs to Burlang Bhanjyang (2,438 metres) then descends past **Chaubas** (2,233 metres) to **Mulkharka** (1,768 metres). There are fine views of the Kathmandu Valley from here. The forests of rhododendron, pine and oak around here are the source of much of Kathmandu's wood fuel and in the mornings hundreds of villagers can be seen going to cut it. Drop down from the ridge to a dam and then continue through forest to **Sundarijal** (1,285 metres) where you can easily get transport back to Kathmandu (13 kilometres).

Short Trek:
Sundarijal-Chisopani-Nagarkot

If you are limited for time, there is a pleasant little trek that takes you just beyond the rim of the Kathmandu Valley through Sundarijal and into the hills to the north, then east to Nagarkot and back to Kathmandu. You can do it over two or three nights.

Sundarijal to Chisopani Walk or take a taxi to Sundarijal (see also page 303). Taxi drivers are sometimes reluctant to drive as far as Sundarijal, so you could go to Bodhnath and walk the rest of the way. The Sundarijal road forks left from the main road about one kilometre east of the Bodhnath stupa and almost immediately the scenery becomes more pastoral. The road – barely a track in parts – skirts around the north of Gokarna and continues through villages to Sundarijal where basic accommodation and refreshment is available.

Sundarijal means 'beautiful water' and is notable for the massive and not so beautiful water pipe which supplies Kathmandu with much of its water. Sundarijal to Chisopani is a walk of around six and a half hours. The route follows this pipe up the interminable steps until you reach an attractive reservoir. Nearby are a couple of places where you can stop for breakfast or lunch and is the last place for stocking up with mineral water before Chisopani. You have now moved out of the predominantly Newar villages of the Kathmandu Valley and are in Gurung country. The route continues uphill through attractive forest and the occasional village. After around five hours of walking, the route levels out briefly and there are wonderful views of the Helambu and Langtang mountains to the north. The remainder of the day is a gentle descent to **Chisopani** (2,194 metres).

The village is one of numerous 'Chisopanis' ('Cold Water') in Nepal. It is perched on a ridge with terraced slopes tumbling down all sides to the valley several hundred metres below. There is a handful of places to stay and a couple of shops to stock up with provisions. *Dorje Lakpa Lodge*, T01069283, nine rooms, one bath and separate toilet. Dining room does reasonable food, small shop. *Mountain Lodge*, T01069284, seven rooms, two bathrooms and two separate toilets. *New BBC Lodge*, T01069309, 11 rooms include a dormitory, two baths and two separate toilets. Food and a small shop. *Golden Guest House*, three rooms, one bath and separate toilet. At Rs 10 a night, this is Chisopani's cheapest place to stay.

Chisopani to Nagarkot The walk from Chisopani to Nagarkot is gentler than yesterday. Most of the route has excellent mountain views. The main path you left yesterday continues east towards Nagarkot, with a cross country section which probably requires a guide. The walk takes around five hours, including the final steepish climb to Nagarkot itself. Nagarkot has a good range of quality accommodation. From Nagarkot you can walk back to Kathmandu via Bkaktapur, or take the northerly route via Sankhu and the picturesque **Changu Narayan Mandir**.

Day 1

Day 2

Trekking

Trek 10 Langtang: Syrabru to Tarke Ghayang

KATHMANDU

This is an extension of the Helambu trek . It is a difficult trek which fits in between Days 3 to 6 of the above description and should not be done without an experienced guide. From Syabru, you follow the Langtang Khola to the east before turning south to cross the Ganja La pass towards Tarke Ghayang. Much of this route is spent above 3,000 metres (10,000 feet), so mountain sickness is a constant factor. We have repeated this information. It is, of course, possible to carry on to Kathmandu.

Briefing

Access: This area is relatively accessible, especially from Kathmandu. It does involve trekking for the first 2 days through Helambu.

Trailhead: Syrabru

Duration: 9 days including 2 days from Kathmandu.

Best Trekking Season: Possible all year as long as you do not make crossings out of the Langtang valley

Altitude: The trek climbs rapidly from under 2000m to 5,122m at the Ganja La Pass.

Equipment: Take all equipment, although it is possible to get provisions

along the trail and at the trailhead.

Organization: Parts of the trek should not be attempted without a guide. The use of firewood is prohibited within the park, so remember to take all supplies with you.

Permit Cost: US$5 per week. Langtang National Park entrance fee Rs 650.

Maps: Mandala's Helambu-Langtang-Gosainkund (1:100,000) is in colour and covers the whole region as far north as Langtang Lirung and from the Trisuli River in the west to the Bolephi Khola in the east. Schneider Helambu-Langtang (1:100,000). US Army Map Service sheets NH45-13 ('Jongkha Dzong') and NG45-1 ('Kathmandu').

Langtang National Park is Nepal's largest and the first of the Himalayan regions to be so designated in 1976. Its vegetation ranges from alpine to subtropical. Within its area of 1,710 square-kilometres are 45 villages as well as a rich flora of over 1,000 plant species in addition to 30 species of animal and 160 varieties of bird. The forests of fir, pine, birch, maple, oak and rhododendron harbour leopard, Himalayan black bear, red panda and monkeys, while musk deer and tahr inhabit higher altitudes. The migratory birds use the Bhote-Kosi-Trisuli Rivers to travel between Tibet and India.

Langtang Lirung (7,245 metres) towers over the valley. The technically difficult **Ganja La** pass (5,122 metres) connects the upper valley with that of the Ripal Khola and Malemchi Khola in Helambu. The region's inhabitants are of Tibetan stock with many having intermarried with Tamangs from Helambu.

Kathmandu to Dhunche Dhunche (1,966 metres) is the trailhead, about Day 1 four hours' drive from Kathmandu. From near Rani Pauwa (29 kilometres) there are good views of Annapurna II, Ganesh Himal and Manaslu. Up to about 1,500 metres, the valley is inhabited by Brahmins and Chhetris; the houses have shingle roofs weighted down with stones. Tamangs live in the higher altitudes. Barley is cultivated on terraces. Dhunche is a compact village with a few hotels, a police checkpoint where you have to show your trekking permit and a park office where you pay the entrance fee of Rs 650, and where you can get an insight into the park's ecology. Keep your ticket, as you will probably have to show it again later.

Dhunche to Syabru A short distance from Dhunche, the trail crosses the Day 2 Trisuli River. This is followed by a short stiff climb to the intersection of the Langtang Valley and Gosainkund trails. Take the left hand trail which leads to **Bharku** (1,860 metres). From here, there is a fairly new trail which climbs over the ridge to **Syabru** (2,130 metres), situated on a spur a few 100 metres below the pass. Many of the village houses offer basic accommodation. The other trail is longer and heads north alongside the Trisuli River to **Syabru Bensi** (1,462 metres), situated at the confluence of the **Trisuli, Bhote Kosi and Langtang** Rivers and continues through **Syarpa Gaon** (2,581 metres). The former route saves a day and climbs steeply above Bharku to a 2,300 metres pass from which you can see **Langtang Lirung, Ganesh Himal** and into the **Tibetan mountains.**

Syabru to Chomgong Walk through forest to the Langtang Khola (1,860 Day 3 metres), then follow it upstream gaining height rapidly. After some distance you cross the river by a bridge to the north bank and the thinner, drier forest. **Chomgong** (2,380 metres) is a small hamlet with accommodation and a camping site.

Chomgong to Langtang Village Climb above the village, then follow the Day 4 trail around the cliffs. Ghore Tabela (3,048 metres) has a police checkpoint where you will probably be asked to show your permit and park entry receipt. The valley becomes wider and you pass some Tamang villages. **Langtang** (3,307 metres) has Tibetan style houses with stones weighing down the shingled roofs and walled fields. There is a choice of accommodation, including the Tibetan run *Hotel Langtang View* which has excellent, reasonably priced and surprisingly varied food served in a kitchen by the fire, a warm and friendly atmosphere. There are also no holes in the walls! The airstrip nearby is for charter flights.

Langtang Village to Kyanching Ghyang The valley continues to become Day 5 wider. Kyanching Gompa (3,049 metres) has a monastery and a yak cheese factory established by the Swiss in 1955. It only takes half a day to reach the village, but it is not wise to continue higher in order to acclimatize. Some five kilometres to the south are the peaks of Naya Konga (5,846 metres) and, to the southeast, **Ponggen Dopku** (5,930 metres).

The Tibetan Lama of Tarke Ghayang

Kathmandu was once in the grip of a great plague. The plague claimed countless lives and the king was deeply disturbed. So he sent some of his men to ask the help of a well known holy man who lived in a small village high in the mountains of Tibet. Upon hearing their plight, the lama took pity and accompanied the king's men to Kathmandu. Within seven days of his arrival, the plague was contained. So grateful was the king that he asked the lama what gift he could give in return. A horse, thought the lama, would be useful for getting around his village in Tibet. The king then presented him with 100 horses. But before long, the horses became a burden to the lama, so the king instead gave him a plot of land in the mountains near Kathmandu on which he could build a ghayang. The temple the lama built was soon known as Tarke Ghayang, which in Tibetan means the temple of a hundred horses.

Day 6 **Kyanching Ghyang to Naakhang** You make a relatively short but steep ascent to Naakhang (4,100 metres), a seasonal (monsoon) yak pasture. Much of this is through rhododendron and juniper forest.

Day 7 **Naakhang to Keldang** You climb steeply towards the Ganja La pass and will probably encounter snow fairly early on. The last few 100 metres are precarious, so the utmost care is needed. From the pass, there are spectacular views of **Langtang Lirung** and the Tibetan peaks beyond. The descent is on a steep and dangerous scree slope for over one kilometre: again care is needed. After some distance, you reach the basin of **Ganja La Chuli** (5,846 metres). Further down you reach the **Yangri Khola** which you follow until you reach a few stone huts at **Keldang** (4,270 metres).

Day 8 **Keldang to Dukpu** Start early for the long undulating grind along the ridge. All of today's walk is along the Dukpu Danda at elevations of between 4,000 metres and 4,500 metres and the ridge follows a course between the **Melamchi Khola** to your right and the **Yangri Khola** on your left hand side. The **Yangri Danda** ridge begins just before you reach **Dukpu** village (4,023 metres) which has accommodation. (Note the Thai Airways cutlery in the lodge!) The local 'sightseeing' is to the nearby site of an air crash for which the owners' children are keen to act as guides. Apart from the post monsoon months of October and November and during the monsoon itself, water is very scarce in this area.

Day 9 **Dukpu to Tarke Ghayang** You first have to cross a 4,020 metre pass which offers good views before descending along the ridge through rhododendron to pine forest. Some stretches are quite steep. There is a sharp descent of almost 800 metres on your final approach to Tarke Ghayang. Above the village at 3,020 metres is **Gekye Gompa** where masked dances are performed during the full moon festival in March.

Trekking in the Everest Region

Everest is the magnet of Nepal. Many are attracted by the mountain itself, others by the Solu Khumbu region – the home of the Sherpas – and some by both. The Everest Base Camp trek is the second most popular in Nepal and is the longest established.

The classic trek to Everest Base Camp from Jiri takes around three weeks. You move from the predominantly Hindu Middle Hills to the Tibetan Buddhist High Himalaya. Mountaineering expeditions enjoyed the trek as a way of getting fit as well as acclimatizing. Some trekkers fly to and from Kathmandu, but most walk in and fly out from Lukla. Delays at Lukla are common, so allow a few extra days for flexibility. Because of its popularity, the trail and the Sagarmatha region is well endowed with guest houses and *bhattis*, though rather less luxurious than in the Annapurna region.

The Base Camp trail involves many ascents and descents as you move from one north-south valley to another. You must be really fit to enjoy the trek. Many trekking companies worldwide offer the Base Camp trek in their programme, so you will pass numerous trekking parties of all nationalities. Popular campsites can be congested and water sources polluted, so infection is a hazard.

It can get extremely cold north of Namche Bazaar, so appropriate clothing is necessary. You can hire down jackets in Namche Bazaar for around Rs40-70 per day; this saves hiring and carrying them from Kathmandu. Clothes made of synthetic materials can be very light and warm. It is worthwhile keeping a set of dry clothes in which to sleep.

Yak **attacks** do occur. Give these creatures a wide berth and if you are passing them on a slope, go around them the higher way. Downhill walks can be tough on the **knees** and ankles: a stick or knee support can help. Begin walking early in the morning, as fog often descends from early afternoon.

The following few hints on social behaviour will help you to appreciate Sherpa culture and to avoid local faux pas. Out of courtesy to Sherpas, don't attempt to climb Khumbi-yul-lha, the mountain directly behind Khunde and Khumjung, as this is the sacred abode of the deity that protects the Khumbu region. The name of a dead person should not be mentioned to his close relatives or in his house as this may attract his reincarnated spirit. Many Sherpas do not allow whistling in their homes for the same reason. Do not write a Sherpa's name in red ink, as this symbolizes death and is used for inscriptions at funeral ceremonies. Do not ask a Sherpa to kill a wild animal for you. If you offer food or drink to a Sherpa and it is politely refused, you should offer it twice more. Traditional Sherpa hospitality requires that you offer something three times. The Sherpa word for 'thank you' is *tuche*.

Cultural Interaction

Begging, especially by children, has been on the increase over the last few years. If you give, you will be encouraging others to beg. *Maagnu karap cha* means 'begging is bad'!

Health & Rescue Because of the region's popularity and the unstinting efforts of Hillary's Himalayan Trust, there is a hospital at Khumjung. There are small hospitals at Jiri, Phaplu and Khunde which are staffed by a doctor and Sherpa assistants.

The Himalayan Rescue Association maintains a **Trekkers' Aid Post** at **Pheriche** staffed by a physician and trained Sherpa assistants during the two trekking seasons. They advise about the problems of altitude and, when necessary, arrange rescues and treat victims. If a member of a group is severely affected, one or two others should go on ahead to the Trekkers' Aid Post where staff may decide to **evacuate** the victim by helicopter. On no account should the affected person be left on their own. Helicopter evacuation is the last resort. It may take up to 24 hours to arrive and then only if some guarantee of payment is made. Trekking companies may arrange for this contingency for their clients. If a person is having problems above Pheriche, come down immediately carrying or assisting the affected person. Always accompany anyone with severe symptoms of mountain sickness. Descent invariably brings about a marked improvement.

Sagarmatha National Park Mount Everest, or **Sagarmatha** ('Mother of the Sea') in Nepali and **Chomolungma** in Tibetan, is part of the 3,104 square-kilometre **Sagarmatha National Park**, established in 1976 with the help of the New Zealand government. Visitors must abide by a few simple rules, the most important being that they must carry in their fuel and dispose of their rubbish carefully. In 1979, Sagarmatha National Park was declared a UNESCO World Heritage Site.

In terms of animal conservation, Sagarmatha has proved an outstanding success. In its sheltered environment, the numbers of many creatures have increased. It has the largest population of Himalayan tahr and the similar serow and ghoral. The sure-footed tahr, the size of an American mountain goat, can be seen on seemingly unscalable hillsides. Nepal's national bird, the **Impeyan Pheasant** (the male, beautifully coloured), is also fairly common, although farmers regard it as a pest. In the mountain forests are **red panda**, **wolves** and the prized **musk deer**, the latter safe from poachers. Only the males, which have two fang-like canine teeth, produce the musk from a small glandular sac under the skin of the abdomen. Valued in China as a folk medicine and aphrodisiac, a small quantity of 30 g can fetch a year's earnings for an average Nepali.

Overall, the park has been only a partial success. Deforestation continues, although alternative **energy** sources such as small scale hydro-electricity schemes are being developed to meet the needs of the growing Sherpa population and the many thousands of trekkers who travel here each year. **Sir Edmund Hillary** had noted on the 1953 British expedition a forest of junipers around Pangboche which had practically disappeared just 30 years later. He felt a sense of responsibility, knowing that the expedition had paved the way for others who had recruited small armies of porters who attacked the forests. To rectify the destruction, he set up the **Himalayan Trust** which, as an independent non-governmental organization, has undertaken extensive building works in the region. The Trust has been careful to provide the services that the Sherpas themselves have asked for, namely schools and hospitals. By 1973, Hillary realized that some kind of control was needed if the Khumbu region was not to become a treeless desert. Responding to his overtures, the New Zealand government assisted with the creation and management of the park.

Trekking

Some Park Regulations

*It is prohibited to carry arms or explosives or to remove anything from the park, including rock samples and specimens of flora and fauna. You are also forbidden to scale a mountain without permission, or to climb any sacred peak of whatever elevation. Keep to the main trails and carry sufficient fuel for your trip. Buying firewood from the local population is forbidden; this also applies to porters. Park personnel are empowered to arrest anyone suspected of infringing these regulations and may search a trekker's or porter's belongings. **Kerosene** is often available at Namche Bazaar's Saturday market. A filter is required to sift out pieces of dirt which can clog up a stove and render it inoperable.*

Weather conditions can change very rapidly at high altitude, particularly as a result of unforeseen changes in the western jet stream. The region's climate is dominated by the mountains that enclose the valleys. They deflect much of the **wind** coming off the Tibetan High Plateau and act as a wall against the rain-bearing monsoon clouds brought in from the Bay of Bengal.

Heavy frosts are common in Namche Bazaar from late October onwards and gradually the ground freezes to a depth of around 500 millimetres. There is light snow in **Autumn**, while **December, January** and **February** are the coldest months with heavy falls of snow occuring after **December**. From **January** to **March**, the weather is fairly settled with periods of clear weather lasting for up to three weeks at a time. These are broken by short stormy periods lasting a few days.

Between November and **March**, the average daily temperature is only a few degrees above freezing. At night it can fall to -15°C at Namche Bazaar and below -20°C beyond Lobuche. These temperatures rise steadily from **March** onwards until the onset of the monsoon. This is a period of little rain and increasing heat and haziness.

The monsoon arrives in **mid-June**. Rain clouds form rapidly to cover the peaks and fill the valleys by midday. Light mist turns into heavy rainfall by nightfall and, at higher altitudes, this turns to snow. Visibility is poor and clinging mists can hang around in valleys for weeks. From **mid-September** the clouds and rain withdraw. Some 75 percent of the annual rainfall of 1,000 millimetres comes during the monsoon. The peaks receive most of their snow at this time and the snow-line comes down to 5,500 metres.

Climate

Trekking

KATHMANDU

Trekking

Trek 11 Everest Base Camp

The classic trek to the Everest Base Camp from Jiri takes about three weeks. You move from the predominantly Hindu Middle Hills to the Tibetan Buddhist High Himalaya. Because of its popularity the trail is well endowed with guest houses and bhattis, although campsites can be crowded. The Base Camp Trek involves many ascents and descents as you move from one valley to another. You must be really fit to enjoy the trek. The trek also goes through the Sagarmartha National Park, from which you can get a fantastic view of the local mountains and Everest. Within the National Park you have to carry all your own cooking fuel and the use of firewood is prohibited.

 Briefing

Access: You can walk all the way to Sagarmatha National Park from Kathmandu. Flying **to Syangboche** (Namche Bazaar) is not recommended, as it allows no time for acclimatization. **Lukla** is a STOL (short take off and landing) airstrip; the approach and landing is interesting, though can be unnerving for some. Book and reconfirm your return flight in Kathmandu; this can save your being bumped when you check in at Lukla. From Lukla (2,886 metres), it is a walk of several kilometres along the Dudh Kosi Valley to Namche Bazaar (3,446 metres). The flight to **Jiri** is preferable, as the walk in allows the body to acclimatize gradually and it's a very scenic route.

Trailhead: Kathmandu

Duration: 20 days

Best trekking season: Late September-early November and March-April.

Altitude: Most of the route after Namche Bazaar is above 3,000m.

Equipment: Accommodation and provisions available throughout the trek. Warm clothing, sunblock cream and sunglasses are essential equipment.

Organization: Go in groups, largely due to the problem of altitude sickness.

Permit cost: US$5 per week for the first 4 weeks, thereafter US$10 per week.

Maps: The Schneider series (1:50,000) is the best. Their Tamba Kosi & Likhu Khola map covers the route from Jiri to Junbesi; Shorung/Hinku covers the stretch from Junbesi to between Lukla and Namche Bazaar; Khumbu Himal covers the area from north of Lukla to Mount Everest; and if you are trekking from Lamidanda, the Dudh Kosi map covers the area from there to Lukla. Locally produced maps include Nepa's Rolwaling Himal & Solu Khumbu (1:110,000) covering the Sagarmatha National Park from Jiri in the west to the Hunku Khola in the east and north to Mount Everest.

Kathmandu to Jiri (via Lamosanga) Buses leave Kathmandu throughout   Day 1
the day for Jiri. It takes 12 hours by public bus, much less by private. The route
passes through Bhaktapur, Banepa and Dhulikhel. Trekkers going into the
Helambu region get down at Panchkal. The others continue to Lamosanga, a
market town approximately 50 kilometres from the Tibetan border and 78
kilometres from Kathmandu. **Jiri** (1,905 metres) is some 110 kilometres from
Lamosanga and has a STOL airfield so you can fly in, though this is expensive.
There is a choice of accommodation.

Jiri to Bhandar Changma Start early. The Solu Khumbu trail begins at the   Day 2
head of the road behind the hospital and climbs through forest and the occasional hamlet to cross an open ridge at **Chitre** (2,400 metres). You then
descend into the **Khimti Khola** valley through **Dovan** to **Shivalaya** (1,767
metres), a large village with a market.

From Shivalaya you ascend to a 2,705 metres pass, passing through
Sangbadanda (2,240 metres) and **Buldanda**. You will notice the first *mani*   *Walk to the left of*
walls of the trip which marks your moving from a predominantly Hindu   *mani walls and*
region into regions inhabited by the Tibetan Buddhist Tamangs and Sherpas.   *chortens*

The pass is approached through forest. You then get a good view of the
Likhu Khola and Bhandar Changma ahead of you. A short distance below the
pass, the path forks. The right goes to the Solu region via Roshi. Continue on
towards **Bhandar Changma** which you reach after crossing pasture and the
cultivated area. Bhanda Changma has a gompa and two striking chortens. The
village has a number of guest houses and a good camping ground about 15
minutes beyond the settlement.

Trek 11: Jiri to Namche Bazaar

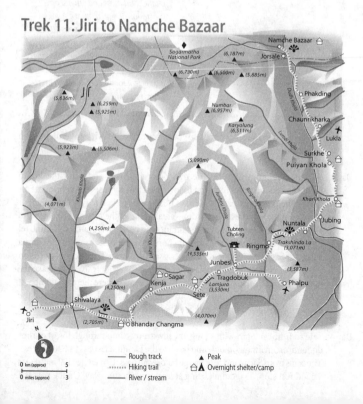

—— Rough track	▲ Peak	
⋯⋯ Hiking trail	🏠▲ Overnight shelter/camp	
—— River / stream		

0 km (approx) 5
0 miles (approx) 3

The Yak...

Nothing quite characterizes the Tibetan dominated, higher reaches of the Himalaya like the yak. Indeed, with the appearance of the yak at altitudes of 3,000 to 6,000 metres, you know that you have arrived in the ethnic Tibetan area. The animal has been closely associated with Tibetan groups since antiquity and its use as a pack animal – carrying loads rather than passengers – has contributed to the wealth and livelihood of nomadic herders as well as traditional farming communities. It also forms an important part of the diet, providing meat, milk, butter, curd and cheese, all high in protein. Its hide, meanwhile, is used for footwear, and its coat for clothing.

The yak (Bos grunniens – literally, 'grunting ox') is a member of the bovine family and has the same number of chromosomes as the common dairy cow. The word yak comes from the Tibetan gyag and is in fact the male of the species,

while the female is known as a nak by Sherpas and dri by the Bhotias. It has been successfully cross-bred with the domestic cow to produce the dzo, a strong ploughing animal which is also renowned for the richness of its milk.

The yak is well adapted to its lofty habitat. Its coarse and long wirey outercoat covers a fine though shorter undercoat, which together provide protective warmth against the extremes of high altitude temperatures. The skin is thick and has very few sweat glands which further conserves heat by reducing perspiration, although this can become a liability at lower elevations. Its lungs are larger and the blood contains up to four times as many red blood cells as other bovines, enabling the maximum utilisation of available oxygen. Its digestive system has become highly efficient at metabolising low quality fodder, while its tongue and short teeth allow it to graze off the short grass and other scarce vegetation of high altitudes. A yak's normal lifespan rarely exceeds 20 years. Curiously, this is largely due to that last adaptation to its environment; for one of the main causes of yak mortality is insufficient food intake resulting from worn out teeth.

This is a very long day's walk, so you may want to break it by overnighting in Shivalaya.

Day 3 **Bhandar Sangma to Sete** The trail descends to Baranda and the **Likhu Khola** (1,580 metres) which you follow then cross by suspension bridge. Following the river upstream to **Kenja** (1,634 metres), you may see grey langur monkey troops in the forest. From Kenja, home of the Newars, Sherpas and Magars, where there are shops, restaurants and hotels, it is a fairly stiff climb up to the **Lamjura ridge**. At the trail junction, the left fork leads up to the Sherpa village of **Sagar** (2,440 metres). There is a Himalayan Trust school here and some small guest houses. People often camp in the schoolyard. If you take the main right hand fork, you reach **Sete** (2,575 metres) where there is a gompa. It is difficult for camping, but there are a number of hotels. From here all the remaining villages along the trek are Sherpa.

Day 4 **Sete to Junbesi** Start with a long, mostly steady climb through forest of rhododendron, magnolia, maple and birch to the Lamjura La pass (3,530 metres). The trails from Sagar and Sete merge before the pass. **Goyem** (3,300 metres) is a good rest stop, Tragdobuk being at least three hours away. On the pass is a

...and Yeti

He is hairy, has big feet, is of large humanoid appearance, consumes an omnivorous diet and smells of garlic and rotten eggs. He is also extremely elusive. But the yeti, or abominable snowman, features strongly in Sherpa mythology in which he is endowed with various supernatural qualities including the capacity to become invisible, which Hillary considers to be just as important a feature as his alleged physiognomy.

The yeti is often held responsible for sporadic vicious attacks on yaks, an occupation which has not endeared him to yak herders. He apparently kills by grabbing the unfortunate yak by the horns and using them to twist its neck. In 1974, a village girl was reportedly assaulted by a yeti in Macchermo, two days walk north of Namche Bazaar towards Gokyo. The local police confirmed the attack, but failed to apprehend the suspect. It was this kind of antisocial behaviour, combined with his decidedly

malodorous aspect, which led to the epithet 'abominable' being bestowed upon this abstruse creature. The word yeti, meanwhile, seems to have entered the English language in the 1920s and is thought to derive from the Tibetan me t'om k'ang mi, meaning 'man/bear snowfield man'.

The existence of an abominable snowman was first suggested to the world in 1898 by Wassell who discovered a series of large and inexplicable footprints in Sikkim. There have been numerous subsequent reported sightings either of the creature himself or of his 'footprints', notably by Shipton in 1951. Yet he has continued to thwart all efforts to locate him or verify his existence. Footprints in the snow are written off as those of another animal which have been enlarged by the warmth of the sun, while an analysis of a yeti skull from a Khumbhu monastery revealed it to be that of a humble serow.

---

cairn topped with prayer flags marking the highest point between Jiri and Namche Bazaar. On the far side you descend gradually, first through forest then through meadows and fields to **Tragdobuk** (2,860 metres) which has a few hotels.

Climb again to a huge rock at the head of the valley, then go over the ridge to Junbesi (2,675 metres), known simply as **June** in the Sherpa dialect. The village has a monastery and several large hotels. Camping is below the village on the river bank. Around the village are a few sights worth seeing. To the north, two hours walk away, is the large monastery of **Tubten Choling** (Mopung on the *Schneider* map), and there is a Sherpa art centre at **Phukmoche**. The monastery, situated at 3,000 metres, with about 200 Tibetan refugee monks, was founded in 1960.

Junbesi to Nuntala From Junbesi, you can cross the Junbesi Khola and continue on the direct route towards **Ringmo**, or take the trail heading south along the Junbesi Khola to **Phaplu** where there is an airstrip, the **Himalayan Trust Hospital** and the local style *Hostelerie des Sherpas*. The route then climbs to cross the ridge at 3,080 metres, giving the first view of Everest, Chamlang (7,317 metres) and Makalu (8,463 metres). Descend through **Salung** (2,980 metres) to the **Ringmo Khola** (2,650 metres). This is a good place for washing, as the next river, the **Dudh Kosi**, is much colder. Climb to **Ringmo** village (where you join the improved trail to Namche Bazaar) and then to the **Trakshindo La** pass (3,071 metres). Drop down past the impressive Trakshindo monastery and through rhododendron forest to **Nuntala** (2,350 metres) which has reasonable accommodation.

Day 5

Om mani padme hum

Day 6 **Nuntala to Khari Khola** Descend to the Dudh Khola. Cross then turn north and begin to follow the river up towards Namche Bazaar. The trail then climbs to **Jubing** (1,676 metres) inhabited by Rais (a group recruited into the Gurkha regiments), who have adopted both Hinduism and Buddhism. It continues up to the village of **Khari Khola** (2,050 metres) by the Khari River which has good accommodation. The campsite is beyond the village across the bridge.

Day 7 **Khari Khola to Puiyan** Drop to cross the Khari Khola at 2,100 metres where there are some mills, then climb up to Bupsa (Bumshing) where there is a white chorten and some accommodation. Continuing, you climb steadily to the ridge. The **Dudh Kosi Canyon** is very precipitous here. From the 2,900 metre pass, you descend along an impressive (scary for some) section of the trail into the side canyon of the **Puiyan Khola**. The village is situated at 2,835 metres and has accommodation.

Day 8 **Puiyan to Phakding** You climb for about one hour to the 2,800 metre ridge opposite Puiyan from where you can see the airfield at Lukla, recognized by the roof of the Sherpa Co-operative Hotel and possibly still some wrecked aircraft. The trail descends to just above Surkhe (2,339 metres), situated on the **Surkhe Khola**, a tributary of the Dudh Kosi. From Surkhe you climb for about 15 minutes to a trail junction. **Lukla** airfield is about one hour's steep climb up a stone staircase to the right. The Khumbu trail continues north to **Chaunrikharka** (2,713 metres). There is accommodation here, but you can continue on through terraced fields to **Choplung** (2,660 metres) where the path is joined by the one from Lukla.

The village of Ghat (2,550 metres) is the next village, followed after an undulating section of the trail, by **Phakding** (2,640 metres) which is spread across both sides of the river.

Day 9 **Phakding to Namche Bazaar** The trail climbs up the Dudh Kosi Canyon, crossing from side to side passing the villages of Benkar and **Chomou** and through forests of blue pine, fir and juniper. Between 3,600 metres and 4,200 metres birch and rhododendron predominate. Solid villages with long dry stone walls of the type so common in the English Yorkshire Dales and the Lake District can be seen running down from the high meadows. Many of the huge boulders are carved with the now familiar Buddhist mantra, *Om mani padme hum*, the six sacred syllables. The entrance to the national park is just beyond Chomou, at **Jorsale**. All trekkers must register here.

Beyond Jorsale, the trail undulates along the valley up to the confluence of the Bhote Kosi and **Dudh Kosi**. This part of the trail is virtually sunless and notoriously cold and windy, the wind funnelling down the gorges of both rivers. Camping in this spot, however, may be rewarded with sighting a red panda. From here you begin the final steep climb up to Namche Bazaar. From a couple of places along this trail you can see **Everest, Nuptse** and **Lhotse,** but by the afternoon, these are usually covered in cloud.

Namche Bazaar (3,446 metres) is situated in a sheltered horseshoe shaped basin high above the **Bhote Kosi Gorge.** Terraced houses cling to the hillside. There is plentiful accommodation here with many guest houses having hot showers – a great luxury when trekking in the Himalaya. The friendly *Tawa Lodge* has five rooms and a nine bed dorm, though it is better to eat out. The *Sherpa Guest House* and *Khumbu Lodge* are recommended. The latter has good food and a host of Jimmy Carter memorabilia – the owner was the former US president's guide in 1985. The restaurants serve exotic delicacies such as banana cake, cinnamon roll and apple pie. There is also a bank, a police checkpoint, a bakery and the park office. In the bazaar you can hire Sherpas; the village men are often away so the women do the trading in this matriarchal society.

Namche Bazaar A rest day should be spent relaxing in Namche Bazaar for acclimatization. Another day should be built into your programme if you are going to the Base Camp. It is important that you allow two nights at the same place twice between Lukla and Lobuche.   **Day 10**

The weekly (Saturday) market is usually colourful and noisy. Traders from lower altitudes, mostly Tamangs and Rais, carry in baskets of rice, millet and other produce, often having been on the road for up to a week. Sherpas from surrounding villages converge to make their purchases and to socialize in the local tea shops.

Trek 11: Namche Bazaar to Everest Base Camp

You have to present your trekking permit and park entrance receipt at the police checkpoint. Above it is the Sagarmatha National Park Headquarters, which has a Visitors' Centre for information and a good presentation on the park's ecosystem and the impact of tourism on the region.

The **A** *Everest View Hotel,* Kathmandu T224854, F227289, in Syangboche claims to be the highest hotel in the world, and has superb views of Everest Lhotse and Anadablam. 12 rooms, all with bath (no running hot water) and a heater. All meals included in the price. Located 50 minutes walk from Syangboche air strip.

Namche Bazaar to Thyang-boche There are two routes to Thyangboche: the direct one from Chorkung and a slightly longer but interesting one via Khumjung and   **Day 11**

👉 *Mount Everest*

*For 13 years after it was found to be the highest mountain in the world, **Peak XV** had no European name. In 1865, the then Surveyor General of India suggested that it be named after his predecessor, **Sir George Everest** (1790-1866), the man responsible for the Great Trigonometrical Survey, completed in 1841, which ultimately determined its height. Everest himself, though honoured, was privately unhappy, as it was official policy that mountains be given their local vernacular name. However, an exception was made and the name stuck.*

*Everest has been climbed many times and by many routes since 1953. The route taken by **Hunt's** expedition is the 'Ordinary Route', disparagingly called the 'Yak Route' by Sherpas. Following his achievement on Annapurna's Southern Face, Chris **Bonnington** led two expeditions to tackle Everest's SW face and succeeded in 1975. The Americans traversed it in 1963. In 1970, Yuichiro **Muira** tried to ski down the Lhotse Face*

*from the South Col, but spent most of it airborne and out of control, ending unconscious on the edge of a crevasse! Rheinhold **Messner** climbed without oxygen and then solo. Ang **Pertember** has been there twice as well. Peter **Hillary** followed in his father's footsteps and stood on the summit in 1990. In April 1988, two teams of Japanese met on the top, having scaled the north and south faces. And there, to record the event, was a television crew!*

On 29 September 1992, a GPS survey using signals from satellites determined the height of Everest as 8,846.1 metres. Although this is two metres lower than previously believed, Everest is still higher than K2, despite claims to the contrary made in the New York Times in March 1987. In April 1993, the team that first climbed Everest trekked to the Base Camp for a 40th anniversary re-union: they found 1,500 other climbers waiting their turn to climb to the top of the world.

Khunde, described here. In all there are four trails that splay out from Namche following the major valleys of the park: the Bhote Kosi, the traditional trading route to Tibet; the **Dudh Kosi**, leading to the Ngozumpa Glacier, Gokyo Lake and Mount Cho Oyu; the **Imja Valley** running up under Nuptse and Lhotse, Baruntse and the back of Ama Dablam; and the main **Khumbu Valley** leading up to Everest Base Camp. (See **Options**.)

From Namche Bazaar, it is a steep one hour climb to Shyangboche (3,720 metres). There are good views of Ama Dablam and Everest from here, and a short airfield built to service the Japanese built *Everest View Hotel*.

The trail descends from the hotel to the village of Khumjung (3,790 metres). The gompa claims to possess the skull of a yeti, though tests show it to be that of a humble serow (a goat-like antelope). The mixed forest of rhododendron, birch and silver fir contrasts with the bare slopes of the gorge and you may see musk deer and Impeyan pheasant. The village of **Khunde**, with its Himalayan Trust school and hospital, is a short distance away. Across the canyon from Khunde and opposite the confluence of Imja Khola and Dudh Kosi Rivers is **Thyangboche** (3,867 metres) with its famous monastery rebuilt after fire damage in 1989 and a Sherpa Cultural Centre. The trail to it from **Khumjung** goes down the valley, past chortens and mani walls and soon meets the direct Namche Bazaar to Thyangboche trail. Just beyond is **Kenjoma** with a few hotels. Further on, you descend to Teshinga and lower still to **Phunki Tenga** (3,250 metres), noted for its water driven prayer wheels.

Climb steeply at first through forest and then more gradually to the Thyangboche saddle. At dawn the view is magnificent: Kwangde (6,187 metres), **Tawachee** (6,542 metres), **Everest** (8,848 metres), **Nuptse** (7,855 metres), **Lhotse** (8,616 metres), **Ama Dablam** (6,856 metres), **Kangtega** (6,779 metres) and **Thamserku** (6,608 metres), all arrayed in a stunning panorama. There is accommodation here. Certain campsites are reserved for individual companies. The monastery has been rebuilt following a fire in 1988. A donation of around Rs20 is expected (receipted by a monk) for camping in the grounds.

At the November/December full moon, the *Mani Rimdu* festival takes place. The colourful masked dances depict the triumph of Buddhism over the old Bon faith of Tibet. You will be expected to pay an entry charge, with an additional movie camera surcharge.

Thyangboche to Pheriche Descend through forest to Devuche where there   Day 12 are a few travellers' lodges and a nunnery. After crossing the **Imja Khola** on a steel suspension bridge, climb up past some mani stones to **Pangboche** (3,860 metres), the highest all year settlement in the valley with the **Himalayan Rescue Association's Trekkers' First Aid Post** and some accommodation. The gompa claims to have a yeti scalp and hand (see previous **Yeti** box), which you can view for a small fee. The lower village can be visited on the way to Everest Base Camp, the upper on the return.

From Pangboche, the trail initially remains fairly steady above the Imja Khola, then climbs through a small group of houses called Shomare. Continue on past the village of Orsho and along a broad terrace to the confluence of the Imja Khola and the **Lobuche Khola**. To your right, less than its own height away from you, is **Ama Dablam** (6,856 metres) and the **Tsuro Glacier** cradled below the mountain's sharp ridges. **Ama Dablam** is considered by many to be one of the most beautiful mountains in the area, easily surpassing Everest in the aesthetic stakes.

The track diverges at the confleunce of the river, the right hand one running up to Dingboche, the producer of high quality barley for *tsampa*. Instead, take the left hand trail which passes above some houses, mounts a shoulder, then descends to cross the river. The valley is wide and flat until it reaches the terminal moraine of the **Khumbu Glacier**. The village of **Pheriche** (4,243 metres) is at the lower end and consists mainly of hotels and teashops plus a shop selling expedition leftovers.

Pheriche Spend a rest day here, even if you are feeling in good condition. A   Day 13 side trip can be made up to **Nagkartshang Gompa** (approximately 4,600 metres) which also offers a good view of Makalu. There is another, more strenuous, side trip to **Chhukung** (4,700 metres), a small summer settlement where you get excellent views of **Island Peak, Lhotse** and **Ama Dablam**. Climb the hill to Dingboche, then follow the Imja Khola to Chhukung (see **Options**).

Pheriche to Lobuche The first part of the route passes up the long scrubby   Day 14 flat bottom of the valley to Phulung Kharka. It rises steadily, then drops down, crosses the river and enters **Dughla** (4,620 metres) with its tea shops. From here the trail climbs higher and onto the moraine. A row of chortens in memory of the Sherpas who have died on Everest marks the top of the climb. Follow the small valley and stream bed on the left hand side of the moraine. **Lobuche** (4,930 metres) has a range of accommodation, including the *National Park Lodge*. Everything in Lobuche is expensive, hardly surprising considering its location. The views of **Taweche** and **Nuptse** are spectacular.

Lobuche to Gorak Shep Continue up the grassy valley beside the Khumbu   Day 15 Glacier moraine until the terminal moraine of the **Changri Nup** and **Changri Shar** glaciers on your left. It then becomes steeper and rougher as you climb to the top of the moraine. As it crosses an unconsolidated slope, the route changes from season to season. Usually there are small stone cairns and tell-tale signs of yak droppings to indicate the way. Then it is a short descent to the dry sandy area of **Gorak Shep** which has a small lake beyond. **Pumori** (7,161 metres) is easily seen and if you follow the south ridge down, you can see **Kala Pattar** (5,545 metres), the commom vantage point for viewing Everest.

You can reach Gorak Shep by lunchtime. It has little accommodation. If you leave Lobuche early, you can climb Kala Pattar ('Black Rock') and then return to Lobuche at the end of a tiring, but immensely satisfying, day. If you are in a party, you do not need to strike camp and can travel fairly light. However, be sure to take plenty of clothing for the bitterly cold mornings, as well as some emergency rations. It is tiring, because of the altitude, the grass slope and the steepness of the ascent, but from the top you can see the south face of Everest off to the east (in winter you may be surprised at how little snow there is on Everest's south face), and the west ridge running down to the Lho La pass (6,026 metres). To the southwest is **Nuptse**.

Day 16 **Gorak Shep to Everest Base Camp** To do this trip, you have to stay at Gorak Shep and make a day trip. Most prefer not to, being quite content with the view from Kala Pattar. Everest Base Camp is to the east of the Khumbu Glacier. After leaving the head of the lake at Gorak Shep, you climb through a boulder strewn area, some of the rocks having inscriptions to the many climbers and Sherpas who have died in pursuit of the summit. The trail then crosses the moraine wall and descends to the Khumbu Glacier which you cross. Cairns mark the route which changes constantly. Take great care.

The Base Camp area is at 5,400 metres and if there are expeditions in residence you may not be welcome: some put signs up to dissuade calls. The round trip from Gorak Shep takes over six hours and is not as rewarding as the Kala Pattar walk, as Everest is not in view from the camp. Continuing beyond the base camp requires mountaineering skills.

Days 16-19 **The Return to Namche Bazaar and Lukla** Allow three or four days for the return. You will probably be pleasantly surprised that as you descend you feel great rushes of energy. Going down can be done at any speed, but care is needed and on long descents it can be quite tiring on the knees and calves. From Namche Bazaar to **Lukla**, you retrace your steps as far as **Chablung**, then turn off above **Chaunrikarka** towards Lukla. There are some good hotels, including the *Sagarmatha*, possibly one of the most pleasant and the *Sherpa Co-Operative*. The RNAC office in Lukla is usually open 1700-1800, sometimes one hour later, for you to re-confirm your flight. Failure to do this can mean loss of your seat. Check-in begins early in the morning and can be chaotic, especially when there is a backlog of passangers. Your hotel will have all the relevant information.

Options

From Day 14 From Pheriche, it is possible to take the right hand trail leading up the **Imja Khola Valley** to **Island Peak** (6,189 metres), the most popular of Nepal's designated 'Trekking Peaks'. You need a permit and a guide if you are not very experienced. You climb above the river to some terraces and a low ridge. **Dingboche** (4,360 metres) is on a wide alluvial terrace and near the stream is a chorten and some hotels. **Bibre** (4,571 metres) is the next village and, after a further climb, you reach **Chukhung** (4,730 metres), a summer grazing village. Food and accommodation is available here in season. From Chukhung, the

Sherpa Tenzing

Tenzing Norgay (c1914-1986) is remembered as the quintessential Himalayan mountain guide who accompanied Sir Edmund Hillary in the first Western expedition to reach the top of Everest. Tenzing began his career as the companion and guide of the Italian Tibetologist, Guiseppe Tucci. After being a member of Shipton's unsuccessful British expedition to Everest in 1935 and the Swiss expedition of 1952, which very nearly made it, he and Hillary finally reached the summit of Everest at 1130 on 29 May 1953. Unable to write, he dictated his biography to Malcolm Barnes. He became an honorary Indian and as Director of the Himalayan Mountaineering Institute in Darjeeling, he was an inspiration to thousands. Without Tenzing and his Sherpas, it is doubtful that the 1953 expedition, or many others afterwards, would have been successful.

The Sherpas have received considerable help to set up schools and small hospitals from a foundation named after Sir Edmund Hillary, who felt he had a debt to repay the Sherpas. Thyangboche, on the Everest Base Camp trek, has an informative Sherpa Cultural Centre.

route ascends and follows a moraine ridge before descending to a wide open area between the Imja and Lhotse moraines. Beyond is the terminal moraine of the **Imja Glacier** and near its base is an old lake bed, a suitable place for a base camp.

An interesting variation is to visit Dingboche (4,360 metres) at the mouth of **On the Return** the **Imja Khola Valley**. Take the uphill route to **Dugha** on the opposite side of the valley, then past yak pastures to a chorten and Dingboche. It is a typical summer village with some accommodation. The view of **Island Peak** (6,189 metres), at the head of the valley and south of Everest and Ama Dablam and Makalu in the distance, is impressive. To reach the main route back to Namche Bazaar, you can either cross to **Pheriche** on the west side, or follow the Imja Khola down to its confluence with the Khumbu Khola.

Trekking

Trek 12
Gokyo Lakes

*The **Dudh Kosi Valley** does not see as many visitors as the Khombu Khola to Kala Pattar area. But it is no less spectacular and, if anything, even more so. From Kala Pattar (5,483 metres) you can see four of the world's eight highest mountains.*

Briefing

Trailhead: Namche Bazaar

Duration: 6 days

Best trekking season: Late September – early November, and March – April.

Altitude: The majority of the trek is above 3,000m so it is crucial to allow yourself to acclimatize.

Equipment: You should have basic mountaineering equipment in case conditions become difficult, eg an ice axe, rope and preferably crampons. Note that yaks and heavily laden porters cannot negotiate sections of the terrain.

Organization: It is recomended that you take a guide especially on the more difficult sections of the trek.

Permit cost: US$5 per week for the first 4 weeks, thereafter US$10 per week.

Maps: The numerous locally produced maps include Nepa's Rolwaling Himal & Solu Khumbu (1:110,000) covering the Sagarmatha National Park from Jiri in the west to the Hunku Khola in the east and north to Mount Everest. Mandala's Khumbu & Mt Everest sheet (1:75,000) has a trekking map covering Lukla and the national park.

Days 1-2   **Namche Bazaar to Luza** The same requirements for acclimatisation apply, so you should allow at least two days before you actually enter the valley at Phortse, then if possible another rest day is recommended.

From Namche Bazaar, follow the main route up the **Dudh Kosi** to some tea shops at **Sarnasa** where there is a junction with the Phortse trail, above which the trail divides. You can follow either way: the right is wider and suitable for livestock, the left climbs the bluffs on a staircase, through a cleft. Near the top of the ridge, the two trails rejoin and continue towards a chorten. This ridge runs down from **Khumbi-yul-lha**, the Sherpas' guardian mountain. **NB** You should not climb this on any account.

Beyond Phortse village, the track on the west side of the valley offers a good choice of campsites. It then climbs steeply through rhododendron forest and past the Sherpa summer settlements of **Tongba** (3,950 metres), **Gyele** (3,960 metres), **Dole** and **Lhabarma** (4,220 metres). **Luza** (4,360 metres) is situated in another side valley by a perennial water source. There are good views of **Tawachee** and **Khumbila**.

Trek 12: Gokyo Lakes

To Everest Base Camp (Trek 11)

Lobuche
Chhugiema La (5,420m)
Kala Pattar (5,433m)
Phulung Kharka
Gokyo Lakes
Dughla
Tawachee (6,501m)
Pangkha
Pheriche
Kyajori (6,186m)
Maccermo
Pangboche
Luza
Sagarmatha National Park
Lhabarma
Dole
Phortse
Dudh Kosi
Khumbi-yul-lha (5,761m)
Thyangboche
Khumgung
(6,608m)
Khunde
Namche Bazaar

To Island Peak (Trek 11)

N

0 km (approx) 5
0 miles (approx) 3

—— Rough track
·········· Hiking trail
= = = = Optional route

—— River/stream
▲ Peak
⌂▲ Overnight shelter/camp

Luza to Pangkha From Luza, a gentle climb high above the river brings
you to the wide **Macchermo Valley**.
Cross the stream and veer back
towards the Dudh Kosi. Opposite
Pangkha village is the terminal
moraine of the **Ngojumda Glacier**,
the longest in Nepal. You climb the
moraine to the first lake at 4,650
metres and the trail levels off. After
the second lake is **Gokyo Lake** at
4,750 metres. The fourth and fifth
lakes are beyond Gokyo.

Day 3

**Pangkha to Kala Pattar to
Pangkha** Many of those who have
been to both Kala Pattars reckon that
the one from Gokyo, which takes two
hours in each direction, offers the
better views.

Day 4

Pangkha to Namche Bazaar The
return should take only two days. It is
also possible to go over the **Chhugiema La** pass (5,420 metres) to **Pheriche**.
Whilst not technically difficult, you should have basic mountaineering equipment is case conditions become difficult, for example an ice axe, rope and preferably crampons. Note, though, that yaks and heavily laden porters can not
negotiate the terrain, but take the main Khumbu trail and meet up after 2-3 days.

Days 5-6

Trekking

Trek 13
Lukla Escape

*It is essential to be prepared for delays getting back to **Kathmandu** from **Lukla**. If you are really **desperate** for an alternative, with a five day trek you can reach **Lamidanda**, the air traffic control point for this region, with flights to **Kathmandu** and **Biratnagar**.*

Day 1   **Lukla to Bupsa**   The trail begins appropriately at the end of the Lukla airfield and descends to join the main trail to Kathmandu. At Surkhe, you begin to climb across the pass at **Phuiyan** (2,835 metres) and descend to **Bupsa** (2,300 metres) where there is a choice of accommodation.

Day 2   **Bupsa to Wobsa Khani**   A short, steep descent brings you to the important market village of Khari Khola (2,070 metres) where you can stock up with provisions. The trail climbs above it and after some 30 minutes it divides. The right hand fork continues towards Junbesi and Jiri. Take the left hand route and cross the ridge to **Jule** (2,100 metres). Descend and cross the **Thana Khola** and ascend a side valley. After about two hours you reach **Wobsa Khani** (1,800 metres), a Rai village below which there is a copper mine and smelter.

Day 3   **Wobsa Khani to Lokhim**   From Wobsa Khani, descend through Waku (1,500 metres) and Suntale (1,100 metres) to the Hinku Khola (980 metres). Cross it and climb to the 1,590 metres ridge, passing **Utha**. There are stone huts here and camping areas. **Lokhim** (1,800 metres) is about one and a half hours further on.

Day 4   **Lokhim to Ilim**   The trail contours around the Dudh Khola valley before climbing steeply to **Deorali**. Go over the pass, descend to the Sherpa village of **Harise** (2,300 metres), then drop down to **Aiselukharka** (2,100 metres). From here a wide track leads to **Ilim** (1,450 metres).

Day 5   **Ilim to Lamidanda**   The trail descends through sub-tropical vegetation to the Ra Khola, then ascends to **Pipal Danda**, afterwards following the hillside around to **Lamidanda**.

Eastern Himalaya

This region of Nepal has been opened quite recently to trekkers and there are a number of possible longer treks. Facilities along the routes have yet to be developed to the same extent as in the neighbouring Everest region, so trekkers here will have to be virtually self-sufficient.

Some people are deterred from trekking here because of the distance and the expense of getting there from Kathmandu. But this could also work to the advantage of the intrepid trekker, as it is an environmentally and culturally diverse region which remains relatively unaccustomed to Westerners, allowing a reasonably unaffected insight into traditional communities and attractive trails not littered with previous trekkers' garbage.

Trek 14
Makalu Base Camp

The east of Nepal has only recently opened to trekkers and facilities along routes have yet to be developed. However it is a culturally and environmentally diverse region and well worth a visit. This trek passes through the Makalu national Park and ends at the Base Camp from which there are fantastic views of Everest, Makalu and Lahotse. Due to the altitude of this trek mountain sickness is a hazard and adverse weather conditions may limit or prevent further progress.

Tumlingtar to Khadbari Tumlingtar (937 metres) is situated on the east bank of the Arun Khola which you will be following by an ancient trade route during the first three days of this trek. **Khadbari** (1,067 metres) is a bazaar town around three hours walk from Tumlingtar and has accommodation, shops, a hospital and a police checkpoint. **Day 1**

Khadbari to Sakurate From Khadbari, the trail heads due north while the river veers slightly to the northwest. You climb up the ridge to the village of **Mane Bhanjyang** (1,158 metres) and on up through terraced fields through **Pangma** to **Bhotebas** from where there are the first really spectacular views of the mountains to the north. The route undulates through more small settlements and a stretch of rhododendron forest to camp just beyond **Sakurate** (1,893 metres). **Day 2**

Sakurate to Num The trail continues climbing along the ridge, with rhododendron forest now dominant. You then begin a gentle descent through Mude. The erstwhile forest on the slopes has been denuded to make way for **Day 3**

👉 *Briefing*

Access: The **Makalu** trek described here begins at **Tumlingtar** which has regular flight connections with Kathmandu. However, if you are travelling up from the Terai, you could take the bus from Biratnagar/Itahari via Dharan and Dhankuta to **Basantpur** and start from there. There is also a daily flight between Biratnagar and Tumlingtar (US$33). Curiously, the Kathmandu to Tumlingtar sector is one of the cheapest in Nepal (US$55), possibly because few Westerners come here. Nevertheless, the three or four weekly flights get fully booked quickly, so it is worth making your reservation well in advance. There are a couple of flights a day from Kathmandu to **Biratnagar** (US$77) and you should have no trouble in securing a reservation the day before (one of the private airlines operates a raffle on its flights: the prize, a free flight).

You should also book early for flights from Kathmandu to **Taplejung** (US$110), as there is just one flight a week. There are daily flights between **Biratnagar** and **Taplejung** (US$55). It is also possible to begin the **Kanchenjunga** trek from **Ilam**, the town at the centre of Nepal's tea growing region and walk along the **Tamur Khola** to **Dobhan** and **Taplejung**. To get to Ilam, you can hire a vehicle from Kakarbhitta, or there are daily (slow) bus services from Birtamod and Charali on the Mahendra Highway.

Trailhead: Tumlingtar.

Duration: 16 days.

Best Trekking Season: March-April, and October-November.

Altitude: Much of the route is above 3,000m.

Equipment: You must be self-sufficient as use of firewood is prohibited. Be prepared for varied weather conditions. Potable water is difficult to get along the trail.

Organization: Guides are essential.

Permit Cost: US$5 per week for the first four weeks, then US$10 per week. Also Makalu National Park entrance fee Rs 650.

Maps: Nepa has a good 1:175,000 colour map, Trekking Routes Around Kangchenjunga, by Paolo Gondini covering the area from Everest to Kanchenjunga and Bhojpur and Phidim to the south. Mandala's Makalu and the Arun Valley. US Army Map Service sheets NG45-2 and NG45-3.

•••

cultivation. There is accommodation at **Num** (1,524 metres).

Day 4 **Num to Sedua** It is a fairly steep descent with many bends from Num to cross the Arun Khola (690 metres) by suspension bridge at **Runbaun**. It is then a stiff, rocky climb up the other side of the river to **Sedua** (1,500 metres), with its shops and guest houses.

Day 5 **Sedua to Tashigaon** For the next couple of days, the trail steers a middle course below the ridge-line between the Kasuwa and **Iswa Kholas**. From Sedua, climb to the north across cultivated terraces. The trail continues a continuous though reasonably gentle climb past the settlements of **Navagaon** and **Kharshing Kharka** to **Tashigaon** (2,063 metres), the last major village along the trek. A guide is essential from here onwards.

Day 6 **Tashigaon to Kauma** Start early and begin a steep climb through forest, which can be magical in the early morning mist. The climb continues through Unshisa to **Kauma**. You should consider allowing a **rest day** for acclimatization.

Kauma to Mumbuk The trail twists and turns steeply, passing through forest before emerging on to a ridge with mani walls, numerous prayer flags and fine mountain views, including Kanchenjunga to the east. You traverse the Shipton La pass via the **Keke La** pass (4,230 metres) and the **Tutu La** pass (4,200 metres) where there is a chorten. From here it is a fairly gentle descent through rhododendron and pine forest to level off at **Mumbuk** (3,500 metres). *Day 7*

Mumbuk to Nehe Kharka The day begins with a sharp descent down a wooded ravine and continues on to cross the Barun Khola just beyond **Tematan Kharka**. The trail is indistinct along much of the route. It can also be slippery with numerous rock falls, so extra care is necessary. You are now *Day 8*

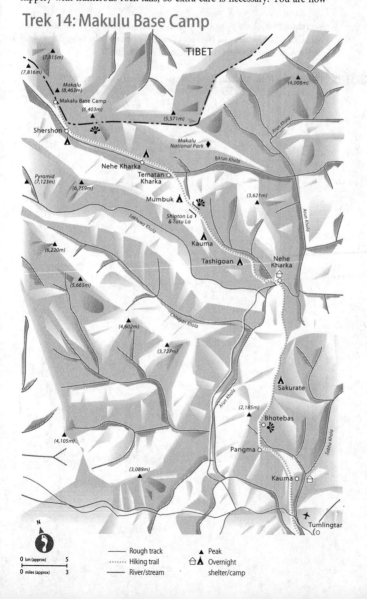

Trek 14: Makulu Base Camp

Trekking

following the Barun Khola along its northern bank. Pass the seasonal settlement of **Yangri Kharka** and on to the campsite a little way beyond **Nehe Kharka** (3,660 metres).

Day 9 **Nehe Kharka to Shershon** With a gain of over 1,500 metres along today's route, the danger of altitude sickness is very real. Soon after Nehe Kharka, you cross the Barun Khola by wooden bridge and climb through forest. The river valley becomes increasingly (and spectacularly) steep, with waterfalls gushing picturesquely down sheer rock faces. The trail continues its climb past the tiny settlements of Jhark Kharka, Ramara and **Mera** before reaching **Shershon** (4,720 metres).

Day 10 **Shershon to Makalu Base Camp** It is a walk of about one hour to Makalu Base Camp (4,853 metres). It's a rocky barren place with the large **Barun Glacier** beyond, but there are superb views of Makalu itself.

Days 11-16 **The Return from Makalu Base Camp** You can retrace your steps in around half the time it took on the way up.

Trek 15 Kanchenjunga Base Camp

Taplejung
KATHMANDU

Trekking

Tucked into the northeastern corner of Nepal, the area has a very high concentration of high peaks but is dwarfed by Kanchenjunga (8,586 metres). There are fine views as you ascend first over the Dhupi La and then through Tserem to Ramje (4,580 metres). The Yalung Glacier gives an added dimension. You have to be very fit to do this trek. There are two main trails from Taplejung: one follows the Tamur Khola and continues around to the north of Kanchenjunga, while the other, described here, runs roughly parallel to the south end at Kanchenjunga Base Camp.

....

Briefing

Access: One flight a week from Kathmandu (US$110). Book early. Daily flight from Biratnagar (US$55). It is also possible to begin the Kanchenjunga trek from Ilam, the town at the centre of Nepal's tea growing region and walk along the Tamur Khola to Dobhan and Taplejung. To get to Ilam, you can hire a vehicle from Kakarbhitta, or there are daily (slow) bus services from Bitarmod and Charali

Trailhead: Taplejung

Duration: 15 days

Best trekking season: March-April and October-November.

Altitude: Much of the later stages of the walk are over 3,000m and going as high as 4,580m at the base camp.

Equipment: All equipment and

provisions must be taken. Nothing can be bought along the way. Supplies at the trailhead are likely to be very limited.

Organization: Organized, escorted groups only.

Permit Cost: US$10 per week for the first 4 weeks, then US$20 per week. In theory, trekking permits for Kanchenjunga can be issued at the Immigration post in Kakarbhitta, but officials there may be unwilling to issue them and instead refer you to the Kathmandu Immigration Office.

Maps: Nepa has a good 1:175,000 colour map, Trekking Routes Around Kangchenjunga, by Paolo Gondini covering the area from Everest to Kanchenjunga and Bhojpur and Phidim to the south. Mandala's Makalu and the Arun Valley. US Army Map Service sheets NG45-2 and NG45-3.

....

Taplejung to Tambawa From Taplejung airport (at nearby **Suketar**; 2,020 metres), you can start walking without having to go into Taplejung itself. The

Day 1

trail begins with a gentle climb through forest before levelling out, crossing several streams and then descending to join the main trail from Taplejung. Turn right onto this path and continue to **Tambawa** (2,000 metres) which has accommodation and a campsite.

Day 2 **Tambawa to Khesewa** There is a climb followed by a steep descent through the village of Pokara to a river which you cross by suspension bridge. This is followed by another steep climb as you pass through the villages of **Kunjuri** and **Shikhaicha** just before you get to **Khesawa** (2,120 metres).

Day 3 **Khesewa to Mamamkhe** The route undulates through the hamlets of Funfun (or *Phunphun*) and **Anpan** (2,040 metres) at which point you are walking above the **Kabeli Khola**. After crossing a stream, it is a climb to **Mamamkhe** (1,920 metres).

Day 4 **Mamamkhe to Yamphudin** By distance this is a short day, but the trail is rocky and uneven which makes the going rather slow. Soon after Mamamkhe, you cross a tributary of the Kabeli Khola, then climb steeply to a ridge and continue along the undulating path to Yamphudin (1,990 metres), which has limited accommodation and a police checkpoint.

Day 5 **Yamphudin to Chittre** Leaving Yamphudin through cultivated land and having crossed a couple of rivers, the trail begins a fairly long and steep ascent to traverse the Dhupi La pass (3,430 metres). Descending from the pass, you cross a stream and climb steeply to the next ridge beyond which is the Simbua Khola Valley. Before you enter into the valley proper there is a campsite just south of **Chhitre**.

Day 6 **Chhitre to Torontan** The trail twists and turns through forest as it descends the Deorali Danda into the **Simbua Khola Valley**. Follow the river in a northeast direction to the village of **Torontan** where there are caves and camping grounds. You might consider spending a rest day here in order to acclimatize.

Day 7 **Torontan to Tseram** Today's walk gains almost 1,000 metres. Climb through rhododendron forest and continue along past Whata and **Anda Phadi** before reaching **Tseram** (3,980 metres).

Day 8 **Tseram to the Yalung Glacier/Ramje** Another climbing day,

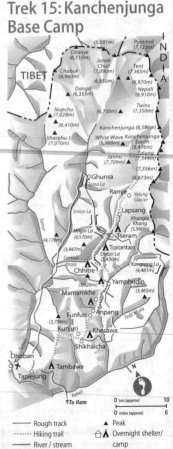

Trek 15: Kanchenjunga Base Camp

— Rough track
•••••• Hiking trail
— River / stream
▲ Peak
⌂▲ Overnight shelter/ camp

0 km (approx) 10
0 miles (approx) 6

although the gain is considerably less than yesterday. Soon after leaving Tseram you come across the first of two trail junctions. The left hand one leads up over the Sinion La pass to Ghunsa and continues a route to the north of Kanchenjunga. Follow the right hand trail which effectively goes straight ahead, still following the Simbua Khola. Climb to a clearing at Yalung and on towards **Lapsang** where you meet another trail junction, this crossing the Lapsang La pass (5,932 metres) also *en route* to Ghunsa. You are now coming level with the bottom end of the **Yalung Glacier**. Follow its northern edge to reach **Ramje** (4,580 metres). It is a difficult and rarely trekked route to Kanchenjunga Base Camp (5,400 metres).

You can retrace you steps back to Taplejung in six days or less.   Days 9-14

Trekking

Mountaineering and mountain biking

Mountaineering is the mother of trekking. Nepal's innumerable peaks provide climbers with some of the most challenging mountaineering in the world. Mountaineering as a sport began in Nepal in the 1920s, though it was not until after Hillary had conquered Everest in 1953 that expeditions began coming to Nepal in large numbers. Some mountains hold a sacred position in the religion of certain communities and climbers are prohibited from attempting these. Spring and autumn are the best times for most mountaineering. Expeditions have to get a permit from the Nepal Mountaineering Association in Kathmandu and royalties are payable. These can be very high – that for Everest is now US$50,000! Because of the huge quantity of rubbish that now litters Base Camp, restrictions have been placed on groups attempting Everest and there is a long waiting list. Among a long list of rules and regulations, a registered guide must accompany every mountaineering expedition and he along with the porters must be insured. There are a number of lesser peaks known as *Trekking Peaks* (see the **Trekking** section) which may be climbed without a mountaineering permit, though many do require mountaineering skills and equipment.

The country's undulating landscape offers plentiful scope for mountain biking, though you have to be fit! If you are a serious cyclist, you should think about bringing your own bike to Nepal; if not, Kathmandu, and to a lesser extent Pokhara, both have several places where you can hire multi-geared bikes. Long distance cycling is not recommended during the monsoon, when smaller roads often get washed out and everything is muddy and slippery. The 150 kilometres-long Tribhuvan Highway combines fantastic scenery, little traffic, some serious ascents and descents and, from Daman, one of the very best Himalayan panoramas. Some trekking routes may allow biking. There are a number of opportunities also within the Kathmandu Valley. In a single day you can easily get off the beaten trail and either explore the rural countryside or try scaling some of the surrounding 'hills', whilst never being too far from a main road heading back to town. The *Mountain Biking shop*, in the *Kathmandu Guest House*, operates organized guided biking tours for reasonably fit beginners to extremely fit experts. On- and off-road tours around the Kathmandu Valley and beyond. For the not-so-fit, there is also the appealing 'Down Hill Ride'! All tours include hire of American brand bikes and helmets. Occasional biking tours in Tibet are also organized, advance booking normally essential. T418286, F419815, dtd@frontier.wlink.com.np. Try also *Himalayan Mountain Bikes* (next to *Ultimate Descents* in Thamel) T419295, F411933, bike@wlink.com.np (Pokhara T23240).

Rafting

The rivers of Nepal are increasingly recognized as among the very best in the world for rafting and kayaking, with many runs providing the thrill of some of the world's least known but finest rafting rivers while passing through unrivalled scenery covering a wide range of alpine and sub-tropical environments. The superlatives are not misplaced.

Origins of rafting

As the sports of trekking and mountaineering in Nepal emerged as a variation on the traditional theme of two and four-legged transport, so her rivers also are being adapted to recreational use. Considering the country's abundance of rivers that drain the Himalaya together with the spectacular scenery of which they form a part and the sense of adventure inherent in most travellers, it is perhaps surprising that leisure rafting and kayaking have not caught on more than they have until now. Although organized rafting and kayaking tours have been going since the late 1970s, recent years have seen them being heavily promoted especially in Kathmandu, but also in other towns and overseas. As with the trekking industry before it, it is rapidly developing into big business.

This may or may not be a good thing from the perspective of environmental and cultural protectionism, but is a certain consequence of Nepal's continuing efforts at increasing its revenue from tourism and, as long as organizers and tour operators maintain a respectful and responsible approach, there is no reason why its effects need be any more harmful than the censorship of institutional protectionism.

With rivers previously off-limits to foreigners being opened up by the government for commercial exploitation – with, it should be added, encouragement from leading operators – river rafting in the late 1990s may be seen to bear some comparison with the extraordinary increase in mountaineering activity that took place in Nepal in the 1960s. This amounts to a unique opportunity for the traveller to be part of the first generation of leisure rafters to navigate these rivers and to experience at first hand their centuries' old local cultures and often spectacular natural environments.

Of course, the physical demands of rafting are not for everyone, but aficionados maintain that once the bug takes root, it's there for life. There are various levels of difficulty – or ease – according to the stretch of river and the season (see below) and you certainly don't have to be an expert, or indeed have had any previous experience of rafting, to be able to enjoy and take competent part in an organized, lower grade run. What is required is at least moderate physical fitness and some affinity for water.

For more information on rafting in Nepal, various bookshops in Nepal and abroad stock 'White Water Nepal' (David Allardice and Peter Knowles, Rivers Publishing, UK; Menasha Ridge Press, USA), probably the best available rafting guide. Pilgrims bookshop in Thamel, Kathmandu, also occasionally have other rafting literature.

Best rafting seasons

Rafting conditions depend largely on rainfall and temperature, so the best times are from March until the end of May or early June, and again from mid-October until the end of November. At other times, it is either too cold or monsoon run-off leads to very high rivers which make rafting dangerous and impractical for all but the most experienced. The winter, however, can still be a pleasant time for shorter rafting trips at lower elevations and it will usually be possible to find reputable rafting companies that do offer such trips.

The warmer weather generally begins in March (although still at this time the water can be rather chilly), with low water levels and therefore relatively gentle rapids. April and early May bring good rafting weather, although the effects of melting snow on the mountains from mid-May onwards lead to rising water levels and consequently faster and more difficult rapids in many rivers. The end of May also marks the end of season for a number of organized rafting trips. During the monsoon period, from late June until late September, rivers become torrents capable of carrying well over 50 times their dry season flows. Nepal's most popular rafting season extends from mid-October through to the end of November, when the climate is ideal and generally stable and rivers have their best range of flows.

Preparations

Ways of rafting **Independent rafting** On the more challenging rivers this is not recommended unless you are experienced in rafting or kayaking, but it is possible to hire equipment (mainly in Kathmandu and Pokhara) and some rivers would be ideal for independent rafters. Generally, though, it is far easier in terms of getting permits, hiring the equipment and arranging porterage and transport to go as part of an organized group. Just as every aircraft pilot checks the *en route* weather before a flight, so also it is important to consult one of the reputable rafting companies in Nepal for current conditions of the rivers you are intending to raft before setting off: Himalayan rivers are more active than most.

Organized Rafting Trips Most rafting companies are based in Kathmandu and some have offices in Pokhara. It is also possible to book your rafting trip through a specialist travel agency abroad, but the only real advantage of doing it this way is if you have limited time in Nepal and want to be sure of having all the arrangements made before leaving home. Otherwise Kathmandu has a good choice of trips and you will be able to compare and contrast what is on offer as well as getting recommendations from people who have just returned from a trip.

Prices vary dramatically, but are considerably cheaper than their equivalents in the West. They do, however, reflect the product that you are buying and start at about US$20 per day rising to US$80 or more per day. At the bottom end, equipment and transport are likely to be basic and the food can be awful. It is important to remember that there is no regulatory body or minimum safety standards for rafting in Nepal, so no legal obligation on the part of operators to comply with any international codes of practice. The more expensive operators, though, will usually take a serious approach to safety and their trips generally include all permits, private transport to and from the river, professional, qualified and trained guides, good hygienic food, and modern rafts and safety equipment.

In 1992 there were about 50 rafting operators in Kathmandu. By 1997 this figure had doubled, an increase in line with the growing popularity of the sport. Some, though not all, of the newer operators, encouraged by the demand, have set up without the experience or material and human resources necessary to guarantee first class levels of service and safety. When booking a rafting trip, do ask questions and find out what is and what is not included in the package on offer. There is also a difference between rafting *operators* and *agents*. You can book your trip through both, but many companies act as agents for the operators. While entirely legitimate, their talents may be more conspicuous in the sell than in knowledge of what exactly they are selling. *Himalayan Encounters*, T432632, F417133, Kathmandu Guest House, Thamel, is one of the oldest established companies. It is a well run outfit with qualified staff and quality equipment. There is little to distinguish it from *Ultimate Descents*, T229389, F411933, North Field Café, Thamel, another professionally run company with good staff and equipment and seemingly boundless enthusiasm for rafting. Other leading established operators offering a professional service include *Equator Rafting*, T414803, F411933, Tukche Peak Guest House, Thamel; *Himalayan River Exploration*, T418491, F414075, Hattisar, Kathmandu; *Himalayan Wonders*, T414049, Thamel; and *Raging River Runners*, T214712, F229983, Jyatha.

Most companies have publicity material outlining the trip. Again, it is worth studying these and asking questions to find out what is included. For the first-time rafter, some reading between the lines may lead to the conclusion that, for example, 'exhilarating rapids' actually means an alarming stretch of river. Additionally, find out what will be expected of you during the trip, for example who does the carrying, fetching and cooking?

Insurance

Due to the inherent risks involved, it is important to ensure that you have an insurance policy that specifically covers rafting in Nepal. There may be an additional premium to pay. Currently, there are no insurance policies available in Nepal that cover rafting.

Rafting permits

Rafting permits are required. These cost US$5, a passport photo and proof of insurance and are available from the Ministry of Tourism at Tripureshwar. If you go as part of an organized trip, these permits should usually be included in the price, but it is still worth checking to make sure that the operator has indeed got the permits. Some operators, especially the cheaper ones, have occasionally been known not to bother which could create major difficulties if

Nepal's major rivers

0 km 100
0 miles 60

Major rafting rivers

Trekking

you happen to encounter checkpoints during the trip. If you are combining rafting with trekking, you will also require the appropriate trekking permits.

NB If you intend to raft independently and not as part of an organized trip, the process of acquiring a rafting permit can be a lengthy and laborious one in which you may have to demonstrate your considerable command of the Nepali language. It is very worthwhile, therefore, to get a reputable operator to do this for you. Most will oblige, usually at cost price plus a small service charge.

Equipment
All of the top companies should provide the safety equipment mentioned above. In addition to the safety aspects, the differences in various operators' prices lie in the non-essential desirables which create the distinction between an experience and a really enjoyable experience.

Alloy or hardened plastic paddles are lighter and easier to use than the traditional wooden varieties. Check the types of tents that will be used. What are the cooking arrangements? Will the kitchen be constructed above sand level and will there be a separate eating tent? In recognition of the appetite generated by a day on the river, some leading operators make a considerable effort in their catering, bringing fresh vegetables and meat, fruit juices, porridge and even paté, honey and marmite.

Personal equipment is best kept to a minimum, but should include a sleeping bag, a set of dry clothes for the evening (also a sweater in winter), a camera and a pair of strong canvass shoes or Teva type sandals.

Rafting & the environment
Many of these rivers flow through Nepal, continuing into India and Bangladesh before reaching the Bay of Bengal and, although waste from an individual rafting trip may not in itself greatly damage the ecological infrastructure of the Himalaya and beyond, it does contribute, is an eyesore and degrades the environment. In respect of the environment, it is important to adhere to the Himalayan Trust Code of Practice (see the Trekking section) so that in the future other people too will be able to enjoy the rivers and their magnificent surroundings. Use natural gas or kerosene for cooking, or only as much driftwood as is needed and only if it is surplus to local people's requirements.

Safety
With no prescribed minimum standards, ensuring safety on a rafting trip assumes even greater significance. The Nepal Association of Rafting Agents (NARA), based at Kamaladi near Durbar Marg, is supposed to be an umbrella organization for the trade, but, although it has pushed for the establishment of operating standards, it remains largely ineffective. While the company you go with should have their own safety equipment, training and procedures, there are a number of things that you can do to make your trip as safe as possible.

In selecting an operator, ask about the types of rafts used and their age. Makes such as Avon, if well maintained, can safely be used for many years. Modern self bailing rafts are essential particularly on the more testing rivers. They operate by having a system of manufactured holes below an inflated floor by which a ton of water will drain in about 45 seconds instead of the six or seven minutes that it would take doing it manually by bucket. The raft should also be equipped with a first aid kit and throw lines, cylindrical sacks attached to the raft and containing a brightly coloured coiled rope.

The quality of life jackets is important. 'Americas Cup' and 'Maravia' are both good makes and, when new, have US Coastguards' certification. Exposure to the sun, however, deteriorates their outer shell, but are still river-worthy if they are properly re-covered. The quality of locally produced life jackets is improving rapidly, but they have been known to rip easily and have a useful life of only a few months. Helmets should have approval for the type of rafting they are being utilized for. You can ask the operator to see a sample helmet: some operators have been known to use poor quality, motorcycle type helmets which, in an emergency, are more likely to sink than to float!

The quality and experience of accompanying guides is crucial in ensuring a trip's safety. The guide leading the trip should ideally have 10 years' constant river experience including five-years' training and at least five trips on the river being rafted. Training includes competence in first aid and in cardiac-pulmonary resuscitation (CPR). For a three raft trip, the top rafting companies would normally employ one guide on each raft and perhaps three manning the safety raft. A reasonable level of spoken English will also help with communication. Nepal has about 20 of the world's top rafting guides, most of whom will be working with the leading operators.

The number of rafts on a trip is another important consideration. An accompanying safety raft is there to help in an emergency and can carry much of the equipment avoiding overload in the others. Some companies also use experienced safety kayakers who are more manoeuverable and therefore more able than a raft to reach a stranded person in difficult parts of a river.

Rafting trips

The following are outlines of some of the more popular organized rafting trips. Itineraries may vary among different operators according to budget and time available, but are governed by the rivers. They are arranged from west to east, and (with the exception of the Marshyangdi), allow for transport to and from Kathmandu. Generally, they assume an average of about five hours actual rafting per day, which is probably enough for most people and allows time for cooking, socializing and taking in some of the local scenery.

Karnali River

Grade: 4-5; **Duration**: 11 days

This is undoubtedly one of the best trips available in Nepal, beginning with a lowland forest trek and combining magnificent forest scenery, spectacular rock formations, waterfalls, deserted white river beaches and wildlife (including monkeys, birds, reptiles and the occasional large cat), with classic whitewater rafting. It is Nepal's longest river and also offers opportunities for fishing for, for example, *masheer* and giant catfish.

Depart Kathmandu for the 20-hour bus journey to Surket in the far west of Nepal.   Days 1-2

Trek through sal forests and bamboo groves via the Swat Kola valley to arrive at the Karnali by late afternoon on Day 4. Local porters carry equipment.   Days 3-4

Days 5 and 6 pass through many smaller rapids. Day 7 is a rest day. Days 8 and   Days 5-10

9 are spent negotiating the trip's more challenging rapids which have acquired names such as Jail House Rock and Flip 'n' Strip, while passing through some spectacular steep wooded canyons. The Karnali's major rapids and whitewater are left behind as the river joins the Seti, and Day 10 allows for gentle rafting and observing the river's abundance of wildlife.

Day 11 The final day is an easy drift to the small town of Chisopani, from where there is a bus to Nepalgunj for the flight to Kathmandu.

River Grades

1-2 *Easy, generally flat water, little current, floatable*

3 *Moderate, narrow channels, waves, swift currents, some physical effort required*

4-5 *Challenging, steep drops, constricted channels, powerful water, possibility of overturning, physically strenuous*

6 *Unrunnable*

Kali Gandaki River

Grade: 3-4+; **Duration**: Seven days

Named after Kali, the goddess of creation and destruction, the Kali Gandaki winds its way down from Mustang, in the north of Nepal, through the Annapurna and Dhaulagiri mountain ranges where it carves out the world's deepest river gorge, before veering abruptly east to join with the Narayani River. This trip has magnificent mountain views and much of its course also passes through popular trekking territory. Numerous temples, shrines and burning ghats along its banks testify to its significance as a holy Hindu river. Look out for a stunning 19th century deserted palace at Rani Ghat, the former home of a government minister exiled there for plotting a coup. This trip's most powerful rapids are encountered on the first two days, while the final day also has some challenging stretches of fast flowing water. With a combination of pre-monsoon rains and sun-melt from the end of May, the water gets colder, changes colour and becomes, in the words of one rafter, "an absolute raging torrent".

Day 1 Fly from Kathmandu to Pokhara.

Days 2-6 Bus ride from Pokhara to the river at Baglung. Gentle rapids in the first mile give way further along to grade 4 and 4+ rapids. On Day 3 the river descends through a deep gorge, while much of the following day is spent floating in preparation for the final day's strong rapids in which newly acquired skills can be tested.

Day 7 Return to Pokhara, then by air to Kathmandu.

Marshyangdi River

Grade: 4-5; **Duration**: Seven days

Said to be one of the world's greatest whitewater rivers, this is not a trip for the faint-hearted. Meaning 'raging river', it is also popular among guides, which may or may not be a good thing for the casual rafter, but the trip is remarkably scenic with some superb views of the Annapurnas. The trek on Day 2 has fine views of Mount Manaslu. Only opened for tourists in 1995.

Bus from Pokhara to the overnight stop at Besisahar, then a pleasant six-hour trek on the second day along the river valley to camp at Ngadi.   Days 1-2

The rapids start almost immediately and continue, often powerfully, through-out the trip. The route has many steep sections, a constant reminder to partici-pants of the origin of the river's name. Day 5 is a rest day. The trip ends with an hour's bus journey back to Pokhara.   Days 3-7

Trisuli

Grade: 2-3; **Duration**: 2-4 days

By virtue of its duration, grading and proximity and ease of access to Kathmandu, this is by far the most popular (and, indeed, commercialized) rafting trip in Nepal. It is almost unique among Nepal's rafting rivers in that it is able to be run in all seasons. It is thus also among the cheaper trips available. Just about every rafting company will offer a Trisuli trip, but will vary as to their put-in and take-out points. These are worth checking, as the best whitewater sections are upstream of Mugling. Most trips end at Narayanghat and can be combined with a trip to the Royal Chitwan National Park. The main disadvan-tages of the Trisuli also lie in its popularity, which usually means an absence of the sense of wilderness and isolation and in the main road which runs beside it for much of the way. Nevertheless, it has some fine scenery and provides a con-venient and economical introduction to rafting in Nepal.

Sun Kosi

Grade: 4-5; **Duration**: Nine days

Scenically, this is probably the most diverse rafting trip in Nepal as well as being the longest river trip currently available. Starting some 60 kilometres from the Tibetan border, from where a clear day allows panoramic views of the mighty Himalaya and Mount Everest, it finishes a similar distance from the border with the Indian state of Bihar, a total distance of about 270 kilometres winding through the Mahabharat mountains and into the Terai plains. The river has some excellent whitewater, especially after the monsoon and is con-sidered by many to be among the world's 10 classic river journeys. It is the cheapest of the main rafting rivers to raft on a daily basis.

Travel three hours by bus to the put-in point at Dolaghat village. Two hours rafting gives an introduction to the river.   Day 1

Days 2 and 3 are mostly concerned with lesser rapids, but from then on the trip is best defined by the names given by previous expeditions to some of the more powerful rapids: Meatgrinder, High Anxiety and Rollercoaster, for instance. Overnighting on white sand beaches. One rest day.   Days 2-8

After negotiating the last major rapid and joining the Arun and Tamur Rivers,   Day 9 a gentle cruise leads to the take-out point at Chatara. Road to Biratnagar for the flight to Kathmandu.

Other rafting rivers

Arun The Arun River does not attract many leisure rafters, mainly because there are so many other rivers that are easier to reach. Nevertheless, good three-day trips can start from the put-in point at Tumlingtar.

Bheri An easy grade 2-trip passing through forests and the Royal Bardia National Park.

Bhote Kosi Only opened to commercial rafting in 1995, the Bhote Kosi offers a short two-day trip that can also be run in the winter months. It is, however, a very steep river with conditions ranging from grade 3 to grade 5 rapids at times of high flow. Convenient from Kathmandu. **NB** This can be an extremely challenging trip which should be done only with an experienced rafting company.

Seti Gandaki Conveniently located for most visitors to Nepal. Pleasant and relatively easy two-day trips start from Damauli on the Prithvi Highway and continue through forest for about 30 kilometres until the Seti Gandaki joins the Trisuli between Narayanghat and Mugling. **Warning** Do not attempt to raft the upper part of this river without having first consulted a reputable rafting company, as a section of the river flows below ground.

Tamur The usual trip would involve about six days on the water. Following a punishing drive from Kathmandu to Basantpur (or a flight to Biratnagar and then by road to Basantpur), a three-day trek through delightful rhododendron forests and with views of Kanchenjunga, Makalu and Everest, brings you to the put-in point at Dobhan. The rafting itself is among the most challenging to be found in Nepal, with classic whitewater, occasionally steep and almost continuous rapids of grades 4-5. As with the Sun Kosi trip, the take-out point is Chatara.

Upper Sun Kosi An easy two-day, grade 2 trip with fine scenery.

The Kathmandu Valley

4

The Kathmandu Valley

The Valley
173 The land
176 People & culture

178 Kathmandu
178 Ins and outs
181 Durbar Square Area
191 Northeast from Durbar Square
192 Central and Eastern Kathmandu
192 South Kathmandu
193 Southwest Kathmandu
193 Thamel and Chhetrapati
194 East of Kantipath
197 Pashupatinath
201 Swayambhunath
204 Bodhnath Stupa
209 Museums
211 Sleeping & eating
226 Entertainment
228 Festivals
230 Shopping
238 Local transport
239 Long distance connections
243 Directory

250 Short walks
250 Royal Kathmandu Walk
252 Teku to Tripureshwar
257 Swayambhunath
258 Whole day walks

260 Patan
260 Ins & outs
261 Durbar Square
264 Royal Palace
268 Kumbheshwar Mandir
269 Golden Temple
274 Ashokan stupas
275 Jawalakhel
276 National Bronze Museum
277 Sleeping
277 Eating
278 Festivals
279 Shopping
281 Transport

282 Bhaktapur
282 Ins & outs
283 Durbar Square
288 Taumadhi Square
290 Dattatraya Square
292 Buddhist Bhaktapur
293 The Ghats
293 Kumha Twa – Potters Square
295 National Art Gallery
296 Sleeping
296 Eating
297 Festivals
297 Shopping
298 Transport

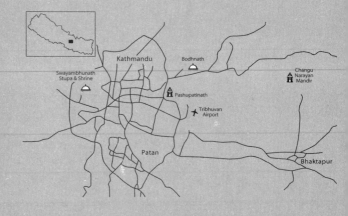

Surrounded by terraced hills, set in magnificent surroundings, the Kathmandu Valley is the cultural and political heart of Nepal. Centred around three cities, Kathmandu, Patan and Bharktapur, the valley is easily accessible.

Buddhist Sites *The stupa of **Swayambhunath** stands high on a hilltop to the west of Kathmandu and marks the spot of the Valley's legendary 'self arising' which led to the former lake being drained of its waters through the attractive **Chobhar Gorge**. The **Bodhnath** stupa, just east of Kathmandu, is the largest in Nepal. The remains of four stupas in **Patan** are said to have been erected by the great Indian emperor, Ashoka, in the 4th century BC.*

Hindu Temples *The three cities of **Kathmandu**, **Patan** and **Bhaktapur** each have a Durbar Square full of spectacular temples and other monuments. The **Pashupatinath** temple on the banks of the Bagmati River, home also to hundreds of monkeys, is one of the most sacred sites in the Hindu world. The impressive and mysterious temple of **Dakshinkali**, where regular sacrifices are offered to the goddess Kali, is in the southwest corner of the Valley, while a huge, ancient statue of Vishnu lies placidly at **Budhanilikantha**. The **Changu Narayan** temple, north of Bhaktapur, is set in beautiful surroundings and has origins dating back to the 5th century.*

Mountain Views *The hilltop retreats of **Nagarkot**, **Dhulikhel** and **Kakani** offer stunning panoramic views of the snowcapped **Himalaya**. On a clear day, you have vistas extending from Dhaulagiri in the west as*

far as Everest and Kanchenjunga in the east.
(**NB** *The best months for viewing the Himalaya are from November to February. During and around the monsoon months, ie April to September, the mountains are almost permanently hidden by cloud.*)

Walking and cycling If you don't have the time or energy for a full Himalayan trek, there are endless opportunities for short **excursions** throughout the Valley. Probably the best way of seeing and experiencing at first hand the Valley's **rural culture**, its timeless villages and traditional agriculture. Pass through delightful tracts of evergreen and rhododendron **forest**, with routes to the north and to the south of the Valley known for their abundance of flowers that blossom in spring.

Roughly oval in shape, the fertile valley is neatly and attractively enclosed by terraced hills. Little more than 30 kilometres in circumference at its widest, it contains not only the cities of Kathmandu, Patan and Bhaktapur – each with their own rich cultural heritage – but also many smaller villages, traditional cultivating communities that give the Valley its lush patchwork appearance, and a concentration of important Hindu and Buddhist religious sites. It is the extraordinary blend of developing urbanism, continuing traditional lifestyles and an historic and prominent religious culture which still retains a high level of contemporary relevance, all set in magnificent surroundings and combined with a genuinely friendly people, that gives the Kathmandu Valley its dynamism and universal appeal. Slightly offset to the west from the geographical centre of the valley, Kathmandu now has roads extending out to all cardinal points, making the Valley easily accessible by car, cycle or on foot.

Geography

At 1,340 metres above sea level, the Kathmandu Valley covers an area of some 351 square kilometres (estimates vary according to boundary demarcations) in the broadly latitudinal midland zone of Nepal, between the Mahabharat Mountain ranges to the south and the high Himalayan massifs to the north. The region is affected by its location at the junction of two of the world's major geological plates. The northward movement of the South Asian landmass towards the Central Asian plate, which began some 100,000 years ago and resulted in the building of the Himalaya, continues to make the whole region vulnerable to significant seismic activity. The last great earthquake occurred in 1934 and caused immense devastation both within the Valley and further afield. It is estimated that the region is hit by major earthquakes on average every 150 to 200 years. Since the late 1970s, two seismic monitoring stations have been established in the Valley: at Phulchowki to the south, and at Kakani to the north.

The orginal Valley lake created by the Himalayan uplift of the late Pleistocene became the focus of a centripetal **drainage** system, in which a network of rivers from the north converged upon the Valley. Later seismic activity led to the breaching of the Valley wall at Chobhar, allowing the lake to drain out to the south through the Bagmati River. The resultant lacustrine **soils** were highly fertile, permitting cultivation and human settlement. Soils vary considerably with altitude, but include a range of red soils in addition to the alluvial deposits.

Temperate and subtropical wet hill vegetation dominates the Valley's **flora**, with species of pine, cedar, fir, spruce, bamboo and rhododendron especially conspicuous. There are few species of large mammals among the Valley's **fauna**, but deer are not uncommon in the broader tracts of forested slopes. Monkeys (including the Rhesus Macaque and Common Langur) are also prevalent in some areas. The Valley's main rivers have now become so polluted that they are unable to support any significant populations of fish. Commonly visible birds include species of kite and egret. Colourful species, such as parakeets and kingfishers, are concentrated in the forested periphery.

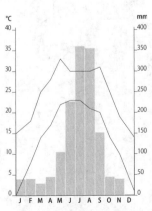

Kathmandu climate:
A monsoon shower is often preceded by a few minutes of windy weather immediately followed by a similar and contrasting period of stillness. This is the time to take refuge.

The Kathmandu Valley

Kathmandu Valley

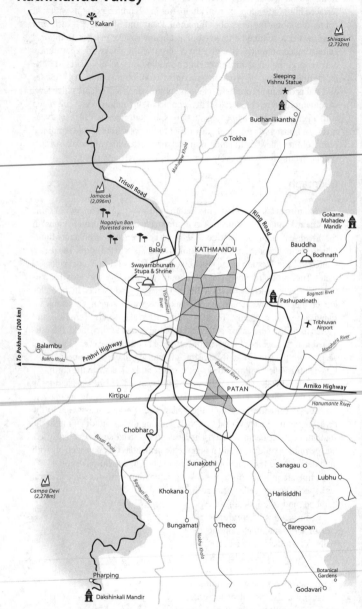

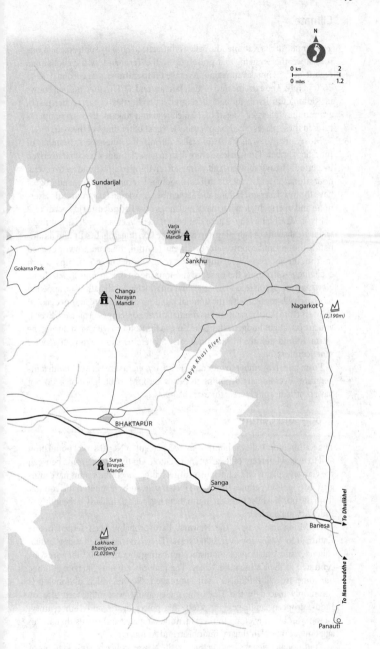

Climate

The climate of the Kathmandu Valley is influenced both by subtropical, monsoonal weather systems that prevail up to the Terai and by the cool alpine regime of the Himalayan region. Average **temperatures** range from 10°C to 26°C in July. The extremes are -3°C in January and 37°C in July. It never snows in Kathmandu itself, though there are winter flurries in the higher places around the Valley, eg Nagarkot, Phulchowki and Kakani. Evening temperatures in these places are also noticeably lower at other times of the year.

Most of the Valley's **rain** falls during the monsoon months of June-September. Though less severe than in lower latitudes, it is characterized by periodic **heavy** showers and storms of anything from 5 minutes to several hours duration and can result in local flooding. The months of July and August have the heaviest rain. In June and September, most rain falls from early afternoon and overnight, leaving many mornings dry. **Thunderstorms** occur regularly in April and May. These can be quite spectacular, especially at night when great shafts of lightning dart across the sky, lingering briefly and illuminating the city and countryside. By the end of April, moist air is being pushed in from the southeast. The **humidity** remains for the next 5 months. Much excitement surrounds the onset of the monsoon rains in mid to late June. Newspapers speculate as to the exact day on which it is officially proclaimed to have arrived, though with the gradual build up of humidity and occasional showers from April it is rather less dramatic than sometimes professed. Even if you are on a tight budget, taking the time to find a room with a fan during the warm, humid months of May until early September can make your stay far more comfortable.

From mid-November to the end of February, nights are very cold with temperatures occasionally dropping to below zero. Most budget hotels do not have central heating, so ask for extra blankets.

People and Culture

The Kathmandu Valley is home to some 5 percent of Nepal's total population and to over 34 percent of its urban population. On the trading route between the Gangetic plains and China, two entirely different ethnic strains have mingled. Mongoloid peoples from the Tibetan plateau have entered the country from the north whilst from the south there has been a similarly large influx of Indo-Aryan people.

Of Mongolian origin, the **Newaris** have probably been settled in the Kathmandu Valley for over 2,000 years. They have absorbed many Indian characteristics, including Hinduism. Numbering about 700,000, they are concentrated in the Kathmandu Valley. The majority are now Shaivite Hindus, but some are still Buddhist. Their **language** is Newari which, although it is commonly placed in the Tibeto-Burmese family, was influenced also by Indo-European languages. Despite losing power in the mid 18th century, Newaris stubbornly clung to their identity, language and rituals that are an agglomeration of Hinduism, Buddhism and Animism.

Traditionally Nepal's leading traders, the Newaris once organized trains of basket-carrying porters over the trans-Himalayan passes to Tibet. They are also successful craftsmen and developed the unique building style that successfully blends influences from India, China and Tibet, with carved wood beams and pagoda-like temple roofs.

Festivals Innumerable festivals are celebrated in the Kathmandu Valley

The Goddess Kumari

*One ancient Newari **belief** is that the goddess **Kumari** temporarily resides in the bodies of selected Newari girls. Nearly a dozen communities have Kumaris and each is worshipped with offerings of ornaments, food and money. Most give up this holy post on reaching puberty, although comparatively recently the Kumari of Patan retained hers until well over 20. Since her feet were not allowed to touch the ground, a relative had to carry her. Newari tradition holds that the Kathmandu Valley was a deep lake until the bodhisattva Manjushri swung his mighty sword to create a huge cleft in the encircling mountains.*

throughout the year. Many are colourful, joyful and accompanied by a carnival atmosphere. Some are national festivals, others may be specific to a particular temple or location. As well as providing an interesting spectacle, they also offer a fascinating insight into the culture of the Valley, often incorporating Buddhist and Hindu practices and attracting adherents of both. The dates of the festivals are usually set according to the lunar calendar, so change each year.

The Kathmandu Valley

Kathmandu

Population: 675,341
Area: 395 sq km
Altitude: 1,370m
Phone code: 01
Colour map 2, grid B5

Kathmandu is the capital of Nepal, its largest city and the arrival point into the country for most visitors. Nestled at the heart of the Kathmandu Valley, it manages to combine an air of laid back confidence and the genuine friendliness of its people with urban expansion and the hussle and bustle typical of any city. Its cultural wealth – most apparent in its innumerable and often quite awe-inspiring temples and stupas – includes four UNESCO World Heritage Sites (Durbar Square, Swayambhunath, Bodhnath, and Pashupatinath) and co-exists with the increasing manifestations of modern global living: satellite dishes, Japanese cars, fax and email bureaux and, of course, the ubiquitous hoardings that promote international brands of soft drinks and beer.

Aside from its cultural gems, Kathmandu's tourist heartland, Thamel, is renowned for its amazing number of budget hotels and quality restaurants offering cuisines from around the world at reasonable prices. Particularly gratifying if you've just arrived from elsewhere in South Asia.

Although government tourist assistance and information is limited, Kathmandu is nevertheless a city very much geared towards meeting the demands of tourists. There are hotels catering for every budget and restaurants make a commendable effort to satisfy all culinary preferences while the city, as the hub of Nepal's tourism, also has an abundance of tour operators and allied services arranging trekking, rafting and wildlife trips.

There is, however, a down side to this. Motor vehicle pollution is on the increase, sewerage systems seem perilously close to being unable to cope with rising demand, and the gap between rich and poor is widening. Most of all, though, the effects of a growing tourist industry – construction of new hotels contrasting starkly with traditional architecture and an increasingly consumerist society, to name but two – are rapidly changing the character and ethos which have contributed much of the city's tourist appeal until now. Whether or not Kathmandu becomes a victim of its own success in promoting tourism will remain to be seen.

Ins and outs

Getting there Most people arrive in Kathmandu by air. The runway is aligned approximately NNE-SSW (020° and 200°). You get a fine view over the city after take-off or before landing, particularly on southbound departures when some older jet aircraft have to fly an additional small circuit in order to gain sufficient height to clear the hills. The approach to Kathmandu airport is an interesting one requiring some good old fashioned visual navigation as you enter the valley. Diversions (and, consequently, delays) are not uncommon in poor visibility. If you are continuing on to one of the more remote airstrips in the Himalaya, however, Kathmandu may seem relatively flat in comparison.

Tribhuvan Airport is situated to the east of the city and has separate domestic and international terminals. An ordinary taxi from central Thamel will charge about Rs 100 and takes about 20 minutes. There are pre-paid taxi booths as you leave both terminals, but these charge the airport taxi syndicate rate of Rs 150 to Rs 200 into central Thamel as do taxi drivers waiting outside as you leave the terminal.

Kathmandu's rapid development as an international centre of tourism followed a long period of isolation throughout the 19th and early 20th centuries. The first surfaced road to reach Kathmandu, that from Raxaul Bazar, was completed only in 1956. Now it also has direct road connections with Uttar Pradesh, Bihar and West Bengal in India, Lhasa in Tibet, and Pokhara to its west. Thus, in recent years, Kathmandu has become one of the important gateway cities for travel to and from **Tibet** (along with Chengdu, Lanzhou, Kunming and Kashgar). Apart from the Kathmandu-Lhasa air route, there are two main land routes – via the Arniko Highway (Kathmandu – Dhulikhel – Lamosangu – Barabise – Tatopani – Kodari) and via west Nepal (Kathmandu – Nepalganj – Simikot – Til – Khojarnath).

Getting around

By South Asian standards, Kathmandu is a fairly small and compact city. Many of its highlights and tourist attractions and within easy reach, either on foot or by a short taxi or rickshaw ride. The airport is around 20 minutes by car from the tourist heartland, and there are always taxis and auto-rickshaws available outside as well as hotel

Kathmandu

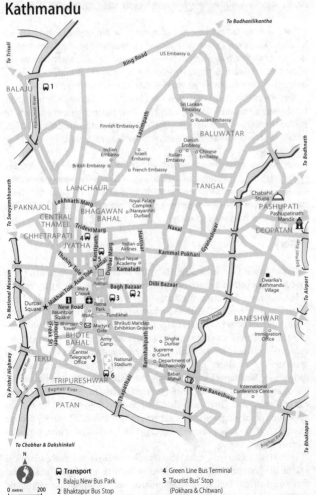

Related maps
Central Thamel, page 212
Chhetrapati, page 215
Durbar Marg area, page 223
Durbar Square, page 182
Jhocchen (Freak Street), page 222
Jyatha & Kantipath, page 217
Lazimpath, page 225
Paknajol, page 220

🚌 Transport	
1 Balaju New Bus Park	4 Green Line Bus Terminal
2 Bhaktapur Bus Stop	5 'Tourist Bus' Stop
3 City Bus Park	(Pokhara & Chitwan)
	6 Trolley Bus Stop

0 metres 200
0 yards 219

Pollution

The phenomenal growth of Kathmandu, especially over the last decade, has brought with it the new problem of pollution, one that is exacerbated by the seeming inability of the city's narrow streets to disperse the fumes of daytime traffic congestion. It is particulary difficult for asthma sufferers. By 1999 there were over 100,000 motor vehicles on the 341 kilometres of roads in the valley, most concentrated in the capital itself. Since the early 1990s, more and more pedestrians and cyclists have taken to wearing protective masks. While anti-pollution laws do exist, they are often ambiguously applied. A vehicle's maximum permitted carbon monoxide emission is three percent. In June 1996, the Prime Minister's Mercedes failed a routine, though high profile test. The penalty: fix it within two months, or be banned from driving in the valley!

vehicles offering a free ride in if you stay at their establishment. The main long-distance bus station is a 10 minute drive from Thamel, and again there are always taxis and rickshaws available.

There are two distinct areas of Kathmandu. The **old city** is located between Kantipath ('King's Way'), which runs north-south, and the Vishnumati River. Immediately east of the Kantipath is the Tundhikhel, a long parade ground, with the **new city** beyond. At its south end, the highway crosses the Bagmati River to Patan. Today, although the river separates the two cities, they have merged imperceptibly.

After the earthquake of 1934, New Road (Juddha Sadak) was constructed from Tundhikhel west to Durbar Square. Today, New Road is the city's commercial axis. The old trade route from Tibet crosses diagonally across the northern half of the Old City, running in a northeast-southwest direction through Durbar Square.

Climate Winter temperatures often fall to around freezing with highs of about 15°C. It is hottest in May when the temperature can climb to 34°C or higher. The monsoon lasts from mid-June to mid-September when most of the 1,306 mm falls. The best time to visit is immediately after the monsoon before it gets too cold in December and in February to April when it is warming up again.

History

Kathmandu was founded in 723 AD by the Licchavi king Gunakamadeva at the confluence of the Bagmati and Vishnumati rivers. The hub of the city is the oldest building, the Kasthamandap, which stood at the crossroads of two important trade routes. The name Kathmandu is itself derived from this temple, but did not enter customary usage until after Prithvi Narayan Shah's conquest in 1768; previously it was the Valley and surrounding areas were known as *Nepala* or *Nepal Mandala*. Later, following Jayasthiti Malla's 14th century unification of the three medieval Newar towns (Kathmandu, Patan and Badgaon or Bhaktapur) which occupy the Valley, Kathmandu became an important administrative centre, but the medieval character of the three towns was well preserved. Then, in the late 17th century, following on the Gorkha unification of the kingdom by King Prithvi Narayan Shah, it naturally became the capital of the newly formed country. This sparked off a long period of expansion.

In the 19th century, the ruling Rana family travelled frequently overseas, as a result of which new European building styles were introduced. The palaces that Jung Bahadur built from 1850 onwards were European in concept and contrasted sharply with the indigenous Newari style. Singha Durbar, a palace

Kathmandu Valley

with 17 courtyards and over 1,500 rooms, was built within a year (1901). Reputed to have been the largest contemporary building in Asia, it was severely damaged by fire in 1974. Other palaces were built at Patan and Kathmandu, but with the eclipse of the Rana family's power in 1951 and the strengthening of the monarchy, these became neglected. Many are now used as offices.

Durbar Square Area

This astonishing area of religious and regal architecture and monuments is the spiritual and cultural heart of Kathmandu. It emerged from the crossroads of important trading routes. The old royal palace was at the centre of the city, surrounded by temples and other important buildings. The Durbar Square area in fact comprises three large open areas or squares and contains more than 50 monuments, the oldest dating back over 800 years. Many of the old buildings were rebuilt after the 1934 earthquake, but not always to the original design. Visit it early in the morning to see men start work and Hindu women arrive to make their offerings of flowers to the gods; or after dark, when candles, small electric lights, shadows and wisps of incense give the temples an altogether different perspective. (**NB** *Mandir* = Temple.) Numbers correspond to the map.

In the southwest corner is one of Kathmandu's most famous buildings, the **Kasthamandap** Kasthamandap (*Kastha*, wood; *mandap*, platform or pavilion) which strad- **(1)** dles the crossroads of the ancient trade routes, and is one of the grandest temples in Kathmandu. This is the real central point around which the city developed. Widely believed to have been built in 1596 by King Lakshmina Narasimha Malla from the wood of one enormous sal tree (*Shorea robusta*), it is now known to have a much earlier origin, as references to the temple have been found in a manuscript dating from the 12th century. It was originally a resthouse or community centre for merchants trading with Tibet and so has an open ground floor. Later it was made more ornate and converted into a temple dedicated to Gorakhnath. His shrine is at the centre of a small enclosure, although the temple also houses a few smaller shrines to other deities. For some years Tantric devotees lived here using the temple for Tantric *chakra puja*. The Malla kings greatly embellished it. Nowadays, two bronze lions guard the entrance, scenes from Hindu epics are portrayed along the cornices

Delia Denman

of the first floor, and at the four corners there are figures of Ganesh. People gather to recite devotional songs, although the early morning is the time of greatest activity.

Mahadeva Mandir (2) (*Maju Deval* or *Shiva Mandir*) Just behind the Kasthamandap to the north-west, the smaller *shikhara* style Mahadeva Temple is considered to be especially auspicious for singers and dancers who come to worship here. Built in around 1690 by Queen Riddhi Laxmi, the terracotta edifice contains an image of the *linga*, symbolizing the creative male force of Shiva, in its usual combination with *yoni*, symbol of the feminine genitalia. Local lore has it that a golden image of Natyeshwar was stolen from the temple. Natyeshwar is the name given to the many-armed dancing Shiva enclosed in a circle of fire, and is particularly revered by Newars as patron of music and dance.

Kathmandu Durbar Square

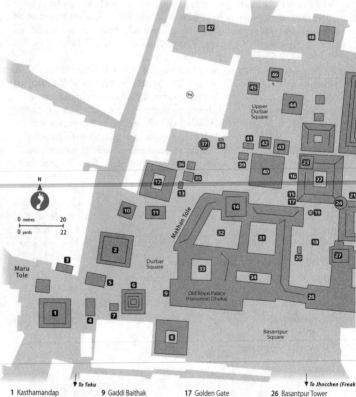

1 Kasthamandap	9 Gaddi Baithak	17 Golden Gate	26 Basantpur Tower
2 Mahadeva Mandir	10 Narayan Mandir	18 Nasal Chowk	27 Kirtipur Tower
3 Ashok Vinayaka	11 Asta Yogini Mandir	19 Narasimha Statue	28 Lalitpur Tower
4 Kabindrapur Mandir	12 Nuwakot Bhagawati	20 Coronation Platform	29 Bhadgaon Tower
5 Lakshmi Narayan Mandir	Mandir	21 Sundari Chowk	30 Lohan Chowk
6 Trailokya Mohan Narayan	13 Great Bell	22 Mohan Chowk	31 Dahk Chowk
Mandir	14 Degutaleju Mandir	23 Mohan Tower	32 Masan Chowk
7 Garuda Statue	15 Hanuman Statue	24 Panch Mukhi Hanuman	33 Hunluche Chowk
8 Kumari Bahal & Chowk	16 Stone Inscription	25 Mul Chowk	34 Lam Chowk

To Teku

To Jhocchen (Freak

Kathmandu Valley

Singha Satal Immediately to the south of the Kasthamandap, the Singha Satal is said to have been built from wood remaining after the construction of the Kasthamandap. *Singha*, or *Singh*, means lion, and the temple takes its name from the the four lions guarding it at each corner. Inside, the four handed image of Vishnu in his incarnation as Hari Krishna is considered to be among the finest in Nepal. Vishnu is riding Garuda, the half-man half-bird god, on his way to slaying Bhaumasur, the demon king of Assam, and releasing 1600 captive girls.

Also known as the Maru Ganesh Temple, this is dedicated to Ganesh (Vinayaka/Ganapati). As the god of wisdom, success and good fortune, Ganesh is propitiated by departing travellers at this small but important golden temple, which has a continual flow of worshippers especially on Saturday and Tuesday. The gilded roof was added in 1874 by King Surendra Bikram Shah Dev, and each new King of Nepal comes to worship Ganesh here immediately following his coronation.

Ashok Vinayaka (3)

(*Natyeshwar* or *Nasal Devta* or *Dhansa Deval* temples) Opposite the Kasthamandap to the east, this temple is dedicated to Shiva in his (Natyeshwar) dancing form and is another temple favoured by Kathmandu's dancers. The broad, three-storeyed structure was renovated in the mid 1980s. The ground floor is enclosed by wooden latice screening through which you can see various images of the dancing Shiva which constitute the temple's focal point. The second floor in particular has some finely carved wooden struts supporting a protruding verandah whose seven windows testify to equally skilled and intricate craftsmanship. The smaller top storey is surmounted by three white vase-type pinnacles.

Kabindrapur Mandir (4)

Offset to the north between the Kasthamandap and Kabindrapur Mandir, the Lakshmi Narayan Mandir is a two-storeyed temple conspicuous by its decorative banality in Durbar Square's concentration of artistic and architectural masterpieces. Like the Kasthamandap, it was built as a rest house for pilgrims and travellers and only later did it assume religious significance. Inside there are two shrines which can be seen from

Lakshmi Narayan Mandir (5)

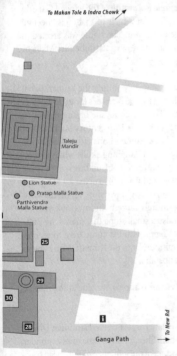

To Makan Tole & Indra Chowk ↗

Taleju Mandir

Lion Statue

Pratap Malla Statue

Parthivendra Malla Statue

25

29

30

28

To New Rd

Ganga Path

St)
35 Stone Vishnu Mandir
36 Saraswati Mandir
37 Krishna Mandir
38 Great Drums
39 King Pratap Malla's Column
40 Jagannath Mandir
41 Kala Bhairava
42 Indrapur Mandir
43 Vishnu Mandir
44 Kakeshvara Mahadeva Mandir
45 Kotilingeshwar Mahadev Mandir
46 Mahavishnu Mandir
47 Kot Square
48 Mahendreshwar Mandir

the northern facing entrance: one appropriately dedicated to Lakshmi Narayan riding his vehicle, Garuda, while an image of Avalokiteshwara (*Tib* Chengrisek) representing the infinitely compassionate aspect of God occupies the other. Today, souvenir vendors have also established themselves inside and around the temple.

Trailokya Mohan Narayan Mandir (6) This temple directly to the east of the Kasthamandap is dedicted to Vishnu and was built in the 1680s by King Parthibendra Malla as a memorial to his elder brother, Nripendra. A five-stepped platform supports the three-tiered building which has finely carved roofs, struts and window screens. Carvings illustrate the 10 incarnations of Vishnu – fish (*Matsya*), tortoise (*Kurma*), boar (*Baraha*), man-lion (*Narasingha*), dwarf (*Vaman*), Brahmin (*Parasuram*), Rama and Krishna (respectively the central protagonists of the Ramayana and Mahabharata), Buddha, and destroyer of sinners (*Kalaki*) – and these have given the temple its other name, Das Avtar Dekhaune Mandir ('Ten Incarnation Views Temple').

On the Kasthamandap side of the temple is a **statue** of the winged **Garuda (7)**, exquisitely sculptured in stone. The faithful vehicle of Vishnu is kneeling with hands folded in prayerful homage of Vishnu. The statue was erected in about 1689 either by Queen Riddhi Lakshmi, widow of Parthibendra Malla or by her son Bhupalendra.

Kumari Bahal & Chowk (8) To the southeast of the Trailokya Mohan Narayan Mandir is the Kumari Bahal and Kumari Chowk, where a living goddess (Kumari) resides for up to a dozen years until reaching the age of puberty. The stucco façade has a number of intricately carved windows on its three floors. This 18th century building and monastic courtyard is guarded by two large painted lions either side of the entrance. Note how the lintels are carved with laughing skulls while deities, doves and peacocks decorate the balcony windows. The building is in the style of the Buddhist monasteries of the valley, and was constructed by King Jaya Prakash Malla who instituted this tradition of virgin worship, reputedly as an act of penance. Inside, four large and beautifully carved windows look over the quadrangular courtyard where there is also a small stupa that marks the Buddhist worship of the Kumari as Vajra Yogini. Hindus come here to receive *darshan*, a glimpse considered to be propitious, from the Kumari. Non Hindus are allowed into the courtyard, but not upstairs.

NB You may not photograph the Kumari who appears on cue at the middle window. ■ *Entrance Rs 10.*

Gaddi Baithak (9) To the north of the Kumari Bahal, this palatial annex of the Hanuman Dhoka complex was built in 1908 by Chandra Sham Sher, a Rana prime minister under King Prithvi Bir Bikram Shah Dev. A product of the influence of European travels on the Nepali aristocracy of the time, it is a large white colonaded building in the European neo-classical style and, although magnificent in its own right, sits uncomfortably amidst the area's indigenous Nepalese architecture. It houses a royal throne together with life sized portraits of all the Shah kings, and large chandeliers complete the opulence. It is used for state functions and the royal family come here to pay their respects to the Kumari and other deities.

Narayan Mandir (10) To the north of the Mahadeva Mandir, the much smaller Narayan Mandir is three-storeyed and built on a three-stepped platform. Each roof is tiled and small bells dangle from the top roof, ringing gently in a breeze.

The 'Living Goddess'

Hindus worship the Kumari as the living reincarnation of Shiva's consort, Parvati, Buddhists as Tara. The cult was instituted just over 200 years ago by Jaya Prakash Malla. All Kumaris are drawn from the Newar Shakya clan of gold and silversmiths and are initiated into the role at the age of 4 or 5. They must meet 32 requirements, including being at least 2 years old, walking, a virgin, in immaculate health, and having an unblemished skin, black or blue eyes, black hair with curls turning to the right, a flawless and robust body, soft and firm hands, eye lashes 'like those of a cow', slender arms, brilliant white teeth and 'the voice of a sparrow'. Her horoscope must also be consistent with that of the king.

The final examination is a test of nerve. Each suitable candidate is led to the Taleju Temple at Kalrati in the dead of night and must remain calm and fearless as she walks amidst severed buffalo and goat heads. She confirms her divine right by identifying the clothes of her predecessor from a large assortment of similar articles. The installation ceremony is private. Astrologers then match her horoscope with the king's and she is ensconsed in the bahal. The Royal Family consult her before important festive occasions. The bahal is her home until she menstruates or loses her perfection through haemorrhage from a wound or from losing a tooth. To maintain her purity, she is only allowed to leave the bahal for religious ceremonies when she is carried through the streets on a palanquin or walks on cloth. Her feet must not touch the ground, as this would be polluting. Whenever she appears she is dressed in red and has a 'third eye' painted on her forehead. When her reign ends, she leaves the temple with a handsome dowry, is free to marry and live a normal life. Nowadays she is taught to read and write to prepare for the future.

(*Shiva Parvati Mandir*) Next to the Narayan Mandir, the wooden images of Shiva and Parvati observing life from an upper window have given this temple its alternative nomenclature. Asta Yogini refers to the eight mother goddesses whose images are contained within the rectangular building, and two large painted, stone lions guard it from the bottom of the steps. Built in 1750 by the grandson of the great King Prithvi Narayan Shah, its architecture is similar in style to a traditional Newari house. Wonderfully carved ornamental doors and latticed windows allow a glimpse of the interior, while Shiva and Parvati look out arm in arm from the shade of the temple's overhanging tiled roof adorned by three decorative pinnacles. The eminent Nepali scholar, Prof TC Majupuria, considers the temple "one of the finest examples of Nepalese architecture". **Asta Yogini Mandir (11)**

Directly to the north of the Asta Yogini Mandir, this small temple has some of Durbar Square's most beautiful wooden window and balcony carvings – if you can ignore the gaggle of souvenir sellers beneath. The upper two roofs are gilded while the first floor is tiled. Wooden figures of various female deities lavishly decorate the struts supporting each roof. Built during the first half of the 18th century by King Jagatjaya Malla in honour of his grandfather Mahapatindra whose image it contained. But the image was stolen in 1766 and the shrine remained empty for more than a century until it was again occupied, this time by a small image of the goddess Bhagawati installed at the behest of King Prithvi Narayan Shah. The image is taken to the village of Nuwakot, 57 kilometres north, for an annual festival. A ceremony takes place each morning in which sweet cooked rice is offered to the deity. **Nuwakot Bhagawati Mandir (12)**

Proceeding up Makhan Tole, on your left is the **Great Bell (13)**, installed by Bahadur Shah in 1797 which is rung whenever ceremonies are held at the **Makhan Tole**

Kathmandu Valley

adjacent **Degutaleju Mandir** (see below). It is popularly believed that the ringing of the bell wards off evil spirits, and in its early days it was used also as a general alarm. Suspended by metal chains from its decorative pagoda-style roof shade, it arrived in Kathmandu some 50 years later than similar bells in the Durbar Squares of Bhaktapur and Patan.

Ivory Windows and Sweta Bhairava Mask Opposite the Great Bell on Makhan Tole, the beautifully carved **windows** giving onto the corner balcony are another example of the fine craftsmanship concentrated in this area. The middle window is of polished copper while those flanking it are carved from ivory. The six wooden struts supporting the balcony are embellished with figures of Shiva and other deities. It is said that this was a perch from which early Malla rulers of Kathmandu would watch as processions passed through Durbar Square.

Adjacent to the balcony and behind a large wooden grill is a huge and fiercely grimacing mask of Shiva in the form of **Bhairava**. Although also depicted in black or dark blue, Bhairab is most often portrayed in white (hence *sweta*, *seto* or *seti*) as, allowing for the addition of golden hues, is the case here. Wearing an elaborate crown of skulls and jewels, Bhairab is associated with tantric worship, has fanged teeth, a red tongue, wild eyes and the all seeing middle eye and his purpose is to ward off devils and evil spirits, a task for which he has been well endowed by the artist's skill. The mask was commissioned by Rana Bahadur Shah in 1796. The wooden grill is removed only during the Indra Jata festival each September (approximately), though at other times you can see it through the grill. During the festival, *jand*, a rice based liquor, is offered to the deity and having thereby become *prasad*, the consecrated liquor flows through the image's mouth to be eagerly consumed by worshippers.

Degutaleju Mandir (14) Beside the Bhairab Mask to the east, this three-tiered pagoda style temple is a smaller and visually less impressive version of the huge Taleju temple dominating the northeast of the square. Standing some 15 metres high, it is built on top of a house and the wooden struts below its gilded roofs are once again decorated with elaborate carvings.

Hanuman Dhoka (The Old Royal Palace)

The Old Royal Palace is a collection of buildings which takes its name from the **Hanuman Statue (15)** at the entrance, installed by Pratap Malla in 1672. The monkey god is wrapped in a red cloak, his face smeared with red vermilion powder and mustard oil, and has a golden umbrella above. Hanuman, a hero of the Hindu epic *Ramayana*, is worshipped to bring success in war. Nearby, outside the palace wall, is a **stone inscription (16)** in 15 languages, including French and English, in praise of the goddess Kalika. It was carved on 14 January 1664 during the reign of Pratap Malla, a talented poet and linguist.

The palace was originally built around more than 30 courtyards (*chowks*), but the addition of new buildings by successive royals through the centuries have left just 10 today. The site is believed to date back to the late Licchavi era. Mahendra Malla started the present buildings in the 16th century, and during the 17th century Pratap Malla added many temples. The south wing was added by Prithvi Narayan Shah in 1771, and the southwest wing by King Prithvi Bikram Shah in 1908.

The **Golden Gate (17)** of the palace is brightly painted in green, blue and gold and is flanked by two stone lions, one carrying Shiva, the other his consort

Parvati. The door itself is thought to have been installed by King Girvana Yuddha Bikram Shah in 1810, while the entrance dates back to the Mallas. In the niche above the gate is Krishna in his ferocious tantric aspect, flanked by the more gentle, amorous Krishna surrounded by the *gopi* (cowgirls), and by King Pratap Malla (believed to be an incarnation of Vishnu) playing a lute, and his queen. ■ *1030-1600 daily, Rs 10.*

In the west wing of Hanuman Dhoka is the Tribhuvan Museum dedicated to the king who led a revolt against the Ranas who built it. (See also under **Museums**.)

Sundari Chowk

The Golden Gate (Suvarnadvara) leads to Nasal Chowk, meaning the 'courtyard of the dancing one', after the small figure of the dancing Shiva (Natyeshwar or *Nasaleshwar*) in a white temple on the east side of the courtyard; it is the largest of the 10 palace courtyards and is where coronations take place. Malla rulers used Nasal Chowk as both a theatre and a forum where the king would meet his subjects. Immediately on the left as you enter, a wooden door with exquisitely carved panelling leads to the former Malla living quarters. Images of the Mallas' protecting deities, Jaya and Vijaya, stand on either side. An interesting story lies behind the framed, dark and animated statue of the half-man – half-lion god **Narasimha (19)** in the act of destroying the demon Hiranyakashipu: the silver-inlaid stone image was placed there by King Pratap Malla in 1673 as penance for publicly dancing while dressed in Narasimha costume. Just beyond the image, there is a line of portraits of all Shah kings, the **Sisa Baithak**, beneath which is a ceremonial throne used by the King during official functions – a sword takes the monarch's place in his absence. The present king, Birendra, was crowned on the **Coronation Platform (20)** in the centre. The image of Indra which is usually kept in the Degutaleju Mandir (see above) is brought here during the Indrajata festival and stands on the platform.

Nasal Chowk, along with the **Sundari Chowk (21)**, **Mohan Chowk (22)** and the **Mohan Tower (23)**, was originally built by Pratap Malla in the 17th century. Mohan Chowk, to the northwest of Nasal Chowk, was renovated by Rajendra Bikram Shah in the early 19th century and was used exclusively by the king to entertain visiting royalty. It is said that the occasional recalcitrant royal would be brought here to spend a little time at His Majesty's pleasure behind bars. Carved wooden **verandahs** illustrating the exploits of Krishna look down on the chowk on three sides. Intriguingly, there are also some depictions of figures in Western costume along the north wall. The decorated golden waterspout named **Sundhara** was also built by Pratap Malla, who brought cool clear water from Budhanilakantha to a bath 3.5 metres below ground level. Sculpted portrayals of the mythical Indian king, Bhagirath, who is credited with bringing the Ganges River from Heaven to its earthly course, adorn the waterspout, while various deities decorate the surrounding walls. Thus Pratap Malla was able to combine bathing with daily puja.

In the northeast corner of the complex is the **Panch Mukhi Hanuman (24)**, a round five-storeyed building which only the temple priests may enter for

Nasal Chowk (18)

worship. The five faces (*panch mukhi*: monkey, the winged Garuda, boar, ass and man-lion) of Hanuman are portrayed on the mid-17th century structure.

Mul Chowk (25), beside this round tower and at the northeast of the complex, is unfortunately not open to visitors, but contains numerous statues, images and carvings, and was used for coronations by the Mallas. Mass animal sacrifices apparently take place here during Dasain.

You can climb to the top of the 18th century **Basantpur Tower (26)**, or Kathmandu Tower, that overlooks the square. It is the nine-storeyed palace in the southwest corner of Nasal Chowk with beautiful wooden windows and superb carvings on the roof struts. Prithvi Narayan Shah renovated many of the earlier buildings and from 1768 onwards extended the palace to the east. He introduced the fortified tower to Durbar Square, adding the smaller towers which are named after the ancient cities of **Kirtipur (27)** to the northwest with its superb copper roof, **Lalitpur (28)** to the southeast, and **Bhadgaon (29)** to the northeast. It once overlooked beautiful gardens with a clear view of the Taleju Temple, all set around the **Lohan Chowk (30)**.

The area west of Nasal Chowk was built in the latter half of the 19th century. This includes the **Dahk Chowk (31)**, **Masan Chowk (32)**, **Hunluche Chowk (33)** and **Lam Chowk (34)**. The **Degutaleju Temple**, dedicated to the Mallas' personal goddess, was erected by Shiva Singh Malla who reigned from 1578-1620.

Running south from Basantpur Square is **Jhocchen**, or **Freak St**, where cheap hotels, restaurants and hashish retailers made it a centre for hippies in the 1960s. The dope peddlars are still active, here and throughout the wider Thamel area.

Stone Vishnu Mandir (35) Returning to the west of Hanuman Dhoka, next to the Great Bell stands the Stone Vishnu Mandir, a square red columned structure supporting a grey stone and bell shaped upper portion, and standing on a three-tiered platform. The temple was badly damaged in the 1934 earthquake and has only recently been fully restored. Its origins are unknown. An image of Vishnu atop Garuda stands in the earth floored interior.

Saraswati Mandir (36) Also recently renovated after earthquake damage, this small single-storeyed temple has an image of Sarawati, goddess of knowledge and education, flanked by four armed Lakshmi, goddess of wealth, and Ganesh, the elephant headed god of wisdom and success.

Krishna Mandir (37) This is one of the few eight-sided temples here and was built by King Pratap Malla in 1648, either in response to the impressive Krishna Mandir in Patan, or as a religious consolation for his earlier failure to conquer the city, or in memory of his two wives, or a combination of all three. The three-tiered traditional Newari building is supported by stone columns around the circumference of the base. The image of Krishna inside the temple is accompanied by his two wives, Satyabhama and Rukmani, all of which, according to a Sanskrit inscription, bear deliberate resemblance to Pratap Malla and his own two queens. Beside the temple, a pair of **Great Drums (38)** mark worship at the temple. Added by King Girbana Yuddha Bikram Shah in 1800, they were formally used in combination with the Great Bell (see above) to sound alarm or as a call for people to congregate, but are now used only twice a year and accompany the sacrifice of a goat and a buffalo.

(*Pratap Dhwaja*) Opposite the Krishna Mandir to the east, this beautifully decorated column with statues of Pratap Malla, his two wives and four sons, was modestly erected by Pratap Malla himself in 1670. It shares a platform with several smaller religious objects, while the figures on top of the column are seated and looking directly into the prayer room used by Pratap on the third floor of the Degutaleju Mandir.

King Pratap Malla's Column (39)

This two-storeyed temple is the oldest in Durbar Square. Built on a three-tiered platform in 1563 by King Mahendra Malla, it contains images of Vishnu and Jagannath. A total of 48 wooden struts support the tiled roofs and are decorated with an amazing variety of sexually explicit carvings. Eight miniature shrines are affixed to the ground floor walls, but the deities they once contained are missing.

Jagannath Mandir (40)

Opposite the Jagannath Mandir and immediately to the north of the Pratap Malla Column, the Kala Bhairava (Black Bhairava) is a fearful image of Shiva the destroyer, carved out of a single stone. Opposite and to the west, the Durbar Square police station now stands on a site formerly occupied by law courts.

Kala Bhairava (41)

Standing to the northeast of the Kala Bhairava, this temple is recognizable by the small but typically Newari open balcony of its first floor where an image of Indra was traditionally shown during Indrajata. A Shiva lingam stands inside the temple, but the image of Garuda is conspicuously positioned outside to the south, suggesting that it may once have been a Vishnu temple that was subsequently rededicated to Shiva.

Indrapur Mandir (42)

Immediately adjacent to the Indrapur Mandir to the east, this Vishnu temple is constructed on a four-tiered plinth and its three storeys rise attractively above its neighbour. Its exact origins are also unclear, although it is believed to have existed during Pratap Malla's reign. Its black and gold image of Vishnu as Narayan is seated. Its posture suggests that that it was originally playing a flute.

Vishnu Mandir (43)

This small temple was built in 1681 by Queen Bhubhan Lakshmi and is an interesting combination of Newari and Indian architectural styles. On a two-tiered platform, the ground floor has wooden columns supporting the sloping red-tiled roof, while the upper portion contrasts totally with its bright white shikhara style edifice. The whole is surmounted by the *kalasa*, a vase traditionally held by Hindus to contain the primeval water of Brahma the Creator, while Buddhists believe it holds *amrit*, the elixir of immortality.

Kakeshwara Mahadeva Mandir (44)

In the northwest corner of the Durbar Square, this temple was built by Mahendra Malla in the 16th century and is one of the square's oldest temples. It is dedicated to Shiva and, with a Nandi bull, it differs from the surrounding temples. It is a cube with a bulbous dome in the Gumbhaj style, similar to early Muslim tombs in India. Attractively built of stone brick on a three-tiered platform, it also has a smaller adjoining dome above a square columned porch.

Kotilingeshwar Mahadev Mandir (45)

Heading east from the Kotilingeshwar temple, the Mahavishnu Mandir nearby was built by Jaya Jagat Malla in the first half of the 18th century. The eponymous golden image of Mahavishnu was moved to the Royal Palace following the damage caused by the 1934 earthquake to the temple. It has remained there since, and the Mahavishnu Mandir has no replacement image. The temple has a miniature shikhara-type spire topped by a golden umbrella, a royal insignia.

Mahavishnu Mandir (46)

Shiva the Destroyer

The six-armed black deity wears a crown and has a garland of skulls. He carries a sword, a severed head, a hatchet, a shield and a skull (which has become a bowl for devotees' offerings), and is stamping on a corpse said to be that of Shiva's father-in-law. The image was brought to its present location by Pratap Malla in the second half of the 17th century after being found in a field to the north of the city. A lie told before the image is said to result in instant death. In the past, those suspected of crimes were brought here and forced to touch the feet of the image, stating their innocence.

Kot Square (47) Just off the northwest corner of Durbar Square is the Kot Square. In 1846 Jung Bahadur Rana, the founder of the Rana Dynasty, murdered all his potential opponents from the local nobility before seizing power. As if commemorating that event, during Durga Puja each year, at this spot, young soldiers attempt to cut off a buffalo head with a single stroke of their khukuri.

Mahendreshwar Mandir (48) Just to the east of the Mahavishnu Mandir, this two-storeyed temple was built by Mahendra Malla in 1561. Steps lead beneath a simple metal arch to its main entrance from where the Shiva image can be seen. The stone deity (Kamadeva) is standing, clearly demonstrating the procreative aspect for which this image of Shiva is worshipped.

Taleju Mandir (49) This is the tallest and the most magnificent of all the temples in the Durbar Square area, and stands in **Trishul Chowk**, a courtyard named after Shiva's trident which is stationed at its entrance. It stands 36 metres high, soaring above the Hanuman Durbar complex. The Taleju Mandir is closed to the public except on the ninth day of the annual Dasain festival in autumn when Hindus may enter. It was built in 1564 and only the royal family and important priests are allowed regular access. **Taleju** was a patron goddess of the Malla kings from the time of Jayasthiti Malla in the late 14th century. The image is said to have come from Ayodhya. One story recounts how it was damaged by an unnamed king in his fury at not being allowed to marry the wife of his choice, because she was not of his caste. The rulers of **Bhaktapur** and **Patan** followed suit and established their own Taleju temples beside their palaces, though neither could match this original for beauty and grandeur.

The entrance on the east side, on **Indra Chowk**, has a large peepul tree (often found by Hindu temples and religious sites) which gives shade to an image of **Vishnu** accompanied by his vehicle, **Garuda**. The main entrance (**Singha Dhoka**) on the south side of the temple has two stone lions guarding it and its arched frame is decorated with numerous brightly painted terracotta carvings some of which were apparently pillaged from Bhaktapur by Pratap Malla in 1663. On the broad eighth stage of the elaborate 12-stage plinth a wall providing additional protection has 12 miniature two-storeyed temples outside it, while another four are placed at each of the four corners within. At the top of the platform are two large **bells**, one installed by Pratap Malla in 1564, the other by Bhaskar Malla in 1714, which are rung during temple worship. Smaller bells hang from the edges of all three roofs and ring gently in the breeze. Metal **flags** engraved with portraits of various deities are suspended from the corners of the first two roofs, while four *kalasas* hang from the corners of the top roof. It has ornately carved wooden beams, brackets and lattices, and superb wood and engraved bronze window decoration on each side. The extensive use of copper gilt makes it an even more attractive sight at **sunset**.

Kathmandu Valley

The peak decoration, in keeping with the lavishness of the rest of the temple, has four small bell shaped spires surrounding a larger central spire of gold which is topped by a golden umbrella.

Tanu Deval Mandir In the northeast extremity of the square, this small temple is comprised of two shrines, one dedicated to Vishnu, the other a Newari style house complete with brightly coloured carved window struts and a five point spire, which was formerly used for tantric worship.

Northeast from Durbar Square

From the northeast corner of Durbar Square, you can walk to Indra Chowk, Asan Tole and the Rani Pokhari tank. This thoroughfare is the old artery of the city. An enclosed old stone image of the **Shiva linga** and **yoni** is supposed to be a smaller replica of the one at Pashupatinath. It is referred to as a five faced image, but only four are visible. On your left in the corner of the square is a statue of **Garuda**.

Makhan Tole was the start of the trade route to Tibet and is lined with interesting temples and shops. After the earthquake, much of its traffic was diverted along **New Road**. There are medieval houses with colourful façades, overhanging carved wooden balconies and carved windows. Many of the shops sell thangkas, clothes and paintings.

Indra Chowk, the first crossroads, is at the intersection of Makhan Tole and Shukra Path. The southwest corner has a small brass **Ganesh** shrine. The **Akash Bhairava Mandir** to the west has a silver image of the rain god which is displayed outside for a week during the Indrajata festival. Two large lions flank the entrance and the walls are decorated with red and white chequered tiles, while the balcony is of attractive gold and blue. Two roof vents allow incense smoke to escape. This Bhairav is used by Royal Nepal Airlines as their logo. Non Hindus are not allowed in. The square was a textile market and many shops still specialize in blankets, shawls and cloth. In the northeast corner is a **Shiva Mandir** as the street runs towards Khel Tole, another market square with Tibetan carpet shops.

Off to the west past a small shrine often smeared with fresh blood, almost halfway between Indra Chowk and Asan, is the **Sweta Matsyendranath Mandir** (or *Jana Bahal*), one of the most venerated Buddhist shrines in Kathmandu but one that is equally popular with Hindus. It has a two-tiered bronze roof and two brass lions guard the entrance. The courtyard is filled with small shrines, carved pillars and statues. The white (*sweta*) faced image inside the elaborately carved shrine is **Padmapani Avalokiteshwara**, a form of the compassionate and benevolent divinity Matsyendra. There are an astonishing 108 paintings of Avalokiteshwara throughout the temple. A colourful procession of the main image around town takes place during the **Rath Yatra**, or chariot festival, in March/April. The pagoda Hindu temple next door on the left is the

Dragon, the winged monster, depicted on the walls of Akash Bhairava Mandir and often woven into Tibetan carpets.

Lunchun Lumbun Ajima, a *shakti* temple with erotic carvings. Dedicated to Ajima, protecting goddess of children, it also contains an image of Ganesh.

Leave Khel Tole and continue walking northeast until you reach the next square, **Asan Tole**. Three temples dedicated to Annapurna, Ganesh and Narayan line the square which is regarded as the commercial heart of the old city with the rice market and bicycle and rickshaw repair shops. The **Annapurna Mandir**, also known as Yoganvara, is an attractive three-storeyed temple with copper gilt roofs whose rounded up-turning corners give a distinctly oriental impression and have copper birds attached to the end of each. Lions once again stand guard at the entrance and the divinity (an abstract silver form of *pathi*, a unit of weight) is worshipped by local traders for success and prosperity. On the opposite side of the square to the east, the **Ganesh Mandir** is a two-storeyed temple with a fine golden bell-shaped spire topped by an elaborately carved umbrella. It is also a shrine popular with Buddhists. The smaller **Narayan Mandir** is slightly offset from the centre of the square and is considered less significant locally than the above two. Its main image of Vishnu as Narayan is accompanied by those of Uma Maheshwara and Lakshmi Narayan. A tiny temple or shrine dedicated to **Uma Maheshwara** stands beside the Ganesh temple, while on the east side of the square a small water **tank** contains a statue of a **fish**. The fish is one incarnation of Vishnu and is venerated accordingly. Various legends compete with one another to explain its origin. One of the most mind boggling has it that the tank was placed here after a fish fell from Heaven, the exact place where it landed having been foretold by a father and son, both Tantrics, though the son's prophecy turned out to be the more accurate as he remembered to allow for the bounce as the fish crashed to the ground!

Central and Eastern Kathmandu

Durbar Marg runs parallel to Kantipath, extending southwards from the Royal Palace as far as the Army Camp at the southeast corner of the Tundikhel. At its northern end, the road forms a T-junction with **Tridevi Marg** heading towards the Immigration Office and Thamel to the west, and towards Nag Pokhari and Bodhnath to the east. Proceeding southwards along Durbar Marg, you pass the magnificent *Yak and Yeti* hotel at the end of a lane on your left, and the somewhat less grand *Annapurna* hotel on your right. At the crossroads ahead of you, Jamal Road cuts southwest towards Rani Pokhari, while to the east lie **Kamaladi and Bagh Bazaar** leading on to the Naxal and Maitidevi districts respectively. In this area there are a number of upmarket hotels and expensive restaurants, various airline offices and travel agencies.

South Kathmandu

The area of South Kathmandu, extending from Jhocchen (**Freak Street**) towards the Vishnumati and Bagmati rivers is predominantly an untouristed area, where Hindu traditions thrive. There are temples dedicated to Bhimasena, one of the five Pandava brothers whose epic tales are recounted in the *Mahabharata*; the *Jaisi Deval* (dedicated to Shiva), and Panchali Bhairava near the ghats of the Bagmati River.

New Road, extending southeast from Durbar Square, was constructed in the aftermath of the devastating 1934 earthquake, and is now the city's main commercial thoroughfare. Here, there are supermarkets, textile and clothing stores, jewellers, the **Nepal Bank**, and **Royal Nepal Airlines** on its intersection with

Kantipath. Heading north along Kantipath from this intersection, you pass the **Bir Hospital** on the left, and **Ratna Park** on the right. If you turn south, you pass the **GPO**, Bhimsen Tower, Sundhara bathing area, and the **Central Telegraph Office** to the right, with the Martyr's Gate and the **National Stadium** on the left. Beyond the Martyr's Gate, at the south end of Ratna Park and the Tundikhel, there is a large and well kept military camp, the **Singha Durbar** government buildings, the Supreme Court, and the **Archaeology Department** which must issue certificates before antiques or apparent antiques can be exported.

On the right side of the Bagmati River lies the **Tripureshwar Temple**. Built in 1818 by Queen Lalitatripurasundari Devi Shah, this is a three-storey temple in pagoda style, surrounded on four sides by small temples dedicated to Vishnu, Surya, Ganesh and Devi. In the centre of the main temple is a shapeless Shiva lingam without any facial features, which is circumambulated by worshippers.

Southwest Kathmandu

Although the **Bagmati River** has been abused and neglected in recent years, it has traditionally been a major source of irrigation for the valley's agriculture and of domestic water for its settlements, in addition to its historical religious significance to which various Nepali sacred texts (eg the Baraha Purana, the Pashupati Purana and the Nepal Mahatmya) bear witness. But the city's rapid growth has led to its transformation into a repository for sewage and other urban waste. Nevertheless, there is a multitude of temples, shrines, relics and other monuments along its northern bank, from **Teku** to **Tripureshwar**.

See also Short Walks in Kathmandu, page 250

Thamel and Chhetrapati

Heading west from Asan Tole, you will reach the crossroads of Bangemudha on Shukra Path. Continue south to return to **Indra Chowk**, or north to reach the tourist heartland of the old city. If you head north you will pass on your left a recessed square containing the large **Kathesimbhu Stupa**, and soon reach **Thahiti Tole** where the traffic moves around yet another stupa. From here you can turn east along Jatha Road to Kantipath, passing on the right the entrance to the **Chusya Bahal**. Alternatively, proceeding north from the stupa you will enter the **Thamel** area, which takes its name from a former Buddhist monastery and rest house here (*Tham Bahal*) and has become the undisputed focal point of the city for tourists. Or, heading west, you will reach the frenetic intersection of **Chhetrapati** where traffic converges from six directions. This is the city's tourist centre with numerous budget hotels and exotic restaurants featuring cuisines from the four corners of the world. The intersection of Thamel Chowk can be reached from the **Thahiti Stupa** in the south via Kwa Bahal Road, or from Tridevi Marg and the Royal Palace to the east. Two parallel north-south running roads are particularly geared to the tourist industry: Kwa Bahal Road to the east and Thamel Road to the west. The former has more shops, selling Nepalese, Tibetan and Bhutanese handicrafts and second hand trekking equipment, while the latter has many hotels, guesthouses and restaurants. Heading south, east or north from the junction near the Kathmandu Guest House, you will be mesmerized by the density of facilities available for the budget tourist – far removed from the ancient culture of the surrounding city. By contrast, at **Bhagawan Bahal** in Northeast Thamel, there are three

See map, page 212

Where the cockerel landed

When the hiti spring in the grounds of the Royal Palace ran dry, astrologers advised the king, Vikramajit, that only the sacrifice of the most righteous person in the land would restore the waters. The distraught king reflected and resolved that only he himself fitted the description. So one dark night he commanded his son Manadeva to go to the dry spring at midnight and, with a single stroke, decapitate the shrouded figure he would find lying there. Manadeva dutifully carried out the king's instructions and watched in utter dismay as his father's head flew up into the air and continued over the city before landing at Vajra Yogini. Consulting the Vajra Yogini deity, Manadeva was told that the only way he could redeem himself was by releasing a cockerel and building a stupa for his father's remains where the bird landed.

active Newar Buddhist shrines which are particularly colourful during Dasain.

Around **Chhetrapati** there are many more low priced guesthouses, interspersed with authentic street life. This area is also interesting as the neighbourhood of brass bandsmen who are in demand during local festivals and Nepalese weddings, especially in February. Heading south from the Chhetrapati intersection, you will eventually reach the Kasthamandap at the southwest end of Durbar Square.

East of Kantipath

The Royal Palace Returning to the intersection of Prithvi Path and Durbar Marg and heading north you reach the southern gate of the Royal Palace at the top end of Durbar Marg. Its official name is **Narayanhiti Durbar**, after a Vishnu (in the form of Narayan) temple to the east and the adjacent waterspout (*hiti*). The original palace buildings were constructed in 1915 for Rana Bahadur Shah and are situated behind the ultra modern pagoda extension seen from Durbar Marg which was completed for the wedding of King Birendra Bir Bikram Shah (then heir to the throne) in 1970. The grounds cover more than 30 hectares and are guarded on all sides. ■ *1000-1700, Rs 300. There is no admission to the private residence, though parts are open to visitors on Thursday during the winter.* Look out for the throngs of giant bats hanging from the trees all along the northern extension of Kantipath to the east of the palace. A little further south along Durbar Marg, a prominent statue of **King Mahendra** in full ceremonial attire gazes down on Kathmandu's most exclusive thoroughfare.

Tridevi Mandir (or Thamel Bahal) Returning towards central Thamel and diagonally opposite the immigration office on Tridevi Marg, the cluster of three small but attractive temples give the road its name (*tri* is three, and *devi* refers to feminine divinity) and are dedicated to the goddesses Dakshinkali, Jawalamai and Mankamna. An almost Biblical legend is associated with the site's origins. A rich man named Bhagawan Bal (who, in the way of things, has reached demi-god status in the minds of many) was on a pilgrimage to Tibet when he had a dream. The dream warned him to leave the place where he and his travelling companions were staying at once and not to look back, for there were demons there. A white horse was sent to spirit them away. After some time they reached a river and were about to cross it when a group of beautiful women appeared. They begged the men to stay, but their horse continued through the water. The women continued to urge them back and so appealing were their cries that all but Bhagawan Bal turned to see them one last time. To their horror, they saw not women but demons who consumed the men. After many adventures, the good Bhagawan Bal eventually returned to Kathmandu and stayed in the house of a peasant in Thamel. But even here the demons would not leave him. After killing the poor peasant, they entered battle with Bhagawan Bal. Our hero fought valiantly and killed many of the demons before those remaining, now resigned to defeat, promised to leave and never to return to Thamel.

Nag Pokhari

On the north side of Tridevi Marg about one kilometre east of Durbar Marg towards Pashupatinath, Nag Pokhari is a water temple where people have traditionally prayed to Naga, the serpent deities, for rainfall. A fine gold serpent image stands atop a tall narrow plinth in the centre of the tank.

Rani Pokhari

Following the road east of Asan, you reach Kantipath and Rani Pokhari (*Queen's Pond*), a huge tank with a white temple dedicated to Shiva in the middle. The Rani in question was Pratap Malla's queen who in 1667 commissioned its construction in memory of their son, **Chakravartendra**, who, following his father's abdication in favour of his four sons each of whom would rule for one year, died on the second day of his reign, apparently having been trampled by an elephant. The pagoda temple originally installed by the Mallas fell into disrepair and was replaced by the current edifice in 1908 by Jung Bahadur Rana. The water with which the pond was originally filled was taken from 51 sacred rivers throughout Nepal, thus ensuring its sanctity.

If you can ignore the fumes, the hooting, beeping, buzzing and other vehicular distractions (these are reduced if viewed from the east side), Rani Pokhari can be magical in the sunset, while a moonlit night gently illuminates the temple to contrast beautifully and mysteriously with the calm water.

Access to the temple is along a white stone walkway from Kantipath, but the area is kept locked except for one day during the Tihar festival (October-November). The **temple** has a domed roof reminiscent of classical Indian Mughal architecture and is surmounted by a copper spire. The main **image** is of the Shiva lingam, but other deities also feature. Four small **shrines** at each corner contain images of Bhairava, Harishankar, Shakti and Tarkeshwari. On the southern embankment is a statue of an elephant carrying three passengers on its back, thought to be three of the male members of the Pratap Malla family, while a fourth person is held in its trunk.

Not surprisingly, various myths and legends have come to be associated with Rani Pokhari over the years. It is said to be haunted by ghosts, including one especially seductive female spectre which managed to unnerve even the great Pratap Malla. The pond was also used for a time for 'ducking': suspected criminals were immersed and if they drowned they were guilty, but their innocence was proven if they survived. Fortunately, it seems that most suspects were innocent.

The large clocktower (**Ghantaghar**) to the east of Rani Pokhari stands in the grounds of a college and serves as a useful local landmark. The tank contains fish whose numbers are said to be increasing following their serious depletion in the 1960s when toxic chemicals were emptied into it. The pond also attracts small numbers of ducks, herons and the occasional migratory waterfowl, as well as snakes, otters and frogs.

Tundikhel

Immediately to the south of Ratna Park and about one kilometre south of Rani Pokhari, Tundikhel means literally 'open grassy field'. The Royal Pavilion is to its north and has statues of six Gurkha recipients of the Victoria Cross, awarded for outstanding bravery during the two world wars. The Tundikhel has traditionally been used for army parades and major ceremonies (eg National Day in February, and Dosain in October/November) which are often attended by the King, who may use the opportunity to impart a Message to the Nation, by the Prime Minister, military leaders and other senior civil servants. Many thousands of people throng the Tundikhel on such occasions, but if you

Parachutes and politicians

An oft recounted tale concerns the 19th century prime minister, Jung Bahadur Rana, who allegedly jumped from the top of the Bhimsen tower astride a horse. Sadly, but not unexpectedly, his mount expired immediately upon landing, while the prime minister survived by virtue of an umbrella under which he was able to parachute gently to safety. No account explains either what inspired Jung Bahadur to attempt this feat in the first place or how he managed to get the horse to the top.

can find a strategic viewing place (standing on a wall has been recommended) the colour and pageantry is well worth the effort. Army drill sessions take place here early most mornings, when much of the Tundikhel is off limits.

Mahakal Mandir On the west side of the Tundikhel, this attractive three-storeyed pagoda temple is venerated by Hindus and Buddhists alike. Hindus worship the image as Bhairava while Buddhists consider it as Amitabha ('endless light'). Gilded copper covers all three roofs which have divine images carved on the beams. The main entrance is an arched gate topped by a *kalasa*.

Bhimsen Tower **(Dharahara)** South of the Tundikhel and the GPO, this 60-metre tall column was built as a watchtower, one of two erected by Bhimsen Tappa in 1832. The other collapsed soon after construction, but this, although damaged in the 1934 earthquake, still serves as one of the city's most prominent landmarks. It resembles a Muslim minaret and the design seems to have been strongly influenced by Calcutta's Ochterlony Monument (now renamed *Shahid Minar*) which was constructed in 1828 as a memorial to Sir David Ochterlony who led East India Company troops against the Nepalese in the war of 1814-1816.

The revered **Sundhara**, a below ground level quadrangle with spring water flowing from the mouth of a gilded crocodile statue, is located beside the base of the Bhimsen Tower.

Shahid Smarak **(Martyr's Gate)** On Prithvi Path just east of the GPO, this memorial arch encloses a statue of King Tribhuvan and is dedicated to those who fell or were executed during the struggle for democracy and against the Ranas in 1940. Black marble statues portray four eminent martyrs: Dharma Bhakta, Dasarath Chand, Ganga Lal and Shukra Raj Shastri. Wreaths are customarily placed here by visiting foreign dignitaries. Just to the east is the **Bhadrakali Mandir**, a small temple dedicated to the goddess Kali. Its alternative name, *Lunmari Mandir*, is derived from a popular legend which tells of how bread (*mari*) baked by a local baker turned into gold (*lun*).

Singha Durbar Heading east from the Shahid Smarak, you reach this magnificent former Rana residence set in a 30-hectare complex which, since 1951, has been used as the central government's bureaucratic headquarters. Built by Chandra Shamsher Rana in 1901, the splendid neo-classical façade reflects the influence of the Ranas' newly found taste for European sojourns. The palace contains over 1,000 rooms and a similar number of servants were retained for its upkeep. Inside, the huge marble floored Durbar Hall was used to host lavish receptions: illuminated by giant crystal chandeliers, its walls were hung with ornate mirrors and portraits of previous Rana rulers, while stuffed tigers stood in each corner and richly embroidered carpets were rolled out for the guests. In July 1973 much of the eastern part of the building was destroyed by fire and has since been only partially restored. The complex also includes the Supreme Court.

Pashupatinath

Some four kilometres northeast of central Thamel and near the airport, Nepal's most important Hindu pilgrimage site is located on the banks of the Bagmati River, in the dry season no more than a trickle of badly polluted water. It covers an area of more than 260 hectares with almost as many temples and religious monuments. Pashupatinath has been designated a World Heritage Site by UNESCO and its location allows a visit to be combined with a trip to Bodhnath. There is a Tourist Information Unit. Radio Nepal begins its daily transmission with a hymn to Pashupatinath, while the god's name is frequently invoked in the course of a royal blessing.

A telephoto camera lens is a good way to get a closer view of the temple's magnificent architecture and decoration as well as of the activity within.

Pashupatinath belongs to **Shiva**, here in his peaceful form as Pashupati, the shepherd or lord of beasts, and to Narayana. Shiva is known by many names, of which Pashupati is one. *Pashu* means 'living beings', and *Pati* means 'lord'. The temple is one of the most important to Hindus in the subcontinent and has been closely associated with orthodox south Indian Shaivism since the visit of Shankaracharya. The linga representation is the form in which Shiva is perhaps most widely depicted and venerated, a potent image implying life, fertility and regeneration. The **Pashupati linga**, over one metre in height, is among South Asia's most important linga sites for Hindu pilgrims and, in keeping with Nepali tradition, there are numerous abstruse legends explaining its origin. One version from the Vedas has it that Shiva, living in the nearby Shleshmantaka forest as a deer, was captured by the gods who broke one of his horns in the process. The broken horn was transformed into a linga by Vishnu and buried. In due course, a sacred cow named Kamdhenu began to visit the spot every day and issued her milk upon it. An intrigued herdsman began to dig and discovered the linga which became a centre of worship.

The original temple was reputedly built by a Licchavi king, **Supuspadeva**, 39 generations before Mandadeva (AD 464-505), but later underwent considerable repair and reconstruction. The main temple was renovated by Queen **Gangadevi** during the period 1578-1620, turning it into a pagoda of brass and gilt with silver plated gateways. Upon her death the Pashupati linga is said to have emitted a cry of lamentation so loud that local residents were deafened. **NB** Non Hindus, which in practice usually also includes Western converts to Hinduism, are not allowed into this 17th century temple, but from the

Kathmandu Valley

The ghats of Pashupati viewed from the Shiva Shrines on the east bank of the Badmati

Kathmandu Valley

southern entrance you may get a glimpse of the gilt **Nandi** bull, Shiva's vehicle. It is thought to be around 300 years old, though was not placed here until 1879. The black, four headed image of Pashupati inside the temple is older, and it replaced one destroyed by Muslim invaders in the 14th century.

The temple courtyard For non Hindus the best views of the main Pashupatinath Temple are from the steps rising above the east bank of the Bagmati which overlook the eastern gate. The row of 11 shrines, each containing a stone linga, were placed to commemorate those widows who came here to commit *sati* and are dedicated to Shiva. The two-storeyed pagoda temple dominates the complex, its gold and silver bedecked roofs rising majestically from the centre and supported by wooden struts carved with portraits of various deities. Adorning the pinnacle are Shiva's trident (*trishul*), axe and drum.

The Pashupatinath Temple and inner courtyard are administered by a *guthi* or a trust of priests, while the rest of the complex has been managed since its inception in 1987 by the Pashupati Area Development Trust (PADT). Under the joint patronage of the King and Queen, it aims to conserve and develop the complex as a place of pilgrimage and a tourist destination.

In the northeast of the courtyard is the **Vasuki Temple**, dedicated to the image of the *naga* king Vasuki, whose lower body appears as an intricate tangled body of snakes. Devotees generally circumambulate the Vasuki Temple before worshipping Pashupatinath, as Vasuki is considered the main temple's protector. It was constructed by King Pratap Malla during the Malla period. In the northwest corner, images of Shiva's consort Parvati decorate the **Tandav Shiva Temple**, while to the southeast the **Kotilinga Temple** is a three-storey circular building surrounded at its base by a large number of linga-yonis. Just to the west of the main temple, a large white building with a sloping grey roof (visible from the east bank of the Bagmati) houses a collection of religious images. Elsewhere in the courtyard numerous statues stand freely, including those of Hanuman, Unmatta Bhairab, Vishnu and Garuda, King Mahendra, and a large Shiva trident.

Outside the temple courtyard Surrounding the main Pashupatinath temple complex are numerous structures and temples which are open to non Hindus. Just west of Pashupatinath is a cluster of white temples called **Panchadeval** ('five temples'). Built in 1870, the central temple and the four surrounding it all have Shiva lingas as their central shrines. The pilgrim resthouses around the temple are used for homeless

Eastern Gate, Pashupatinath

old people, and outside vendors sell an array of puja accessories including a colourful selection of powdered dyes which entrepreneurial traders push as paint dyes to tourists. To the south and near the river is the 6th century **Parvati** (or **Bacchereshwari**) **Temple**, another two-storeyed pagoda with a crescent moon unusually forming part of the pinnacle. This contains a number of erotic Hindu tantric carvings and it is thought that in the past human sacrifices were made here during the Shivaratri festival. The adjoining **Narayan Temple** is said to have been constructed in the course of a single night in 1929, a memorial to the late prime minister Chandra Shamsher Rana. Nearby is a fine but neglected 7th century Buddha statue while a little further down the river is the **Raj Rajashwari Temple**, notable for its carved windows and roof struts, and where many congregate during the Shivaratri celebration. It contains life sized images of Rama, his consort and three brothers, and at the entrance is a huge Shiva linga image. The upper floor has five dome-like structures with gilt finials and commands a very good view of Kathmandu.

Along the western riverbank are the **Royal Cremation Ghats**, four on either side of the footbridge by the Parvati Temple. Cremations follow prescribed rituals and are presided over by a *pandit*, or Hindu priest, with family members also playing an active role in the ceremony. You can observe ceremonies from the opposite bank or from the roof above the southern ghats.

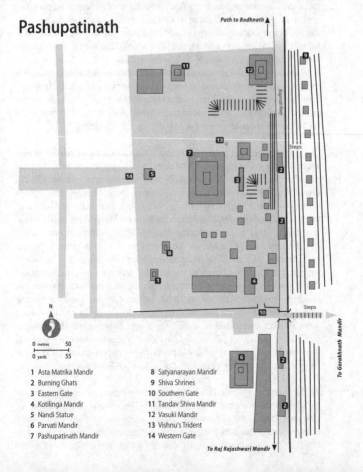

Pashupatinath

Path to Bodhnath ▲

Bagmati River

Steps

Steps

To Gorakhnath Mandir

N

0 metres 50
0 yards 55

1 Asta Matrika Mandir
2 Burning Ghats
3 Eastern Gate
4 Kotilinga Mandir
5 Nandi Statue
6 Parvati Mandir
7 Pashupatinath Mandir
8 Satyanarayan Mandir
9 Shiva Shrines
10 Southern Gate
11 Tandav Shiva Mandir
12 Vasuki Mandir
13 Vishnu's Trident
14 Western Gate

To Raj Rajashwari Mandir ▼

Although conducted in the open air, a funeral is, as in the West, a profoundly emotional occasion, so sensitivity to the grief of the mourners is recommended. Conspicuous photography of a cremation is intrusive and is considered, at best, impolite.

Near the top of the stepped ghats on the eastern bank of the Bagmati is the **Hermit's Cave**. Further up is the **Gorakhnath Temple**, a tall brick *shikhara* structure with a brass trident in front, surrounded by lingas. This is one of the oldest temples dedicated to Gorakhnath, a semi-mythical figure who is considered a guardian deity of the Nath sect. The temple was built by Jayasthiti Malla in the late 14th century on a site dating several hundred years further back and is believed to contain the footprints of Gorakhnath. A track leads off to the right past the **Mankamna Temple** to the **Vishvarupa Temple** (non Hindus are not allowed inside). Inside the onion domed edifice is a huge image of Shiva in union with his Shakti, almost six metres high. Beyond the Gorakhnath Temple and down by the Bagmati River on the other side of its meandering loop is the **Guheshwari Temple**, built in the 17th century and dedicated to Kali, the goddess of destruction and re-birth. It is closely identified with the original **Sati**, the remains of whose reproductive organ, according to legend, fell here following her sacrificial self immolation. The arched tubular metal construction covers the main temple. Near the top, four gilded snakes support the roof apex illustrating the *yantra* diagram (geometric triangle). In the centre of the temple is a pool covered at the base in gold and silver. At the head of the pool is a jar which is worshipped as the goddess Guheshwari and the water from the pool is accepted as her offering. Again, only Hindus are allowed inside to see the gilded shrine room. Thousands of devotees visit Guheshwari daily.

Warning The 400 or so **monkeys** living in the area should be treated with caution. Rabies is not unheard of. Keep a tight hold of bags and avoid tempting them with food, as they will not hesitate to assert their perceived right to your packed lunch. In the late afternoon they are fed inside the temple courtyard – the sight of the advancing simeon mob is memorable indeed.

Festivals In addition to the other major Hindu festivals, the following are celebrated with special ardour at Pashupatinath. The dates of each vary according to the lunar calendar, and all attract large numbers of pilgrims and visitors. **Chhaya Darshan**, which takes place in January/February, means literally 'sacred sight of the shadow' and is marked by the laying of a cloth crown on the head of one of the Pashupatinath images. Pashupati is the focus for **Maha Shiva Ratri** (February/March), a Shaivite festival during which small fires are lit throughout the city and the king leads a parade on the Tundikhel. The Pashupatinath temple remains open all night. **Teej** (August/September) is celebrated in honour of women. Traditionally, unmarried women have prayed for good husbands and married women for a happy conjugal life. In theory, women are supposed to maintain a total fast on this day and it has been customary for women to bathe and wash 365 times in the Bagmati River, but today a symbolic contact with the water is often considered to suffice for many. **Balachaturdashi** (November/December) honours those who have died during the preceding year and their families. A 24-hour vigil is kept with worshippers taking a dip in the Bagmati and distributing a number of propitious seeds in the forest.

Getting there You follow an ancient road which in medieval times linked the old royal palace in Durbar Square with the temple complex, crossing the Dhobi Khola by a steel bridge. The road then traverses the Pashupatinath plateau which was the probable site of the Licchavi capital of **Deopatan**. You will pass a large pilgrims' rest house and a small village before reaching the temple to the right of the road. From the Royal Palace, head east towards the airport which, with Pashupati, is well signposted. Allow one hour by foot. Auto-rickshaws charge about Rs 50 and taxis Rs 90 from Thamel.

Buddhist Kathmandu

Early traditions

In the previous aeon, when the Kathmandu Valley was a huge lake, the Buddha Vipashyin came and cast a lotus seed into its waters. The flower grew and blossomed with a thousand petals and a hillock arose from its centre, the 'self-arisen' *Swayambhu*. Later, the *bodhisatva* Manjushri came from the mountains of Tibet to fulfil the prophecy of the Buddha Vishvabhu and drained the lake of its waters by cleaving the hills to the south with his mighty sword during an earthquake, creating thereby the Chobhar Gorge and, eventually, a fertile valley fit for human habitation. Successive Buddhas, including Gautama Siddhartha (following his enlightenment at Bodhgaya), came to the valley to pay homage at the great Swayambhunath, to meditate and to preach.

Religious influences

The valley is dotted with monuments, stupas large and small, and other Buddhist sites reflecting its long and rich association with the faith. Buddhist legends and practices have influenced and have been influenced by Hinduism in a manner unique to Nepal, with followers of either readily venerating at the shrines of the other and observing their festivals with respect. The Swayambhunath complex, for example, includes a number of shrines and small temples dedicated to Hindu deities, while the marvellous Pashupatinath complex, one of Hindu Nepal's most important pilgrimage sites, is also included among the country's sacred Buddhist sites. In addition to the following which are the best known of Kathmandu's primarily Buddhist sites, many other temples and shrines in the city are jointly venerated by Hindus and Buddhists.

Swayambhunath

From Thamel and Chhetrapati you can head west to the banks of the Vishnumati River and on to one of the most sacred sites of the Kathmandu Valley on its far bank. The Swayambhunath Stupa (*Tib* Phakpa Shangku) is revered as the oldest and one of the two most important sites of Buddhist worship in Kathmandu. It is a major landmark, towering above **Padmachala Hill**, 175 metres above the valley and three kilometres west of the city centre. According to legend, the hill and stupa occupy the site where the Buddha of the previous aeon, Vipashyin, is said to have thrown a lotus seed into the lake which then filled the valley, causing it to bloom and radiate with a 'self-arising' luminosity, identified with that of the primordial Buddha, Vajradhara. The *bodhisatva* Manjushri is believed to have made this lotus light accessible to worshippers by using his sword to cleave a watercourse for the rivers of the valley, and thereby draining the lake. Newar Buddhists hold that the primordial Buddha Vajradhara is even now embodied in the timber axis of the stupa.

You pass the National Museum on the south approach to the stupa: leave time to visit it. See page 210 for further details.

The earliest historical associations of the site are linked to **Vrishadeva**, the patriarch of the Licchavi Dynasty, who is said to have built the first shrine, perhaps using a pre-existing projecting stone. Later inscriptions attribute the stupa's construction to his great-grandson King **Mandeva I** (c. AD 450) and its reconstruction to the Indian master **Shantikara**, a contemporary of King **Amshuvarman**. It became a focal point for Indian pilgrims and was frequented by Padmasambhava, Atisha and others. By 1234 it had become an important centre of Buddhist learning, with close ties to Tibet. In 1349 Muslim

Kathmandu Valley

troops from Bengal ravaged the shrine, but it was soon rebuilt with its now familiar tall spire. In 1614 additions and renovations were made by Zhamarpa VI during the reign of Pratap Malla. Access from Kathmandu was improved with the construction of a long stairway and a bridge across the Vishnumati. Pratap Malla also added two new temple spires and a large vajra placed in front of the stupa. Later repairs were carried out by Katok Tsewang Norbu (1750), Pawo Rinpoche VII (1758), and the Shah kings (1825 and 1983).

The famous stupa is the centre and focal point of the complex which also includes numerous chaityas, shrines and decorative religious art.

The Eastern Stairway
The numerous **monkeys** *here can be aggressive: treat with caution and take care of bags.*

The climb up the 400 stone steps is more impressive than the modern road. At the bottom are three painted images symbolizing the Three Precious Jewels of Buddhism, which were erected in 1637 by Pratap Malla and his son, Lakshmandra Singh Malla. A large **footprint** in the stone is said to be that of either the Buddha or Manjushri. At regular intervals are pairs of eagles, lions, horses and peacocks, the vehicles of the peaceful meditational buddhas.

Swayambhunath

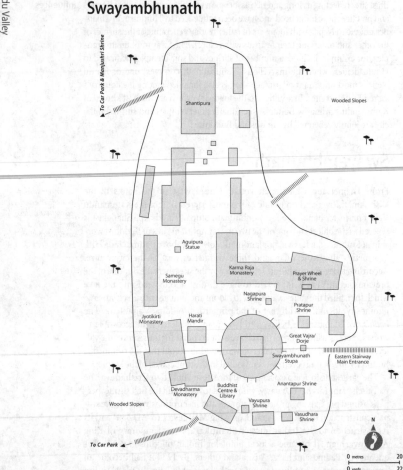

Shantipura

Wooded Slopes

To Car Park & Manjushri Shrine

Aguipura Statue

Samegu Monastery

Karma Raja Monastery

Prayer Wheel & Shrine

Nagapura Shrine

Pratapur Shrine

Jyotikirti Monastery

Harati Mandir

Great Vajra/ Dorje

Swayambhunath Stupa

Eastern Stairway Main Entrance

Devadharma Monastery

Buddhist Centre & Library

Anantapur Shrine

Wooded Slopes

Vayupura Shrine

Vasudhara Shrine

To Car Park

N

0 metres 20
0 yards 22

On entering the compound from the main stairway, you see the **Great Vajra** set upon its drum base, symbolizing male skilful means, and the **Bell** alongside, symbolizing female discernment. Around the pedestal are the 12 animals from the Tibetan calendar: hare, dragon, snake, horse, sheep, monkey, bird, dog, pig, mouse, ox, and tiger.

The Stupa

With a diameter of 20 metres and standing 10 metres high, it has been a model for subsequent stupas constructed throughout Nepal. It was seriously damaged by a storm in the summer of 1816, coinciding with the instalment of an official British Resident in Kathmandu, an association not lost on the suspicious Nepalis. Repairs were carried out a decade later. The various tiers of its base and dome respectively symbolize the elements: earth, water, fire, air, and space. Above the dome is the square *harmika*, each side of which has the eyes of the Buddha, gazing compassionately from beneath heavy black eyebrows, fringed by a curtain of blue, green, red and gold material. The shape of the nose is considered by some to represent the number '1' in Nepali script, symbolizing unity. The 13 steps of the spire surmounting the *harmika* represent the successive bodhisatva and buddha levels and the crowning canopy represents the goal of buddhahood. On each of the four sides of the stupa, at the cardinal points, there is a niche containing a shrine dedicated to one of the meditational buddhas, each with its distinct posture and gesture, deeply recessed and barely visible within a richly decorated gilded copper repoussé. Aksobhya is in the east, Ratnasambhava in the south, Amitabha in the west, and Amoghasiddhi in the north. Vairocana, the deity in the centre, is actually depicted on the east side, along with Aksobhya. The female counterparts of these buddhas are located within the niches of the intermediate directions. The faithful turn the prayerwheel as they walk clockwise around the shrine. The vajra at the top of the stairs is flanked by the two white *shikhara* temples, known as Anantapur (southeast) and Pratapur (northeast), which were built by Pratap Malla in 1646 to house the protector deities Bhairava and Bhairavi. Circumambulating the stupa clockwise, on the south side you will pass Newar shrines dedicated to Vasudhara and the Nagas (rebuilt in 1983). On the west side, after the rear entrance, there is a museum, a Bhutanese temple of the Drukpa Kagyu school, and Newar temples dedicated to Manjushri and Ajima Hariti. Lastly, on the north side, is a Newar temple dedicated to Chakrasamvara, and a Karma Kagyu temple of the Zhamar school, built in the 1960s by Sabchu Rinpoche.

Kathmandu Valley

Della Denman

Swayambhunath
Stupa

An International Buddhist Library and Pilgrim Guest House are located on a side pathway. On a neighbouring hill is another stupa dedicated to Saraswati, the Hindu goddess of discriminative awareness and learning.

Festivals The two most popular festivals celebrated at Swayambhunath mark the Tibetan New Year (Losar) in February or March, a time of joyous revelry, and Buddha Jayanta in April or May which commemorates the Buddha's birthday. Both are very crowded, but colourful and worth a visit.

Getting there
If you hire a cycle, it is worth paying Rs 1-Rs 2 to have it 'minded' by one of the small boys hanging around: this avoids tyres being let down.

Swayambhunath is a comfortable one-hour walking distance from Durbar Square, along Maruhiti Tole to the river which you cross by a footbridge. There are cremation ghats on the riverbank. The path then leads through a built-up area with a sizeable Tibetan carpet weaving community, to a meadow. Or take a taxi or rickshaw to the south entrance at the bottom of the hill. From Thamel, taxis and auto-rickshaws charge around Rs100. (Buddhists believe that higher merit is attained by walking.) See also **Short Walks in Kathmandu**, page 250.

Chabahil

Heading east from the city centre towards Bodhnath, you reach **Goshala** (where there is a road leading south towards Pashupati and the airport). Continue eastwards from this crossroads, and you pass through **Chabahil** where there is a small but elegant stupa known as **Dhanju Chaitya**. Believed to pre-date the Bodhnath stupa, it is widely thought to have been built by King Dharmadeva who also contributed to the early growth of the Pashupati complex. During Licchavi times, Chabahil was a village at the crossroads of a major trade route between India and Tibet. Ashoka's daughter, **Charamuti**, is said to have lived here and, with her husband Devapala, founded two monasteries. Some sources also credit her with construction of the stupa itself, which is occasionally still known locally as **Charamuti**. Tantric Buddhist monks were based here during the early 9th century. The stupa was rebuilt during the 7th century and again renovated during the 17th century, and stands over 12 metres high. There are even now some old chaityas, their form possibly influenced by that of the Shiva linga, and statuary at the site, including a 9th century free-standing Bodhisattva. Unusually, the stupa has no prayerwheels. Images of Dhyani Buddhas are found on each of the four sides around the stupa. On the northern side of the stupa is a 3½-metre statue of Buddha in *bhumiparsha mudra* pose. It is said that the copper gilt in which the stupa was originally plated was removed and sold by the Mallas to raise funds for their ultimately futile defence of the valley against the invading forces from Gorkha.

The Chabahil area is also well known for its **Ganesh Temple**, which is one of the four Ganesh temples protecting the Kathmandu Valley. For the local people, this temple has the reputation of curing sores and pimples. The Ganesh image is reputed to date from the 8th-9th centuries and once a year is taken around locally in a chariot. Tuesdays are the most popular days for devotees.

Bodhnath Stupa

About one kilometre east of Chabahil, the Bodhnath Stupa is 38 metres high and 100 metres in circumference, and looms above the road dominating the ancient trade route between Kathmandu and Lhasa. It is the largest stupa in Nepal and is revered by both Tibetan and Newar Buddhists.

Tibetans believe the stupa to contain the bone relics of the past Buddha **Origins**
Kashyapa and to have been built by a lowly poultry keeper and widow four
times over named **Jadzimo**. Wishing to utilize her meagre resources in an
offering to the Buddha, Jadzimo sought and received permission from the king
to begin construction. When they saw what was being built, the local nobility
became jealous and resentful that such a great stupa was being constructed by
one of such humble social standing. They demanded that the king order its
immediate destruction, but the good hearted monarch refused with the words
'*Jarung Kashor*' ('The permission given shall not be revoked') from which
comes the stupa's Tibetan name, Chorten Jarung Kashor. Jadzimo's sons are
said to have been subsequently reborn as King Trisong Dtesen, Shantaraksita,
and Padmasambhava, who together established Buddhism in 8th century
Tibet, while the widow herself is said to have attained buddhahood and is
known as the protectress Pramoha Devi.

Newar chronicles, in contrast, hold the stupa to have been constructed by
the Licchavi king **Manadeva** in the latter half of the 5th century AD in order to
atone for his crime of patricide. Thus, according to Newari legend, construction began. The stupa's Newari name, Khasti Chaitya (Dewdrop Stupa),
comes from the drought that accompanied its construction when workers put
out cloths at night to be able to drink the dewdrops which accumulated. Other
versions maintain that the name comes from the Khas Mallas, a dominant ruling house of the time of the stupa's construction, or from the relics contained
within Khasa, the name both of a village on the Tibet-Nepal border and a
Tibetan Lama, or from Kasyapa, a previous Buddha.

The structure was subsequently restored (some sources say re-constructed)
by the Nyingmapa lama Shakya Zangbo in the early 16th century. Later, following the 1852 treaty between Nepal and the Manchus, which ended the

Kathmandu Valley

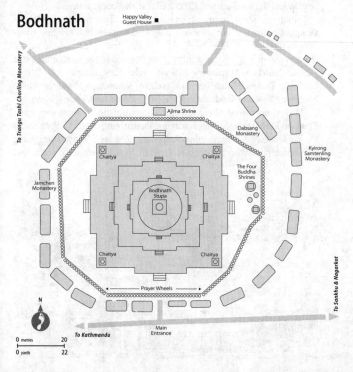

Bodhnath

Tibeto-Nepalese border wars, the abbotship of Boudha was granted in 1859 to a Chinese delegate whose descendants, known as **Chini Lamas**, continued until recently to hold a privileged position in local affairs.

The stupa By its sheer size, the Bodhnath stupa may seem even more impressive than that at Swayambhunath. It too has a hemispherical dome symbolizing the emptiness from which everything emanates, topped by a square *harmika* painted on each side with the eyes of the Buddha symbolizing awareness, above which rises the spire with its 13 steps or stages to the canopy which symbolizes the goal of Buddhahood. However, it is now almost hidden from distant view by the surrounding buildings, which create an attractive courtyard effect for the stupa itself.

Around the octagonal three-tiered base of the stupa there is a brick wall with 147 niches and 108 images of the meditational buddhas, inset behind copper prayerwheels. Each section of the wall holds four to five such prayerwheels. The main entrance to the stupa is on the south side, and the principal shrine dedicated to the female protectress Ajima/Hariti on the west. Around the stupa there is a pilgrim's circuit which is densely thronged in the early mornings and evenings by local Tibetan residents and by pilgrims from far flung parts of the Himalayan region and beyond. Numerous shrines, bookstores and handicraft shops surround the circuit, the speciality being Newar silverware cast by the *ciré perdue* ('lost wax') process.

In recent years Boudha, once a remote village, has become a densely populated suburb of Kathmandu. There is a particularly high concentration of Tibetans here, alongside the older Newar and Tamang communities, and this is reflected in the prolific temple building in which the various Tibetan traditions have engaged since the late 1960s. These shrines and monasteries are too numerous to describe here, but a few of the most important among them can be mentioned, some with well structured **teaching programmes**.

The only temple of importance on the south side of the main road is **Orgyen Dongak Choling**, the seat of the late Dudjom Rinpoche, a charismatic meditation master and scholarly head of the Nyingmapa school, whose mortal remains are interred here in a stupa. Those located to the **west** of the stupa include **Jamchen Monastery** (Sakya; under the guidance of Chogyel Trichen), **Sharpa Monastery** and Trulzhik Rinpoche's Monastery (both Nyingma), **Tsechen Shedrubling** (Kagyu), and **Shelkar Chode** (Geluk).

Heading **northwest** of the stupa, the following are the most important: **Tharlam Monastery** (Sakya), **Karnying Shedrubling** (Karma Kagyu; under the guidance of Chokyi Nyima Rinpoche), **Zhechen Tenyi Dargyeling** (Nyingma; under the guidance of the late Dilgo Khyentse Rinpoche and

Kathmandu Valley

Bodnath Stupa in 1877
Source: Ed. Wright, D, History of Nepal, CUP: Cambridge.

Zhechen Rabjam Rinpoche); Bairo Khyentse Rinpoche's monastery (Kagyu), and **Marpa House** (Kagyu; under the guidance of Khenpo Tsultrim Gyatso).

Close to the stupa on the **north** side are: **Dabsang Monastery** (Kagyu), **Trangu Tashi Choling** (Kagyu), and **Kyirong Samtenling** (Geluk).

To the **east** are: **Tashi Migyur Dorje Gyeltsen Ling** (Sakya; under Tarik Tulku), **Dezhung Monastery** (Sakya), **Leksheling** (Sakya/Kagyu; under Karma Trinle Rinpoche), **Thubten Ngedon Shedrubling** (Kagyu), and **Karma Chokhor Tekchen Leksheling** (Kagyu).

Further **north** on or near Mahankal Road are: **Mahayana Prakash Pelyul Dharmalaya** (Nyingma; under Penor Rinpoche), **Pullahari** (Kagyu; under Jamgon Kongtrul Rinpoche), **International Buddhist Academy** (Sakya; under Khenpo Abe), and the **Drukpa Kagyu Monastery** (under Tsoknyi Rinpoche). Mahankal Road extends **northeast** to **Kopan Monastery** (Geluk; under Lama Zopa and Lama Yeshe), and **Ngagi Gonpa** (Kagyu; under Tulku Orgyan). To the extreme east of Boudha, on the north side of the main road, is **Chubsang Monastery** (Geluk; under Tsibri Chubzang Rinpoche).

All the major festivals are fixed according to lunar patterns. A lively procession **Festivals** carrying the goddess Mamla around the Bodhnath area is the main attraction of the **Mamla Jatra** festival (January/February). The Tibetan New Year, **Losar** (usually February) is celebrated here on the third day of the new moon with special prayers, processions, masked dances and a feast. The Tamang festival of **Timal Jatra** (March/April) attracts Tamangs from throughout the country and begins with an all night celebration of music and dancing before a procession heads for ritual bathing at Balaju and continues on to Swayambhunath. Though honouring in particular those who have died during the past year, the vivacious **Gonai** festival (July/August) is celebrated with processions and much revelry and humour by Tamangs. Bodhnath's largest festival attracts Tibetans from all parts and takes place on the day of the first full moon of the year of the bird which next falls in 2005.

C *Padma*, T479052, F481550. 10 rooms all with bath and TV. Small restaurant and bar. **Sleeping &** Major credit cards accepted. Located just to the west of the stupa. **D** *Maya Guest* **eating at** *House*, T470866. Has good, expensive rooms, but wonderful garden and trekking ser- **Bodnath** vice to Langtang. *Stupa Hotel*, T470400. Is large with a spacious garden. **E** *Snowlion Lodge*, T447043. Large building with two blocks and restaurant facilities. *Lotus Guest House*, clean but simple rooms in excellent location. The *Hotel Tashi Delek*, T471380, and *Bir Restaurant*, T470790, are both located close to the noisy bus stand.

Crowded buses to Boudha leave from Ratna Park and Bagh Bazaar. Better to take a taxi **Getting there** (about Rs 150 by meter from central Thamel), or an auto-rickshaw (Rs 80). Alternatively, to walk from the Guheshwari Temple at Pashupati, head to your left downstream to the bridge, or from Pashupatinath Temple upstream along the west bank. Both paths meet on the north side of the bridge. A footpath leads off the northeast to Boudha, 1½ kilometres.

Continuing some three kilometres northeast of Boudha, on the banks of the **Gokarna Park** Bagmati River, the royal game reserve at Gokarna used to be a favourite picnic spot, but since the mid 1990s is being developed into an exclusive hotel and golf resort. Work was expected to have been completed by 1999. Meanwhile, the park sadly remains closed to visitors.

To the west of Ratna Park and near the Bir Hospital, this impressive stupa **Mahabuddha** standing in the centre of a busy market square measures over 10 metres in **Stupa**

Kathmandu Valley

height. Entrance to the square through arches on the west and east sides. Four statues of Buddha, each in a different pose, stand around the stupa at the cardinal points. Beside the east entrance arch, a three-pinnacled shrine built by Newari Buddhists encloses another statue of Buddha and its wooden porch is decorated with carvings of Buddha and various mythological animals.

Parks

Balaju Water Gardens Some two kilometres north of Paknajol, this small park was created by Rana Bahadur Saha in the last century as a place of recreation easily accessible from Kathmandu, but the city's recent expansion and the building of the Ring Road has effectively brought it within the bounds of Kathmandu itself. Paths lead around numerous small fountains in the centre of the park. Statues commemorate Nepal's foremost poet **Bhanu Bhakta**, and King **Mahendra** with his **queen** overlooking a pool of exotic fish. By the tank is a typical Nepalese temple flanked by a row of images of Hindu deities including one of the three supine Narayana images attributed to King Vishnugupta (7th century). At three metres in length it is smaller than – and, some say, a copy of – the one at Budhanilikantha.

Along the whole of the north wall, natural **spring** water gushes from 22 open jawed crocodile taps, while the nearby seating area is shaded by a large peepul tree and surrounded by aromatic beds of rose and jasmine. At the far side a path leads up a small hillock wooded with pine, sal and bamboo. This is a popular spot for birdwatchers – 450 species are said to congregate here – and offers good **views** of the valley. The park also encloses a large **swimming pool**, formerly for the exclusive use of the Royal Family, but now open to the public, admission ■ *Rs 20.*

Saturdays are especially crowded. Best time to visit is from April to June when flowers are in bloom. Refreshments available. Pleasant, but too popular to be really peaceful. ■ *0700-2000, Rs 2, plus Rs 2 if accompanied by a camera.*

Nagarjuna Hill Overlooking Balaju is Nagarjuna Hill (2,188 metres). It offers a fabulous view of the entire valley and a partial vista of the Himalaya which are somewhat obscured by the Shivapuri range. There is a Buddhist shrine and look-out tower at the summit. The whole hill is densely wooded providing a refuge for deer, pheasant, leopard and wild pigs. Woodcutting is prohibited and penalties are strictly enforced. The hill is revered in the Tibetan tradition as the site where the Buddha delivered the *Prophetic Declaration of Goshringa*, although other sources locate this peak in Ghotan.

Getting there You can drive to the summit via a dirt road, or go to Balaju by bicycle or bus (from Rani Pokhari) and hike about 2 hours on a trail. From Balaju below the hill a road heads northwest towards the Trisuli Valley.

Ratna Park About one kilometre east of Durbar Square and established in the 1940s by King Mahendra in honour of his wife. Some flower beds, a fish pond containing specimens from around the world, and a snack shop. It is circumscribed by a main road and its position at the centre of Kathmandu makes it busy, noisy and polluted.

Exhibition Ground Separated by Durbar Marg to the west of Tundikhel, the Exhibition Ground (or *Bhrikutimandap Mela*) plays host to occasional fairs, especially during the major festivals, when it is full of handicraft shops, food stalls, and popular games, including a type of bingo! At other times it has a market, **Sastobazar**,

Beggars

In striking contrast to many Indian cities, there are relatively few beggars in Kathmandu. Most of those that are there concentrate their efforts in the Thamel and Durbar Square areas. It is said that the majority of Kathmandu's beggars come from the Terai with some even making their way up from the Indian states of Bihar and Uttar Pradesh. Whether or not to give is a dilemma faced by every visitor. The official line is **don't give to beggars**, but an active conscience may suggest otherwise. If you do give, you will be helping that person in a small way for a short time, but the effect may be to encourage others. Some people prefer to give to aid/development organizations which work to alleviate poverty.

renowned for cheap clothes, electronic items and other bargains. This has given rise to a local saying, '*Sastobazar ma kinmal kolagi*' ('Let's go to Sastobazar'), used when one is short of cash.

Museums

See also **Patan** and **Bhaktapur**, pages 276 and 295.

Located within the grounds of the Ministry of Education on the corner of **Keshar Library** Kantipath and Tridevi Marg, the Keshar (or *Kaiser*) Library occupies a wing of the former palace of **Field Marshal Keshar Shamsher Jung Bahadur Rana** (1891-1964). A small newspaper reading room leads to the library proper which is guarded by a huge stuffed **tiger** of menacing disposition, a trophy from one of Keshar's hunting expeditions. Shelves on two floors are dominated by books on military strategy and the Second World War, but there are also volumes on European history, philosophy and religion, some League of Nations and early UN year books, as well as several finely bound collections of Hardy, Tolstoy, Chesterton and Dickens including a large white leather bound *David Copperfield* illustrated in colour by Frank Reynolds and signed by the artist, which was published in London then sold by a Bombay bookseller in 1915. Keshar also collected books on Nepal, India and China, but many of these are kept in closed metal cupboards on the first floor.

The field marshal was as eclectic in his collection of portraits which now hang alongside a couple of suits of armour and trophy heads of antelope, wild buffalo and more tigers as well as the skull of a rhinoceros. Among them are those of Nelson and Napoleon, Gandhi and Churchill, Tolstoy and Lenin, Shakespeare and Mao, and George V and Kaiser Wilhelm. There is also a large photograph of the Delhi Durbar of 1902, and a smaller, signed photograph of a young Lord Mountbatten, later to be India's last viceroy, presented in 1921 when he visited Nepal during his ill-fated tour of the subcontinent with the future King Edward VIII, then Prince of Wales. On the ground floor, a silver frame encloses a mysterious photograph of one Mrs Smith, but sadly without accompanying elaboration. Truly fascinating for its reflection on the priorities, pursuits and interests of a bygone age, it is the kind of library a well read (and connected) colonial colonel might have kept, and is highly recommended. ■ *1000-1700, Sunday-Thursday, 1000-1430 Friday, free.*

The gardens too, though not enormous, are worth a visit and have much to interest the ornithologist and amateur botanist. From the entrance (an unmarked opening in the wall on the right after leaving the library) a path leads to an out-house or shelter at one end surrounded to a surprising extent by tall

Kathmandu Valley

and overgrowing grass and weed, and is reminiscent of the type of scene that may have been envisaged by Paul Scott when he created the Bibighar Gardens in his *Raj Quartet*. A sunken pool in the middle is shaded by fir trees and palms which are a home to giant bats and, seasonally, to a noisy and rather smelly flock of egrets. An umbrella or hat is recommended.

National Museum Situated just outside the Swayambhunath complex (you pass it on the way up from the south approach), this small museum houses an eclectic collection of antiquities of national importance, most dating from the early 18th century onwards. On display are vestments of previous rulers and prime ministers, including the personal drinking pot of Bhimsen Thappa, Nepal's first prime minister, military uniforms, coins from the 14th century, khukuri knives, pistols, rifles and other weapons, many associated with the **Gurkhas**. An art gallery, immediately on the left as you enter, has a collection of some wonderful thangkas. Especially memorable are those featuring a series of scenes from the Ramayana and Mahabharata epics. The museum also has a collection of sculptures going back over 2,000 years, some exquisite wood carvings, a poorly maintained display of taxonomy and even a sample of moon rock.

Security has been a problem in recent years with items having been stolen, allegedly to order, for European and American collectors.

Rather than being run down, the museum gives the impression of never seriously having been run up, but it is worth a visit as part of a day at Swayambhunath. Allow up to three hours for a complete tour. ■ *1000-1700, Friday 1000-1430. Rs 10. Local guides offer their services outside. After negotiation, expect to pay between Rs 50-100.*

Natural History Museum Near the National Museum, this is run by the Tribhuvan University and has a notable collection of butterflies, as well as displays of birds, reptiles and mammals. ■ *1000-1700, Sunday-Friday, free.*

Tribhuvan Museum Inside the old Royal Palace on the west side of Nasal Chowk, this museum houses a small but interesting collection of the chattels of King Tribhuvan, grandfather of the present King Birendra, including bicycles, clothes and ceremonial dress, as well as Tribhuvan's study and bedroom. Allow one hour. ■ *T215613. 0800-1600, Wednesday-Monday. Rs 10.* Also includes the *Mahendra* and the recently added *Birendra* museums.

Inside the old Royal Palace: Tribhuvan Museum

Della Dennan

Essentials

Hotel names The names of Kathmandu's hotels and restaurants have been changing with bewildering regularity over recent years, so that as well as new additions to the city's tourist landscape, many existing establishments have also undergone changes of identity. Much of this practice is apparently down to non payment of either statutory dues or of *baksheesh* to keep officials sweet. A place may be forced to close down for a time before being allowed to re-open under a new name. Reluctant to lose their good reputation, many owners have simply prefaced their former title with the word *New*. What happens when the *News* start to be closed down is anyone's guess.

The hotels are grouped by area together with places to eat which are close at hand. During the **monsoon** (June-September), some roads remain flooded after prolonged periods of heavy rain, resulting in difficulties of access. These include a stretch of **Lekhnath Marg**, near the *Malla Hotel*, some of the lanes running off **Lazimpath**, the road leading south from the main **Chhetrapati** intersection towards Durbar Square, and the north-south **Bhagawan Bahal** road linking Lekhnath Marg with central Thamel. Other areas remain very muddy and slippery. Central Thamel is not usually affected seriously.

Sleeping and eating Central Thamel

This is Kathmandu's tourist heartland, a mass of hotels, restaurants and shops densely concentrated along narrow lanes and often congested. This is the place to stay if you want the closest proximity to the rest of the transient population and to the steaks and cakes for which the area has become renowned, not to mention the perennial wallahs of tiger balm, khukuri knives, hashish and more. You won't go far wrong with most of the hotels and guest houses here.

Sleeping

■ for hotels &
● for restaurants
on map, page 212

Price codes: see inside front cover (under flap)

C *Centrepoint*, T424522, F426320, cenpoint@wlink.com.np. 44 rooms, all with a/c, bath and TV. Restaurant is best for Indian food, but also has other offerings. A modern and spacious hotel. **C** *Excelsior* T411566, F410853, exel@wlink.com.np 50 rooms all with bath, some with tub, very central but reasonably quiet, lift, continental restaurant. **C** *Horizon*, T220904, F423855. 20 comfortable and well furnished rooms, breakfast served on the terrace. **C** *Karma*, T417897. 15 rooms all with bath, some with tub, breakfast only in restaurant. **C** *Kathmandu Guest House*, T413632, F417133, kgh@thamel.mos.com.np www.nepal-hotel.com 115 comfortable rooms including some larger rooms, most with TV and some with a/c, relaxed restaurant with pleasant shaded garden sitting area, it even has a small 'business centre', one of the first hotels to open in Kathmandu and a Thamel reference point for many, prices reflect its reputation, so you can get a similar room nearby for a third of the price. **C** *MM International*, T411847, F412945. 31 rooms all with bath, Indian and continental restaurant, around the corner from supermarket. **C** *Marco Polo*, T25194. 30 comfortable rooms all with bath and TV. Popular with groups. **C** *Newa Guest House*, T415781, F420055. 20 rooms all with bath and phone, good Indian restaurant, comfortable and helpful.

C-D *Garuda*, T416340, F413614. 34 rooms, all with bath, some a/c, continental restaurant and deli counter.

D *A-One Guest House*, T229302, F227333. 9 rooms some with bath, no food. **D** *The Earth*, T228850, F228890. 14 rooms all with attached bath and TV, and a large dorm, snacks available, credit cards accepted. Recommended. **D** *Fuji Guest House*, T/F229234. 14 rooms, some with bath, good food nearby. **D** *Himal Cottage*, T229187.

Central Thamel

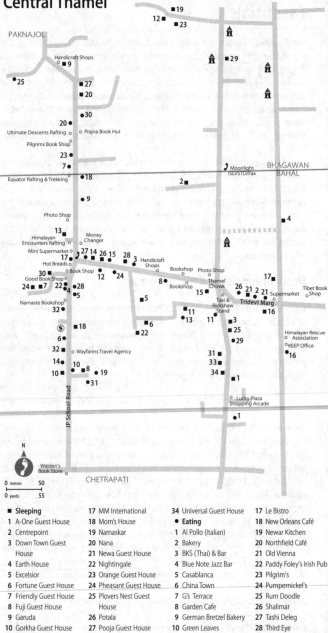

Sleeping	17 MM International	34 Universal Guest House	17 Le Bistro
1 A-One Guest House	18 Mom's House	**Eating**	18 New Orleans Café
2 Centrepoint	19 Namaskar	1 Al Pollo (Italian)	19 Newar Kitchen
3 Down Town Guest House	20 Nana	2 Bakery	20 Northfield Café
4 Earth House	21 Newa Guest House	3 BKS (Thai) & Bar	21 Old Vienna
5 Excelsior	22 Nightingale	4 Blue Note Jazz Bar	22 Paddy Foley's Irish Pub
6 Fortune Guest House	23 Orange Guest House	5 Casablanca	23 Pilgrim's
7 Friendly Guest House	24 Pheasant Guest House	6 China Town	24 Pumpernickel's
8 Fuji Guest House	25 Plovers Nest Guest House	7 G's Terrace	25 Rum Doodle
9 Garuda	26 Potala	8 Garden Cafe	26 Shalimar
10 Gorkha Guest House	27 Pooja Guest House	9 German Bretzel Bakery	27 Tashi Deleg
11 Guest Palace	28 Sagarmatha Guest House	10 Green Leaves	28 Third Eye
12 Karma	29 Sonna	11 Green Vegetarian	29 Tibetan
13 Kathmandu Guest House	30 Star	12 Helena's	30 Tom & Jerry's Pub
14 King's Land Guest House	31 Tashi Dhele	13 Himalayan Steak House	31 Typical Nepali
15 Kunal's Guest House	32 The Earth	14 In Himalayan	32 Ying Yang
16 Marco Polo	33 Thorung Peak	15 KC's	
		16 Kilroy's	

10 rooms, some with bath, credit cards accepted. **D** *Lovers' Nest*, T220541, F227795. 15 rooms some with bath, rooftop restaurant with movies, rates highly negotiable. **D** *Mont Blanc*, T222447. 17 rooms, food on request. **D** *My Home*, T231788, F224466. 20 rooms all with bath, no food, expensive. **D** *Nightingale*, T225038. 25 rooms most with bath, cheaper rooms with common bath, breakfast only. **D** *Puska*, T225027, F227795. 22 rooms most with bath (small), 'Big Belly Restaurant', clean and pleasant. **D** *Sonna*, T418399, F471375. 20 rooms all with bath, movies shown in restaurant, helpful staff. **D** *Star*, T411004, F411442. 55 rooms, restaurant, carpeted but gloomy. **D** *Tashi Dhele*, T217446. 24 rooms, restaurant, clean and comfortable. **D** *Thamel Guest House*, T411520. 13 rooms all with bath, good restaurant also shows videos, very central. **D** *Thorung Peak*, T224656, F229304. 27 rooms some with bath, rooftop restaurant tries everything, quiet, off road location. **D** *Universal Guest House*, T240930, F227333. 32 rooms most with bath, restaurant downstairs.

D-E *Down Town Guest House*, T224189, F419870. 19 rooms all with bath, no food, close to many handicraft shops. **D-E** *Gorkha Guest House*, T214243, F240292. 10 rooms, some with bath and tub, also *Johnny Gorkha Restaurant*. Recommended. **D-E** *Guest Palace*, T/F225593. 8 rooms, some with bath, attached steak house also does breakfast. **D-E** *Namaskar*, T421060, F420678. 12 rooms all with bath, no food, clean and good value. **D-E** *Range Guest House*, T410182, F420678. 10 rooms some with bath, no food. **D-E** *Sagarmatha*, T410214. 28 rooms some with bath.

E *Cosy Corner Lodge*, T411957, F417799. 14 rooms, all common bath, no food, central. **E** *Fortune*, T411874. 4 rooms all with bath, no food, cheap. **E** *Friendly Guest House*, T414033. 12 rooms, no food, good value. **E** *Kunal's Guest House*, T411050. 21 rooms a few with bath and some with TV, comfortable and reasonably priced. **E** *Memorable Guest House*, T243683. 12 rooms, forgettable. **E** *Mom's House*, 10 rooms some with bath, no food. **E** *N Pooja Guest House*, T416657. 12 basic but good rooms, reception on 2nd floor above Red Rock restaurant. **E** *Pheasant Guest House*, T417415. 15 rooms all common bath, no food, impressive entrance with old Gurkha family weapons and some pet pheasants. Recommended. **E** *Potala*, T416680, F419317. 25 rooms all common bath, some with balcony, no food, clean and friendly, bookshop on 1st floor. Recommended.

Central Thamel has the bulk of the restaurants that have made Kathmandu famous for culinary excellence. Sticking to the restaurant's speciality can avoid disappointment. **Eating**

Austrian: *Gourmet Vienna*, T419183, F415488, gourmet@vienna.wlink.com.np Has one branch just north of Pilgrim's Bookshop, a deli counter for takeaway sandwiches, salamis and cakes, and a couple of tables for eating in; a similar branch towards Tridevi Marg at the front of the outstanding *Old Vienna Inn*, a superior Austrian restaurant and one of Thamel's best. Recommended.

Chinese: *Oriental Kitchen*, T416683. For average Chinese food, central.

Indian: *Shalimar*, T423606. Indian restaurant, try the Kathi rolls. *Third Eye*, T227478. Has excellent Indian food, also some continental, huge club sandwiches, more expensive than average, credit cards accepted.

Italian: *Al Pollo Pizzeria*, some excellent Italian food using home grown herbs, proprietor lived in Florence, also herbal teas, south of Thamel Chowk near Chhetrapati. Recommended. *Mamma Mia*, does pizzas and some of the best and most reasonably priced Italian food in Kathmandu, candlelit tables, located at the west end of a lane leading off from JP School Rd about 300 metres south of Kathmandu Guest House.

Kathmandu Valley

Recommended. *Pizzeria Panorama*, T216863, shows free movies in separate 'jungle room'.

Japanese: *Aji No Silk Road*, T423681, just north of Thamel Chowk. For Japanese food, set meals, relatively expensive. *Fuji Restaurant*, T225272, Kantipath, near Grindlays Bank. Lovely Japanese restaurant in a peaceful off road location, surrounded on 3 sides by a small moat, set meals from Rs 500, regular customers keep their unfinished bottles of Scotch in locked glass cabinets, expensive. Recommended.

Multi-cuisine: *Kilroy's*, T250440. Much hype surrounded the first few months of this restaurant's existence in late 1998. Unusually, it was entirely justified, for Kilroy's quickly established itself as Thamel's finest 'continental' restaurant. The eponymous Kilroy is Mossiman trained whose past clientele reads like a Who's Who of the great and the good. The slightly obscure entrance is 50 yards from Thamel Chowk. Attractive indoor and outdoor seating. The food is excellent, with the desserts particularly worthy of mention. Prices are higher than the Thamel average, but it's worth it. *Casablanca*, T260187. A smart modern restaurant with Indian and continental food. Good vegetarian and non-vegetarian Thalis, and sandwiches. *Hotel Marshyangdi's* Cozy Garden restaurant, specializes in open-air barbecues and grills, elegant rooftop *Palace* restaurant has an eclectic menu, expensive. *Manang Hotel's* Jewels of Manang, in basement, exclusive, intimate atmosphere, continental, Italian, Chinese, Indian food, live bands play Western and Indian music, dinner only, expensive. Recommended. The *Holiday Inn* has 3 speciality restaurants, an expensive *Al Fresco* for authentic Italian food, *Gurkha Grill*, despite the name, for candlelit *haute cuisine française* and a live band, and *Himalchuli* for the best of Nepali and Indian food accompanied by live music and dance; *Berale* is opposite *Helena's* and does continental and Israeli style (not Kosher) food. *Le Bistro*, T411170, F419734, right in the heart of Thamel, good breakfasts, sandwiches, apple pie, and continental food, avoid the steaks. Recommended. *Green Leaves*, T224067. Multi cuisine, live Nepali folk music every night. *Helena's*, T412135. Continental food and cakes in congenial rustic surroundings, very central. *In Himalayan*, jack of all foods, master of none, also Nirula's ice cream. *KC's Restaurant and Bambooze Bar*, T416911. Is an established favourite in the middle of Thamel, good breakfasts, salads and continental dishes, sandwiches on a variety of breads, cheese and meat fondu for minimum 4 persons, Rs 250, spectacular but indifferent sizzlers, more expensive than average, pleasant bar upstairs. *New Orleans Café*, T416351, F418436. Mexican and continental food, outdoor and indoor seating, jazz. About 200 metres south of the *Kathmandu Guest House*, opposite the *Hungry Eye* restaurant, the *Ying Yang Restaurant*, T227478, F425510, amma@apsons.mos.com.np A smart Thai and continental restaurant with delightful courtyard seating area, excellent food and buffet breakfast at Rs 200, quality bakery stand has excellent lemon meringue pie, highly recommended, perhaps Thamel's best restaurant but expensive.

Nepali/Tibet: *Thamel House*, T410388, is a charming, traditional Newari house, extensively renovated, and has a comprehensive excellent Nepali menu, a huge 9-course set meal costs Rs 500, bar, some floor cushion seating, credit cards accepted, expensive. Recommended. *Newar Kitchen*, simple but good Nepali food, at the east end of a small lane off JP School Rd, near *Green Leaves* restaurant; *Tashi Deleg*, is centrally located opposite Namche Bazaar building, Tibetan food. *Typical Nepali Restaurant*, near the *Green Leaves* restaurant, small and friendly, typical tourist prices.

Northfield Café, T424884. Does snacks, excellent Mexican food, good sandwiches, free chips with beer during nightly happy hour, next to *Pilgrim's Bookshop*; *Old Spam's Space*, T412713, good English breakfast, snacks and light meals, Thamel's version of a British pub, 100 metres north of *Pilgrim's Bookshop*; *Roadhouse Café*, T229187. Snacks, meals and bar.

Vegetarian: *Skala*, T223155, F229459. Does good vegetarian food.

Thai: *BKS Restaurant*, T415420. For Thai food, opposite *Helena's*.

Sleeping and eating Chhetrapati

This area south of central Thamel takes its name from the busy intersection of 'six roads' where there is now a bandstand and a large city map. From here, the road heads south to Durbar Square. Most hotels here are situated along the main east-west road where there are also a number of good restaurants to choose from.

B *Marshyangdi*, T414105, F410008. 60 rooms, modern, courteous, well located, fine views from roof terrace, 24-hour coffee shop, 'Palace' restaurant has extensive menu, bar, popular with groups. Recommended.

C *Harati*, T226527, F223329. 59 rooms, good restaurant with Indian and continental menu, reasonably priced, bar, attractive garden, popular with groups. **C** *Lai Lai*, T240419. 32 rooms, restaurant, very clean, excellent views from rooftop, peaceful. **C** *Nirvana Garden*, T/F222668. 55 rooms, some with a/c, TV, balcony and bathtub, good Chinese food in restaurant, tastefully decorated, also quiet garden with small waterfall. Recommended. **C** *Tibet Guest House*, T260383, F260518, tibet@guesths.mos.com.np 42 comfortable rooms all with bath and TV, most with a/c. Tibetan and continental restaurant. Friendly, professionally run and always helpful. Long established, and probably the best accommodation in this category. Highly recommended.

Sleeping

■ for hotels &
● for restaurants
on map, page 215

Price codes: see inside front cover (under flap)

Kathmandu Valley

Chhetrapati

■ **Sleeping**	9 Norling Guest House	● **Eating**
1 Base Camp	10 Park	1 Bro-Sis
2 Harati	11 Potala Guest House	2 Everest Steak House
3 Kathmandu Holiday	12 Shambala	3 La Cimbali
4 Kathmandu View	13 Tara Guest House	4 La Menagerie
Guest House	14 Tayoma	5 Narayan's Steak House
5 Lai Lai	15 Thahity Guest House	6 Nepalese Kitchen
6 Lucky Guest House	16 Tibet Guest House	7 Paradise Café
7 Marshyangdi	17 White Lotus Guest	8 Rainbow Steak House
Mandala	House	9 Silk Road Café &
8 Nirvana Garden	18 Yak Lodge	Gemini

C-D *Park*, T214053. 36 rooms all with bath, small rooftop eating area, 2 adjoining buildings, clean and comfortable. **C-D** *Shambala*, T225986, F414024. 32 rooms, most with bath and phone, water filters on each floor, restaurant does good Tibetan food, bar, clean and modern. Recommended.

D *Base Camp*, T212224, F221344. 17 rooms, some with bath, small restaurant, also 2 simple apartments, one with an occasionally functional sauna. **D** *Kathmandu Holiday*, T220334, F229459. 18 rooms all with bath, tiny restaurant. **D** *Potala Guest House*, T220467. 60 rooms all with bath, some have TV and phone, one of Kathmandu's long standing favourites, popular restaurant for steaks, Italian and Mexican. **D** *Tara Guest House*, T220634, 24 rooms. Many with bath, some triples and good value cheaper rooms, boiled water available, roof terrace, breakfast only. **D** *Tayoma Guest House*, T242356, F245323. 16 rooms some with simple bath, no food, central location. **D** *Thahity Guest House*, 15 rooms all with bath, small restaurant for snacks and light meals, between the Chhetrapati bandstand and Thahity Tole. **D** *White Lotus Guest House*, T224563, F229967. 16 comfortable rooms most with bath, restaurant shows videos daily.

E *Norling Guest House*, T221534. 16 simple but clean rooms, common bath, very reasonable Tibetan food on request.

Eating

Chhetrapati has some excellent eateries spilling over from Central Thamel

Nepali/Tibetan: *Nepalese Kitchen*, near the *Base Camp hotel*, has good Nepali dishes, also Tibetan and continental, also some interesting alcoholic hot drinks, stunning black and white photographs of Nepali life throughout, central fireplace, music and dance programme on alternate evenings from 1830-2100. Recommended. *Yulo* in the eastern part of Chhetrapati is small, but does good and reasonably priced Tibetan food. More Tibetan food at the *Tibet Canteena*, T212224, in the *Base Camp hotel*, at the *Tibet Guest House*, and at the *Yak Lodge*.

Indian: *Cabin* restaurant, T214769, on the eastern side of Chhetrapati towards Thahiti Tole. Does cheap Chinese, Nepali and Indian food, including a plate of Dal-Bhad-Tarkari at Rs 25.

Steaks: *Everest Steak House*, T217471. Has by far the best steaks in all Nepal, a carnivore's dream, superb fillet steak and grilled chicken, the Chateaubriand for two (Rs 650) is magnificent and enough for four, also Italian, Tibetan and Mexican, but stick to the steaks. Recommended.

Sleeping and eating Jyatha and Kantipath

Sleeping

■ *for hotels &*
● *for restaurants*
on map, page 217

Price codes: see inside
front cover (under flap)

There is a scattering of hotels in the Jyatha area and a couple on Kantipath, slightly removed to the southeast from central Thamel, and close to the pick-up point for tourist buses to Pokhara and Chitwan. One or two superb eating places are located on Kantipath which makes the walk there or back a little shorter; otherwise, head into central Thamel for food.

B *Mountain*, T246744, F249736, mountain@vishnu.ccsl.com.np Kantipath. 56 comfortable rooms in modern building, expensive coffee shop, restaurant and small bar, lovely rooftop lawn with seating and fine views of city and surrounding areas, but service is unexceptional. **B** *Yellow Pagoda*, T220337, F228914, Kantipath, 56 rooms and 3 rooftop apartments, Indian restaurant, lobby bar and 24-hour coffee shop, also a small gift shop, central location, but like its neighbour, the *Hotel Mountain*, expensive and pretentious.

C *Gautam*, T244515, F228467. 20 rooms all with bath and some a/c, restaurant does

Indian, Chinese and continental food. **C** *Nepa International*, T251368, F256306. 30 rooms, all with bath and TV. Restaurant. Modern and smart. **C** *Rara*, T222436, F229158. 32 rooms all with bath (and tubs) and TV, some a/c rooms, unexceptional restaurant and bar, rooftop beer garden, credit cards accepted. **C** *Paradise Plaza*, T255153, F255152, paradise@pacific.wlink.com.np www.info-nepal.com/members/paradise Modern, smart-ish hotel, popular with Indian visitors. 25 rooms some with a/c and TV. Restaurant is best for Indian dishes.

D *Himalayan View*, T216531, F221656. 24 rooms all with bath, small restaurant. **D** *Jagat*, T250732, F227701, jagat@ccsl.com.np 13 rooms all with bath. No restaurant. Some good value cheaper rooms. **D** *Kohinoor*, T213930. 25 rooms all with bath, no food. **D** *Kailash*, T232819. 40 rooms all with bath, chaotic restaurant for Indian food.

Old Vienna Delicatessen Centre, T419183, F415488, gourmet@vienna.wlink.com.np on Kantipath. Excellent Austrian deli with seating, cheeses, breads and pastries, cold meats. Light meals including Bratwurst and chips, and fish and chips. Smoked salmon also available. Recommended. *Café Lungta*, T217804, F227600. Around the corner from the Yellow Pagoda hotel, reasonable but rather expensive pizzas and continental food. *Royal Kasturi Restaurant*, T212082, in Jyatha. For Thai, Chinese, Indian and continental dishes, moderately priced.

Eating
A couple of fine restaurants on Kantipath, but nothing exceptional in the Jyatha area.

Kathmandu Valley

Jyatha & Kantipath

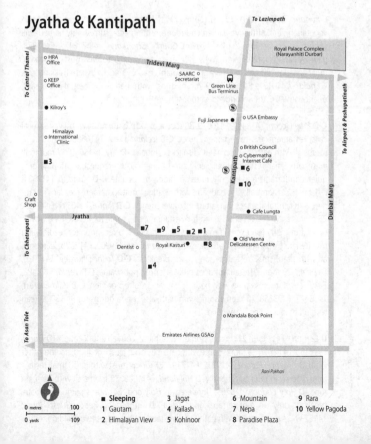

■ **Sleeping**	3 Jagat	6 Mountain	9 Rara
1 Gautam	4 Kailash	7 Nepa	10 Yellow Pagoda
2 Himalayan View	5 Kohinoor	8 Paradise Plaza	

0 metres 100
0 yards 109

Sleeping and eating Paknajol

Sleeping

■ for hotels &
● for restaurants
on map, page 220

Price codes: see inside
front cover (under flap)

To the northwest of central Thamel, has a number of good value, mid-range hotels and guest houses. It is, for the most part, less congested than central Thamel with one or two quiet corners (a distinct advantage if you want some distance from overflowing, narrow laned commerciality), but is easily accessible and has some good restaurants. The word Paknajol is a combination of this area's ancient name, *Pakna*, and *jol*, from the Sanskrit for water, after a natural spring that provided water to the locality. The spring still exists, albeit usually in a rather uninspiring puddle-like form, just off the Paknajol road as it turns northeast towards Lekhnath Marg.

A *Malla*, T410620, F418382, Lekhnath Marg near the Royal Palace. 125 rooms and 20 apartments for long-stay guests, 3 restaurants, including Chinese and the pleasant garden terrace looking out across well kept lawns and a raised Buddhist stupa. Modern bar.

B *Manang*, T410993, F415821, Ehtlmanang@vishnu.ccsl.com.np www.travel-nepal. com/ hotel/manang 35 comfortable rooms, 2 restaurants. Popular with groups. **B** *Marshyangdi*, T414105, F410008, htlgold@mos.com.np www.catmando. com/marshyangi 55 rooms, 2 restaurants and bar, small conference room. Modern and comfortable.

B-C *Norbhu-Linka*, T414799, F419005. 40 rooms, 24-hour coffee shop, restaurant, rooftop bar and snacks, nicely decorated.

C *Buddha*, T413366, F413194. 37 rooms all with bath, restaurant (vegetarian and non vegetarian), bar, attractive garden and rooftop sitting area, surprisingly named, will confirm reservations by fax. **C** *Gauri Shankar*, T417181, F411878, gauri@asianadv.mos.com.np www.asian-trekking.com 36 rooms most with bath, quiet location off Lekhnath Marg, restaurant, bar, owned by Asian Trekking Ltd. **C** *Shakti*, T410121, F418897. 39 rooms most with bath, continental restaurant, opened in 1976, the second oldest tourist hotel in Kathmandu.

C-D *Blue Ocean*, T418499, F410079. 30 rooms all with bath, most with TV, free local calls, restaurant and roof garden, quiet. **C-D** *Iceland View*, T416686, F420678. 16 rooms all with bath, rooftop bar and snacks, central. **C-D** *Lily*, T415640. 17 rooms all with bath, small restaurant will serve almost anything on request, rooftop garden, quiet, comfortable and friendly, rates are highly negotiable. **C-D** *Mandap*, T413321, F419734. 23 rooms all with bath and with heating, rooftop garden, pleasant restaurant with central fireplace, bar, attached travel agency. **C-D** *Rimal*, T410317, F417121. 28 rooms all with bath and TV, rooftop restaurant, bar, some rooms have exotic fish tanks, but many fish expire if room key is not handed to reception for feeding and maintenance during guests' absence. **C-D** *Shree Tibet*, T419902, F412026. 25 rooms, all with bath, small restaurant only does breakfast. **C-D** *Tashi Dhargey*, T417030, F423543. 22 rooms, restaurant does breakfast only, poor value. **C-D** *Tenki*, T414483, F412571. 35 rooms some with bath, restaurant, rooftop garden. **C-D** *Villa Everest*, T413471, F423558. 10 rooms some with bath, also 3-bed dorms for Rs 150, Korean restaurant, quiet. Recommended.

D *Capital*, T414150. 21 rooms some with bath, convenient location. **D** *Florid*, T416155, F412747. 25 rooms some with bath, basic but clean, no food, no entry after 2330. **D** *Greeting Palace*, T417212, F417197. 27 rooms most with bath, small restaurant, gloomy interior but friendly. **D** *Holyland*, T411588. 15 rooms all with bath, no food. **D** *Holy Lodge*, T416265. Unrelated to *Holyland*, 24 rooms some with bath, breakfast only on roof terrace, good value. **D** *Kathmandu Peace Guest House*, T415239. 24 rooms most with bath, small restaurant, comprises two buildings either

Kathmandu Valley

Kathmandu Valley

side of the end of the track, good views across valley, friendly, popular with travellers so early booking advised in season. Recommended. **D** *Mount Fuji*, T413794. 16 rooms all with bath, quiet but expensive. **D** *Namche Nepal*, T417067, F229459. 32 rooms most with bath, restaurant does Indian/Nepali food, average. **D** *Prince*, T414456, F415158. 13 rooms all with bath, pleasant rooftop garden restaurant. Recommended. **D** *Shikhar*, T415558, F220143. 15 rooms all with bath, 2 restaurants (Indian and Chinese), rooftop garden, quiet, friendly. **D** *Souvenir*, 8 rooms some with bath, small restaurant, friendly. **D** *Tibet Peace Guest House*, 19 rooms some with TV and bath, all with phone, restaurant which expands to include 'traditional' floor seating at peak times, attractive garden, good views, despite the name is run by a Bengali. Recommended. **D** *Tridevi*, 14 rooms most with bath, restaurant, best rooms at the back.

E *Ajanta*, 8 rooms, no food. Recommended only for the experienced budget traveller. **E** *Annapurna*, 15 rooms, dark but cheap, isolated. **E** *Arumdaye*, small and noisy, very basic. **E** *Chitwan Tulasi Peace Guest House*, 6 rooms, spartan, best avoided. **E** *Earth House*, 15 rooms most with bath, rooftop garden restaurant, clean. Recommended. **E** *Green Peace Guest House*, T420333. 12 rooms some with bath, breakfast on rooftop terrace, friendly, quiet. **E** *Kalika Lodge*, small, noisy and very basic. **E** *Lonely Planet*,

7	Chitwan Tulasi Peace Guest House	18	Life Guest House
8	Country Villa	19	Lily
9	Earth House	20	Lonely Planet
10	Florid	21	Manang
11	Gauri Shankar	22	Mandap
12	Green Peace Guest House	23	Marshyangdi
13	Greeting Palace	24	Mona
14	Holyland	25	Mount Fuji
15	Holy Lodge	26	Namche Nepal
16	Kalika Lodge	27	Nippon
17	Kathmandu Peace Guest House	28	Norbhu Linka
		29	Rimal
		30	Shakti

■ **Sleeping**
1 Ajanta
2 Annapurna
3 Aramdaye Lodge
4 Blue Ocean
5 Buddha
6 Capital

31	Shikhar
32	Shree Tibet
33	Souvenir
34	Tenki
35	Tibet Peace Guest House
36	Tridevi
37	Valentine Guest House
38	Villa Everest

T418918. 14 rooms some with bath, small restaurant not recommended, has what claims to be a 'Tibetan Ayurvedic Yoga Massage Clinic', unexceptional. **E** *Mona*, T422151, F415158. 4 rooms all with bath, no food, good views from rooftop terrace. **E** *Mustang*, T/F419361. 15 rooms, 24-hour room service, rooftop garden. **E** *Nippon*, 5 rooms, basic. **E** *Yeti*, T419789. 14 rooms some with bath, reasonable rates.

Although nowhere near as extensive a selection as in central Thamel, there is nevertheless a reasonably good range of restaurants in Paknajol. Some of the better hotels in particular are worth trying for ambience and variety.

Eating

Delima Garden Café, T414456, F415158. Continental, Chinese and Indian meals and snacks in a quiet pleasant setting. *Hungry Eye*, next to *Capital Guest House*, reasonable Indian, Chinese and continental food. *Pradhan's San Francisco Pizza Restaurant*, T412314. Pizza, pasta and ice cream, popular among travellers, actual size paintings of menu items on the wall. Recommended. *Rum Doodle*, T414336, F227068. Among Kathmandu's best known eating and drinking spots, excellent steaks, continental, Mexican, Chinese and Indian food, wonderful rum and raisin cheesecake, cocktails, named after WE Bowman's account of the conquest of the 40,000 ft fictional mountain available for purchase at Rs 150, signatures of mountaineering expeditions and eminent visitors on display including Sir Edmund Hillary and Jimmy Carter, considered by a 1985 edition of *Newsweek* magazine as among the world's best drinking places but this has increased prices, large fireplace. Recommended.

Sleeping and eating Jhocchen (Freak Street)

Leading off from the southeast corner of Basantpur Square, near Durbar Square, this area has attained minor celebrity status (or notoriety) as the place where budget travellers of the hippie generation stayed and has occasionally been compared to another point on the previously popular overland route from Europe, Chicken Street in Kabul, Afghanistan. Although Freak Street's popularity decreased markedly with the emergence of central Thamel as the travellers' heartland from the late 1970s, there are still several smaller hotels and restaurants along its length with some of the cheapest rooms in town. It is convenient for the temples of Durbar Square and the Basantpur Square market and the area has its share of reasonable eateries, though the best are 20 minutes walk away in Thamel. The long hair and flares of the hippie days may be long gone, but the ghost remains in the respectable 50-something year olds sauntering with evident nostalgia through former haunts, in the tunes of the Beatles and the Byrds still drifting with the smoke from the windows of a cheap bar, and in the style and shades of nihilism in the post modernist descendants of the original 'freaks'.

Sleeping

■ *for hotels &*
● *for restaurants*
on map, page 222

Price codes: see inside front cover (under flap)

D *Eden*, T213863. 16 rooms all with bath, tall narrow building with lift, located at the southern end of Freak St, good views from the rooftop. **D** *Sugat*, T216656, F241576. 11 rooms most with bath, attractive wooden carved reception area, at the top end of Jhocchen overlooking Basantpur Square and the Hanuman Dhoka palace. Recommended.

E *Annapurna Lodge*, T213684. 20 rooms some with bath, its *Diyalo* restaurant does reasonable Indian and continental food, large portions. **E** *Buddha Guest House*, T240071. 8 rooms all common (squat) bath, cheap, basic and clean. **E** *Century Lodge*, T247641. 25 rooms all common (squat) bath, cheaper dorm, parrots and budgies in reception, a traditional favourite also popular with cockroaches. **E** *Himalaya's Guest House*, T246555. 16 rooms, 3 with bath, basic and sometimes clean. **E** *Pagoda Lodge*, T212029. 17 rooms all common bath, boiled and filtered water on request. **E** *Pokhara Guest House*, T241773. 14 rooms all common bath, cheap and awful. **E** *Traveller's*

Kathmandu Valley

Paradise, T240602. 8 rooms all common bath, with good vegetarian *Paradise* restaurant.

Eating

A few restaurants in and around Freak St, popular with budget travellers.

Tibetan: *New Mandarin Tibetan Restaurant*, opposite the Eden hotel to the south of Freak St, is small, dimly lit, and serves Tibetan food to Western music.

Multi-cuisine: *Diyalo* restaurant in the Annapurna Lodge does generous portions of Indian and continental food. *The Meeting Place*, T244984. Does Chinese, Indian and continental food, some low seating. *Meggi Restaurant*, T213643. On the first floor, for Japanese and continental dishes.

Vegetarian: *Oasis*, T214392. Towards the south of Freak St, is good for vegetarian food, indoor and courtyard seating. *Paradise Restaurant*, T240602. In the Traveller's Paradise Guest House is good for vegetarian food.

Fastfood: *Carpe Diem Music Café* is a small trendy place for snacks, lassis, juices and beers. *The Old Palace Café*, T225246. On the southern side of Basantpur Square does most types of food at very reasonable prices, also snacks and cocktails, some floor cushion seating, pleasant, friendly and helpful. Recommended.

Jhocchen (Freak Street)

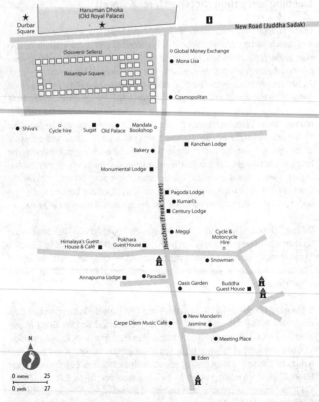

Sleeping Durbar Square/New Road

AL *Holiday Inn Crowne Plaza*, T272555, F272205. Pagoda style building, formerly the Oberoi and the first and largest 5-star hotel in Nepal, 286 rooms most with excellent views of mountains, suites at US$675 per night, swimming pool, tennis court, 24-hour casino, 4 restaurants including French, Italian, Indian, good Indian and Western buffet breakfast in coffee shop, located at Tahachal, 10 minutes southwest from Durbar Square, free bus service to New Rd and Durbar Marg at 1000, 1230, 1500, 1800 and 1930, all returns 30 minutes later.

B *Classic*, T222630, F224889, New Rd. 84 rooms, superb views of the city and mountains from the top floor *Tower* restaurant, and live music in the *Natraj*, large building in the centre of the city's main shopping and commercial area, near Durbar Square.
B *Crystal*, T223636, Shukrapath, corner of New Rd, near Durbar Square. 52 rooms, all a/c, good views of town from roof terrace and convenient for temple visits, price reflects location, restaurant (Indian and continental).

E *Kumari Guest House*, basic, hot showers, but no safes for luggage, hence insecure, unsatisfactory laundry.

A *Royal Singi Hotel*, T424190, F424189, hotel@rsingi.wlink.com.np 83 rooms, 2 restaurants, 24 hour coffee shop does breakfast, lunch, dinner buffets, bar. Excellent views of Kathmandu, Patan and Kirtipur from the 7th floor Chinese restaurant.

Kamaladi

Durbar Marg area

Sleeping Durbar Marg

AL *Yak and Yeti*, T248999, F227782, sales@yakandyeti.com, www.yakandyeti. com 270 rooms include an executive floor, 8 suites, set in charming landscaped gardens. The older rooms compare with Thamel's 3-star offerings, but at 5-star prices. *Sunrise Cafe* coffee shop does good buffet breakfast, lunch and dinner, with occasional jazz evenings. *Naachghar* restaurant for good Nepali and Indian food in a delightfully extravagant setting. *Chimney* restaurant does continental food with alleged Russian influences, a meal for two would cost around Rs 3,000. Fitness club, also open to non residents, with sauna, jacuzzi and steam. Swimming pool. Expensive shopping arcade. A new conference centre, Nepal's largest, was due to have opened in December 1999. The reservations system can be unreliable, so make sure you get the class of room you booked. One of Nepal's best hotels, but no longer in a class of its own.

Sleeping

A central area with some excellent hotels and fine restaurants.

Kathmandu Valley

AL *Radisson*, T411818, F411720, radkat@mos.com.np www.radisson.com 172 rooms including 'business class' rooms, conference rooms, swimming pool, health and fitness centre, two good restaurants. Comfortable and modern. Located at the southern end of Lazimpath, close to the diplomatic areas and to central Kathmandu.

A *Hotel de l'Annapurna*, T221711, F259596, apurna@taj.mos.np www.yomari.com/taj-annapurna Durbar Marg. 159 rooms, the best overlooking garden and pool, good Indian restaurant and coffee shop for buffet breakfast, swimming pool open to non-residents at Rs 850, also tennis court and billiards room at Rs 450 per hour, live Nepali and Western music every evening in foyer/bar, exclusive shops and cultural centre, extensively remodelled in 1993, refurbished rooms recommended. **A** *Dynasty Plaza Woodlands*, T220623, F223083, Durbar Marg. 125 rooms, restaurant and bar, health club, sauna, squash courts, and pool open to non-residents at Rs 250. **A** *Sherpa*, T227000, F222026, sherpa@mos.com.np www.info-nepal.com/members/sherpa Durbar Marg. 83 rooms and 2 restaurants: *Sherpa Grill* for Indian and continental food, evenings only, and *Café de la Paix* coffee shop with breakfast, lunch and dinner buffets, hours 0700-2300, rooftop swimming pool open to non-residents at Rs 300, regular Sherpa and Tamang cultural programmes.

D *Mayalu*, T223596, F220820. With 28 rooms all with bath, Punjabi restaurant also does some continental dishes.

Eating **Indian**: *Golden Gate* T225938. For the best Indian food, live ghazals every evening 1930-2130. Recommended. *Niramar Restaurant and Bar* on the corner of Jamal Rd, near the statue of King Mahendra. Does good South Indian vegetarian food, ghazals every evening 1900-2200, 'no dancing', also has coffee house. *Taj*, T240744. In a basement at the southern end of Durbar Marg, near the two Mosques, good tandoori Indian and Chinese food at reasonable prices.

Nepali/Tibetan: *Bhanccha Ghar*, T225172, on Kamaladi, off Durbar Marg. Excellent authentic Nepali food. *Saino Restaurant*, T230682, at the northern end of the road. Set Nepali and Tibetan meals include local rice wine at US$10, also Indian, continental and Chinese food.

Fastfood: *Hot Breads*, T221331, F228816. For fresh bread, cakes and pastries, also ice creams. *Wimpy*, T220299, F414184. For lamb burgers, fries and shakes.

Sleeping and eating Lazimpath

Sleeping

■ *for hotels &*
● *for restaurants*
on map, page 225

Price codes: see inside
front cover (under flap)

Leads north from the Royal Palace, almost as an extension of Kantipath. The road passes through the main embassy area before continuing on towards the statue of the sleeping Vishnu at Budhanilikantha. There are a couple of luxury hotels here as well as some in the middle price range. Central Thamel is about 20 minutes' walk. Offices of a number of foreign NGOs are also located in this area, as well as some excellent supermarkets and a few restaurants and bookshops.

AL *Shangri La*, T412999, F414184, Lazimpath. 82 rooms, best face garden, Tibetan style décor, cultural programmes, good French and Chinese restaurants, garden café and small pool open to non-residents at Rs 250, conference facilities include tiny library/meeting room with Desmond Doig sketches, shopping arcade.

A *Kathmandu*, T410786, F416574, Maharajganj, Embassy area. Modern, clean, friendly, all Nepali staff. **A** *Shankar*, T410151, F412691. Located at the southern end of Lazimpath, 94 rooms, delightfully converted Rana palace, sumptuous, intimate and atmospheric, one large restaurant serves all types of food, comfortable bar with fireplace, lovely exterior and gardens. Recommended.

C *Ambassador*, T414432, F413641. 44 rooms all with TV, phone and bathtubs, small restaurant does continental, Indian and Chinese food, bar, modern hotel at the southern end of Lazimpath, popular with groups. **C** *Lion*, T419395, F415307. 26 rooms all with a/c, TV, phone and bathtub, restaurant and bar does good Chinese and continental food, rooftop terrace. **C** *Manaslu*, T410071, F416516. 56 rooms, multi-cuisine restaurant, bar, modern décor, peaceful though somewhat inconvenient location at the end of a small lane that can get very muddy in the monsoon.

China Town for Chinese food, bar. *Himtai Restaurant*, is 100 metres north of the Ambassador hotel and does good Thai food. *New Peace Restaurant* is small, but has a reasonable Chinese and continental menu. The *Tandoori Fast Food Café* is cleanish and has good tandoori meat preparations, 'burgers', 'pizzas', and momos also available to take away.

Eating
In addition to the major hotels here, there are a couple of smaller restaurants and fast food outlets.

Kathmandu Valley

Sleeping and eating other areas

AL *Everest*, T220567, F226088, New Baneshwar, near the airport. 162 large rooms and 9 restaurants including *The Café*, all day coffee shop, *Sherpaland* for Tibetan and Chinese food; and Indian cuisine in *The Far Pavilion* on the 7th floor with classical Indian music and excellent views, 2 bars, swimming pool and disco, tennis courts, international conference centre next door.

East of the city

B *Dwarika's Kathmandu Village*, T470770, F472328, Batisputali, near Pashupatinath. 32 rooms all individually decorated with hand carved, traditional Newari windows, won PATA Heritage Award for cultural sensitivity, excellent Nepali restaurant, 9 courses, reservations essential. **B** *Manang*, T410993, F415821. 39 rooms, coffee shop, 360° views of valley from rooftop terrace lawn, bar, elegant '*Jewels of Manang*' restaurant does dinner only, but has live Western and Indian/Nepali music.

Lazimpath

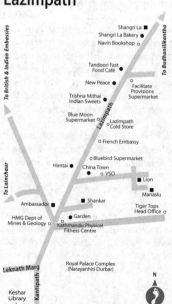

A couple of good hotels in Lainchaur, the area north of Lekhnath Marg, near the Royal Palace and about 10 minutes' walk to central Thamel. **D** *Namaste*, T410459, F418578. Has 17 comfortable modern rooms all with bath, multi cuisine restaurant is best for Indian dishes, bar facilities, TV lounge area, rooftop terrace, and helpful and friendly staff, good value. Recommended. *Sungawa*, T418217, F424457. Opposite the *Namaste* and has 15 rooms some with bath, small dining room does Nepali/Indian food.

Lainchaur

Bhagawan Bahal Bhagawan Bahal is the area between central Thamel and Kantipath and has a couple of decent places to stay. **D** *Shakti*, T410121, F418897. Has rooms with bath, restaurant. *Earth House*, T418197, F416351. Comfortable rooms some with bath.

Tripureshwar A few hotels also in Tripureshwar, along the main road running parallel to the Bagmati River in the south of the city. This area can be noisy and is removed from the principal places of interest. **B-C** *Bluestar*, T228833, F226820. 106 rooms, coffee shop (0700-2200) and 2 restaurants: *Vaishali* for Indian and continental food, and *Gompa* for Chinese, bar closes at 2200, conference facilities.

Swayambhunath Going across the Vishnumati River towards Swayambhunath, try **E** *Catnap*, T272392, and *Peace Lodge* at Chauni. Both are fairly quiet.

Bhote Bahal **D** *Janak*, large rooms, restaurant. *Sayapatri*, T223398. Breakfast, pleasant garden. **E** *Valley View*, T216771. Some rooms have bath, terrace, clean.

Bag Bazaar There are a few very basic guest houses in the Bag Bazaar area to the east of the city centre, but they have little experience of foreign visitors.

Naxal *Mike's Breakfast* (T424303) is one of Kathmandu's longest established and most popular eateries, with portions as substantial as the menu.

Entertainment

Bars There are few pub-type bars in Kathmandu, though just about every restaurant has its own bar. *Paddy Foley's Irish Pub* (T432593), in Central Thamel, has daily happy hours from 1700-2000. No food, but free popcorn. Green walls, Irish memorabilia and music, bottled Guinness and other beers, and comfortable modern seating, but more Paddy O'shrestha than Foley. All the big hotels have bars, including that at the *Malla Hotel*, peacefully looking across at a Buddhist stupa in the middle of its well maintained gardens. The *Yak and Yeti's* bar has a fireplace and an atmosphere of old world comfort. Recommended. The *Shankar* hotel at the southern end of Lazimpath has a cosy bar delightfully decorated with traditional Newari carving and fireplace. Also, try upstairs at the ever popular *Rum Doodle's*. *Tom and Jerry's*, opposite Pilgrim's Bookshop in central Thamel has regular theme nights and happy hours. In Paknajol, try the *Himalayan Cocktail Bar* for a range of surprisingly good cocktails (including the 'Thamel Tiger'!). Special offers during happy hour, free popcorn but no other food. 'Cold stores' throughout the city sell good locally produced beers (including Tuborg, Guinness, San Miguel, Carlsberg) at around Rs 60, and awful (though cheap) locally produced spirits.

Beauty parlours & massage All the '**AL**' and '**A**' hotels have in house beauty parlours for ladies (open to non-residents) with Western trained staff and the latest equipment. Appointments not always necessary. Others include *Enigma Beauty Parlour*, T411131, *Hotel Garden*, Naya Bazaar. *Sipi Beauty Club*, T244768, Putali Sadak, Kamaladi (closed Monday); and *Veena's Hair and Beauty Clinic*, with branches at Hattisar (T422095) and Old Baneshwar (T473511).

Kathmandu's luxury hotels also have qualified masseurs. Many of the numerous massage parlours to have emerged in Thamel are set up in a family home, are unqualified and mercenary. There are, however, a few formal establishments such as *A-One Massage Centre*, T246544, at Kwabahal. Quality hairdressers often do excellent and hygienic head massage. If you want to learn massage techniques, check the noticeboards around Thamel for courses.

Cinemas The city has five cinemas, all showing hugely popular Bombay produced **Hindi**

Hot air ballooning

Hot air ballooning arrived in Kathmandu in 1996, the latest in Nepal's ever increasing range of tourist attractions and undoubtedly one of the most stunning visual experiences the city has to offer. The balloon, or 'envelope', is made of 3,000 square metres of fabric and when inflated stands over 100 feet high with a volume of 260,000 cubic feet. It is powered by four burners and the gondola can carry up to 12 passengers, although this does make it rather cramped – six to eight is probably a comfortable maximum. Weather permitting, the one-hour ride leaves from Kirtipur. Its course and speed is determined largely by the winds. The ride reaches heights of up to 1,500 metres above ground level (about 3,000 metres above sea level) with stupendous 360° views across the Himalaya, the Kathmandu Valley and south. On a clear day there are views of Dhaulagiri in the west, across the Annapurnas, Manaslu, Ganesh Himal, Langtang, and as far as Everest and Kanchenjunga in the far east, which probably makes it the finest viewing platform in all Nepal. The ride also takes in much of the Kathmandu Valley as it floats over Patan and Bhaktapur. A camera is essential.

The flights leave early in the morning when weather conditions are most favourable. Daily during the main tourist season. At US$195 per person the one hour ride is not cheap, but the price includes a post flight breakfast and transport from the set down point to Thamel. Discounts available for groups of 10 or more. **NB** Contact the operator the day before the flight to confirm departure times and details. The usual meeting place is the Kathmandu Guest House, times depend on weather conditions. Full refunds are given if the ride has to be cancelled. Currently there is just one company operating the balloon: Balloon Sunrise Nepal, c/o Nepal Air Services, PO Box 1273, Lazimpath, Kathmandu, T424131, F424157, balloon@sunrise.mos.com.np www.travel-nepal.com/other/ balloonsunrise

movies as well as occasional **Nepali** films. Although geared principally to the local market, the anthropologically minded visitor will find an afternoon spent watching a Bombay ('Bollywood') movie an unusually memorable experience. Many are a variation on a set formula: helpless beauty pursued and captured by repugnant villain, rescued in the nick of time by dashing hero. Car chases, gun battles, fist fights and songs throughout. Audience participation is the other major ingredient, with plenty of unabashed oohs and aahs, vociferous encouragement for the hero and vehement condemnation of the villain. A knowledge of Hindi is not always necessary. *Biswajyoti*, T221837, in Jamal, east of Rani Pokhari and near the clock tower. *Gopikrishna*, T479893, in Chabahil, on the east side of town. *Jai Nepal*, T411014, near the Royal Palace. *Kumari*, T414932, in Putali; and *Ranjana*, T221191, New Rd. Most have shows in the late morning, early and late afternoon and, occasionally, an evening showing. Tickets from Rs 2 to Rs 25. Buy in advance or queue.

An increasing number of restaurants in **Thamel** have begun showing Western videos in an effort to attract more customers. Their menus can be slightly more expensive. Titles range from fairly recent Hollywood blockbusters to an eclectic selection of enduring favourites, including *The Wall*, various 007's, *Pulp Fiction* and *The Sound of Music*. **NB** Choose a place that has a generator to reduce power cut disruptions.

The *Hotel Mandap* has programmes of Nepali classical music every evening Tuesday-Sunday, 1900-2130, including flute, sarangi, harmonium and musical drama, free admission. Nepali music and dance at *Hotel Marshyangdi* twice a week, check days and timings. The *Soaltee Holiday Inn* also has a good dance and music programme every evening in the Himalchuli restaurant, 1900-2245, but you have to eat and

Cultural events

transport to central Kathmandu can be problematic late in the evening. The **New Himalchuli Cultural Group** is one of the country's leading groups and has performed extensively in south Asia as well as in Europe and has nightly music and dance shows at the *Hotel Shankar*, 1900-2000 in summer and 1830-1930 in winter (Rs 250). The **Gandharba Culture and Art Organization** has programmes of music (including sarangi, maadal drum, basuri flute and uniquely the traditional Gandharba arbas), song and dance every day at *Spam's Restaurant* from 1500. The **Everest Cultural Society**, T228787 has Nepali folk dances at the *Hotel de l'Annapurna* at 1830 (Rs 300). The *Hotel Everest* has a programme of Indian classical music most nights, while there are also nightly performances in the magnificent setting of the *Yak and Yeti's* Naachgar restaurant (recommended). The **Chimal Cultural Group** in the *Manaslu Hotel* and the *Hotel Vajra* also organize regular shows. **Ghazal** programmes are good at the *Amber Restaurant* on Durbar Marg (most evenings), and at the *Jewels of Manang* restaurant in the Hotel Manang in Paknajol, 1900-2200 Tuesday-Sunday.

Regular theatre performances are staged at Kantipath and Rani Pokhari. Details from Rashtriya Naach Ghar, Kantipath, near Rani Pokhari (T211900). A further possibility is the **Royal Nepal Academy** at Kamaladi and the City Hall, opposite the Exhibition Ground. The **Arniko Cultural Society** is in Dilli Bazaar.

Gambling   Kathmandu has 4 casinos, all open 24 hours and especially popular with Indian tourists. *Anna*, at the *Hotel de l'Annapurna* on Durbar Marg; *Everest*, at the Everest Hotel, New Baneshwar, near the airport; *Nepal*, at the *Soaltee Holiday Inn*; and *Royale*, at the *Yak* and *Yeti Hotel* off Durbar Marg. Games include roulette, blackjack, poker and slot machines. All have bars where drinks and food are reasonably priced or free. If you have flown into Nepal within the past week, you can get Rs 100 worth of free chips on production of your passport and ticket or boarding pass. US dollars and Indian rupees accepted. Free transport to your hotel or the centre of town is provided from 2300 to 0300. Nepalis are not admitted – a visit to any of the casinos will confirm this to be an insignificant deprivation.

Music & dance   For performances of traditional Nepali dances and music, see below. Otherwise, Kathmandu offers little in the way of late night entertainment. The *Dynasty Plaza Woodlands Hotel*, T225650, on Durbar Marg has a **nightclub**, *Woody's Place*. The *Everest Hotel* also has a **disco**, *Galaxy*, supposed to be for foreigners only, open 2200-0400. Some Thamel restaurants have live **bands**. *Amber Restaurant* on Durbar Marg has live **ghazals** on some evenings. Recommended.

Theatre   With occasional drama performances and concerts, the **National Theatre** (Rashtriya Nach Ghar) on Kantipath, is Kathmandu's only theatre.

Festivals

More than 50 festivals covering a total of over 100 days are celebrated in Kathmandu. Many are occasions for brightly coloured processions and gatherings, offering the visitor a vivid insight into the Valley's culture and customs. Festivals are set according to the lunar calendar and dates therefore vary each year. The most important include:

January-February   *Magh*, the 10th month of the Nepali calendar, is marked by women who dedicate their month long 'fast' of one meal per day to Shiva.

Ghyo Chaku Sanlhu, on the winter solstice, takes its name from the clarified butter (*ghyo*) and molasses (*chaku*) which are essential ingredients in the festival meal that also includes yams and sesame seeds.

Basanta Panchami at the Hanuman Dhoka palace, Swayambhunath, Budhanilikantha and other Vishnu shrines, marks the coming of spring and is dedicated particularly to Saraswati, goddess of learning and creativity.

Losar, the Tibetan new year at Boudha and Swayambhunath.

Maha Shivaratri at Pashupatinath and other Shiva shrines, the most important Shiva festival of the year, attracts pilgrims from throughout Nepal and India to an all night vigil at Pashupatinath.

Holi celebrates the victory of Narasingha over the demon Hiranyakashipu. Its most conspicuous feature is the coloured water and powders which are thrown over friends, acquaintances and passers by – beware!

March-April

Buddha Jayanti (or *Swanya Punhi*) at Swayambhunath and Bodhnath, commemorates the birth, enlightenment and nirvana of the Buddha and is marked throughout the Valley by colourful processions and burning candles. At Bodhnath, an elephant is elaborately decorated and paraded around the stupa, while musicians gather at Swayambhunath and the stupa is surrounded by thousands of small ghee lamps.

May

Jya Punhi at Swayambhunath, where devotees offer rice and flowers to mark the Buddha's departure from his family and the start of his quest for spiritual enlightenment.

June-July

Tribhuvan Jayanti at Tripureshwar.

Trishul Jatra, a Tantric Shaivite festival, processions and music to Deopatan, near Pashupatinath.

Guru Purnima is held in honour of teachers, celebrated by Buddhists as *Dilla Punhi*, marking the conception of the Buddha, Siddhartha Gautama.

Gathemangal marks the end of monsoon rice planting and exorcizes evil spirits.

August

Pancha Dan at Swayambhunath, Boudha and elsewhere, a Buddhist festival of charity when rice and other consumables are ritually offered to Buddhist monks.

Bahidyo Bwoegu, a Buddhist festival meaning 'displaying the gods'.

Gunhi Punhi (or *Janai Purnima*) takes place throughout the Valley and is the day when Hindus ceremonially bathe before tying their new sacred thread for the coming year.

Gaijatra (or *Saparu*) is marked by recently bereaved families who trek around the city with a decorated cow which is believed to assist the departed into their next life.

Indrajata, one of the most dynamic and colourful celebrations, marks the passing of the summer monsoon. Masked dances and processions of chariots and lamps start from Durbar Square. The Kumari begins her two day procession through the city streets on the third day.

September

Krishna Janmastami, in honour of Krishna. Processions to the Krishna Temple in Patan's Durbar Square.

Teej, the festival of women, at Pashupatinath and other Shiva shrines. A huge feast is followed by a 24-hour fast during which many women wear red wedding saris.

Dasain, the major festival of the year, celebrates the triumph of good over evil as represented by the goddess Durga's victory over the demon Mahishasur. Gifts, especially of clothing, are exchanged and numerous rituals observed in the home. Animal sacrifices at many temples. Mechanical devices are venerated during the final days – if you are at the airport at this time, watch as Nepali aircraft become the objects of *puja* worship. Government offices remain closed for a week and the city is very busy and crowded.

October

Accommodation and transport are difficult during Dasain.

Tihar, the festival of lights (approximating *Diwali* in India). Each of the five days has a special theme. The first day is dedicated to crows, and the second to dogs. The third is the Day of the Cow on which Lakshmi, the goddess of wealth and prosperity, is propitiated by

November

Kathmandu Valley

candles and small lamps placed in every household. The Nepali new year is celebrated on the fourth day, while sisters honour their brothers on the final day.

Ekadasi at Budhanilikantha and Pashupatinath.

December *Bala Chaturdasi* at Pashupatinath.

Indrayani Jatra, in honour of a mother goddess is celebrated at Kirtipur with musical processions, animal sacrifices and a feast.

Yomari Punhi marks the end of the rice harvest. Yomari is a sweet made of rice flour, sugar and sesame seeds.

Shopping

Basantpur Square is popular among tourists, so tourist prices prevail and are usually absurdly inflated. If you can get a Nepali or Indian friend to do the bargaining for you, you can pick up some memorable gifts and souvenirs at a reasonable price. Stand well away during negotiations!

Eventually, it is said, you can find anything you are looking for in Kathmandu. From an astonishing array of handicrafts sold in the huge Basantpur Square market and hundreds of smaller shops throughout the city to Western fashions and imported luxury goods in the expensive Durbar Marg and New Road stores, as well as imported foodstuffs in the increasing number of supermarkets on Lazimpath and New Road. First thing in the morning try wandering around the colourful and hectic local markets – Asan Tole, Indra Chowk and Bagh Bazaar for instance – and watch as the locals haggle with stallholders for the best prices of vegetables, clothes and pots and pans. Most markets are open from dawn to dusk, though shops (especially in the Thamel area) often don't open until after 0900. Saturday is the main weekly holiday and many shops open late or remain closed.

Antiques Reliable antiques are available from the *Tibet Ritual Art Gallery* above the Sunkosi Restaurant, and from the *Potala Gallery*, opposite the Yak and Yeti Hotel, off Durbar Marg. There is also a thriving trade in fake antiques, with masks, woodcarvings, metalwork etc made to look considerably older than they actually are. **NB** Genuine antiques require a clearance certificate from the Dept of Archaeology (National Archives Building, Ramshah Path) permitting them to be exported. All reputable dealers will help in getting this.

Bakeries Numerous bakeries claiming various national identities throughout **Thamel**. The *Bretzel Bakery*, opposite Kathmandu Guest House, always has fresh bread in the morning and is recommended. *Hot Breads*, under Le Bistro restaurant in the heart of Thamel, as well as the *Hot Bread* shop opposite, both have good fresh and cakes, as well as savouries and sandwiches. Good for an awayday packed lunch. *Ying Yang* restaurant, 200 metres south towards Chhetrapati, has an excellent bakery stall (lemon meringue pie a speciality). *Helena's*, in central Thamel has an alluring window display, but the cakes can flatter to deceive. Good apple pie at *Le Bistro*, and excellent cheesecake at *Rum Doodle's*. Try *Old Vienna Delicatessen*, in Thamel and on **Kantipath** for apple strudel and good sandwiches. The *German Bakery* in **Jhocchen** (Freak St) has a good line in bread and cakes. On **Durbar Marg**, *Hot Breads* has fresh bread and pastries. The *Annapurna Bakery* in the Hotel de l'Annapurna has a good selection. The nearby *Nanglo Bakery and Café* is apparently the hip place for Kathmandu's bright young things to hang out and be seen, but the food is unexceptional. On **Lazimpath**, the *Shangri La* hotel has a good bakery. Other shops recommended for cakes, bread and pies along **Maru Tole** ('pie alley').

Bookshops There are a number of bookshops in and around Thamel with a wide range of fiction and non fiction, maps, postcards, guidebooks and second hand. Surprisingly, prices vary considerably, so it is worth shopping around and bargaining. Most stay open until late and will buy back books at half the selling price. For those desperate for news from home, you can get *Time* and *Newsweek* as well as one day old Hong Kong editions of the

Wall Street Journal in some Thamel shops. The latter's Monday edition usually includes **results** from the weekend's European **football, cricket** and other sports.

Central Thamel: *Barnes and Noble Book House*,T435844, next to Le Bristo, has one of the best selections including a substantial second hand section. They will buy back a book at half the price you bought it for. *Pilgrims Book House*, T424942, F424943. Nepal's largest bookshop with a superb range of books, especially on Nepal and South Asia, as well as a few small handicraft items, hand made paper and paintings, expensive but recommended, nice coffee shop at the back. *Prajna Book Hut*, opposite Pilgrims, manages to pack a surprising amount of stock into its small premises, good for maps and Himalaya and philosophy books, postcards; *Kathmandu Book House*, T412367, next to Helena's restaurant, and further along, the *Global Book Centre*, T412180, have mostly travel and Nepali culture titles, maps, also tapes and CDs. Two shops next to Le Bistro restaurant have an excellent selection of fiction, new and second hand, and guide books. Head south along this road and you pass another couple of smaller book sellers. *Walden's Bookshop* faces you when you reach Chhetrapati and also has one of Kathmandu's widest range of new and second hand fiction and they will also buy books. The cash counter keeps a copy of the out of print *Birds of Nepal* (external inspection only), a snip at US$150.

Tridevi Marg: *Tibet Book Store*, T415126, has the city's best selection of Buddhist titles, as well as books on other religions and guidebooks. Recommended. *Bookland* is opposite the Immigration Office and has a smaller range.

Other areas: *Kailash* by the Yak and Yeti Hotel's main entrance is good but rather expensive. *Mandala*, Bidhur, Kantipath. *Himalayan Booksellers*, near Clock Tower, small but good range. *Everest Books* and *Asia Book House*, off Durbar Marg near National Theatre and Rani Pokhari. *Ratna Books*, Bagh Bazaar, near French Cultural Centre, wide range, informed, helpful. *Educational Bookshop*, Kantipath, opposite New Rd, excellent for educational books. There are also a couple of smaller bookshops on **Lazimpath**.

There are two main types of carpet on the market: Tibetan woollen and the better **Carpets** quality Kashmiri silk. Manufacture of the woollen ones is concentrated in Patan where they can be bought directly from the makers, but there are numerous shops in Thamel, Indra Chowk and Durbar Marg stocking a wide range of sizes, designs and qualities. Also at Bodhnath. The best of these use handspun yarn, sometimes with a mix of Tibetan and New Zealand wools. Traditional Tibetan designs are characterized by their strong patterns and bright colours, though in recent years weavers have favoured floral and animal pastel coloured designs on undyed wool. Some retailers issue quality guarantee certificates with each purchase, but quite how these would be honoured is unclear. Expect an average carpet to last up to 15 to 20 years with normal usage. Despite international labour agreements, it is thought that child labour is still extensively used in carpet production in Nepal and throughout South Asia.

Since the increased political instability all but decimated Kashmir's tourist industry, there has been something of a minor influx of Kashmiri carpet emporia to Kathmandu, resulting in a degree of hostility aimed towards Kashmiris here. Nevertheless, Kashmiri silk carpets are among the finest in the world, and the best ones will last well over a hundred years and are sometimes bought as investments. Although it is possible to buy a top quality carpet in Kathmandu, the risk of being seriously overcharged for an inferior product is ever present. Shops on Durbar Marg. In Thamel try *Worst Arts*, T223778, F419419, next to the Al Pollo restaurant, 2 minute walk south of Thamel Chowk, and *Q Enterprises*, T214940.

In addition to the ubiquitous tee shirts, you can get good quality clothing, ready to **Clothing &** wear and tailor made, often at very reasonable rates. Jackets, sweaters and casual **textiles** trousers can be especially good value. **NB** Cheaper clothes have been known to fall

Kathmandu Valley

apart within days, so check the seams for strength. Sweater designs can be as eclectic as their tee-shirt equivalents: in 1996, a scowling woolly Mona Lisa remained on view but unsold in central Thamel for 8 months!

Pashmina shawls: a lightweight but very soft and insulating kid's wool from the Nepalese and Tibetan Himalaya or from Kashmir, are a speciality. The best quality are so delicate that they can be passed through a ring, and, it is claimed, so warm that an egg wrapped in a shawl overnight will be partly boiled the following morning! Lambswool shawls are also popular. Best bargains at Asan and Indra Chowk. **Blankets** and **bedspreads** are sold throughout the city and are much cheaper outside Thamel. There are a couple of non profit making, fixed price shops on Lazimpath: *Women's Skill Development Project*, near the French Embassy, and *Community Craft Centre*. Elsewhere, try the UNCF's *Hastakala*, opposite *Himalaya Hotel*, and *Mahaguthi*, on Durbar Marg.

Attractive and excellent quality embroidered **cushion covers** are best value in numerous shops in the Kamaladi area, to the east of Rani Pokhari.

You can buy **saris**, **salwar kameez** (Indian style loose trousers and top for women) and **topis** (traditional Nepali hat worn by men, an essential part of the national dress) made from a variety of material in most parts of the city, but try Asan Tole and the areas around Indra Chowk. Bottom end saris start at around Rs 200, while at the top end gold embroidered silk saris can sell for many hundreds of dollars. A decent salwar kameez will cost between Rs 300 and Rs 1,000, while you can get a nice little topi for Rs 30. For top of the range clothing, South Asian and Western, try the various department stores on Dharmapath, near New Rd.

Confectioners

Chewing paan can leave your mouth a deep red colour!

European and Indian confectionery is available from supermarkets in Thamel, Lazimpath and in the New Rd area. Opposite the entrance to Bishal Bazaar (New Rd) is an Indian confectioners, where *gulab jamons* (syrupy sponge balls) are especially good. Also try *Trishna Mithai* on Lazimpath for quality Indian sweets. For enthusiasts of *paan*, a mixture of chopped betel nut and sweet Indian masalas wrapped in a betel leaf then chewed (some use it as an aid to digestion), there is a Bengali *paan* wallah just south of the *Thamel House* restaurant.

Foreign goods

The area around New Rd is the centre of Kathmandu's upmarket shopping, with modern Western style department stores and shopping malls appearing in total contrast to the nearby Durbar Square. On one side of New Rd, on the corner of Shukrapath, is *Bishal Bazaar*, a 4-storeyed shopping centre. Close by are **Dharmapath**, **Kicha Pokhari** and **Bhugol Park**. All have shops selling imported Western brand name goods and give the impression of an expansive duty free shopping complex where you can get French perfumes and fashion, cosmetics, electronic items, foods, etc. Prices are competitive and appeal especially to Indian tourists. *Bishal Bazaar Supermarket*, T222423, New Rd. *Bluebells Fashion Wearhouse*, T217501, and *Central Department Store*, T222028, Kicha Pokhari. *La Dynasty*, T220859, Bughol Park.

In addition to the shops in Thamel which sell mainly European and North American foods, there are a few supermarkets along **Durbar Marg** and **Lazimpath** well stocked with familiar consumables, wines and trekking food. On Lazimpath, try the excellent *Bluebells*, T415181, which has another branch in Tripureshwar, T245726.

Handicrafts

Handicraft shops abound in central Kathmandu; indeed, Thamel consists of little other than hotels, restaurants and myriad handicraft shops spilling into one another, each competing with its neighbour for space and custom. There are stalls around Thamel Chowk impressively laid out with khukuri knives of all sizes, with Buddhist prayer bells, wheels and flags, with masks of Bhairab, and paintings, puppets, coins and carpets. Just about all of Nepal's indigenous handicrafts are represented here, together with imported Indian varieties dressed for the Kathmandu tourist market.

The Rug Trade

The origin of decorative carpets can be traced back to the beginning of the second millennium when, records show, they were made by Persian gypsy women for use as wedding ornaments. In the course of the next centuries the idea caught on and spread from Persia, gradually being adopted as a trade. One fine specimen found its way to the court of the Kashmiri King, Zani ul-Abddin, who, dazzled by what he saw, sent some of his finest craftsmen to Persia to learn the skill. The returning expertise led to this region of northern India becoming a major carpet producing centre. Possibly the greatest innovation to come from here was the introduction of a new form of interlocking knots which effectively doubled the life of a carpet. Meanwhile, new combinations of wool, cotton and silk, together with a move away from the traditional Persian reliance on maroon, red, blue and black dyes, and the banning of child labour during the time of the last Shah, led to the emergence of Kashmir as the world's major quality silk carpet manufacturer. The state is rightly proud of the quality of its silk, a product of a climate in which the mulberry tree thrives.

The best carpets involve fantastic workmanship. They are always hand knotted with up to 1,200 knots per sq inch and use vegetable dyes, including maroon (from the cockscomb flower), rust (pomegranate) and saffron, a mere 10 grammes of which is enough to dye 1 kg of silk! Traditional techniques and designs, usually of geometric or floral patterns, are often maintained by being passed through generations of a single weaving family using a secret coded language which can be read only by members of that family. Such is the intricacy, that a top quality silk on silk carpet measuring 3' by 2', with 1,100 knots per sq inch and using up to 15 colours, would take 18 man months to make and retail at around US$1,500!

Very few shops have the real, high quality Kashmiri silk carpets, where prices are determined by the number of knots per sq inch and begin at around US$1,100 for a 4' by 6' silk on cotton carpet. Any decent shop will have a magnifying device which you hold to the back of the carpet to count the knots. You can also get much cheaper synthetic silk carpets, or those combining silk and cotton. In some cases, the latter have silk attached to ends of cotton threads to give the impression of pure silk. The best way to test whether a carpet is of real silk or of cotton chemically made to shine is to pull out and burn a knot from the centre – but **not** from the silk-rich border. Real silk burns like a human hair, curling to form a charcoal like crust and producing an ugly sulphurous smell, while artificial silk has a less unpleasant smell and burns with a straight flame.

Upmarket shops are concentrated on Durbar Marg. Many of these specialize in jewellery and in precious and semi-precious stones and though you are more likely to get the genuine article, prices here are also significantly higher than elsewhere. For metalwork and woollen carpets, you could try Jawalakhel, near the zoo in Patan, while Bhaktapur is the place for terracotta pottery and for watching small scale craftsmen at work creating smaller trinkets. As usual, all prices are ripe for negotiation.

Jewellery Ranges in both style and quality, the latter being largely concerned with trinkets and semi-precious stones. If you are continuing on to India, it may be better to postpone any major gem purchases until you arrive in one of its main cities, though silver items

Kathmandu Valley

can be good value in Kathmandu. Typically, gem stones and turquoise and coral are used in settings. Thamel shops and the stalls in Basantpur Square offer everything from coral necklaces to aquamarine animal figures. The *Namkha Craft Collection*, T243636, F423543, 100 metres west of Walden's Bookshop on Chhetrapati is good for advice and is recommended for some of the most honest prices for its trinkets, silver and necklaces. The purity of gold and silver has been questioned, though the upmarket jewellers on and near New Rd are generally reliable.

Markets
Beware of pickpockets, especially as evening approaches.

Basantpur Square, in the shadow of Durbar Square; this busy market area has many shops and stalls selling handicrafts, precious and semi-precious stones, statues, khukuri knives and jewellery. Also *munga*, coral necklaces worn by married women, and jewellery favoured by women of the Gurung caste.

Indra Chowk is one of the city's 3 ancient centres of trade (with Asan and Bhotahiti), its reputation as a place of commerce dating as far back as the 14th century. Situated on the old trade route that linked India with Tibet, probably Malla Kathmandu's equivalent of today's New Rd. The market supplies the local populace with fruit and vegetables and its tourist interest is now mainly anthropological and historical.

Asan, on a busy thoroughfare linking Kantipath with Durbar Square, has shops and stalls selling everything from souvenir khukuri knives to cucumbers.

Putalisadak, meaning 'street of butterflies', is near the City Bus Park and is known for its quality furniture and foreign clothes shops. It takes its name from the hordes of butterflies which descended annually on an erstwhile park at this site.

Bagh Bazar is a typical example of a bustling urban South Asian market area. Here you can watch as all the ingredients for dal-bhad-takari are bargained for; look out for the many varieties of rice being sold. There are also a number of private language institutes along the road offering courses in English, Japanese, Spanish, etc.

Kicha Pokhari extends along Exhibition Rd from the Bhimsen Tower to New Rd, with shops selling 'fancy goods': decorations, curios, ready made garments and cosmetics. The name means 'dog pool'.

Metalwork
The word 'bronze' is often used as a general term for any bronze coloured metal.

Patan is the centre for bronze casting by the *ciré perdue* ('lost wax') process. Metal figures of deities, gameboards and pieces for the traditional Nepalese game *bagh chal* are also available. Buddhist **prayer bells** are popular. Though touted as being made of 7 or even 9 metals, most contain only 2 or 3 and should be sold with a *vajra*, the sceptre like symbol representing the male principle to the bell's female principle. You should also get a short wooden rod which, when rubbed continuously around the base of the bell, produces an intriguingly loud resonance. Another favourite is the miniature Buddhist **prayerwheel**, a hand held device containing a scroll with hundreds or thousands of the 'Om mani padme hum' mantra which, when rotated, enables the believer to offer this prayer very much more rapidly than vocally. Basantpur Square and Thamel once again have the widest ranges, but you can probably get the best prices from individual stalls, particularly in Chhetrapati. Otherwise, try Jawalakhel in Patan.

Paintings

Thangkas, traditional Tibetan Buddhist religious paintings on cotton scrolls, together with *paubhas*, their Nepali equivalent, are available in most handicraft shops. In some shops, notably in the vicinity of Durbar Square, you can watch as they are painstakingly painted, but prices here are relatively high. Today, most thangkas are made expressly for tourists, a fact that is reflected by the colours and designs used. Quality is determined by the intricacy, eg look for detail in the hands and facial features, and (more difficult for the untrained eye to tell) by the quality of the pigments used. Traditionally, thangka artists have used ground stone and natural pigments along with powdered gold and silver. If you are considering a higher quality purchase, it is well worth while spending time in different shops comparing, contrasting, asking questions and generally getting your eye in before making a choice. All the top class hotels have shops where you can get advice as well as seeing some stunning examples. Durbar Marg has a number of thangka retail outlets, including *Dawa Arts*, T228938, and *Mannies Arts*, T223715, in Sakya Arcade. In Thamel, try *Amrita Craft Collection*, T244345, in Chhetrapati, and *Tibetan Thangka Treasures*, T418177. On Lazimpath, the *Tibetan Thangka Gallery*, T417300, is near the *Ambassador Hotel*. Try also Jhocchen (Freak St). **Rice paper prints** are available in Thamel, near the Kathmandu Guest House. *The Print Shop* has a good selection of batik, small oil paintings, and greeting cards made of peepul leaf are popular and reasonably priced. The *Kathmandu Handicrafts* shop, opposite the *Malla Hotel* on Lekhnath Marg, also stocks *Mithila art*, a traditional form of painting from the Janakpur area.

There are a couple of small shops ('museums') selling excellent **watercolours** by local artists on the road leading from the main Chhetrapati intersection to Durbar Square. These shops do not yet feature on the main tourist shopping circuit and if you are lucky you can pick up something really impressive here for around Rs 500 or less.

Papier mâché

Masks and puppets made from a combination of rice paper, cotton rag paper, ordinary wood paper, brush shavings and newspapers are widely available in all three of the valley's cities. **Thimi** is the manufacturing centre for masks (Ganesh, Bhairab and the Kumari are popular), and Patan's artisan district of **Jawalakhel** also produces puppets and masks. Some come from Kashmir and other parts of India. The best are water resistant and hand painted, sometimes decorated with gold and silver or with brass dust or bronze powder, though the two latter will eventually blacken through oxidation. Some masks are used in the traditional masked dances during the Indra Jata festival in September/October.

Photography

Kodak and Fuji films are readily available in Kathmandu and developing and printing can be done with confidence. There are numerous processing labs in the Thamel area. Film costs about Rs 110 for 24 exposures and Rs 160 for 36. Developing the negatives costs about Rs 40 with an additional Rs 10 per print. Most shops will give discounts in the region of 20 percent for processing a 36 exposure film, more for bulk orders. Single use disposable cameras are also available at about Rs 400 for 36 exposures. Send pre-paid processing films home.

T-shirts

Kathmandu has acquired something of a reputation for its made-to-order logo tee shirts, and you can find any number of shops in the central area displaying their newly embroidered products while sewing machines tick away inside. You can create your own design and enlarge it, if required, by photocopy; the options are limited only by the bounds of good taste. Prices depend on the amount of embroidery involved, but are generally very reasonable and start at around Rs 120, including the price of the shirt, for simple embroidery and go up to Rs 300 for intricate, multi-coloured designs. Orders placed in the morning are usually ready by the same evening or the following morning. The 'Double Apple' and 'Shangri la' makes have been recommended.

Terracotta pottery

This is particularly good in Bhaktapur and Thimi (en route) which specialize in little flower pots, often in animal shapes. You can also get the increasingly popular clay pipes. One variety is alleged to result in less harmful smoking by passing the smoke through a water filter. Decorative wall designs are also available.

Trekking equipment
See also Trekking section, page 82

You can get everything you need for a trek in Kathmandu. Numerous shops in Thamel and along Freak St stock clothing including warm jackets, sleeping bags, rucksacks, footwear, rainwear and other supplies. You can also rent many larger and more expensive items, for which a deposit is required. Some shops demand a passport as deposit, but this is not advised. Rates increase in peak season. If you buy cooking

Kathmandu Valley

equipment, you can usually sell it on to other trekkers when you return. **NB** Large shoe sizes can be difficult to obtain.

Woodcarvings Miniature replicas of carved windows and doors are popular souvenirs and are available in all the city's tourist areas. You can also get some superb furniture, including beautifully carved screens, writing desks, coffee tables, etc, from the upmarket shops on Durbar Marg and on and just off Kantipath. The best will be made from seasoned hardwoods such as teak and walnut, both of which are long lasting but expensive. Try Basantpur Square for masks and jewellery boxes, or Bhaktapur for miniature windows, picture frames and screens. You can also get small exquisitely carved **statues** made of heavy yak bone.

Sports

Billiards *Hotel de l'Annapurna*, Rs 100 per hour.

Chess A chess club meets occasionally at the British Council library on Kantipath, T221305.

Fishing With its wealth of rivers, it is surprising that fishing has not yet caught on as a major tourist activity in Nepal. In theory, you are supposed to get a fishing permit from the National Parks and Wildlife Conservation Department at Babar Bahal. They may also be able to provide up to date information on angling opportunities. Bring your own tackle or, better still, learn local techniques which include the use of nets, spears and poisonous plants. *Mahseer*, which can grow up to 40 kilogrammes, and *asla*, a kind of snow trout, and other fish are found in Terai rivers and valley lakes. For fishing in Karnali, Rapti and Narayani rivers, contact *Tiger Tops* and *West Nepal Adventures*, Hattisar, T222706, February-March and October-November are the best months.

Golf The 18 hole *Royal Nepal Golf Club*, T472836, is next to the airport and is the country's only major golf course. Temporary members, any handicap, are welcome. 1 month membership costs around Rs 2,500, but can take 2 or 3 days to arrange. Club hire costs Rs 500 per day. Alternatively, a 1 day visitor can pay about US$40 which includes temporary membership, clubs, balls and caddy. Facilities include a small club house with bar, changing room and showers. The course is frequented by numerous monkeys from the nearby Pashupatinath Temple with a propensity for making off with flags and balls. Ongoing plans exist to build a new 18 hole course on the other side of the airport.

There is also a new 9 hole course in **Tansen**, between Pokhara and the Indian border town of Sunauli. Tansen T(075) 20183, Kathmandu T228506. Temporary membership and equipment available, rates negotiable.

Rafting
See the Rafting section, page 391

Rafting and kayaking along Nepal's rivers is becoming increasingly popular. There are now over 100 rafting tour operators, but no effective regulatory body to ensure safety standards which makes it important to choose one that can demonstrate a practical (rather than merely rhetorical) commitment to safety. Also, check that your travel insurance covers you for rafting – this insurance was not available in Nepal in 1997. Some operators hold regular informative and entertaining slide shows in central Thamel to whet the appetite. These provide a good opportunity to ask questions. **NB** Try to read between the lines of the publicity blurb: the ultimate adventure for some may be a complete nightmare for others.

Squash *Dynasty Plaza Woodlands Hotel* on Durbar Marg.

Swimming The *National Stadium* at Tripureshwar has a large pool, open daily except Sunday for

Ayurvedic medicine

Ayurveda (science of life/health) is the ancient Hindu system of medicine – a naturalistic system depending on diagnosis of the body's 'humours' (wind, mucous, gall and, sometimes, blood) to achieve a balance. In the early form, gods and demons were associated with cure and ailment; treatment was carried out by using herbs, minerals, formic acid (from

ant hills) and water, and hence was limited in scope. Ayurveda classified substances and chemical compounds in the theory of panchabhutas or five 'elements'. It also noted the action of food and drugs on the human body. Ayurvedic massage using aromatic and medicinal oils to tone up the nervous system has been practised for centuries.

members (temporary membership is available – enquire) and guests, Monday, women only, open 1000-1230 and 1330-1600 daily (Friday opens at 0830), Rs 30 women, Rs 35 men. There is also a large public pool by the *Balaju Water Garden*, formerly the Royal family's private pool, northwest of the ring road, open 1000-1600 daily, Rs 20, modest swimming costumes recommended. The *Yak and Yeti*, *Everest*, *Narayan* and *Soaltee Holiday Inn* hotels all have private pools which are open to non-residents on payment of a fee.

See the Trekking section.

Trekking

Yoga is concerned with systems of meditation that can lead ultimately to release from the cycle of rebirth. Several establishments in and around Kathmandu offer meditation courses and retreats that are suitable for Westerners. The *Kopan Monastery*, beautifully set in quiet surroundings about 3 kilometres north of Bodhnath, is a popular centre for short residential courses giving a theoretical and practical introduction to the Tibetan Mahayana tradition of Buddhist philosophy. These combine lectures with meditation practice and informal discussion groups, and are jointly led by Tibetans and Westerners. Some retreats are silent and some involve fasting. Courses and retreats are generally of 7 to 10 days' duration, but visitors are also welcome to come for the day. Also an annual 1 month meditation course, suitable for beginners. Accommodation is simple, but clean. Bring a sleeping bag, blanket and warm clothes for the winter. **NB** Courses and retreats are not restricted to Buddhists – practising Christians also attend and can adapt techniques to their own beliefs (see also any of the outstanding and eminently readable books by William Johnson, an Irish Jesuit priest living in Japan). Early booking is usually essential. PO Box 817, Kathmandu (T226717, F290742, franz@komonpc.mos.com.np). Accommodation and short courses also available at its affiliated *Gaden Yiga Chozin Guest House*, Lakeside, Pokhara. See also under **Bodhnath**.

Yoga, meditation & spiritual retreats

The *Himalayan Yogic Institute* is affiliated to Kopan and also offers short courses. Baluwatar, Kathmandu (T413094). The *Kathmandu Buddhist Centre* holds talks and courses in Thamel and Patan (PO Box 5336, Kathmandu). Retreats and organized meditation at the *Osho Tapoban Retreat Centre*, north of Balaju, T271385. Yogic meditation classes and courses at *Patanjali Yoga Centre*, near Swayambhu, T272321, F229459. Also, the *Vipasana Centre*, Kantipath, T225237. Classes at *Yoga House*, T417900. The *Holistic Yoga Ashram*, T419334, near the *Hotel Star*, 400 metres south of the *Kathmandu Guest House*, conducts classes and also does reflexology, acupressure, etc.

Yoga, meditation and **ayurvedic** therapies (see above) are combined at *Himalayan Herbs*, Tangal Durbar, T413462, F418515. The *Arogya Niwas Clinic*, T249227, F249475, goes several steps further and incorporates astrology, gem and magnet therapy and even 'tele-therapy' in its catch all approach. **NB** From the perspective of some in Western science, quackery has been a prominent characteristic of ayurvedic practice, but with the resurgent popularity of herbal and homeopathic remedies in the West, ayurveda is also enjoying increased acceptance. Many now appreciate it as complementary, though not an automatic substitute, to 'Western' medicine. You can get ayurvedic preparations at any of the numerous ayurvedic pharmacies throughout the city. Some also sell English language herbal formularies and diagnosis/treatment manuals.

Local transport

Five main highways converge on Kathmandu: the Tribhuvan Raj Path linking Kathmandu with Birgunj and Raxaul Bazaar at the Indian border (200 kilometres); the Arniko Highway linking Kathmandu with Kodari on the Tibet border (114 kilometres); the Prithvi Highway linking Kathmandu and Pokhara (206 kilometres); the Mahendra Highway covering the Terai from east to west (1,000 kilometres); and the Kathmandu city Ring Road built by the Chinese in 1975 (32 kilometres).

Auto-rickshaws These also have meters which they should use and are a good way of getting around the narrow streets and alleys of the city. They are more manoeuvrable than cars and can often squeeze through impossible gaps in Kathmandu's traffic jams. The meter starts at Rs 1.50 and increases by 50p for each 50 metres. Fares are highly negotiable, but should be fixed before starting the journey if not using the meter. A long trip across town costs about Rs 50 by meter, with a journey from Thamel to the airport roughly the same. Prices rise sharply in wet weather and late at night.

Bus Local buses are cheap but very crowded and do not allow good views of the journey.
Last buses leave at There is little point in taking a bus within Kathmandu, as most parts of the city are eas-
about 2000. Fares are ily accessible on foot. To **Patan**, **Bhaktapur**, **Dhulikhel**, **Kirtipur** and other parts of the
cheap; to Bhaktapur Rs valley, buses leave from the City Bus Park and from Shahid Gate. Regular departures
10, and to Patan Rs 4. from 0600 and throughout the day. Buses leave when they are full. **Trolley buses:** An intriguing cross between a bus and a tram, link Kathmandu with Bhaktapur. Their slow journey begins near the National Stadium at Tripureshwar.

Car hire Car hire is available in Kathmandu. Most come with a driver. Private car hire can be expensive – upwards of US$50 per day, and it is usually cheaper to hire a taxi for the day. If you do this, negotiate with the taxi driver in advance, explaining where you want to go and for how long you want the vehicle. There are official government set rates for certain routes and distances which the driver will show, but with discussion these can be substantially reduced.

Cycle & Available from numerous points in Thamel and elsewhere. Prices are always negotia-
motorcycle hire ble, but increase in peak season. You can get a very basic and old bike for about Rs 30 a
Check tyres, pump, day; this increases to about Rs 90 for a mountain bike. Deposit not usually required.
gears, lock, etc before **Motorcycle hire**: from Rs 400 to Rs 600 per day. Japanese and Indian models avail-
setting off. able, including the excellent Indian made Enfield. You should carry your international driving licence with you. **NB** Make sure that your travel insurance covers you for motorcycling, liability, etc. This is not available locally.

There are several private hire companies in Kathmandu offering a variety of vehicles from the Indian made Premier (similar to an ancient Fiat) to Land Rovers and Toy-
ota Land Cruisers. Book through your hotel or direct. They include Prajapati Transport
Services, Bhagawan Bahal, T424692, and Transportation Mediator Services, Kamaladi,
T610220, F220161.

Cycle rickshaws An interesting way to cover short distances. Fares are negotiable, but should always be fixed **before** setting off. Rates are generally Rs 3 per kilometre, but rickshaw wallahs have become accustomed to extracting considerably more from tourists, particularly if the journey starts or ends in Thamel. Some may find it an uncomfortable means of transport. An annual rickshaw race through the streets of Kathmandu provides much amusement for participants and onlookers alike, and allows the winner to proudly paint 'Rickshaw Wallah of the Year' on his vehicle!

Kathmandu has numerous taxi companies, although there is little to differentiate **Taxis** between any of them. They will go anywhere in the city as well as to Patan, Bhaktapur and elsewhere in the valley. They are supposed to use the meter at all times, but if you are going a longer distance it is usually possible to negotiate a fixed rate before setting off. In early 1999 the meter started at Rs 7 with an additional Rs 2 for each 200 metres. Radio controlled taxi companies are beginning to make an appearance in Kathmandu and include Dial-a-Cab (T417978) and Kathmandu Yellow Cabs (T420987). Fares increase dramatically after 2230 and when it is raining, and it can be difficult to find a taxi after midnight. A long trip across town costs in the region of Rs 80, while from Thamel to the airport (but **not** vice versa, see **Airport** section, below) is about Rs 100.

Long distance connections

Kathmandu is the centre of Nepal's air transport system which essentially consists of a **Air** hub and spoke operation mainly from the capital. It has the country's only international airport and is the base for most domestic operations.

Airport Although it is standard procedure for almost every airline in the world to overbook their flights, both RNAC and Indian Airlines as well as Nepal's domestic airlines are renowned for taking this practice well beyond the bounds of reason. This can be especially problematic during peak tourist seasons, so it is advisable to re-confirm your flight at least once and preferably twice. It has been reported that some out-stations will not confirm a flight on a busy route unless it has already been done in Kathmandu, an absurd situation that can leave you the only option of travelling by road or waiting for the next available flight. Check the current situation with a good travel agency before leaving Kathmandu. Check-in times for domestic flights are 1 hour, and 2 hours for international departures.

Auto-rickshaws are not supposed to drive right up to the airport terminal entrance, but a minute's walk to the right after you leave either terminal will take you to an auto-rickshaw pick up point where you can get to central Thamel and elsewhere for less than half of the normal taxi fare. Agree a price before leaving or insist on the meter being used.

On arrival: there are separate queues for those with and without **visas**. Visa forms are available here and the fee is payable at the counter. **NB** Only US dollars are accepted. Ironically, the 'Without Visa' queue can be quicker than that for those who already hold a visa.

If you have a new passport but already hold a valid visa in your old one, you can get it transferred. Both passports will have to be surrendered and an official receipt given. After the inevitable form filling and payment of US$1, it will be ready at the Immigration Office in Baneshwar the following day. **NB** Be sure to change money at the bank counter in the immigration hall before surrendering your passport.

Departure formalities: are relatively straightforward. Before checking-in for Royal Nepal Airlines flights, the **departure tax** (Rs 600 within South Asia, Rs 700 for all other destinations) must be paid for which two coupons are issued, one of which is retained at check-in. (Official figures show that revenues from this tax constituted the 15th highest single source of government receipts in 1994!) For other airlines, this tax is payed at the check-in counter itself. Some baggage handlers have been known to ask for a tip after you have checked in. An embarkation form is required to be filled out and this is handed to the immigration official when entering the departure lounge. For security reasons you usually have to identify your checked-in luggage before boarding the aircraft, either behind the check-in counters or beside the aircraft.

Your airline ticket

*On your flight coupon, the 'Status' box should read '**OK**' if you are booked on that sector. '**RQ**', meanwhile, indicates that you are on a wait list ('**WL**') for the flight, but have no reservation. '**RR1**' on a computer print-out of your reservation means that you have reconfirmed. The airline or travel agency should **stamp** the coupon once you have reconfirmed. Although in practice dollar fares are usually given priority, it has become standard practice for those desperate to get on a fully booked flight to pay 'under the table' money to ensure a reservation, but this* *should not be left until the last minute. The amount payable depends on the demand for the flight and on how desperate or wealthy the person you are dealing with thinks you are. One knowledgeable travel agent in Kathmandu suggested that Rs 100 or Rs 200 is normally enough to secure a seat during off-season, while a maximum of Rs 500 may be demanded at peak times. **NB** These are neither definitive bribery rates, nor should they be used as guidelines to encourage propagation of corrupt practices.*

Duty-free: there is a small duty-free shop in the departure lounge. It stocks a limited range of alcohol, tobacco and perfumes as well as handicrafts. Prices are competitive for tobacco and alcohol, but are otherwise expensive. The shop accepts Nepalese and Indian Rupees, Sterling, US Dollars and some other major currencies. Amex, Mastercard and Visa credit cards (except those issued in India, even if printed 'Valid in India and Nepal') are also accepted. It is possible to make duty-free purchases on arrival as well as when leaving.

Banks: you can change money in the arrivals' hall where there is an efficient Nabil Bank counter. Another Nabil Bank is located in the main terminal concourse, but this has unreliable opening hours. **NB** Remember to keep the exchange certificate so that you can change back any unused money when you leave.

International 11 international airlines operate regular scheduled services to Europe and Asia. **NB** It is essential to reconfirm your return or onward flight at least 72 hours before departure (see also below).

Schedules vary slightly according to season. The following applied in 1999:
Aeroflot Russian Airlines (SU), one weekly flight to Moscow (Tupolev 154), Kamaladi, Kathmandu (T227399). *Austrian Airlines* (OS) weekly flights to Vienna (Airbus A310), Kamaladi, Kathmandu, T241470, F241506. *Biman Bangladesh Airlines* (BG), 5 flights to Dhaka per week (Fokker 27), Kamal Pokhari, Kathmandu (T434740). *China Southwest Airlines* (SZ), twice weekly services to Lhasa (Boeing 757), Kamaladi, Kathmandu (T419770, F419778). *Druk Air* (KB), twice weekly flights to Paro (Bhutan) (BAe 146), Durbar Marg, Kathmandu (T225166, F227229). *Gulf Air* (GF) twice weekly flights to Abu Dhabi (Airbus A340), Hattisar, Kathmandu. T430456, preintl@mos.com.np *Indian Airlines* (IC), daily flights to Delhi and Varanasi, 4 times a week to Calcutta (Airbus A300, A320 and Boeing 737-200), **reconfirm** your flight at the Indian Airlines/Air India office, Hattisar, Kathmandu (T419649). **Ticket sales**: at World Travels, Durbar Marg, Kathmandu (T226275, F226088). *Pakistan International Airlines* (PK), 4 flights a week to Karachi (Boeing 737), Durbar Marg, Kathmandu (T227429). *Qatar Airways* (Q7), 1 weekly flight to Doha (Boeing 727), General Sales Agent: High Mountain Tours, Durbar Marg, Kathmandu (T417812). *Royal Nepal Airlines* (RA), daily flights to Delhi, 4 times a week to Bangkok, 3 flights a week to Patna, Hong Kong, Frankfurt and Dubai, twice weekly to Calcutta, Bombay, Singapore, Shanghai, Osaka and London, and weekly flights to Paris (Boeing 757 and Boeing 727), Kantipath, Kathmandu (T220757,

Kathmandu Valley

F225348). *Singapore Airlines* (SQ), 2 flights a week to Singapore (Airbus A300), Durbar Marg, Kathmandu (T220759, F226795). *Thai Airways* (TG), 5 flights a week to Bangkok (Airbus A300), Durbar Marg, Kathmandu (T221316, F221130). *Transavia Airlines* (HV), weekly flights to Amsterdam (Boeing 757), Heritage Plaza, Kamaladi, Kathmandu. T247215, F244484.

The following fares applied for one way flights in 1999: *Bangkok* US$220. *Bombay* US$257. *Calcutta* US$96. *Dhaka* US$96. *Frankfurt* US$575. *Hong Kong* US$310. *London* US$630. *Osaka* US$500. *Paris* US$575. *Patna* US$70. *Shanghai* US$320. *Singapore* US$310. *Varanasi* US$96.

Several airlines not flying to Kathmandu also have offices or representatives here where you can make reservations, amend or confirm flights, etc.
   Air Canada, Durbar Marg (T222838). *Air France*, Durbar Marg (T223339). *Air India*, Kantipath (T211730). *British Airways*, Durbar Marg (T222266). *Burma Airways*, Durbar Marg (T224839). *Cathay Pacific*, Kamaladi (T411725). *China Airlines*, Hattisar (T412778). *Dragon Air*, Durbar Marg (T227064). *Emirates*, Kantipath (T220579). *Gulf Air*, Durbar Marg (T228288). *Japan Airlines*, Durbar Marg (T222838). *KLM*, Durbar Marg (T224895). *Korean Airlines*, Kantipath (T212080). *Kuwait Air*, Kantipath (T222884). *Lauda Air*, Hattisar (T419573). *Northwest Airlines*, Lekhnath Marg (T410089). *Philippine Airlines*, Durbar Marg (T226262). *Qantas*, Durbar Marg (T220245). *Royal Brunei Airlines*, Kamaladi (T410208). *SAS*, Kupondole (T524232); TWA, Kamaladi (T411725). *Saudia*, Kantipath (T222787). *Swiss Air*, Durbar Marg (T222452).

Domestic 3 private carriers in addition to Royal Nepal Airlines operate 'fixed wing' domestic services. All offer the popular '**Mountain Flight**', a tour of the Himalaya, from Kathmandu at US$99. All domestic fares are set by the government and are identical. Those under the age of 26 qualify for **discounts** of 25 percent; a valid passport or student identity card is required. Children under 12 years old pay 50 percent of the adult fare, and infants below 2 years pay 10 percent. **Refunds**: a 5 percent charge is made for refunds submitted more than 48 hours before departure; this increases to 10 percent up to 24 hours before and 33 percent up to 1 hour before the flight. **NB** No refunds are given after the flight has left or for lost tickets. No **airport tax** is payable on dollar fare domestic flights. On flights longer than 1 hour, a couple of the private airlines have a lucky dip with the prize of a free flight.
   (**Denotes non all weather airport, seasonal services.*)
   Necon Air (3Z), regular scheduled flights on HS748 and Cessna Caravan aircraft from Kathmandu to Bhairahawa, Biratnagar, Janakpur, Nepalgunj and Pokhara. Kalimatidole, Kathmandu (T480565, F471679, reservation@necon.mos.com.np, www.neconair.com
   Lumbini Airways, based at Bhairahawa with regular scheduled flights by Twin Otter from Kathmandu to Pokhara and Jomsom, Nepalgunji, Bhairahawa (for Lumbini), Bharatpur, Meghauli, Simara, Tumlingtar, Lukla and Phaplu. T221523, F483380, lumbini@resv.wlink.com.np
   Buddha Air (BA) has emerged as one of Nepal's favourite airlines. Operates modern Beechcraft 1900 aircraft from Kathmandu to Pokhara, Nepalgunji, Bhairahawa and Biratnagar. It claims to have the only aircraft in Nepal able to climb above the monsoon clouds allowing mountain flights even during the rainy season. T418864, F429739, buddha_air@wlink.com.np, www.nepalonline.net/buddhaair
   Cosmic Air, scheduled flights between Kathmandu and Pokhara, Jomsom, Bharatpur and Bhadrapur on Dornier 228 aircraft. T427151, F427084, soi@worldink.com.np
   Gorkha Airlines, sheduled flights from Kathmandu to Pokhara, Tumlingtar and Bharatpur on Dornier 228 aircraft. T435121, F435430, gorkha@mos.com.np,

Kathmandu Valley

www.travel-nepal.com/airline/gorkha

Yeti Airways (YA), regular scheduled flights on Twin Otter and Brasilia Embraer aircraft from Kathmandu to Pokhara, Lukla, Simra, Lamidanda, Biratnagar, Nepalgunj and Phaplu. T421147, F420766, yetiair@vishnu.ccsl.com.np

Royal Nepal Airlines (RA) Nepal's most extensive network of regular scheduled flights on HS748, Twin Otter and a Pilatus Porter aircraft from Kathmandu to Bajura, Bhadrapur, Bhairahawa, Bharatpur, Bhojpur, Biratnagar, Dang, Janakpur, Jomsom, Jumla, Lamidanda, Lukla, *Meghauli, Nepalgunj, *Phaplu, Pokhara, *Rajbiraj, Ramjatar, Simara, Surkhet, *Taplejung, Tikapur and Tumlingtar. From its smaller base at Nepalgunj, there are connections to several lowland and mountain destinations in the far west.

Reservations for Pokhara, Bharatpur and Lukla are handled by the RNAC head office on Kantipath (T220757), while the New Rd office deals with all other domestic destinations (T224497). It is easiest to book through a reliable travel agent.

The following fares applied for one way flights to selected destinations from Kathmandu in early 1997: **Bhadrapur** US$99; **Bhairahawa** US$72; **Bharatpur** US$50; **Biratnagar** US$77; **Janakpur** US$55; **Jomsom** US$110; **Lukla** US$83; **Nepalgunj** US$99; **Pokhara** US$61; **Taplejung** US$99; **Tumlingtar** US$48.

Helicopters There are several companies operating helicopters. Their great advantage lies in their adaptability which allows them to reach some of the more remote parts of the Himalaya where fixed wing aircraft are unable to land. Most companies use the sturdy Russian MI-17 helicopter which can carry up to 22 passengers. The French Ecureil machines, meanwhile, are smaller, holding just 5 passengers, but are rather more comfortable and can reach altitudes of up to 19,000 ft. Helicoptor operators are increasingly targeting the top end of the tourist market, offering tailor made group charters. This can be an excellent way for a group to arrange their own itinerary, eg for trekking or sightseeing (including Everest), particularly if you are on a tight schedule. As ever, there is room for negotiating rates, but reckon on about US$1,000 per block per hour for the MI-17, and proportionately more per person on the Ecureil. Always arrange directly with the company or through an approved, recommended broker.

Asian Airlines, regular charter flights to Everest, Lhotse and Simikot. Also ad hoc charters (MI-17), Tridevi Marg, Kathmandu (T410086, F423315). *Dynasty Aviation*, tourist charters (Ecureil), Lazimpat, Kathmandu (T414626, F414627). *Everest Air*, tourist charters, emergency flights (MI-17), Babar Mahal, Kathmandu (T477174, F228266). *Gorkha Airlines*, tourist charters (MI-17), tourist and cargo services, new Baneshwar, Kathmandu (T471136, F414102). *Himalayan Helicopters*, tourist charters mainly to Langtang, Everest, Annapurna and Lumbini (Ecureil), Durbar Marg, Kathmandu (T414596, F225150). *Karnali Air* (Ecureuil 350), has a range of set tours from an aerial trip around the Kathmandu Valley at $99 to a 4 hour visit to Everest at an absurd $749. T473141, F488288, karnaair@mos. com.np www.travel-nepal.com.karnaliair *Manakamana Airways*, tourist charters (MI-17, Bell 206), Lazimpat, Kathmandu (T416434, F420422). *Nepal Airways*, tourist charters (MI-17 and Ecureil), Lal Durbar, Naxal, Kathmandu (T420421, F411610).

Buses Tourist buses to **Pokhara** and Chitwan leave from Kantipath, opposite Grindlays Bank,

A video coach is one that shows an uninterrupted series of Bombay movies, usually at maximum volume.

all long distance Sajha government buses go from the new central bus station near Balaju. You can make reservations either at your hotel or from any of the innumerable travel agents in the city. By far the best bus service to Pokhara and Chitwan is the *Green Line* company, which has a/c buses, individual music systems and complementary refreshments. Kathmandu to Pokhara fare Rs 600, Kathmandu to Chitwan Rs 480. They leave from their private terminal on Tridevi Marg (next to the SARC building). T253885, nanglo@vishnu.ccsl.com.np The Swiss Travels bus company, on Tridevi Marg, has also been recommended. During peak seasons it is essential to book early – at least a couple of days in advance is usually enough – particularly for the more popular destinations such as Pokhara and Tadi Bazaar (Chitwan). Fares on **tourist buses** are always subject to commission, so are negotiable. Freelance baggage loaders are often loitering around the Kantipath bus stop and have been known to demand (and get) ludicrous sums from tourists for putting their bags on the roof: Rs 5 is about twice as much as a local would pay and is reasonable. **NB** Beware of pickpockets.

Buses leave either from the **New Bus Park** at Balaju, or from the **City Bus Park**, east of Ratna Park on the southern extension of Durbar Marg.

Pokhara (202 kilometres): several tourist buses run daily from Kantipath, departing at around 0700 for the 8-hour journey, Rs 200. (See also **Prithvi Highway**, page 334.) When you book, ask for a seat on the right hand side of the bus for best views. Cheaper government buses leave at the same time from the central bus station, but are slower and less comfortable than tourist buses, Rs 110. Night buses also operate from here, but miss out on the breathtaking scenery en route.

Tadi Bazaar (for Chitwan) (156 kilometres) Also served by tourist buses leaving the Kantipath stop at about 0700. The 8-hour journey goes through Mugling and Narayanghat and costs Rs 175.

The following destinations are all served by Sajha government buses departing from the new central bus station near Balaju. **Biratnagar** (541 kilometres): mid-afternoon departure, 16 hours, Rs 275. **Birganj** (270 kilometres): early morning and night buses, 10 hours, Rs 140. **Dharan** (539 kilometres): mid-afternoon departure, 16 hours, Rs 275. **Janakpur** (375 kilometres): evening departures, 12 hours, Rs 190, a good place to break the long Kathmandu to Kakarbhitta journey. **Kakarbhitta** (610 kilometres): early afternoon departures, 18-20 gruelling hours, Rs 341. **Kodari** (114 kilometres): departures from early morning, 6 hours. **Mahendranagar** (713 kilometres): morning departures, 24 arduous hours, Rs 397. **Narayanghat** (146 kilometres): several buses leave from early to mid morning, also night buses, 8-9 hours, Rs 90. You can also take a tourist bus to Tadi Bazaar (Chitwan) and get off at Narayanghat. **Nepalganj** (531 kilometres): mid-afternoon departures, 16 hours, Rs 275. **Sunauli (Belahiya)** (282 kilometres): early morning and night buses, 9 hours, Rs 150.

Directory

There are several banks and authorized money changers in the Thamel area. Rates and commission may vary, so check if you are changing a lot of money. (The *Nepal Rastra* bank often has better rates and/or lower commission than *Grindlays*.) Bank rates are always better than those offered by hotels. You will need your passport to change money. Normal banking hours are 1000-1400 Sunday-Thursday, 1000-1230 Friday, closed Saturday. The main branch of *Grindlays Bank* is on Kantipath, with a Thamel branch, T233128, F228692, 100m south of Le Bistro restaurant, Mastercard and Visa withdrawals, telegraphic money transfer, open 1000-1600, Sunday-Friday, closed Saturday. Most of Thamel's various authorized money changers are open daily, 0800-2000. **On Kantipath:** *Nepal Bank*, T227375, Saturday 0930-1230, closed Sunday; and *Nabil Bank*, T227181. **On Durbar Marg:** *Everest Bank*, T214878. *Nepal Indosuez Bank*, T228229; and *State Bank of India*, T225326. **On New Rd:** *Nepal Bank*, T221185, is open daily, 0800-1900. *Himalayan Bank*, T224787, at Bishal Bazaar, 0800-2000 Sunday-Friday, closed Saturday. *Rastra*

Bus travel

You can ask for a particular seat at the time of booking. Many long distance buses have maximum leg room in the front row of seats behind the door. Try to avoid the back row of seats which do not recline at all. If there is a choice, ask for a 2x2 bus (ie 2 seats on either side of the aisle); if it has 2x3 seating, ask for a seat on the '2' side, and if it is a 3x3 you might think about waiting for the next 2x2. A cushion or inflatable pillow is recommended for long journeys.

Banks

Keep your exchange certificates which are required to change money back when you leave.

Kathmandu Valley

Banijya Bank, T228335, at Bishal Bazaar. **Credit cards: *American Express*,** T226172, has an office in Jamal, between Durbar Marg and Kantipath. Also deals with Amex TC enquiries and travel services. Open 0800-2000 Sunday-Friday, 0930-1600 Saturday. *Mastercard* and *Visa* are at *Alpine Travel*, T225020, on Durbar Marg, 0800-2000 Sunday-Friday, 0930-1600 Saturday.

Communications

Kathmandu area code:
1 (01 if dialling from within Nepal).

Dozens of public call offices have sprung up in Thamel and throughout Kathmandu and offer international direct dialling, fax and, increasingly, email facilities. **Phone** calls from Nepal are set by the government and are expensive by international standards. In 1999, a call to **India** cost Rs 40 per minute, and Rs 180 to **Europe** and **North America**. Similar rates apply for faxing. **NB Calls are charged per minute**, not per second, so 1 min and 1 sec is charged as 2 mins – dial with care! **Telecommunications:** Nepal country code: T977. To send **email** costs about Rs 50/Kb (approx 1,000 characters), and Rs 25/page to receive. Some places accept credit cards, but a surcharge is made. You may be able to negotiate a small discount as a regular user – try the friendly and obliging *Moonlight Communications* (T424854, F426966, scenic@ccsl.com.np) quietly located near the Rainbow Guest House 200m north of Thamel Chowk. Most are open until 2230 and you can also receive calls ('callback'), at Rs 5-10 per minute. The *Central Telegraph Office* at Tripureshwar, 200m south of the GPO, has an international telephone service counter open 24 hrs and is a little cheaper than the private bureaux, but charges a minimum of 3 mins, even if answerphone. Phone calls, telex and fax messages may be sent. For international calls, T186, domestic information T197, and domestic trunk calls T186.

Internet and email: email and internet cybercentres have blossomed in Thamel. Most charge Rs 5-6 per minute for internet access. Email is an excellent way to stay in touch. If you don't already have an email address, there are several free email services available. You can easily and quickly acquire an address from anywhere in the world. Try the free Hotmail service by logging on to the internet address www.hotmail.com and follow the instructions on your screen. Even dyed-in-the-wool technophobes will find this simple.

Make sure that cards and letters are franked in your presence.

Post Offices: are open 1000-1430 Sunday-Thursday, 1000-1230 Friday, closed Saturday. **GPO:** at Sundhara, near Bhimsen Tower, open Sunday-Thursday 1000-1700, Friday 1000-1500, closed Saturday. There is a small post office in Durbar Square, often overlooked by visitors and therefore quicker. Major hotels sell stamps and have letter boxes. **Poste Restante:** at the GPO (not efficient for forwarding mail), and a philately counter. The American Express office on Jamal has a poste restante service for cardholders. **Courier and Freight Services:** *Das Worldwide Freight International*, T244097, Thamel. *DHL*, T223222, F220215, Kamaladi. *Ritual Freight*, T241842, F220842, Thamel. *Speedway Cargo*, T410595, F412679, raju@speedway.mos.com.np Thamel. *United Parcel Service* at Nepal Air Courier Express, T221588, F225915, Putali Sadak.

If using the poste restante, have your mail addressed with your surname in capitals and underlined and bring your passport for identification.

Cultural centres

Alliance Francaise, Dillibazar, Kathmandu, T410193/411076, F417694 (Postal address: c/o French Embassy, Lazimpat, PO Box 452, Kathmandu). *The British Council*, Kantipath, PO Box 640, Kathmandu, T221305/223796, F224076. *The Goethe Institut* (Germany), Ganabahal, PO Box 1103, Kathmandu, T220528, F222967. *Russian Centre of Science and Culture*, Kamalpokhari, PO Box 1433, Kathmandu, T415453/410503, F412249. *United States Information Service*, Gyaneshwore, PO Box 58, Kathmandu, T415845, F415847. Additionally, the following organization promotes Nepali culture and conducts cultural tours for visitors: *International Community Services*, Lazimpath, Kathmandu, T415353.

Embassies & consulates

Indian Visas: getting an Indian visa can be a lengthy and complicated affair. Rules and regulations can change frequently, but go early and be prepared for a week-long wait. Some nationalities may additionally require a letter of recommendation from their embassy, though exactly what this seeks to achieve is unclear. If you are about to enter India for the first time, you should have no problem in getting a tourist visa valid for 1, 3 or 6 months, but some travellers who have just left India and are applying for a new visa to return have been granted a much shorter one than they had applied for. No hard and fast rules are apparent, however, and regulations may be interpreted differently at other times and by Indian Embassies in other countries. **Chinese Visas:** in 1999, visas for Tibet (and for entry into the rest of China through Tibet) were theoretically granted only as part of a group package tour and not for individual travel. Your tour operator should arrange this and can also help with general visa enquiries.

Embassies & consulates

Australia, T411578, Bansbari

*Austria, T410891, Hattisar

Bangladesh, T414943, Maharajganj

*Belgium, T228925, Durbar Marg

*Canada, T415193, Lazimpath

China, T411740, Baluwatar

Denmark, T413010, Baluwatar

Egypt, T524844, Pulchowk, Patan

Finland, T471221, Lazimpath

France, T418034, Lazimpath

Germany, T416832, Gyaneshwar

*Greece, T233113, Tripureshwar

*Hungary, T525015, Pulchowk, Patan

India, T414990, Lainchaur

Israel, T411811, Lazimpath

Italy, T412280, Baluwatar

Japan, T226061, off Durbar Marg

South Korea, T270172, Tahachal

*Maldives, T223045, Durbar Marg

*Mexico, T412971, Pani Pokhari, Lazimpath

*Netherlands, T523444, Kumaripati, Patan

Pakistan, T411421, Pani Pokhari, Lazimpath

*Philippines, T474409, Shinamangal

*Poland, T221101, Ganabahal

Russia, T412155, Baluwatar

*Spain, T472328, Batisputali

Sri Lanka, T417406, Baluwatar

*Sweden, T220939, Kicha Pokhari

*Switzerland, T523468, Jawalakhel, Patan

Thailand, T420410, Bansbari

*Turkey, T232711, Bijuli Bazaar

United Kingdom, T411590, Lainchaur

USA, T411179, Pani Pokhari, Lazimpath.

* Consular service

Kathmandu Valley

If you fall ill, there are numerous **pharmacies** throughout Kathmandu where you can buy medicines without prescription. If you require a stool, blood or urine **test**, it is advisable to get this done at a reputable clinic. Results are usually ready the same day or by the following morning. For vaccinations, lab tests, health information and surgical or GP consultations, the **The Travel Medicine Centre (Yak & Yeti Rd, off Durbar Marg)**, has been recommended, T228531, F224675, advice@ciwecpc.mos.com.np www.bena.com.ciwec **Himalayan International Clinic**, T225455, F220143, is in Chhetrapati; the **Mt Everest International Clinic**, T421540, F412728, is 400m west of the Immigration Office in Thamel; and the **Synergy International Clinic**, T415836, is tucked away opposite the Excelsior Hotel in central Thamel. These are private clinics aiming to provide Western standards of care and travel medicine.

Government hospitals include the *Bir Hospital*, T221988, on Kantipath near the Tundikhel; the Japanese assisted *Teaching Hospital*, T412303, and the *Kanti Hospital*, T411550, are both in Maharajaganj.

If you fall sick whilst **trekking** and require evacuation, the **Himalayan Rescue Association** (T416828) can advise on helicopter rescue. This is expensive and requires proof of sufficient insurance or a written guarantee of full payment.

Hospitals & medical services
Remember to keep receipts for insurance claims

The **National Library** houses a collection of about 70,000 books, many in English but with a small and useful Sanskrit section. It is situated in Pulchowk, Patan (T521322). ■ *Sunday-Friday, 1000-1700*. The **National Archives** on Ramshah Path and the smaller **Asa Archives** (*Asa Saphu Kuthi*), T223817, at Kulambhulu in the city's western suburbs have scholarly collections of historical manuscripts in Sanskrit, Nepali and other regional languages. Elsewhere, the **Nepal Bharat Sanskritik Kendra** in the RNAC Building is on New Rd, and the imaginatively named **Book Library** is on Ramshah Path. The **Keshar Library** (see page 209), in the HMG Ministry of Education premises on the corner of Kantipath and Tridevi Marg, is more of a museum than a library, but is definitely worth a visit. The **SAARC** headquarters on Tridevi Marg has a small library, containing reference materials and newspapers from the seven SAARC countries. You can also buy SAARC publications from here. Temporary membership may be available at some of the foreign cultural centre libraries, see below.

Libraries

Places of worship
There are few **churches** in Kathmandu. Catholics can attend Mass at St Xavier's School in Jawalakhel, Patan, and at the Hotel de l'Annapurna on Durbar Marg. There is a Protestant church on Ramshah Path. For further information on Evangelical services, contact the Evangelical Christian Alliance of Nepal, PO Box 3230, Kathmandu, T522267, or the Foursquare Gospel Church, T525303. Two **mosques** (*masjid*) are located half way along Durbar Marg, to the west of Rani Pokhari, near the clock tower and the Bhothahiti/Bagh Bazaar crossing. There are no **synagogues** in Kathmandu.

Tour companies & travel agents
Check all tickets, travel documents, etc, carefully

Many agencies in *Thamel. Tiger Mountain*, T411225, F414075, www.tigermountain.com operate some of the best (and more expensive) hotels and lodges throughout the country. They also have hiking and rafting companies. *Wayfarers*, T229110, F245875, wayfarer@mos.com.np 50m south of Le Bistro restaurant is efficient, trendy and good for advice, with a branch in Pokhara. Recommended. Credit cards accepted.

Many quality agencies on **Durbar Marg**. *Adventure Travel*, T223328. *Everest Express*, T220759, F226795. *Himalayan Travels*, T223045, F224001. *Karthak*, T227223. *Modern Travels*, near Yak and Yeti Hotel, T244357, F242388. *Natraj*, Ghantaghar, T222014. *President*, T220245, F221180, a first class travel service. Recommended. *Shambhala*, T225166, F227229, specialists in Bhutan. *Team Tours*, T227057, F243561. *Wonderland*, near Yak and Yeti Hotel, T244643, F231116. *World Travels*, for Indian Airlines reservations, T226275, F226088. *Yeti*, T221234.

Tridevi Marg: *Sita World Travel*, T418363, F227557, sitaktm@sitanep.mos.com.np *Swiss Travels*, T412964, F423336, has branch in Pokhara. *Tibet Travel and Tours*, T231130, F228986, leaders in Tibet tours, all arrangements made. Recommended.

Elsewhere: *Everest*, Ganga Path, T222217, F249896 (Kantipath T249216). *Holy Land Travels*, Bodhnath, T479019, F478592. *Kathmandu Travel and Tours*, Tripureshwar, T222511, F471379. *Marco Polo*, Kamal Pokharai, T414192. *Namaste*, Maitighar, Ramsha Path, T227484, F226590. *Nepal Travel Agency*, Ramshah Path, T413188, F420203. *Paramount Nepal Tours*, Lazimpath, T/F415078. *Pashupati Travels*, Kantipath, T248598, F224695.

NB Making reservations on *Indian Airlines* is best done early and in Kathmandu, as there is no Indian Airlines office outside Kathmandu.

Numerous other travel agents on Durbar Marg, Thamel and Kantipath where you might find very competitive rates. Half day tours to city and surroundings, and overnight trips to Dhulikhel. (See also **Trekking** section for specialist trekking operators.)

National Parks and 'Jungle Safari': packages to **Chitwan** and **Bardia** National Parks and to **Koshi Tappu** Wildlife Reserve are offered by almost every tour operator and travel agent in Kathmandu. At Chitwan, the lodges **inside** the park mostly offer 5-star accommodation in 'jungle style' buildings, while all the mid range and budget accommodation is concentrated in the village of Sauraha just **outside** the park boundary. Chitwan is also the most developed for tourism with Bardia a distant though preferable second. It is possible to combine a visit to both with a rafting trip down the Trisuli or Karnali rivers. Most packages are for either 2 or 3 nights duration. Compare packages and check what is and what is not included, eg transport (from Kathmandu or from Tadi Bazaar), food, park entry (Rs 650), elephant rides (Rs 650), etc. It is best to book directly with the tour operator rather than through an agent. **NB** If you are going to stay in Sauraha, you do not have to go as part of an organized tour. It may be cheaper, if marginally less convenient, to make your own arrangements.

Chitwan: (*Inside the park*): *Chitwan Jungle Lodge*, T440918, F228349, Durbar Marg; *Island Jungle Resort*, T226002, F223184, Durbar Marg; *Gaida Wildlife Jungle Camp*, T220940, F227292, Durbar Marg; *Machan Wildlife Resort*, T225001, F220475, Durbar Marg; *Tiger Tops*, T222706, F412920, Durbar Marg. **Chitwan** (*Sauraha, outside the park*): *Alka Resort Camp*, T224771. *Hermitage*, T/F424390, Tridevi Marg, near Immigration Office. *Jungle Camp*, T/F222132, Thamel. *Rainforest Guest House*, T60235. *Rhino Lodge*, T420316, F417146, Thamel. *Royal Park*, T229028, F412987, Thamel. **Bardia National Park**: *Tiger Tops* (see above), *Bardia Jungle Lodge*, T417395, F229459. *Forest Hideaway*, T423586, F226763, Thamel. **Koshi Tappu Wildlife Reserve**: *Koshi Tappu Wildlife Camp*, T226130, F224237, Kamaladi. **Sukla Phanta Wildlife Reserve**: *Silent Safari*, T520523, F536941.

Tourist offices
There are two government **tourist information offices** in Kathmandu, one at the airport (T470537), the other just off Basantpur Square (T220818). Open 0900-1700 Sunday-Thursday, 0900-1500 Friday, closed Saturday. They have free brochure handouts and maps, but are otherwise largely ineffectual. The Department of Tourism headquarters (T523692) is situated behind the National Stadium in Tripureshwar and also has a supply of leaflets. Open

Kathmandu Valley

Sunday-Thursday 1100-1600, Friday 1100-1500, Saturday closed.

There are a number of free **magazines** for tourists which carry interesting articles on various aspects of Nepali life as well as maps and compendious lists of useful and useless phone numbers. Titles include *Adventure Nepal, Image Nepal, Nepal Visitor* and *Travellers Nepal* and are available at the airport and in good travel agents.

Noticeboards at various locations in Thamel are a good way to find out about any special events, as well as courses (eg language, yoga, massage), lost and found, travel companions wanted, trekking gear for sale, etc.

Officially registered **tourist guides** can be hired, rates start from US$5 for half a day. *Himalayan Rescue Association (HRA)*: a non profit organization promoting safety in trekking and mountaineering. The HRA office is 100m west of the Immigration Office on Tridevi Marg (T419755). Open 1000-1700, Sunday-Friday, closed Saturday. Knowledgeable and friendly staff can provide practical advice on most aspects of trekking. Regular talks are held on the avoidance and treatment of Acute Mountain Sickness (altitude sickness). The office also has useful reading material related to the Himalaya, and a useful and informative notice board. Recommended. *Kathmandu Environmental Education Programme (KEEP)*: this excellent organization was established to promote awareness of environmental problems facing the Himalaya and to reduce the negative impact of tourism on their ecology and culture through education and by maintaining a high profile for its wider agenda of conservation and development. Its publications include the informative *Himalayan First Aid Manual* and *Trekking Gently in the Himalaya*, both of which are recommended reading for all trekkers. There is a small library and regular presentations, video and slide shows are held at its office and travellers' information centre is located on Bhagawan Bahal in the eastern part of Thamel, PO Box 9178, Tridevi Marg, Kathmandu, T410303, F411533, grt@greatpc.mos.com.np In the UK, contact KEEP (UK), 3 Bangor Rd, Holywood, Co Down, Northern Ireland B18 0NT. *Himalaya Dog Rescue Squad*: supported by British, Dutch and German volunteers, use German Shepherd dogs to assist in searching for lost trekkers. T/F371066, Shanti Marg, Bansbari. *Himalayan Explorers Club*: small organization aiming to provide travel assistance. It also helps co-ordinate a *Home Stay Programme* for visitors wishing to stay with a Nepali family. Prices from US$40 per week. Office in the KEEP premises, T424698, tour@keep.wlink.com.np In USA, call *Helping Hands*, T303-4494279.

Useful addresses

Aid and Development Agencies: Nepal is one of the world's highest per capita recipients of aid and there are numerous foreign funded NGOs (Non Governmental Organizations) working in Nepal running social, agricultural, medical, education and training projects as well as organizations and firms engaged in construction and technological development. There are also many thousands of small Nepalese NGOs throughout the country whose work does not depend on foreign contributions. **Volunteering:** NGOs generally have enough staff to cover the work they do, but some organizations may appreciate help, either skilled or general, at certain times. If you want to spend a length of time volunteering, it is best to get in touch with the organization before you set off for Nepal and find out about visa requirements, costs, living conditions, language, etc. **NB** In recent years, a small number of NGOs in Nepal have been used as a front for decidedly non charitable activities or have otherwise abused their status for financial or political gain. This has resulted in NGOs being widely perceived with suspicion and having to operate in a sensitive and highly politicized context. Also, the activities of religious (especially non Hindu/Buddhist) organizations are monitored closely and the entry into Nepal of foreign religious organizations is strictly regulated.

There are a number of publications available in bookshops and public libraries in Europe and North America with up to date lists of organizations working in Nepal. The following is a selection of some NGOs which may be of interest. Most of these are the head office addresses who can help with enquiries; many of the project sites may be located in remote areas.

Action Aid, PO Box 3198, Lazimpath, Kathmandu, F419718. Various aid and development projects. *Amnesty International*, PO Box 135, Bagbazaar, Kathmandu, F225489. Works on behalf of political prisoners. *Ananda Kuti Vihar Trust*, PO Box 3007, Swayambhu, Kathmandu, promotes Buddhism and Buddhist education. *Arniko Society*, Maitighar, Kathmandu, Alumni society of China returnees. *Biodiversity Conservation Project*, PO Box 3923, Kathmandu. Crocodile conservation in Chitwan National Park. *Bouddha TB Control and Primary Health Care Project*, PO Box 1313, Bouddha Tusal, Kathmandu. TB and primary health care in the Tibetan community. *Britain Nepal Medical Trust*, PO Box 9, Biratnagar 16. Medical research and field work. *Canadian Centre for*

International Studies and Co-operation, PO Box 4574, Lazimpath, Kathmandu, F410422. Supports community development programmes. *Care International in Nepal*, PO Box 1661, Krishnagalli, Pulchowk, Patan, F521202. Various aid and development programmes. *Centre for Rural Technology*, PO Box 3628, Tripureshwar, Kathmandu, F225212. Promotes appropriate rural technology through education. *Child Workers in Nepal Concerned Centre*, PO Box 4374, Kalimati, Kathmandu, F224466. Child rights activists, research, training, education and development programmes. *Development Communication Production*, PO Box 1230, c/o INC Sanepa, Patan. Produces health education materials. *Dilaram House*, PO Box 1119, Kathmandu. Assists Western travellers with drug addiction, mental breakdown and loneliness. *Environment and Public Health Organization*, PO Box 4102, Jayabageshwari, Kathmandu, F474946. Water studies, quality testing, air pollution studies. *Green Energy Mission Nepal*, PO Box 10647, Ghattekulo Anam Nagar, Kathmandu, F410857. Research and development of natural resources as substitute for fossil fuel. *Institute for Sustainable Development*, PO Box 4006, Pulchowk, Patan, F26467. Research and information. *Kathmandu Environmental Education Project (KEEP)*, PO Box 9178, Thamel, Kathmandu. Himalayan environmental and education programmes. *King Mahendra Trust for Nature Conservation*, PO Box 3712, Jawalakhel, Patan, F526570. Nature conservation and development. *Mothers' Club Central Committee*, PO Box 2463, Kathmandu. Women's development, including maternity and child care, family planning, literacy programmes. *Natural History Society of Nepal*, Rampur Campus, Chitwan, botanical and biogeographical research. *Nepal Agroforestry Foundation*, PO Box 916, Kathmandu, F222026. Aims to reduce deforestation by promoting agroforestry. *Nepal Heritage Society*, PO Box 1041, Bhadrakali, Kathmandu. Promotes conservation of Nepali culture. *Nepal Red Cross Society*, PO Box 217, Kalimati, Kathmandu, F271915. Aid and development projects. *Nepal Water for Health (Wateraid)*, PO Box 4321, Thapathali, Kathmandu, F227730. Water and hydrology projects. *Oxfam Nepal*, PO Box 2500, Lagankhel, Patan, F525620. Aid and development projects. *Seto Surans Community Child Development Centre*, PO Box 4103, Jhamsikhel, Patan. Early child care and education programmes for under-privileged children. *SOS Children's Village*, PO Box 757, Sanothimi, Bhaktapur, F612091. Children's education and development. *Unicef*, Lekhnath Marg, Kathmandu. Child education. *World Education*, PO Box 937, Bhagawati Bahal, Kathmandu. Literacy projects. *World Neighbours*, PO Box 916, Bishalnagar, Kathmandu. Healthcare, self-sufficiency programmes. *Worldview Nepal*, PO Box 2912, Kalikasthan, Dillibazaar, Kathmandu, F225915. Promotes indigenous technologies encouraging sustainable use of natural resources. For further information about these and other NGOs, contact the *Social Welfare Council*, Lekhnath Marg, Kathmandu, T418111, F410279. A booklet, NGO Profile, listing the activities and contact addresses of 42 NGOs is published by IUCN and USAID, and is available from the KEEP office in Thamel.

Emergency Phone Numbers: Emergency: T100. **Police:** T216999. **Tourist Police:** (Babar Mahal) T211293. **Fire:** T221177. **Ambulance:** Bishal Bazaar T211121. **Nepal Chamber:** T230213. Bhimsenthan T211959. **Red Cross:** (Brikhuti Mandap) T228094.

Government Offices: *Dept of Tourism*, Babar Mahal, T223581. *Immigration Office*, Tridevi Marg, T412337. *Kathmandu Municipality*, Dharma Path, T221280. *Ministry of Tourism and Civil Aviation*, Singha Durbar, T211286.

Miscellaneous: *Cargo Agents Association of Nepal*, Thamel, T419019. *Central Carpet Industries Association*, Kamal Pokhari, T413135. *Handicraft Association of Nepal*, Thapathali, T212567. *Himalayan Rescue Association*, Tridevi Marg, T418755. *Hotel Association of Nepal*, Thamel, T412705. *Kathmandu Environmental Education Programme*, Thamel, T410303. *Nepal Association of Fine Arts*, Naxal, T411729. *Nepal Association of Rafting Agents*, Kamaladi, T221197. *Nepal Association of Travel Agents*, Naxal, T411764. *Nepal Chamber of Commerce*, Gangapath, T228733. *Nepal Mountaineering Association*, Hattisar, Naxal, T411525, F416278. *Sagarmatha Pollution Control Committee*, Durbar Marg, T410137. *Tourist Guide Association of Nepal*, Kamaladi, T225102. *Trekking Agents Association of Nepal*, Naxal, T419245. *UNDP Quality Tourism Project*, PO Box 107, UNDP Building, T413991.

Short walks in Kathmandu

Kathmandu is relatively small and very compact with almost endless opportunities for walks both within the city and further afield to other parts of the valley.

Royal Kathmandu Walk

Allow 2½ hours This triangular walk starts and finishes at **Durbar Square** and takes you past **Singha Durbar** and Narayan Hiti, the **Royal Palace**.

South of **Hanuman Dhoka**, the old Royal Palace, you enter **Basantpur Square** where every type of handicraft made by the Kathmandu Valley's artisans is sold in a vast market area. **Jhocchen** (**Freak Street**), the road named after some of the more outlandish travellers of the hippie generation, leads off the square to the southeast. In contrast, **New Road** (Juddha Sadak) proceeds to the east and, lined with fashionable stores and supermarkets, is the city's upmarket shopping area. Continue along here, passing through the large and decorative Juddha Gate (named after the man responsible for rebuilding this district after the 1934 earthquake) to the end where the road meets **Kantipath**,

Kathmandu walks

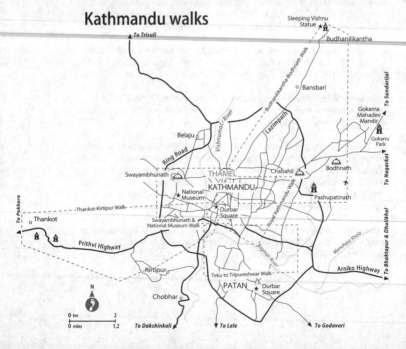

with the green expanse of the **Tundikhel** opposite. This is used by the army for drill and physical exercise in the mornings. Turn right (south) down Kantipath, then left (east). You pass the **Martyr's Gate** in a roundabout on **Prithvipath**. Continue along here for 200 metres and you arrive at the crossing with **Ramshahpath**. Opposite is **Singha Durbar**, the magnificent former Rana palace, now headquarters to several government departments and the site of the **Supreme Court**. You can wander around the grounds and if you can manage to get inside, you can get a taste of this palace's former splendour.

Proceed north along the busy Ramshahpath. The first major crossroads you reach is that of **Bagh Bazaar** to your left and **Dilli Bazaar** on your right which leads eventually to the airport. Both are busy market areas where traditional life thrives. Continuing north through the **Kamaladi** and **Kamal Pokhari** areas and along **Hattisar**, the road meets the eastern continuation of Tridevi Marg. Turn left (west) and, after five minutes, you reach **Narayan Hiti**, the Royal Palace. The modern palace you can see from the southern side was built for the wedding of the present king, while the name of the complex comes from a small spring in the western part of the grounds. (If you walk a little further west, at the junction of Tridevi and Durbar Margs is the **Keshar Library**, in the HMG Ministry of Education complex. The trees lining either side of

Kathmandu

Royal Kathmandu Walk

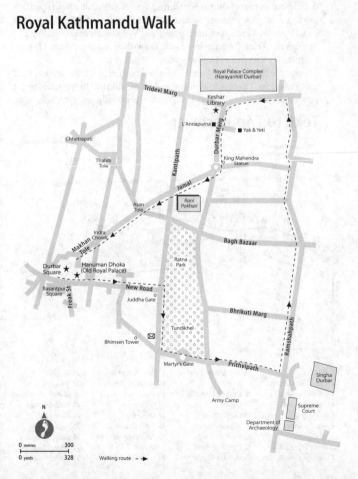

Kantipath, to the west of the Royal Palace, are home to thousands of giant bats, an unusually impressive sight.) Returning to the southern entrance of the Royal Palace, turn right (south) down **Durbar Marg**, where there are several opportunities for a good tea break. At the first roundabout where an imposing statue of King Mahendra stands tall, turn right (southwest) along **Jamal Road**. Continue in a southwest direction along this road. On your left is **Rani Pokhari**. Cross **Kantipath**. This is the ancient trading route and oldest artery of the city (leading to/from the **Kasthamandap**). You then pass through the **Asan** and **Indra Chowk** market areas with numerous small temples, stupas and shrines on either side of the road. Just beyond Indra Chowk, you enter Durbar Square from the northeast, with the magnificent Taleju Mandir ahead of you.

Teku to Tripurshwar – Southwest Kathmandu

The northern bank of the **Bagmati River** has not featured prominently in tourist guides of the city and is overlooked by many visitors, but a host of temples, shrines, relics and other monuments line its length, a reflection of the river's traditional importance and sacredness. Unfortunately, the area is very run down and little effort appears to have been made to prevent its further decline, but if a tour of Durbar Square has not resulted in cultural overload, it is worth a stroll along the approximately two kilometres of narrow lanes and paths from the junction of the Bagmati and Vishnumati rivers heading east through the **Teku**, **Tripureshwar** and **Thapathali** localities where life contrasts starkly with that of Durbar Square.

From the **Kasthamandap** in the southwest corner of Durbar Square, head south (downhill) along **Chikamugal** and follow this road through two major crossroads, for as far as you can go. You will eventually reach the **Teku** area,

Teku to Tripureshwar

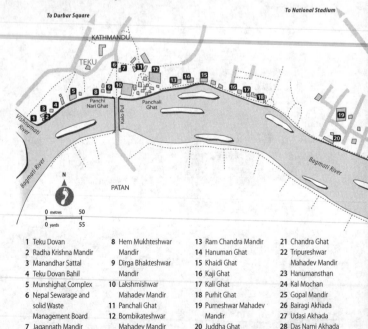

1 Teku Dovan	8 Hem Mukhteshwar	13 Ram Chandra Mandir	21 Chandra Ghat
2 Radha Krishna Mandir	Mandir	14 Hanuman Ghat	22 Tripureshwar
3 Manandhar Sattal	9 Dirga Bhakteshwar	15 Khaidi Ghat	Mahadev Mandir
4 Teku Dovan Bahil	Mandir	16 Kaji Ghat	23 Hanumansthan
5 Munshighat Complex	10 Lakshmishwar	17 Kali Ghat	24 Kal Mochan
6 Nepal Sewerage and	Mahadev Mandir	18 Purhit Ghat	25 Gopal Mandir
solid Waste	11 Panchali Ghat	19 Purneshwar Mahadev	26 Bairagi Akhada
Management Board	12 Bombikateshwar	Mandir	27 Udasi Akhada
7 Jagannath Mandir	Mahadev Mandir	20 Juddha Ghat	28 Das Nami Akhada

and the following description goes from west to east starting at Teku Dovan, the point where the Bagmati and Vishnumati rivers join.

Teku Dovan (1) This junction of two holy rivers is regarded as an especially sacred place by both Hindus and Buddhists, and is known as *Chitamani Thirtha* by the latter. Several small shrines and statues of Hindu deities stand attractively alongside Buddhist stupas and chaityas. Cremation ghats line the riverbank and it is said that some Malla kings were cremated here. As you approach from the north, you pass three sattals, or pilgrim rest houses, freely decorated with more images, including those of Bhairava, Ganesh, Harihar, Mahadev and Surya.

Radha Krishna Mandir (2) Heading northeast along the riverbank, this shikhara design Vishnu temple was built in 1937, but lack of maintenance makes it look older. It is, nonetheless, interesting and is surrounded by numerous objects of religious significance including, in front of the main entrance, a Garuda pillar from which the eponymous deity has taken flight. The temple itself is built of terracotta and stands on a four-stage plinth. Four images of Vishnu are placed around the base of the shikhara, while beneath, images of Rukmani and Subhadra flank the flute-playing Krishna in the temple's sanctum.

Immediately north of the temple, the larger **Manandhar Sattal (3)** is named after a wealthy 19th century trader, Subbha Ganesh Das Manandhar who, by a twist of fate, was to spend his final days here in relative poverty after the majority of his wealth was 'confiscated' by the then Rana prime minister. The modern building next door is an electric crematorium established in 1971 during the panchayat years, but has remained unused since its construction.

Just to the east is a small monastery, the **Teku Dovan Bahil (4)**, dating from the Second World War and surrounded by recently added chaityas.

Munshighat Complex (5) Moving on, this complex consists of a temple, sattal and cremation ghat. The ghat is used by the Karanjits and is overlooked by the small sattal. The Lakshmi Bhakteshwar Mandir, located in an open courtyard on the northern side of the sattal, is architecturally uninspiring, a square brick structure surmounted by a white bell-shaped dome. To its east are another sattal and the 19th century **Rajendreshwar Mandir**.

Jagannath Mandir (7) From the Rajendreshwar Mandir, turn left and continue along this lane heading north (appropriately passing the *Nepal Sewerage and Solid Waste Management Board* (6) headquarters on your left) until you arrive at Teku's main traffic intersection. Diagonally

opposite to the right is a courtyard containing the Jagannath Mandir, one of the oldest and largest temples along this stretch of the Bagmati. The buildings to its north and east are sattals, the northern one being home to the head priest. Another, on the western side, has fallen into disrepair, but used to have a uniquely carved window depicting a hugely popular scene from the Ramayana of Krishna accompanied by a number of *gopis*, village cow-girls with whom he would cavort. An image of Vishnu as Narasimha remains in front.

The Vaishnavite temple was built in 1792 by Bhava Singh Pradhan and, though damaged in the 1934 earthquake, it has been restored to its former state. An octagonal porch is supported by 28 wooden pillars; the top third of each have decorative carvings. Inside, an image of Krishna is flanked by those of Subhadra and Balaram. Above the porch roof, four balconies are attached to the base of the brick shikhara.

Twin Temples Returning to the riverbank and continuing east you reach the twin temples of **Hem Mukhteshwar (8)** and **Dirga Bhakteshwar (9)**. These identical shrines were built by the wife of an army general in the mid-19th century and stand within a partially walled compound. Once again, lack of maintenance is leading to their steady dilapidation.

Along the riverside here is the stepped **Panchi Nari Ghat**, historically one of the Bagmati's holiest ghats where locals have traditionally taken a dip in the blessed waters during Dasain. Three nearby sattals, the earliest constructed in 1753, were built to accommodate the pilgrims, but the pollution and gradual drying of the river has led to a decline in the number of devotees.

Kalo Pul, the black coloured **suspension bridge**, links Kathmandu with Patan and was constructed in France then transported, piece by piece, to the city in 1939. On the opposite side are the hot sulphuric spring waters of the **Raj Tirtha**, another holy bathing spot.

Lakshmishwar Mahadev Mandir (10) Beyond the bridge you come to this Shaivite temple. Originally a graceful three-storeyed pagoda construction surrounded by Newari sattals, it is now one of the city's best examples of beauty in an advanced state of decay. Nevertheless, the temple is still richly endowed with finely carved windows, roof struts and doors, depicting a host of deities. An inscription dated 1813 and written by Bani Bilas, the poet laureate of the time, records that the temple and sattals were built by Lakshmi Devi, wife of King Rana Bahadur Shah. The main entrance faces west and in front of it is Nandi, the divine bull-vehicle of Shiva. Shiva's trident, meanwhile, is on the northern side of the building.

Panchali Ghat (11) This astonishing complex, a few metres walk to the east, is a rectangle barely 100 metres in length and contains nearly 100 small shrines and monuments of both Hinduism and Buddhism. A microcosm of Nepal's religious life, there are images of Vishnu (including those of his *Das Avatar*, or ten incarnations – see page 521), Shiva, and a wide variety of other Hindu deities side by side with a large statue of a seated Buddha and numerous chaityas. Most date from the 19th and early 20th centuries. On all but the southern side are sattals, the earliest built in 1795.

To the east of the complex a path heads north. Immediately beyond a sattal with carved wooden window frames is the main entrance to the **Bombikateshwar Mahadev Mandir (12)**. Built in 1850 by Bom Bahadur, appropriately an army general and the younger brother of the Rana's first prime minister, Jung Bahadur, in thanksgiving – one is tempted to surmise – for his *dada's* safe descent from the Bhimsen Tower (see page 196). It is a complex of religious buildings and monuments centred around the **Teen Dewal**, a columned temple standing on a four-stage plinth and surmounted by three shikharas. Two bells and another statue of Nandi stand at the main entrance, while more (especially Shiva) shrines and images of major deities are scattered around the complex, most installed at intervals over the last century and a half.

Other smaller temples lie between this walled compound and the river. Immediately to the south is the **Shiva Mandir** with its onion shaped dome topped by the *trishul*, or trident, of Shiva. The stocky, tower-like structure enclosed in a low slate wall to the east is the 19th century **Panchalinga Mahadev Mandir**, while the three shikhara shrines are dedicated to Balaram, Krishna and Subhadra and were built in 1827 by an army officer, Guman Singh Kharki. Following a failed robbery, the shrines' respective deities were moved to the Bombikateshwar Mandir where they still remain. To the south is the shikhara **Narayan Mandir** whose Narayan image is missing. Alongside the lane leading back towards the river, the long series of arches was built as changing rooms for pilgrims taking to the Bagmati waters.

Six Ghats Returning east along the river, you reach the **Ram Chandra Mandir (13)** and **Hanuman Ghat (14)** which includes a sattal complete with prayer bell and a bedecked statue of Hanuman standing on a covered pedestal. This typical Newari house is one of the few buildings along this stretch of the river in reasonable repair. Daily worship takes place here. The **Radha Krishna** sattal to the east gives its name to the ghat here, while, beyond, the **Khaidi Ghat (15)** (*Prisoners' Ghat*) was intended for inmates wishing to perform puja. Moving on, you come to **Kaji Ghat (16)** where there is a three-storeyed sattal and the octagonal **Krishna Mandir**, a small domed structure standing on an eight-sided, three-stage brick platform and built at the end of the 19th century. Yet again, the temple's original image has been stolen. **Kali Ghat (17)**, beyond, is named after a small Kali Mandir, while the **Purhit** (or **Aryal**) **Ghat (18)** to its east is a more interesting agglomeration of shrines, statues and religious objects. The southern sattal has a beautifully carved five-piece window on the first floor above the main entrance.

Purneshwar Mahadev Mandir (19) and **Juddha Ghat (20)** Five minutes' walk east of Purhit Ghat, a lane heads north to a walled courtyard containing the Purneshwar Mahadev Mandir. Architecturally unexceptional, it was reconstructed after the original temple on this site was destroyed in the 1934 earthquake. The fully occupied sattal on the northern side gives the place life. Like New Road, near Durbar Square, Juddha Ghat on the riverside to the south is named after Juddha Sham Sher, a Rana prime minister, who built the sattal here which is now used as a school. A small temple was installed inside the building in the 1970s and is dedicated to Saraswati, the goddess of learning and wisdom.

Chandra Ghat (21) This long brick terrace was built as a sattal a year after the end of the First World War by the then prime minister, Chandra Sham Sher Rana. Today it is used as police barracks, its occupants perhaps being beneficially influenced by the surroundings in their official duties.

Tripureshwar Mahadev Mandir (22) and **Hanumansthan (23)** A few metres to the east, the Hanumansthan is an interesting little collection of Shiva lingas together with a dominating image of the monkey god Hanuman, an Uma Maheshwar sculpture (the name given to the depiction of a peaceful Shiva with Parvati, or Uma, sitting on the holy Mount Kailash) and a couple of miniature Buddhist stupas. Dating as far back as the late Licchavi period, this is

Kathmandu Valley

the oldest existing religious site along this stretch of the Bagmati.

Take the lane leading north from here to get to the **Tripureshwar Mahadev Mandir (22)**, a three-storeyed pagoda temple and the largest in this area. Named after **Rani Lalit Tripura Sundari**, wife of Rana Bahadur Shah, who was responsible for its construction in 1822, it gives this area of Kathmandu its name, and is one of the finest examples of temple architecture from the Shah era. Several smaller monuments are scattered around the complex, including a statue of Rani Tripura, another of the bull-god Nandi, and pillars supporting a number of deities. The temple itself stands on a four-stage platform with smaller, two-roofed pagoda temples containing images of Bhagawati, Ganesh, Surya and Vishnu at each corner. A large bronze bell hangs beside the main entrance. The lower roof is tiled while the middle and top roofs are copper gilded. The *kalasha* pinnacle is gold plated. Beautifully carved roof struts depict, from top to bottom, the Matrika devis, images of Krishna, and scenes from the Mahabharata.

Kal Mochan (24) Continuing east, you cross the bridge over the small Tukucha River before reaching this temple complex, dominated by the **Jung Hiranya Hem Narayan Mandir** in the centre, the first in a series of neighbouring temple complexes between here and the Thapathali Bridge which links Kathmandu with Patan. A two-storeyed square structure surmounted by an onion shaped dome, its design demonstrates the influence of classical Mughal architecture. The deity is Vishnu in the form of Narayan and in front of the main entrance is a fine bronze statue of his faithful mount, Garuda, while a little beyond a statue of Jung Bahadur Rana, who built this temple in 1874, stands on a column looking over Garuda and into the sanctum. Fierce statues of mythical animals are placed at the four corners above the first floor. Smaller, semi-shikhara style octagonal shrines stand as if in homage to the central temple around the complex.

Gopal Mandir (25) Immediately adjacent, this Vishnu shrine has a stunted bell shaped roof and was built by one of Jung Bahadur Rana's wives.

Bairagi, Udasi and Das Nami Akhadas As if to outdo his wives, Jung Bahadur Rana himself was responsible for the construction of all three of these *akhadas*. The unusual **Bairagi (26)** sattal/temple is the first you come to and was built for Bairagi pilgrims. Near the entrance are two Bairagi tombs and the temple's onion shaped dome stands above a squat pagoda porch. Inside are bronze statues of various deities, with more outside. The **Udasi Akhada (27)** next door was renovated in 1992 and consists of a small Vishnu temple and a sattal for Udasis, followers of a sect founded by Sri Chandra, son of the founder of the Sikh faith, Guru Nanak. Finally, the neighbouring **Das Nami Akhada (28)** is the last religious building before the Thapathali Bridge. Built for followers of the Hindu saint, **Shankaracharya**, the name means 'Ten Names', a reference to the ten different surnames used by this community. Demolished in the great earthquake, it was completely rebuilt in 1935.

From here, you can head back north past the National Stadium towards Thamel, or south over the **Chandra Pul** to Patan. This red coloured bridge is named after Chandra Sham Sher, during whose prime ministership it was constructed in 1902, but is known also as **Tripureshwar Pul** and **Rato Pul** ('Red Bridge'). It replaced another bridge at the same site built by Bhimsen Thapa and Rani Tripura in 1810. The present structure was manufactured in England before being transported in sections and reconstructed here under the stewardship of the first Western trained Nepali engineer, Kumar Narasing Rana.

Swayambhunath and the National Museum

Swayambhunath is a comfortable one-hour walk from **Durbar Square**, from where you head northwest along **Maruhiti Tole** to the **Vishnumati River** which is crossed by a footpath. There are cremation ghats along the river bank. Follow the road to its junction with the main **Dallu Tole** road, then turn left (west) and continue through the houses and gardens of suburban Kathmandu until you reach Swayambhu. Alternatively, head south from the five-point intersection at **Chhetrapati** and, at the first major crossroads, turn right (west) through **Raktakali** and continue along this road which crosses the river to become the main **Dallu Tole** road.

As you near Swayambhunath, the increase in the Tibetan population is apparent. You arrive at the southern side of the **Swayambhunath stupa**, with the long steep stairway to the top of the stupa ahead of you. There are many Tibetan hawkers selling a variety of handicrafts and artefacts around the base, on the way up, and at the top. There are also numerous monkeys in the area who are ever eager to snatch anything that is (and is not) on offer, so beware. Several smaller shrines, Buddhist and Hindu, surround the stupa (see the **Swayambhunath** section, page 201). There are also wonderful views from here of the valley and the mountains, especially the snowcapped peaks changing colour in the sunset.

From the stupa, head south past the military hospital and follow the road to **Chauni** and the **National Museum**, about 20 minutes' walk from the stupa. Nearby is the *Soaltee Holiday Inn* at **Kalimati**, which has a coffee shop. From the museum, take the road heading east, going through **Tankeshwar** before crossing the **Vishnumati River**. Continue along this road in a northeast direction and you will arrive at the Kasthamandap and Durbar Square after about 40 minutes.

Kathmandu Valley

Swayambhunath & National Museum Walk

Whole day walks

Thankot-Kirtipur This trip involves a cross country walk from Thankot to Kirtipur which is not suitable for cycling. You can either push the bike along this stretch or, better, take a taxi or a local bus from Ratna Park to Thankot and walk to Kirtipur or all the way back to Kathmandu.

From **Durbar Square**, follow the road heading southwest. Immediately after crossing the **Vishnumati** River to **Kalimati**, take the left hand fork and continue in a southwest direction. After two kilometres, you cross the **Ring Road**. Continue along here – this busy main road becomes the Prithvi Highway and reaches Pokhara 200 kilometres later. Some four kilometres beyond the Ring Road, you will see the small **Vishnu Devi Mandir** on your left (south), then a footpath leads to the **Mahalakshmi Mandir** a little further on your right (north). After another two kilometres, past another small temple on your left (south), there is a police checkpost before the small village of **Thankot**, where an old fort (*kot*) used to stand.

Just before this checkpost, take the footpath on your left (south) and climb for five minutes to a Shiva shrine. Here the path veers southeast and continues in this direction for about four kilometres, undulating through attractive countryside, and passing another shrine/temple in less than pristine condition before passing north of **Macchagaon** village and its **Narayan** shrine. There are good views of the Himalaya to the north. Just beyond Macchagaon, the path forks: take the less distinct left hand fork heading northeast. The trail then descends for about three kilometres towards **Kirtipur**. Home to **Tribhuvan University**, Kirtipur is an attractive, old town, relatively untouristy and spread across two hills and their valley. The main university campus is situated to the northeast of the town. On the way to the university is the bus stop for Kathmandu and a taxi stand. You can also walk back to Kathmandu: from the bus stop by following the road east for 1½ kilometres until it meets the road from Dakshinkali. Turn left (north) at this junction and follow this road along the west bank of the **Bagmati River** as it crosses the **Ring Road** after one kilometre. After another 1½ kilometres it crosses the lower **Vishnumati River** into **Teku** to join **Tripureshwar Marg**.

Thankot-Kirtipur walk

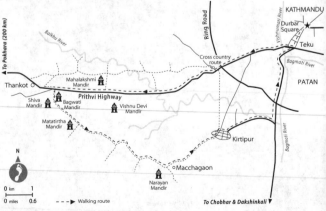

This trip takes in two of the valley's most important religious sites and there is the option of continuing from Budhanilikantha into the hills to the north.

Local buses run hourly from the Ratna Park bus stand to **Bansbari**, from where it is about an hour's walk up to **Budhanilikantha** and its statue of the supine Vishnu (see page 302).

From Budhanilikantha you can continue on a trail up towards **Shivapuri** mountain from where there are spectacular views across the **Ganesh** and **Langtang** Himal. **NB** This is a steep ascent of about three and a half hours from approximately 1,500 metres at Budhanilikantha to the peak at 2,732 metres. The trails can be steep and indistinct at times and you should carry sufficient food and water with you. But it is also a beautiful walk through lush evergreen and rhododendron forests, past small hamlets, terraced fields, springs and streams.

From Budhanilikantha, take the trail heading east towards the **Naga Gompa** monastery. After almost one kilometre, turn right (south) and continue downhill for about two kilometres until you reach a small **Kali Temple**, on the steep eastern bank of the Dhobi Khola River. Here, you are about one kilometre east of the main Lazimpath to Budhanilikantha road. From this Kali Temple, continue walking south for a further one kilometre along the narrow road to the timeless Newari village of **Tupek**. The road continues down from here for about three kilometres to **Bodhnath**. From Bodhnath you can take a bus back to the city centre or, if you cross the main road opposite the entrance to the stupa, it is about a one kilometre walk along a lane that passes through cultivated fields to the **Bagmati River** and **Pashupatinath**.

Budhanilikanth-Bodhnath Walk

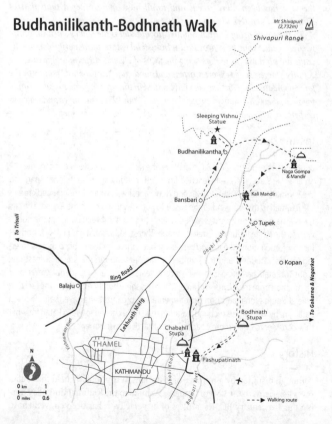

Patan

Patan has a unique atmosphere which is due to its compact scale and the remarkable vivacity of its Malla temple architecture. With a Durbar Square more densely packed with Hindu temples than either Kathmandu or Bhaktapur, and a total of 55 major temples and 136 monasteries, Patan is the artistic and architectural centre of the Valley.

Also known as **Lalitpur** ('beautiful town'), Patan (pronounced Paa-tan, with the emphasis on the first, long, syllable) is officially the Valley's second largest city, although it has now been effectively absorbed into Kathmandu, separated from the capital by the Bagmati River. It has a long history and has traditionally been an important centre of Newar Buddhism. The four earth and brick directional stupas at its four corners are attributed to Emperor Ashoka.

Like Kathmandu, the development of the city centred around its Durbar Square which marks the point at which all major roads to the city converge and around which a grid of other roads has been built. This is the oldest, most traditional and lively area of the city, while the growth of the newer residential area to the west has been more recent and, until now, more ordered than that of Kathmandu's eastern districts.

To the southeast of Durbar Square, **Jawalakhel** is the Valley's artisan centre where, together with the nearby **Patan Industrial Estate**, the majority of its handicrafts are produced as well as being the focus of Nepal's carpet manufacture, the country's largest single export. Carpets and handicrafts are produced mainly by the large population of Tibetans who have settled in this area, a former refugee camp, following their migration from their homeland from 1959. You can go and watch as carpets are woven and see statues take shape in the smiths' workshops.

Ins and outs

Population: 257,086
Area: 385 sq km
Phone code: 01
Colour map 2, grid B5

Bounded to the north by the Bagmati River, the Ring Road effectively encloses the city on all other sides. It is easily reached from Kathmandu with three bridges spanning the Bagmati to Teku, Tripureshwar and New Baneshwar, while the Ring Road crosses the Bagmati to the west and to the east into Koteshwar and on to the airport. The city is easily navigable on foot: it is about 3 kilometres from the Teku bridge in the northwest to the Patan Industrial Estate to the southeast. Although it has far fewer options for accommodation than its northern neighbour, there are a number of hotels catering for most budgets and the number of travellers choosing to spend at least one night in Patan has increased over recent years. There are wonderful views over Kathmandu from the **Kopundol** area, which has some hotels. Apart from the fact that several international and non governmental aid organizations have their offices in Patan, many Westerners working in Kathmandu have chosen to live in Patan for what they consider to be its more peaceful and attractive environment.

History

Although disputed by a number of historians, it is popularly held that Patan owes its origins to the visit of Emperor **Ashoka** to the Kathmandu Valley during the 3rd century BC. Regardless of its veracity, it has been convenient to believe that such a pilgrimage did indeed did take place and this has served to promote the city's worthiness as an historical Buddhist centre, a perception which assumes added significance in the context of the cultural heritage of the Valley's other two cities. Patan was probably founded during the early Licchavi period, from the 5th century AD, when it was known as **Yupagrama Dranga**. Amongst the earliest written records, there are allusions to a 5th century 'palace' belonging to one of the **Mangaladhipati** kings, after which **Mangal Bazaar** to the south of Durbar Square may have been named. There is, however, little or no archaeological evidence to confirm either its existence or exact location, though there is a natural spring (**Manga Hiti**) in Durbar Square which may have provided drinking water to early residents. Inscriptions dating from the 7th century refer to changes made by the Licchavi king **Narendra Deva** to the taxation system, which suggests that the town had been fully established by then.

The medieval period brought political changes with the **Mallas** assuming a hegemony in the Valley in about 1200, while the town's old name was replaced by **Lalitpur**. During the rule of **Yaksha Malla** in the mid-15th century the Valley was divided into three city states, with Patan ruled by Yaksha Malla's son and daughter, respectively named **Dharmavati** and **Ratna**. There followed a

Patan

■ Sleeping
1 Aloha Inn
2 Café de Patan
3 Greenwich Village
4 Himalaya
5 Narayani
6 Summit
7 Youth Hostel

● Eating
1 Ashoka & Bar
2 Café Pagoda
3 Café de Temple
4 Downtown
5 Hot Breads
6 Pumpernickel
   German Bakery

7 Second Step Kitchen
8 Serene Hut Café
9 Taleju & Bar
10 Three Sisters

period of unprecedented growth for the city, by now the Valley's largest. Many of Durbar Square's magnificent temples, monuments and other architecture were built during the reigns of three generations of Malla kings: **Siddhi Narasingha Malla** (1618-1658), **Sri Nivas Malla** (1658-1685) and **Yoganarendra Malla** (1685-1706).

Patan remained one of the Valley's three independent kingdoms until discord and rivalry between the ruling Mallas of Kathmandu, Patan and Bhaktapur allowed their eventual conquest and the unification of Nepal by the King of Gorkha, **Prithvi Narayan Shah**, in 1768. Patan's political importance decreased with the choice of Kathmandu as the Shah capital.

Durbar Square

NB Mandir = Temple More compact, more concentrated and more the city's focal point than either of its namesakes in Kathmandu and Bhaktapur, Patan's Durbar Square is a celebration of Newari architecture, its distinct character a product of the traditionally pivotal role of religion in society combined with the rivalry that existed between 17th and 18th century Malla rulers of the Valley's three city states for the most resplendent reflection of their authority. It ranks between Kathmandu and Bhaktapur in both size and number of monuments, although there are similarities in conception insofar as most temples and structures are built facing the Royal Palace complex which completely dominates one side of the square, separated by an avenue or tangible open space. Further temples and Buddhist monuments are located to the north and south of Durbar Square.

Bhimsen Mandir (1) This three-storeyed marble and gilt-faced building at the north end of Durbar Square has twice been restored: once by King Sri Nivas Malla in 1682 after a fire and again in the late 1960s following the damage it suffered in the 1934 earthquake. In front of the temple stands a pillar surmounted by a lion. Bhimsen in the *Mahabharata* is the exceptionally strong god of traders and the temple is propitiated accordingly by local businessmen.

Vishvanath Shiva Mandir (2) Standing on a three-stage plinth, this two-storeyed temple is dedicated to Shiva and was built in 1627 by King Siddhi Narasingha Malla. It has a large linga-yoni throne and the beams and brackets are profusely carved with erotic motifs. Two stone elephants guard the entrance to the east, while a statue of the Nandi bull stands to the west.

Patan Durbar Square

Standing beside the Vishvanath Shiva Mandir and set further back from the main thoroughfare, this is one of two temples in the square dedicated to Krishna and is sometimes referred to as the Krishna-Radha Mandir. This impressive shikhara design structure, built by King Siddhi Naransingha Malla and completed in 1637, is unlike the other Malla temples in using stone in a combination of early Mughal and Nagara architecture. It is one of the best known temples in Nepal, noted for the high quality of its stonework. The first three floors have *chattri* pavilions and open colonnaded sides reminiscent of the great Emperor Akbar's Panch Mahal at Fatehpur Sikri in India. On the second floor is a Shiva linga. Capping it is the curvilinear Hindu shikhara which contrasts with the traditional pagoda temples dominating most of the square and is similar to those in the Kangra Valley of Himachal Pradesh. A golden **Garuda**, the faithful bird headed vehicle of Vishnu, faces the temple from atop a pillar on the east and was erected on completion of the temple by King Narendra Malla. Inside are superb stone bas relief carvings of scenes from the

Krishna Mandir (3)

Kathmandu Valley

Patan Durbar Square

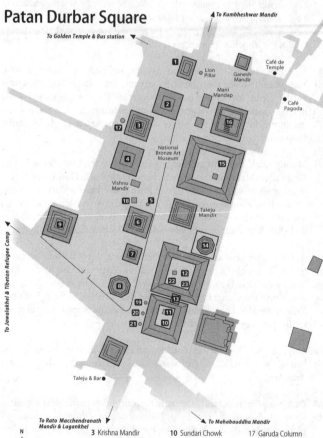

To Kumbheshwar Mandir

To Golden Temple & Bus station

Lion Pillar
Ganesh Mandir
Café de Temple
Mani Mandap
Café Pagoda
National Bronze Art Museum
Vishnu Mandir
Taleju Mandir

To Jawalakhel & Tibetan Refugee Camp

Taleju & Bar

To Rato Macchendranath Mandir & Lagankhel

To Mahabauddha Mandir

N
Not to scale

1 Bhimsen Mandir
2 Vishvanath Shiva Mandir
3 Krishna Mandir
4 Jagannarayan Mandir
5 Yoganarendra Pillar
6 Hari Shankar Mandir
7 Taleju Bell
8 Krishna Mandir (Chyasim Deval)
9 Bhai Dega Mandir
10 Sundari Chowk
11 Tusha Hiti
12 Mul Chowk
13 Taleju Bhavani Mandir
14 Degu Taleju Mandir
15 Mani Keshab Chowk
16 Manga Hiti
17 Garuda Column
18 Narsingha Statue
19 Vishnu Statue
20 Ganesh Statue
21 Hanuman Statue
22 Ganga Statue
23 Yamuna Statue

Hindu epics with fine details, with stories from the *Mahabharata* depicted on the first floor and from the *Ramayana* on the second. A popular festival is held on Krishna Janmastami in August/September when devotees gather to pay homage to Krishna.

Jagannarayan Mandir (4)
(or Charnarayan Mandir)

Also dedicated to Vishnu (as Narayan), this is said to be the oldest temple in the square dating from about 1566, although some scholars date it from the late 17th century. Two stone lions proudly guard the entrance. The red brick edifice contrasts attractively with the beautifully carved wooden doors, windows and roof struts. The latter are abundantly illustrated with erotic carvings.

Yoganarendra Pillar & Statue (5)

To the south of the Jagannarayan Mandir, a bronze statue of King Yoganarendra Malla, complete with headwear, sits in a gilded basket on top of a six-metre tall stone pillar gazing into the Taleju Mandir opposite. A bronze *naga*, or cobra, rises behind him, its head forming a protective umbrella for the king, on which stands a small bird. A local legend recounts how the godfearing Yoganarendra left his palace one night for the ascetic life and that as long as the bird remains, the king may return to his palace. A window is kept open for his return, and a hookah (pipe) ready for his use!

Hari Shankar Mandir (6)

The three-storeyed Hari Shankar Mandir was built by Yogamati, King Yoganarendra Malla's daughter, and was completed in 1705. The temple is notable for its roof struts whose carvings recall Dante-esque images of the inferno, which local wits suggest to be a warning to mere mortals against over-indulgence in some of the scenes depicted on the struts of the nearby Vishvanath Shiva Mandir.

Taleju Bell (7)

Moving south, this large bell hanging between two thick pillars was cast by King Vishnu Malla and his wife Rani Chandra Lakshmi in 1736. It was the first of the great bells to be installed in all three of the Valley's Durbar Squares. Although now largely ceremonial, it was rung during worship at the temples and could also be used to sound an alarm. Some accounts assert that by ringing the bell, citizens could draw the king's attention to injustices suffered by them.

Krishna Mandir (8)
(or Chyasim Deval)

At the southern corner of the main thoroughfare, this is the only octagonal temple in Durbar Square and was built by Yogamati, daughter of King Yoganarendra, in 1723. Made completely of stone with some fine sculpting, it stands on a three-stage base and is considered the lesser of the square's two Krishna temples. The columns of the ground floor are topped by small minaret-like structures from which the shikhara spire emerges.

Bhai Dega Mandir (9)

This is a small Shiva temple containing an image of the linga and is situated behind the Taleju Bell. A Mughal style dome surmounts the cube-like main structure.

The Royal Palace

Occupying the entire area to the east of the main thoroughfare is the Royal Palace which gives the square its name. The exact origins of this magnificent complex are unclear, but date back as far as the 14th century which makes it the first of the Valley's Durbar Square palaces to be built. The bulk of its construction occurred during the 17th century in the latter Malla period when the palace complex is said to have been comprised of at least seven *chowks*, or courtyards: Agan Chowk, Dafoshan Chowk, Kisi Chowk, Kumari Chowk, Nasal Chowk, Nuche Agan Chowk, and Sahapau Chowk. The complex was badly damaged during Prithvi Narayan Shah's conquest of the Kathmandu Valley in 1768 and

The Deities of Durbar Square

Ashta Matrika	*Eight mother goddesses.*
Avaloketeshvar	*From Buddhism, also known as Padmapani and portrayed holding a lotus. Newaris also recognize Avaloketeshvar in the protector deity, Macchendranath, who has an important shrine in the village of Bungamati, south of Patan.*
Bhairab	*A fearful Tantric form of **Shiva**.*
Garuda	*The winged, snake devouring and occasionally bird headed vehicle of **Vishnu**. Usually portrayed kneeling with hands folded in a namaste gesture, with statues often placed in front of Vishnu temples. Also the name of the national airline of Indonesia.*
Hari Shankar	*A combination of **Vishnu** (Hari) and **Shiva** (Shankar).*
Ganesh	***Shiva's** son, the elephant headed and pot bellied god of wisdom and material success is one of Hinduism's most popular deities. His vehicle is the shrew, Murshika.*
Ganga	*From Tantrism.*
Hanuman	*The monkey god created in the epic Ramayana in which he helped Rama to destroy the demon Ravana. Revered as the model of a strong and faithful servant and one of the most widely worshipped minor deities.*
Narayan	*One form of **Vishnu**, also portrayed in a supine state as at Budhanilikantha.*
Krishna	*The eighth incarnation of **Vishnu** and worshipped as perhaps the most human of the gods. His advice on the battlefield of the Mahabharata is one of the major sources of guidance for the rules of daily living for many Hindus today. Usually portrayed with blue skin.*
Kurma	***Vishnu's** second incarnation as a tortoise who carried Mount Kailash on his back when rescuing the ambrosia of eternal youth and other treasures that were lost when a great flood covered the earth.*
Lakshmi	*The wife of **Vishnu**, daughter of **Shiva** and Durga.*
Nagas	*Serpent deities, **Shiva's** companions, invoked for abundant rainfall.*
Nandi	***Shiva's** vehicle, a bull often found in front of a Shiva temple.*
Narasimha	*Half man, half lion. The fourth incarnation of **Vishnu** who destroyed the demon Hiranyakasipu.*
Parvati	*The wife of **Shiva**.*
Radha	***Krishna's** consort.*
Shiva	*One of the trinity of all powerful Hindu gods. Interpreted as both creator and destroyer.*
Taleju	*The patron goddess of the Malla rulers.*
Vishnu	*One of the trinity of all powerful gods. Frequently perceived as the god with the human face, especially in the form of **Krishna**, the eighth of his 10 incarnations. Followers of Vishnu ('Vaishnavites') believe Vishnu to have taken these different forms to save the world from impending disaster.*
Yamuna	*From Tantrism, a benevolent Shakti aspect.*

Kathmandu Valley

👉 *Shakti*

*The images of Ganga and Yamuna flanking the main entrance of the Taleju Bhavani Mandir are two expressions of the creative energy of Shakti. Traditionally, practising Hindus were divided into two main sects, **Vaishnavas** and **Shaivas**, worshipping Vishnu or Shiva respectively as the supreme deity. **Tantric** beliefs within Hinduism led to the development of Shakti cults which stressed that the male could be activated only by being united with the female in which sexual expression and spiritual desire were intermingled. Its origin has been traced to the persisting worship of the Mother Goddess from the Indus Valley civilization in the 3rd millennium BC, which has remained a feature of Hinduism in South Asia. Since this could not be suppressed, it was given a priestly blessing and incorporated into the regular ritual. Until this century, many temples kept devadasis, women whose duty included being the female partner in these rituals.*

again in the 1934 earthquake. Some renovations were made by the early Shah occupants, but today there are three main chowks (Sundari Chowk, Mul Chowk and Mani Keshar Chowk) each enclosed by a palace building.

Sundari Chowk (10) The name means 'beautiful courtyard' and it is the smallest and southernmost of the three chowks. The entrance is guarded by stone statues of Narasimha, Ganesh and Hanuman. The fine three-storey palace has carved roof struts and windows. The central window above the entrance was originally gold plated, while those on either side are of ivory. The ground floor *dalans*, or open areas, surrounding the courtyard were used by the Malla kings for official functions. The numerous pillars here are ornately carved. Seventeen images of Hindu deities carved from wood are set in niches around the courtyard.

The centre of the chowk is occupied by the magnificent **Tusha Hiti (11)**, a sunken royal bath decorated with fine stone and bronze carvings. There is an incomplete set of carved stone Ashta Matrika deities, eight divine mother goddesses who attend Shiva and the god of war, Skanda; the eight Bhairabs, incarnations of Vishnu; and the eight Nagas, serpent gods. The bath is shaped as a yoni. The bronze plated water tap is formed in the shape of a conch shell and has a small figure of Lakshmi Narayan on it. Beside it are stone statues of Hanuman and Krishna. Sadly, the source that supplied water to the bath dried up in the 1970s. The stone block by the steps leading down into the bath was used by King Siddhi Narasimha Malla, who is credited with the construction of this part of the palace and chowk in 1670, and his descendants for meditation and prayer following ritual bathing.

Mul Chowk (12) The construction of this building and chowk was started in 1627 by King Siddhi Narasimha Malla. A major fire destroyed much of the building and it was left to Siddhi Narasimha's son, King Sri Nivas Malla, to complete his father's work in 1666. The chowk forms the core of the Royal Palace complex and has a small gilded **Vidhya Mandir** at the centre dedicated to the family deity and placed there to commemorate the completion of construction. The cloister is a two-storeyed building, comprising the Patan royal family's erstwhile residence, with three **Taleju** temples around the courtyard. The smallest of these, the three-storeyed Bhutanese style **Taleju Bhavani Mandir (13)** on the south side of the chowk, is considered to be the most important. It was built at around the same time as the rest of this section of the palace and the main entrance is flanked by two brass images of the *shakti* (see box, page 266) Ganga on Kurma, a tortoise, and Yamuna on the mythical *makara*, a crocodile. The main courtyard was used by the Mallas for the performance of religious ceremonies and is still used today when, during the Dasain festival, the image of the goddess of the Taleju Bhavani Mandir is carried into the chowk to be worshipped and offered sacrifices of buffaloes and goats. There are, once again, many examples of fine Patan craftsmanship throughout, including statues of various deities, metalwork and roof struts carved with images of Bhairav.

To the east of the chowk, but not open to visitors, is the **Bhandarkhal Garden**, dedicated to the family deity and containing a pond of lotuses and a number of images. On the northern side, meanwhile, the original structure of the **Degu Taleju Mandir (14)** was built in 1640, then destroyed by the great fire of 1662 before being renovated four years later. Just to the north, the large five-storeyed **Taleju Mandir** soars majestically above Durbar Square and is the largest and most spectacular of the palace's temples. A late addition to the main palace buildings, it was constructed in 1736 and rebuilt following its destruction by the 1934 earthquake.

Mani Keshab Chowk (15) (or **Keshab Narayan Chowk**) The most northerly chowk and, according to some sources, the most recent, though its exact dates are not known. Records show that a structure of some sort on this site was used for a gathering of the Kathmandu Valley's religious leaders in 1631 (which could actually make it the oldest of the three chowks) and that the chowk was renovated or rebuilt in the mid 1670s. Substantial alterations were carried out again in 1733 and much of the building dates from then. Following the conquest of Patan, this chowk became the residence of Dalmardan Shah, Patan's first Shah king and, by consummate chance, brother of Prithvi Narayan Shah.

The main entrance to the chowk is through the splendid **golden gate** from Durbar Square's main north-south thoroughfare. An inscription on the gate chronicles its restoration under Jung Bahadur Rana in 1854 at a cost of Rs 321. Above the gate is a fine golden *torana* engraved with images of Shiva and Parvati, while a **golden window** shows Avalokateshvar. A small shrine dedicated to Keshab Narayan stands in the courtyard and gives the chowk its name. Since the mid 1990s, the chowk has been home to the **National Bronze Museum**.

Manga Hiti (16)

Directly to the north of the Royal Palace complex is the Manga Hiti, the conduit of spring water which may have existed at the time of the founding of Patan from the 5th century. Steps lead down to the pool shaped as a lotus and water comes from three stone spouts carved in the shape of crocodiles. The **Mani Mandap**, or Royal Pavilion, built in 1700, stands beside it.

Beyond Durbar Square

Radha Krishna Mandir

Just to the north of Durbar Square, this three-tiered temple has recently been renovated by a trust concerned with the conservation and restoration of the Valley's architectural heritage. The attractive entrance leads to the shrine dedicated to that most popular of Vishnu's incarnations, Krishna, and his lover Radha, an incarnation of Lakshmi.

Uma Maheshwar Mandir

Continuing north from Durbar Square, about 300 metres beyond the Radha Krishna Mandir you reach this two-storeyed temple on your right. A black stone frieze inside the shrine depicts the Uma Maheshwar, the name popularly given to this peaceful representation of Shiva and Parvati sitting closely together on Mount Kailash. Strictly speaking, Uma is one of 108 names used for the wife of Shiva – in this case, Parvati – while Maheshwar (*Maha* and *Ishwar*) means 'Great God'.

Vishvakarma Mandir   Leaving Durbar Square to the south, this three-tiered temple is situated on the first road on the right after about 200 metres. Vishvakarma means 'Creator of the World' and is the patron deity of this locality's artisans whose own creations on and in the temple pay seemly homage to the god. The temple's frontage is lavishly screened with embossed copper plate, while suspended bells flank the entrance and a large stone lion stands guard just outside.

Kumbheshwar Mandir   Some 300 metres along the road which leads north from Durbar Square stands this imposing five-storey temple. Dedicated to Shiva, it is the oldest existing temple in the city and, with Bhaktapur's Nyatapola Mandir, is the other of the two detached five-storeyed temples in the Valley. Construction of the original temple on this site is credited to Bhaskar Deva in 1392. A small tank on the northern side of the temple is said to be fed by an underground stream having the sacred Lake Gosainkund in the Himalaya (about a week's walk in each direction from Patan), as its source: immersion is believed to confer great merit upon the bather. This is the *kumbha*, literally a pot carrying holy water for use during temple worship, which gives the temple its name. *Ishwar* is a Sanskrit word for God. During the Janai Purnima festival in July/August, large crowds of pilgrims take a ritual bath and worship a silver and gold linga, placed in the tank. Brahmins and Chhetris replace their sacred threads at the festival amidst frenetic dancing by strikingly dressed *jhankri*, witch doctors.

A Shiva linga is enshrined in the temple and some people believe that the temple is Shiva's dwelling place during the six months of the year that he is away from Mount Kailash. There are also different forms of Shiva carved in wood around the temple, as well as statues of Shitaladevi, Suriya and even Vishnu. Some are said to date from the late Licchavi period. The whole structure is acclaimed for its dimensional equivalence, an asset which doubtless helped it survive the earthquake which destroyed many other older buildings throughout the Valley and beyond in 1934.

To the south of the temple is the **Baglamukhi Mandir**, a Newari house in which devotees implore the eponymous crane-headed goddess for succour in times of adversity.

Buddhist Patan

Patan is steeped in Buddhist history, tradition and legend, stretching back as far as the disputed visit of the great emperor Ashoka in the 3rd century BC. More than half of the city's population is Buddhist. Shrines and temples were often built to become the geographical focus of the local community. Many of the temples and bahals are open to visitors, their monks happy to explain their traditions and to show the exquisite craftsmanship which decorates some of the buildings. A number of other Buddhist monasteries not mentioned here are located throughout the city which, sadly, have fallen into disrepair and now lie as defunct relics of a former age. With the exception of the Ashokan stupas and the Golden Temple, all of the following are situated south of Durbar Square.

Also known as **Kwa Bahal** and **Suvarna Mahavihara**, this Buddhist temple and monastery is two minutes' walk north of Durbar Square and its fabulous craftsmanship and lavish decoration should not be missed. Though first documented in 1409, it was renovated by the 11th century King Bhaskaradeva. It was presumably constructed some time before then – some sources say by a local trader in gratitude for the wealth he had accumulated in Tibet.

The Golden Temple (or Hiranyavarna Mahivihara)

Behind the inconspicuous entrance (look for the street sign) guarded by a pair of decorative stone lions, the complex is surprisingly compact. The central courtyard contains a small but spectacular shrine dedicated to Swayambhunath. Mythical, griffin-like creatures stand on pillars at its four corners, and each side has wooden lattice windows. The golden pagoda roof is brightly polished and four *nagas* combine to support the *kalasa* at its pinnacle. On one side is a rack of prayerwheels. This shrine is a late addition and, because it is no longer possible to view the fine façade of the main temple from across the courtyard, is considered by some purists to have diminished the earlier aesthetic appeal of the complex. The courtyard, circumambulated in a clockwise direction, is surrounded on three sides by lines of prayerwheels which form the inner enclosure of a continuous verandah. Several shrine rooms used by Buddhist monks for prayer are located off this verandah, their dim candle lit interiors, wisps of incense and murmured venerations exuding the essence of devotion. The second floor is similarly arranged.

NB The temple is open to visitors, but leather items, including belts and watch straps, are not allowed inside.

For an explanation of the images in the Golden Temple, see overleaf.

A large bell hangs beneath a gilded canopy near the entrance to the main temple, while above the entrance is a series of 12 carved images of the Buddha. On either side, the eyes of the Buddha are engraved into the bronze border and two richly decorated elephants stand guard. The temple itself is a marvellous three-storeyed pagoda building with each roof covered in copper whose colour gives the temple its popular name. Small statues of birds in flight are attached to the four corners of each roof, while bells hang along the length of their rims. Latticed window screens and carved roof struts are found on the first two floors. The 13 steps forming the pinnacle represent the Buddhist stages on the path to enlightenment. Two bronze lions shown carrying the goddess Tara flank the entrance to the sanctum. Tara, it is said, was created from a teardrop of Avalokiteshwar, the Bodhisatva of compassion, and provides protection in the journey through the ocean of existence. Directly in front of the sanctum are a number of broad oil lamps, some hanging from the ceiling, which help to illuminate the many engravings and rich golden hues of the interior. The shrine has a frieze depicting the life of Shakyamuni Buddha where a strong Hindu component of some images indicate the extent of religious cross-fertilization in the Valley.

Heading southwest from Durbar Square, you reach the Rato Macchendranath temple, another major religious site revered by both Hindus and Buddhists. It also known as **Taha Bahal** and **Bungadhya**, the latter name linking it with Bungamati, regarded as the 'home village' of Macchendranath. The construction of the original temple is attributed to Narendra Deva in 1408, though the present temple dates from 1673. It is venerated as an abode of the Bungamati Macchendranath, also called Karunamaya Avalokiteshwar or, in Tibetan, Bukham Lokeshwar. Legend has it that when Gorakhnath, a disciple of Karunamaya, visited Kathmandu, he was not shown due respect. In his anger he cursed the people and consequently they suffered drought and famine lasting 12 years. When Karunamaya learnt of this, he told Gorakhnath to pardon the people and lift the curse; this was done and rain poured down. In

Rato Macchendranath

Kathmandu Valley

Tibetan Buddhist images in the Golden Temple of Patan

Kathmandu Valley

Deities	In contrast to the understandings of Judeo-Christian or even Hindu traditions, deities in the Buddhist sense are not regarded as concrete or inherently existing beings, but rather are revered as pure expressions of buddha-mind who are to be visualized in the course of meditation in their pure light forms: a coalescence of pure appearance and emptiness. Through such meditations, blessings are obtained from the mentors of the past, spiritual accomplishments are matured through the meditational deities, enlightened activities are engaged in through the agency of the dakinis, and spiritual development is safeguarded by the protector deities.
Avaloketeshwar	(Tib Chenrezik) One of the eight major bodhisattvas and the patron deity of Tibet, white in colour, symbolizing the Buddha's compassion and sense of taste, and holding a lotus untainted by flaws. There are various forms of this most popular bodhisattva: the 11 faced and 1,000 armed Mahakarunika, the four armed Chenrezik Chak Zhipa, the two armed Kharsapani, the lion riding Simhanada, the soothing form called Mind at Rest (Semnyi Ngalso) or Jowo Lokeshwar, and the standing Padmapani.
Buddha Shakyamuni	(Tib Shakya Tupa) The historical Buddha (6th-5th centuries BC), known prior to his attainment of buddhahood as Siddhartha or Gautama, and is also revered as the fourth of the thousand buddhas of this aeon. He is depicted in diverse forms, seated, standing, or reclining (at the point of his decease), and with diverse hand gestures symbolizing past merits, generosity, meditation, teaching, fearlessness and so forth. The Jowo form depicts him as a bodhisattva prior to his attainment of buddhahood, and the form Munindra depicts him as he appears among devas.
Dalai Lama	(Tib Gyelwa Rinpoche) Revered as the human embodiment of Avalokiteshwar. Since the mid 17th century, the successive Dalai Lamas have assumed both spiritual and temporal authority in Tibet.
Macchendranath	An aspect of Avalokiteshwar ('lord of fish') which is revered in Nepal, the white form known as Jamali being enshrined in Asan, Kathmandu, and the red form, Bukham, in Patan.
Tara	(Tib Dolma) A female meditational deity, who is identified with compassion and enlightened activity. There are aspects of Tara which specifically offer protection from worldly tragedies and fear of the elements. Among these, the most popular are Green Tara (Tib Doljang) who is mainly associated with protection, and the White Tara (Dolkar) who is associated with longevity. In addition, the form known as Chintamani (chakra) Tara is a meditational deity of the Unsurpassed Yogatantra class.
Vajradhara	(Tib Dorje Chang) An aspect of the buddha-body of actual reality (dharmakaya), appearing in a luminous form complete with the insignia of the buddha-body of perfect resource (sambhogakaya). He is dark blue in colour and holds a vajra and a bell in his crossed hands.

**Avaloketeshwar
Eleven-faced/Thousand-
armed Mahakarunika**

Green Tara

**Shakyamuni
Buddha of the Three Times**

Vajradhara

**Dalai Lama XIV
Tendzin Gyatso**

Iconographic line drawings are taken from
Chandra, Lokesh (1988) *Buddhist Iconography*,
Aditya Prakashan

Kathmandu Valley

Kathmandu Valley

Patan's Sakhya Artisans: casting in God's image

The art of metalcasting in the Kathmandu Valley stretches back to at least the 2nd century AD and possibly further, to pre-Buddhist times. Earliest references to the craft are traced to the community of Sakhya artisans in Boku Bahal in southeast Patan where the Rudravarna Mahavihara now stands and which remains an important centre for the manufacture of fine metal images, intricate designs from the pantheon of Nepali deities their speciality.

The reign of King Amshuvarman in the 7th century witnessed the acme of metalcasting in Patan: the Minanath Mandir's image of Lokeshwar is said by some to date from that time. Others maintain that the dissemination of Buddhism to Tibet was advanced by the huge quantity of statues and images brought by Amshuvarman's daughter, Bhrikuti, as part of her dowry for her marriage to Prince Songtsen Gampo. So beautiful were the statues that Songtsen, together with Bhrikuti, constructed the Jokhang Temple in Lhasa, now Tibet's most sacred shrine, to house them. The main temple gate faces Nepal, its design is based on a Newar model and the images

Bhrikuti brought (including those of Amitabha, Akshobhya, Maitreya, Mahakarunika and Shakyamuni Achalavajra) were installed in the building according to a strictly geomantic system.

The casting process begins with the shaping of the figure in bees wax. A combination of cow dung and clay (chira) is then applied to the figure with another layer added when the chira is dry. Then a mixture of damp rice husks and yellow mud is applied and left to dry. The wax is removed and the mould is ready. The metal is heated to about 1,200°C and poured into the mould. It is crucial that this is done in completely still conditions, as any breeze can disfigure the image. Once cooled, features are painstakingly chiselled into the figure. The figure is then coated with a mixture of mercury and gold dust to which a strong flame is applied which leaves a golden complexion. Finally it is polished.

The tradition of excellence has endured and Patan's accomplished community of Sakhya artisans continue to produce skilled works of art, statues and images of deities with both local and worldwide commissions.

honour of Karunamaya's kindness, King Narendra Deva built this temple. He also instigated the annual chariot race.

A number of pillars supporting statues of various creatures related to the Tibetan calendar stand in front of the elaborately decorated main north entrance, and a large bell hanging from a Tibetan style shaft is to the left. The revered image is made of sandalwood and clay, is repainted in red (hence *rato*) before each annual chariot race, and is further embellished with jewellery and garlands. It is worshipped as a god of rain and Hindus also believe that simply seeing the chariot festival of Rato Macchendranath is enough to attain salvation. The courtyard is filled with sculptures of animals including horses, lions and bulls. For several weeks from April onwards (in the month of Baisakh), the deity is trundled through the streets of Patan in an enormous chariot. This culminates in the Boro Jatra festival, strategically timed prior to the onset of the monsoon, when the chariot reaches Jawalakhel. The lower roof of the temple is tiled, while the upper two are overlaid with copper. Carvings on the struts of each roof depict various deities with lesser beings placed deferentially at their feet.

Minanath Mandir On the main road leading south from Durbar Square, the Minanath Mandir is smaller than the Rato Macchendranath Mandir opposite, but both are dedicated to forms of Avalokiteshwar and the bronze image of its deity, Bodhisattva Lokeshwar, also has a place in the annual Boro Jatra festival. Various legends explain the personage of Minanath, including this almost Biblical account: Minanath was a fisherman who plied his trade in southern Bengal where the Ganges meets the open sea. One day he hooked a whale, but Minanath was engulfed by the whale. He remained in its stomach for 12 years until the whale happened to overhear a sermon preached by Mahadeva which prompted it to release Mininath who built the temple in thanksgiving.

A temple was first built on this site during the Licchavi era. Two bronze lions stand guard on either side of the entrance and a large prayerwheel stands beneath a canopy to one side. Like its neighbour, the lower roof is tiled while the upper is overlaid with copper.

Mayurvarna Mahavihara

Dedicated to Maya Devi, the revered mother of the Buddha Gautama Siddhartha, this temple and monastery is located at Bhimcche Bahal, near the Rato Macchendranath Mandir. Feline guardians at the entrance are flanked by two suspended bells and the bronze torana above the main entrance depicts scenes from the lives of Maya Devi and the Buddha. Inside are three stupas. Both roofs are tiled. Legend has it that the group of chaityas here were commissioned by the emperor Ashoka.

Mahabouddha Mandir

To the southeast of Durbar Square, and along a southwest leading alleyway, is the 16th shikhara style Mahabouddha Mandir, dedicated to the thousand buddhas of the auspicious aeon (*Tib* Sangye Tongsta) whose names are enumerated in the *Bhadrakalpikasutra*. Among these, Shakyamuna Buddha was the fourth, and the next to appear in the world will be Maitreya. Tightly hemmed in by surrounding buildings, the terracotta and tile building is difficult to locate. It is somewhat reminiscent of the great Mahabodhi Temple at Bodhgaya in India. This is a masterpiece of terracotta and each of the 9,000 or so bricks is said to carry an image of the Buddha, and the face of Buddha is portrayed on blocks of the shikhara structure. In the centre is a gold image of the Buddha, which, some sources maintain, was brought here from Bodhgaya. Surrounding the shrine are numerous friezes depicting scenes from the Buddha's life, while the many oil lamps here are lit also in honour of Maya Devi. A narrow staircase leads to the upper part. Although it was completely destroyed in the 1934 earthquake, it has been rebuilt exactly like the original. The small shrine standing behind the main temple is said to have been built with bricks remaining from the post earthquake reconstruction. The temple is surrounded by Newar Buddhist craft shops, most of them selling images of Buddhist deities fashioned in the renowned *ciré perdue* ('lost wax') process. The temple, whose name means 'Great Bouddha' (sometimes translated as 'One Thousand Buddhas') was completed by 1585 by Pandit Abhaya Raja in the reign of Mahendra Malla.

Rudravarna Mahavihara (or Oku Bahal, or Bankali Rudravarna Mahavihara)

About 100 metres south of the Mahabouddha Mandir, this temple and former monastery is one of the – if not the – oldest in Patan. The use of the site for religious purposes probably dates back to the early Malla period and some of the fixtures of the present building are said to be from the 13th century. The main temple rises from the centre of the monastery buildings. The tiled lower roof of the two-storeyed pagoda temple is topped by five decorative stupas and small statues of peacocks, and the copper upper roof has beams trimmed with images of demi-gods. Above the richly adorned entrance are bronze friezes with various Buddhist representations, including Maya Devi. Inside the rectangular complex are courtyards alive with reflections of the culture of Patan, with bronze and stone statues of elephants, peacocks, Garudas and (remarkably many) lions, as well as mirrors, woodcarvings, bells, *vajras*, minor deities

Kathmandu Valley

and a statue of the Rana prime minister responsible for rebuilding much of Kathmandu after the earthquake, Juddha Shamsher. The courtyard also contains a central statue of the Buddha and a line of oil lamps.

Ratnakar Mahavihara (or Ga Bahal) Southwest of Durbar Square, this attractive three-storeyed temple and monastery is notable for the double row of Buddha images above the main entrance and, either side, the guardian lions which carry statues of the Buddha. Patan has its own 'living goddess', the *Kumari*, though the role does not have the profile of Kathmandu's Kumari nor does it come with palatial accommodation. Patan's Kumari is chosen from amongst the daughters of the priests of the Ga Bahal and lives with her family. Her major duty of the year is to take part in the Boro Jatra festival of Rato Macchendranath.

Haka Bahal West of Durbar Square, this monastery includes a small temple and a Buddhist shrine contained in an inner courtyard.

Ibaha Bahal Located to the south of Durbar Square, between the square and the Rato Macchendranath Mandir, this monastery has recently been renovated with Japanese assistance and now includes a school.

Ashokan Stupas The remains of four stupas, their construction attributed to the Mauryan emperor Ashoka in the 3rd century BC, are located approximately at the cardinal points delineating the ancient boundaries of Patan. All but the Northern stupa are now mostly grassed over, though still recognizable.

Northern Stupa (Bahai Thura) Located north of Durbar Square, beyond the Uma Maheshwar Mandir on the road towards the bridge to Southeast Kathmandu, this is the best preserved of the four stupas. A lotus shaped adornment supports the *kalasa* pinnacle above the spire's 13 steps, and a group of chaityas form part of the circumference wall at the base of the stupa. A natural spring, active only during the monsoon, is said to exist on one side. A small shrine dedicated to Saraswati, the Hindu goddess of knowledge, stands on the northern side. The exterior of the stupa has recently been renovated.

Eastern Stupa (Bhate Thura) This is the most out of the way of the four stupas and lies beyond the Ring Road to the southeast of Durbar Square at Imadole. Four chaityas are fitted into the brick perimeter wall at the cardinal points and a small stone structure, the remains of the pinnacle, projects from the top of the grassy hillock. The stupa is a landmark of sorts, but outwardly is otherwise undistinguished and attracts few visitors.

Southern Stupa (Lagan Thura) This, the largest of the four, is situated by a lotus pond just to the east of the main road leading south from Durbar Square and gives this area of Patan (Lagankhel) its name. Protruding from the top of the stupa is a small hemispherical stone edifice painted with the eyes of Buddha, replacing an earlier wooden structure, and supporting a compact spire representing the 13 stages on the path to enlightenment. The circumference wall is interesting for its inset hewn images of Buddha. A stone mandala, representing the 'palace' of the meditational deity, stands beside the eastern chaitya, while the western chaitya has a shrine containing images of Amitabha (*Tib* Opame), one of the five peaceful meditational buddhas forming the buddha-body of perfect resource. Amitabha is red in colour, symbolizing the purity of perception and the discerning aspect of buddha-mind. He holds a lotus to symbolize the purification of attachment and the altruistic intention.

Ashoka, beloved of the Gods

The greatest of the Indian dynasty of Mauryan emperors took power in 272 BC. He inherited a full blown empire based in Patna in modern day Bihar, but extended it further by defeating the Kalingas in what is now Orissa, before turning his back on war and preaching the virtues of Buddhist pacifism. Ashoka's Empire stretched from Afghanistan to Assam, and from the Himalaya to Mysore. He inherited a structure of government set out by Chandragupta Maurya's Prime Minister, Kautilya, in a book on the principles of government, the Arthashastra. The state maintained itself by raising revenue from taxation on everything from agriculture to gambling and prostitution. He decreed that 'no waste land should be occupied and no tree cut down' without permission, not out of a modern 'green' concern for protecting the forests, but because all were potential sources of income for the state.

Described on the edicts as 'Beloved of the Gods, of Gracious Countenance', Ashoka left a series of inscriptions on pillars and rocks across the subcontinent. Apart from that at Lumbini, two of the most accessible for modern visitors to South Asia are in the Indraprastha Fort in Delhi, where Feroz Shah Tughluq had it taken in the 14th century, and in the Asiatic Society's small museum in Calcutta. Over most of India, these inscriptions were written in Prakrit using the Brahmi script, although in the northwest they were in Greek using the Kharoshti script. They remained unintelligible for over 2,000 years after the decline of the Mauryan Empire until James Prinsep, one in a line of distinguished amateur Oriental scholars attached to the Asiatic Society, deciphered the Brahmi script in 1837.

Through all the edicts, Ashoka urged all people to follow the code of Dharma, or Dhamma, translated by the Indian historian Romila Thapar as 'morality, piety, virtue and social order'. He established a special force of Dharma officers to try and enforce the code which encouraged tolerance, non-violence, respect for priests and those in authority and for human dignity. In addition to exercising a liberal domestic policy, Ashoka had good relations with his neighbours. However, Romila Thapar suggests that the failure to develop any sense of national consciousness, coupled with the massive demands of a highly paid bureaucracy and army, proved beyond the ability of Ashoka's successors to sustain. Within 50 years of Ashoka's death in 232 BC, the Mauryan Empire had disintegrated, and with it the whole structure and spirit of its government.

Western Stupa (Pulchowk Thura) Situated in Pulchowk, about one kilometre along the main Mangal Bazaar road heading west from Durbar Square. A large mound topped by a stone structure painted with the eyes of Buddha and with four chaityas in the base. This is where the annual Boro Jatra festival of Rato Macchendranath begins its procession.

Jawalakhel

This area of Southeast Patan, pronounced *Jowl-a-kel*, is renowned for its large Tibetan community and the **Tibetan Refugee Camp**, now occupied by only the poorest of the exiles. Nepal's only **zoo** is also located here.

The refugee camp, with those in Pokhara and at Bodhnath is one of three major camps established by the Red Cross to accommodate the influx of Tibetans from the early 1950s, developed from a transit camp into a focus for the manufacture of **handicrafts** and **carpets**. With further help from the Swiss Association for Technical Assistance, the production of Tibetan carpets blossomed, growing so rapidly that by the early 1990s carpet export accounted for more than half of Nepal's total export earnings. You can watch all stages of their production, from the dyeing and spinning of yarns to the weaving and final trimming. There are fixed price shops where you can buy the carpets made here along with blankets, jackets and pullovers.

From Durbar Square, you can get here by following the road south of the square, then turn right (west) onto the main road just past the Rato Macchendranath Mandir. Continue along here for about one kilometre until you reach a major crossroads with a roundabout, just beyond the Haka Bahal. Turn left and follow this road south and past the zoo for less than one kilometre and the Tibetan Refugee Camp and handicraft centre on your left, just inside the Ring Road. If you continue south along this route, you will reach the village of **Bungamati**, the other home of the Rato Macchendranath deity, after about four kilometres.

Zoo

Vendors of peanuts (you may feed the animals) congregate outside the zoo, where there are also small snack stalls and even fortune tellers.

Just south of the busy Jawalakhel Chowk is Nepal's only zoo (frequently pronounced *joo*). If you have visited a zoo in India you will have an idea of what to expect, but it is as well to remember that perceptions of animal (and, indeed, human) welfare are different in South Asia and that the conditions in which the animals are kept could be worse. The small zoo is not recommended as a special trip, but has pleasant gardens and its inmates include tigers, lions, leopards, rhinos, elephants, deer, monkeys, antelopes, snakes and an aviary. Elephant rides are available at Rs 100 inside the park and at Rs 2,000 for a stroll through the streets of Patan. ■ *1000-1630, daily. Saturday is very busy with long queues. Rs 20, camera charge Rs 10, video camera charge Rs 50.*

Museums and Libraries

National Bronze Art Museum

This is situated inside **Mani Keshab Chowk**, the northernmost of the three courtyards comprising the Royal Palace complex in Durbar Square. Refurbishment of the museum was completed in the mid 1990s and it houses a total of almost 900 exhibits. Most are religious ornaments and statues of national importance. The oldest are believed to date back to the Licchavi era and, although precise dating is virtually impossible due to the absence of either written records or inscriptions indicating the maker's name or the origin of the commission, some are certainly 7th century masterpieces of Patan's celebrated *Sakhya* community of metalsmiths. Images of Avalokiteshwar, the Buddha, Shiva and Vishnu dominate in a collection which also includes many other representations of images from Nepal's Hindu-Buddhist pantheon. ■ *1000-1600, Wednesday-Monday (1000-1500 Friday), closed Tuesday. Rs 10.*

National Library

This contains Nepal's national collection with a total of approximately 70,000 volumes. Most are in English, but there are also a few Nepali and Hindi titles as well as some in Nepal's regional languages. There also exists a small and scholarly collection of books in Sanskrit, the ancient language of the northern areas of South Asia, known by some as the 'Latin of the subcontinent'. The library's oldest books (in English and Sanskrit) date from the 17th century. To get there, follow the main Mangal Bazaar road west from Durbar Square for about one kilometre until you reach a T-junction at Pulchowk. Turn right (north), then left (west) near the Hotel Narayani. The library is situated inside the Harihar Bhavan building a short walk along this lane. ■ *T521332. 1000-1700, Sunday-Friday.*

Essentials

Patan has neither the abundance nor range of accommodation on offer in Kathmandu, particularly of bottom end budget hotels. Most hotels are situated to the west of Durbar Square. Kopundol is the elevated area of Northwest Patan from where you can get magnificent views of Kathmandu and of the mountains beyond.

A *Himalaya*, T423900, F523909. 95 rooms many with balcony and excellent views across Kathmandu and to the Himalaya, pleasant *Chalet* restaurant for multi cuisine and good views, 1000-2300, *Base Camp* coffee shop, breakfast buffet and à la carte, 0700-2200, bar, business centre and conference facilities, handicraft and book shops, swimming pool (residents only), tennis and badminton, situated some 700 metres from the bridge to South Kathmandu and about 1½ kilometres northwest of Durbar Square.

B *Greenwich Village*, T521780, F526683. 43 rooms, coffee shop, rooftop garden restaurant and larger dining room, bar and swimming pool, small conference room has a wonderfully carved 3-piece wooden window, off season rates are very competitive and are negotiable, situated in Kopundol 'Heights', Northwest Patan. **B** *Narayani*, T525015, F521291, nbe@nbepc.mos.com.np 88 rooms, restaurant and coffee shop (0600-2200), free coffee in reception, pleasant garden and swimming pool (residents only), conference facilities, beauty parlour (ladies only), a tip box in reception is curiously marked 'To improve promptness'! Located in Pulchowk, west of Durbar Square. **B** *Summit*, T521894, F523737. Has 72 rooms and 4 apartments, multi cuisine restaurant, bar, lovely building with traditional Newari touches, and beautiful garden, small swimming pool, some of Patan's best views of Kathmandu, Swayambhunath and the mountains, travel agent and trekking operator in hotel, an old wing has cheaper rooms, common bath, located in the high Kopundol area of Northwest Patan. Recommended.

C *Aloha Inn*, T522796, F524571. 42 rooms all with bath, TV and fridge, restaurant does Chinese, Indian and continental food, in house travel agency, quietly situated in Jawalakhel, near the zoo, there is a good bakery shop opposite and Grindlays Bank next door. Recommended.

D *Café de Patan*, T525499. 14 rooms most with bath, situated on the Mangal Bazaar Rd just west of Durbar Square, this is one of Patan's favourite budget guest houses and has an excellent restaurant downstairs.

E *Mahendra Youth Hostel*, T521003. The Valley's only youth hostel, situated in Jawalakhel 200 metres north of the zoo, this uninspiring establishment has the cheapest accommodation in Patan: double rooms with bath, a 4-bed dorm and another with 32 beds, no food, arrivals accepted only between 1700-2200, check out by 1000, closed from 1000 to 1700, lights out at 2200, no smoking, no alcohol, 10 percent discount for YHA members.

Once again, there are far fewer options for eating than in the capital. Durbar Square has a smattering of small restaurants and there are a couple more along the road leading to the bridge to Thapathali, South Kathmandu.

Expensive restaurants: the *Summit Hotel* has excellent Nepali, Indian, Western and Tibetan cuisine, and the neighbouring *Hotel Greenwich Village* has an attractive terrace restaurant by its garden and swimming pool. The *Chalet Restaurant* in the Hotel Himalaya overlooks Kathmandu and the mountains and does good Indian and continental food.

Sleeping

■ *for hotels &*
● *for restaurants*
on map, page 261

Price codes: see inside
front cover (under flap)

Eating

Budget Restaurants: on the main Mangal Bazaar road just west of **Durbar Square**, the *Café de Patan*, T525499, has a small outdoor 'garden' area while various masks of Bhairab peer down as you eat indoors. Excellent Indian, Newari and Tibetan food, good salads. Large portions. Chilli chicken and momos with mint sauce are recommended. The *Café Pagoda*, T536629, is tucked away in the northwest corner of Durbar Square and has good views from the first floor, it does a bit of everything including light meals, drinks and ridiculously overpriced dal-bhad-tarkari. Just opposite is the Café Pagoda, and with marginally better views of the square, the *Café de Temple*, T527127, does good snacks and meals, and cheaper dal-bhad-tarkari. On the south side of the square, the *Taleju Restaurant and Bar*, T525558, is a Tibetan restaurant, but also does a few continental dishes. The third floor section has traditional floor cushion seating, while tables and chairs are on the fourth floor which has excellent views of Durbar Square and the Valley.

In **Jawalakhel**, *Hot Breads*, T524359, has seating and does good cakes, breads, ice cream, soft drinks and hot snacks. The *Pumpernickel German Bakery*, is just north of the main Jawalakhel crossroads towards **Pulchowk** and sells breads, good doughnuts (Rs 4) and rum and raisin balls (Rs 10). Diagonally opposite is the *Serene Hut Café*, T522568, which does reasonably priced grilled sandwiches, pizzas, steaks, and Chinese food. Further north and on the left hand side (west), the *Three Sisters Restaurant*, does reasonable pizzas and pastas, closed Sunday. Next door is the *Second Step Kitchen*, T535311, which has good value Chinese and Indian food, and has a bar. Heading downhill towards the main junction and the *Hotel Himalaya*, the *Downtown Restaurant*, T522451, is on your left, is clean and does relatively cheap Chinese and Indian food. The *Ashoka Restaurant* is next door.

Bars All the large hotels have their own bars. Most of the restaurants mentioned above have bar facilities.

Festivals **February**: *Ilhan Samyek*, is held every 4 years in Patan (next in 2000), every 12 years in Kathmandu and annually in Bhaktapur. It celebrates the role of alms giving in Buddhism and is marked by devotees offering rice and coins to images of the Buddha especially at Nag Bahal.

April-May: *Rato Macchendranath* is the month long festival when the red faced image of the patron deity of the Valley, the god of rain and harvest, is taken around the city. His chariot moves by daily stages and may not return for some months. The image is prepared for the event in Pulchowk, when it is washed and repainted awaiting the assembling of the remarkably tall chariot. The procession through the streets is accompanied by musicians and soldiers and the nightly halts are marked by worship and feasting. The arrival in Jawalakhel several weeks later is witnessed not only by the royal family but also by Patan's Kumari, the 'living goddess'. Every 12 years the procession continues on to Bungamati, a village 5 kilometres south of Patan where the image is ensconced in a second home for 6 months. This next occurs in 2003.

July: *Janai Purnima* celebrates the annual changing of their sacred thread, the *janai*, by Hindus. At the Kumbeshwar Mandir the occasion is marked by the placing of a linga on the platform in the centre of its holy tank. Rice is also offered symbolically to frogs here following the monsoon rains.

August/September: *Krishna Janmastami* (or *Krishnastami*) celebrates the birth of Krishna, the eighth incarnation of Vishnu. It centres around the Krishna Mandir in Durbar Square, where, on the 'eighth day of the dark moon', an all night candlelit vigil is held by devotees from throughout the Valley and prayers recited. Much of Durbar

Square is beautifully illuminated. *Mat Ya* is a Buddhist festival in which processions carrying candles and incense tour the city's Buddhist sites, accompanied by musicians. Patan residents are expected to partake at least once during their life.

Patan is regarded as the best place for handicrafts in the Valley. It has a long metal working tradition and produces fine statues of the Buddha, various bodhisattvas and the Buddhist tantric deities. Prices for gold plated bronze figurines range from Rs 2,000 to over Rs 10,000. There are 3 main areas that concentrate on handicraft retail: Jawalakhel, the Patan Industrial Estate with some of the best prices in town, and the old city area south and southeast of Durbar Square.

Bookshops: Patan has surprisingly few bookshops. Try the large hotels. The *Christian Bookshop* is located on the main road between the large Jawalakhel intersection and the crossroads south of the Rato Macchendranath Mandir.

Carpets: the centre for carpet manufacture is the Tibetan area of Jawalakhel where you can watch the entire production process.

Jawalakhel retailers include *Carpet Trading Company*, T521241, F527727, among the first businesses to export carpets from here; *Senon Carpets*, T522665, F524029; and *Sharma Carpet Manufacturing Co*, T525147, also has a showroom in Thamel.

At the Patan Industrial Estate, *Mahabaudha Carpet Industry*, T526110, F522291. Try also around the Durbar Square area and along Mangal Bazaar.

Jewellery: trinkets are available in and around Durbar Square as well as Jawalakhel, Patan Industrial Estate and Oku Bahal.

Metalwork: the **Patan Industrial Estate** is a collection of manufacturing units and retail outlets in **Lagankhel**, about 2 kilometres south of Durbar Square, and you can watch craftsmen creating images and decorative items in their workshops. Try *Nepalese Crafts*, T521412.

The **Mahabaudha (Oku Bahal)** area, south of Durbar Square, has a tradition of high quality metallurgy. Here you can get some of the best bronze, brass, copper and other metallic images and idols available in the Valley and also high quality goods not usually available from Thamel's itinerant handicraft wallahs. Various outlets include *Ganga Handicrafts*, T525857; *Goodwill Handicrafts*, T521912, F522406; *Gyan Hastakala Udhyog*, T525051; *Kishor Handicrafts*, T522294, F525098; *Mahabaudha Art Concern*, T522431, F226590; and *Mahabaudha Art Enterprises*, T526229, F522431.

For **khukuri knives**, the best are available from *The Khukuri House*, T522116, F526185, at the Tibetan Refugee Camp in **Jawalakhel**.

Painting: Thangkas are available in the Oku Bahal area. Try *Mahabaudha Art Enterprises*, T526229, F522431. The area around the Golden Temple, north of Durbar Square, also has a number of shops dealing in thangkas as well as other Nepali paintings and arts. A smaller selection in Jawalakhel.

Woodcarvings: there are few outstanding woodcarving shops in Patan (see Bhaktapur), but try *Om Woodcarving Industries*, T426710, in the Patan Industrial Estate.

Other Shopping: there are a small number of 'supermarkets' scattered around the western part of the city which also sell some foreign foods. On the road heading east from the large intersection at **Jawalakhel**, there is the *Lalitpur Shopping Centre*. Some 300 metres north of this intersection, where the road forks, is the *Namaste*

Traditional Tibetan carpet designs

Although also sold locally, the majority of carpets (95%) are made for export. The export of Tibetan-Nepali carpets did not begin until 1964, but the industry has grown rapidly to become Nepal's largest single export. It now constitutes some 10% of world carpet exports and provides employment for about 200,000 people. Germany is by far the country's largest single customer, its imports accounting for about 80% of the total. Most of the wool is imported either from Tibet or from New Zealand. Weaving is usually by the traditional Tibetan double knotting system which helps to increase the pile, or thickness, of the carpet. In recent years modern colours and designs of carpets have started to replace the traditional, Buddhist inspired, designs and, although natural vegetable dyes are still used, manufacturers are increasingly favouring imported chemical dyes. The standard size of a Tibetan carpet has traditionally been approx 6' x 3' (c 183 x 91 cm), but global demand for the carpets has led to a variety of sizes being woven and you can now get anything from a tiny rug to a large, room sized carpet.

All the traditional designs of Tibetan carpets include images derived from Buddhist lore. The most common are:

Buddhist Knot
Symbolizes the attenuation of enlightenment

Snow lion
a legendary guardian of the earth. Two appear on the Tibetan flag supporting a gemstone (symbolism of Buddhism) and a gkhyil (symbolic of prosperity).

Dragon
The ruler of the seas who commands the life-giving rains

Swastika
An auspicious Buddhist/Hindo symbol included among the 32 'excellent major marks' of a buddha's body

Lotus flower
Represents purity and immortality

Phoenix
Represents peace and eternal life

Supermarket. If you take the right hand fork, just to the north is the *Dai Chi Supermarket* and, diagonally opposite, the *Landmark Supermarket*.

Local All areas of Patan are within walking distance of each other. **Taxis** as well as **cycle**- and **auto-rickshaws** are readily available. A taxi from Durbar Square to Thamel in Kathmandu will cost around Rs 180 one way. There is a regular and cheap **bus** service from Patan Gate to Kathmandu City Bus Park (last departure at around 2000). There are few cycle hire places in Patan; better choice in Kathmandu. **Transport**

Long Distance Connections Government *Sajha* buses link Patan with all major destinations. The Patan Central Bus Station is located near the UN complex and bookings are made here. Most long distance buses go via Kathmandu's new bus station at Balaju, departures are 1 hour earlier.

Communications Post Office: the main post office is situated at Patan Gate, northwest of Durbar Square. **Speedway Cargo Service:** Jawalakhel, T525930. **Telecommunications:** there are a number of places in the Durbar Square area where you can make international phone calls. **Directory**

Embassies & consulates *Norwegian Consulate*, Jawalakhel, T521646. *Swiss Consulate*, Jawalakhel, T523468.

Hospitals & medical services *Patan Hospital*, Lagankhel, T522266.

Useful addresses Aid and development agencies: a number of NGOs, national and international, have Patan as their administrative base in Nepal: *Care International in Nepal*, PO Box 1661, Krishnagalli, Pulchowk, Patan, F521202. Various aid and development programmes. *Development Communication Production*, PO Box 1230, c/o INC Sanepa, Patan. Produces health education materials. *Institute for Sustainable Development*, PO Box 4006, Pulchowk, Patan, F526467. Research and information. *King Mahendra Trust for Nature Conservation*, PO Box 3712, Jawalakhel, Patan, F526570. Nature conservation and development. *Oxfam Nepal*, PO Box 2500, Lagankhel, Patan, F525620. Aid and development projects. *Rotary Club of Kathmandu*, c/o Hotel Narayani, Pulchowk, Patan. Member of Rotary International, philanthropic professionals. *Save the Children*, North Pulchowk, Patan. Child oriented education and development programmes. *Seto Surans Community Child Development Centre*, PO Box 4103, Jhamsikhel, Patan, T512447. Early child care and education programmes for under-privileged children. *United Nations* (various agencies): North Pulchowk, Patan, T523200.

Kathmandu Valley

Bhaktapur

*Bhaktapur ('city of devotees'), or Bhadgoan, lies some 10 kilometres east of Kathmandu. Built on a plateau (1,400 metres) on the northern banks of the **Hanumante River**, it is the smallest of the Valley's three cities. Its geographical separation from Kathmandu is deceptive, for it retains a simplicity far removed from the trappings of 20th century life which pervade the capital. The city exudes a sense of the past which is not so much medieval as traditional and, despite the gradual emergence of satellite dishes and other contemporary icons, gives the impression that little has changed here for centuries, that little is set to change and, happily, that it is a city at ease with itself. In its Durbar Square, Taumadhi Square and Dattatraya Square, it has arguably the Valley's finest panoply of Newari temple architecture, including the magnificent five-storeyed **Nyatapola Mandir**, the tallest pagoda temple in Nepal.*

Earthy red colours dominate the cityscape and the architecture is, almost without exception, traditional Newari: typically, two or three storey wooden or brick houses with protruding upper floors or roofs, decorative window frames, and a low entrance leading to a small courtyard perhaps containing a shrine or small image. The German funded Bhaktapur Development Project has led to much new building taking place, though traditional styles have successfully been maintained.

You can spend hours strolling through these uncrowded streets without getting either bored or lost, and can capture the unique flavour of the place in the natural courtesy of the people, in the women eternally chattering as they lay quantities of chillis and grains out to dry, in the grand and innumerable not-so-grand temples and shrines, and in the many expressions of personal devotion which give the city its name. All lead to the overwhelming impression of a village-city, that you are in an urban setting without the urbanism.

Ins and outs

Getting there

Population: 172,952
Area: 119 sq km
Altitude: 1,400m
Phone code: 01
Colour map 2, grid B5

Bhaktapur is approached from Kathmandu via the Ring Road, passing to the south of the airport and along the undulating, marijuana lined road and past the walled city of Thimi. Entering Bhaktapur from the west, you pass through a lovely pine grove on a low hill where two tanks once supplied the population with drinking water. The bus stop is near the walled tank known as **Siddha Pokhari**, considered holy by both Hindus and Buddhists. Beyond this, the road divides, the left fork continuing into Durbar Square.

Getting around

With Durbar Square less unequivocally a nucleus than its namesakes in either of the Valley's other two cities, the three squares together form the point from which all other areas have developed and are connected by a newly paved main road, the city's central artery. Either side is a network of narrow, occasionally cobbled but mostly earthen, lanes proceeding through the main residential areas down to the river to the south and to open countryside to the north.

The city's **tourist facilities** are minimal, consisting largely of a handful of guest houses and restaurants catering mainly to the budget traveller. Most people come for the day from Kathmandu, an hour away by bus.

Newars of Bhaktapur

In contrast to the greater variety of ethnic groups found in Kathmandu and Patan, Bhaktapur's population is dominated by **Newars** who constitute more than 90 percent of its people. The independent development of Bhaktapur within the Valley has resulted in a strong sense of identity for its people which is illustrated in the use of a dialect of Newari distinct from that spoken in Kathmandu and Patan. More than half of the population is directly or indirectly involved in agriculture.

The city is renowned for its curd (yoghurt) which, as vendors will not hesitate to tell you, is made from full cream milk (cow or buffalo), unlike some varieties, alleged to be made of powdered milk, sold in Kathmandu. It is known as juju dhau, or 'king of curds'. Rich and creamy it is, but not a scratch on the mishti dhai (sweet curd) of Bengal.

History

The early history of Bhaktapur is vague. Its origins lie in the Licchavi period, but credit for its founding is widely attributed to King Ananda Malla in the late 9th century AD. The city began as a trading centre known as **Khopring** and was renamed *Bhaktagram* ('village of devotees') in the early Malla period. Its steady growth led to the replacement of the suffix *gram* with *pur* ('city'). The city is said to have been laid out in the shape of a conch shell and the main road which still winds its way through the centre of the city may (with a little imagination) be thought to resemble the outline of a conch shell. It will be noted, however, that the road also approximately parallels the course contours of the Hanumante River to the south.

The peak of the city's influence was between the 14th and 16th centuries when it became the Valley's *de facto* capital. It was fortified in the 15th century. Many sources suggest that the royal palace was originally situated in Dattatraya Square before being relocated subsequently to its present Durbar Square location. Internecine rivalry among the Valley's Malla rulers from the 17th century was expressed also in the arts with each city striving to exalt itself and endorse the authority of its rulers through the character and splendour of its architecture. Many of the temples and monuments adorning the three squares date from the late 17th and early 18th centuries, during the rule of King **Bhupatindra Malla**. With the Gorkha unification of Nepal and the selection of Kathmandu as the national capital by Prithvi Narayan Shah in 1768, Bhaktapur's influence declined dramatically and the city's development continued largely independently from then.

The city's architectural heritage was significantly damaged by the 1934 earthquake. Some restoration has taken place. A major development project was initiated with German funding in 1974. This resulted in further restoration and renovation of many of Bhaktapur's buildings as well as road construction and improvement and the establishment of sewerage and drinking water systems.

Durbar Square Area

The 1934 earthquake caused considerable damage to buildings in the square which consequently appears more spacious than its two namesakes in Kathmandu and Patan. It is still an architectural showpiece, exhibiting numerous superb examples of the skills of Newari artists and craftsmen over several centuries.

Kathmandu Valley

Shiva/Parvati Mandir As you approach Durbar Square from the west, in front of you is this small, two roofed temple dedicated to Shiva who is depicted with his consort, Parvati. The main **gate** to the square is just beyond. Erected by King Bhupatindra Malla in the early 18th century, it is elaborately decorated with various auspicious symbols, images of Kartikkaya, a son of Shiva and god of war, as well as large carved images of Bhairab on the left and Hanuman on the right.

Statues of Ugrachandi Durga & Bhairab (1) On your left after entering the square a pair of large stone lions stand either side of the entrance to a school and guard these fine stone statues representing the 18-armed goddess Ugrachandi Durga and the 12-armed Bhairab. Durga is the furious form of Parvati, Shiva's consort, and is shown plunging her trident into the prostrate body of the demon Mahishasur whilst maintaining an air of remarkable serenity. Bhairab is a Tantric deity, a terrible form of Shiva. Both are garlanded with human heads and were commissioned in 1707 by Bhupatindra Malla. So pleased was the king with these sculptures, and so concerned that neither Kathmandu nor Patan should acquire their equal, that he ordered the hands of the unfortunate sculptor to be cut off.

Rameshwar (2), Bhadri (3) & Krishna Mandirs (4) Opposite the two statues are three temples of lesser importance, dedicated respectively to incarnations of Shiva (Rameshwar), Vishnu/Narayan (Bhadri) and again Vishnu as Krishna. The Krishna Mandir is the largest of the three, a two-storeyed simple pagoda design with a statue of Garuda, Vishnu's faithful vehicle, placed on a column facing the main entrance.

Shiva Mandir (5) Heading on towards the middle of the square, this shikhara style temple was constructed in 1674 by King Jita Mitra Malla. Images of various deities adorn the exterior on all sides.

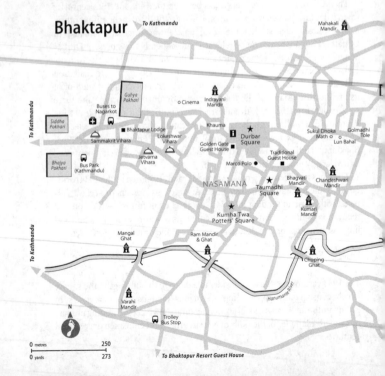

Kathmandu Valley

The original Royal Palace, built in 1427 by King Yaksha Malla, was situated in Dattatraya Square but was reconstructed in Durbar Square during the reign of Bhupatindra Malla (1696-1722). It was completed by King Jaya Ranjit Malla in 1754 and the result bore little resemblance to the original structure. The complex is said to have consisted of no fewer than 99 *chowks*, or courtyards. It was badly damaged in the 1934 earthquake and, despite extensive renovations, much of the artwork was lost and only six chowks remain (Bhairab Chowk, Igta Chowk, Kumari Chowk, Malagti Chowk, Mul Chowk and Siddhi Chowk). The palace is renowned for fabulous **55 carved windows** (after which it is sometimes known) as well as its **Golden Gate** (Sun Dhoka), **Taleju Mandir** and the **National Art Gallery** (see under **Museums**).

The Royal Palace (6)

Widely regarded as one of the most important artefacts in the Valley's heritage, this stunning portal to the middle section of the complex and the Taleju Mandir was commissioned by Ranjit Malla in 1745. Actually made of brass, it is set into and contrasts attractively with the main brick edifice. A pair of small gilded lions stand on their own miniature plinths either side of the remarkably small door, which is surrounded by images of six deities engraved in each side of the vertical brasswork. The large tilting torana above the door has a central image of a multiple limbed Taleju, above which it is crowned by a dynamic image of Garuda, vehicle of Vishnu. The surrounding masonry is framed with brass, with the upper portion having small finials of elephants and lions, flags, three central *kalasas* and a larger *kalasa* rising to form the pinnacle.

The Golden Gate (7) (Sun Dhoka)

Completing the trio of major temples dedicated to the Malla patron deity, Taleju, in the Valley's three Durbar Squares, this temple has its origins in the early 14th century which makes it the oldest of the three. It and the courtyard (Mul Chowk) in which it stands are not open to visitors, although the guard may allow you to look from the open entrance. Hindus may enter only on one day of the year, during Dasain. The temple itself is a lavishly decorated, one-storey structure, and is considered to be Bhaktapur's holiest religious site. It is believed to have some of the Valley's finest artwork. There are statues of various deities. One window of the temple is said to have been carved by Bhupatindra Malla himself. Squeezed between Taleju Chowk and Sundari Chowk is the tiny **Kumari Chowk**, again richly decorated.

Taleju Mandir

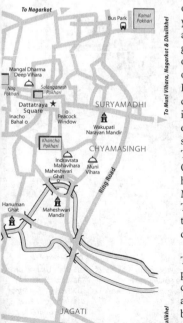

This is the eastern section of the complex and is named after the superbly carved balcony of windows in the red and black outer wall of the large Durbar Hall, the centre of what remains of the original Royal Palace after the 1934 earthquake. They are widely

The Palace of Fifty Five Windows (8)

considered to be the finest examples of decorative woodcarving in the Valley and were commissioned in the early 18th century by Bhupatindra Malla.

Sundari Chowk (9) This is the westernmost chowk of the palace complex. The name means 'beautiful courtyard'. Like its namesake in Patan, it contains a bathing tank used by the ruling Malla family, but is bigger than the one in Patan. An upright brass *naga*, or serpent deity, is situated on your right as you enter, with another fixed to the base of the tank. The sides of the stone tank are elaborately adorned with carvings of various deities.

King Bhupatindra Malla's Column (10) The mastermind behind the major development and beautification of Durbar Square is immortalized in brass opposite the Golden Gate. Reverentially seated in a bushel atop a stone pillar, the lifesize statue of the king wears a turban-like headpiece, while a shield and sword lie at his side. His gaze is directed towards the Taleju Mandir within.

Taleju Bell (11) This large bell, like those in Patan and Kathmandu's Durbar Squares, was used during temple worship and could double as an alarm. It was installed in 1737 by King Jaya Ranjit Malla, apparently in an attempt to thwart the nightmares that plagued him. It is also known as the 'Barking Dogs Bell', because its timbre seemingly incites the local canine population to collective bellowing.

Bhaktapur Durbar Square

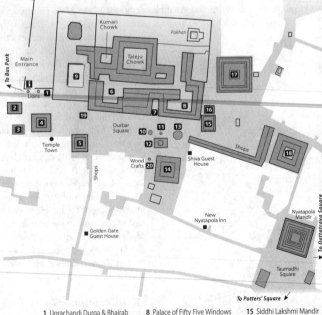

Not to scale

1 Ugrachandi Durga & Bhairab Statues	8 Palace of Fifty Five Windows
2 Rameshwar Mandir	9 Sundari Chowk
3 Bhadri Mandir	10 King Bhupatindra Malla's Column
4 Krishna Mandir	11 Taleju Bell
5 Shiva Mandir	12 Vatsala Durga Mandir
6 The Royal Palace Complex	13 Chayasilin Mandapa
7 The Golden Gate (Sun Dhoka)	14 Pashupatinath Mandir

15 Siddhi Lakshmi Mandir
16 Vatsala Mandir
17 Fasidega Shiva Mandir
18 Tadhunchen Bahal
19 National Art Gallery
20 Small Nandi Pillar

Durbar Square entry fee

In 1996 the entry fee payable by visitors to the Durbar Square was dramatically raised from Rs 50 to Rs 250. The reason given for this steep increase was the cost of continuing maintenance and restoration of the square. With cheap labour in Nepal, it was difficult to imagine benevolent contractors paying substantially higher than average wages to their workers. Local hoteliers, apart from wondering just how all of this extra revenue would be utilized (and to whose benefit), feared that the increase would seriously affect their business. "It's all right for the 5-star tourists", remarked one, "but overnight budget travellers will no longer come". Another quiped philosophically that a new age must be about to dawn on Durbar Square, with the authorities of the later 20th century continuing where the Mallas left off more than 200 years ago.

Vatsala Durga Mandir (12)

Beside the Taleju Bell is this shikhara style temple, one of two dedicated to Vatsala in Durbar Square. Steps flanked on either side by five stone animals lead to the shrine which is attractively surrounded by a pillared porch or verandah. Towards the top of the shikhara are further stone representations of minor deities. The temple was built in 1737 by King Jaya Ranjit Malla.

Chayasilin Mandapa (13)

Standing in front of the Palace of Fifty-Five Windows and beside a small tank is Durbar Square's only octagonal structure. The original pavilion was probably used by members of the ruling Malla family to sit and watch Durbar Square life, but it was destroyed in the 1934 earthquake. The present pavilion, an attractive double-storeyed pagoda, was a gift from Germany in the 1990s. It was modelled from a 19th century photograph and is an exact replica of the original. It is one of the few structures here to contain steel rather than brass or copper.

Pashupatinath Mandir (14)

The exact origins of this temple are disputed: some say it dates from the late 15th century, a posthumous tribute to King Yaksha by his widow and son, while others maintain it was built much later, in 1682 by King Jita Mitra Malla. The design of the two storeyed pagoda is based on the central shrine of the more famous Pashupatinath Mandir on the banks of the Bagmati River in Kathmandu. The roof struts have carvings depicting scenes from the *Ramayana* as well as some erotic themes. The shrine contains a Shiva linga.

Siddhi Lakshmi Mandir (15)

Returning to the eastern corner of the Royal Palace, this stone temple has statues of various animals as well as of men, women and children either side of the steps leading up to the entrance. The eponymous deity is the same as that to whom the shrine of the magnificent Nyatapola Mandir in Taumadhi Square is dedicated. Its construction was started by King Jita Mitra Malla and completed by Bhupatindra Malla after the death of the former in 1696.

Vatsala Mandir (16)

The second Vatsala temple in Durbar Square stands on a three-stage plinth beside the Siddhi Lakshmi Mandir. It is again of shikhara design and was built by King Jaya Ranjit Malla in 1737, an especially productive year in the history of Durbar Square. The central shikhara is surrounded by three smaller shrines. Southeast of the temple is a pair of stone lions.

Fasidega Shiva Mandir (17)

To the north of the Vatsala Mandir, this temple stands prominently on a six-stage plinth. Steps leading up to the main entrance are once again flanked by elephants and other animals. In contrast to the surrounding monuments, the shrine itself is plain, a cuboid structure topped by a small dome. It contains an image of the linga and yoni, which apparently replaced the originally intended deity, Macchendranath.

Tadhunchen Bahal (18) From the Fasidega temple, the square narrows to become an alley leading southeast to the neighbouring Taumadhi Tole. On your right (south) after the line of shops is this large 15th century monastery, the only Buddhist building here. The shops occupy what were dharamsalas, pilgrims' rest houses. Its design is classical Newari, and has some finely carved supports. If you continue west from the bahal, this paved road, the city's central artery, leads to Dattatraya Square after about one kilometre.

Taumadhi Square

From Durbar Square's Pashupatinath Mandir, follow the alleyway round to the south of the Tadhunchen Bahal and after 100 metres you arrive in Taumadhi Square. It is effectively an extension of Durbar Square to the southeast and, though much smaller, it contains Bhaktapur's finest and most impressive temple, the Nyatapola Mandir. From here you can head south to the city's famous pottery area, or east to join the road leading to Dattatraya Square. Around the Nyatapola Mandir is a small bazaar, or market area, where various handicrafts as well as local produce are sold.

Nyatapola Mandir With a height of 30 metres, this is the tallest free-standing pagoda temple in Nepal, and is unquestionably the city's most superb example of temple architecture. It stands in the northern part of the square and completely dominates the area. The five-storeyed temple was constructed by King Bhupatindra Malla in 1708 and, remarkably, emerged almost unscathed from the 1934 earthquake, the only damage being experienced by a section of the uppermost roof. Some say that Bhupatindra built the temple as a foil to the terror of Bhairab, to whom a neighbouring temple is dedicated.

The successive tiled roofs are supported by fabulously carved and painted beams and struts, with equally decorative windows. Five pairs of stone carved figures line the steps of the five plinths. Each figure is considered to be 10 times stronger than the one below. The images of the fabled Bhaktapur wrestlers, Jaya Malla and Phatta Malla, who are reputed to have had the strength of 10 men, kneel at the base and are followed in ascending order of strength by elephants, lions, griffins, and finally the goddesses Baghini and Singhini respectively depicted in the form of tiger and lion. The metaphor of strength serves to underline the power of the temple deity. Some people also come here to worship the goddess Bhairabhi, in a belief which

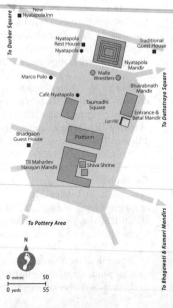

Taumadhi Square

- To Durbar Square
- New Nyatapola Inn
- Nyatapola Rest House
- Nyatapola
- Marco Polo
- Café Nyatapola
- Malla Wrestlers
- Nyatapola Mandir
- Traditional Guest House
- Bhairabnath Mandir
- Taumadhi Square
- Lun Hiti
- Entrance & Betal Mandir
- To Dattatraya Square
- Bhadgaon Guest House
- Platform
- Til Mahadev Narayan Mandir
- Shiva Shrine
- To Pottery Area
- To Bhagawati & Kumari Mandirs
- N
- 0 metres 50
- 0 yards 55

Quick nip to Taumadhi Square

You can get to Taumadhi Square without having to enter Durbar Square. At the main entrance gate to Durbar Square turn right and continue downhill along this lane as it bends first left then right. When you reach the junction at the end, turn left. From here you can either continue until you get to the southern end of Taumadhi Square or, after 50 metres, turn left. This narrow lane leads up to the centre of Durbar Square. If you wish, you can make a contribution to the continuing maintenance and restoration of the square at the information centre by the main entrance.

has Tantric origins. The interior, accessible only to priests, is Sino-Thai in character. It contains a shrine (but no idol) dedicated to the Hindu Tantric goddess Siddhi Lakshmi who is also carved into the 108 roof struts. The temple has a well planned geometry, with the size of each roof smaller than the one beneath by a constant proportion. Similarly, extrapolations of lines drawn to connect the corners of the supporting plinths will meet at the top of the entrance doors on each side.

To the southeast of the Nyatapola Mandir and contrasting markedly with it, this three-storeyed temple owes its rather stocky appearance to its unusual rectangular base and to its originally intended design as a single storeyed place of worship. It was built during the reign of King Jagat Jyoti Malla (1613-37). The second and third roofs were added by King Bhupatindra Malla in 1718. The whole building collapsed in the 1934 earthquake; the present structure is a replica which used those pieces of masonry and wood that could be salvaged from the remains of the original. A large prayer bell is suspended in front of the main entrance. The nearby image of Bhairab is surprisingly small, standing just 30 cm high, and is the focus of worship during the chariot processions of the annual *Bisket* festival. The main entrance to the temple is through the small **Betal Mandir**, located behind the temple. Betal is a protecting deity. There is a raised **platform** in front of the temple covering most of the southern part of the square which was used for performances of dance and drama, and shrines dedicated to **Shiva** and **Narayan** behind. Immediately south of the Bhairabnath Mandir is a small spring and tank, the **Lun Hiti**.

Bhairabnath Mandir

Inconspicuously situated in the southeast corner of the square, this two-storeyed temple is one of the oldest in Bhaktapur. Its curious nomenclature (*til* means sesame) is attributed to a travelling salesman who, upon setting up his stall on this spot, found an image of Narayan in his sack of sesame seeds. A stone inscription refers to this as a site of religious importance since 1080. The image of Narayan in the shrine is said to date from the 12th century. A statue of Garuda, vehicle of Vishnu (Narayan), stands on a pillar in front of the entrance, as does a *chakra* (wheel) and a delicately poised representation of a conch shell, both images associated with Vaishnavism. Next to it is a shrine dedicated to **Shiva** which includes a linga and yoni, the former being carved with four faces while the 'fifth' is 'invisible'. To get here, take the lane south of the Bhairabnath Mandir and turn right into the courtyard behind the block of red houses.

Til Mahadev Narayan Mandir

This popular restaurant now occupies a former pagoda temple. Renovated in the late 1970s as part of the Bhaktapur Development Project, it has some fine carved wooden beams and lattices. The roof strut carvings are dominated by erotic imagery.

Café Nyatapola

Walking east from Taumadhi Square Leaving Taumadhi Square by a lane at the northeast end of the square, you join the main road through Bhaktapur which leads to Dattatraya Square after barely one kilometre. The road is unusually and attractively paved with red brick, again a result of the Bhaktapur Development Project. Although many of the buildings along here have also benefited from restoration, you nevertheless get a reasonable impression of the city's life, with activity in and around the lines of traditional Newari houses, the men and women sitting all day long on 'their' piece of pavement and selling rice and vegetables, and groups of men engrossed in board games. Here and there you will also see tiny workshops where artisans chip away at a wooden or metallic sculpture, or are busy counting the beads onto a necklace. This is also the city's main commercial thoroughfare where most consumer items are available.

As the road bends to the right after Taumadhi Square, there is the **Sukul Dhoka** on your right. The *math* is home to some of the local temple priests, and was built as a monastery by King Jaya Ranjit Malla in the mid 18th century, Bhaktapur's last Malla king before Prithvi Narayan Shah led the Gorkhas to victory over the Valley's cities. It was renovated in the late 1980s and the first floor in particular is decorated with some accomplished woodcarving. The **Lun Bahal** just beyond was built as a Buddhist monastery in the 16th century, but in 1592 was transformed into a Hindu temple dedicated to Bhimsen, a deity of exceptional strength and courage. A little further on you arrive at **Golmadhi Tole**, a minor square with a small three-storeyed temple dedicated jointly to Ganesh and Bhairab who feature on the carved roof struts. There is also a *chaitya*, or small Buddhist shrine, small Shiva and Vishnu shrines, and a sacred water tank. Continuing along the main road and just before it veers north, there is a good view south to the burning ghats on the **Hanumante River** and beyond. You then pass the small and variously decorated **Inacho Bahal** on your left. From here it is a short stroll into **Dattatraya Square**. The road continues on through Bhaktapur's eastern suburbs and Nagarkot before it eventually arrives at Kodari on the Nepal-Tibet border.

Dattatraya Square (Tachupal Tole)

The easternmost of Bhaktapur's three main squares is also the oldest. It is widely thought that the original Royal Palace was built here in 1427 by King Yaksha Malla and later relocated to its present location in Durbar Square. The square is dominated by the large **Dattatraya Mandir** and has a good restaurant with excellent views across the square. In an alley southeast of the square is the remarkable and justifiably celebrated **peacock window**, a masterpiece of woodcarving. It also has two interesting museums (see **Museums**) with exhibitions of bronze and woodcarving.

Bhimsen Mandir This 17th century rectangular temple sits at the western end of the square in front of a small spring and tank. The ground floor is open while lattice windows enclose most of the middle floor. The much smaller second roof appears like an afterthought and is copper covered. In front of the temple to the east is a raised brick platform which was used, like that in Taumadhi Square, for performances of drama and dance.

Salan Ganesh Mandir Behind a large, old house on the northern side of the square, this small temple has roof struts carved with images of Ganesh and Bhairab as well as representations of the *Ashta Matrika*, or eight 'mother-goddesses'. It also dates from the 17th century. Its main image is a rock said to be a likeness of the elephant headed Ganesh.

Dominating Dattatraya Square from the eastern side, the construction of this **Dattatraya** temple was started by King Yaksha Malla in 1427 and completed in 1458. The **Mandir** temple is dedicated to Dattatraya, a syncretistic deity believed to be either an incarnation of Vishnu, a teacher of Shiva or a cousin of the Buddha. The presence of the winged Garuda standing on a tall pillar opposite the main entrance and, beside it, of a conch shell atop a smaller column, indicate that in this case the deity is worshipped primarily as Vishnu. The structure of the temple is reminiscent of the Kasthamandap in Kathmandu's Durbar Square and, similarly, the Dattatraya Mandir is said to have been built from the wood of a single tree. Its original purpose is unclear, but a further parallel with the Kasthamandap is suggested by those who argue that it was built as a pilgrim's rest house and was only later developed into a temple by the addition of the second and third floors. Its unique and somewhat ungainly second floor protrusion seems to serve only as embellishment. A large bell hangs suspended at the southwest corner of the temple and two huge painted statues of Jaya Malla and Phatta Malla, Bhaktapur's legendary wrestlers, stand guard at the main entrance.

Forming the southeast corner of the Square is a complex of former *maths* (reli- **Pujari Math &** gious houses where prayers and other religious activities take place, usually **the Peacock** according to a set schedule, and which can provide accommodation for celi- **Window** bate men at various traditional stages of Hindu life. The term is also used in the Jain religion). *Pujari* means those who perform *puja*, so the establishment therefore served as a semi-monastic residence for local priests. The original *math* dates from the 15th century. It was renovated and further buildings were added by King Jaya Ranjit Malla in 1763, five years before the Mallas were ousted from power by Prithvi Narayan Shah. The complex now houses the Woodcarving Museum. It was once more renovated in the 1980s as part of the German funded Bhaktapur Development Project.

Kathmandu Valley

Dattatraya Square

To Royal East Inn

To Wakupati Narayan Mandir

Salan Ganesh Pokhari

Salan Ganesh Mandir

Bronze & Brass Museum

Café de Peacock

Dattatraya Mandir

Bhimsen Mandir

Garuda Column

Dattatraya Square

To Taumadhi Square

Dattatraya Guest House

Pujari Math

Peacock Window

National Woodcarving Museum ★

Taja Math

N

0 metres 30
0 yards 33

To Khancha Pokhari

To Khancha Pokhari

Hawkers are invariably on hand on the street below to offer some surprisingly good miniature replicas of the window.

Of the many examples of magnificent woodcarving here, the **peacock window** is the best known. It is situated on the first floor of the east facing façade, a few metres along the narrow street leading off from the southeast corner of the square. The small window depicts a peacock displaying its fan of 19 feathers in a circular arrangement, surrounded by foliation and cherubic figures in the top corners. Thirty-five smaller birds form a border on three sides while deities are carved into the base. Three delicately carved eaves form the vertex. The (live) chickens belonging to the neighbouring household provide a humorous diversion by regularly parading along their own windowsill.

Buddhist Bhaktapur

Although Bhaktapur has a predominantly Hindu tradition, a Buddhist presence is maintained in the city's shrines and monasteries (*viharas*). Unfortunately, many show the signs of years of neglect and the Bhaktapur Development Project has largely passed them by. Some have been converted and others have fallen into disuse. The following description runs from west to east.

Sammakrit Vihara Two *vyala*s, or lion-like statues, guard the front entrance of this shrine and the expansive metal door frame is ornately engraved. Inside is a modern statue of the Buddha. The surrounding walls have attractive representations of episodes of his life and were given by a group of Buddhist monks from Thailand. To the right after you enter are the monastic living quarters. The tiled roof is supported by carved struts. The vihara is located on the next street running south after the bus stop.

Jetvarna Vihara Heading into town from the bus stop, take the right hand fork just east of the bus stop and after about 300 metres there are two Buddhist sites on opposite sides of the road. In a courtyard on the right hand side (south), the Jetvarna Vihara has a raised platform on which two small chaityas, or shrines, stand. Two *vyala*s are placed at the front corners. The pagoda-like shrines contain images of Shakyamuni and Avalokiteshwar. Squeezed between the two is a small white chaitya and behind it stands an ornamental pillar.

Lokeshwar Vihara On the northern side of the road, this is probably the city's most attractive Buddhist structure and its only three-storeyed pagoda temple. In front of the entrance, a Buddha statue is surrounded by several smaller chaityas and other objects. Two large bells are installed on either side of the main doorway which is also guarded by stone lions. The temple is noteworthy for the *jangha*-like arrangement of household utensils between the first two floors, which are symbolically offered to the temple deity with the petitions of the faithful.

Mangal Dharma Deep Vihara Located on a side street just southwest of Dattatraya Square, the name means 'holy (or blessed) religious flame', but this small vihara is memorable only for its ornately attired image of Dipankar.

Indravrata Mahavihara South of Dattatraya Square and on the northeast side of Khancha Pokhari, is this uniquely designed vihara. Below the small upper pagoda roof, the square building has three floors. The middle one is compressed, giving the whole an almost sandwich-like appearance. The decorative main entrance has the ubiquitous lion guardians which in turn are flanked by racks of prayerwheels. A beautifully carved window frame above the architrave is the centrepiece of the stunted second floor.

Following the main road as it leaves Dattatraya Square to the east on its way to   **Muni Vihara**
Dhulikhel and eventually Tibet, you arrive at this active monastery after about
700 metres. It has an attractively columned verandah. Inside, the shrine has a
large statue of the meditating Buddha accompanied by two smaller Buddha
statues in different poses.

The Ghats

There is no actual footpath that follows the slender Hanumante River, but you
can reach its ghats along streets leading from the centre of town. **Mangal Ghat**,
the westernmost of the main ghats, is surrounded by a number of small buildings and religious monuments. You can cross the river here and after 200 metres
there is the small Vaishnavite **Varahi Mandir**. **Ram Ghat** is about 200 metres
downstream. It is used for cremations and bathing and has a temple, the **Ram
Mandir**. If you arrive from Kathmandu by trolley bus and head northeast from
the bus stop, you will cross a bridge beside Ram Ghat. This road continues north
through the pottery area and on towards Taumadhi and Durbar Squares.

If you leave Taumadhi Square heading east (near the entrance to the Til
Mahadev Narayan Mandir) the road passes two temples (**Bhagvati Mandir**
and **Kumari Mandir**) as it loops south and crosses the river to **Chuping Ghat**,
a *mélange* of small rundown monuments and a cremation site.

You can reach the largest and busiest ghat, **Hanuman Ghat**, from either
Taumadhi Square or Dattatraya Square. The ghat is used for bathing, washing
and burning. It is surrounded by numerous small monuments and lingas, and
there is an image of Hanuman beside a Rama shrine. On one side is a
dharamsala, a pilgrims' rest house. The site also marks the junction of two
channels of the Hanumante River and is thus considered to be endowed with
greater holiness.

Getting there   Leave Taumadhi Square at its northeast corner, by the Nyatapola
Mandir, then take the first right turning. This road (southeast) continues straight to
the ghat after some 700 metres. From Dattatraya Square, take the road heading south
from the centre of the square. After 100 metres turn right then left around the rectangular Khancha Pokhari. Follow this road in a SSW direction for a further 400 metres.

Furthest northeast is the much smaller **Maheshwari Ghat**, situated on the
northern bend of the river. There is the small **Maheshwari Mandir** over the
bridge. Leave Dattatraya Square as above for Hanuman Ghat. Just south of
Khancha Pokhari, take the left hand fork leading to the ghat after 100 metres.

Kumha Twa – Potters' Square

Bhaktapur has earned a reputation for its pottery and produces much of the
Valley's terracotta pots, vases and souvenirs. The main pottery area (*Kumha
Twa*, or Potters' Square) is south of Durbar Square and you can go there to
watch the wheels go round in its open courtyards and verandahs. A visit is well
worthwhile and you can buy souvenirs – anything from an ornamental candle-
stick to the traditional round water containers used by women in villages
throughout the subcontinent – both in the square and from hawkers lining the
street from Taumadhi Square.

As you enter the square from the north, there is a shrine dedicated to
Ganesh, the patron deity of the local potters. Built by a Kumha Twa potter, the
two-storeyed **Jeth Ganesh Mandir** dates from 1646 and tradition has it that its
priest comes from this potter community.

Kathmandu Valley

A tradition in clay

The art of pottery is almost as old as civilization itself and traditional methods have been maintained by Bhaktapur's kumha potter community. Like the Sakhya community of metalsmiths in Patan, the trade is largely hereditary, its skills handed down through generations of the same families, with workshops and studios remaining in one locality. A major factor behind Bhaktapur's terracotta success has been the quality of clay found particularly in areas to the south of the city. The village of **Sipadol** lies some three kilometres south by a small river, the Sipadol Khola. Its clay soil, known as dyo cha or 'black clay', is highly valued by Kumha Twa potters who barter their earthenware products for clay from the village farmers.

Once the clay arrives in Bhaktapur, it is kept covered and away from the sun to avoid loss of moisture and malleability. Before it is used it must be kneaded, any stones removed and more water added if necessary to obtain just the right consistency. It is then ready for the wheel. Traditionally made of wood, some interesting alternatives have recently been introduced including a converted, old lorry tyre. The potter's proficiency is applied with the turning of the wheel as the clay rises and takes shape in his adroit hands. It does not always work out right first time, as any of the young apprentices here will involuntarily demonstrate. After it has joined a multitude of others drying in the sun, the pot is slowly fired in the brick kiln, a process that takes several days. Finally it is removed, cleaned, polished and sent to market.

Bhaktapur's potters have not escaped the consequences of 'new' technology, with local preferences steadily turning to plastic as the favoured medium for tableware and containers. Tourism, however, has come as an unexpected boon and now terracotta candlesticks, masks, ashtrays and other small decorative items are being produced to be sold locally as well as exported.

Getting there follow the street leading downhill from the southwest corner of Taumadhi Square and take the first turning on your left (southwest). After about 100 metres, the square opens to your right. You can continue along this street for a further 400 metres and arrive at the small **Ram Mandir** and **Ram Ghat** (bathing and cremation) by the **Hanumante River**.

Other areas

While the splendour of Bhaktapur lies most conspicuously in its three major squares, its rustic charms extend both north and south of the city's central artery. Just before the main western entrance to Durbar Square, you can turn left (north) down a long set of steps with small houses on either side and agricultural countryside beyond. Half way down on your left (west) is the **Indrayani Mandir**, dedicated to the king of gods and god of rain. After 150 metres you reach the junction of the road that heads east to Nagarkot and west to Kathmandu. Turn right (southeast) and this street leads back towards the eastern side of Durbar Square, but if you head east on the Nagarkot road, you will see the raised **Mahakali Mandir** on your left (north) after 400 metres. Just beyond and again on your left is a dirt road that leads north to Changu Narayan (seven kilometres).

From the Changu Narayan road junction, you can turn right (south) and after 300 metres turn left (southeast) at the second crossroads you come to. This road leads to Dattatraya Square after 300 metres, passing the **Nag Pokhari**, a small holy tank dedicated to the serpent deities which control rainfall and another indication of the strong link between nature, agriculture and religious expression. You can continue through the maze of narrow streets north and northeast of Dattatraya Square and the large **Kamal Pokhari** is at the northeast corner of the city. There are lovely views across both sides of the valley from here. From the pokhari, head south to join with the city's main central thoroughfare after 300 metres. Turn right (west) and the **Wakupati Narayan Mandir** is ahead of you. This is an attractive two-storeyed pagoda temple with a shrine containing an image of Vishnu as Narayan. Facing the entrance are numerous pillars with images of Garuda, a *chakra* and a conch shell.

Museums

This small museum is in the restored **Pujari Math** in the southeast corner of Dattatraya Square. It has some fine examples of Newari arched windows, roof struts, statues and ornamental carvings from throughout the Valley. Most date from the 17th century onwards. The small courtyard is enclosed by fabulously carved windows. On the ground floor is a mask of Jaya Malla, one of the pair of Bhaktapur's legendary wrestlers. The recently renovated main staircase faces north in accordance with local geomantic practices which prescribe that a staircase must never face south. The **peacock window** is actually an exhibit, but is viewed from the outside (see under *Dattatraya Square*). **NB** The museum is closed on Tuesday, but if the main door is open you may be able to persuade the security guards to let you in. ■ *1000-1530, daily except Tuesday and holidays. Friday closes at 1430. Rs 10, camera charge Rs 10, T610005.*

National Woodcarving Museum

Located on the first floor of the old part of the Royal Palace ('Palace of Fifty-Five Windows') in Durbar Square and opened in 1961, this is the most recent of the Valley's 'national' museums. Its collections include some especially fine displays of **thangkas** and **paubhas**, palm leaf **manuscripts** and examples of Bhaktapur's **craft** heritage. The entrance is flanked by statues of Hanuman in the Tantric form of Bhairab, and Vishnu as Narasimha. These were commissioned in c 1698 by King Bhupatindra Malla, who purportedly wanted to combine the deities' respective powers in an effort to maintain law and order in the city. On either side of the entrance are **inscriptions** in stone: one dates from the Licchavi king, Shiva Deva, the other is more recent and was carved during the reign of one of the first Malla rulers, King Yaksha Malla (1428-82). Many of the paubhas are strongly influenced by Tantrism and have depictions of various *shaktis*.

National Art Gallery

Stunningly painted **manuscripts** include an opus of Buddhist *Prajnaparamita* (a class of Mahayana literature focusing on the bodhisattva paths which cultivate the perfection of discriminative awareness) penned in golden ink and lavishly illustrated throughout. There is also a hand painted/written 'biography' of the much revered **King Pratap Malla** (reigned in Kathmandu 1640-74) who was responsible for the construction of many of the temples and monuments in Kathmandu's Durbar Square. It is thought to be Nepal's oldest existing biographical manuscript. The collection of strange, colourful 17th century Newari **animal paintings** on the second floor should not be missed. ■ *T610004. 1000-1530, daily except Tuesday and holidays, Friday closes at 1430. Rs 5, camera charge Rs 10.*

Located in a 15th century math on the northern side of Dattatraya Square, opposite the Pujari Math, this offers a collection of domestic and religious metalware. Exhibits include *kalasas* (the vase-like pots often used as temple finials), *hookahs* (or 'hubble-bubble', a smoking vase in which the smoke is drawn through water by sucking on a long flexible pipe), and spittoons. ■ *T610448. 1000-1330, daily except Tuesday and holidays, Friday closes at 1430. Admission Rs 5, camera charge Rs 10.*

The Bronze & Brass Museum

Kathmandu Valley

Essentials

Sleeping Although Bhaktapur has even less accommodation than Patan, there are still a few places where you can stay in reasonable comfort. All are in the lower price range, catering for the budget traveller, and most are fairly central. It is not really an alternative to Kathmandu for a longer stay, but the advantage of staying overnight is that you get to see the place in its stimulatingly natural state, unencumbered by daytime touts and tourist buses.

C-D *Bhaktapur Resort Guest House*, T610670, F610267. Located outside Bhaktapur, on a hill overlooking the city from the south, follow the road south from the trolley bus stop. 20 rooms most with bath, restaurant does Nepali and Chinese food, pleasant grounds, parking area, traditionally decorated hall.

D *Bhadgaon Guest House*, T610488, F610481. 9 rooms all with bath, some with tub, good rooftop restaurant for all types of food, modern, clean, comfortable and bright, excellent location in the southwest corner of Taumadhi Square. **D** *Dattatraya Guest House*, no phone, 10 rooms all common bath, large modern building on the west side of Dattatraya Square, bright and clean, rooftop restaurant has Bhaktapur's best views looking out over the Dattatraya Mandir and the southern valley. **D** *Golden Gate Guest House*, T610534. 15 rooms some with bath, clean, basic Indian, Chinese, continental food, rooftop terrace. **D** *Nyatapola Inn*, T611323. 9 rooms all with bath, small eating area, clean and comfortable, luminous green bed sheets throughout, small handicraft shop, prices ripe for negotiation, Taumadhi Square. **D** *Royal East Inn*, no phone, 18 rooms some with bath, same food as *Café de Peacock*, northeast of Dattatraya Square, near the Dhulikhel bus stop. **D** *Shiva Guest House*, T610740, F(Kathmandu) 228600. 10 rooms (including 3 triples) all common bath, good Chinese and continental food, basic but clean, friendly family atmosphere, excellent views over Durbar Square from dining room and roof. Recommended.

E *Bhaktapur Lodge*, no phone, 10 rooms all common bath, very dark and basic, simple eating area downstairs, no English spoken, near the bus stop. **E** *Nyatapola Rest House*, 5 basic rooms all common bath, attached restaurant, superb location just north of the Nyatapola Mandir, but the only view from the rooms is of a brick wall. **E** *Traditional Guest House*, T611057. 10 basic rooms all common bath, a typical large Newari house built around a sociologically intriguing courtyard containing a number of small shrines and an extremely large satellite dish, some food available, rooftop terrace, located between Durbar Square and Taumadhi Square.

Eating Bhaktapur is by no means overburdened with restaurants, but there are enough in and around the three main squares to cater for most tastes.

Bhadgaon Kitchen Restaurant and Jom Bar, T610094. Located on the main road just west of Dattatraya Square. Clean and bright, reasonably priced Nepali, Chinese and continental food. *Café de Peacock*, T610684. Probably the best place to eat in Bhaktapur, a popular restaurant on the first floor of a well maintained Newari wooden building with commanding views of the Dattatraya Mandir and square. Good menu including continental, Mexican and Nepali food, Kathmandu prices, cheaper liquor. *Café Nyatapola*, T610346. This is the large pagoda building (sometimes confused for a temple) in the middle of Taumadhi Square, and is said to have been built using materials remaining from the reconstruction of the Bhairab Mandir opposite, popular for snacks and meals, also sells Kodak film and Western cigarettes. *Marco Polo*, is at the northwest corner of Taumadhi Square and there are good views over the square from the balcony, Italian, Indian, Chinese. *Nyatapola Restaurant*, just north of the

Nyatapola Mandir in Taumadhi Square, reasonable Nepali and Indian food, some 'continental' snacks, top floor has views of the square. *Temple Town*, T/F610782. Situated in the southwest corner of Durbar Square. Semi-Thamel menu including Chinese, continental, Indian snacks and meals, more expensive than average, good views over Durbar Square from roof.

Cinema: a cinema showing mainly Bombay produced Hindi films is located northeast of the Kathmandu minibus stop, west of Durbar Square.

Entertainment

January: *Basant Panchami* Marks the coming of spring and is dedicated to Saraswati, the goddess of knowledge. In Bhaktapur it is celebrated particularly by craftsmen.

Festivals

April: *Bisket* (Snake Slaughter) Special celebrations to commemorate the great battle in the Hindu epic *Mahabharata*. Chariots carrying Bhairab and Bhadrakali are drawn through the narrow streets. A tug-of-war between the upper and lower parts of town decides who will be fortunate for the coming year. A tall wooden pole (sometimes up to 20 metres high) is erected near the riverside at Chuping Ghat with cross beams from which two banners, signifying snake demons, are hung. On the following day (New Year), it is brought crashing down after another tug-of-war. There is dancing and singing in the streets over four days.

May: *Sithi Nakha* celebrates the victory of Kumar, god of war, over the demons, as well as marking the onset of the monsoon rains. A palanquin carrying an image of the goddess Bhagawati is the focus of a procession through Taumadhi Square.

August: *Gathan Muga* (or *Ghantakarna* or *Gathe Mangal*) This festival derives from Tantrism and marks the completion of the season's rice planting by a sort of mass celebratory 'exorcism' of evil spirits which may affect the crops' growth. Effigies of the demon, Gathan Muga, are made of straw or dried rice stalks and in the evening are immersed in the river. Offerings of cooked rice are placed along the streets to placate the demons and iron nails (the Newari equivalent of 'Transylvanian' garlic) are driven into the horizontal beam above the doorway of each house.

August/September: *Gai Jatra* A folk dance unique to Bhaktapur is performed during this festival. Families which have been bereaved during the past year are supposed to send a cow to join the procession, in the belief that the sacred cow will assist the departed soul in its onward journey. Alternatively, they will attire themselves in fancy dress resembling a cow. The procession is jovial and accompanied by music and dancing. Evening feasts centre around *kwati*, a type of bean soup.

September: *Panja Dan* A Buddhist festival of charity when rice and other consumables are ritually offered to Buddhist monks. Uniquely in the Valley, Bhaktapur celebrates the day with colourful processions carrying five images of the Dipanker Buddha. The festival is also marked at Swayambhunath and Bodhnath.

Most of Bhaktapur's handicraft shops are concentrated around the three main squares. If you wander along the side streets leading off from the main road that runs through the centre of the city, you will come across numerous small shops where artisans demonstrate a remarkable degree of dexterity by simultaneously using hands, feet and tools to fashion metal **statues**, pieces of **jewellery** and other souvenir handicrafts – follow the gentle tapping noises. You can find the wonderful **woodcarvings** for which Bhaktapur is acclaimed sold on the street below and near the peacock window, off Dattatraya Square. Try also *Antique Wood Carving* in Dattatraya Square. (**NB** Genuine antiques require certified permission from the Dept of Archaeology, Singha

Shopping

If you can't find what you're looking for in Bhaktapur, it's all available in Kathmandu as well

Durbar, Kathmandu, in order to be exported.) Miniature reproductions of the window are popular, but if you want a full size replica carved to order by a skilled craftsman, this can be done within 25 days for Rs 20,000!

The large spherical water containers used by village women throughout South Asia are attractive and inexpensive, but may have difficulty in surviving the rigours of a flight home.

For **terracotta** and **earthenware** products, the best place to go is the pottery area, south of Durbar Square where you can buy direct from the potter. Although the mainstay of the area's output has traditionally been water pots and other household containers for local sale, attractive ornamental items are increasingly being produced. You can get anything from decorative candlesticks to masks of various deities here. As always, expect to bargain hard. Try also the various streetside vendors between Dattatraya Square and Hanuman Ghat, and along the main road heading east from Dattatraya Square.

Puppets: made in Bhaktapur often show tribal people with tools of their trade or many armed deities clutching little wooden weapons in each hand. Try the *Handicrafts Centre*, near the Dattatraya Mandir. For **cushion covers**, **napkins**, etc, try *S Laxmi Crafts*, T611323, in the *New Nyatapola Inn*, in Taumadhi Square. *Radha Krishna Dhaubhadel*, T612002, is at Suryabinayak, west of Dattatraya Square, and has export quality **pashmina shawls**, **rice paper prints** and textiles. You can get good **thangkas/paubhas** in Durbar Square, and **topis** (traditional Nepali caps worn by men) from shops near the Bhairabnath Mandir in Taumadhi Square. A range of locally produced handicrafts at *Valley Handicrafts and Workshop*, T610946, in Durbar Square.

Transport   The only long distance route operated from Bhaktapur is via Dhulikhel to **Kodari** on the Nepal-Tibet border, but this begins its journey in Kathmandu.

Local Minibus: the terminus for minibuses to and from **Kathmandu** (Bagh Bazaar, City Bus Park and Martyrs' Gate bus stops) is at **Siddhi Pokhari**, about 800 metres west of Durbar Square. Regular departures throughout the day at approximately 15-minute intervals or when the bus is full. Last bus leaves Bhaktapur at about 1900 – check. Fare Rs 5. Journey time approximately 50 minutes. **Trolley Bus**: this is an intriguing cross between a bus and a tram and runs only between **Kathmandu** and Bhaktapur. It is slow and can be unreliable. It leaves Kathmandu from Tripureshwar, near the National Stadium. The Bhaktapur terminus is south of the Hanumante River: head south from Durbar and Taumadhi Squares, through the pottery area and across the river at Ram Ghat. Regular departures. Fare Rs 3. Journey time approximately 2 hours. **Taxi**: the official rate set by the government for the journey from Kathmandu is about Rs 800 each way, but this can be substantially reduced with negotiation. Hiring a taxi for the day is usually cheaper than going to a car rental firm. It allows flexibility and you can easily combine Bhaktapur with Thimi (en route), Dhulikhel or Nagarkot on a whistle stop tour of the eastern valley. Make sure that you fix the price with the taxi driver before setting off.

Directory   **Hospitals & medical services**   There is a hospital at Doodh Pati, T610676. Several pharmacies in the centre of town, no prescriptions required.

Public toilets   Serviceable ladies and gents WCs in the tourist information office at the western entrance of Durbar Square. (Gents has an impractically high urinal.) Wash basins sometimes have water. Two more public WCs opposite here, next to the *Temple Town* restaurant.

Tourist offices   There is a small tourist information office at the western entrance to Durbar Square, but you will only get photocopied city maps here.

Kathmandu Valley
beyond the three cities

5

Kathmandu Valley
beyond the three cities

302 Budhanilikantha & Baghdwar

302 Gokarna & Sundarijal

304 Sankhu, Vajra Jogini & Changu Narayan Mandir

307 Nagarkot

310 Kathmandu to Dhulikhel

311 Dhulikhel

316 Arniko Highway from Dhulikhel to Tibet

319 Bishanku Narayan, Godavari & Phulchowki

320 Bungamati, Chapagaon & Lele

322 Chobhar, Pharping & Dakshinkali

326 Kirtipur

328 Ichangu Narayan Mandir, Nagarjun & Bani Bans

329 Kakani & the Trisuli Road

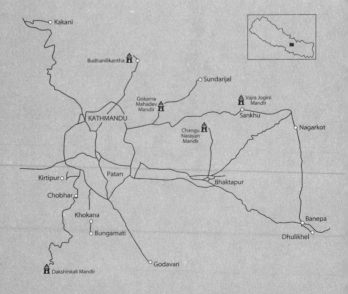

Within easy reach of the three cities, the Valley still has more to offer. Stupas and temples encircle the three cities with the impressive and mysterious temple of Dakshinkali in the southwest and the more peaceful and beautiful Changu Narayan in the north particularly outstanding. Cultured out? Why not relax in the hilltop retreats of Nagarkot or Dhulikhel: sit back and admire the views.

NB *Since most of the Valley's major roads fan out from Kathmandu, this section is arranged in a clockwise order from the capital.*

Budhanilikantha and Baghdwar

Colour map 2, grid B5 *Heading northwest from the Royal Palace along Lazimpath, you enter Kathmandu's diplomatic enclave. Turn left at the Hotel Ambassador to reach the British and Indian embassies, or right on Lazimpath to reach the US embassy. Continuing along, you will eventually reach Budhanilikantha, some nine kilometres north of the city centre, which is one of the valley's most photographed sites.*

Budhanilikantha
(Budhanilkantha)

Revered as an emanation of Avalokiteshwara by Newar Buddhists, and by Hindus as Narayana, an incarnation of Vishnu lying on a bed of Naga spirits or snakes, this remarkable supine image is the largest stone sculpture of the Kathmandu Valley and one of three fashioned by King Vishnugupta in the seventh century. Another lies at Balaju, while the third was installed in the old Royal Palace for King Pratap Malla. It draws large crowds at Haribodhini Ekadasi and Kartik Purnima. The five metres monolithic statue is in a small tank at the foot of the Shivapuri Hills and is thought to have come from beyond the valley. In his four hands the deity holds the four attributes: a discus (symbol of the mind), a mace (primeval knowledge), a conch shell (the five elements), and a lotus seed (the universe). Pilgrims descend to the tank by a stone causeway. A priest washes the god's face each morning at around 0900. Jayasthiti Malla revived the Vishnu cult at the end of the 14th century, pronouncing himself to be an incarnation of Vishnu, a belief held by successive rulers to the present day. Since the time of King Pratap Malla (17th century), who dreamt that his successors would die if they were to visit the image, no king of Nepal has ventured into its presence. According to legend, Vishnu sleeps for four months of the year and the festival of Budhanilikantha, held in November, celebrates the deity waking from his monsoon repose.

Getting there: Buses run from the City Bus Park to Bansbari. From here it's about an hour's walk. Alternatively, you can walk from Kathmandu or cycle. Further north, the road heads from Budhanilikantha into the Shivapuri hills.

Baghdwar

This small Buddhist site is actually situated outside the Valley, beyond the Shivapuri Hills to the north of Budhanilikantha. It is revered by Buddhist legend as the place where the Buddha Krakuchhanda preached and effected the origin of the Bagmati River. The word bagmati means 'stream of words'.

Gokarna and Sundarijal

Gokarna
Colour map 3, grid A3

Some seven kilometres northeast of Kathmandu, Gokarna is best known as a 'safari park' or 'royal game reserve'. The park's forested hills are home to deer, antelope and boar, as well as numerous species of bird and butterfly. Since 1996, however, the park has sadly remained closed while construction of a new luxury hotel and golf complex continues. This was scheduled to have been completed by 1999. The entrance to the park is on the main road heading east from Kathmandu, about two kilometres beyond Bodhnath.

To the north of the park, standing on the west bank of the Bagmati River in its early stages, is the Gokarna Mahadev Mandir. This three-storeyed pagoda temple dates from the late 16th century and is built on an ancient sacred site. It is dedicated to Shiva and the shrine contains a linga. Above the main eastern entrance is a torana, or metal plaque, depicting Shiva with his consort, Parvati. Leading to the temple and surrounding it is an unusual collection of religious

Gokarna Mahadev Mandir

statuary, the extent of which is possibly unique in Nepal. In addition to several representations of Shiva plus appendages, there are also images of Vishnu including one 'footprint', as Narasingha the man-lion incarnation, and in the form of Narayan. To complete the Hindu trinity, Brahma is also portrayed – as a bearded figure – in a rare representation of the Hindu god of creation. In August-September each year, thousands of people come here to pay homage to the memory of their forefathers.

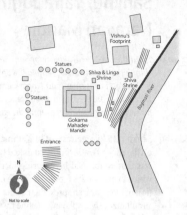

Getting there: Gokarna is a good cycling destination. From Kathmandu, follow the road east from Chabahil. You pass the Bodhnath stupa on your left (north). After a further 1 kilometre, the road forks. Take the left hand fork (northeast) which becomes the Sundarijal Road. Climb for about 2 kilometres until you arrive at the temple. On your right is the small Bagmati River valley and on the opposite slope is the Gokarna park. Buses run regularly from City Bus Park to Bodhnath from where it is a pleasant walk. Alternatively, auto rickshaws will charge about Rs 120 from central Thamel, and taxis about Rs 220 by meter. Kopan, with its monastery and spiritual retreat centre (see page 207), can be reached by turning left (northwest) along a track just before the Gokarna temple. Follow the track for about 800 metres to the tiny village of Jagdol from where a path leads south to Kopan.

Sundarijal

This is a popular starting point for treks heading into the Helambu region, but also makes for an accessible excursion from Kathmandu. The name itself means 'beautiful water' (sundari jol) in reference to the early stages of the Bagmati River. The river is actually no more spectacular than a stream here, though there are a series of small waterfalls which are particularly attractive during and after the monsoon. If you continue some kilometres north of Sundarijal you will reach a reservoir which supplies much of Kathmandu's drinking water. A large and unsightly overland pipe channels the water from the watershed to the capital. Although it rather spoils the picturesque environment, it does serve as a useful landmark for walkers.

Getting there: From Gokarna, the Sundarijal Road continues in a northeast direction for about three kilometres until the road becomes a track.

Short Walks In addition to the longer treks heading up into the mountains, there are several possibilities for shorter walks from here. If you head east along one of the trails that lead from the Sundarijal Road before you reach Sundarijal, you will link into a web of other trails that connect various small villages and settlements on the way to Sankhu. From Sankhu, there is a minor road that climbs east to Nagarkot where there are superb views of the Himalaya as well as accommodation. Leaving Sundarijal to the west is a trail which veers sharply to the north, a steep climb, to join a minor road which approximately follows the contours west to the Naga Gompa monastery after about three kilometres. From here there is another trail for about two kilometres west to Budhanilikantha and its renowned statue of the reclining Vishnu.

Sankhu, Vajra Jogini and Changu Narayan Mandir

From the old Newari village of Sankhu on the road from Kathmandu you can climb up to the attractive temple site of Vajra Jogini.

The road continues onto Nagarkot which perhaps offers the best views of the Himalaya from the Kathmandu Valley as well as being the start or finishing point for several possible walks around the eastern Valley.

Sankhu   Sankhu, 15 kilometres east of Kathmandu, emerged as a result of its position on the ancient trade route that linked India and Tibet. A permanent settlement was first established here during Licchavi times. Today, Sankhu is a village which in many ways typifies rural life in the Kathmandu Valley: an agglomeration of old Newari houses, their structural woodwork often dilapidated whilst simultaneously displaying the fine carvings which seem to have been taken so much for granted in traditional Newari architecture. The village is surrounded also by fertile agricultural land, the basis for the village's existence. Particularly to the east and northeast, this is arranged in a series of gentle terraces which enables farmers to make the most of natural water run off from the hills with which to irrigate their paddy. This makes for a spectacular scene dominated by bright lush green as the crops begin to mature. If you are here either at harvesting or sowing, it is worth taking time to watch as all those who are physically fit join together to plant or reap.

A large and colourfully decorated arched gateway marks the village limits. There are a couple of shops in the village selling cold drinks and snacks, but there are no restaurants. From Sankhu, you can head north to the temple of Vajra Jogini, or continue east towards Nagarkot.

Getting there: Sankhu is 14 kilometres from Kathmandu on the main road heading east from Chabahil past Bodhnath. There are irregular bus services from Kathmandu's City Bus Park – it is a slow journey of about 2 hours and the fare is Rs 10. If you hire a car or taxi, it is possible to combine a visit to Vajra Jogini with an excursion to Nagarkot. Negotiate the rate in advance. Alternatively, you can hire a mountain bike, though it is a long and steep climb onwards to Nagarkot, and the condition of the road deteriorates east of Sankhu. You can also take the bus as far as Sankhu then walk to and spend the night at Nagarkot.

Vajra Jogini Mandir   This delightful three-storeyed pagoda temple, built by King Prakash Malla who was responsible for many of the buildings and monuments standing in Kathmandu's Durbar Square, is situated some two kilometres north of Sankhu and commands magnificent views of the Valley. The uppermost roof is said to be of gold, while the two lower roofs are copper gilded. The struts of all three roofs are lavishly carved with depictions of various deities and mythical animal figures. The main entrance of richly engraved copper is guarded by two large and brightly coloured stone lions. Just below and on plinths on either side of the steps are two smaller metallic lions. The site has long been associated with religion and, although the current temple structure dates from the 17th century, it is widely believed that the location was used as a place of worship even during Licchavi times. The deity, a fearsome shakti aspect which normally remains out of sight, derives from Tantric traditions and, as part of a local festival, is carried in an annual journey to Sankhu every April.

Around this main temple is a variety of statuary and religious icons and to the west another smaller temple with some fine woodcarvings is dedicated to one of the Buddhist Taras. Beware of the numerous monkeys here. Basic dharamsala accommodation is available for devotees.

Getting there: From Sankhu it is a 30-minute (2 kilometres) uphill walk. North of the village, you can either follow the bumpy but more or less motorable road or, after 1 kilometre, take the footpath that forks off to the right (northeast) and parallels the road. En route you will pass an old dharamsala, or pilgrims' rest house, and just before you reach the stone steps that lead to the temple courtyard there is a site where sacrifices take place. There are several trails leading from Vajra Jogini to the north and west. It is possible to climb to the top of the ridge that encloses the Valley to the northeast, but although only about 4 kilometres as the crow flies it involves an ascent of some 800 metres through dense woodland in parts. You can also head northeast and join up with trails that will eventually reach Budhanilikantha. Sufficient supplies of food and water as well as a local guide are recommended.

The ancient Hindu temple of Changu Narayan ranks as one of the finest and **Changu** most dramatic of all sites in the Valley and is a UNESCO designated World **Narayan Mandir** Heritage Site. Perched on the Dolagiri hill some 125 metres above the valley floor and 13 kilometres east of Kathmandu, it has superb views across the Valley. Its origins are widely believed to date back to the fifth century AD. Some sources suggest an earlier beginning and that it was built by King Hari Dutta Varma in AD 325, while others say the temple was built on an erstwhile animist place of worship. Before the 18th century unification of Nepal it was part of the independent Malla kingdom of Bhaktapur. The temple is acknowledged to be the oldest extant example of the Nepalese style of pagoda architecture, though much of the present structure dates from 1702 when it was rebuilt following a

Kathmandu Valley: beyond the three cities

Changu Narayan Mandir

N

Not to scale

1 Changu Narayan Mandir	5 Inscription	9 Ganesh Statue
2 Garuda Statue	6 Garuda / Vishnu	10 Shiva Shrine
3 Bhupatindra Malla Statue	7 Shiva Linga	11 Vishwarup
4 Pillar	8 Vishnu Shrine	12 Lakshmi Narayan Mandir

fire. A programme for its conservation and development was initiated in 1985 under the auspices of HMG Dept of Archaeology.

The main temple (1) is a two-storeyed building standing slightly off centre in a rectangular courtyard which also contains two smaller temples and numerous statues. The shrine contains a gold image of Vishnu as Narayan which is said to date from the seventh century, but is not open to visitors. Each of the four entrance doors is ornately decorated. The north door is guarded by a pair of winged lions; the east door by griffins; the south door by elephants; and the west door by lions. The torana and lavishly engraved brasswork surrounding the main west door is particularly memorable for its intricacy and detail. Each of the roof struts of both floors is a masterpiece of Newari woodcarving. Caryatid-like figurines of the various incarnations of Vishnu, characteristically painted with blue skin, form the centre piece of each below which are depictions of other deities all in seated posture.

Standing just in front of the west door are statues of Garuda (2) and of Bhaktapur's King Bhupatindra Malla (3) with his queen in a gilded cage. That of Garuda, Vishnu's winged vehicle shown here in reverential pose, is believed to have been sculpted in the fifth or sixth century and is one of the Valley's most important works of art. Two pillars (4) stand at the temple's western corners, supporting a sankha, Vishnu's conch shell, on your right, and the chakra, Vishnu's discus, to your left. Near the chakra pillar is the Valley's oldest inscription (5). Dating from the mid fifth century, it is credited to the Licchavi king, Manadeva, and chronicles how he successfully deterred his mother from committing sati by going to battle. Garuda (6) appears again in more dynamic form in the northwest corner of the courtyard. He is shown carrying Vishnu in a representation which is reproduced on the back of the Nepali Rs 10 note.

In the northeast corner is a Shiva linga (7) and between it and the temple are more images of Vishnu (8). The eastern gateway leads to the small village of Changu Narayan. Moving to the southeast corner, there is a statue of Ganesh (9), Shiva's elephant headed son, with a shrine to Shiva (10) beside it. Continuing clockwise, you next come to the Vishwarup (11) which portrays Vishnu in his full, multi-limbed and multi-headed splendour as protector of the universe set upon the naga.

Beyond is the two-storeyed Lakshmi Narayan (12) temple/shrine with two important eighth century arch shaped stones containing bas-relief images of Vishnu. One shows the god in his fifth incarnation as the dwarf Vikrantha (or Vamana) who, in order to save the world, appeared in this form before the demon Bali and asked him for as much land as he could cover in three strides. Once granted, Vishnu became a giant, covering the earth in three strides and leaving only hell to the demon. The other is of the half-man half-lion god Narasimha, Vishnu's fourth incarnation, who came to destroy another demon, Hiranyakasipu, who could not be killed either by day or night, nor by god, man or beast. Reminiscent of the denouement in Shakespeare's Macbeth, the demon's riddle of immortality was summarily solved by Vishnu as neither man nor beast, at sunset when it was neither night nor day.

Getting there: Although there are no bus services directly to Changu Narayan, it is relatively simple to get there. Either hire a car or take the bus from Kathmandu towards Sankhu and get down 2 kilometres after Gokarna, just past the village of Thali. From here it is a walk of 1 kilometre along a footpath that crosses the Manohara River. Alternatively, it is a 6 kilometres walk along a motorable road from Bhaktapur. It is also possible to walk from Nagarkot – see page 307.

Nagarkot

At the far east of the Valley, 32 kilometres from Kathmandu and at an altitude of *Colour map 3, grid A6* *2,190 metres, Nagarkot is widely considered to have the best views of the Himalaya from the Kathmandu Valley. On a clear day, there are panoramas extending from the Annapurnas – Annapurna S (7,273 metres), Annapurna III (7,557 metres), Annapurna I (8,090 metres) and Annapurna II (7,937 metres) – in the west, to Everest (8,848 metres) and Kanchenjunga (8,597 metres) in the east. The best months for viewing are from November to February. In October and March views may be obscured, while at other times the mountains remain concealed for most of the time by clouds. The views can be exceptional at sunrise and sunset when the mountains are bathed in perceptibly changing hues of pink, red and crimson. To the east, the Indrawati and Chok rivers are visible.*

Nagarkot itself is barely a village, though it has an army camp, a shrine and an increasing number of small hotels of varying standards. The army camp is a legacy of history: Nagarkot's strategic location allowing clear lines of vision through almost 360° led to a military presence being established here several centuries ago, a fact to which the suffix kot (fort) is attributed. Its recent growth – especially in the number of hotels – is almost entirely the result of tourism. A visit is highly recommended and the place is particularly relaxing after Kathmandu. Due to the altitude, temperatures are invariably lower than in Kathmandu (by as much as 10°C) and warm clothing is advised outside the hot summer months. It can also be very windy, so popular with kite flyers. The spring flowers and unusual rock formations make short and undemanding treks from Nagarkot particularly attractive. It is also a popular picnic spot for Nepalis and you may come across groups singing and dancing in traditional Nepali style.

There are several excellent walking opportunities ('short treks') from Nagarkot. You can even walk all the way back to Kathmandu, an all day hike, without having to spend too much time on main roads. Trekking through the Valley is also an agreeable substitute for the more demanding mountain treks, especially for those who do not have time for longer treks, and does not require trekking permits. Always make sure that you take enough water and food with you. A compass will also be useful.

Walks from Nagarkot

To Sankhu and Vajra Jogini Leaving the mountain views, you can follow the lesser used road from Nagarkot, a rather bumpy route that leaves Nagarkot to the north for about two kilometres. You will pass the small Mahakal shrine on your right and then, near the Niva guest house, the road veers to the west. Continuing downhill, it is a seven-kilometre walk to Sankhu. The road twists and turns, you cross a few small streams and walk through the tiny villages of Bishambhara and Palubari. Just before you reach Sankhu, the road crosses the small Sanadi River and on your right is a temple dedicated to Vishnu. Turn right (north) at Sankhu and continue through the village; the Vajra Jogini temple complex is a 30 minute (two kilometres) climb from here. There are irregular bus services from Sankhu back to Kathmandu, but the village has no formal guest houses. You can also follow a cross country trail for part of the way. Both head in a northwest direction, one leading off from near the Floral Hill hotel, the other from north of the Club Himalaya Nagarkot Resort hotel, and meet the road about halfway between Nagarkot and Sankhu.

To Changu Narayan and Bhaktapur This is an attractive way to get to Bhaktapur and a good alternative to taking the bus or following the road all the way. Leave Nagarkot along the road heading south to Bhaktapur for about four kilometres at which point the road bends sharply to the right into a hairpin bend where it doubles back on itself. You might think about hitching a lift in a bus or taxi for this portion. Three trails lead off from the northern point of this hairpin bend. Take the left trail, a dirt track climbing through the forested slope then heading west along the contour. Continue along here for about three kilometres until it narrows to become a winding path which leads to Changu Narayan after approximately another three kilometres. You walk through a couple of small villages on the way where you can get directions if you get lost. From the Changu Narayan temple, it is a six kilometres walk to Bhaktapur. Start by going back the way you came but stay on the road which climbs to the south. After you cross the ridge, it's downhill all the way, through the village of Pikhel and alongside the small Khasyang Khusyung River. There are several guest houses in Bhaktapur and the last bus for Kathmandu leaves from the Siddhi Pokhari bus stop at around 1900.

To Banepa and Dhulikhel This is the longest of these three walks and covers a distance of about 16 kilometres. Leave Nagarkot along the ridge road heading south from the army camp. After a gentle climb of about three kilometres you reach a junction where the road effectively comes to an end and several paths lead off to the south. From here trails are indistinct, but you should continue heading south. If you get lost there are occasional houses where you can get directions – ask for the village of Nala. After a descent of three kilometres the terrain evens out again and you join a dirt road for two kilometres to Nala. This attractive village has a Buddhist shrine to the west and a four-storeyed temple dedicated to the goddess Bhagawati in the centre around which the village fans out. The road continues through Nala to the south and meets the main Bhaktapur-Dhulikhel road (the Arniko Highway) after three kilometres at Banepa. You can either follow the main road as it climbs the four kilometres up to Dhulikhel or walk the trail through terraced fields south of the main road.

Essentials

Sleeping Nagarkot has a range of accommodation to fit in with most budgets. Most hotels are within a 30 minute walk of the bus stop, though rooms are also available in private residences on both the approach from Bhaktapur and from the northern route. Most visitors come for an overnight stay, arriving in the afternoon. All hotels are accustomed to catering for early risers. Although there is usually more than enough capacity to cope with demand, in peak season it is advisable either to book in advance or to find a room immediately upon arrival. At all times (and even in peak season) it is

Nagarkot

To Farm House Hotel & Sankha

The Niva
Country Villa
Himalayan
Madhuban Village
The Fort
Peaceful Cottage
At The End Of The Universe
Viewpoint
Galaxy   Chautari
Space Mountain

o Cheese Factory

To Changu Narayan

Bus Stop   Tea House

Club Himalaya
Nagarkot Resort

To Bhaktapur

Nagarkot
Cottage

Flora Hill

Army Camp

N

0 metres   300
0 yards   328

To Viewing Tower

worth negotiating room rates. If you are staying in one of the cheaper establishments, you might think about bringing a sleeping bag.

B *Club Himalaya Nagarkot Resort*, T413632, F417133, clubhim@mos.com.np www.nepal-hotel.com 42 rooms, coffee shop with panoramic views, good Tea House restaurant next door does buffet lunches and dinners, bar, facilities include indoor pool, sauna and gym, modern building that sticks out like a sore thumb in a central location, but with superb views, has its own helicopter landing pad (10 minutes from Kathmandu's Tribhuvan airport), most guests come on a 1 night/2 day package from Kathmandu, inclusive prices from US$130 per person (one published itinerary finishes with "Departure for Kathmandu by helicopter and drop at hotel"), book through the Kathmandu Guest House in central Thamel. **B** *Chautari*, T419718, 30 rooms, restaurant. **B** *Country Villa*, T228014. 28 rooms some with verandah, restaurant, Japanese style bar and prices. **B** *The Fort*, T290869. An extensive modern building traditionally decorated, good views, popular with groups. **B-C** *Space Mountain Holiday Resort*, T290871. 20 rooms, restaurant, modern, expensive, inexplicably built to face away from the mountains.

C *Flora Hill*, T226893. 13 rooms, restaurant. Government owned, modest but relatively comfortable, though inconvenient location to the south, on the road to Bhaktapur. **C** *Nagarkot Farm House*, T228087. 9 rooms all with bath (best room: No 9), restaurant, conceived and built by an American in conjunction with a Tibetan, open fireplace in dining room, good food, 3 meals included in room rate, small hall for yoga, meditation or small conferences of about 20 people, solar heated water, about 10,000 trees have been planted, including 2,000 peach and apple trees, delightful and secluded location to the north, good value, reservations through Hotel Vajra in Kathmandu (T272719, F271695). Highly recommended.

D *Nagarkot Cottage*, T222532, F227372. 15 rooms in individual cottages, restaurant, hot water available in buckets, remote location 15 minutes walk south of bus stop, simple but clean. **D** *Taragaon Resort*, T221768. Government owned, 8 minutes walk south of bus stop, recently re-opened. **D** *View Point*, T290870. Clean if basic rooms with bath in cottages on a hillside, restaurant, electricity, hot water, excellent views from some rooms, now partially blocked by The Fort hotel, heavily booked in season, offers bus service from Kantipath, depart 1330, return 1030 the following morning.

E *At The End Of The Universe*, TBhaktapur 610874. Cottage/hut accommodation, dining room, good views, another of Nagarkot's hotels whose name is inexplicably influenced by astronomy – to attract star trekkers? **E** *Galaxy*, T290870. 9 rooms some with bath, cheaper dorm accommodation, food available, electricity, better views from upstairs rooms. **E** *Madhuban Village*, rooms in bamboo cottages/huts, has electricity. **E** *The Niva*, cottage/hut accommodation, dining room. **E** *Peaceful Cottage*, T290877. 8 rooms some with bath, excellent views from dining room. Recommended.

Eating All hotels and guesthouses have some dining facilities, but Nagarkot is by no means known for culinary excellence. The one, shining exception is the *Tea House*, T413632, F417133. Operated by and in a separate building next to the Club Himalaya Nagarkot Resort hotel. Good Nepalese, Indian and Chinese buffet lunches and dinners are available most days in season, as well as an à la carte menu, snacks and set teas. The restaurant has superb panoramic views of the mountains and an outdoor terrace seating area. Open 0600-2000. The Fort hotel has a good restaurant. Try also the *Flora Hill*, and the *Nagarkot Farm House* has good vegetarian dishes.

Sports **Cycling**: a popular option, though it should not be taken lightly. The road from

Bhaktapur is good, but it is a continuous and fairly steep climb to the top. You can also approach Nagarkot from Sankhu to the north. Leave Kathmandu via Chabahil and Bodhnath. After Sankhu, however, the condition of the road deteriorates markedly, so this route may be left for the bumpy downhill journey. A possible cross country route that is walkable and just about manageable by bike leads from the Changu Narayan temple north of Bhaktapur to join with the Bhaktapur-Nagarkot road about 5 kilometres west of Nagarkot.

Transport   **Buses**: run to irregular schedules from Bhaktapur, leaving the Siddhi Pokhari stop when they are full. From Kathmandu, buses leave from the City Bus Park and go via Bhaktapur. With plenty of stops en route this can be a very slow journey of up to 4 hours, Rs 15. There is also one tourist bus service leaving Kantipath (near the British Council) at lunchtime for its 3-hour journey, Rs 60 each way. The return leaves Nagarkot after breakfast. Book in advance through your hotel or any good travel agent.

The official **taxi** fare from Kathmandu is around Rs 800 each way, but a little bargaining will normally reduce this by half. The journey takes about 1 hour. You can usually find a taxi to take you back to Kathmandu just below the Club Himalaya Nagarkot Resort hotel.

A **helicopter** service from Kathmandu is operated by the Club Himalaya Nagarkot Resort hotel as part of their 1 or 2 night package deals. Book through the Kathmandu Guest House.

Directory   **Tourist office and travel agents** Package tours are widely available at travel agents in Kathmandu and include transport and overnight accommodation. Prices start at around US$20, but as always there is room for negotiation. Many hotels in all of the Valley's three cities run their own half day tours to catch the sunrise from Nagarkot, but these usually involve a horribly early start and are subject to cancellation if there are not enough bookings to make it worth their while.

Kathmandu to Dhulikhel

The road from Kathmandu passes just to the south of Thimi and Bhaktapur before continuing through Banepa and climbing on up to the old Newari hilltop village of Dhulikhel. There are some interesting stop-offs en route. Dhulikhel has a reasonable variety of accommodation available and also offers some fine walking opportunities.

Thimi   Thimi is the first town you come to after leaving Kathmandu, some three kilo-
Colour map 3, grid A3   metres before Bhaktapur, and although often overlooked it is actually the fourth largest in the Valley. It is renowned for its craftsmanship, especially pottery and papier mâché masks. Indeed, its name is a derivation of the Newari for 'capable people'. The majority of the masks sold in Kathmandu are produced here, though some are also used during local festivals. The surrounding land is a rich source of clay and, as in Bhaktapur, it is fascinating to watch as potters throughout the town prepare then turn the clay on large manually operated wheels. You can buy their wares – anything from practical water pots to ornamental candlesticks – direct from the potters themselves or from the several shops scattered throughout the town. With a little bargaining, prices are amongst the cheapest that you will find, though these are assuredly set to rise as the number of visitors to Thimi also increases.

The architecture is very much Newari in character, but the town is rather run down and there are few buildings of general tourist interest. The Balkumari Mandir in the square at the southern end of town is a 16th century structure and is dedicated to the kumari in her child form, but the temple has no 'living goddess'. A main road runs through Thimi and links the Arniko Highway to the south with a minor road running from the airport to Bhaktapur to the north. Just north of this smaller road lies the three-storeyed Ganesh Mandir which you can reach via a stone stairway. Less than one kilometre further north towards the Manohara Khola is the village of Bode with its 16th century Mahalakshmi Mandir.

Getting there: You can get to Thimi by trolley bus which leaves Kathmandu from Tripureshwar and runs along the Arniko Highway and on to Bhaktapur. Public buses from the City Bus Park stand are quicker. You can cycle to Thimi either along the Arniko Highway or by turning left (north) just after you pass the southern end of the airport. After 1½ kilometres turn right (east) for the 3 kilometres ride which takes you to the northern end of Thimi with the Ganesh Mandir on your left.

This shikhara temple is located on a ridge about one kilometre south of Bhaktapur. The temple is dedicated to Ganesh. Two bells are suspended on either side of the entrance and the image (usually daubed in red sindur by devotees) is believed to help cure children of learning disabilities. Surya means 'sun', apparently because the temple was built to catch the sun's first morning rays. The site has good views of Bhaktapur and across the Valley. To get there from Bhaktapur, follow the road leading southwest from the potters' area and cross the river at Ram Ghat. Continue down over the Arniko Highway past the trolley bus stop and a stone stairway leads up to the temple.

Surya Binayak Mandir
Colour map 3, grid B4

Banepa is a small, uninspiring town 24 kilometres from Kathmandu at the base of the Valley's southeast hills. It was briefly a capital of the Kathmandu Valley during the 14th century. A large statue of King Tribhuvan forms a roundabout in the eastern part of town, an ideal point from which to view the numerous police check points along this stretch of the Arniko Highway. The town has a number of small guest houses and restaurants serving Nepali food and light refreshments. The nearby three-storeyed Chandeshwar Mandir is pleasantly situated in woodland about one kilometre to the northeast and connected to Banepa by a dirt road. The temple is named after a Shiva shakti who, legend has it, came here to destroy a demon named Chand. The temple's brightly coloured exterior depicts some of the injurious exploits of the Tantric deity, Bhairab, who is also carved onto the roof struts along with representations of the eight (ashta) matrikas, or mother deities.

Banepa
Colour map 3, grid B6

Dhulikhel

Dhulikhel is the last major village in the Kathmandu Valley through which the Arniko Highway passes on its way to Kodari on the Nepal/Tibet border. About 30 kilometres from Kathmandu, it stands on the southeast slopes of the Valley at an altitude of 1,585 metres and is a popular daytrip and overnight destination with good mountain views. In contrast to Nagarkot with which it is often compared, however, Dhulikhel is an established village with a history of settlement that goes back to its days as a stopover on the India-Tibet trade route. Its people are predominantly Newaris. The main part of the village lies to the west of the Arniko Highway, where the winding street leads up through the laid back, old and rustic residential areas before descending down towards Banepa. The Arniko Highway continues its eastward progress, but a major police checkpoint just after the road begins to dip outside Dhulikhel ensures

Colour map 3, grid B6

often lengthy traffic queues. Views of the Valley from here, though, can be magnificent, particularly if your visit coincides with the expanse of fields below appearing as a glorious patchwork of lush green and golden crops. To the east you can see the Indrawati River meandering down from the Himalaya towards the Terai. As elsewhere, mountain views are dependent on the weather. The best months to visit are from October to March. During and around the monsoon time you will be lucky to get a glimpse of the mountains, though the otherwise entirely occlusive cloud cover is most likely to break in the early morning and late afternoon.

Entering the village from the east, you come to a junction and square where roads branch off to the southeast and northwest. A small pokhari, or tank, of rather forlorn appearance lies beside a statue of King Mahendra and the square is used as something of a local meeting point. Heading southeast the road climbs and you will pass a couple of budget guest houses. Continuing directly along here you will reach an open space from where there are good mountain views, recommended for sunrise and sunset visits. After about one kilometre a road to the southeast leads up to a small temple/shrine standing on a hillock, another popular viewpoint. If you continue downhill to the bottom of the gorge, there is a small Shiva Mandir standing beside a stream. The shrine contains an image of the linga and the kalasa is supported by four nagas. Around the temple are a number of statues of deities in various states of repair, including the remains of some others which have been stolen.

If you take the northwest road from the square, you pass the architecturally unimpressive Ganesh Mandir partially hidden by trees to your right before entering another square, again with a small pokhari and two three-storeyed pagoda temples dedicated to Vishnu. The Harisiddhi Mandir is the first on your right, while just beyond is the colourful Narayan Mandir with two distinctive statues of Garuda, the bird headed vehicle of Vishnu, in front.

Essentials

Sleeping There are several hotels and guest houses along the road from Banepa, but with ample accommodation usually available in Dhulikhel there is really nothing to be gained by staying at any of these.

A *Himalayan Horizon Sun-n-Snow*, T011-61260, F011-61476. Reservations from Durbar Marg, Kathmandu T/F225092, 28 rooms (deluxe or standard), 2 restaurants,

Dhulikhel

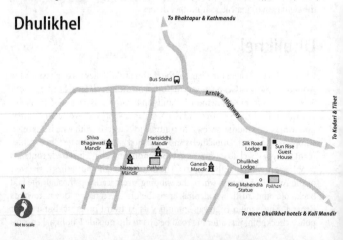

bar, excellent mountain views from all rooms and good food, room only and full board tariffs available. **A** *Himalayan Shangri La Resort*, T/FKathmandu 423939. 16 large rooms all with mountain views, restaurant, bar, conference room, modern building in a secluded location south of the main village, all rooms attractively decorated in traditional Newari style.

B *Dhulikhel Lodge Resort*, T011-61114. Reservations from Kamaldi, Kathmandu T247663, F222926, 25 rooms, Nepali, Tibetan and continental restaurants, bar, large and comfortable with good views of valley and peaks.

C *Himalayan Mountain Resort*, T011-61158. Reservations from Tridevi Marg, Kathmandu T225388 ext 358, F220161, 18 rooms, restaurant and bar. Traditional Chhetri décor, pleasant terraced gardens with seating and fine views. **C** *Royal East Inn*, large hotel near bus stop, comfortable, good restaurant, bar.

D *Dhulikhel Lodge*, T61114. Large building centrally located and the oldest budget hotel in Dhulikhel, reasonable food in restaurant with floor cushion seating, hot water in common bathrooms, ISD facilities, top floor rooms recommended, photocopies of the 1 day trek to Namobuddha available from reception. **D** *Peace Paradise*, 8 rooms some with bath, restaurant, modern red brick building with some good value rooms.

E *Nawranga*, T61226. 6 rooms all common bath, small but good budget restaurant, sells postcards and the paintings of a self taught local artist. **E** *Silk Road*, T61269. 6 rooms some with bath, food available, central location but basic. **E** *Snow View*, T61229. 6 rooms all common bath, food available. **E** *Sun Rise*, T61482. 4 rooms all common bath.

Eating

All of Dhulikhel's eating places are attached to its hotels and guest houses. If you are here on a day trip, the *Royal East Inn*, conveniently situated near the bus stop, has a good restaurant serving Nepali/Indian and continental food. The upmarket hotels are further from the centre, but since all have good mountain views each makes for an excellent lunch destination. Although most of the budget restaurants offer continental food, it is usually best to stick to what they know best, namely variations on dal-bhad-tarkari. The *Nawranga* guest house has a small restaurant serving huge portions of Nepali food and has several excellent tarkaris and pickles. The custard pie also just about lives up to its claim as 'the best in the Kingdom of Nepal'. Try also the *Dhulikhel Lodge* restaurant for good, tried and tested Nepali food. Seating is on floor cushions.

Transport

There are regular bus services leaving from the City Bus Park in **Kathmandu** from early morning. The journey goes via Bhaktapur and takes 2 hours or more, Rs 15. The bus stop is on the main road east of the village. To get into the village either turn right just after the bus stop or walk 200 metres and turn right as the road bends. You can make the journey in less than half the time by taxi. Once again, negotiation is essential after which expect to pay around Rs 450 one way and Rs 800 for a return trip with 2 hours waiting. **NB** Check that the taxi has the necessary documentation to allow it to go as far as Dhulikhel. There are numerous police check points along the Arniko Highway and the administration of on-or-near-the-spot fines can be a lengthy affair.

Walks from Dhulikhel

There are numerous interesting walks around Dhulikhel. For the more adventurous, there are trails leading all the way to Budhanilikantha via Nagarkot, Sankhu and the Vajra Jogini temple (see under Nagarkot), or eastwards beyond the Valley.

Walk 1 to Banepa As part of a day trip, you can walk the four kilometres from Dhulikhel down to Banepa from where you can catch the bus back to Kathmandu. Leave Dhulikhel along the main road that goes northwest through the village. When you get to the junction at the end of the village, turn left (west). Continue all the way down this attractive trail as it cuts through the wooded slopes and leads into Banepa where the bus stop is on the main road near the statue of King Tribhuvan.

The following two walks, to Panauti and Namobuddha, can also be combined.

Walk 2 to Panauti Leave Dhulikhel along the road leading southwest from near the Dhulikhel Lodge which joins a trail. The trail continues downhill and you walk through some delightful rural scenery before meeting the road between Banepa and Panauti some three kilometres from Dhulikhel. The road follows the Punyamata Khola River for three kilometres into Panauti.

The village is typically Newari in character and has several examples of finely carved windows. Its location at the confluence of Punyamata Khola and Roshi Khola bestows it with special sanctity. Legend has it that the Buddha in a previous incarnation gave his life for a hungry tigress (see boxed feature, opposite). A monument to this sacrifice was built at Namobuddha. To the southwest of the village is one of Nepal's oldest Hindu temples, the three-storeyed Indreshwar Mahadev Mandir, believed to date from the 13th century. The temple has some magnificent woodcarvings and, in contrast to later composite caryatids, the roof strut figures are each carved from single lengths of wood. Two other temples, the Krishna Mandir and Brahmayan Mandir, stand at the northeast end of the village.

There are several options to go on from Panauti. To return to Kathmandu or Dhulikhel, you can either take the bus or walk the six kilometres north to Banepa from where there are regular local buses in both directions. It is also possible to cycle to Dhulikhel, though this is hard work: the way down is considerably more gratifying. You can walk from here to Namobuddha along an

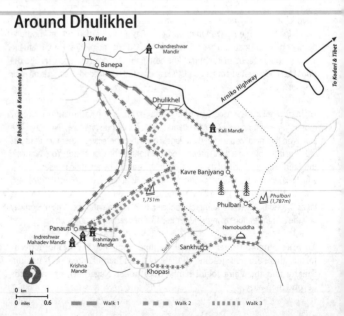

Around Dhulikhel

The Buddha and the Hungry Tigress

This touching and almost Biblical legend, recounted by the Buddha to his chief disciple Ananda, is believed by Newari Buddhists to have taken place at Panauti. Many years ago there lived a strong, wealthy and wise king named Maharatha. The king had three sons, Mahapranada, Mahadeva and Mahasattva. One day the king and his sons went to a park to walk and relax. The park was beautiful and there were colourful flowers growing everywhere they looked. After they had walked for some time, they came upon a large bamboo grove where they rested. As they sat, Prince Mahapranada told his brothers of his fear that wild animals might be hiding in the grove. Prince Mahadeva, too, was anxious. But Prince Mahasattva, the youngest, said:

> "No fear feel I, nor any sorrow either,
> In this wide, lonesome wood, so
>   dear to Sages.
> My heart is filled with bursting joy,
> For soon I'll win the highest boon."

Having rested, the princes got up and carried on walking. Before they had gone far they noticed a tigress and her five cubs lying forlornly only a short distance away from them. The poor tigress had not been able to find any food or water for days and now lay exhausted on the ground, unable to feed her young and close to death. The three princes felt great pity for her. "Tigers live on fresh meat and warm blood," said Prince Mahapranada. "And who would sacrifice himself to preserve her life?" asked Prince Mahadeva. After some time Prince Mahasattva, who had not yet spoken, replied: "It is difficult for people like us, who are so fond of their lives and bodies, and who have so little intelligence. It is not at all difficult, however, for others, who are true men, intent on benefiting their fellow creatures, and who long to sacrifice themselves. Holy men are born of pity and compassion. Whatever the bodies they may get, in heaven or on earth, a hundred times will they undo them, joyful in their hearts, so that the lives of others may be saved."

The princes carefully edged towards the tigress. As they did so, Prince Mahasattva contemplated the situation and decided to sacrifice himself for the sake of the tigress and her cubs. "For long I have served this putrid body," he reflected. "And given it beds and clothes, food and drink, and conveyances of all kinds. Yet it is doomed to perish and fall down, and in the end it will break up and be destroyed. When I have renounced this futile body ... then I shall win the perfectly pure Dharma-body, endowed with hundreds of virtues, full of such qualities as trance and wisdom, immaculate, free from all substrata, changeless and without sorrow." The prince then went to the tigress and lay down before her. But the animal was too frail to fight. So he took a sharp piece of bamboo and cut his throat. Smelling the fresh blood, the tigress ate the prince and in this way saved herself and her cubs.

When the Buddha had finished the story, he turned to Ananda and said: "It was I, Ananda, who at that time and on that occasion was that prince Mahasattva."

Adapted from Dr Edward Conze's 1959 translation, 'Buddhist Scriptures', Penguin Books, London.

Kathmandu Valley: beyond the three cities

attractive though indirect trail which leaves Panauti to the east.

Alternatively, you can cycle all the way back to Kathmandu either via Banepa and the Arniko Highway, or, more interestingly, along the cross country trail that heads west from near the Indreshwar Mahadev Mandir and leads eventually to Patan after 30 kilometres. Some three kilometres out of Panauti, the trail meets the Roshi Khola valley and follows the small river for the next 10 kilometres. The trail undulates, twists and turns, and there are some wonderful views both across the Valley and (on a clear day) of the mountains beyond before you reach the attractive village of Lubhu 12 kilometres further on. Lubhu is one of the Valley's spinning and weaving centres and almost as many of its inhabitants are employed on the looms as on the surrounding fields. Another five kilometres and you pass Patan's eastern Ashokan stupa before crossing the Ring Road. The road continues straight to Mangal Bazaar at the southern end of Durbar Square.

Walk 3 to Namobuddha (or Namura) There are two ways to get from Dhulikhel to Namobuddha. You can walk both as an all day circuit. The shorter route (nine kilometres) leaves Dhulikhel for the Kali Mandir. After the temple the trail descends into the Kavre Valley and past the village of Kavre Banjyang, four kilometres from Dhulikhel. You can either walk along the motorable road that continues south or along one of the paths at the side. After another three kilometres through pine forest you reach the Tamang village of Phulbari from where it is a further three kilometres to Namobuddha. Returning to Dhulikhel by the longer route (11 kilometres), leave Namobuddha to the west for two kilometres to the village of Sankhu (from here there is a cross country trail via Khopasi to Panauti). At Sankhu follow the trail to the right (north) as it goes downhill. You reach Batase after about three kilometres. Continuing north, the trail veers right at Mirchatar before arriving at Dhulikhel three kilometres later.

   Namobuddha is one of Nepal's holiest Buddhist sites and commemorates the supreme compassion of the Buddha in his legendary self-sacrifice to a starving tigress at Panauti. The origins of the hilltop site are unknown, though some sources suggest that the architectural style is indicative of construction in the 17th or 18th centuries. It is dominated by a large stupa (Dharma Dhatu) to which many prayer flags and banners are attached. It is surrounded by numerous chaityas, bells, prayerwheels and other Buddhist accoutrements. To one side is a small monastery which contains images of the Buddha. A little way beyond is a more recent monastery and meditation centre with more representations of the compassionate Buddha. Beneath a nearby tree, a plaque illustrates the Buddha and the tigress. The main festival of the year takes place in March when pilgrims, especially Mahayana Buddhists, come to offer prayers.

The Arniko Highway from Dhulikhel to Tibet

The Arniko Highway connects Kathmandu with Kodari, 81 kilometres northeast of the Valley on the Nepal-Tibet border, and continues on to the Tibetan capital, Lhasa. For most of its journey north, the road runs along first the Sun Kosi ('golden river') then the Bhote Kosi ('Tibet river') valleys. The scenery is often spectacular with the clear waters flowing through ancient, deep cut gorges. It is especially vulnerable to landslides during and after the monsoon, however, and these can leave sections of the road (particularly north of Barabise) unpassable for days at a time. The road was built with assistance from China in the 1960s and it remains the only official land route into Tibet for tourists. The Chinese aid should be seen in the context of the prevailing political climate following its war with India in late 1962. The construction of the Arniko Highway after the Chinese victory provided the first direct road access from China (Tibet) to India through Nepal and was greeted with much suspicion by India. Today it is used by tour groups, by rafters making for the Sun Kosi River and trekkers heading into the Helambu, Solu Khumbu and Everest regions.

The road descends from Dhulikhel into the Panchkal Valley, a picturesque expanse of scattered agricultural communities. A patchwork of fields dominates the valley floor while innumerable minutely terraced fields cover the slopes. The road winds its way northeast from Dhulikhel to reach the village of Panchkal after 21 kilometres. From here it is eight kilometres east to Dolalghat, a small town where the Indrawati and Sun Kosi rivers meet, where the Sun Kosi rafting trips put in and some Helambu treks begin. The road then continues northeast following the Sun Kosi River valley. Just beyond the village of Baliphi, 16 kilometres from Dolalghat, is the turn off for the road to Jiri, a stunningly beautiful though arduous 65 kilometres to the east. The area around Baliphi is effectively an ethnic transition zone where you leave behind the Newari dominated area to the south for the peoples of the mountainous

Arniko Highway: the road to Tibet

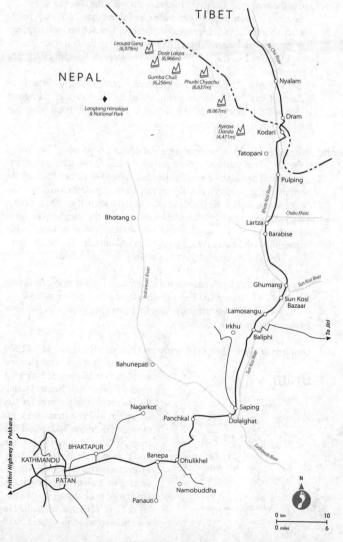

☞ Dust on the highway

The sealed road ends just north of Barabise to become a motorable dirt road. This can get extremely dusty, a fact that is no fun whatsoever if your bus is stuck behind a lorry or convoy of lorries for any length of time. Take a supply of handkerchiefs to cover your nose or, if you can get one, a face mask of the type used by some pedestrians in Kathmandu.

country to the north. Lamosangu is five kilometres north of Baliphi, a quiet Sherpa village with a few shops and a basic guest house. Next comes Barabise, a functional town and the final destination for many buses from Kathmandu. For those continuing to Kodari it is a popular refreshment stop. Although it has several basic guest houses, the town offers little else of tourist interest. Just before you reach Barabise you pass the confluence of the Sun Kosi and Bhote Kosi rivers. The source of the Sun Kosi lies in the mountains to the east and for the rest of the journey to Kodari the road runs alongside the Bhote Kosi.

Some 24 kilometres north of Barabise and about three kilometres before Kodari is Tatopani, a relaxed village which takes its name from the hot springs here (tato hot, pani water). To get to the springs, follow the road heading north from the central market for 700 metres. The steps to the springs are then signposted.

NB Modesty is the rule and nude bathing is prohibited. The village has a number of small basic guest houses including the Sherpa Lodge, the Sonam Lodge and the Tibet Lodge. All do simple Nepali food. Local buses run between Barabise and Tatopani.

Tibetan border Balanced on one side of the deep gorge that separates Nepal from Tibet, Kodari is the last village you reach before passing through Nepali immigration and crossing the Friendship Bridge (Tib. Dzadrok Zampa) into Tibet. Although the views from here are spectacular, Kodari itself is a motley assortment of huts and houses and its interest lies mainly in its strategic location. If no buses are running, you may have to walk the eight kilometres from the Friendship Bridge to reach the Chinese immigration and customs checkpoint at Dram (Chin Zhangmu; North Khasa). Porters are available on both sides. The border is currently Tibet's most important land border with the outside world.

Immigration The Dram customs and immigration posts open at 1000 Beijing time (GMT +8; Nepal = GMT +5.45), while those at Kodari open at 0930.

It is advisable to cross early in the day. Dram has a bank and post office both located in the upper end of town.

Onwards to Tibet The sprawling town of Dram stands at an altitude of 2,300 metres and extends down the hillside for over four kilometres through a series of switchback bends. During the monsoon, motor vehicles are sometimes unable to reach the town from the Friendship Bridge (and also from Nyalam, 31 kilometres to the north) owing to landslides which are a constant hazard to the local population. Nonetheless, the people of Dram tend to be among the wealthiest in Tibet. Black market trading in assorted commodities, gold and

Dram

To Nyalam
Army
Tibet Foreign
Trade Shop
Foreign
Registration Office   ✉
Cemetery
Nepalese
Transport   Ⓢ   Ⓟ   PSB
Station   Himalayan
Guest House   Lodge   ✚
Guest House
New
Monastery   Zhangmu
China Customs & Immigration

N
To Friendship Bridge & Nepal
Not to scale

currency is rife. The Gonpa Sarpa monastery is located at the lower end, beside the China Customs Building.

The *Zhangmu Hotel*, adjacent to the China Customs Building at the lower end of town, has double rooms at US$32 (breakfast US$7; full board US$28). Curiously, this five-storeyed hotel has its reception on the top floor which is at road level, and its restaurant on the lowest floor. Electricity supplies are erratic and the rooms are often damp. There are many small roadside restaurants in town, where Sichuan, Tibetan and Nepali food is available.

Bishanku Narayan, Godavari and Phulchowki

This attractive route to the southeast of Kathmandu leads past one of the Valley's more important Vishnu shrines, Bishanku Narayan, through the small town of Godavari with its botanical gardens, and up through delightful forests and rural scenery to Phulchowki, the tallest of the hills enclosing the Kathmandu Valley.

This Vishnu temple marks the place where Vishnu is said to have delivered Shiva of the malevolent intentions of the demon Bhamasur. The temple, amongst the most revered by the Valley's Vaishnavites, is a natural cave set into the hillside. The entrance is a narrow fissure (**NB** not recommended for those of corpulent configuration) through which you crawl to reach a spiral set of stone steps that lead down to the shrine. Here is a statue of Hanuman and of Vishnu.

Bishanku Narayan
Colour map 3, grid B3

Getting there: Follow the Godavari Rd as far as the village of Baregaon, 6 kilometres from the Ring Road at Patan. Take the dirt road that forks off to the left past a Tibetan carpet workshop and continue for 1 kilometre to the village of Godamchaur. Continue straight over the minor 'crossroads' (northeast) and up the hill. The temple is on your right after another 1 kilometre. There are also regular buses from Kathmandu's City Bus Park and from Lagankhel in Patan.

This small town, 10 kilometres southeast of Patan's Ring Road, is notable principally for its botanical gardens and as a stop off on the way up to Pulchowki. On the approach along the Godavari Road, you will see a large marble quarry on your right (west) just before you get to the town. Though oft berated as an eyesore and pollutant by some environmentalists, its 'pink marble' is of importance to the local economy. St Xavier's College, one of several in the subcontinent with the same name and run by Jesuits, is a useful local landmark. Established in the 1950s, it was the first Catholic school to be opened in Nepal since Catholic missionaries were expelled from the country in the 18th century by Prithvi Narayan Shah.

Godavari
Colour map 3, grid B3

The Royal Botanical Gardens lie to the northeast of Godavari. Follow the main road northeast from St Xavier's for 800 metres then turn left. An inexpensive map together with a guide to the gardens are sold at the main

Godavari surroundings

Kathmandu Valley: beyond the three cities

entrance. Since almost all the plants are unlabelled, these will be useful if you intend to do more than just enjoy the colour and variety. Though not enormous, the gardens are both interesting and appealing with numerous endemic and exotic species. There are several small ponds and streams, a Japanese garden, a rockery and the National Herbarium where research into the medicinal use of plants is carried out. A number of tropical species are on display in the greenhouses, including various cacti and orchids. It is also a popular picnic spot. The best times to visit are March-April and September-November when the gardens are at their most colourful. ■ *1000-1600 daily. Rs 5.*

The Godavari Kunda, a sacred water tank, is located on the main road just beyond the turning to the botanical gardens. Fed by natural spring water, whose source some believe to be spiritually if not physically associated with the Godavari River in India, it is regarded as an important holy bathing place. A special festival is held every 12 years (next in 2003) when pilgrims attain merit by bathing in its waters.

A large fish farm is situated 400 metres further along the main road. About 100 metres south of St Xavier's is the Phulchowki Mai Mandir. This is one of two similarly named temples dedicated to the local female deity, Phulchowki Mai. The other is situated at the summit of Phulchowki.

Phulchowki
Colour map 3, grid B3

At a height of 2,762 metres (1,200 metres higher than Godavari) it's a hard walk up, but the rewards are awesome. Phulchowki boasts breathtaking views of the entire Valley with a Himalayan panorama beyond which, on a clear day, stretches from Dhaulagiri in the west to Everest and Kanchenjunga in the east.

Forest covers much of the mountain slopes and provides a habitat for deer and other wild animals. It remains relatively undiminished by human settlement. The area is renowned for its flowers – indeed, phul chowki means 'flower place' – and you pass through wide rhododendron tracts on your way up as well as orchids and a host of other wild flowers, most of which bloom from March-April. At the top is a telecommunications tower which serves the Kathmandu Valley, and the area's other Pulchowki Mai shrine. During winter, the summit is usually snow capped.

You can reach the summit by a motorable road. The car journey takes about 45 minutes. There are also a couple of footpaths which can take up to four hours to climb up and about three hours for the way down.

NB This is a steep ascent. If you do walk up, ensure that you start the day early enough and calculate your return to Godavari within daylight hours.

Bungamati, Chapagaon and Lele

The roads heading directly south of Patan lead past some typically Newari villages, including Bungamati with its Rato Macchendranath Mandir and Chapagaon with the nearby Vajra Varahi Mandir, and through forest and open countryside to the tranquil settings of Lele. This is a good mountain biking route. Two parallel roads run from the Patan Ring Road, the western one going as far as Bungamati and the eastern one to Chapagaon. There are a couple of easily walked trails leading from Bungamati to Chapagaon.

Khokana &
Bungamati
Colour map 3, grid B2

Leaving the Patan Ring Road south of Jawalakhel, you first reach the village of Khokana after five kilometres. This is a traditional agricultural community. It has not featured prominently on tourist itineraries, but during harvest it really comes alive as sheaf loads of crops are winnowed and the grain spread across the cobbled streets to dry in broad, though neatly defined, rectangles. The surrounding fields are also used to grow mustard and the village has been a traditional centre for the production of mustard oil, a pungent and distinctively flavoured ingredient used in much of the subcontinent's cuisine. About one kilometre from the main road to the west of the village stands the Shekali Mai Mandir, a three-storeyed temple dedicated to a local female deity.

It is one kilometre from Khokana to Bungamati. Just before you reach Bungamati, you can visit another temple, the Karya Binayak Mandir, about 200 metres to the west of the road. The small temple is one of the four most important Ganesh shrines in the Kathmandu Valley and is attractively set in woodland with marvellous views of the Bagmati River beyond.

Some five kilometres from Patan, Bungamati is a compact village standing on a plateau just above the valley floor, its limits surprisingly precisely demarcated as if by a giant swathe, and surrounded by gently terraced slopes. A traditional farming village it is also noted for its weaving and, more recently, for its numerous tiny woodcarving workshops which supply Kathmandu's shops with interesting souvenirs. It is best known, however, as the other residence of Rato Macchendranath during the six months over winter when this deity's image is not installed in its Patan temple. The practice, which originated in the 16th century, is believed to have derived from a legend that relates how the guru Macchendranath delivered the Valley from years of drought by making Gorakhnath rescind his curse. Much celebration surrounds the annual procession of the image to and from Patan. Every 12 years (next in 2003) the whole village takes part as the god is carried on a huge chariot in a journey which can take weeks. The Rato Macchendranath Mandir is the centre of the village, the focal point to and from which most streets lead. The imposing temple, a large shikhara structure painted white, stands in the middle of a wide courtyard. The courtyard also contains a number of smaller shrines and other religious apparel.

Getting there: There is an irregular bus service from Patan's Jawalakhel bus stop to Bungamati.

The seven kilometres road to Chapagaon leaves Patan's Ring Road southwest of the Industrial Estate. The first village you come to, after three kilometres, is Sunakothi ('beautiful house') with its Jaganath Mandir and Bringareshwar Mahadev Mandir. The latter dates from the 16th century and is a two-storeyed temple. Although in a sadly neglected condition, there remain sufficient indicators to suggest that it was once another fine example of Newari temple architecture. It is renowned for containing the Valley's 64 most holy lingas. Some 600 metres south of Sunakothi there is a footpath heading west to Bungamati (1½ kilometres).

Chapagaon
Colour map 3, grid B2

Theco is another three kilometres further along the road and is the largest settlement in this part of the Valley. Guarding the gates of its two-storeyed Brahamayani Mandir are a pair of lions and, in an unusual portrayal, a statue of a swan stands on a column nearby. In the southern part of the village, a statue of a peacock stands on a column in front of the brightly coloured Balkumari Mandir.

Chapagaon is one kilometre further uphill to the south and marks the end of the sealed part of the road from Patan. The village has three temples of note. The first you come to is a Vishnu shrine, while just to the south is a small shrine dedicated to Bhairab. As you enter the village, a path leads off to your left (east) for some 600 metres to the Vajra Varahi Mandir. The structure, delightfully situated in a clearing amid woodland, dates from the mid 17th century on a site which had traditionally been used for religious worship. The eponymous goddess is a wrathful Tantric shakti deity portrayed in the *nrityamurti asana* position, a posture typical of Tantrism in which the left leg stands slightly bent (in this case, on a prostrate Bhairab) while the right leg is bent in towards the thigh. The temple also contains images of the eight mother goddesses, the *Ashta Matrika*.

Lele   Lele is a small village that lies in a minor valley hemmed in by the 1,774 metres peak of Bhaga Ban and by the southern slopes of Kathmandu Valley. It is a walk of two kilometres from Chapagaon to the base of Bhaga Ban where you have the option of two routes around the peak. There are fine views across the Bagmati River valley from the western route. When you have almost reached the other side of the mountain, you will see the Tika Bhairab Mandir (tika is the red or vermilion powder applied to the forehead as a symbol of the divine) whose main attraction is a large wall painting of Bhairab. A little way to the east is the Lele Kunda, an important but rather dishevelled pool fed by sacred spring water. The village of Lele is one and a half kilometres further east, while another kunda dedicated to the goddess Saraswati lies by a 17th century shrine another one and a half kilometres east.

Chobhar, Pharping and Dakshinkali

This scenic route to the southwest corner of the Kathmandu Valley has plenty to offer for a full day excursion from the capital. With a possible diversion to Kirtipur en route, the road runs alongside the Bagmati River for much of the way and passes the attractive Chobhar Gorge, also an important Buddhist site, before climbing through lush forest with superb views and through the scattered settlements of Pharping before reaching the fascinating temple site of Dakshinkali.

Chobhar   The small village of Chobhar stands on a hill on the west side of the Bagmati
Colour map 3, grid A2   River, four kilometres from the Patan Ring Road. The village is dominated by a three-tiered Adinath Lokeshwar Mandir (or Chu Vihara or Karuna Maya), an unusual Buddhist temple adorned by an extraordinary number of metal pots, pans, mirrors and other household items nailed to wooden boards. These utensils are supposed to have been offered to the temple deity by recently married couples and others in a prayer for domestic contentment. The temple was built in the 15th century and renovated in 1640. Its origins as a religious site, however, are said to date further back to an earlier Hindu temple dedicated to Macchendranath and only later converted to a Buddhist shrine. This may explain the appearance of the deity in current occupation, a red faced image closely resembling the Rato Macchendranath image of Bungamati and Patan. The top roof of the temple is of gilded copper and the copper torana above the entrance to the shrine has six engraved images of the Buddha.

Chobhar Gorge   At the picturesque Chobhar Gorge the Bagmati River narrows to cut its way through the rocky hills. The gorge has an important place in Newari Buddhist lore. Legend recounts how the bodhisatva Manjushri came from the mountains of Tibet and drained the huge lake that was the Kathmandu Valley of its waters by renting the hills to the south with his mighty sword during an earthquake. He thus created the Chobhar Gorge and a fertile valley fit for human habitation. Spanning the gorge is an old iron suspension bridge, built in Aberdeen and installed here in 1903.

Just to the south and standing majestically on the bank of the Bagmati is the beautiful Jal Binayak Mandir. Built in 1602, this is one of the Valley's four most

Walks around Chobhar

If you take a bus or taxi from Kathmandu to the Ring Road at Jawalakhel, this route is short enough for a satisfying and reasonably undemanding day's walk. There are plenty of charming natural diversions on the road south with numerous paths leading off into hamlets, woods and fields. The Bagmati River is never more than two kilometres away from the road (usually less) and the Chobhar Gorge is only two kilometres from the Ring Road. There is a five kilometres' cross country walk from Bungamati up to Chapagaon from where you can catch one of the more regular buses back to Patan.

important Ganesh shrines (Binayak is another name for Ganesh). The main three-storeyed temple is incorporated into the western flank of the complex edifice and has a copper upper roof. In the centre of the courtyard facing the shrine is a rare bronze image of Mushika, the divine vehicle of Ganesh in the form of a shrew. The main image of Ganesh, meanwhile, is a large rock which is believed to resemble the shape of an elephant. There is also an image of Uma Maheshwar, a depiction of Shiva and Parvati, which is thought to have been made in the early 12th century. The pagoda roof struts are carved with images of the eight mother goddesses, the *Ashta Matrika*, and of Ganesh. Steps lead from the main entrance of the complex to the river ghat, and on its southern side is a large cement factory.

Sadly, the Bagmati River carries the pollution of Kathmandu – sewage and other urban waste – for much of its course south. A further two kilometres south of Chobhar, between the Dakshinkali Road and the river, is the small Taudaha Lake. This is the only residue of the Valley's original lake and was the mythical repository of the nagas released during Manjushri's draining of the Valley.

After Chobhar, the condition of the road deteriorates as it climbs the eight kilometres to the village of Pikhel and a number of scattered settlements collectively known as Pharping. The consequent reduction of speed is amply compensated for by splendid views across the Bagmati River as it meanders a rugged course through the verdant countryside. Better still are your immediate surroundings: slopes of thick pine, bamboo and evergreen forest, home to deer, numerous varieties of birds, flowers and other wildlife. There are occasional springs and mini waterfalls which feed streams that irrigate the gently terraced paddy fields below. If you can stop for a few minutes en route you will be amply rewarded by the sights and sounds of the wildlife around you, especially memorable in the early morning mist.

From the small village of Pikhel (ask your driver or bus conductor to point it out), there is a walking trail

Pharping

Southwest from Kathmandu

Kathmandu Valley: beyond the three cities

heading four kilometres northwest to Champa Devi, a 2,278 metres peak with excellent views across the Valley and to the Himalaya beyond. About one kilometre along this route is the (**B**) *Himalayan Heights Hatiban Resort Hotel*, T290623, F418561, in a delightful setting and with excellent views. From Pikhel, it is another three kilometres along the main road to Pharping which, before the 18th century unification of Nepal, was an independent kingdom.

The Shekha Narayan Mandir stands below a steep limestone cliff at the first of Pharping's settlements. This Vaishnavite temple, dedicated to the fifth incarnation of Vishnu as the dwarf Vamana, contains statues said to date from the seventh century and has several water tanks at road level below the colourful main temple building. The current structure dates from the 17th century, though the site itself is believed to have been used as a place of worship for considerably longer. There are a couple of shops and tea stalls here.

The place is also sacred to Buddhists to whom it is known as Yanglesho. The cave alongside the temple is revered as the place where Padmasambhava attained his realization of the Mahamudra teachings. Legend relates how snakes came to disrupt Padmasambhava during meditation. The guru reached up and turned them all to stone, an act commemorated by the stone images of snakes hanging here today. Adjacent to the Shekha Narayan Mandir and approached via a flight of steps is the Buddhist Monastery under the guidance of Chatrel Rinpoche Sangye Dorje, one of the greatest living masters of the Nyingma school who maintains the Katok and Longchen Nyintig traditions, among others.

On a ridge a few hundred metres beyond, there is an ancient Newari pagoda site dedicated to Phamting Vajra Jogini. This 17th century temple is one of the four main Vajra Jogini sites of the Valley. Higher up the hillside, there is the Astura Cave, where Padmasambhava attained realizations by propitiating the meditational deity Vajrakila combined with Yangdak Heruka. The cave is venerated by Hindus as an abode of Goraknath. There are several Tibetan Buddhist temples and monasteries which have been constructed on the hillside around and below this cave in recent decades and which principally represent the Nyingma and Kagyu traditions. Among them are those under the guidance of Zatrul Rinpoche and Lama Ralo. An exquisite 'self arising' rock image of the Tantric deity, Tara, which was not so long ago exposed to the elements, has now been incorporated within a large temple complex.

Dakshinkali Mandir
Colour map 3, grid B1

Leaving Pharping, the road snakes down the hill for three kilometres towards the Dakshinkali Mandir (*dakshin* = 'southern'). Just before you get there, the (**D**) *Ashoka Hotel* on your left is popular with Indian tourists and offers basic accommodation if you want to stay overnight. A car park at the bottom of the hill charges Rs 8 for cars and Rs 2 for cycles and motorbikes. From here you can get to the temple by walking along the road lined by vendors of red *sindur* and other coloured powder dyes, fruits, vegetables, chickens and lucrative souvenir carvings and paintings. Uncastrated black male goats without deformation, the most common sacrifice for those who can afford it, are brought by the worshippers, though chickens are a popular alternative. You can also go through the green gate near the car park and walk down along the riverside to the temple. There are other ways also which can be combined with some wonderful short walks around the area: if you get lost, aim downhill to the river or follow the noise.

The temple complex straddles the banks of a small river in a ravine surrounded on three sides by steep, densely wooded slopes. The combination of the location's natural grandeur with the devout, though oft seemingly brutal, worship of a demanding goddess imbues the whole area with a remarkably intense atmosphere that is not soon forgotten.

Kali sacrifice

The goddess Kali (literally 'black'), described in the Mahabharata as "born of anger ... the cruel daughter of the ocean of blood, the drinker of blood", is the terrifying form of Durga, the consort of Shiva, one of the trinity of 'all powerful' Hindu gods. Kali is perhaps the best known of all the Tantric shakti divinities and is seen as representing, or controlling, destruction and death in the unending cycle of life. Often known affectionately as Ma ('Mother') Kali by devotees for her other, protective qualities, her propitiation in the past occasionally involved human sacrifice; in the modern era it continues to include, inter alia, animal sacrifice. This practice, which emerged as a prominent feature of Hindu worship during the late Vedic period (c 900-500 BC), is seen as continuing the process of creation by repeating the first great sacrifice in which the world was created. There are specific rites and rituals associated with it and the value of the sacrifice depends upon their correct performance by a priest. Kali is usually portrayed with multiple arms, a protruding tongue, wearing a garland of skulls and treading on the prostrate figure of Shiva.

The temple was built by a Malla king in the 14th century to appease Kali with a great sacrifice of buffaloes when the country was in the grip of a cholera epidemic. The path down from the car park crosses a bridge leading to the temple guarded by a pair of stone lions. The gilded canopy roof is supported by four bronze nagas, while the shrine beneath contains the image of the goddess formed of black stone. Tuesday and Saturday are the busiest days when pilgrims and visitors come by the busload and when the sacrificial knife is at its most active. Worshippers ritually wash in the river before and after puja. The sacrifices take place on a mosaic stone floor beside the shrine. They are mercifully quick: a single swing of the knife is usually enough. The streams of blood flow along drains and into the river below where they mingle with huge quantities of chicken feathers before disappearing with the drift of the besmirched, ruby waters. Although visitors are not allowed into the shrine, there are walkways on both sides of the river from where you can view proceedings.

Getting there: There are frequent bus services on Tuesday and Saturday from the City Bus Park from 0600 for the 2-hour journey, Rs 20. You can also join a group or hire a taxi. There are hourly bus services daily as far as Pharping and it is a 3 kilometres walk on to Dakshinkali. Most of Kathmandu's travel agencies offer bus tours. By taxi, the journey from Kathmandu takes a little under an hour. Expect to pay around Rs 500 for the return trip. You can also make your way by mountain bike, but it is uphill all the way to Pharping and much of the road is in poor condition. Allow 2½ to 3 hours with time to take in the scenery, but avoid Tuesday and especially Saturday when the road is full of buses. It is best to arrive by 0800 when the temple is at its busiest.

Kirtipur

Colour map 3, grid A1 From Kalimati in the western suburbs of Kathmandu, the main Prithvi Highway to Pokhara extends westwards. Turning southwest from this highway, a side road leads from Kalimati one and a half kilometres west of the confluence of the Bagmati and Vishnumati rivers to the medieval hilltop town of Kirtipur (1,400 metres). Formerly classed as one of the four cities of the Valley, and with a predominantly Newar Buddhist population, Kirtipur has a proud though bittersweet place in the history of the Valley and its name means 'glorious city'.

Its origins are traced back to the 12th century when it belonged to the kingdom of Patan. By the 15th century it had broken its links with Patan and was established as an independent Malla kingdom. Its hilltop location gave Kirtipur a strategic advantage over attackers and its defence was increased by the building of a fortified wall around the town, the remains of which can still be seen today. The wall had 12 gates which opened to each of the town's precincts. It was the last of the Valley's towns to fall to the invading and ultimately unifying armies of Gorkha under Prithvi Narayan Shah. So fierce was the town's resistance, aided by its strategically high location, that it withstood the Gorkhas three times before eventually falling in 1769, a year after the submission of Kathmandu, Patan and Bhaktapur. Retribution for the town's opposition came swiftly, however, as Prithvi Narayan Shah famously ordered the noses of all men to be cut off, save those who could play wind instruments. It was reported that the severed noses filled two baskets with a combined weight of 40 kg! An erroneous, though amusing piece of hearsay has it that the noses of Kirtipur's men are still shorter than average.

Kirtipur is often considered to be among the most quintessentially Newari of the Valley's towns. In some ways it bears comparison with old Bhaktapur: an undulating maze of narrow cobbled streets typically hemmed in by terraces of three-storeyed earthy-red houses often with fabulously carved windows and doors. Unlike Bhaktapur, however, many of its buildings are in an advanced stage of disrepair and this sad example of floccinaucinihilipilification has only recently been addressed with efforts aimed at restoration and development of infrastructure. The town's people have traditionally been involved in agriculture though the manufacture of handicrafts, particularly carpets and textiles under the auspices of the Kirtipur Cottage Industry Centre, increasingly occupy many.

The town offers some fine views of Kathmandu and the mountains as well as a number of pleasant walking opportunities from and including Kirtipur (see also Whole Day Walks from Kathmandu, page 258).

Sights **Uma Maheshwar Mandir** This temple stands on a high point on the western side of the town from where you have marvellous views of Kathmandu. Two elephants stand guard on either side of the impressive stone stairway that leads up from the east. The three-storeyed temple was built in the 17th century. The smaller Vaishnavite shrine nearby is dedicated to Vishnu as Narayan together with his consort Lakshmi in an interesting complement to the Uma Maheshwar image of Shiva and Parvati.

Bagh Bhairab Mandir In the centre of town, just north of the main square, this is Kirtipur's best known temple. Bagh means tiger and the clay image of Bhairab is shown with the mask of a tiger, which underlines the deity's ferocious character. This image has no tongue, a deliberate absence derived from the story of a Kirtipur boy who once made a clay model of a tiger and, upon returning from the wood to fetch a leaf for the tongue, discovered that his model had come to life. The site has been used as a place of worship for as long as Kirtipur has existed, though the three-storeyed temple was built much later. Its principal attractions are the swords and shields which adorn the temple, fascinating vestiges of the battle in which Kirtipur fell to Prithvi Narayan Shah. The Bagh Bhairab festival takes place in autumn when the image is carried on a palanquin through the village and down to the river. Sacrifices are offered to Bhairab on Tuesday and Saturday.

Chilancho Vihara Also known as Chilandev Bahal and Jagatpal Mahavihara, this stupa stands in a square on Kirtipur's southern hilltop. Like those of Patan, its construction is widely attributed to the emperor Ashoka, though it is strongly disputed whether Ashoka ever actually visited the Kathmandu Valley. The oldest known reference to the stupa, pertaining to its enlargement and renovation, dates to 1509.

The central stupa is 11 metres high and above the dome 13 circular brass steps lead to the chhatra. A bamboo structure supports an additional umbrella above the stupa. At the cardinal points around the base are smaller chaityas and between these are other shrines, some containing images of Dhyani Buddhas and various depictions of Tara. A bell, installed here in 1755, is suspended on one side. Typical of the idiosyncratic nature of religion in Nepal, images of various Hindu deities, including those of Ganesh and Sita, are placed as you enter the site. Around the stupa are a number of dharamsalas as well as the buildings of a disused monastery.

Leaving the stupa, a path leads south towards the market area of Naya Bazaar. Just beyond is the new Nagara Mandapa Kirtivihara, a temple gifted to Kirtipur by the Thai government in the 1980s and built in the Thai style. At the extreme western end of town is the Kirtipur Cottage Industry Centre.

Tribhuvan University The main campus of Nepal's only university occupies the area to the north of the town. With more than 5,000 students, it was established in 1959 and named after King Tribhuvan (d 1955). The university also has affiliated institutions in other parts of Nepal. Library facilities are available. To get there, follow the main road out of Kirtipur towards the Dakshinkali Road. About 200 metres outside the built up area of town, take the left hand turning which takes you to the campus.

Getting there: See map, page 323. From Kathmandu's Durbar Square, it is a 5 kilometres walk or bike ride to Kirtipur. Take the main road (which becomes the Prithvi

Kirtipur

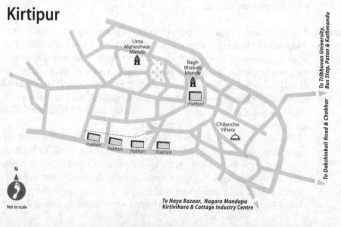

Highway) out of the city. At Kalimati, 1½ kilometres after crossing the Vishnumati River, take the left hand turning (southwest) and follow this road all the way to the northern side of Kirtipur. From Patan, follow the Ring Road and immediately after crossing the Bagmati River turn left (south) onto the Dakshinkali Rd. Continue south along here for just under 1 kilometre then turn right (west) for the 2 kilometres into the town past the road leading up to Tribhuvan University. There are regular buses throughout the day from Kathmandu's City Bus Park. The Kirtipur bus stop is on the link road between the town and the Dakshinkali Rd at the junction of the road leading to the university.

Thankot Thankot is a largely uninteresting village at the extreme western end of the Valley where the police checkpoint frequently results in lengthy queues of traffic heading to and from Pokhara. It is not recommended as a destination in its own right, although there is a pleasant cross country walk from Kirtipur through hamlets and past old temple remains.

Ichangu Narayan Mandir, Nagarjun and Rani Bans

Ichangu Narayan Mandir
Colour map 3, grid A1

This small temple site, a good destination for a half day mountain bike ride, lies beyond the village of Ichangu, some three kilometres northwest of the Swayambhunath stupa. The road from Swayambhunath leads uphill towards a Bhairab shine at the village of Halchowk at the top of the hill from where there are excellent views of the stupa with Kathmandu in the background. Beyond Halchowk, the road becomes a dirt track as it descends the one kilometre to Ichangu village. The temple lies at the far end of the village and is one of the quartet of the Valley's most important Vishnu/Narayan shrines (with Changu Narayan near Bhaktapur, Bishankhu Narayan at Chapagaon, and Shekha Narayan at Pharping). In October/November each year, many thousands of Vaishnavites begin a one-day pilgrimage of all these sites with a visit to the Ichangu Narayan Mandir.

The two-storeyed temple was built in the 18th century on a site which has been associated with Vishnu worship since the fourth century. Attractively set amid trees and open countryside, a stone wall surrounds the complex. There is a small statue of Vishnu's vehicle, Garuda, as well as stone images of Vishnu's chakra (discus) and conch shell. The sanctum's main image of Narayan is missing, apparently stolen.

Nagarjun & Rani Bans Covering a large hilly area to the north of the Ichangu Narayan Mandir is the delightful forest reserve of Nagarjun Ban (ban = forest) and Rani Ban ('Queen's Forest'). The wide expanse of forest is virtually unspoiled by the latter-day urbanization of Kathmandu and provides a natural habitat for a range of wildlife, including deer, pheasant, leopard and wild pigs. There are some lovely walks through tracts of rhododendron and oak, and the higher you climb the better are the views of both Kathmandu and the Himalaya to the north. There is a view tower near the stupa.

Bring your own supply of water, as none is available either on the way up or at the top.

The hill, standing 2,128 metres above sea level, is an important Buddhist site named after Nagarjuna, a Buddhist philosopher and saint who is said to have lived in the caves inside the hill. At the top is the stupa of Jamachu which marks the location of the legendary first sermon given by the Buddha in the Valley. Legend also has it that prayers for rain made from here are particularly efficacious. The stupa is a simple white structure standing on an exposed stone

Caves of Nagarjuna Hill

A honeycomb of caves inside Nagarjuna Hill, for the most part as yet unexplored, gives rise to numerous tales related to Nagarjuna. One, with continuing allegorical relevance, tells of the buffalo herdsman who regularly supplied Nagarjuna with milk. Nagarjuna suggested the herdsman to join him in meditation. But the herdsman, forever preoccupied with his livestock, declined and was promptly turned into a buffalo. The Mahe Buddha Gufa (gufa = cave) is located on the north side of the hill, about 500m from the Trisuli Rd. Nearby is the Lakshmi Gufa, known to Tibetans as Guru Rinpoche Gufa, another of Nagarjuna's reputed abodes. The main hollowing contains an image of the Buddha and is reached through a very narrow passage. Two chaityas inside the Acharya Vasubandhu Gufa on the northeast slope are thought by some to contain reliquaries of the Buddha's parents.

platform. The numerous prayerflags attached to it amply demonstrate how windswept the site is. A dharamsala offers simple accommodation for pilgrims.

The main entry gate is just to the north of Balaju. ■ *0700-2200. Rs 10 (including bike), Rs 20 (motorbike), Rs 50 (car).*

Getting there: You can drive to the summit by a long and winding dirt road, cycle to Balaju or take the bus from Ratna Park, then hike about 1-2 hours on an easy trail. **NB** Trails can be very slippery during the monsoon. From Balaju below the hill, a road leads northwest into the Trisuli Valley.

Kakani and the Trisuli Road

With breathtaking views of the Annapurnas, Ganesh Himal, Langtang Himal and the southern peaks of Tibet, the village of Kakani stands on a 2,067 metres ridge in the northwest corner of the Valley, 23 kilometres from Kathmandu's Ring Road. Like Nagarkot, with which it is frequently compared, Kakani appears on the tourist map almost exclusively for the views. Though spectacular, these are impeded somewhat by the Valley's northern hills and are considered by many to be inferior to those from Nagarkot. Nevertheless, the road from Kathmandu passes through beautiful countryside and there are some pleasant short walks around Kakani.

The tiny village of Kakani is connected by a paved road two kilometres east of the main Trisuli Road. Accommodation is limited, though the sunrise and sunset are rewards enough if you do stay the night. There are a couple of trekking standard guest houses, but almost all visitors make for the government run (C/D) Tara Gaon Hotel, T290812, which has a reasonable restaurant and a delightful garden. The village was chosen as an official residence by the British Resident during the 19th century Rana era and the quaint old house still stands next to the Tara Gaon Hotel. From here you have fabulous views not only of the mountains but, equally magnificent, of the hillside, its wooded slopes cascading rockily down to the distant river valley below. Continuing on the road through the village, a road to the north leads up to the Kakani Memorial Park, where a hilltop monument commemorates the victims of a 1992 air crash. To the east of the village is an army camp. Kakani was famously the entry point into the Valley for the armies of Prithvi Narayan Shah in the mid 1760s.

Kakani
Colour map 2, grid B5

Getting there: Kakani is easily accessible from Kathmandu via the Trisuli Rd. Buses bound for Trisuli and Dhunche have regular morning departures from the City Bus Park for the 2 hour journey. Ask to be dropped off at Kaulia from where it is a 2 kilometre walk east along a paved road. The views from here are fabulous: on your left you have the mountains and on your right the valley and its wooded slopes. By taxi, the drive up takes less than an hour. Negotiate the fare in advance and expect to pay in the region of Rs 450 each way. Kakani is often recommended as a good route for (dedicated) mountain bikers, though it is uphill all the way from Kathmandu. Join the Trisuli Rd at the northwest Ring Road and continue through Balaju. From Balaju, the road runs alongside the Nagarjun Ban for 6 kilometres before twisting the rest of the way up through lush paddy terraces and forest, particularly attractive in spring and late autumn when a wide variety of flowers are in bloom.

The Trisuli Road   From the Kakani turn off, the road meanders dramatically first west out of the Kathmandu Valley then north for a total of 42 kilometres to the town of Trisuli Bazaar, previously a popular starting point for treks into Langtang. Most of these treks now start at Dhunche, 50 kilometres further north. Beyond Kakani, the road descends steeply to meet with the Tadi Khola River valley. The Tadi runs southwest to join the Trisuli River. The road then veers in a northerly direction and, for one hour or so before reaching Trisuli Bazaar, follows attractively to the east of the Trisuli River. There are numerous police checkpoints along the road where you may be required to show your trekking permit.

Nawakot   Just to the south of Trisuli Bazaar, this small village is set high on a ridge overlooking its neighbour and also has majestic views of the mountains and surrounding valley. The kot, or fort, was another of Prithvi Narayan Shah's encampments between Gorkha and the Kathmandu Valley. Like all great military tacticians, Prithvi always chose such locations for strategic reasons and for the ease with which they could be defended. Three towers dominate the ruins of the walled fort, one of which is open to visitors. The village also has a two-storeyed temple dedicated to Bhairab.

Trisuli Bazaar   As an old trailhead for treks into Langtang, Trisuli Bazaar served to amplify the contrast between the beauty to come and that which was left behind. It is known for the dam and Trisuli River Hydroelectric Project on the river beyond the main bridge. It is one of several which have been constructed with foreign aid (in this case, from India) and have helped to provide electricity to many parts of the country previously without. The town is very much a functional centre, a market town where buses from Kathmandu to Dhunche stop for tea. It is possible to follow in reverse the steps of the Gorkha conquerors of the Kathmandu Valley by trekking from here to Gorkha. No longer accustomed to catering for large numbers of visitors staying overnight, accommodation is limited to a few trekking standard guest houses, including the Pratistha Lodge, Shakyar Lodge, Ranjit Lodge and the Trisuli Guest House, all located on the other side of the bridge. All food available here is Nepali – the Ranjit Lodge has been recommended. (See the Trekking section for places north of Trisuli, page 167.)

Getting there: From City Bus Park, there are regular morning departures by bus. Because of the poor condition of the narrow road and its constant twists and turns, the 65 kilometres journey takes around 4½ hours (longer in the monsoon), Rs 50.

Kathmandu to Pokhara

6

335 Mugling

336 Gorkha

341 **Pokhara**

344 Sights

344 Phewa Tal

346 Tibetan Villages

347 Sarangkot

350 Museums

351 Rupa and Begnas Tals

351 Sleeping and eating

363 Shopping

365 Transport

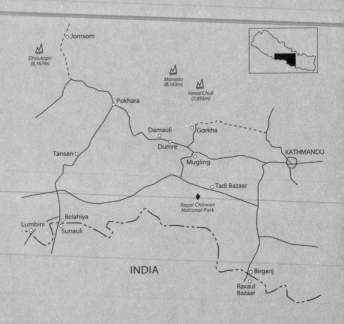

Probably the stretch of road most travelled by tourists in Nepal, the Prithvi Highway links the country's two main centres of tourism in a nine-hour bus journey. This is Gurkha country. Once out of the Kathmandu Valley, the journey enters the attractive Middle Hills. Precarious at times but also graceful, the road winds its way across hills and valleys, passing grassy, rocky countryside dotted with small springs and picturesque villages. For much of the time, the spectacular snow-capped peaks of the Annapurnas form the northern horizon. Pokhara has an air of laid-back easiness which greets new arrivals with a casual embrace leaving them to unwind in one of the myriad cafés and restaurants surrounding the lake with its reflection of Macchapuchere, the 'Fish-Tail' Mountain, appearing as an almost perfect pyramid.

Prithvi Highway

Colour map 2, grid B1-B5

From Kathmandu, best mountain views are fom seats on the right hand side of the bus, and on the left hand side from Pokhara

The 206 kilometres long road was built from Kathmandu to Dumre with Indian Government help and from Dumre to Pokhara with Chinese assistance. It is a slower journey than the distance suggests, particularly because landslides have caused damage and sections are in a poor state just out of Kathmandu and again west of Mugling. Tourist buses take between eight and nine hours to complete the trip – including what can often be a painfully slow departure from Kathmandu where numerous unscheduled pick-ups are invariably accompanied by confusion of some sort, before the onset of traffic jams in the western suburbs and further stops for tea and the completion of morning ablutions.

Once out of the Kathmandu Valley, though, the journey enters the attractive **Middle Hills**. The road follows the **Trisuli River** to **Mugling** (110 kilometres from Kathmandu), the confluence of the Trisuli and **Marshyangdi** rivers, which together form the **Narayani** or Sapt Gandaki which flows south to the plains. The point of confluence is attractive and unmistakable, joining the brown water of the Trisuli with the milky-white and green of the Marshyangdi. For two kilometres or so, these two streams of water flow side by side in one river before merging gradually. If you turn left at Mugling, the road brings you to Narayanghat and the Chitwan National Park. Continuing west from Mugling you reach **Dumre** after 42 kilometres with the small village of **Damauli** a further 20 kilometres away. Close to Damauli is a regular stopping point for tea and snacks for tourist buses whose drivers are said to be offered incentives for stopping there. One establishment, *The Highway Restaurant*, does tea, soft drinks and some excellent channa and onion bhaji, but

One member of its staff openly (and accurately) jokes of it as The Highway Robbery

Kathmandu to Pokhara (central Nepal)

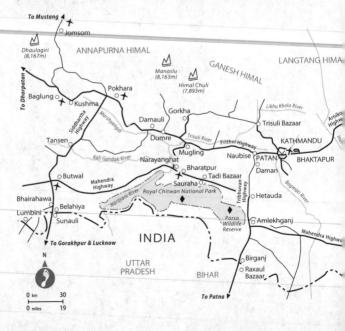

at hugely inflated prices for tourists. If you can persuade one of the friendly Nepali conductors on your bus to buy for you, you can reduce your bill by up to 75 percent!

The **Pokhara Valley** is entered just beyond and below **Khairani**. At the east end of the valley are the **Rupkot** and **Begnas Tals** (lakes).

Mugling

The small town of Mugling (pronounced *Moogling*) owes its existence to its position at an important junction linking the Prithvi Highway from Kathmandu to Pokhara with the main road heading south to Narayanghat, where it joins with the Mahendra Highway which extends east-west across the entire Terai. Almost all buses running between Kathmandu and Pokhara stop at Mugling for tea. Owing to the poor state of the Siddhartha Highway, on paper the shortest distance between Pokhara and the border crossing of Sunauli, several tourist buses connecting these towns actually take a considerably longer route, first running east from Pokhara to Mugling then south to Narayanghat before returning west to Butwal to complete the final part of the journey along the Siddhartha Highway's only section of well constructed road. Given the preoccupation with thrift which features prominently in many of the region's commercial activities, such a major diversion, with the extra fuel required, is a striking reflection on the condition of the Siddhartha Highway.

Colour map 2, grid B3

Mugling has little to recommend it as a destination in its own right. It is a purely functional place, a small collection of houses, shops, eating places and a few small hotels flanking the main road. The junction is on the western edge of the main road, marked by a lopsided sign pointing in the direction of Narayanghat. Most buses pull in outside a restaurant where the driver thinks he is most likely to enjoy a free lunch, but there is no pressure to eat or drink at any particular place. There are several reasonable **tea** and **dal-bhad** establishments along this northern central section of the road and some also offer beer, cold drinks, crisps and other snacks such as pakhora and chana. Itinerant fruit sellers and corn-on-the-cob merchants patrol the footpath outside. Accustomed to high prices unwittingly paid by some tourists (including Rs 15 that someone was once charged for a banana!), your bargaining skills may be well tested here.

Mugling marks the lowest and warmest point along the Kathmandu-Pokhara highway, and a short distance to the west of the town is the confluence of the **Marshyangdi** and **Trisuli** rivers. The highway runs attractively alongside the Marshyangdi as far as Dumre, passing the huge concrete **Marshyangdi Hydroelectric Project** Control Centre. Completed with World Bank assistance in 1990 at a cost of over US$200 million, it is responsible for generating a large proportion of Nepal's electric energy and is a forerunner of a number of proposed mega hydroelectric projects using natural resources to supply the country with electricity into the next century.

Mugling is also the start point for the country's most popular rafting trip along the lower Trisuli River, as well as the finishing point for trips **rafting** down the Marshyangdi and Seti rivers.

There are a few small hotels in the central part of Mugling. A number of these cater for transiting long distance drivers. Mugling also has a reputation for prostitution, so some of these hotels may prove to be less than ideal places to stay. About 1 kilometre outside Mugling to the west is the **B** *Motel du Mugling* (reservations from Kathmandu, T225242). Pleasantly situated on an isolated bend of the main road, it has a restaurant and is Mugling's only decent hotel.

Sleeping

Kathmandu to Pokhara

Transport Although no tourist buses start or end their journey in Mugling, the town is well served by local transport. There are regular buses throughout the day to **Narayanghat** (2 hours, Rs 10); **Dumre** (1 hour, Rs 5); **Damauli** (1¾ hours, Rs 12); **Naubise** (3½ hours, Rs 20); and **Gorkha** via Abu Khaireni (1½ hours; Rs 12).

If you are stuck in Mugling and are wanting to get to either **Kathmandu** or **Pokhara**, most tourist buses will allow you to join for between Rs 60 and Rs 100, but this will probably involve standing or sitting on your backpack in the aisle.

Manakamana

Altitude: 1,302m
Colour map 2, grid B3

The Manakamana temple, six kilometres north of Mugling and 12 kilometres south of Gorkha, is the most important Hindu site in western central Nepal. Situated on a conspicuous ridge, the temple attractively overlooks the Trisuli and Marshyangdi rivers, with views of the Annapurnas also. It attracts around 500,000 visitors – almost all of them pilgrims – every year. The first shrine was built on this site in the 17th century by one Lakhan Thappa. When the Gorkha King Rama Shah died in 1636, his queen committed sati on his funeral pyre on the Manakamana River. Some time later, a farmer discovered blood and milk pouring from a stone in a nearby field. When Lakhan Thappa heard about this, he was convinced it was a sign from the dead queen, and constructed a temple in her honour. The present temple in a 19th century replacement, a two-tiered pagoda with numerous carved roof struts. Tradition has it that the temple priest must be a descendant of Lakhan Thappa. Goats and chickens are regularly sacrificed to the deity queen, Manakamana Devi.

Organized tours are operated by Manakamana Darshan, Naxal, Kathmandu T434960, F434515, rajesh@cc.wlink.com.np

Sleeping Manakamana has a number of small and basic guest houses, but there is no tourist standard accommodation.

Transport Buses run from Kathmandu and Pokhara to Mugling (around Rs 150 each way) from early morning. From Mugling take a local bus to Cheres (6 km), where a modern cable service runs regularly to the Manakamana shrine (Rs 250 each way).

Gorkha

Altitude: 1,145m
Colour map 2, grid B3

Gorkha is an optional starting point for treks in the Annapurna region and along the Buri Gandaki in the Manaslu region

Gorkha (or *Gurkha*) is 20 kilometres north of the village of Abu Khaireni on the Prithvi Highway along a good all-weather road, 136 kilometres west of Kathmandu and 106 kilometres east of Pokhara. Probably Nepal's most famous village, it is the ancestral home of the Shah dynasty, the birthplace of King Prithvi Narayan Shah after whom the Prithvi Highway is named, and was at the heart of the recruiting area for Gurkha regiments. The modern village is a steepish walk to the south of Prithvi Narayan's Gorkha Durbar headquarters and, considering its role in the history of Nepal, surprisingly small. It has a bus terminus, a bank, post office, *tundhikel* (parade ground), and a small number of budget hotels and eating places.

Surrounding the Rani Pokhari, a tank in the square 100 metres north of the bus stand are a number of locally important buildings. The temples are to Vishnu, Krishna and Ganesh. There is also a column with a statue of the great king. Veering right, you pass the Tallo Durbar on your right. This pre-dates the conquest of Kathmandu and was the royal palace. 100 metres further on, steps lead off to your left. Gradual at first but steeper towards the end, these bring you to the Gorkha Durbar.

King Prithvi Narayan Shah

Regarded as the founding father of the modern state of Nepal, Prithvi Narayan Shah was born in 1723 and, at the age of 20, succeeded to the Gorkha throne established in 1560 by Dravya Shah. He soon demonstrated an unusual proficiency in leadership, and his rule was noted for its justice, efficiency and tolerance. Under his command, the Thakuri, Tamang and Magar soldiers became known collectively as the Gurkhas. Myth has it that the legendary saint Gorakhnath, appearing disguised as an old man, foretold that Prithvi Narayan would rule wherever his feet would take him. And indeed Prithvi succeeded where his father and forefathers had failed, bringing all the passes that bordered with Tibet under his control and, helped by the feuding of the respective Malla rulers of Kathmandu, Lalitpur and Bhadgaon, conquering the states of the Kathmandu Valley on the day in 1768 when the valley was celebrating the Living Goddess Kumari, thereby uniting the entire kingdom of Nepal for the first time. It is said that the Kumari placed a tikka on Prithvi's forehead, interpreted as ritually bestowing on him the divine right to rule. A steely but ultimately fallible aspect of Prithvi's character, however, is illustrated by his order to sever the noses of all males – except those with a talent for playing wind instruments – in the village of Kirtipur following the latter's successful defence of the Kathmandu Valley in the face of his invading army in 1767. With his eventual success he moved his capital from Gorkha to Kathmandu where it has remained ever since. Prithvi Narayan Shah died in 1775, Nepal's present king, Birendra Bir Bikram Shah is a 10th generation descendant.

A steep one kilometre walk from the bus stand is Gorkha Durbar. Strategically located to overlook the village and beyond, thereby allowing an early warning of any approaching aggressors, this impressive complex comprising fort, temple and palace was built by Prithvi Narayan Shah to celebrate his conquest of the Kathmandu Valley. Views from the Durbar are quite spectacular: to the south is the lush Trisuli valley, while a 200 kilometres stretch of the Himalaya forms a majestic northern horizon.

Gorkha Durbar

Photography within the complex is prohibited and access to most parts is barred to all but the king and certain appointed Brahmin priests. Nevertheless, there are many fine examples of Newari woodcarving and craftsmanship on view. The path from the village approaches the complex from the west from where you can see the impressive set of steps leading to the entrance. The first building you come to is the **Kalika Mandir**, one of the most important Hindu temples in the region. Dedicated to the goddess Kali, wrathful consort of Shiva, the temple is the focus of Gorkha's principal festivals of Dasain in October and Chaitra Dasain in April when sacrifices of goats and chickens are made near the entrance. The exterior of the temple has some intricately carved window frames. Beside the temple and central to the complex is Prithvi Narayan's birthplace, the **Dhunipati** durbar, again with examples of window decoration exquisitely carved by Newari craftsmen originating from the Kathmandu Valley. This is regarded as the ancestral home of the Shah dynasty, and although not open to the public it contains the eternal flame commemorating King Prithvi and the throne on which he was crowned. Just beyond the Dhunipati are stairs leading down to a shrine that marks the cave where **Gorakhnath**, the village's eponymous patron saint and traditionally spiritual mentor to the Shahs, lived.

Elsewhere, numerous Hindu deities and small shrines with attendant priests and devotees lend a sense of added legality and authenticity to the role of the complex as a historical and spiritual centre of the rule of royalty in the modern era.

Kathmandu to Pokhara

Tallokot An indirect route back to the village heading west along the ridge from Gorkha Durbar takes you past a Shah monument before reaching the small disused fort-watch tower of Tallokot. From here a path leads south through terraced fields to Gorkha.

Upallakot At over 1,500 metres this is the highest point of the ridge, about 40 minutes walk to the east of Gorkha Durbar. There are stunning views through 360°, and from the Annapurnas to the Ganesh Himal. The TV tower also takes advantage of the altitude. Sunrise and sunset from Upallakot have been recommended.

Sleeping **B** *Gorkha Hill Resort*, reservations in Kathmandu T227929, F471630. 25 rooms most with panoramic views over the valley, good restaurant, comfortable but inconveniently situated some 5 km south of Gorkha village itself. **D** *Bisauni*, T20107. 10 rooms some with bath, cheaper dorm accommodation, ISD facilities and hot water, small eating area does reasonable snacks and meals, the best of Gorkha's budget places. **E** There are a few very basic lodges in the area leading to the bus stand. Most have cold running water though buckets of hot water are usually available on request. They include: *Pamper*, *Park Lodge*, *Thakali Lodge* and, beyond the bus stand, the *Sugat* where food is available with advance notice.

Eating There are Nepali and Tibetan food outlets near the bus stand. Non-residents can eat at the *Bisauni*. The restaurant in *the Gorkha Hill Resort* is expensive, but has the neighbourhood's best range of food.

Transport Gorkha is well connected by local buses which go regularly throughout the day to and from Abu Khaireni and on to Mugling. A number of buses link the village with key tourist centres, including Kathmandu, Pokhara and Tadi Bazaar (for Sauraha and the Chitwan National Park), as well as to the southern border crossings of Birgunj and Sunauli. Frequency varies with season. Most departures to **and** from Gorkha, especially on the longer routes, leave in the morning. Tickets are available from the bus stand.

Gorkha

The Gurkhas

The Gurung, Magar, Rai and Tamang among the Tibeto-Nepalese people have together contributed the bulk of the famous Gurkha regiments of the British army. The Gurung live in the shadow of the great Annapurna Massif, and have a reputation for strength, endurance and fearlessness. As early as the 16th century they were much sought after by Indian princes and in the late 18th century formed the martial stock which created the Gurkha Kingdom. Many enlisted in the British army in India in the 19th century. Then the name Gurkha was applied to the people, although it is really a geographical term referring to the Gurung who came from the fortress town of Gorakhnath.

Numbering about 300,000, Gurkhas have played distinctive and gallant roles in British wars and campaigns since 1815. With 26 Victoria Crosses for gallantry and numerous other battle honours, they came to be regarded as an intrinsic element in Britain's army. Some villages derived over 75 percent of their income from military service and became dependent on it. The Magars and Rais are large groups who also enlisted into the Gurkha regiments. Most are subsistence farmers living in the Middle Zone hill country from the high mountain down to the Terai.

They all have markedly mongoloid features. Each group has its own mythology. The Tamangs, for example, believe that the first mother of the Tamangs was a cow who bore three sons, the youngest of whom, Tolgu, founded the race. The Tamangs practise a religion which outwardly resembles Tibetan Buddhism blended with Hindu teachings, but also incorporate elements of their 'old' religion based on shamanism. They live just beyond the Newari-Hindu area of the Kathmandu Valley. While most are subsistence farmers, the name is apparently Tibetan for 'horse trader' which suggests a past somewhat similar to the Sherpas. There are approximately 1 million Tamangs.

British Gurkha regiments have been based in Hong Kong and in recent years have seen action in the Falklands, during the Gulf War and most recently in East Timor. With the return of Hong Kong to Chinese administration in 1997 and the changing face of modern military strategy, plans were announced in 1992 to reduce the Gurkhas in the British army to a total of 2,500 men, amalgamated into two infantry battalions and support units. Although redundancy packages and 'resettlement training' is being provided, the reduction will have a significant bearing on the local economies of communities traditionally reliant upon remittances.

Kathmandu to Pokhara

Dumre

Dumre is another of those small towns to have emerged since the 1960s and 1970s as a direct result of the construction of new roads, in this case the Prithvi Highway. Its growth has also been due partly to its location at the point where the Marshyangdi River veers sharply from its southbound course to parallel the Prithvi Highway eastwards. About two and a half to three hours by bus (70 kilometres) east of Pokhara, and between five and six hours (136 kilometres) west of Kathmandu, Dumre is a small, chattering bazaar town, the urban focus for the area between Mugling and Damauli that also serves tea and snacks to occasional transiting buses. What the town lacks in aesthetic appeal, it compensates for as a traditionally popular starting point for treks heading into the Annapurna region and those following the Marshyangdi River. There are a couple of shops selling trekkers' provisions and, to the west of the town centre, there is a telephone kiosk. If you are staying in Dumre, there is a possible excursion to the attractive village of Bandipur which overlooks the valley from about five kilometres south of the highway.

Colour map 2, grid B2

Sleeping It is best to arrive early in the day so that you can begin trekking without having to spend a night in Dumre. If you are staying here, though, there are a handful of basic places to stay, but all are rather spartan and noisy because of the main road. They include: **E** *Annapurna*, *Chandrag*, *Jomsom*, *Mustang*, and *Ravi*.

Transport Local bus services provide Dumre with regular connections to and from **Pokhara** (2½-3 hours, Rs 50) and **Mugling** (1 hour, Rs 5). From **Kathmandu** there are also public bus services, but these take longer than the tourist buses. The most comfortable way of getting to or from Kathmandu is to take a tourist bus to Pokhara and tell the conductor to drop you off in Dumre. A ticketing and reservation counter for buses to Kathmandu and Pokhara is located between the Jomsom and Marpha hotels, just west of the road that heads north towards Besisahar.

Damauli

Colour map 2, grid B2 Damauli is situated close to the confluence of the Seti and Madi rivers and is a functional, administrative centre. There are some pleasant walks along the riverbanks and one traveller recommended it for birdwatching. Otherwise it has little of general tourist interest. There is a small tea and snack stop popular with Kathmandu-Pokhara bus drivers nearby (see also page 334).

Pokhara

Population: *55,000 approx*
Altitude: *884m*
Phone code: *061*
Colour map 2, grid B1

Nestled in a valley in the shadow of the Annapurna mountains and on the shore of the Phewa Lake, Pokhara is Nepal's most popular tourist destination after Kathmandu. There are two Pokharas. One is the traditional Nepali town of narrow streets, bazaars and noise. The other is the relaxed, laid back agglomeration of hotels and restaurants in a stunningly beautiful setting along the shore of Nepal's second largest lake and in the shadow of the awesome Annapurna mountains. The small airport and main bus station are neighbours between these two faces of Pokhara. It is a 10 minute taxi ride to both Lakeside and Damside, and you can be sure of a crowd of competing taxi drivers awaiting your custom as you step off the plane or bus.

Like Kathmandu, there is an abundance of accommodation to suit all expectations and budgets, and most offer excellent value. Gastronomically, Pokhara is not quite as well endowed as Kathmandu, but there is still a wide range of places to eat good food. You can easily get around the main tourist areas on foot, while taxis are readily available to take you further afield.

Ins and outs

Getting there Both the airport and bus terminal are located more or less in the centre of town at the end of the Prithvi Highway, very close to the lake. The flight takes about 30 minutes from Kathmandu while it is a long eight hour trip by bus. The views are fairly spectacular though. Try to sit on the right hand side when travelling from Kathmandu.

Getting around Most parts of Pokhara are within walking distance of each other. Local buses during the day connect the lake area with the bazaar. There are no rickshaws, pedal or auto, in either Lakeside or Damside. Taxis, however, are readily available. The main taxi rank in the southern part of town is at a sleepy intersection at the southern end of Ratna Chowk, between Lakeside and Damside. All taxis should use their meters, but bargaining for a fixed rate is not unusual. From here, the fare to the airport should be about Rs 30, to the main bus station it is around Rs 40, and to the central bazaar area about Rs 100.

Climate Winter daytime temperature never falls below 10°C and reaches 20°C. Summer temperatures rise to 36°C or higher, when it is hot and humid. The monsoon lasts from mid-June to mid-September. Best time to visit: October to April.

Location

The Pokhara Valley is situated in the centre of Nepal. 400 metres lower

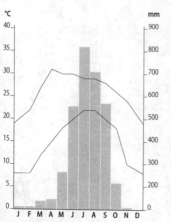
Pokhara climate

than Kathmandu, the valley is hemmed in far more closely by the Himalayan giant peaks. Dominated by the Annapurna massif to the north, the valley is dotted with lakes, of which the Phewa Tal (lake) is the largest. Its stunningly beautiful setting first attracted tourists in numbers during the late 1960s and early 1970s when it became particularly popular with hippies, and much of the town has been transformed since then into a travellers' retreat of hotels, small family run guest houses and restaurants. A small airport was built in the mid 1950s which provided the most direct link with the outside world – in this case, Kathmandu. The construction of a hydroelectric plant followed 10 years later, and work began on roads connecting Pokhara with Kathmandu to the east and with the border towns of Bhairawa and Sunauli to the south during the 1970s.

The town of Pokhara itself on the Seti Khola River is overshadowed by the towering Macchapuchere (6,997m), the Fishtail Mountain. Reflected in the still waters of the Phewa Lake it is one of the most beautiful mountains in the world, from Pokhara appearing as an almost perfect pyramid. The twin peak

Pokhara

from which it takes its name only appears after some days travelling to the west. Annapurna, just 30 kilometres to the north, towers more than 7,000 metres above the valley, flanked by a range of superb and sometimes daunting mountains. The sheer majesty and enormity of the Himalaya is especially apparent when viewed from the lake, and you can often see people downing oars in a rowing boat in the middle of the Phewa Lake to gaze at the snowcapped peaks in wonder.

Its magnificent natural scenery, contrasting environments and proximity to unaffected rural life ensures that Pokhara neither has nor requires many artificial attractions, and some consider the area as among the most beautiful places in the world. As with Kathmandu, however, the town's undoubted success as a tourist resort has resulted inevitably in further development of new hotels, restaurants and other tourist facilities. While such development contributes to the local and national economies by drawing in more foreign exchange, it also affects the character of the town. Two and three story concrete hotels, often remarkably similar in design but offering comfortable rooms and Western bathrooms, are increasingly replacing traditional homes with more basic facilities converted into guest houses that offer a valuable insight into the Nepali way of life. Comparisons with the early development of some Mediterranean resorts inevitably come to mind which, if allowed to continue, would consign an important part of Pokhara's charm and appeal to the past.

About 40,000 people live in the valley around Pokhara, while the mountains are left to snow leopards, blue sheep and innumerable species of birds. From the snow covered peaks, vegetation grows ever more luxurious with the drop in height, passing through one of the largest rhododendron forests in the world to the humid lowlands, where many of Nepal's native plants thrive, including over 100 varieties of orchids. At a lower elevation than Kathmandu, it is a warmer climate. It is also the town with Nepal's highest annual rainfall, concentrated during the monsoon, which has led to it being referred to as the 'Cherrapunjee of Nepal'.

Annapurna Conservation Area Park Headquarters is at Ghandruk, Kaski District, and an Annapurna Information Centre is at Prithvi Narayan Campus Museum in Pokhara. The King Mahendra Trust for Nature Conservation is a non-profit, non-governmental organization dedicated to conserving natural resources in Nepal. The Trust supports the project for conservation, education and participation to revitalize villagers' independent initiatives.

It is fitting that the origins of settlement in Pokhara can be traced back to its time as a stopover for travelling merchants plying ancient trading routes from the plains to the Himalaya. During the Middle Ages the Pokhara Valley was known as Kaski and ruled by a king from Kaskikot, or Kaski fort, built on a high ridge north of the town in the 15th century near the present day village of Sarangkot. During the 17th century, the region's traditional Gurung and Magar communities were joined by Newars from the Kathmandu Valley who came at the invitation of the king as traders.

The bazaar, to the north of the Phewa Lake, is the oldest established part of Pokhara and in sections its architecture reflects the influence of the Newars who came from Kathmandu and settled here three centuries ago. Although endless street (as Giuseppe Tucci called it in 1950) still forms the main north-south thoroughfare, the area has expanded greatly since, in line with the town's overall increase in population. A seemingly haphazard maze of smaller lanes now backs off the main road to the east and west; in character the area is considerably further removed than the actual five kilometres separating it from the tranquil settings of Lakeside and Damside.

Sights

Phewa Tal

Take care of where you swim: poisonous snakes, including cobra and green mamba, as well as other non poisonous varieties, are known to inhabit especially the areas where trees and undergrowth extend down to the lake shore. Leeches can be a problem in summer and often attach themselves to the side of the boat.

The Phewa Tal is the focus of tourism in Pokhara and around it have grown the town's two principal concentrations of hotels and restaurants. It is Nepal's second largest lake after Rara in the west. It is fed from the west by the small Harpan Khola while to the southeast it narrows to become the Pardi Khola for 2 kilometres which in turn feeds into the Fusre Khola. The hydroelectric dam was built with Indian aid in 1968. It has traditionally been a rich source of fish for local communities, but over-exploitation during the last decade in particular has led to a serious depletion of reserves, so that the fish that are widely advertised on Lakeside and Damside menus as coming 'fresh from the lake' now usually come fresh from the Begnas and Rupa lakes to the east of Pokhara.

There are a number of places along Lakeside and – but to a lesser extent – Damside where you can hire rowing boats by the hour and half- or full day. Rates are always negotiable. They vary according to demand, but are generally cheaper the further you go from the central area. In peak seasons, operators may demand Rs 70 per hour or Rs 250 for a full day, but in summer you can get this down by half or more.

Seen from both Lakeside and Damside, the lake reflects the richly wooded hills to the south, appearing emerald green across a crystal surface disturbed only by the ripples of boats and swimmers. But more magnificent still is the sight from its western and southern banks. Take a boat from Lakeside and row diagonally across towards the other side. From here you can see the mighty Annapurnas rising high above the town and northern ridge, geological enormities whose lofty, snowcapped elegance shimmers on the now blue water.

In addition to some pleasant walking opportunities either side of the lake, it is also possible to swim. Although many people do swim along the Lakeside and Damside shores, these areas are not recommended because of the sewage and other waste that is pumped directly into the lake at strategic intervals here. It is better to swim from the northen bank or from a boat in the middle of the lake.

Temples

As a relatively new town and in complete contrast to Kathmandu, Pokhara has little in the way of an architectural heritage. There are, however, four minor temples of interest.

The **Varahi Mandir** is situated in the Phewa Lake, approximately level with the main Lakeside road as it veers from the north to the east. It is reached by boat and is dedicated to Varahi, the Hindu god Vishnu's third incarnation in the form of a boar.

In the Bazaar area in the northern part of town is a small Newari style temple dedicated to **Bhimsen**, while further north still is the **Bidhyavasini Mandir**. Set on a shady platform, this shikhara style temple is dedicated to the goddess Durga in her Bhagwati manifestation. The shrine is a saligram (marine fossil) of local black ammonite, providing a link to an earlier and warmer geological age when the valley was submerged by water. About 20 minutes walk to the northwest of the main bus stop, the small **Bhadrakali Mandir** sits attractively atop a green hillock with pleasant views to the east.

'Peace Temple' Construction on this new Buddhist centre began in 1994 and was scheduled for completion by 2000. A joint venture with Japan, it has an idyllic location on the high ridge overlooking the Phewa Lake opposite Lakeside, from where views of the lake and the mountains to the north, as well as over the Fusre and Seti rivers to the south, are simply unsurpassed. (A dawn view is especially recommended.) To get there, you can either take a boat to the

Prayer flags

Any prominent place exposed to the wind may be adorned with multicoloured prayer flags (darchok), permitting the natural power of the wind to distribute the blessings of their inscribed prayers as they flap to and fro, for which reason they are known also as 'horses of the wind' (lungta). Domestic rooftops and monastery compounds often have large poles to which these flags are attached, and renewed annually on the 3rd day after the Tibetan New Year. Similarly, most mountain passes (la-tse) are marked by cairns of stones (some inscribed with mantras), to which sets of prayer-flags are attached. Wherever public buses or private jeeps cross over a major pass, the passengers will invariably disembark to add a stone to the cairn, or tie a newly prepared set of prayer flags and burn incense as an offering to the spirit of the mountain, who would have been tamed and appointed protector of Buddhism by Padmasambhava back in the 8th century. Some will cast paper prayer flags into the air from the bus window, rejoicing loudly in the ancient paean: "Kyi-kyi so-so! May the gods be victorious!" (lha-gyel-lo).

A single set of cotton prayer flags is ordered in the sequence: blue, white, red, green and yellow, respectively symbolizing the five elements: space, water, fire, air and earth. In each corner of the flag there may be a protective animal: garuda (top-left), dragon (top-right), tiger (bottom-left), and lion (bottom-right), while the mantra-syllables forming the main part of the inscription may vary according to the preferred meditational deity of the devotee. Those of the three bodhisattvas: Avalokiteshvara, Manjughosa, and Vajrapani are commonplace, as are the mantras of the female bodhisattva Tara, who protects travellers from the diverse dangers of the road.

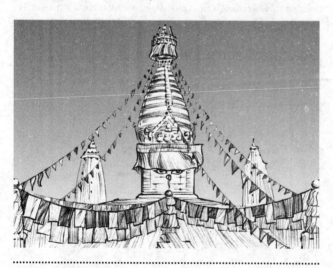

shore directly opposite Lakeside for a steepish climb of about 45 minutes to the top, or from the *Gurkha Haven Hotel* crossroads at Damside take the road heading west, cross the two bridges over the Pardi Khola and begin a relatively gentle climb of about one hour through forest to the top of the ridge. A climb to the temple makes for an excellent half day excursion. The Rani Ban forest is home to numerous species of exotic birds - Hari K.C. at the *Fish Tail Lodge* is an excellent and qualified guide. From Lakeside, the temple is clearly visible by its solitary twinkling lights at night.

Devi Falls Some two kilometres southwest of the main concentration of hotels at Damside, the Devi Falls is a sink hole (waterfall) where the Pardi Khola disappears from view, emerging 200 metres to the south just in time to join the Fusre Khola. Known locally as *Patale Chhango*, it is best visited during or in the months following the monsoon; at other times, the Pardi Khola may be no more spectacular than a trickle of water. A popular local legend ascribes the name *Devi Falls* to an unfortunate tourist named David or Devi who, whilst peering down, was unwittingly made to obey the laws of gravity with devastating consequences. ■ *An admission fee of Rs 5 may be charged at peak times.*

Pokhara's Tibetans Following the Chinese liberation of an already free Tibet in 1950, refugees flooded into Nepal. Many settled in the Kathmandu Valley, but some also found their way to Pokhara. While not as conspicuous a population here as in Kathmandu, there are nonetheless several prominent Tibetan owned and run hotels and restaurants where portraits of the Dalai Lama hang proudly indoors and prayer flags flutter optimistically in the breeze outside. Few Tibetans are directly involved in retail, but groups of women are often to be found wandering the Lakeside and Damside streets offering their varied handicrafts for sale to tourists.

Tibetan villages Several Tibetan settlements are dotted around the Pokhara area. The **Tashiling Tibetan Village** is probably the best known, because it is the most accessible. Just to the south of the Devi Falls, it is about 30 minutes walk or a 10 minute cycle ride from Damside and the airport, and has a population of some 600. North of the town, at Hyangja on the Pokhara-Baglung Highway some five kilometres from the lake, is the village of **Tashi Palkhel** with over 1,000 inhabitants, where there is also a monastery (*gompa*) of about 70 monks. The village also has some excellent views of the Annapurnas. Both villages

Pokhara & surrounding areas

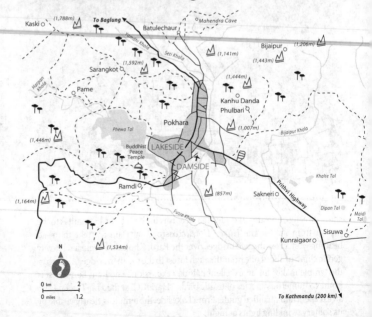

originated as refugee camps and are now bustling centres for the manufacture of woollen carpets and handicrafts for export, and at both you can watch as carpets are woven. Not surprisingly, local sales of carpets and handicrafts are enthusiastically promoted by residents; alternatively, there is a small shop selling the locally produced wares in each village. **NB** Quality of handicrafts and souvenirs is variable, so check.

A 20-minute cycle ride northwest of the airport brings you to the **Karma Dhuligiya Nyeshang Kirti Monastery**, about one kilometre north of the Bhadrakali Temple. Built by Tibetan speaking people from Manang in the 1960s, it is pleasantly situated on a small hill surrounded by woodland, and is home to about 40 monks.

Short excursions and walks from Pokhara

The real charm of Nepal lies outside its tourist quarters. If you don't have the time, inclination or energy for a long trek there are a number of shorter, one-day walks that can be made from Pokhara which, in addition to the pleasure derived from the natural beauty of the surrounding countryside, allow for an insight into the area's environmental and ethnic diversity as well as a first hand appreciation of a rural culture that may otherwise be available only in the glossy pages of a geographical magazine. Treks from Pokhara, including those of 'shorter' three and four day duration, are described in the Trekking section; the following, meanwhile, are suggestions for walking excursions and do not require trekking permits.

Sarangkot

Some people make the walk to Sarangkot as preparation for a longer trek, but the village makes a wonderful destination in its own right either as a day excursion or for an overnight stay. The absence of motor vehicles contributes to Sarangkot's peaceful atmosphere. At an elevation of just under 1,600 metres, it is perched on a high ridge to the northwest of Pokhara and has panoramic mountain views from Dhaulagiri and across the Annapurnas to Manaslu, as well as south over the Pokhara Valley. Nearby is the valley's ancient capital of Kaski.

Two main routes lead from the town to Sarangkot. Some people take the gentler path from the Bazaar area on the way up and descend via the steeper route to Lakeside.

From **Lakeside**, follow the road north, continuing along it as it becomes a track before turning right and beginning the steep climb up a long stone stairway. The steps ascend through cultivated land and rocky scree. Blue painted arrows point towards the top. This is a steep walk and can be tiring and although there are shortcuts they are just as

strenuous. Views are mainly to the south with the full range of mountains not visible until you have almost reached Sarangkot. Allow three hours.

From the **Bazaar** area, take the road heading west from the Bidhyavasini temple. Turn left and a stone stepped path brings you to Sarangkot. A taxi from Lakeside to the end of the sealed road costs about Rs 500 from where it is a 30 minute walk. This is less physically demanding than going from Lakeside and there are better views of the mountains as well as of the milky-white Seti Gandaki as it gorges its way towards Pokhara and beyond. From Bidhyavasini temple, you can make the walk in about two hours.

A few lodges and small restaurants line the road through Sarangkot. Just west of the *Peaceful Lodge*, a path climbs steeply north to a viewing area where there are also the remains of an old walled fort, a shrine and a TV tower. The village has no ISD facilities, but you can make calls within Nepal from the radio phone at the TV tower.

Sleeping Sarangkot's guest houses are all basic, trekking standard lodges. Food supplies are limited in range: there is very little fresh fruit available, but vegetables are brought up most mornings. Lemon tea is popular, but its taste has been likened to that of a flu remedy. All lodges have double rooms with common bath and 'bucket showers' and all fall in our **E** range: Didi Lodge, 9 rooms, bright and clean, front rooms have best view, good shop. Recommended. Mountain View, 3 rooms, good views of valley and mountains. Peaceful Lodge, 5 bed dorm only, open plan, traditional house. Rising Moon, 4 rooms, all rather stuffy, the village's cheapest menu. Sarangkot Lodge, 4 rooms, clean but no great views. Sunrise, 2 rooms, cramped. Tourist Lodge & Restaurant, 6 double rooms, small shop. Trekking Lodge, 4 rooms, dark and very basic, expensive food. View Top Lodge, 6 rooms, some with excellent views, small garden.

Kaski The region's former capital is now a small village about 45 minutes walk along the southern side of the ridge due west of Sarangkot, passing the village of Kaule on the way. A couple of small shrines either side of the path mark your arrival into Kaski where the ruins of its 200 year old fort, Kaskikot, can also be seen. If you want to climb to the top of the ridge (there are no set paths), you can get a fine view over its steeply wooded northern slope and across to the villages that dot the confluence (Puranchaur village) and valleys of the Mardi and Seti rivers. About one kilometre east of Kaski, a 1,788m hillock is the highest point along the ridge between Sarangkot and Kaski.

Kahnu Danda This is an alternative to Sarangkot, situated on a ridge to the northeast of the town with views from a slightly lower elevation over the valley and, though more obstructed than from Sarangkot, to the Annapurnas. You can get a clear view of the magnificent Macchapuchere from here.

From Mahendrapul, two kilometres north of the airport, cross the bridge over the Seti Gandaki and follow the path in a northeast direction. The trail is indistinct at times, but

Sarangkot

Not to scale

takes you past a Buddhist monastery and through the small hamlets of Phulbari. Aim for the lookout tower from where you get the best views of the mountains and across the valley. There are also the remains of a 250 year old fort, Kahnukot. Allow three hours for the walk up.

Although these lakes feature prominently on several of Pokhara's organized sightseeing itineraries, it is quite possible to visit them independently. At about 15 kilometres from the town they are too far to walk in a day, but make for an excellent day's cycle trip. Alternatively, public buses depart regularly from the bus stop at Chiple Dhunga (near Mahendrapul) to Begnas village.

Rupa Tal & Begnas Tal

From Prithvi Chowk, the intersection just north of the bus station, follow the main road east as it becomes the Prithvi Highway. After about eight kilometres you pass a police checkpoint. Then take a left turn along a sealed road which brings you to the village of Sisuwa after a further one kilometre. From here a two kilometres trail passes through the bazaar village of Begnas and leads on to Pachbaiya, the ridge separating the two lakes.

Begnas is the larger of the two and has rowing boats for hire. Commercial fishing takes place on both lakes and their fish are acknowledged to be the ones described simply as 'fresh from the lake' on Pokhara restaurant menus. There are many fine and picturesque walking opportunities in the area around the lakes. It is an especially good place for birdwatching, with varieties of water-fowl always in evidence. From Sisuwa a trail leads northeast to the northern shore of Begnas. Between Begnas and Pokhara there are a couple of small lakes including the Dipan Tal and Khalte Tal.

It is the destination rather than the walk that is the attraction here, although once you have seen the cave there are options for some pleasant walking. The cave itself is a limestone cavity whose dark interior is enlivened by the presence of a number of stalagmites and stalactites ('-mites' go up, '-tites' come down).

Mahendra cave

Take the main road heading north from the bazaar, crossing the bridge over the Seti Gandaki (KI Singh Pul) before passing the Gurkha Camp on your right. After five minutes the road forks, take the right hand fork (Batulechaur) and continue the climb along here for another two and a half kilometres until you reach the entrance to the site.

Many of the cave's original stalactites have been removed, but it is still an interesting place to visit. There is electric light, but it is worthwhile taking a torch with you in the event of a power cut. Limestone, which characterizes much of the area's geology, is porous and the caves are a product of the gradual erosion by underground streams of water flowing down from the mountains over thousands of years. The stone is also responsible for the Seti Gandaki's adjectival nomenclature – Seti means white. Only a section of this subterra-nean cavern has been explored and it is believed that a honeycomb of more caves and hollowings lie beyond. An entry fee of Rs 10 is charged and local guides are ever on hand to lend their expertise.

One of the Seti Gandaki's many tributaries flows past the Mahendra cave and you can join a trail that leads attractively north along its bank. Another path leads east into the hills from Batulechaur (a village traditionally associated with minstrels and itinerant folk singers, just south of the cave) for about four kilometres before veering north and then west to form a small circuit, eventu-ally joining the trail alongside the tributary back to Mahendra cave.

This walk takes you around the Phewa Tal and over the ridge towering above its southern bank. Taken at a leisurely pace it is a good all day outing, but involves a steepish ascent and descent. It also crosses two small rivers as well as

Phewa Tal circuit

Pokhara: from bazaar to bizarre

Much of today's Pokhara is a creation of the tourist industry whose history, if it can be called such, barely stretches back a quarter of a century. Until the 1960s, it was a seasonal market town for the Gurungs and Newaris, where traders from Mustang on the Tibetan border and merchants from Butwal on the Terai exchanged goods. Although it is in the region of the Gurungs, the majority of the inhabitants today are Brahmins and Chettris from Kathmandu, and Tibetan settlers. One early traveller, the Italian Giuseppe Tucci, visiting Pokhara in the early 1950s en route to Mustang, considered it "not a town at all, [but] an enormous bazaar winding along one endless street". This changed dramatically over the course of the next two decades with the arrival in large numbers of budget travellers who gave Pokhara its enduring reputation as a popular retreat for chilling- and chilled-out hippies.

passing through some muddy land and is best avoided during the monsoon and after, while in spring water levels are at their lowest. Alternatively, the following can be done as two semi-circular walks, to the north and south of the lake respectively.

Follow the road north from Lakeside as it becomes a track. Exchanging the modern hotels and restaurants for the gentle lapping of water, you continue along the lake shore. After about one kilometre, a path to the right leads up towards Sarangkot. After a further two kilometres, the trail hits a 'crossroad'. The right hand path follows a steep ascent again to Sarangkot, while the left hand turning veers southwest. An option here if you don't want to walk the whole way round is to follow the path straight ahead towards the west. This brings you to the small village of Pame after two kilometres set amid cultivated fields at the base of the northern ridge, where there are a couple of tea shops. From Lakeside, allow two to two and a half hours to walk to Pame. Returning to the 'crossroad' of paths, the trail veering southwest goes through two small rivers (traverse with care) feeding into the lake and continues at some distance from the lake. **NB** This is not recommended during or after the rainy season. After one kilometre the path begins its ascent up the southern ridge, passing through attractive and at times dense woodland, home to wild deer and a variety of birdlife including pheasants and parakeets. This is a steep climb of almost two kilometres and has worn out those alleged to be in full fitness! The climb ends at the village of Pumdi where you can stop for tea. The path is horizontal along most of the ridge. From here you get outstanding views of the mountains from Dhaulagiri right across the Annapurnas, and of much of the Pokhara Valley. There is a Buddhist centre, the Peace Temple, which has been constructed with Japanese assistance. The wooded descent brings you to Damside about 100 metres south of the dam. Turn left when you meet the road to bring you onto the main road through Damside.

Museums

Pokhara Museum Prithvi Chowk, north of the bus station. A government sponsored museum with mediocre displays of costumes, artefacts and cultures of various ethnic groups (including Gurungs, Magars, Thakalis and Tharus) living in central Nepal and the Pokhara area. There is also a display of an 8,000-year-old settlement from Mustang. ■ *1000-1700, daily except Tuesday. Admission Rs 10, camera charge Rs 10, T20413.*

Nadipur Bagar, three kilometres north of bus station. Noted for its collection of butterflies – the largest of its kind in Nepal. Also has some interesting displays on the ecology of the Annapurnas, past and present, as well as on the work of the Annapurna Conservation Area Project (ACAP) and on the contemporary challenges facing the area's environment. ■ *0900-1700 (closed from 1300-1400), daily except Saturday, free, T21102.*

Natural History Museum (Annapurna Regional Museum)

Essentials

Pokhara's hotels are concentrated in 4 localities: Lakeside, Damside, around the airport, and in the bazaar area. For the majority of travellers, the choice is one simply between Lakeside and Damside, areas which are themselves almost linked and where many hotels are so similar in their design, facilities and service as to defy distinction but in name – a distant echo of Kathmandu's Thamel area. There are, of course, shining exceptions to this generality, and finding a hotel that really stands out can add much to your stay in Pokhara. The greatest difference in staying at either Lakeside and Damside lies in the respective views. From many of the Lakeside hotels you can see at least part of the Phewa Lake, but the ridge to the north obscures most of the Annapurnas. Best mountain views from Lakeside are from the hotels east of the Royal Palace. Damside, meanwhile, offers little in the way of lake views, but is far enough from the northern ridge to allow superb mountain vistas – on a clear day it is possible to see Dhaulagiri and a Himalayan panorama stretching as far east as Ganesh Himal. **NB** From April until the monsoon gives way to dry weather, mountain views are severely restricted by cloud.

Taxi drivers know most of the hotels in Lakeside and Damside, so when you arrive in Pokhara there should be no problem in asking to be taken to any one particular hotel.

Touts 'Beware of touts' is a maxim as applicable in Pokhara as elsewhere. The arrival of each bus from Kathmandu, Chitwan or one of the border towns is invariably greeted by a gaggle of eager touts on commission from one or more of the Lakeside or Damside hotels. You may be offered a free taxi ride to a 'recommended' hotel, or be shown brochures or be assured that your driver is quite independent of any residential establishment. It is more likely, though, that anyone offering their services either at the bus station or at the airport will receive a payment for every passenger successfully introduced to a hotel. Despite all the warnings against using touts, if you do arrive in Pokhara with only an idea of the area in which you intend to stay it may be possible at times to negotiate a reasonable room rate in a decent hotel with the tout. If you do, make sure that there is a clear understanding that you will only stay at 'his' hotel if you are satisfied with it on arrival and, if not, that the taxi driver will wait and take you elsewhere at an agreed fare. Finding reasonable accommodation in Pokhara, however, is simple and does not require touts. You have just as much (if not more) of a chance of negotiating a good room rate directly with the owner.

Sleeping and eating outside Pokhara

AL *Fulbari Resort Hotel*, T23451 (Kathmandu T527588, F523149), www.yomori. com/fulbari A luxury resort perched spectacularly on the edge of a canyon high above the Seti River. 165 rooms, multi-cuisine restaurant, coffee shop, bar, swimming pool, tennis court, fitness centre, sauna, shopping, pony rides. Extensive landscaped grounds, resident peacocks. 8 kilometres and 20 minutes drive from Pokhara airport along a winding road, with regular shuttle services to Lakeside, the bazaar and airport. Much thought was clearly given to the design and the interior incorporates many traditional Newari aspects, including a fantastically carved replica window and an indoor hiti. The stunning mountain views amply compensate for the distant location. The hotel stands above all its competitors locally, and most nationally.

Kathmandu to Pokhara

A *Shangri-La Village*, T22122, F21995, hosangp@village.mos.com.np 5 minutes drive from Damside. 65 comfortable rooms all with a mountain view. Attractive landscaped gardens, swimming pool and jacuzzi, health club, and a 'Yoga Meditation Centre'. 24-hour coffee shop does breakfast, lunch and dinner buffets. Oriental restaurant.

Sleeping and eating Lakeside

Sleeping Lakeside (or *Baidam*) extends along almost the entire eastern shore of the Phewa Lake, a right-angular sprawl of budget and mid-range accommodation with by far the greatest number of hotels, guest houses, restaurants, bars and shops to satisfy the various corporeal wants and desires of most travellers. A few smaller and relatively basic hotels are spread out along the northern fringe of Lakeside. While these are 10 or 15 minutes walk from the area's main concentration of eating places, they do offer peace and quiet together with some of the best views of the lake. The main north-south road runs alongside the lake and, together with the five roads leading off it to the east, is the centre of Lakeside's activity. A couple of very basic guest houses taking in occasional visitors lie further east than is included on the map – although attractively set, the only advantage in staying in one of these is if you really want the greatest distance between yourself and the rest of civilization.

Lakeside **B** *Fish Tail Lodge*, PO Box 10, T20071, F20072, fishtail@lodge.mos.com.np 62 rooms
expensive (12 are deluxe), restaurant does good buffet lunches and dinners, also bar especially cosy in winter with its glowing central chimney-fireplace, hotel is situated on a semi-island in the Phewa Lake and is reached by wooden pontoon raft from eastern Lakeside, accommodation is divided into 4 circular bungalows set in attractive gardens, winner of international award in 1993, nightly cultural programmes, reservations can be made at Kathmandu's *Hotel de l'Annapurna*.

B *Base Camp Resort*, T21226, F20903. 30 rooms in separate thatched cottages, set in attractive gardens, most rooms have reasonable mountain view, good restaurant does all types of food, popular with groups but expensive for individual travellers. **B** *Pumori*, T21462, F(Kathmandu) 418919. 20 rooms in 3 buildings, Bhanccha Ghar restaurant is recommended for its fish while the other vegetarian restaurant has established itself as one of Pokhara's best.

Pokhara Lakeside north & west

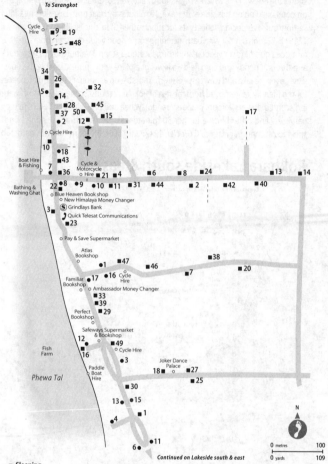

Kathmandu to Pokhara

■ Sleeping

1 Alka Guest House
2 Alpine Villa
3 Amrit Guest House
4 Asia
5 Banana Garden Lodge
6 Buddha
7 Butterfly Lodge
8 Canary Guest House
9 Chhetri Sisters
  Guest House
10 Comfortably Numb
11 Diamond
12 Eden Guest House
13 Everest
14 Evergreen Guest House
15 Eyeball
16 Fewa
17 Full Moon
18 Future Way Guest House
19 Gaden Yiga Chozin
  Guest House

20 Green Palace Guest
  House
21 Hong Kong
22 Hotel Marigold
23 Hotel Tibet
24 International Guest
  House
25 Keiko's Cottage
26 Laxmi Guest House
27 Lubbly Jubbly Guest
  House
28 Maccapuchare Guest
  House
29 Monal & Zorba
  Restaurant
30 Mountain Top
31 Mountain Villa
32 New Excellent Lake
  View Guest House
33 New Skyline
34 Pinky Lodge

35 Pleasure Home
36 Prince Guest House
37 Pushkar Guest House
38 Quiet View Home
39 Rainbow
40 Sagarmatha
41 Shiva Guest House
42 Silent Peak
43 Silvery Moon Guest
  House
44 Sitara
45 Tibet Home
46 Tranquility Lodge
47 Trans Himalaya
48 Utopia Home
49 Yeti Guest House
50 Yokohama

● Eating

1 7-11
2 Al Pollo E-Pizzeria

3 Bamboostan
4 Beam Beam
5 Don't Forget Me
6 Elegant View
7 Enlightened Yak
8 Lama Ma
9 Little Tibetan Tea
  Garden
10 Marco Polo
11 Maya & Pub
12 Mike's
13 Monsoon
14 New Tea Room
15 Nirula's Ice Creams &
  Fast Food
16 Old Blues Night Club
17 Pyramid & Pokhara
  Cyber Café
18 Reggae

C *Fewa*, T/F20885. 10 rooms most with bath, this is the orange building on the other side of the Phewa Lake which is mysteriously allowed to remain despite an official ban on hotel building on this side of the lake, 10 minutes by boat from Lakeside, beautiful setting but overpricing reflects its location rather than the facilities. **C** *Full Moon*, T21511. 12 rooms most with bath including some good value cheaper rooms, restaurant does good Indian vegetarian dishes, located a steep 3-minute climb up a track and through paddy and corn fields, a jewel of a place with unquestionably the finest views over the lake and town especially memorable on a moonlit night; quiet, peaceful and friendly, far removed from the rest of Pokhara's tourist scene; gardens of hanging scented flowers, lemon, orange, mango, lychee and papaya trees frequented by parakeets and other birds; a further 30-minute walk to the top of the ridge brings spectacular mountain views; **C** *Glacier*, T21722, F22164. 18 rooms all with bath, tub

Pokhara Lakeside south & east

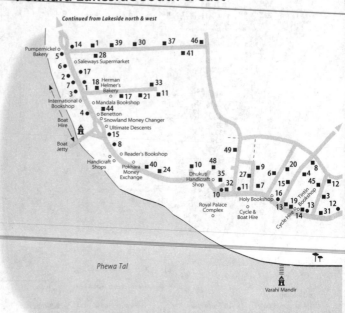

■ Sleeping	6 Gauri Shankar Guest House	20 Mountain King
1 Avocado	7 Glacier	21 Mount Fuji
2 Base Camp Resort	8 Hill Top Lodge	22 Mount Kailash Guest House
3 Bedrock	9 Holy Lodge	23 Namtse Tibetan Guest House
4 Blue Heaven Guest House	10 Hotel Angel	24 Nasa Guest House
5 Garlic Garden Guest House	11 Iceland	25 Nepal Guest House
	12 Kiwi Guest House	26 New Annapurna Guest House
	13 Lake View Resort	27 New Friendly Home
	14 Lakeside	28 New Namaste Lodge
	15 Lonely Guest House	29 New Star Lodge
	16 Marco Polo	30 New Tourist Home
	17 Mayur	31 Nightingale Lodge
	18 Meera	
	19 Moonlight Resort	

32 Nirvana	
33 Noble Inn	
34 Orient	
35 Osho	
36 Pokhara Lodge	
37 Pokhara Peace Home	
38 Pumori	
39 Quiet View Lodge	
40 Sacred Valley Guest House	
41 Sarangkot View	
42 Snow Hill Lodge	
43 Snow View Guest House	
44 Snowland	

Kathmandu to Pokhara

and TV, some a/c, attached restaurant, comfortable, spacious and obliging family run establishment in a good location overlooking the lake and with some of Lakeside's best mountain views. Recommended. **C** *Khukuri*, T21540, F21670. 19 rooms all with bath (some tubs), new hotel notable for its high standards of cleanliness, owned by former British Army Ghurka officer, good restaurant and bar; comfortable, bathrooms even have air fresheners; best rooms at the front with views of both the lake and Macchapuchere; one of Pokhara's better rooftop gardens. Recommended. **C** *Lake View Resort*, T21477. 18 rooms all with bath, attractive and reasonably priced hotel close to lake, pleasant outdoor restaurant, cultural programme every evening from 1900. **C** *Meera*, T21031, F20852. Modern, 18 rooms all with bath, restaurant does good Indian food, rather expensive. **C** *Moonlight Resort*, T21704, F22094. 26 rooms all with bath, restaurant, rates can be negotiated. **C** *Mountain View*, T/F20779. 23 rooms most with bath, all with own balcony and most with lake and mountain view, room windows are specially low so that you can see the mountains while lying down, restaurant serves breakfast only, room service available at other times, lower level rooms can be good value. **C** *Sahana*, T21229. 15 rooms all with bath, TV and phone, restaurant and bar; clean and modern but better value elsewhere. **C** *Snowland*, T20384, F20958. 34 rooms all with bath, ultra-modern in a 1960s way, restaurant next door. **C** *Thorung La*, T241311, F271303. 24 rooms in 2 adjacent buildings, all with bath, some with tubs, a/c and TV, corner rooms have best views, small restaurant.

C-D *Alpine Villa*, T20872, F20897. 22 rooms most with bath; a rarity – probably Pokhara's best value hotel, clean, friendly and efficient, welcome drink of fresh juice from its own garden; rustic outdoor *Harlequin* restaurant with thatched roof, trained waiters, open kitchen breeds confidence and does excellent fish and steaks, you're more likely to hear Ravi Shankar or Hari Prasad Chaurasia from the loudspeakers than Bombay's latest offerings; monthly parties with prizes including air tickets, Chitwan visits or free drinks, generator installed, cultural programmes every Saturday in season (1800-2030). Recommended. **C-D** *Bedrock*, T21876, F21587. 22 rooms all with bath, restaurant does good Indian food, garden. **C-D** *Broad Walk*, T21934. 10 rooms most with bath, small restaurant. **C-D** *Diamond*, T22871, F21451. 16 rooms all with bath and tubs, chalet type hotel, mediocre restaurant, some good value cheaper rooms. **C-D** *Fairmount*,

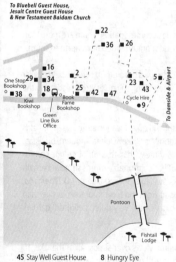

To Bluebell Guest House,
Jesuit Centre Guest House
& New Testament Baidam Church

One Stop Bookshop
Kiwi Bookshop
Green Line Bus Office
Book Fame Bookshop
Cycle Hire
Pontoon
Fishtail Lodge

To Damside & Airport

45 Stay Well Guest House
46 Teacher Krishna Home
47 Trekkers' Lodge
48 United
49 Villa Papillon Guest House

● **Eating**
1 Billy Bunter
2 Boomerang
3 Club Amsterdam
4 East Meets West
5 Elegant View
6 Everest Steak House
7 Fewa Park

8 Hungry Eye
9 Kanitpur
10 Lan Hua Chinese
11 Laxman
12 Le Bistro
13 Lhasa Tibetan
14 Maya & Pub
15 Moondance
16 Peacock
17 Rice Bowl Tibetan
18 Sa Rangsan

Kathmandu to Pokhara

T21252, F21451. 18 rooms all with bath, restaurant, reasonable but overpriced rooms. **C-D** *Hungry Eye*, T20908, F23089. 23 rooms all with bath, TV and phone, some a/c, well equipped and comfortable, occasional cultural programmes in season, popular restaurant, cycle hire, expensive. **C-D** *Lake Side*, T20073. 17 rooms all with bath, restaurant. **C-D** *Mountain Villa*, T21954. 15 rooms all with bath and TV, small restaurant, comfortable and pleasant, top floor rooms have bath tub and mountain and lake views. **C-D** *Nightingale Lodge*, T20338, F21704. 10 rooms all with bath, small restaurant, exceptionally clean establishment, friendly, helpful and professional management, personal hygiene kit in each bedroom, body massage by qualified physiotherapist (women only). Recommended. **C-D** *Shamrock*, 18 double rooms all with bath, so named because the owner once visited Ireland, inevitably attracts Irish visitors but especially popular with Indian groups, restaurant claims to do all kinds of food but concentrates its efforts on Indian vegetarian. **C-D** *Shikhar*, T21966, F22201. 14 rooms all with bath and balcony, small restaurant serves mostly Indian food reflecting the bulk of its clientele, extortionate laundry charges, better value elsewhere. **C-D** *Sitara*, T21579, F21022. 20 rooms most with bath, seemingly redundant restaurant, modern and lacking somewhat in character. **C-D** *Temple Villa*, T21203. 8 rooms all with bath, front rooms have balcony with mountain views, modern, family run, pleasant garden. **C-D** *Tranquility Lodge*, T/F21030. 8 rooms all with bath, no food, modern, clean and comfortable rooms, pleasant garden with some lychee trees, friendly and reasonably priced. **C-D** *Trans Himalaya*, T20917, F21022. 19 rooms some with bath, small restaurant serves Indian food, some good value cheaper rooms. **C-D** *United*, T20874, F21179. 12 rooms all with bath, small restaurant, clean, modern and quiet.

Lakeside cheaper **D** and **E** hotels constitute the bulk of Lakeside accommodation. There are more than 100 hotels here; the following are recommendations arranged from north to south.

The very **northern part of the main Lakeside road** has a group of basic but popular guest houses, while there are some better hotels along the quiet street leading to the shaded square.

D *Tibet Home*, 7 rooms all with bath, pleasant and quiet location surrounded by fields and a wooded hill, run by the accommodating Mrs Dickey Dolma, modern, breakfast and drinks only. **D** *Eyeball*, T21431. 15 rooms some with bath, a curious name considering the lack of mountain or lake views, but has comfortable rooms some at bargain prices, food intermittently available, drinks available always; also the **D** *Tropicana*, T22118. 9 rooms all with bath, best rooms at front, no food, more expensive than most. **D** *Yokohama*, 16 rooms most with bath. Clean, very quiet, delightful garden. **D** *Eden*, 10 small rooms.

E *Banana Garden*, T21880. 6 rooms, wonderful views over almost all of the lake, 10 minutes walk to restaurants and shops, food and drinks available. **E** *Chhetri Sisters Guest House*, 5 rooms most with common bath, clean and friendly, thatched rooftop eating area does 'fine breakfasts' and has a karambot game if you get bored with the lovely lake views. Recommended. **E** *Gaden Yiga Chozin*, no phone, F21022. 8 rooms including 1 'delux', no advance bookings, entrance via a path leading through gardens and up a slope, a Tibetan Buddhist meditation centre and guest house open to travellers, caters for private retreats and runs occasional 2 day courses/retreats in peak season, guests must follow the 5 Buddhist precepts of no killing, stealing, lying, sexual contact, or intoxicants (but couples are allowed to stay together), said to have 'the cleanest toilets in Pokhara', Western breakfast and good dal-bhad evening meal, huge prayerwheel by the entrance. Recommended. **E** *Lonely View*, T21224. 8 rooms some with bath, common bathroom is outside, secluded. **E** *Utopia Home*, a block of 3 rooms with common bath, set off the road and partially obscured by high growing garden, look out for small sign just north of the New Pleasure Home Guest House, basic. **E** *New Pleasure Home*, T21224, 6 rooms, Mellow Fellow café has board games, cycle hire. **E** *Venus Home*, T23132. 7 rooms all common bath, no food. **E** *Pinky Lodge*, 6 rooms some with bath. **E** *New Excellent Lake View*, 8 rooms some with bath, attractive, clean and quiet. **E** *Guru Lotus*, 8 rooms all common bath, one of the few places on the west side of the Lakeside road directly overlooking the lake – also one of the cheapest here, trendy and popular with many types of traveller, small 'restaurant'. **E** *New Laxmi*, 15 rooms most with bath, run by a helpful and friendly growing family, no food but cold drinks available, good value. Recommended. **E** *The Comfortably Numb*, T21747. 16 rooms all with bath, best rooms are furthest from noisy reception, no food but drinks available to assist in attaining eponymous state. **E** *Macchapuchare*, 6 rooms most with bath. **E** *Samrat* (24) T23217, F22614. 16 rooms some with bath, small dining room.

The **northernmost perpendicular road** is littered with hotels on either side.

D *Asia*, T21159. 10 rooms all with bath, best rooms on top floor, rates are always negotiable. **D** *Buddha*, T22123. 25 rooms most with bath, clean and cheerful. **D** *Cordial*, T22652, F21022. 22 rooms some with bath, Indian restaurant, small but good bookshop adjacent to the restaurant (the owner used to work for Pilgrims Bookshop in Kathmandu), runs occasional courses in 'oriental massage', advance bookings by fax will be acknowledged, major credit cards accepted. Recommended. **D** *Dreamland*, T22600. 12 rooms all with bath, very average. **D** *Fishtail View*, T20996. 13 rooms all with bath, corner rooms recommended, not to be confused with the upmarket Fish Tail Lodge. **D** *Hong Kong*, T21202. 25 rooms some with bath, those with common bath especially good value, simple but clean eating area. **D** *Lake Mist*, 8 rooms most with bath, basic but clean. **D** *Motherland*, T23025. 10 rooms some with bath, 'typical Nepali dinner' available at typical tourist price, car, motorbike and cycle hire. **D** *Pancha Koshi*, T21429. 8 rooms some with bath, popular with budget travellers. **D** *Potala*, T/F21941. 11 rooms all with bath, entrance via a path to the rear, eating area in reception, massage by 'Western qualified' masseur. **D** *Sagarmatha*, T22146. 12 rooms most with bath, undistinguished. **D** *Silent Peak*, T21237. 12 rooms all with bath. **D** *Woodland*, T22609. 13 rooms most with bath, unimpressive.

E *Canary*, 6 rooms most with common bath, if unattended the owner may be found selling rice on the street outside. **E** *International Guest House*, T20432. 12 rooms some with bath.

Bottom end accommodation dominates between here and Lakeside's next perpendicular road, though there is a scattering of better budget places.

D *Amrit*, T22882. 16 rooms most with bath, conveniently close to Grindlays Bank. **D** *Bees Hive*, T22085. 8 rooms most with bath, comfortable but on the expensive side. **D** *Butterfly Lodge*, T22892. 14 rooms most with bath, attractive building set in peaceful surroundings.

E *Century Lodge*, 5 rooms all common bath, pleasant verandah. **E** *Tibet Lodge*, T21022. 8 rooms most with bath, congenial.

The heart of Lakeside is convenient for all services, including restaurants, money changers, cycle and boat hire, shops, etc.

Heart of Lakeside

C/D *Lake Palace*, T21027, 20 rooms all with bath, a/c and TV. Small restaurant best for

Indian dishes. Some nice lake views, but only from the top floor can you see the mountains.

D *Vimal's*, T22306. 14 rooms most with bath, no food, there are better places to stay including all of the following: **D** *Alka*, T23357, F21729. 12 rooms most with bath, some credit cards accepted. **D** *Fewa*, T20151, F20885. 20 rooms some with bath and hot water geyser, situated right on the lake shore – you can't get any closer, marvellous location influences prices. **D** *Keiko's Cottage*, T23521. 10 rooms all with bath, separate 'cottage' style rooms in front of the main building, restaurant offers all types of food by chef trained in Mughlai and Kashmiri cooking, fishing tackle available for hire, also has a few board games, guitars, a couple of bookshelves known as the library and some pet parrots and peacocks, run by a family who really make an effort to look after their guests. Recommended. **D** *Lubbly Jubbly*, 14 rooms some with bath, run by friendly and helpful family. Recommended. **D** *Mandala Rest House*, T21478. 10 rooms all with bath. **D** *Monal*, T21459. 15 rooms all with bath, comfortable rooms, well run and above average hotel at the heart of Lakeside activity, good though slightly expensive *Zorba* restaurant within grounds.

E *Future Way*, 7 rooms all common bath, popular with Japanese visitors, recommended for budget travellers. **E** *New Skyline*, T22142. 10 rooms all with bath. **E** *Rainbow*, T21238, F21451. 7 rooms most with bath, sitting room overlooks lake. **E** *Yeti*, 6 rooms all common bath, no food, cheap.

Central Lakeside to Royal Palace There are few hotels in the area between central Lakeside and the Royal Palace, but the road is lined with small shops and stalls hiring trekking equipment as well as selling and producing handicrafts.

D *Avocado*, T21183. 11 rooms all with bath, one of the best hotels of its type, spacious building, friendly service, breakfast only. **D** *Iceland*, T23082. 12 rooms most with bath, pleasant rooftop terrace restaurant, peaceful location away from main road but only 3 minutes walk to restaurants and shops, some good mountain and lake views from top floor front facing rooms. **D** *Mayur*, T22285. 10 rooms all with bath, good rates can be negotiated. Recommended. **D** *Mount Fuji* (134) T23274. 13 rooms most with bath, wall poster has only view of eponymous mountain. **D** *New Tourist Home*, 12 rooms some with bath, average. **D** *Noble Inn*, 12 rooms, most with bath, restaurant. **D** *Pokhara Peace Home*, T23205. 10 rooms most with bath, comfortable. **D** *Pushpa*, T20332. 7 rooms some with bath, well maintained, some good value cheaper rooms. **D** *Sarangkot View*, 10 rooms some with bath, modern.

E *New Namaste Cottage*, 7 rooms all common bath, 24-hour hot water, comfortable and among the cheaper places in this part of Lakeside. **E** *Quiet View*, 8 rooms some with bath, no food, attractive and amiable. **E** *Teacher Krishna Lodge*, 8 rooms all common bath in 2 blocks (the newer block is better), extremely basic converted agricultural buildings, probably the cheapest rooms in Pokhara and possibly the closest you can get to experiencing 'genuine' Nepali rural life, little English spoken but very friendly, the kind of place you would want to recommend but shouldn't.

Gaurighar The area north and east of the Royal Palace, has a concentration of better hotels both along the main road as it heads east and on the small maze of streets and tracks to the north. There are a couple of good restaurants here as well as cycle and boat hire (probably Lakeside's most expensive) and a popular bathing and fishing ghat. Much excitement surrounds a big catch, but more often the talk is of the one that got away.

D *Blue Heaven*, T21435. 8 rooms all with bath, quiet. **D** *Fewa*, T20885. This small hotel is located on the opposite side of the lake and runs a boat service regularly from the Varahi temple ghat, 4 rooms all shared bath, restaurant and bar, superb views over the lake. **D** *Garlic Garden*, 8 rooms some with bath in quiet location, garden has more pot plants than garlic. **D** *Gautama*, T20422. 15 rooms some with bath, efficient and amenable. Recommended. **D** *Giri*, T21435. 8 rooms some with bath. **D** *Heaven's Gate*, T21435. 8 rooms some with bath, breakfast and drinks. **D** *Hotel Angel*, 10 rooms most with bath, restaurant, some good mountain views. **D** *Marco Polo*, T23154. 8 rooms all with bath. **D** *Mountain King*, T21792. 12 rooms most with bath, simple comforts. Nanohana Lodge and **D** *New Star Lodge*, T22478. 10 rooms, some with bath, comprises 2 buildings either side of the road. **D** *Nirvana*, T23332. Very clean rooms some with balcony, rooftop garden, quiet. Recommended. **D** *Orient*, 8 rooms some with bath, has connections with the Youth Hostel Association, owners endeavour to please. **D** *Osho*, 12 rooms most with bath, small restaurant.

E *Nasa Guest House*, 5 rooms some with bath, good value. **E** *New Friendly Home*, T21792. 6 rooms some with bath. **E** *Holy Lodge*, T21435. 8 rooms some with bath, quiet. **E** *Villa Papillon*, 5 rooms some with bath, food 'sometimes' available, peaceful and friendly, surrounded by gardens, banana and fruit trees. Recommended.

Lakeside is a distant but indisputable second to Thamel in Nepal's gastronomic stakes. In quality if not in range its restaurants bear favourable comparison and some, especially those with thatched seating in gardens sloping down to the gently lapping waters of the lake shore, rank among the country's most pleasant places to enjoy a meal. Fish, fresh from one of the valley's lakes, is a speciality while the influence of Pokhara's Tibetan communities is represented by a couple of excellent eating places and interpretations of popular continental and Mexican dishes are also widely available. Outside the main tourist season, some restaurants reduce the price of their menu, and if you are staying longer than a few days some will also give a discount if you eat there regularly.

Eating

Nepali/Tibetan: *Rice Bowl*, roof top Tibetan restaurant also does continental food. *Lhasa Tibetan*, large airy place looking across to the lake and Varahi temple, excellent Tibetan as well as continental and Chinese food. Recommended. *Typical Nepali*, located in the Fewa Hotel across the lake from Lakeside.

Chinese: *Lan Hua*, T26847, near the Royal Palace, has a huge menu including 'Toothpick Chicken'. *New Tea Room*, Chinese and continental, good breakfasts, popular with budget travellers. *Sa-Rangsan*, continental, Chinese and Indian, also some Korean dishes.

Indian: *Khukuri*, upmarket Indian restaurant, excellent food but expensive.

Multi-cuisine: *Bamboostan*, continental and drinks, enduringly popular despite or because of the décor, music and aromas characterizing a chronic hangover from hippydom. *Beam Beam*, central location beside the lake, all types of food and drink. *Boomerang*, continental, Mexican, Indian, etc, pretty garden, has acquired a following in recent years, slightly more expensive than average. *Elegant View*, probably the most authentically Western food in Pokhara, also good Nepali and Indian dishes, Lakeside's only lake side garden restaurant where you can eat and drink to South Asian classical music, indoor fireplace for winter, moderately priced. Recommended. *Fewa Park*, next to and similar to *Boomerang*. *Green Garden*, thatched roof with garden beside the lake, standard eclectic menu, Tibetan style section with floor cushion seating; *Little Tibetan Tea Garden*, friendly restaurant, outdoor seating in the shade of extensive bamboo, Tibetan and continental menu is illustrated by accompanying photo album, service can be slow but excellent 'Trekkers Breakfast' and fruit momos, reasonably priced and probably the largest helpings in town. Recommended. *Maya*, usual menu reasonably priced, roof top is quietest and has fine views over the lake, popular. *Mike's Restaurant*, T20151, has a wonderful dreamy location right at the lake shore, beside the *Hotel Fewa*. The same good menu as *Mike's Breakfast* in Kathmandu. *Monsoon*, T27221, is another pleasant place and has an extensive menu with all the usual favourites. *Moondance*, rustic and unexceptional but good food. *New Billy Bunter*, another popular establishment, standard continental and Chinese fare. *Peacock* thatched roof, continental and Indian. *Pyramid*, easy holiday bistro, home made pasta, good sandwiches make a full meal. Recommended. *Zorba*, an unusual name given that moussaka is the sole Greek offering in an otherwise standard continental and Mexican menu, more expensive than most but high quality. Recommended.

Steak House: *Everest Steak House*, far and away the best steaks in Pokhara, lovely lake views from its thatched rooftop.

Fast food: *Nirula's*, a branch of the Indian ice cream and fast food chain, also pizzas, burgers and sandwiches, popular with more affluent local residents.

Sleeping and eating Damside

Sleeping 10 minutes walk to the southeast where the Pardi Dam marks the effective transition of the Phewa Lake into the Pardi Khola, Damside has been described as Lakeside's younger cousin. Although there are fewer hotels, restaurants and shops here, it has the unmistakable scent of development potential, and new hotels are indeed constantly under construction – as at Lakeside, these are usually 3-storey concrete affairs built to one of the 3 or 4 architectural designs to which almost every new hotel in Pokhara seems obliged to conform. The great charm of staying here, however, and one which renders the above discussion largely irrelevant, lies in the spectacular mountain views. If your room does not have a north facing window, many hotels have a roof terrace or garden where you can sit. Published room rates in Damside are similar to those at Lakeside, but it is often possible to bargain the price down to rock-bottom rates, especially during the monsoon months when views are obscured most of the time. **NB** Accommodation is arranged from north to south.

C *Gurkha Haven*, T22527, F23272. 8 rooms, smart hotel, clean and well run, restaurant, run by army family and their friendly pet dogs, above average. **C** *Twin Peaks*, T22867, F21587. 8 rooms, small restaurant, clean, comfortable with fine mountain views, owned by former British Gurkha, efficient and very obliging. Highly recommended. **C** *Dragon*, T/F20391. 30 rooms all with TV, well decorated and stands out from Pokhara's tourist uniformity but overpriced, good restaurant, Indian style. **C** *City Annapurna*, T21241, F21878. 10 rooms, restaurant has Thamel-style menu, rates include breakfast. **C** *Mount Manaslu*, T23312. 13 rooms, restaurant, comfortable. **C** *Tragopan*, T/F21708. 36 comfortable rooms, restaurant and coffee shop, unattractive concrete exterior, but pleasant garden with seating, restaurant, coffee shop and 'Rovers Return Pub'.

D *Pokhara Prince*, T19. Rooms most with bath, restaurant and bar, overpriced. **D** *Try Star*, T20930. 12 rooms all with bath, restaurant/bar has extensive but standard menu, popular with budget travellers, communal sitting room with satellite TV. **D** *Bermuda*, T23541. 15 rooms all with bath, restaurant. **D** *New Nascent*, T21719. 15 rooms all with bath, eating area, solar water heating. **D** *Peaceful*, T20861. 7 rooms some with bath, reasonable. **D** *Garden*, T20870. 16 rooms most with bath, eating area, standard. **D** *Himali*, T22930. 10 rooms some with bath, rates always negotiable. **D** *Salinas*, Tas

Alisha above. 6 rooms most with bath, eating area, basic and clean, recommended for budget travellers. **D** *Bangala*, 5 rooms some with bath, friendly Bengali run place, cheap. **D** *Himalayan Vision*, T(Kathmandu) 411847, F423442. 14 rooms all with bath, standard modern. **D** *Himalayan*, T21643. 7 rooms all with bath, meals in family dining room, immaculately maintained front lawn. **D** *Super Lodge*, T21861. 11 rooms some with bath, eating area, ISD facilities. **D** *New Anzuk*, T21845. 8 rooms some with bath,

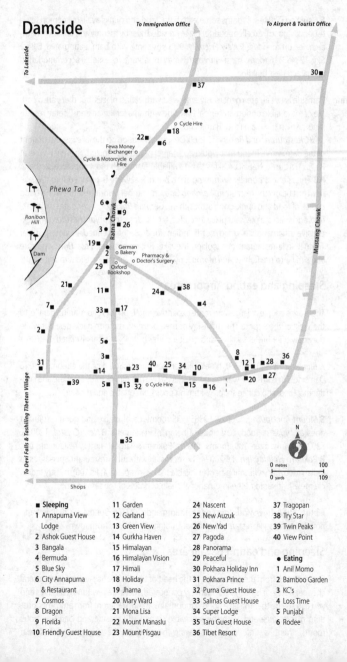

Damside

To Immigration Office

To Airport & Tourist Office

To Lakeside

To Lakeside

Phewa Tal

Raniban Hill

Dam

Ratna Chowk

Fewa Money Exchanger
Cycle & Motorcycle Hire

o Cycle Hire

German
o Bakery
Pharmacy &
o Doctor's Surgery
o Oxford
Bookshop

Mustang Chowk

To Devil Falls & Tashiling Tibetan Village

Shops

o Cycle Hire

N

0 metres 100
0 yards 109

Kathmandu to Pokhara

■ **Sleeping**	11 Garden	24 Nascent	37 Tragopan
1 Annapurna View Lodge	12 Garland	25 New Auzuk	38 Try Star
2 Ashok Guest House	13 Green View	26 New Yad	39 Twin Peaks
3 Bangala	14 Gurkha Haven	27 Pagoda	40 View Point
4 Bermuda	15 Himalayan	28 Panorama	
5 Blue Sky	16 Himalayan Vision	29 Peaceful	● **Eating**
6 City Annapurna & Restaurant	17 Himali	30 Pokhara Holiday Inn	1 Anil Momo
7 Cosmos	18 Holiday	31 Pokhara Prince	2 Bamboo Garden
8 Dragon	19 Jharna	32 Purna Guest House	3 KC's
9 Florida	20 Mary Ward	33 Salinas Guest House	4 Loss Time
10 Friendly Guest House	21 Mona Lisa	34 Super Lodge	5 Punjabi
	22 Mount Manaslu	35 Taru Guest House	6 Rodee
	23 Mount Pisgau	36 Tibet Resort	

dining room with TV, attractive garden with papaya and lemon trees. **D** *View Point*, T21787. 15 rooms, all with bath, rooftop café, solar heating. **D** *Mount Pisgah*, 5 rooms all with bath, dining room, average. **D** *Green View*, T21844, F21587. 12 rooms all with bath, some excellent value cheaper rooms, restaurant and bar, parking and camping facilities, rent tents at Rs 40 per night. **D** *Taru*, T20930. 9 rooms most with bath, small restaurant, rates highly negotiable.

E *New Yad*, T20468. 8 rooms some with bath, food and drinks available (lemon tea is especially good), excellent budget place presided over by friendly and talkative matriarch. Recommended. **E** *New Friendly*, 9 rooms some with bath, eating area. **E** Blue *Sky*, T23433. 16 rooms most with bath, small restaurant, reasonable accommodation in characterless building.

Eating Damside is not an area generously endowed with eating places, but there are a couple of reasonable options in central Damside with smaller Indian and Tibetan restaurants also on the main road (Ratna Chowk).

KC Restaurant and Bakery, T21560. Delightful location on the lake just out of sight of the dam with a menu that would do Thamel proud even including French wine at Rs 1,200 a bottle, Nepali breakfasts also available, Damside's most popular restaurant. **NB** This is also a popular swimming spot, but raw sewage is pumped into the lake from just below the restaurant. *Bamboo Garden*, another favourite haunt with a good choice of food and drink, good atmosphere. *German Bakery*, concentrates on breakfasts and snacks, a pleasant place for coffee, lime sodas, etc. *Punjabi Restaurant*, inexpensive dharbar with good north Indian food. Recommended. Rodee, popular Thamel style restaurant overlooking the lake. Recommended. *Loss Time*, opposite and similar to the Rodee. *Anil Momo*, tiny Tibetan restaurant, excellent momos.

Sleeping and eating Airport area

There are a couple of larger and more expensive hotels on the road running parallel to the west of the airport. The mainstay of their business is group packages, but while they may offer better facilities and greater comfort they are rather isolated.

A *Bluebird*, T25480, F26260, hotel@blustar.mos.com.np South of the airport, close to Damside. 78 rooms, half with mountain views. Two restaurants offer Japanese and continental food, also coffee shop. Swimming pool. Comfortable and modern.

B *Mount Annapurna*, T20027, F23852. 35 rooms, comfortable and good restaurant does all types of food, bar, under Tibetan management. **B** *New Crystal*, T20035, F20234. With over 100 rooms this is Pokhara's largest hotel, restaurant, bar. **B** *Pokhara Holiday Inn*, T/F20094. 17 rooms all with tubs, restaurant specializes in Indian food, bar, swimming pool (available to non-residents at Rs 100), mostly Indian clientele, unrelated to the international chain of hotels of the same name.

Further out **A** *Tiger Mountain Lodge*, TKathmandu 222706. Bungalows built in traditional Gurung style, restaurant, bar, pool, riding, 30 minutes from town.

Sleeping and eating Bazaar area

Further north from the airport and at the heart of town is the Bazaar area with several cheaper hotels. It is noisy and relatively congested, there are few tourist facilities and you can see neither the lake nor the mountains. It is no different from any other bustling market area and, with the invariable surplus of Lakeside and Damside hotel rooms, there is little point in staying here when the experience of similar accommodation is abundantly available in any Terai or Indian town. The area is noisy and congested. There are, however, several cheap guesthouses, including the **E** *Mandala*, *Shankar*, and **Home Guest House** as well as the Tibetan run *New Asia* and *Mandar*.

The Bazaar area is cluttered with small eating places, most of the dal-bhad-tarkari variety, as well as countless tea shops and soft drink outlets. You can eat here very cheaply, but aside from this budgetary aspect there is otherwise nothing to recommend it as a culinary destination. **Eating**

Entertainment

Pokhara has little in the way of organized entertainment. Some hotels have cultural programmes (see below). The *Hotel Alpine Villa* on Lakeside's northernmost side road holds occasional parties in its outdoor thatched-roof restaurant.

Most restaurants will serve alcohol and many have happy hours when the price of a bottle of beer is reduced or is accompanied by free snacks. Happy hour timings vary but are usually displayed prominently outside. **Bars**

The small, European run Avia Club offers one of Pokhara's more awesome experiences with flights from Pokhara airport in one of the club's two 'Binman-1' microlights (one pilot, one passenger). Flights are of 15 minutes (US$45), 30 minutes (US$90) and 1 hour (US$170) duration, reaching maximum altitudes of 4,000, 10,000 and 12,000 feet respectively. You buzz over Pokhara town, Phewa Lake, Sarangkot, along the Seti valley and seemingly to within touching distance of Macchapuchere. It's windy and chilly up there, so wear warm clothes and keep your camera well secured. The best times are early morning (0630-0930) and late afternoon (1600-1700). Flights do not operate during the monsoon. Recommended, but not an experience for the faint-hearted. T251292/25944, (Kathmandu T412830, F415266), aviaclub@mos.com.np, www.travel-nepal.com/adventure/avia/index.html **Microlight flights**

Reflecting aspects of the folk culture of the region's various ethnic groups are performed regularly in hotels during the main tourist seasons. In most hotels this is free if you also have dinner, otherwise an entry fee of up to Rs 100 may be charged. From north to south, the *Hotel Alpine Villa* on Lakeside's northernmost side road has a cultural programme every Saturday evening in season from 1800-2030. The upmarket *Fish Tail Lodge* is a pleasant venue for nightly programmes performed by the Danfe Dance Company, but charges admission for non-residents, Rs 100, 1800-1900 in winter, 1830-1930 in summer. The *Lake View Resort* in the eastern part of Lakeside has a longer programme of traditional music and dance in its pleasant outdoor restaurant, 1830-2100 nightly in season, occasionally during off-season, admission free if you also eat there. The nearby Hotel Pumori charges Rs 100 for its nightly performance, 1900-2000. There is also live music (sitar, tabla, flute) every evening in the restaurant of the *Kantipur Hotel*, 1900-2100, no admission charge, but expensive menu. **Music & dance programmes**

Shopping

Although Pokhara is not the shoppers' paradise that is Kathmandu, you can still get just about everything you need here as well as luxury and imported items. Two or three 'supermarkets' on the lake side of the main Lakeside road carry a wide selection of consumables, including imported sanitary articles and foreign as well as locally packaged food and drink. (**NB** Check expiry dates.) Nepal's national newspapers are also sold here after the afternoon arrival of buses from Kathmandu.

Kathmandu to Pokhara

Kathmandu to Pokhara

Bookshops There are several small bookshops near the lake. Most specialize in popular fiction and the spectacular, large glossy photo-travelogues usually of the Himalaya and Kathmandu Valley. From north to south, the tiny *Blue Heaven* bookstall in central Lakeside has a good range of postcards and the nearby *Atlas* also carries some French, German and Scandinavian titles. A little further on, the *Familiar* bookshop is the place to go if you are looking for Tintin and Asterix books and it also sells stamps. The *Holy* bookshop has a good selection of general fiction, maps and postcards. Curiously, there are few shops specializing in non-fiction, but *Safeways Supermarket* (no relation) has a small Nepalese culture section. The *Oxford Bookshop* on the main road in central Damside has a small collection of fiction, non-fiction and postcards. English language books are generally more expensive in Nepal than in India, but most shops will buy back books they have sold at half price.

Handicrafts Several handicraft shops line the street that runs north of the Royal Palace and in some you can see artists at work, painstakingly adding more detail and colour to a half finished thangka or mandala. These small shops, along with others in the central part of Lakeside and on its northernmost perpendicular road, also sell a small range of other handicrafts including carpets, papier mâché and masks. Itinerant groups of Tibetan women are a common sight in the tourist areas, offering their wares of decorations and costume jewellery. A wider range of locally produced Tibetan handicrafts is available from the Tibetan villages. Woollen carpets are a speciality of Pokhara's Tibetans, but the greater part of their appeal lies more in the context of their manufacture than in their quality.

L'Ile (sic) *Au Tresor*, T22841, opposite the Royal Palace, has a good selection of handicrafts - both Nepali and from elsewhere in South Asia - which can be reasonably priced after a bit of bargaining.

The *Dhukuti* ('treasure') handicraft shop, on the first floor of a building behind a group of hotels to the east of the Royal Palace, has perhaps Pokhara's best display of quality textiles and handicrafts. It is run by the Association for Craft Producers, a professional group based in Kathmandu providing design, training, marketing and technical support for low income, mainly women, artisans. The association operates on a business rather than charitable basis, focusing on and training poor women in a variety of skills from spinning and weaving to painting and metallurgy. It provides the women with all raw materials and pays them cash on delivery of the finished products. From the 38 producers involved when the organization was founded in 1984, there are now more than 750 'beneficiaries' reflecting the ethnic diversity of the country. The Association for Craft Producers, PO Box 3701, Kathmandu.

Thangka

Rocks & fossils Saligrams, attractive fossilized relics of a warmer geological age when the Pokhara Valley was under water, are common findings in the hills and valleys of the central western region of Nepal. Often containing ammonite, a spiral shaped marine creature, these date back more than 100 million years to a time when the Himalaya were barely hills and when the arrival of mankind was an event not destined to occur for another 99.998 million years or so. The fossilized ammonites are sold in many of the small stalls and curio emporia in Pokhara usually at prices ripe for bargaining.

Although the town is no match for Kathmandu in either the quantity or range of various trekking requisites it offers, there are nonetheless several shops selling and hiring clothing and equipment. Most are concentrated in the central part of Lakeside and along the road running parallel and north of the Royal Palace. Here you can get trousers, T-shirts, jackets and other clothing as well as sleeping bags and, in some shops, tents. Most also offer the services of porters and guides. The 'supermarkets' in central Lakeside have a wide array of packaged food items. If you are embarking on one of the Annapurna treks from Dumre, it is advisable to stock up with everything you are likely to want in Pokhara and not to rely on supplies always being available in Dumre. Trekking maps are also available in most bookshops.

Trekking equipment

Transport

This is a popular option and a good way of getting around Pokhara and further afield without being restricted to set itineraries. There are plenty of cycle hire places in both Lakeside and Damside, renting anything from an old and rusty two wheeler with panniers to the latest generation mountain bikes. Rates vary considerably according to season. In summer you can rent a good bike for as little as Rs 50 per day, but during peak season this can increase to three times as much. It is worth casting a critical eye over the bike's condition before accepting it; take it for a short 'test ride' first and check the tyres, gears, etc. There are a few places that rent motorcycles in Lakeside and Damside. Rates start from about Rs 500 per day, excluding fuel. You will have to produce a valid international licence when hiring, and should carry it with you. Insurance is not included, so check that your own travel insurance covers you for motorcycling and liability.

Cycle & motorcycle hire

Air: There are several daily flights between Pokhara and **Kathmandu**. Royal Nepal Airlines as well as all the privates airlines operate this popular route. Most flights leave either after breakfast or in the early to mid afternoon. The flight takes 30 minutes and costs US$61. During the cloudless months, there are stunning views of the Himalaya from the left hand side of the aircraft on eastbound flights and on the right hand side on flights to Pokhara. There is no seat allocation at check-in, so watch out for the arrival of your aircraft and try to be among the first to board.

In the peak trekking seasons only, there are also flights to **Jomsom**, a popular starting point for treks in the Kali Gandaki Valley, in the Manang and Annapurna regions and heading north into Mustang. Royal Nepal Airlines as well as a couple of the private carriers operate this route and all departures are early morning as local weather patterns in Jomsom favour landing and take-off by mid morning. The recent completion of the road from Pokhara to Baglung has taken a little of the pressure off demand for flights to Jomsom. It is, nevertheless, essential to book early and confirm (and reconfirm) reservations to and from Jomsom, particularly if you have a tight schedule.

Long distance connections

Published flight schedules are notoriously inaccurate, so if you are having difficulty in securing a reservation ask the travel agent to check whether there are any other flights operating but not shown on the timetable.

Mountain Flights: All airlines operate this much hyped but scenic 1 hour flight along the Himalaya during cloudless months. Most depart at around 0730 and the fare is US$99.

Bus: The main tourist trunk route links Pokhara with **Kathmandu** via the Prithvi Highway. Numerous tourist buses make the 8-hour journey every day and most will pick you up from your hotel or from a fixed point nearby, arriving at Kathmandu's new central bus station via a stop on Kantipath. Most departures are in the early morning with pick up times starting from 0600, although a further hour can easily pass by the time you actually leave Pokhara for the open road. Occasionally buses also leave in the early afternoon. The fare is about Rs 150, higher if booked through a hotel. Advance booking is essential in peak season, but can usually be left until the previous afternoon in summer.

The *Green Line Bus company* offers the best service to Kathmandu (Rs 600) and Chitwan (Rs 480) with a/c buses, individual music channels and complimentary refreshments. The office is located opposite the entrance to the *Fish Tail Lodge* in Lakeside, T27271.

There are also regular public bus services to Kathmandu. They start from the main bus station near the airport and are about a third of the price, but are slower and less comfortable.

Chitwan National Park (Tadi Bazaar) Tadi is served by both public and tourist buses. Tourist buses depart in the early morning from the central bus station for the 7-hour journey via **Narayanghat**. Rs 150, less on public buses. Advance booking essential in peak season.

To the border: There are direct buses from Pokhara to **Birgunj** and **Sunauli**. Departures are again in the early morning and many will pick you up from outside your hotel although all go via the central bus station. The journey to Birgunj takes about 9 hours and costs Rs 150, while the fare to Sunauli is Rs 125 by tourist bus. Despite the apparent shorter distance from Pokhara to Sunauli, the poor condition of the Siddhartha Highway means that many buses take the longer route via Mugling, Narayanghat and Butwal with a journey time of between 8 and 9 hours. The direct route due south from Pokhara along the Siddhartha Highway is slow, bumpy and uncomfortable and takes almost as long to get there.

It may be worthwhile checking which route the bus will take when you make your booking – the shorter route is not recommended for those with an upset stomach, and the distance between your head and the ceiling is less at the rear of some buses than in the front seats.

If you are entering India through **Nepalgunj**, there is a direct overnight service from Pokhara. Buses leave in the mid afternoon from the central bus station for the 15-16-hour journey, Rs 271.

Directory

Airline offices *Buddha Air*, T21429. *Necon Airways*, Ratna Chowk, T20028. *RNAC*, Pokhara Airport, T21021.

Banks Pokhara is well endowed with exchange facilities. A branch of *Grindlays Bank* is located on the main road in the northern part of Lakeside, open 0800-1630, Sun-Fri. There are also a number of authorized private exchange counters along the main road. Most are 'open' 7 days, 0800-2000, but may be unattended at times. Exchange rates often vary, so if you are changing a lot it is worth checking for the best rate. The *New Himalayan* is near Grindlays and usually has slightly higher rates. The Ambassador does not charge commission but has lower rates. You can also get money out on Mastercard and Visa here, but at even lower rates. *Snowland* is attached to the hotel of the same name. The *Pokhara Exchange Counter* is the first to open, open 0700-1900.

The *Fewa Money Exchanger* (T23035, F21451) in the northern part of Damside changes TCs and makes advances against Mastercard, Visa and Amex. Pokhara does not have Kathmandu's demand for unofficial currency exchange.

Communications The GPO is on Nadipur Patan Rd at the southern end of the Bazaar area, about 3 km from Lakeside and Damside. Open 1000-1700, Sun-Fri. Some hotels will post your letters for you. Phone, Fax and email: the area code for Pokhara is 061. There are an increasing number of public call offices emerging in Lakeside and Damside and it is usually cheaper to phone from these than from hotels with ISD facilities. International calls from Pokhara are generally more expensive than from

Kathmandu, eg India Rs 60 per minute or part thereof, and Rs 190 to Europe and North America. (**NB** Dial with care, as 1 min and 1 second is charged as 2 mins.) Most will allow call-backs, but may charge Rs 10-15 per minute. Many also have a fax. Check that the correct number has been dialled and that the 'Status' on the transmission report reads 'OK'. Similar rates apply. Email facilities are also available. Operators include *Quick Telesat Communications*, opposite Grindlays Bank (also ISD and fax), an off-shoot of Global Net Communications in Thamel, and *Ambassador Travels* (kumar@att.mos.com.np) in central Lakeside.

Hospitals & medical services

If you get sick and know which medicines you want, there are pharmacy shops in both Lakeside and Damside. Prescriptions are not required, but it helps if you know the name of the drug. If you need more urgent treatment, Pokhara's hospital is about 2 km northeast of the airport, just east of the Seti River. Its official name is the *Western Regional Hospital*, but is commonly referred to as the *Gandaki Hospital*. It is a government teaching hospital, but also receives some international funding and is considered by many to be the best hospital outside Kathmandu. It has 25 doctors, including 5 Western doctors, covering general medicine, surgery, orthopaedics, gynaecology and ENT.

Routine out-patients clinic hours from 0900-1200. Emergency service runs 24 hrs. If you require treatment there is an initial registration fee of Rs 200, with a further Rs 2,000 consultation fee if you want to be seen by a Western doctor. Most routine operations cost in the region of Rs 9,000 plus the cost of materials, eg syringes, medication, blood, etc. The hospital's doctors are chronically overworked, so patience is required as you may not be seen immediately. Standards of hygiene are reasonable by South Asian standards: syringes are reportedly not re-used and the operating theatre is said to be sterile. Nevertheless, you may wish to bring your own syringes and needles, although there is a pharmacy within the hospital which sells these as well as a range of medicines. **NB** Remember to keep receipts to help with insurance claims. The taxi fare from Lakeside is about Rs 100.

As the region's only major medical centre, the hospital covers a huge catchment area and many people needing treatment may be unable to pay for it. The hospital has a Poor Fund which provides assistance to those unable to bear the costs themselves. Contributions are welcome – enquire at reception or ask one of the doctors.

There is a small pharmacy and doctor's surgery on the road heading southeast from opposite KC's restaurant in Damside.

Tour companies & travel agents

You can book treks, river rafting and wildlife packages in Lakeside. There is a branch of *Himalayan Encounters* on Lakeside's northernmost perpendicular road, and the *Ultimate Descents* office is located in the central part. All the main luxury lodges inside the Chitwan National Park also have offices in Lakeside, and are distinct from the many travel agents which sell wildlife packages on commission. Use only registered authorized agents. The same applies to the many small agents to have blossomed in Lakeside, some of whom are simply agents of other agents, and who may sell you bus tickets at an inflated price. **Train:** Many travel agents offer confirmed reservations on Indian Railways to various destinations in India. Treat with caution, as reservations may not always turn out to be as confirmed as you are led to believe, and usually involve your having to pick up your train ticket from an intermediate point on production of a receipt. Train reservations are made only in India. **Flights:** Most of the larger travel agents will make reservations for you on Royal Nepal Airlines (RNAC) and any of Nepal's private airlines. This can be a time consuming process, however, with reservations frequently unconfirmed until the last minute (see also page 27). Where available, payment by credit card can attract a substantial surcharge. Booking a flight to India often takes even more time and most travel agents will only offer RNAC. If all RNAC flights are full, *Indian Airlines* is an alternative. Reservations and payment for Indian Airlines flights, however, is only possible in Kathmandu so go to a travel agent which also has an office in the capital – *Wayfarers Travel*, located on the corner of the main north-south Lakeside road where it veers east near the Royal Palace (and with a branch in Thamel), is helpful and has been recommended.

Tourist offices

The tourist office is located diagonally opposite the airport entrance. Expect no more than a couple of govt tourist handouts from its dark and musty interior, T20028. Open 1000-1700 mid-Nov to mid-Feb, 0900-1600 mid-Feb to mid-Nov. Closes 1500 Fri. Closed Sat and public holidays.

The best way to get accurate up to date information is by talking to other travellers. Most hotel and restaurant owners will also happily oblige.

Useful information   Immigration Office and Permits: the immigration office handles visa renewals and trekking permits and is located between Lakeside and Damside, just off Ratna Chowk. Its remit is narrower than Kathmandu's immigration office, and may issue permits for the Annapurna region only. Applications are accepted between 1000-1300 Sun-Fri, closed Sat, and are usually ready for collection between 1500-1700 the same day. **NB** At peak times there can be long queues, so arrive early.

The Terai and Churia Hills

7

370

The Terai and Churia Hills

Background

374   The land

376   People

377   Economy

378   West Terai

378   Mahendranagar

381   Royal Sukla Phanta Wildlife Reserve

386   Royal Bardia National Park

394   Nepalgunj

398   Central Terai

398   Butwal

401   Bhairahawa & Sunauli

404   Lumbini

409   Tansen

414   Narayanghat & Bharatpur

417   Royal Chitwan National Park

426   Sauraha

431   Tribhuvan Highway north to Kathmandu

432   Birgunj

436   Eastern Terai

436   Janakpur

442   Koshi Tappu Wildlife Reserve

444   Biratnagar

447   Dharan

452   Ilam

450   Kakarbhitta

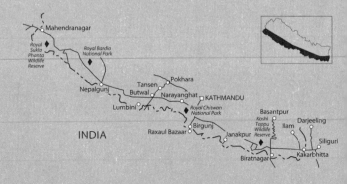

Running for 700 kilometres along the entire southern boundary of Nepal, the Terai is repeatedly crossed by rivers, mostly placid after the tumbling descent from the high peaks as they flow to join the Ganges in the vast plains of the Indian plateau. For the Terai is a transition zone: in a few kilometres, the plains give way to the now largely deforested, malaria-free savannah grasslands before meeting the Churias – the foothills of the Himalaya. Culturally it has been a melting pot as its potentially good agricultural land has been sought alike by hill people and ethnic groups from India. It has immense religious significance too. Lumbini is the birthplace of the Buddha and a major Buddhist pilgrimage site. Archaeological digs are continuing and have unearthed the 'exact' spot where the Buddha was born. Janakpur is a feast of small temples and the Terai's most important Hindu pilgrimage site.

The popular Bardia and Chitwan National Parks are jungle areas teeming with a huge variety of wildlife from tigers and rhinos to deer and monkeys to crocodiles and dolphins. Both have luxury and budget accommodation. Activities include jungle walks and elephant rides. If your schedule allows it, choose Bardia. The Sukla Phanta and Koshi Tappu Wildlife Reserves are renowned for their array of exotic bird life. Ilam combines the quaintness of a traditional Churia hill town with the picturesque surroundings of a seemingly endless carpet of tea gardens. Tansen, meanwhile, typifies traditional Nepali life in its cobbled streets, laid-back meeting places and smattering of temples. The nearby Srinigar Hill has superb Himalayan views.

Terai & Churia Hills

Background

The Terai extends some 700 kilometres from west to east. It includes five of the six approved land **border** crossings for foreigners, namely Mahendranagar, Nepalgunj, Sunauli (Belahiya), Birgunj and Kakarbhitta, and many of Nepal's major rivers flow through the plains on their journey to join the Ganges. The eastern Terai is marginally more developed than the west. It has Nepal's largest industrial town, **Biratnagar** (also the only town/city with a six figure population outside the Kathmandu Valley), and one of the country's major Hindu pilgimage towns, **Janakpur**. The Royal **Chitwan** National Park lies conveniently for most visitors at the heart of the Terai, easily accessible from Kathmandu and from the border crossings of Birgunj and Sunauli (Belahiya). There are, nevertheless, numerous smaller towns and villages where traditional rural life continues and, though off the beaten track, are there for the intrepid traveller to discover.

For many visitors the **Lumbini** district marks the westernmost point of their travels in the Terai, due in large measure to the challenges inherent in travelling onwards from the Buddha's birthplace to the border town of **Mahendranagar**. This lowland area was once densely forested, but agricultural encroachment resulting largely from increasing pressure of population in the mountainous regions to the north and the consequent migration of people

The Terai

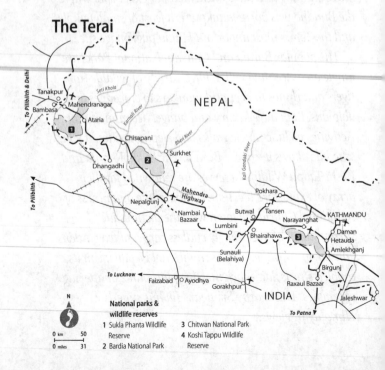

National parks & wildlife reserves
1 Sukla Phanta Wildlife Reserve
2 Bardia National Park
3 Chitwan National Park
4 Koshi Tappu Wildlife Reserve

0 km 50
0 miles 31

to the plains, has led to **deforestation** here on a massive and unprecedented scale. The trend was boosted by a vigorous and partially successful programme of malaria eradication in the region undertaken by the government from the 1950s, so that today its topography bears little resemblance to that of 50 years ago. A giant patchwork of fields and villages, occasionally interspersed with growing urban centres, has replaced the forest's erstwhile predominance and the region now produces a significant part of the country's economic output.

In an age of heightened ecological and environmental awareness this may seem an all too familiar tale, easily and oft condemned as reckless, but as elsewhere concerns for environmental conservation invariably come a distant second behind the instinctive quest for survival as represented by newly opened land.

Travel in the western Terai does have its own particular rewards. The magnificent **Seti**, **Karnali** and **Bheri** rivers all flow through the region from their high Himalayan origins before going on to join the Ganges system in India. If you have time, the **Royal Sukla Phanta** and **Royal Bardia National Parks** cover a combined area of more than 1,100 square kilometres, as yet unspoilt by excessive commercial exploitation, providing a protected habitat for a wide range of birds and other wildlife including a number of endangered species such as the tiger, pygmy hog and swamp deer. Neither park yet features prominently on the main tourist trail, and although individual budget travellers may find getting there more of a challenge than usual, organized inclusive tours are available from Kathmandu. With ever more areas of Nepal being developed for tourism, it is possible that Bardia in particular will go the way of Chitwan before the next century has come of age – until then they remain sanctuaries undamaged by the modern world and allowing an almost undisturbed appreciation of a natural wilderness.

Nepalgunj, near the Indian border some 200 kilometres east of Mahendranagar, is the gateway to Northwest Nepal. This, the area of the country least explored by Westerners, is home to the **Khaptad** and **Rara National Parks** as well as to some spectacular and fascinating – if daunting – trekking regions (see Trekking section).

The Government of India states that the International Boundaries are "neither correct nor authenticated"

The Mahendra Highway Extending across the entire length of the Terai from Mahendranagar in the west to Kakarbhitta in the east is the Mahendra Highway. Mostly single lane in each direction, it scarcely qualifies as a highway by Western understanding, but is the most important single artery for surface transport in Nepal, as it links commercial and industrial centres with the southern border towns and connects conveniently with main roads to Kathmandu, Mugling, Pokhara and Chitwan National Park. Principal bus stops along or just off the highway as it runs through the west Terai are

Terai & Churia Hills

few, but include **Nepalgunj**, a border crossing with India, and **Butwal** from where there is easy access to **Bhairahawa** and **Sunauli**. Unless you are crossing the border through Sunauli, only the town of **Lumbini** offers any kind of incentive for staying in this area. The Buddha's birthplace is one of the most important Buddhist pilgrimage sites and has some truly fascinating archaeological remains.

The Land

Geography   The Terai runs along the northern margin of the Gangetic plain. Formerly a malarial region because of what was dense jungle, together with relatively high rainfall and humidity, it has rich agricultural land and has been used as an overflow area from the increasingly congested hills. The southernmost 15 kilometres wide strip contains the best agricultural land, backing on to a marshy region, while to the north it reaches as far as the first slopes of the Bhabhar and Churia (or *Siwalik*) range of hills. Some descriptions refer to the above as the 'Outer Terai' and include the Churia hills with their *doons*, or broad valleys that extend up to the Mahabharat mountains, as defining characteristics of an 'Inner Terai'. The word Terai itself, however, implies plains or flat areas of land.

The northern Terai lowlands effectively mark the point at which the Indian landmass joined with the central Asian plate more than 100 million years ago, pushing north and creating the Himalayan Ranges from about 35 million years ago. The latest mountain building period, responsible for the Churias, began less than 5 million years ago and is still continuing. There is something of an enduring fascination in seeing and contemplating the abruptness with which the plains give way to slopes, the joining of two landmasses so precisely demarcated along 2,500 kilometres stretching from the Karakoram of Pakistan to the Kuron Range of northern Burma (Myanmar), and so immense and populated that their scale can only truly be conceived of by map.

As a result of the deforestation and malaria eradication in the 1950s, the Terai is now home to almost half of Nepal's population. There are communities representing every ethnic group as well as an increasing number of Indian migrants, many of whom are engaged in cross-border commerce. Many of its towns, including Nepalgunj, Janakpur and Biratnagar, have sizeable Muslim minorities.

Climate   The Terai has a seasonal, humid, sub-tropical climate similar to that of northern Bihar and Uttar Pradesh. The best time to visit is undoubtedly from November to February when it is dry with daytime temperatures in the low to mid 20°s C, when the countryside is lush, when there is rarely anything to obscure a completely clear sky, and when overhead fans are rendered seasonally redundant.

Temperatures and humidity levels rise from March, becoming uncomfortably hot and sticky by late April and into May and June. It is in these months that demand for electricity is usually at its greatest resulting in frequent power cuts. The southwest monsoon prevails from June to September with the Mahabharat hills forcing the moist monsoon airstream to rise, causing heavy rainfall in all parts of the Terai at times, although its influence and strength decreases the further west you travel. The post monsoon period of October and November has mostly settled weather, clear skies, no rain and comfortable to moderately high temperatures. Average maximum temperatures in the Terai are about 40°C in May or early June, with winter nights' temperatures dropping to around 5°C.

Share cropping

A zamindari system of land use and ownership, similar to that found in many parts of the subcontinent, is common in the Terai. Also known as share cropping, it is a system in which plots of land are 'leased' for cultivation by zamindars, or landowners, to landless or land-poor farmers in exchange for either a proportion of the final crop or a pre-determined quantity of crop or cash sum. It is in the zamindar's interest to maximize the yield from his land and many demand up to 50 percent or more of the final crop. Advantages of such an arrangement for poor farmers include the element of control which is able to be exercised over the cultivation process and the choice of which crops are to be cultivated, as well as a social standing perceived as higher than working as a hired labourer.

While the financial rewards in a good year can be significantly more than the accumulated daily wages of a farm labourer, the risks inherent in the system are also considerably higher. In many cases the cultivator must first borrow money to buy seeds and other inputs such as fertilizer and pesticides, ploughs and bulls may have to be rented, additional labour may be required at harvest, and the costs of transport and marketing must also be borne. The failure of the monsoon or of a crop may not be considered sufficiently good reason for waiving, reducing or deferring the payment due to the zamindar. This in turn can result in the cultivator having to resort to borrowing money from a local moneylender (who is often the zamindar) at extortionate rates of interest and thereby falling into a debt trap which can pass through generations.

Vegetation

Although little of the Terai's former forest now remains, it is still the region with the greatest richness and diversity of natural vegetation in Nepal. Tropical moist deciduous vegetation reflects altitude and climate (extending in patches up to the Mahabharat hills) and includes **khair** (*Acacia catechu*), a spring flowering tree with yellow flowers, flat pods and a wood that yields commercial catechu used for dying and tanning; **sissoo** (*Dalbergia sissoo*); and **sal** (*Shorea robusta*). Sissoo provides durable timber and sal produces building timber and resin which has a variety of uses. Sal is a dipterocarp, a tall, straight growing, sub-deciduous tree which is seldom completely leafless and has a reddish-brown or grey bark with smooth longitudinal fissures. The timber is in widespread commercial use and is a durable building material. Its foliage provides food for **lac** insects which deposit lac, a resinous substance used for the manufacture of shellac and other varnishes. After processing, the sal's seed oil is used as a substitute for cocoa butter in the chocolate industry. With the increase in altitude into the Churia Hills, there are sparse forests of **pine** (*Pinus roxburghii*) between 1,000 metres and 2,000 metres, as well as oaks, poplars, larches and walnut.

Both of the western Terai's national parks contain extensive areas of grassland as well as the ubiquitous sal. The Sukla Phanta national park derives its name from the savanna-like, open **phanta** grasslands which once covered large areas of the Gangetic plain region and which themselves provide a natural habitat for some species of endangered wildlife. Sal is also the dominant tree in the Bardia National Park to the west, but riverine forests of acacia together with sissoo and the large, buttressed silk cotton trees are represented in significant numbers too.

Wildlife

Animals The Terai is home also to the country's widest variety of wildlife, including **tigers, rhinos, leopards, gaur, elephants, buffalo** and chital, sambar and swamp **deer**. The Terai encompasses four national parks, areas of protected wilderness, the largest being Bardia (968 square kilometres) in the west, with Koshi Tappu (155 square kilometres) in the east being the smallest. While these provide a protected habitat and therefore the best opportunity to see some of the region's stunning array of animals in the wild, most longer distance bus journeys also pass through wooded areas inhabited by deer, **monkeys** (notably the langur and *Rhesus macaque*) and birds including brightly coloured **parakeets** and **kingfishers**. Large anthills are particularly conspicuous in the far western Terai.

When your bus stops near a wooded area for tea, steal away for a few minutes and listen to the dramatic variety of sounds emanating from the wood – taking care to ensure that you don't miss the bus when it leaves.

Estimates over the number of species of **birds** endemic to the Terai vary. The figure of at least 400 different species is perhaps conservative, and is augmented by many more seasonally migrating varieties. Cranes, storks, herons and egrets are common in wetlands and along river banks. Moist forest and woodland are home to numerous species of cuckoo and pheasant including Nepal's 'national bird', the **impeyan pheasant**.

Although **birds of prey** are more numerous in the higher regions, several species are also found in parts of the Terai, especially from November onwards. These include kites, kestrels and griffons, all of which are occasionally confused with, and referred to, as eagles. There are also communities of vultures, easily recognizable by their awkward and heavy – but strangely mesmerizing – flight. They are usually seen in flocks, rarely alone, circling like a squadron of aircraft waiting to land before coming to perch conspicuously on the tops of trees.

Outside the national parks, the Terai's larger **reptiles, mammals** and other wildlife are generally elusive to the eyes of most visitors, but include many species of lizard and frog as well as snakes, crocodiles, mongooses and jungle cats. An especially attractive sight after dark is the bright flash of light and glow of colour of the **firefly**. There are various species of nocturnal beetles of the Lampyridae family here. The light is produced by the male from an organ at the rear of the abdomen, while the female is lightless and flightless.

People

The extraordinary rate of colonization that the Terai has experienced during the latter part of the 20th century has brought together ethnic groups from throughout Nepal and from some parts of India. Each has brought its own traditions and customs, influenced by religion and environment, to make the Terai something of a cultural melting pot. Ethnic identities, however, together with traditional social structures are maintained. The vast majority of marriages are still arranged strictly according to caste principles: marriage between castes and between ethnic groups is rare.

The Nepali language is as widely understood as Hindi, but a number of regional languages and dialects reflecting the Terai's many different ethnic groups are predominant among local communities. Dialects derived from Sanskrit and related to Hindi are spoken on both sides of the Terai border. Awadhi is the main dialect spoken in Nepalgunj and the western Terai as well as in Uttar Pradesh (UP), while Urdu is also understood in Nepalgunj with its significant minority of Muslims. Bhojpuri is another local language both of UP and of the central Terai area, while Maithili is spoken in the central and eastern Terai as well as in the neighbouring Indian state of Bihar. English is generally only spoken as a second or third language in larger towns and cities, though rarely in villages.

In addition to the movement of people from both the south and the north, the last century has also witnessed a drift of population from the west to the east and a continuous flow into India. The Tharus are believed to be descended from the original inhabitants of the Terai and are distributed along the length of it, but there is a strong affinity with the people of UP and Bihar. The Indian classics suggest that the central region south of the Himalaya already had close cultural contact with the plains of India at least 2,500 years ago. They number around 800,000, are primarily farmers and generally practise a form of Hinduism that is mixed with animist beliefs. Recent Indian migrants are distributed throughout the Terai as well as older established groups who can claim to be Nepali. These include the Danuwars, Majhis and Darais. There are some 400,000 Muslims in the Terai.

The role of the Terai as the country's main food producing region and the reliance of Terai cultivators on a good harvest bestows special significance to **festivals** celebrating or associated with the harvest. The two most important such festivals are Dasain, celebrated over 15 days in October, and the five days of Tihar (or Diwali) usually in early November. The dates of both are determined according to the position of the moon. The full moon marks the final day of Dasain, while Tihar begins with the 13th day of the waning moon. Both are joyous occasions, propitiating respectively the Mother-Goddess Durga in the triumph of good over evil, of light over dark, and Laxmi, Goddess of Wealth.

Economy

Topography, climate, fertility and proximity to India combine to make the Terai Nepal's most important economic region. Agriculture is the principal occupation. The Terai comprises only 23 percent of the country's total land area, but has almost 60 percent of its cultivated land and nearly half of the total population. It accounts for over 80 percent of Nepal's rice production and 65 percent of its wheat. Cash crops like sugar cane, jute and tobacco are also important. A small surplus of grain and industrial products are exported to India. Land holdings are generally larger than in the hills, but average only around two hectares, a figure which is likely to reduce further with the hereditary fragmentation of land.

Terai & Churia Hills

West Terai

Despite containing two important crossings into India, the Western Terai has been difficult to visit as the condition of the Mahendra Highway west of Chisapani has been very poor. Much of it is unpaved as it goes through dense sal forest and fords numerous streams and rivers. This is changing with the construction of the Karnali Bridge at Chisapani and work has again started on upgrading the road. The Royal Bardia National Park is a real gem.

Mahendranagar

Colour map 1, grid B1

On the India-Nepal border and with direct road connections to the capitals of both, Mahendranagar is Nepal's most westerly town, a small and bustling market town of about 65,000 inhabitants lying immediately to the south of the Mahendra Highway. Its role as a transit point means that few travellers get to see beyond its decidedly unappealing façade of shabby shops and dark eateries that line the main road made more dirty, dusty and noisy by the continuous arrival and departure of buses.

Sights From the Mahendra Highway, the town's main road heads south for 600 metres through a bazaar area and past the busy local bus stop and a 'stadium' on your right before reaching the main intersection. Most of the accommodation is concentrated near here, in the grid of streets which make up the town's southeast quadrant. From the intersection the road heading east leads to **Mahendra Chowk**, duly furbished with a large statue of King Mahendra and the focal point for much local activity. There are shops here selling a variety of goods from dress material to electronic items and consumables. A thriving black market also exists. This trade comprises largely of computer chips and other components mostly heading out of Nepal, a result of high prices and perceived questionable quality inherent in India's policy of protection for its own computer and hi-tech industries. Other major commodities finding their surreptitious way across the border here are said to include gold and narcotics, much of which apparently does not originate in Nepal.

Continuing south, the less appealing area of town comes to an abrupt halt with a turn in the main road. The delightful and well maintained **Birenda Park**, on your right, has a central marble monument honouring the restoration of the authority of the monarchy in 1951. A series of paths lined with flowering trees lead through the park. In the southeast corner, the small two-tiered pagoda temple is

Western Terai

NEPAL

Seti Khola

Mahendranagar

Sukla Phanta Wildlife Reserve Ataria

Karnali River

Chisapani

Bardia National Park Surkhet

Bheri River

INDIA Dhangadhi

Nepalgunj

Nambai Bazaar

N

0 km   50
0 miles   31

dedicated to Saraswati, the goddess of learning and wisdom. The main entrance is on the northern side. ■ *Re 1.*

If you have a couple of hours to spare, there is a fine walk down to the northern edge of the Sukla Phanta Wildlife Reserve. Beyond Birendra Park, at the very southern end of town, is a small image of Ganesh set in the concrete base of two peepul trees. Continue past here, then across the stone bridge and follow the path as it heads south. The sudden silence contrasts remarkably with the hectic bazaar life a few hundred metres behind as you pass through several traditional Tharu settlements where a simple *Namaste* is a surprisingly effective response to local curiosity. The bird life for which Sukla Phanta is renowned is conspicuous as you continue along the path, and you can see a variety of exotic species including squadrons of parakeets on regular Jonathan Livingstone Seagull routines. The fenced park boundary is about 40 minutes' walk from Mahendranagar, but entry is through the park headquarters, some 10 kilometres soutwest of the Mahendra Highway by road.

Walk to Sukla Phanta

For full details of the Sukla Phanta Wildlife Reserve, see page 381.

Mahendranagar

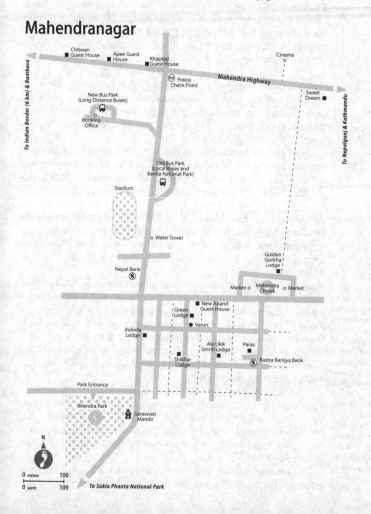

Essentials

Sleeping **C-D** *Sweet Dream*, T22313. 22 rooms all with bath and some with air cooler, restaurant for Indian, Chinese and some continental food, located on the Mahendra Highway, 400 metres east of the town, this is the best hotel west of Nepalgunj, with friendly staff to help with travel arrangements, decent and good value. Recommended.

D-E *New Anand Guest House*, T21693. 17 rooms some with bath, small restaurant does good Indian and Chinese food. **D-E** *Paras*, T21165, F21186. 6 rooms some with bath and TV, dining room with good Indian/Nepali food, STD/ISD facilities. Recommended.

E *Ala Ukik Smriti Lodge*, T21058. 10 rooms all common bath, no food, little English spoken, basic though clean and friendly. **E** *Apee Guest House*, T22107. 10 rooms, some with bath, food on request, some English spoken, STD/ISD facilities, on the main highway. **E** *Chitwan Guest House*, 6 rooms all common bath, no fans, very basic. **E** *Golden Gorkha*, T21576. 9 rooms all common bath. Nepali style eating area, friendly but little English spoken, entrance via outside staircase. **E** *Green Lodge*, T21950. 8 rooms all common bath, no food, basic. **E** *Jhilmila Lodge*, T21535. 6 rooms all common bath, dark. **E** *Khaptad Guest House*, T21645. 10 rooms all common bath, food on request. **E** *Shikhar Lodge*, T22234. 22 rooms some with bath, Nepali food, dreary.

Eating You can get Nepali/Indian food at most hotels and lodges, but it pays to order at least a couple of hours in advance. The *Sweet Dream Hotel* has the town's best restaurant and does good Indian/Nepali food. Aside from the numerous dhabars and street side food stalls, the only other place of note is the *Indian Varun Restaurant* in the grid of streets south of Mahendra Chowk.

Since a women's pressure group succeeded in 1995 in getting a ban on alcohol imposed throughout the Kanchanpur district, all bars have closed down. The main purpose of the police road checks on the way to Mahendranagar is to search for supplies of alcohol brought from Dhangadhi and other neighbouring districts.

Transport **Air** Mahendranagar's airport is situated southwest of the town, 3 kilometres from the entrance to Sukla Phanta Wildlife Reserve. In mid-1997, no airlines were flying to or from Mahendranagar, though both RNAC and Necon Air have operated flights here in the past. The nearest airports are at Dhangadhi, Surkhet and Nepalgunj.

On the Kathmandu and Birgunj buses, the booking office has been known to be reluctant to sell seats for shorter distances, eg to Bardia National Park, and to send travellers off on one of the very slow and uncomfortable local buses to Nepalgunj from the Old Bus Park. In this case, think about buying a ticket on a Kathmandu or Birgunj bus to any destination beyond Nepalgunj: the additional comfort and time saved is well worth the extra expenditure.

Buses There are direct buses from Mahendranagar to **Kathmandu** and **Birgunj** from the **New Bus Park**, situated just off the main north-south road. Kathmandu buses leave at 1330 and 1400 for the 24-hour journey, and there is one daily departure to Birgunj at 1345. Early booking is recommended and, if you are going all the way to Kathmandu, try to get one of the seats behind either the door or the driver.

The busier **Old Bus Park** on the main north-south road is the starting point for local buses to **Nepalgunj** and to **West Nepal**. There are regular departures for Nepalgunj and Dhangadhi throughout the day.

To **Bardia National Park** Buses for Nepalgunj leave regularly throughout the day from the Old Bus Park. Get down to the tiny village of **Ambasa** (journey time approximately 6 hours) and connect with either of the local buses leaving Ambasa at 1600 and 1800 only for the 11 kilometres ride to Thakurdwara. Alternatively, you can try one of the Kathmandu or Birgunj buses which take 3-4 hours and hope to arrive at Ambasa before 1800.

To **Chitwan National Park** Take either the Kathmandu or Birgunj bus and change at **Narayanghat** for any of the numerous local buses to **Tadi Bazaar**.

To **Pokhara**: Take the Kathmandu or Birgunj bus and change at **Butwal** for the slow and scenic journey along the Siddhartha Highway via Tansen, or (on the Kathmandu bus) at **Mugling** for the smoother ride along the Prithvi Highway.

Banks You can change TCs and foreign currency (US$ preferred, no credit card advances) at the *Rastra Banijya Bank*, T21192, 200m south of Mahendra Chowk. Open 1000-1600 Sun-Thur, 1000-1330 Fri, closed Sat. **NB** Allow plenty of time, as transactions can be excruciatingly slow. The *Nepal Bank* on the main north-south road will change Indian rupees only at its dingy first floor office. **Communications** The area code for Mahendranagar is 099. There are a few STD/ISD places scattered throughout the town. Calling Europe or America is fairly straightforward, but it can be extremely difficult to get a line to India or sometimes even to Kathmandu and elsewhere in Nepal. If you want to make an urgent call to India and cannot get through, it can be quicker to phone someone in Europe/America and ask them to relay the message for you. **Directory**

Crossing into India

The border, on the Mahakali River, lies about six kilometres along the tree lined highway from Mahendranagar. Buses leave the old bus park every 30 minutes from 0600-1800, Rs 3. Rickshaws (Rs 20) and tempos (Rs 10) are also available. **Leaving Nepal**

Customs and Immigration on the Nepali side are open 0700-1900. You will probably be able to get through if you arrive later, but will have to ring the doorbell and wait. It is 600 metres to the Indian side where Customs and Immigration are open 24 hours for pedestrians. If you are going through with a vehicle, however, times are restricted to 0600-0700, 1200-1300 and 1800-1900. Ensure that all necessary documents are available and all paperwork has been completed. **At the border**

The State Bank of India in Bambasa should be able to change TCs and foreign currency. Although strictly speaking illegal, changing IC to NC and vice versa is easily done in numerous shops, hotels, etc, in the area. You can change TCs and currency at Mahendranagar's Rastra Banijya Bank (see below).

Rickshaws run between the border and the small town of Bambasa, three kilometres inside India (IC: Rs 5, NC: Rs 8). From Bambasa there are around six buses a day for the eight-hour journey to Delhi (IC: Rs 95 by 'ordinary' bus, and Rs 115 for the 'delux' variant which is faster and more comfortable). Alternatively, you could make for Tanakpur, seven kilometres north of Bambasa, where there is a larger bus park with a greater choice of services to Delhi, Bareilly and Lucknow. Video buses, mercifully, have been banned by the UP Government as a result of their distracting influence on drivers. Trains also operate between Tanakpur, Bambasa and Pilibith where you have to change for connections to Delhi and Lucknow. **Into India**

Royal Sukla Phanta Wildlife Reserve

The most westerly and least visited of Nepal's major wildlife reserves, Sukla Phanta covers an area of 355 square kilometres of forest and grassland. It provides a natural habitat for over 500 species of birds, reptiles and mammals including what is thought to be the world's largest population of swamp deer. In appearance it has been likened to the savannas of sub-Saharan Africa. Colour map 1, grid B1

It is possible to visit the reserve both independently and on a package tour. Its remote location makes it awkward to get to, but also ensures that it remains **Visiting**

Terai & Churia Hills

almost completely uncommercialized. The main entrance and reserve office is located 10 kilometres south of the Mahendra Highway (the junction is two kilometres west of Mahendranagar), and is open daily from 0600 until dusk. The **entry pass** costs Rs 650 and is valid for three consecutive days. The office can provide information about hiring guides. The **best time to visit** is from December-April.

Background Formerly open forest, it was first given protected status as a royal hunting reserve in the 1960s, then redesignated a wildlife reserve of 155 square kilometres in the following decade. The 'extension area' to the east and northeast of the original reserve was subsequently incorporated to bring it to its current size. The name probably derives from the colour of the flowering grasses: *sukila* is a Nepali and Tharu word for white, while *phanta* is the Tharu term for grassland usually occurring in sal forest. It was first mentioned in Western literature in the early 20th century by Baden-Powell in his *Indian Memoirs*. The **Mahakali River** flows to the west of the reserve and is flanked by swamp land.

Unlike any other park in South Asia, the reserve is unique for its grasslands which comprise almost 30 percent of its total area and is the last major area of unspoiled grassland in Nepal. More of the Terai's former forest belt is likely to assume savanna-like form if illegal logging both within Sukla Phanta and, more seriously, beyond its boundaries continues to be tolerated, a practice

Royal Sukla Phanta Wildlife Reserve

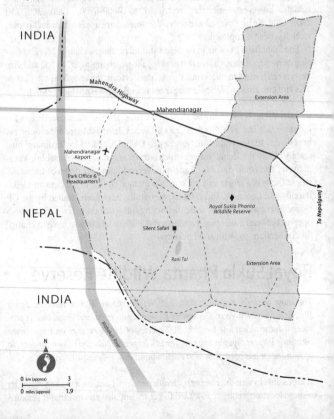

resulting in accelerated erosion, consequent silting up of rivers and a reduced supply of irrigation water for farmers.

See also Royal Bardia National Park, page 388.

Wildlife

Fauna Sukla Phanta shares its fauna with the Bardia National Park to the east and with the forests of Uttar Pradesh extending as far west as Corbett National Park. It lies on the migratory trail between Nepal and India of numerous species of bird as well as several of the larger mammals, including elephants and tigers. Continued deforestation in both Nepal and India, however, is removing the migratory corridors upon which these animals have relied and must lead to decreased numbers and altered behavioural patterns. This is especially serious for a really demanding species, such as the tiger. The open expanse of grassland, meanwhile, increases the confidence of deer and other animals wary of predators, resulting in a high degree of visibility and excellent sighting opportunities.

'Tula Hatti', also known as 'Rajaguj' (see also page 388), said to be the world's largest Asian **elephant** and the subject of a 1990 TV documentary, is perhaps Sukla Phanta's most famous occasional resident. The reserve itself has only a handful of permanent elephants, though herds of up to 24 regularly trample through. Attracted by an ample supply of prey, the tiger population, estimated at a maximum of 35 individuals, is also largely migratory. Although usually shy creatures that hunt mainly by night, there are rare reports of man-eating tigers venturing into Mahendranagar and other surrounding villages. A smaller number of **leopards** are found, but these are generally even more elusive than the tiger. Various species of **deer**, notably the endangered swamp deer and also the spotted, barking and hog deer, abound with sightings of several hundreds at one time a real possibility. Deer mostly inhabit swampy areas by rivers, but are found also at the forest margins. **Monkeys**, especially the common langur (black face, hands and feet, silvery coat and long tail) and the rhesus macaque (reddish face and red-brown body) constitute the reserve's largest population of mammals.

Reptiles include the gharial and marsh mugger **crocodiles** present in prominent numbers in the marshy areas around Rani Tal and along the Mahakali River. There are plans for an FAO sponsored development project to increase the numbers of both. Its proposed conservation centre will include a hatchery and the young will be reared until they can be released back into the wild. **Otters** are common in swampy areas and along river banks where they hunt with speed and great agility for fish, including the large **catfish** (so named after the whisker-like barbels around the mouth).

Birds Most prominent is the reserve's stunning array of bird life, the most diverse of any park in Nepal. The forest, grassland and riverine environments attract a total of almost 500 species, both permanently resident and migratory. They include many exotic, prey, coloured, singing, wading and rare species. The sights as well as the raucous sounds are truly memorable. The reserve is considered by many to be a birdwatcher's idyll; indeed, several species new to Nepal have been identified here.

Flora and environment Between 65 percent and 70 percent of the reserve consists of sal-dominated **forest**, almost 30 percent is *phanta* **grassland**, and the remainder is **swamp** and water.

Although there is a wide range of grasses, the *phanta* comprises three main

Terai & Churia Hills

types of grass: *dhaddi*, a broad leafed variety growing up to two metres and extensively used by Tharu communities for thatching; siru, growing up to 60 cm; and elephant grass (*Typha elephantina*) which can grow up to six metres. The frequent comparisons with a savanna environment are not misplaced, as Sukla Phanta also experiences the seasonal fires characteristic of savanna ecology. Far from damaging the environment as is often perceived, these fires are crucial to its cyclical regeneration. Savanna environments are well adapted to fire and many experts maintain that they are actually dependent upon it.

The tall, straight-growing and broad leafed sal tree is predominant, but there are a number of other varieties, some flowering. The *flame of the forest tree* produces attractive, deep red flowers in March-April.

Viewing The nearest budget accommodation is at Mahendranagar, 12 kilometres to the north, from where you would have to hire a jeep for a tour of the park. Rental will cost upwards of Rs 1,000 per day. Pedestrians are not allowed inside the reserve. Sukla Phanta is not well geared up for independent visitors, though the park office can assist with information and guides.

The beautiful **Rani Tal** in the centre of the park is a popular watering hole and the nearby lookout tower provides a superb vantage point.

Park information **Package tours** are offered by *A Silent Safari* whose luxury tented camp is the only accommodation inside the reserve and is run in the best tradition of nature tourism. Though fully equipped with comfortable beds, furniture, hot showers, Western style bathrooms, bar facilities, and both Nepali and continental food, it has no electricity, telephone or newspapers, and radios are not permitted. It is run by hunter turned gamekeeper, Col (ret'd) Hikmat Bisht, whose knowledge and genuine love for the reserve succeeds uniquely in raising it above a merely commercial undertaking. A large proportion of guests are repeat visitors. Bring insect repellent, binoculars and warm clothing for winter evenings.

Most packages are tailor made and prices include airport transfers and all meals. Options including 'Terai Treks' (eg from Dhangadhi to Sukla Phanta), fishing and specialist birdwatching.

Reservations in Kathmandu: T520523, F536941, or through *Tiger Tops* (Hattisar) T415659, F414075. You may be able to negotiate a good discount by booking direct with *Silent Safari*, PO Box 1, Mahendranagar, T099-21230, F22220. In **India**, book through *Sunshine Travels* (10 Dariyagunj, New Delhi 110 002), T+91-11-3289716, F3277875.

Getting there: As Mahendranagar (page 380). Regular flights from Kathmandu to Nepalgunj and on to Dhangadhi.

Dhangadhi

Colour map 1, grid B1 This small border town between Bardia and Mahendranagar attracts few tourists. Although not listed as one of the recognized border crossings, it is apparently possible to cross the border here. A regional market town, Dhangadhi is also popular with Indians shopping for imported, luxury goods. Situated 12 kilometres south of the Mahendra Highway, the town centres around its main square and has a reasonable choice of budget accommodation. At the northern end of town is an attractive park with a pond, while the border is two kilometres to the south.

A few kilometres into India and bordering the Terai by the **Sarda River** is the Dudhwa National Park, a sanctuary of sal forest, savanna grasslands and large marshy areas supporting a variety of wildlife including tigers, rhinos, deer and waterfowl. The park is open from mid-November to mid-June. **NB**

The area is occasionally disturbed by political activists which may affect border crossings.

D *Afnoghar Guest House*, T22959. 8 rooms all with bath, small restaurant. **D** Kanchan Guest House, T22108. 6 rooms all with bath, Indian/Nepali restaurant. **D** *Top in Town*, 4 rooms all with bath. **E** *Bantistar Lodge*, **E** *Gulshan Guest House* and **E** Sagar Guest House, each have 4 rooms all common bath. **E** *Sangam Guest House*, 11 rooms some with bath, restaurant, probably the best of the bottom end accommodation. **Sleeping**

Air Dhangadhi's airport is 2 kilometres south of the Mahendra Highway. RNAC (T21205) operates flights to/from **Kathmandu** (US$159) via **Nepalgunj** (US$60). **Transport**

    Buses There are regular local buses to **Nepalgunj**, Mahendranagar (3½ hours) and **Chisapani** (3¾ hours) throughout the day, and daily buses to **Birgunj**, **Janakpur** and **Pokhara**, all with early afternoon departures. Long distance buses between Mahendranagar and **Kathmandu** and **Birgunj** stop at the village of Ataria on the Mahendra Highway. Shared auto-rickshaws (Rs 7) and buses (Rs 5) run the 12 kilometres between Dhangadhi and Ataria.

    Into India From **Dudhwa** there are train connections to **Ayodhya**, **Lucknow** and **Mailani**. Transport is not always available at Dudhwa station, so it is advisable to use **Palia** (10 kilometres) and take the hourly bus or taxi. Buses connect Palia with **Lucknow** (219 kilometres), **Shahjahanpur** (107 kilometres), **Bareilly** (260 kilometres) and **Delhi** (420 kilometres).

Banks There are branches of the *Nepal Rastra* and the *Nepal Bank*, but only the *Rastra Banijya Bank*, near the centre, deals in foreign exchange. **Communications** Area code: the area code for Dhangadhi is 091. There are a few STD/ISD places around town, but many experience problems in getting lines to India and further afield in Nepal. **Directory**

Mahendra Highway between Mahendranagar and Nepalgunj

To describe the 140 kilometres of road from Mahendranagar to Chisapani as in bad condition is to do an injustice, for it is considerably worse than bad along much of the route, a dusty or muddy moonscape rollercoaster of a ride to test Tata suspensions to the limit, and relieved only by intermittent, welcome stretches of smooth tarmac where the Terai's sal forest may return to focus. There are also numerous streams and rivers to ford, though bridges are gradually being built. Giant anthills, up to one metre or more high and often appearing as sand-coloured tree stumps, are common alongside this stretch of road.

    An open bid to construct this final western section of the highway was sponsored by the World Bank in the 1980s. The Government of Nepal considered bids on economic criteria and a Chinese contractor was selected, narrowly beating a rival Indian bid. The Goveernment of India, though, still wary of China after its disastrous defeat in the 1962 war, objected to the proposed Chinese presence so close to its own territory and persuaded Nepal to accept a revised, lower Indian bid. Once this had been secured, however, little was done for several years. Only since 1996 has work picked up again and most of the highway should be complete by the turn of the century.

    The large **Karnali Bridge** marks the northwest boundary of the park and most buses stop for tea at the tiny village of Chisapani, on the west bank of the magnificent Karnali River.

    The stretch of road from Chisapani to Nepalgunj is in excellent condition, an easy flat drive of 75 kilometres. For the first 45 kilometres or so, the road runs through the Royal Bardia National Park. This is an especially picturesque drive, perhaps the most attractive section of the entire highway, with dense forest on either side. Sightings of deer, monkeys and wild peacocks foraging along the roadside are not uncommon.

Chisapani

Colour map 1, grid B1

Chisapani is a small though unattractive settlement of thatched huts on the west bank of the **Karnali River**. These provided temporary housing to labourers working on construction of the impressive Karnali Bridge. They have remained since completion and some have been turned into stalls selling tea and snacks (including fried and dried fish from the river) to stopping buses. The bus stop is an occasional hunting ground for touts from the Bardia National Park lodges. Chisapani means 'cold water'. A smaller village also called Chisapani is situated at the southeast corner of Bardia and is sometimes referred to as Purwa (East) Chisapani.

With a span of 500 metres, the **Karnali Bridge** became the longest single tower suspension bridge in the world at the time of its completion, after seven years under construction, in 1995. It provided the first direct road access between the far western Terai and the rest of Nepal to the east, opening the area up to potential development of both industry and tourism, and providing a viable overland trade route between Kathmandu and Delhi.

Surkhet (Birendranagar)

Colour map 1, grid B2

Surkhet is as far north as you can go without a trekking permit.

Attractively set in a valley in the Churia Hills, north of Bardia National Park, Surkhet is rarely visited by tourists, other than trekkers using it as a trailhead for treks to Jumla and Rara. An administrative centre, the town itself has little of general tourist interest. There are, however, several excellent walking opportunities, notably along the **Bheri River**, five kilometres to the south.

Sleeping Basic accommodation near the bus stop and around the bazaar area.

Transport **Air**: Surkhet has an airport with flights from and to Kathmandu and Nepalgunj. **Buses**: leave from early morning to Nepalgunj (6 hours) and from late morning for Kathmandu (15 hours). The road from the Mahendra Highway skirts the eastern boundary of the Bardia National Park and is in good condition until it leaves the plains. Thereafter it begins a bumpy, twisting, undulating course which accounts for the bulk of the journey time.

Royal Bardia National Park

Colour map 1, grid B2

Covering an area of 968 square kilometres, Bardia is the largest of the Terai's national parks. It also emerges favourably from the inevitable comparisons with Chitwan, with a consistent majority of those who have visited both expressing a preference for Bardia.

Bardia has more than 30 species of mammal, over 400 species of bird and several reptiles. Since its designation as a national park, conservation efforts have succeeded in raising the numbers of several threatened and endangered species. Several of the larger mammals and birds are migratory, with individuals and groups trekking between Bardia, Sukla Panta and Corbett National Park in India. It is said to be the best place in South Asia for tiger sightings. Bardia combines dense sal forest, riverine forest and isolated pockets of open grassland, or *phanta*.

You can visit Bardia both independently and by package tour. The main **Visiting**
entrance at Thakurdwara consists of a small complex of buildings, including
the park office (T29712), a visitors' centre, a crocodile breeding centre and an
army camp.

The entry permit costs Rs 650 (Rs 50 for nationals of SAARC countries) and
is valid for three consecutive days. Permits are issued from 0800-1730 daily,
and entry is permitted from dawn to dusk.

NB Ensure that you leave the park in good time, as it may be unsafe to remain
after dark. Overnight camping inside the park is not permitted. The park office
also issues fishing permits, Rs 300 per day.

Best time to visit November-April are the best months. After periods of
heavy monsoon rainfall (June-September) it may be impossible to ford some
of the streams/rivers on the road between Ambasa and Thakurdwara. Most
lodges remain closed during these months. Leeches are present in numbers
and the Khaura River, between the park entrance and the main area of the
park, is also often too high to cross, further restricting visits.

The park is bordered to the west by the Geruwa River, a major tributary of the **Background**
Karnali, and extends into the forested slopes of the Churia Hills to the north and
east. The Mahendra Highway joins the boundary from the south, passing
through the park's 'buffer zone' before veering north to cross the Karnali Bridge
at Chisapani. The Babai River runs an east-west course through the park.

Designated a national park in the 1980s following the extension of the
Karnali Wildlife Reserve, Bardia has been slow to attract tourism on the scale
of Chitwan, due largely to its distance from Kathmandu. Since the 1980s, however, a few lodges have been established in Thakurdwara, the small village near
the park entrance. Thakurdwara has no electricity, a situation considered by

Terai & Churia

Royal Bardia National Park

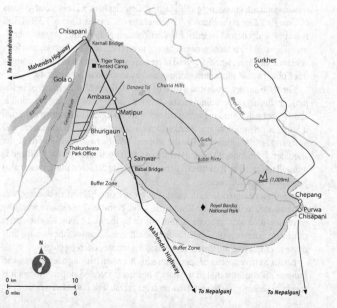

Jungle talk

Evocative, immortalized by Kipling and now widely used to describe realms as diverse as the urban morass and legal double-talk (as well as tracts of dense forest vegetation), the word 'jungle' first entered the English language between *1770 and 1780. Anglicized by early European colonialists in India in true Hobson-Jobson fashion, the word is a derivation of the Hindi* jangal, *or the Pali and Prakrit* jangala, *meaning a rough, waterless place.*

some as crucial in maintaining a pleasing sense of proportion and avoiding the profligate commercialism embraced by numerous Chitwan operators. Activities include 'jungle walks', elephant rides and rafting. Most of the lodges are run either by locals or by those with some years' experience of the area.

King Mahendra Trust for Nature Conservation The KMTNC office is situated one kilometre east of the park entrance. It conducts integrated social and environmental development projects, including reforestation programmes and a regular census of animal populations. It also administers the park's 'buffer zone' to the south of the main area of the park which is designed to be used by locals for building and thatching materials and for the collection of firewood. The Trust has the challenging task of promoting the park's ecology among local communities and explaining the importance of conserving its animal life; it is a challenge that becomes, at best, unenviable following any destruction of crops by elephants or rhinos. Staff can provide information and assistance to students or those interested in Bardia's wildlife and environment.

Wildlife **Fauna** In 1989, only two male elephants (*Elephas maximus*) remained in the wild at Bardia, but a 1996 survey conducted jointly by the KMTNC and Tiger Tops estimated a total number of some 45 individuals. Continuing deforestation in the Terai has removed some of the migratory corridors to India and reduced migration both from and to Bardia. The park is home to the world's largest Indian elephant, known here as 'Rajaguj' ('King Elephant'). He is about 45 years old, stands 3.43m at the shoulder (average height 2.7m with tusks of 1.35m), and is said to be docile and friendly. Elephants occasionally venture into surrounding villages and can cause serious damage to crops. It has also been known for a wild male elephant, when deprived of female company, to make for the domestic elephant stable at the park entrance and mate with a tethered female.

The 1996 survey estimated a total of 75 to 80 tigers (*Panthera tigris*) in the park, including 36 breeding adults. Another endangered species, the adult is about 1.1m tall, 1.8m long with a tail of 90 cm. A shy and often elusive animal, it hunts largely on deer and monkey, and is often found in riverine areas and grassland. More elusive still is the leopard (*Panthera pardus*, 80 cm at the shoulder, 1.5m long, 90 cm tail) which competes with the tiger for food and is not well tolerated by the latter. It generally inhabits the forest margins and also preys on village livestock.

Previously hunted to extinction, the greater one-horned rhinoceros was reintroduced to Bardia from Chitwan in 1986. Numbers have shown a healthy increase with a total of some 40 individuals by the mid 1990s. As elsewhere, rhinos are extremely unpopular with local villagers because of the damage they cause to crops, and are thus often seen as legitimate poaching targets.

Bardia has five species of deer. The reddish-brown barking deer (*Muntiacus muntjac*) is concentrated in the park's northeast forested slopes, though it is regularly seen also in the lowland reverine forest. The name derives from its sharp, dog-like alarm call. The buck has small antlers, while in the doe these are replaced by bristly tufts of hair. It is the smallest of the park's deer. The hog deer (*Axis porcinus*) is a smaller relative of the spotted deer, and is usually found in pairs or small groups. The sambar deer (*Cervus unicolor*) is the largest of South Asia's deer and an adult buck can weigh over 300 kg. These mainly nocturnal animals have a brown coat and thick, three pointed antlers whose full growth is attained at between three and four years of age. It is found in small groups on the forested slopes and along riverine forest margins. The name 'sambar' is a Hindi/Nepali word derived from the Sanskrit sambara. The attractive and immensely graceful spotted deer (*Axis axis*), or chital, has a reddish-brown coat with white spots. It has relatively small antlers and is the park's only deer found in large herds. It inhabits grassland, forest margins and riverine areas. The endangered swamp deer (*Cervus duvauceli*) is one of the tiger's major prey species. It is easily recognizable by its large, multi-pointed antlers after which it takes its local name barasingha, meaning twelve horns. It can be found in small to medium groups, usually in the riverine forest margins.

The nilgai (*Boselaphus tragocamelus*), or blue bull, is actually a large antelope standing 1.4m at the shoulder and 2m long. The buck has small antlers and is a blue-grey colour, while the doe is tawny coloured and without antlers. It inhabits the forest margins and grassland, and may be seen individually or in small groups. The numbers of the smaller black buck (*Antilope cervicapra*, 80 cm tall and 1.2m long) have reduced dramatically in recent years due to poaching, but are found mainly in the southeast area of the park. The buck is black or dark brown in colour with a white underbelly and white eye rings, and has long spiralled antlers of up to 60 cm. The doe is without antlers and is tawny coloured.

Monkeys, notably the common langur (*Presbytis entellus*) and rhesus macaque (*Macaca mulatta*), occupy trees throughout the park and are an important prey species of both tiger and leopard. The word 'langur' is thought to derive from the Sanskrit langulin, meaning to have a tail.

Other mammals include the wild boar (*Sus scrofa*, 90 cm tall, 1.2m long and weighs up to 150 kg). These bristly black-haired creatures feed in the early morning and late afternoon, foraging for roots but also including snakes in their omnivorous diet. The male has sharp tusks. Canids, including the wild dog (*Cuon alpinus*), striped hyena (*Hyaena hyaena*), and jackal (*Canis aureus*) also exist, but are mainly nocturnal and rarely seen. The distant howl of a jackal may be heard at night in Thakurdwara. Various species of mongoose (the Hepestes family) and numerous wild felines are common.

Reptiles include the gharial and marsh mugger crocodiles along the banks of the Geruwa River. The gangetic dolphin (*Platanista gangetica*) is also found in small numbers in the Geruwa.

Birds Among its more than 400 species of bird, Bardia includes six species of stork, 12 species of eagle,

Sambar

👉 *Watching out for the animals ... and also for trees*

The best times to see animals are in the early morning and from mid afternoon when many emerge from the midday heat to drink and eat. Loose, 'jungle coloured' clothing is recommended, and sunblock cream during the day. The most common sightings are of deer, sometimes in herds of up to 100 or more, and monkeys scampering along the ground or swinging adeptly through the trees. Experienced guides know the favoured drinking spots and hunting grounds of tigers, often along or near river banks. The rhino is more elusive here than at Chitwan. It is the animal most feared by guides, who warn against wearing red or orange clothing in case the rhino mistakes you for a tiger and takes pre-emptive action to stop you from making off with any baby rhinos. In the unlikely event of being faced with a charging rhino, guides recommend that you keep a look out for trees in the immediate vicinity up which you can climb to safety!

Signs of elephant life abound in broken branches and trampled trees. They make a spectacular sight drinking at the riverside or wandering across a path. The chances of seeing a dolphin in the Geruwa River are often exaggerated in publicity. Only an estimated 15 to 20 remain and sightings are rare. The best stretches to see them are Gola, Baghaura Pashim and Manau.

Of course, not every visitor will see a tiger or rhino or elephant, but the sense of anticipation as you listen to twigs and leaves being trodden underfoot, waiting for a rhino to approach its watering hole, or hearing the urgent call of monkeys warning of the presence of a tiger, or indeed simply the awareness of being in such an environment, can be just about as thrilling as actually sighting the animals.

vultures, pheasants, peacocks, five species of parakeet, 13 species of owl, 16 species of woodpecker, kingfishers, bee-eaters, hornbills, mynas, and 20 species of flycatcher.

Flora and environment Numerous small rivers and streams, tributaries of both the Karnali and Geruwa rivers, flow through the western areas of the park. In the months preceding the monsoon, many are reduced to minor trickles around large gravel islands, or are totally dry. Riverine forest includes a number of flowering trees such as the silk cotton tree with its delightful scarlet blossoms from March.

Viewing

Soon after you enter the park you have to cross the Khaura River to get to the main area of the park. The bottom is stony and extremely uncomfortable with bare feet, so bring waterproof sandals to change. Flip-flops are available cheaply from the small shop/stall opposite the park entrance. Trainers are best for walking in the park as undergrowth can be thick.

Elephant rides are a popular way of touring the park. Book at the park office, preferably 24 hours in advance, Rs 650 per person per hour (maximum three hours). Rides are available any time from 0630 to dusk. Tiger Tops is the only lodge with its own elephants and also runs jeep tours.

A couple of Thakurdwara lodges have their own **jeeps**, though these may be hired out at extortionate rates. It is usually cheaper to hire one from Nepalgunj for around Rs 2,000 for a full day. Maximum eight passengers, fewer for comfort. Book in advance, or on the same day with at least three hours' notice. Most lodges have a contact in Nepalgunj. There are about 300 kilometres of driveable routes inside the park, but the only real advantage of going by jeep is that you can get further into the park, eg to the Guthi valley to the east, a popular watering hole for rhinos and elephants.

Going on foot (the '**jungle walk**') with a guide is considered by many to be the most exciting way to see the park. With a good and experienced guide, it can be a superb adventure that allows you to get right into the jungle with the minimum of disturbance. **NB** Walking alone in the park can be dangerous and is not advised.

Guides Each lodge has at least one trained guide. Training consists of a short and fairly basic course at KMTNC. The best guides, however, are those with a long experience of Bardia. They will know all the routes as well as the best vantage points, and will have the best overall 'feeling' of the park, its wildlife and safety. Anticipating a boom at Bardia, a number of guides have arrived from Chitwan since the mid 1990s. Although tolerated by locals for their knowledge of tourism and English, they lack local experience and are sometimes believed to guide more by what they think visitors want to hear than by accurate information. The smaller the size of group the better, ideally one to one. For safety and viewing, a group of five is the realistic maximum.

Fishing The Karnali, Geruwa and Babai rivers all offer good fishing opportunities, especially for mahseer. Once caught, the fish should be returned to the river. Organized fishing trips are run by Tiger Tops. **Permits** are required, available from the park office, Rs 300 per day. Bring your own tackle, as the Thakurdwara lodges have none and only homemade bamboo rods are available locally. In theory, you can fish all year round, but the best time is after the monsoon when the rivers are high. Ask your lodge for best places to fish and to arrange transport.

The **crocodile breeding centre** has succeeded in raising the numbers of gharial and marsh mugger in the Geruwa and Babai rivers, which had fallen to about 35 at the time of its establishment in the late 1970s. Recently, the centre has also begun breeding turtles. ■ *Open daily, free admission.*

The **visitors' centre** at the park headquarters has a small but interesting display of photos and maps relating to Bardia.

Rafting It is possible to combine a visit to Bardia with a rafting trip down the Karnali River. These usually finish at Chisapani. Tiger Tops offers a half day raft from Chisapani to the centre of the park, followed by a jeep tour.

Park information

Curiously, it often works out significantly more expensive if you book a package, especially with accommodation at one of the Thakurdwara lodges. With the exception of Tiger Tops visitors and despite anything that Kathmandu travel agents may say, there is no great advantage to booking a package and just about everything that a typical package includes can easily be arranged independently. At peak times, it may be advisable to make reservations at one of the lodges by phone in advance, but there is usually a surplus of available accommodation at Thakurdwara.

What to bring Most essentials are available locally. Bring sunblock cream, insect repellent, torch, camera and film and a jumper or jacket for winter evenings. The stalls around the Thakurdwara bus stop sell fruit and vegetables only. A small stall outside the Bardia Jungle Cottage, opposite the park entrance, sells flip-flops, soap, shampoo and local cigarettes. Occasionally it stocks camera film (check expiry).

Thakurdwara

The tourist enclave extending either side of the park entrance is emerging from the scattered traditional Tharu agricultural settlements collectively known as Thakurdwara. The **bus stop** is about 20 minutes' walk south of the park entrance, and a small temple is nearby.

Activities outside the Park

Cultural programmes Performances of traditional Tharu song and dance can be arranged by all the lodges with at least 24 hours notice. Typically, these consist of choreographed courting routines or festival songs and dances,

Terai & Churia Hills

accompanied by drums (*maadal*) and cymbals (*majura*). The cost is about Rs 1,000 for a group of up to 12 performers.

Cycle hire   Cycling is not permitted inside the park, but there are some pleasant trips through traditional Tharu villages in the surrounding countryside. Basic cycles available from most Thakurdwara lodges at around Rs 15 per hour.

Tharu village tours   These rather tasteless tours can be arranged informally by all the lodges. Alternatively, you can explore some of the countryside by yourself. The small Tharu village on Thakurdwara's western loop, between the Karnali Safari and Rhino Express lodges, is known for its pottery and you can watch as the clay is thrown, moulded and fired.

Essentials

Sleeping   With the exception of the two Tiger Tops camps, all Bardia's accommodation is at Thakurdwara. There are no separate restaurants here, but all lodges do their own food.

A *Tiger Tops Karnali Lodge*, T(Kathmandu) 222706, F414075. 16 comfortable rooms in thatched cottages, restaurant and bar, 2 kilometres from Thakurdwara just outside the park, qualified guides, own elephants, jeeps and rafts, various activities on offer, electricity by generator. Inclusive packages from Kathmandu, open year round.
A *Tiger Tops Tented Camp*, offers the only accommodation inside the park, very comfortable tents beneath thatched roof, some packages include stays at both the lodge and tented camp.

B *Dolphins Manor*, T29717 (Kathmandu T420308, F415401). 13 tents with bucket bath and 5 indoor rooms with bath, restaurant and bar, deals almost exclusively with package tours and is promoted as an alternative to Tiger Tops, facilities and service are a little better than other Thakurdwara lodges, but at US$90 per night it has the distinction of offering by far the poorest value in Bardia. 1 kilometre southwest of the park entrance.

Thakurdwara

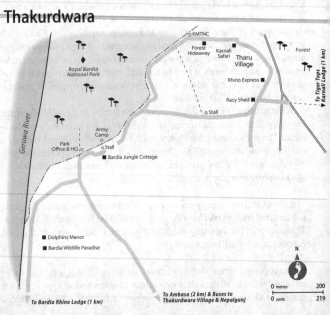

D *Bardia Jungle Cottage*, T29714 (Kathmandu T229459, F417395). 12 rooms in thatched cottages most with bath (hot water available), restaurant does good, large Nepali meals, bar, attractive grounds, the closest lodge to the park entrance, run as a family concern by Bardia's most experienced guide and former ranger, the unassuming Premi Khadka, and even if you are staying elsewhere, you can do no better than a guided jungle walk with him, fishing, short treks and rafting arranged with advance notice, cycle hire, open all year, many repeat visitors, good value, Bardia's best budget lodge. **D** *Bardia Rhino Lodge*, no phone, book through Bardia Wildlife Paradise, 9 rooms in solid brick buildings most with bath, restaurant, a long way from the park entrance. **D** *Bardia Wildlife Paradise*, T29715 (Kathmandu T423367, F424031). 5 rooms all common bath, bar, restaurant menu with a huge selection most of which is unavailable. **D** *Elephant Camp*, on the road between the park entrance and Thakurdwara bus stop, had closed down due to a dispute between the owners, may reopen. **D** *Forest Hideaway*, T29716 (Kathmandu T423586). 8 rooms all common bath (hot water available), good restaurant and bar, attractive gardens, quiet location, jeep rides available but overpriced, Nepali-Scottish owned. **D** *Karnali Safari*, T(Nepalgunj) 081-21359, F21738. 6 rooms all common bath, large though absurdly expensive restaurant with cosy central fireplace, pleasant garden with mango trees, but all rather shabby.

E *Racy Shed*, no phone, 6 rooms some with bath in one terraced bungalow (the 'Shed'), small eating area, quiet location surrounded by fields, basic but adequate. **E** *Rhino Express*, no phone, 6 rooms all common bath, dining room, small and friendly.

Air The nearest airport is at Nepulganj. RNAC and Necon Air operate daily flights to/from Kathmandu, US$99. The 1 hour flight has stunning views of the Himalaya as far east as Dhaulagiri and you can clearly see the twin peaks of Macchapuchare. Best seats on the left hand side for northbound flights and on the right hand side on the southbound. If you are on a package tour, your lodge should meet you and provide transport from and to Nepalgunj. If you are going independently, you can either hire one of the waiting jeeps (2 hours, Rs 700) or take a rickshaw to the main bus stop (Rs 25).

Transport

Buses To Bardia: although there are no long distance buses direct to Thakurdwara, all buses running between Nepalgunj and Mahendranagar stop at **Ambasa**, a tiny village with a tea stall but no phone on the Mahendra Highway, 10 kilometres southeast of the Chisapani bridge. From here, you can catch one of the 2 local buses a day (1600 and 1800 dep) for Thakurdwara (11 kilometres, 45 minutes, Rs 10). **NB** The road to Thakurdwara fords a couple of small rivers. During the monsoon, these can become too high to ford, thus effectively isolating Thakurdwara. These local buses originate in **Nepalgunj**, depart at 1145 and 1445, journey time 3-4 hours, Rs 50. There are numerous local buses from **Mahendranagar** to Nepalgunj, get off at Ambasa, journey time up to 6 hours. You could risk one of the lunchtime buses from Mahendranagar to Kathmandu/Birgunj and hope you reach Ambasa before 1800. From **Kathmandu or Pokhara** take either the Mahendranagar or Nepalgunj bus.

Warning Ambasa is prime hunting ground for touts from the various lodges. Some (notably those from Chitwan) have advanced persuasive skills which may include making unrealistic claims and promises. To avoid their prolonged ministrations, you might think about making a reservation by phone in advance: most lodges will readily send someone to meet you at Ambasa.

From Bardia Local buses to Nepalgunj via **Ambasa** leave at 0800 and 1000 daily. There are numerous local buses stopping at Ambasa for **Mahendranagar**, but it may not always be possible to get a seat on an express bus from Ambasa which means you have to change at Nepalgunj. Buses to **Butwal** leave **Kohalpur** (the bus park on the

Mahendra Highway near the junction with the Nepalgunj road) at 1100 and 1200. Buses to **Kathmandu** and **Pokhara** from Nepalgunj.

Directory **Banks** There is no bank at Thakurdwara. Some lodges may accept payment in foreign currency, especially Indian rupees. Authorized money changing facilities at Tiger Tops and, for small amounts, at Bardia Jungle Cottage. The nearest bank is at Nepalgunj. **Communications** The area code for Bardia is 084. Most lodges have a phone with either STD or ISD facilities. **NB** Phoning from Bardia is more expensive than elsewhere. The nearest post office is at Chitkaiya village, 3 kilometres from Thakurdwara. **Hospitals & medical services** Health: There are two small health posts near the Thakurdwara bus stop. These cater principally to local requirements, but can help with minor conditions, eg snake bites. There are a number of foreign NGOs working in the area, so you may be able to find a Western trained nurse. The army camp at the park entrance also has a medical section. The nearest hospital is at Nepalgunj.

Nepalgunj

Population:
47,819 (1991)
Phone code: 081
Colour map 1, grid B2

Nepalgunj is an important regional centre, the hub of a fairly extensive bus and air network, one of Nepal's six approved land border crossings, and in effect functions as a sort of capital of West Nepal. It is not an especially attractive town, though benign, and offers little of general tourist interest. Some travellers stop here *en route* to Bardia or to break the long journey between Kathmandu and the far west of Nepal. With the anticipated opening of trekking routes through northwest Nepal and on to Mount Kailash and Manasarovar in Tibet, the hotels of Nepalgunj are likely to host an increasing number of overnight visitors in the future. It is popular with foreign aid workers based in some of the more remote areas of West Nepal as a place to stock up with food items brought in from Kathmandu.

Surrounded by open countryside, the town spreads out from two long north-south roads, 11 kilometres south of the Mahendra Highway. The centre is dominated by a **bazaar** area of narrow lanes and side streets, at its busiest early in the morning when fruit, vegetables, meat, textiles and other essentials are haggled over. There is a small and unusually neat **industrial estate** on the town's western flank, with a few more light industrial units to the south *en route* to the border. Here rice and edible oils are processed and there are also saw mills. It is the only Terai town where **tongas**, horse drawn passenger carts, are an important form of local transport. Like many of the larger Terai towns, Nepalgunj has a significant **Muslim** population, the result of long established patterns of migration between the Terai and the Indian states of Uttar Pradesh and Bihar.

Nepalgunj

There are several **mosques** in the town and, with only few isolated exceptions, Nepalgunj has a history of communal harmony.

The **Bagheshwari Mandir**, slightly to the south of the main bazaar area, is the **Temples** largest of the town's temples. A modern, three-storeyed concrete structure of lurid pink, it is dedicated to Kali, the goddess of destruction. A small Shiva linga shrine stands in the courtyard. To the west is a large pokhari where a walkway leads to a central shrine also containing an image of Shiva. The **Janaki Mandir** comprises the two traffic islands either side of Tribhuvan Chowk whose shrines attract worship from passers-by. Adjoining the shrines are a couple of music and clothes shops. 400 metres south of Tribhuvan Chowk and next to the main tonga stop is the small **Hanuman Mandir**.

There are several mosques dotted around town, the largest just north of BP **Mosques** Chowk. Friday is the main day of worship for Muslims.

Essentials

Nepalgunj has a fair choice of budget and mid range places to stay. There are also a **Sleeping** few noisy guest houses near the bus park which are, without exception, awful.

C *Batika*, T21360, F22318. 17 rooms all with bath and either a/c or air coolers, large restaurant, bar, TV room. Attractive grounds include a kitchen-garden, owned by the Nepal Airways group, popular with groups but very high tariff for individual travellers. **C** *Sneha*, T/F20119. 20 rooms all with bath some a/c, good restaurant with walls decorated with Tharu village scenes by local artists, bar, camping facilities, a rather neglected tennis court, delightful and well maintained gardens, helpful staff, the best hotel in Nepalgunj. **C-D** *New Hotel Bheri*, T20213. 10 reasonable rooms some with bath, some a/c, no restaurant though basic food on request, friendly enough but overpriced and a leading contender for Nepal's worst value accommodation; avoid.

D *New Hotel Punjabi*, T20818. 16 rooms some with bath, bar/restaurant does good Indian food, the town's most popular budget place, keep ears closed at night. **D** *Pahuna Ghar*, T22358. 25 rooms some with bath, no restaurant but good vegetarian food in room (order in advance), little English spoken, but good value. Recommended. **D** *Vinayak*, T22138. 10 rooms some with bath, TV and air cooler, basic Nepali/Chinese restaurant, pleasant garden at rear but indoors rather gloomy.

E *Janak*, 10 rooms all common bath, basic. **E** *New Nirala*, 6 rooms all common bath, basic and noisy. **E** *Pooja Lodge*, 16 rooms all common bath. **E** *Sagar Guest House*, 10 rooms some with bath, convenient for the bus park. **E** *Shining Star Guest House*, T20664, F20086. 17 rooms some with bath, Nepali eating area, on the main road, noisy. **E** *Star Lodge*, T22257. 40 rooms some with bath, small Nepali dining room, STD/ISD facilities, in the heart of the bazaar area thus noisy.

The Sneha hotel has the best restaurant in Nepalgunj, with the *Batika* a close second. **Eating** Good Indian/Nepali food at the *New Punjabi Hotel*. The *Cold Corner Café*, T22315, at Tribhuvan Chowk does South Indian food (but dosas are served without chutney), chow mein, 'finger chips', etc, and is the only place of its type. Otherwise, Nepalgunj has only *dhabars* and street side food.

The *Annapurna Supermarket*, 100 metres south of Birendra Chowk, has a good selec- **Shopping** tion of Western foods and is useful for last minute purchases if you are about to embark on a trek.

Terai & Churia Hills

Transport **Local** Cycle **rickshaws** are the easiest way of getting around town. **Tongas** run on set routes. The main tonga stop is 400 metres south of Tribhuvan Chowk. The ride to the border takes around 30 minutes, Rs 5. This is not the most comfortable means of travel and the 'driver' will not leave until as many people as possible are squeezed on to the platform. For longer trips, eg to Bardia, you can hire a **jeep** through any travel agent.

Air Nepalgunj is the hub for air services to some of the more remote areas of **West Nepal**. Most of these flights are operated by RNAC. There are daily flights to/from **Kathmandu** with RNAC and Necon Air, US$99. (In good weather, there are superb views of the Himalaya.) The airport is 3 kilometres north of town. The RNAC office is south of BP Chowk (T20239). The Necon Air, T20307 offices are 200 metres north of Birendra Chowk.

Buses Local buses, including those to Mahendranagar and Thakurdwara (for Bardia), leave from the junction of Surkhet Rd and the road leading east to the main bus park. The adjacent booking office is an unmarked wooden stall just outside the *Hotel New Siddharth* (the signboard is in Nepali; see map). Buses to **Mahendranagar** leave at 0430, 0745 and 0930 (at least 6 hours, Rs 165), best to book in advance. Departures to **Thakurdwara** at 1145 and 1445 (3-4 hours, Rs 50). There are two (Sajha) buses to **Kathmandu**, early morning and late afternoon departures (14 hours, Rs 250), but it is essential to book early.

The **Mahendra Highway** leaves Nepalgunj and continues for 188 kilometres east to Butwal. This drive can be very slow if yours is an old bus, as the road climbs through the Churia Hills. To the south is the **Rapti River** (a different Rapti from that at Chitwan) and beyond are the **Dundwa Hills** for 130 kilometres of the trip.

Directory **Banks** Only the large *Nepal Rastra Bank*, T20227, at Birendra Chowk deals in foreign exchange, TCs and currency. Open 1000-1430 Sun-Thur, 1000-1200 Fri, closed Sat. **Communications Area code**: The area code for Nepalgunj is 081. There are several STD/ISD booths and fax bureaux throughout the town. **Post Office**: The main post office is in the southern part of town, near the hospital. **Hospitals & medical services Health**: The Bheri Zonal Hospital is the largest hospital in southwest Nepal. It has limited emergency facilities. There are numerous pharmacies thoughout the town, prescriptions are not required.

Crossing into India

Leaving Nepal The border lies at **Jamunaha**, five kilometres south of Nepalgunj along a quiet road that cuts through the wide, open tracts of Terai agricultural land. A large arched gate, topped by a miniature pagoda, marks the Nepali frontier and, like all of the country's other land crossings, there is a 'Welcome to Nepal' sign sponsored by a major international soft drinks producer. There is a small temple close to the border as well as a tea stall, a couple of shops selling snacks and drinks, and an STD/ISD phone booth.

At the border **Immigration** This border sees an average of around 700 Western tourist arrivals and departures per year. Nepali Customs and Immigration are about one kilometre inside the border and are open from 0600-2000, though you can get through if you arrive later – ring the bell for assistance. The Indian border is open 24 hours. Formalities are straightforward.

Transport There are usually numerous rickshaws (Rs 15) and tongas (Rs 5) waiting to return to the town centre.

Nambai Bazaar

This small market town on the Mahendra Highway midway between *Colour map 1, grid B2* Nepalgunj and Butwal is a popular tea stop for long distance buses. In addition to the usual peanut and sliced fruit wallahs, there are curiously many vendors of lassi-by-the-glass. The road heading south at the main intersection leads across the Indian border at **Koilabas** and continues south towards Faizabad and Ayodhya. The border is not open to foreigners. Tourists rarely stay here as there is little reason to do so, but there are couple of basic places to stay, including **D-E** *Bhushal Guest House*, Gyanali and, the best of a poor lot, *Lamjung Hotel* with 9 rooms and a restaurant. All are on the main highway, with the bazaar area spreading out to the south.

Central Terai

Flanked by the two most popular crossings to India, the Royal Chitwan National Park maintains its deserved reputation as one of Nepal's most popular tourist attractions. Road access to Pokhara and Kathmandu is good (if a little slow). The Tribhuvan Highway ducks and weaves across the Churai Hills covering 32 kilometres as the crow flies in 107 kilometres! The view from Daman across the valley to the high Himalaya is truly uplifting. Further west, Lumbini, the birthplace of Buddha, is a very important religious site.

Butwal

Population: 44,272
Colour map 1, grid B3

Butwal is one of the Terai's most important crossroads. Equidistant from Tansen and the Sunauli border with easy connections to Lumbini, it is the gateway to West Nepal and lies within a day's bus journey of both Pokhara and Kathmandu. In the early 1950s, Butwal was little more than a village on the west bank of the **Tilottama River** in the shadow of the Churia Hills. With the construction of the Mahendra and Siddhartha Highways, however, it grew rapidly (1991) and most of the town now spreads unprepossessingly to the east and southeast of the river, a product of the laissez-faire growth that increasingly typifies many South Asian towns and cities. The main area with all the town's accommodation lies to the north of **Hospital Chowk**. The Siddhartha Highway continues south from here to Bhairahawa and the border. The innovatively named **Traffic Chowk** is a busy intersection on the Siddhartha Highway and the stop for long distance buses passing through Butwal.

Butwal's main claim to fame is as the site where what was thought to have been the oldest known humanoid bone was discovered in the 1960s. The fossilized bone was of the *Ramapithecus genus* of ape which inhabited the areas around the Indus and Ganges plains between 25 and 10 million years ago. Butwal shares a proud history with Tansen as one of the last territories in central western Nepal to fall to the Gorkhas. The **Sen** dynasty that had ruled from Palpa (Tansen) ended when King Mahadutta Sen, son of King Mani Mukunda Sen, was lured to Kathmandu by Rana Bahadur Shah on the pretext of mutually beneficial discussions, but was arrested upon arrival in the capital and imprisoned. On hearing the news Mahadutta's son and heir, Ratna Sen, fled to Gorakhpur (at that time a part of Nepal and later ceded to British India) where he died without issue.

There are plans to establish a park at **Phulbari**, on the west bank of the Tilottama, on the 10 acre site of the ruins of King Mani Mukunda Sen's

Central Terai

NEPAL
Pokhara
Butwal Tansen
Narayanghat KATHMANDU
Lumbini Bhairahawa Chitwan Daman
National Park Hetauda
Sunauli Amlekhganj
(Belahiya)
Birgunj
Gorakhpur Raxaul Bazaar Janakpur
N Jaleshwar
INDIA
0 km 50
0 miles 31

winter palace. There is an oral tradition, reaffirmed by the town's oldest resident before his death in 1995 aged 98, that there exists an underground tunnel connecting the winter palace with the fort of **Jit Ghar**, also on the west bank of the Tilottama, and with another of Mukunda's forts on **Nuwakot Hill**, eight kilometres west of Butwal. No archaeological investigations to verify the existence of what would have been a major feat of engineering have as yet been undertaken.

Sights Other than its role as a convenient place to rest after a long bus journey, there are few compelling reasons to visit Butwal. There are a couple of minor **temples** in the area north of Hospital Chowk. A small though eyecatching Buddhist **chaitya** on Amar Path is painted as a lotus and has carved images of the Buddha set into the harmika. Some 200 metres south of Traffic Chowk is the **Durga Panchyan Mandir**, dedicated to Durga in the company of four other gods (*panch*, 'five'). The three-storeyed concrete temple contains a huge and lavishly decorated central image of Durga surrounded by smaller representations of Vishnu, Shiva, Ganesh and Surya. There is a small **park** at the northern end of town.

Walks The forested hills around Butwal offer some short, unguided walking opportunities if you find yourself stuck here for any length of time – try heading east from Hospital Chowk. There is a longer excursion to the ruins of King Mani

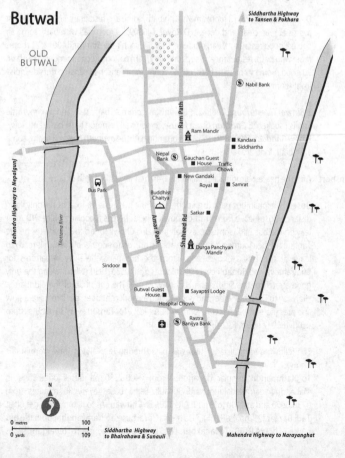

Butwal

Siddhartha Highway
to Tansen & Pokhara

OLD
BUTWAL

Terai & Churia Hills

Mahendra Highway to Nepalganj

Tilottama River

(S) Nabil Bank

Ram Path

Ram Mandir

■ Kandara
■ Siddhartha

Nepal
Bank (S) Gauchan Guest
House ■ Traffic
Chowk

Bus Park

■ New Gandaki

Royal ■ ■ Samrat

Buddhist
Chaitya

Amar Path

Shaheed Rd

Satkar ■

Durga Panchyan
Mandir

Sindoor ■

Butwal Guest
House ■ Sayaptri Lodge

Hospital Chowk

Rastra
(S) Banijya Bank

N

0 metres   100
0 yards   109

Siddhartha Highway
to Bhairahawa & Sunauli

Mahendra Highway to Narayanghat

Mukunda Sen's fort on **Nuwakot Hill**, eight kilometres to the west of Butwal, from where there are also some good mountain views, including of Macchapuchare. From the bridge, allow at least four hours to walk up. A guide is essential – enquire at your hotel. Another option is **Satyawati Tal**, an attractive lake in the hills between Butwal and Tansen. A candle-lit festival attracts pilgrims each October/November when the goddess Satyawati is worshipped with songs and dances throughout the night. *Getting there*: involves a six kilometres bus journey along the Siddhartha Highway to **Jumsa**, followed by a three and a half-hour walk in each direction. Again, a guide is essential.

Essentials

Sleeping & Butwal has a reasonable selection of budget accommodation, the better places also
eating having Butwal's only decent restaurants.

C-D *Siddhartha*, T40380, F40733, 16 rooms all with bath, some a/c, good restaurant and bar, clean, smart and convenient for Traffic Chowk, best rooms at rear. Recommended. **C-D** *Sindoor*, T40381, F40146, 15 comfortable rooms all with bath, some a/c, large restaurant does Indian and reasonable continental food, bar, ISD/STD and foreign exchange facilities, tours to Lumbini arranged, reasonably priced if booking direct, Mastercard/Visa accepted. Recommended.

D *Kandara*, T40175, 13 rooms most with bath, some a/c, restaurant and bar, quietest rooms at rear, clean and decent. **D** *Royal*, T40509, 19 rooms all with bath, some air cooled, good restaurant, bar, modern, STD/ISD, car hire. **D** *Samrat*, T40012, 21 rooms most with bath, restaurant and separate ice cream parlour. Recommended. **D** *Satkar*, 20 good rooms some with bath, dining room, local Tansen buses stop outside, noisy front rooms.

E *Butwal Guest House*, T40532, 11 rooms all common bath, dark and gloomy, little English spoken. **E** *Gauchan Guest House*, 5 rooms all common bath, basic and noisy. **E** *New Gandaki*, T40928, 8 rooms all common bath. **E** *Sayapatri Lodge*, 8 rooms some with bath, food available.

Transport **Air** The nearest airport is at Bhairahawa, 40 minutes drive south of Butwal.

Buses The main bus park, just southeast of the bridge, is for local buses only; long distance buses leave from **Traffic Chowk** where there is a booking office. **NB** After leaving the bus park, some buses wait at Traffic Chowk for up to 30 minutes before continuing their journey. You may be able to hop on to another bus which is ready to leave at the Traffic Chowk stop. From the bus park, there are departures for **Bhairahawa** and **Sunauli** every 20 minutes from 0530-1930 (1 hour along the only good stretch of the Siddhartha Highway, Rs 10). The condition of the Siddhartha Highway to Tansen and beyond is improving as work continues, but it remains a slow and precarious, though scenic, journey. Buses leave for **Tansen** every 30 minutes from 0600-1800 (2 hours, Rs 20).

The following long distance buses all pass through Butwal and leave from Traffic Chowk:
To **Kathmandu**: regular departures from 0400-2330 on buses originating in Mahendranagar, Nepalgunj and Sunauli. Sajha buses every 30 minutes from 0730-0900 and at 1100 (6-8 hours, Rs 120). To **Chitwan** As to Kathmandu, get off at Tadi Bazaar (2½ hours, Rs 65). Also regular local buses to **Narayanghat** from the bus park (3-4 hours, Rs 50). To **Janakpur**: 4 or 5 buses a day (8 hours). To **Nepalgunj**: buses

throughout the day (5-6 hours, Rs 100). To **Pokhara**: most take the longer route via **Mugling**. The journey time (5-6 hours) is the same as along the Siddhartha Highway, though the latter should reduce by 2 hours when the road is completed. Several morning buses (Rs 80 via Tansen, Rs 110 via Mugling) and evening departures (via Mugling only, Rs 120, last bus 2100).

Banks Only the *Nabil Bank*, T41059, on the Siddhartha Highway at the northern end of town deals in foreign exchange. TCs, currency and credit card advances. **Communications** Area **code:** the area code for Butwal is 071. Numerous STD/ISD booths throughout the town. Hospitals & medical services The hospital is just south of Hospital Chowk. **Directory**

Bhairahawa and Sunauli (Belahiya)

The towns of Bhairahawa and Sunauli (Belahiya) are virtually linked and are usually visited only by people crossing the border or by those visiting Lumbini. Jeeps and rickshaws provide easy and regular transport between the two. If you are spending a night here, Bhairahawa is the better place to stay.

Pronounced *Bhy-rawa* and formerly called **Bethari** (now a village five kilometres to the west), the town is also known by its other name of **Siddharthanagar**. It is a laid back, functional industrial and market town that caters to Lumbini tourists and those crossing the border, but with really nothing else of note. There are a number of shops selling imported Western goods, mostly to Indians, and Bhairahawa has a better selection of quality accommodation and eating places than Sunauli. There is also a cinema just north of the main intersection showing exclusively 'Bollywood' films. It has some light industrial units in the surrounding areas, including a distillery and several food processing mills.

Bhairahawa
Population: 39,473
Phone code: 071
Colour map 1, grid B3

Terai & Churia Hills

Sleeping B *Nirvana*, T/F20837 (in Kathmandu T225370, F270048). 40 comfortable rooms, average restaurant, bar, swimming pool, Japanese steam bath house (Ofura), the best hotel in the area, popular with Japanese visitors to Lumbini, 2 kilometres

Bhairahawa

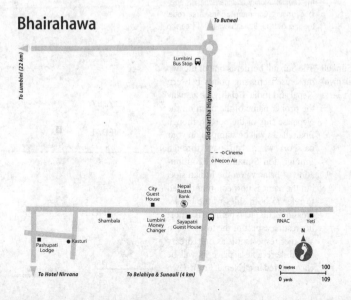

southwest of the main intersection. **C** *Yeti*, T20551, F20456. 18 rooms all with bath some a/c, some better value non a/c rooms, reasonable restaurant, bar, central. Recommended. **D** *Shambala*, T21837, F20961. 15 rooms all with bath, restaurant and bar, a good budget place. **E** *City Guest House*, 6 rooms all common bath, next to Rastra Bank. **E** *Pashupati Lodge*, T20139. 10 rooms some with bath, cheap dormitory beds, food available. **E** *Sayapatri Guest House*, 6 rooms some with bath, central but noisy location.

Eating The *Kasturi Restaurant*, T20680, southwest of the main intersection. Does some of the best Indian food in town, including tandoori. Try also the *Yeti Hotel's* restaurant. The *Nirvana Hotel* has a pleasant restaurant, but the food is unexceptional and service is extremely slow.

Transport Local (See also Sunauli, below.) The best way to get between Bhairahawa and **Sunauli (Belahiya)** (4 kilometres) is by shared jeep or tempo (both Rs 5) which depart from the main intersection. Cycle rickshaws are also available, but take longer and cost more. **Air**: The airport is 10 kilometres north of Bhairahawa and there are daily flights to **Kathmandu**. Necon Air (T21244) and RNAC (T20125) all have offices in Bhairahawa. **Road Bus**: most long distance buses leave from Sunauli (Belahiya). To **Lumbini**: buses leave regularly for Lumbini (22 kilometres, 1½ hours, Rs 18). Alternatively, you could hire a jeep for around Rs 400 after negotiation, but make sure that the price allows for a reasonable waiting time (minimum 2 hours).

Directory Banks A large branch of *Nepal Rastra Bank* deals in foreign exchange, just west of the main intersection, open 1000-1430 Sun-Thur, 1000-1200 Fri, closed Sat; opposite is the *Lumbini Money Changer* which is open longer hours. **Communications** Area code: the area code for **Bhairahawa** is 071 (see also below).

Sunauli (Belahiya)

Colour map 1, grid B3

The Sunauli border is one of the two most used crossing points between Nepal and India. **Belahiya** is actually the proper name of the town on the Nepalese side of the border, though Bhairahawa will be stamped on your passport when you pass through Immigration. **Sunauli** is the continuation of Belahiya on the Indian side, but the name is now commonly used to refer to both sides of the border crossing. This fact is perhaps the most interesting aspect of the town, for in all other respects it is as dull, dreary and disagreeable a place as will be encountered in all Nepal. From dawn

Sunauli (Belahiya)

To Bhairahawa (4 km)

Siddhartha Highway

Mamta

Long Distance
Bus Arrivals

Zorba the Buddhist

New Buddha
New Cottage Lodge
Nepal Guest House

Deep

Jay Vijay
Tanahun

Mukti Lodge

Bus Park

Jeep, Tempo &
Rickshaw Stand
for Bhairahawa

Money Exchange Counter
Paradise

City Money Changer

BELAHIYA

NEPAL

Nepal Customs   Nepal Immigration
Indian Customs   Indian Immigration

SUNAULI

INDIA

N

Niranjana

0 metres   150
0 yards   164

*To Gorakhpur
(90-100 km approx)*

to dusk lorries wait impatiently to complete the paperwork that allows the long bamboo barriers to lift, drivers periodically revving their engines in frustration to release dark clouds of gaseous effluent into the air or directly into the lungs of a passing pedestrian (human or bovine), while cycle rickshaws weave their ringing way through the stationary queues of vehicles, competing for a little business with the ranks of jeeps and tempos; and local hotel touts hover like hungry hawks awaiting the arrival of another bus load of tourists from Pokhara, Kathmandu, Sauraha and elsewhere for whom a night here is about to become an unavoidable blip in their schedule.

Sleeping E *Deep*, T20281. 10 rooms some with bath, small restaurant. E *Jay Vijay*, T20918. 20 rooms most with bath, STD/ISD facilities. E *Mamta*, T20312. 12 rooms most with bath, restaurant, brighter and more spacious than most. E *Mandro*, T20877. 2 clean rooms next to Nepal Guest House. E *Mukti Lodge*, T20405. 15 rooms all with bath (first floor rooms are the least bad), dormitory, dining room. E *Nepal Guest House*, T20877. 34 rooms some with bath, small rooftop restaurant, one of the better places to stay. E *New Buddha*, T20758. 20 cell-like rooms most with bath, small outdoor eating area, dark and seedy. E *New Cottage Lodge*. 11 rooms some with bath, small dining room with a valiant attempt at a good menu. E *Paradise*, 11 rooms all with bath, food available, STD/ISD facilities, inappropriately named. E *Tanahun*, T21995. 22 rooms some with bath, dining room.

Eating Only the *Nepal Guest House* offers anything like reasonable food and has a shop selling biscuits, cold drinks, mineral water and ready packed snack foods at the entrance. The *Zorba The Buddha* restaurant has an extensive menu most of which is unavailable, and is noteworthy more for its extraordinary name than for its fare.

Transport You can buy through-tickets to any destination in India from Kathmandu and Pokhara as well as at Sunauli (Belahiya) itself. These usually involve having to pick up an onward ticket at an intermediate point, an arrangement which offers considerable scope for cheating (see box). All buses leave from the main bus park. There are regular early morning and evening departures, including Sajha buses, to both **Kathmandu** and **Pokhara** (8-10 hours, Rs 150). You can also take either of these buses for **Chitwan** (4 hours, Rs 80), change at **Narayanghat** for local bus to **Tadi Bazaar**.

Directory Banks The nearest bank is in Bhairahawa, but Sunauli (Belahiya) has several authorized foreign exchange places. Knowing that foreign tourists may be unaware of this, some money changers in Sunauli (Belahiya) have been known to off-load quantities of 'reject' notes to tourists, often sandwiched in the midst of a large wad of notes. These may be notes that the dealer himself has unwittingly received or even passed on, but it is also known that damaged notes are available for purchase at less than their face value and, therefore, if unscrupulous dealers are subsequently able to sell them at their full face value, a further profit is made. The *Lumbini Money Changer* at the New Buddha Hotel is a particularly bad offender. **Communications** Area code: the area code for Sunauli (Belahiya) is 071. There are a couple of STD/ISD booths. Except for calls to places in Nepal, it is considerably cheaper to phone (within India and international) from India. If you can persuade both the Nepali and Indian border posts to let you through temporarily without going through the required formalities, there is an STD/ISD booth just after you cross into India.

Crossing into India

The border is immediately adjacent to the built up area of Sunauli. On either side of the road is open countryside. On the Nepal side there is a helpful **tourist office** which has a limited supply of handouts but can help with local information.

Terai & Churia Hills

Through-ticketing: a traveller's woe

"Having booked my bus and train ticket from Sunauli to Calcutta via Gorakhpur, I was given a completed 'Reservation Service' form which I was to hand to the travel agent's so-called 'head office' (Lumbini Travels) on arrival in Gorakhpur in exchange for the train ticket. Lumbini Travels, it transpired, operated from a single room in a down-market hotel near the station. They took the 'reservation service' form, but said that they did not yet have the ticket. I was made to wait for three hours in the corridor along with another traveller waiting to go to Mumbai (Bombay), while the two employees sat in their office and did nothing. Then, 20 minutes before my train's scheduled departure, I was informed that the confirmation had still not come through, that the train was fully booked with no seats available for at least a fortnight.

Before I could protest, the man suggested (with rehearsed inspiration) that perhaps a small amount of baksheesh may secure a last minute reservation, say around Rs 250. At this late stage, he added, it was important to make a decision quickly. I truthfully informed him that baksheesh for this purpose had already been paid to the Sunauli travel agent, but he denied all knowledge of this and suggested that if I was not willing to part with this 'modest' amount, perhaps I would like to return to Nepal and sort the matter out there. Time was ticking by, he reminded me with choreographic precision. So I had no choice but to pay the extra. I left for the station relieved to have a reservation, angry at having allowed myself to have been so manipulated, and wondering how much the traveller hoping to leave for Mumbai in seven hours would be asked to pay."

At the border **Immigration** Formalities are straightforward, though the Indian immigration office has been known to be pedantic in checking visas. It is possible to cross at any time, but you will have to knock and wake the various officials after 2200.

Onward to India There is one reasonable hotel in Indian Sunauli, the UP government run **D** *Hotel Niranjana* which also has a café-style restaurant. The next town in India is Nautanwa, 12 kilometres south. There are regular buses from Sunauli to Gorakhpur. Into India there are day and night buses from Sunauli to Varanasi (0830, 2030 and 2100 dep, 9 hours, Indian Rs 100), and day buses leaving every 30 minutes for Gorakhpur (3 hours, Rs 40) which has train connections to most major destinations in India. There is also a train station at Nautanwa (12 kilometres south of Sunauli) with services to Gorakhpur. (From Nautanwa: train No 96, dep 0910, 2¼ hours; and train No 94, dep 1700, 3¼ hours. From Gorakhpur: train No 95, dep 0615, 2¼ hours; and train No 93, dep 1230, 3¼ hours.) If you leave Gorakhpur after 1400, you will arrive at Sunauli after 1700 and will probably do better to stay overnight on the Indian side in order to maximize Visa days in Nepal.

Lumbini

Colour map 1, grid B3 Buddhist scriptures describe how the Great Maya (deified as Maya Devi), the Buddha's mother, dreamt of a white elephant representing the reincarnation of Buddha into her womb and experienced a pregnancy free from all 'fatigues, depressions and fancies'. When the time came for her to give birth, 'she set her heart on going to Lumbini, a delightful grove with trees of every kind, like the grove of Citraratha in Indra's Paradise'.

The birth of the Buddha, Gautama Siddhartha, in about 563 BC (sources differ) in Lumbini is the best known single event in the history of the Terai, and has had a significant impact on the culture not only of Nepal but on much of Asia and increasingly elsewhere. The Chinese traveller Fa-Hien described the ruins at Lumbini in the 4th century AD, and his compatriot Hiuen Tsang visited the site two centuries later. The ancient Ashokan pillar was not discovered until 1895 by the German archaeologist Alois Führer.

Lumbini today is an unexpectedly tranquil site where ground level archaeological excavations coexist with modern places of worship. Despite the presence of a couple of hotels in the vicinity, the area is relatively untouristed. If you have just entered or are leaving Nepal through Sunauli, an excursion to Lumbini is a good way to break the long journey to or from the major tourist centres. It is easily accessible from Bhairahawa and Sunauli from where you can do a general tour of the site in half a day.

Visiting Lumbini

This small complex lies at the southern end of Lumbini. It marks the place where the Buddha is reputed to have been born and contains all of the area's important historical monuments and archaeological finds.

Sacred Garden

Sections of the **Maya Devi Mandir** are believed to date as far back as the 3rd or 4th century BC, though much of the structure consists of later additions. The temple contained a stone **bas relief** illustrating the Buddha's nativity. It is thought to date from the Malla period, and shows Maya, the largest of the figures, clutching the branch of a tree with the baby Gautama Siddhartha standing at her feet, right arm raised and a halo around his head. Three attendants assist Maya, while groups of celestial beings observe from afar. The original carving is very worn and was removed to a nearby protected location, but a 1950s marble replica by the Nepali sculptor Chandra Man Maskey is the focus for devotees' worship.

In the early 1990s, archaeologists began disassembling the temple brick by brick and relocating it as a result both of its gradual destruction by the roots of a large peepul tree which was itself cut down and beneath which the Buddha was believed to have been born, and because they believed that the original structure was built on top of a still more important site. Excavations continued with great care until 1996 when the experts' predictions and beliefs were vindicated in the most significant of recent finds. At a depth of some five metres and three layers below the original temple, they discovered a series of rooms and a

Lumbini master plan

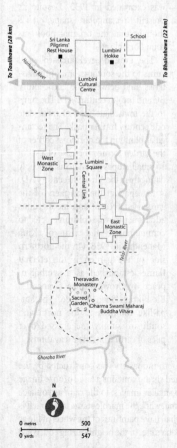

To Taulihawa (28 km)

Horhowa River

Sri Lanka Pilgrims' Rest House

Lumbini Hokke

School

To Bhairahawa (22 km)

Lumbini Cultural Centre

West Monastic Zone

Lumbini Square

Central Link

East Monastic Zone

Telar River

Theravadin Monastery

Sacred Garden

Dharma Swami Maharaj Buddha Vihara

Ghoraha River

N

0 metres 500
0 yards 547

stone slab which is now believed to mark the exact location at which the Buddha was born.

The **peepul tree** that was cut down was almost certainly not the one below which Maya Devi gave birth; the original (considered by some to have been sal) may have survived into the 6th or 7th century AD. Another large peepul tree remains nearby and is honoured by proxy with a number of garlands and prayer flags.

The **Ashokan pillar**, now enclosed by metal railings and bound by metal rings following damage caused by lightning, has a circumference of 2.78 metres and stands at 7.79 metres, though a large section is below ground. It was erected by the greatest of the Mauryan emperors, Ashoka, in 250 BC, 'in the 20th year of his reign'. The inscription is in the Brahmi script and Prakrit language and declares that he made "the village free of taxes and a recipient of wealth". The pillar is Nepal's oldest known monument. As well as marking the extent of his Mauryan empire, Ashoka's inscribed edicts are of unique historical value as amongst the earliest written sources in a region where history and culture were either transmitted orally or were recorded on materials that were unable to withstand the rigours of the climate.

The **Pushkarni** is the pool in which Maya Devi is believed to have bathed prior to giving birth and where the infant Buddha was given his first bath. Terraced steps lead down to the water. It was excavated in 1933. Despite its present rectangular shape, it is thought that the original pool was round or oblong.

The Sacred Garden

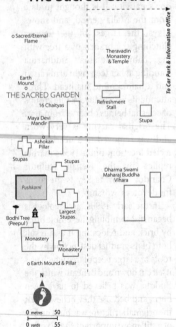

The ground level archaeological **ruins** to the southeast are of monasteries built between the 2nd century BC and the 4th century AD. The ruins to the immediate west of these date one century further back. The rectangular plinth in the northeast corner of the garden formed the base of a set of 16 small stupas or chaityas probably dating from the 8th or 9th century AD.

Set apart at the periphery of the garden is a recent and incongruous addition, a marble **column** erected to commemorate the visit of King Mahendra in 1956. On the northern side of the garden is the **eternal flame**, established as a symbol of peace by Crown Prince Gyanendra Bir Bikram Shah in 1986. The stupa-like **mounds** to the north and south are simply the grassed over piles of earth from the excavations.

Theravadin Monastery Opposite the sacred garden, this modern monastery was constructed by the Government of Nepal. The open arched shrine contains a large bronze image of the Buddha. This is flanked by two smaller images: to the right as you face the shrine is another bronze from Burma, while the marble statue to your left is from Thailand. The walls of the main hall have paintings of the wheel of life as well as depictions of scenes of the Buddha's life. In the neighbouring courtyard are two chaityas, one of which is sacred to the memory of Dharmlok Mahasthavir (d. 1967), a leading campaigner for the restoration of Lumbini. Visitors are allowed into the shrine room, a very peaceful place.

Dharma Swami Maharaj Buddha Vihara

Near the Theravadin Monastery, this Tibetan Mahayana *vihara* was built in 1968 by either (sources differ) the Raja of Mustang or by the well known teacher Chogya Trichen Rinpoche. Popular with Tibetan pilgrims, it has a central image of the Buddha along with numerous smaller representations and other Buddhist artwork. It is home to between 30 and 50 monks.

Lumbini Development Project

The restoration of Lumbini which began in 1895 with Alois Führer received a huge boost in 1967 when the then UN Secretary General, U Thant from Burma, visited Lumbini and inaugurated the Lumbini Development Project. Some 13 countries, including Korea, Japan, India and the USA, contributed to the formulation of a Master Plan under Professor Kenzo Tange, a Japanese architect. The objectives of the plan include development and restoration of the **sacred garden**, the creation of a **monastic zone** and of the '**Lumbini Village**' to provide accommodation and facilities for visitors as well as a Visitors' Centre.

Pipeline plans have become a pipeline reality with the construction of a **museum** and **research centre**, a 420 seat **auditorium** and a **library**, all dedicated to advancing Buddhist learning and practice. All have been built in the same unusual and unmistakable style, like huge concrete tubes stacked beside and on top of each other.

Essentials

Sleeping

It is possible to stay overnight at Lumbini, though most visitors make day trips from Bhairahawa. Both the monasteries described above have *dharamsalas*, though these are meant for Buddhist pilgrims and are extremely basic. More hotels and guest houses are planned for the future. The following are both located 2-3 kilometres northeast of the sacred garden.

A *Lumbini Hokke*, T/F20236. 27 rooms most in Japanese style, restaurant (spotlessly clean kitchen), bar with karaoke, Japanese bath house.

E *Sri Lanka Pilgrims' Rest House*, T20009 (in Butwal T40381, F40146). Over 100 beds, very basic accommodation for the dedicated, food available.

Eating

The *Lumbini Garden Restaurant*, T20815. Opposite the sacred garden and does expensive continental and Indian food. It also has a souvenir shop.

Transport

See Bhairahawa. Buses to/from Bhairahawa stop 1 kilometre north of the sacred garden at the junction with the main road. Check the time of the last bus on your way there.

Around Lumbini

There are a few possible excursions from the Lumbini area to places of historical interest. To visit any of these, it is best to hire a jeep from Bhairahawa.

Leaving Lumbini to the west you reach **Taulihawa**, a busy little market town, after 21 kilometres. The remains of an early pokhari and of four mounds with possible religious significance were discovered at **Kudan**, two kilometres southwest of Taulihawa. Another three kilometres to the southwest is the village of

Gotihawa where the broken remains of an Ashokan pillar remain and which has a large stupa made of bricks believed to date from the third or fourth century BC.

Some three kilometres to the north of Taulihawa is **Tilaurakot**, a small village containing ruins of a fort, a monastery and a stupa, which were possibly part of the ancient town of Kapilvastu. Archaeological investigations have shown **Kapilvastu** to have been a walled city which may have had a well developed culture. It is thought to have been the capital of the Sakya kingdom, from whose royal lineage Gautauma Siddhartha was born and where he lived before embarking upon his search for enlightenment. Just north of Tilaurakot at **Chatradei** are ruins of a medieval settlement where pottery, Sakya coins and other artefacts have been found.

Continuing north, other major sites have been discovered by archaeologists at **Niglihawa** (or Niglisagar). These include two pillars related to Ashoka. The first is not thought to have been placed by Ashoka himself and predates the other and Lumbini's famous pillar by six years. 'Om mani padme hum' is inscribed in the Devanagri script and bears the image of two peacocks. The other has an inscription in Ashoka's more familiar Brahmi script and Prakrit language and refers to a second enlargement of the Kanaka Muni stupa at the emperor's behest. Another four kilometres to the north, in the **Sagarhawa** forest, are the ruins of a Sakya tank, first uncovered by Alois Führer.

The Siddhartha Highway

The Siddhartha Highway (or *Rajmarg*) links Pokhara with Bhairahawa and Sunauli. It leaves Pokhara through the Churia Hills and continues a meandering, undulating path south. Although picturesque for much of the way, the road is for the most part narrow and extremely rough, so much so that most buses running between Butwal and Pokhara take the longer route via Narayanghat and Mugling. From the small village of Syangja, the highway follows the Andhi Khola River valley for about 50 kilometres before it crosses the marvellous Kali Gandaki and snakes its way, often precariously, down towards Tansen. Some 15 kilometres beyond Tansen, it runs alongside the Tilottama

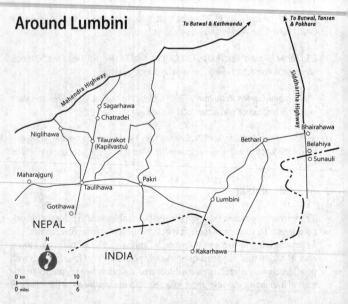

Around Lumbini

River for the remainder of its journey through the Churias. It meets the Terai at Butwal, 158 kilometres south of Pokhara, and continues for 24 kilometres to Bhairahawa along the only well made section of its route.

Tansen (Palpa)

Spread out on a Churia hillside at 1,371 metres, Tansen is something of a rough diamond. Picturesque though not especially pretty, it is one of the most typically Nepali towns on the tourist circuit where Hindu temples, Buddhist shrines and even a mosque coexist easily in a timeless urban setting surrounded by hills and valleys.

Phone code: 075
Colour map 2, grid C1

Tansen is the administrative headquarters of the district of Palpa. It is itself often referred to as **Palpa**, and its people as Palpalis. Until the late 18th century it was the capital of the Sen kingdom, one of the many autonomous regions which made up Nepal before its political unification under the Gorkhas. Indeed, Palpa is renowned as the last kingdom to fall to the Gorkhas, not relinquishing its independence until 1806. Even then it required deceitful means to lure King Mahadutta Sen to Kathmandu where he was arrested, imprisoned and subsequently executed.

The town lies on a small, oval shaped plateau and centres around a former Rana palace, now the seat of local bureaucracy. The surrounding cobbled streets are the focus for the town's commercial activity, notably the production and sale of *dhaka* cloth. Of woven cotton or muslin, this cloth is characterized by jagged, linear designs originally made famous by weavers in Dhaka (or Dacca), Bangladesh (formerly East Bengal, East Pakistan). With principal colours of red, black and white, the cloth is used to make saris as well as *topis* ('Palpali topi'), the hat that is an integral part of the national dress for men. The town is also known for its *Palpali Koruwa*, a brass water jug. You can find these on sale for between Rs 200-500 in shops throughout Tansen.

Forested slopes to the north lead to **Srinagar Hill** from where there are excellent views to all sides. One of the finest views is of the **Mardiphant** valley to the north. See it first thing on a winter morning when it is draped in a thick silvery layer of mist, giving rise to its other name of **Seto Tal** ('White Lake'). There are also a couple of excellent walks from Tansen – see below.

Birendra Phulbari The southwest corner of the **Tundhikhel** is marked by a statue of King Birendra, complete with painted black jacket, *topi* and spectacles. The statue stands on a marble lotus plinth in the shade of a large tree. The surrounding garden (*phulbari*, 'flower garden') contains more than 150 varieties of rose.

Sights

Amar Narayan Mandir This fine three-storeyed Vaishnavite temple was built by Amar Singh Thapa in 1807 and is the oldest and best known of Tansen's temples. Surrounded by a broad stone wall ('the great wall of Tansen'), the roofs are tiled and are supported by struts beautifully carved with images of various deities. There is also some magnificent woodwork on the ground floor. The shrine houses an image of Mahadev and to one side is a natural spring. Daily worship takes place in the early morning and evening.

Immediately to the southwest is another, smaller temple, the **Shankar Mandir**. It is in a sad state of disrepair, with numerous tufts of grass growing from its single roof, but it also has some finely carved woodwork and must have looked beautiful once.

Around Mul Dhoka Built by Khadgar Shamsher Rana as a pilgrims' rest place, the **Shitalpati** is a white pavilion in the centre of the roundabout north of the Tansen Durbar. The originally octagonal structure functions as a local meeting point where men and women sit in casual conversation, with a cigarette or glass of tea, to pass the time of day. The road heading north from Shitalpati leads to Tansen's largest mosque which also serves as the main mosque in the Palpa district.

Mul Dhoka (or **Baggi Dhoka**) is the main gate to the Tansen Durbar, a huge white arch said to be the largest of its kind in Nepal and big enough for elephants to pass through with their mounts. There are lion pillars on either side and, facing the gate, you will see a fantastically carved window on the building to the left, a reminder of the Newari craftsmanship imported from the Kathmandu Valley and which has flourished in this region since the late Middle Ages.

Bhimsen Mandir, the small two-storeyed pagoda temple immediately to the west of Mul Dhoka, has a tiled roof with an attractive copper engraved torana above the shrine entrance.

Tansen Durbar This severe looking red brick building was constructed by Pratap Shamsher Jung Bahadur Rana in 1927 as the local seat of Rana rule. With restoration of effective monarchy in 1951, the palace became the centre of the regional bureaucracy.

Bhagawati Mandir Just to the north of the Durbar, this small temple was built by Ujir Singh Thapa in 1814 to commemorate the Nepali victory over the invading British forces. The event is celebrated by a festival every August when a

Tansen (Palpa)

Terai & Churia Hills

■ **Sleeping**

1 Bajra	5 Lumbini Rest House	9 Srinagar
2 Dhawalagiri	6 New Hotel Siddhartha	10 White lake
3 Gauri Shankar Guest House	7 Pawan Guest House	11 White Lake Guest House
4 Gautam Siddhartha	8 Sherchan	

0 metres 200
0 yards 218

procession parades its deities through the town. It was badly damaged in the 1934 earthquake and several renovations have left it smaller than its original size.

Tansen has a number of Buddhist shrines and monasteries. The best known is the **Ananda Vihara**, near the bus park. It is the oldest monastery in West Nepal, its main chaitya having been built by Sunder Sakya in 1806. It contains images of the 'Panch Buddha' ('five Buddhas') and two more of the Buddha himself, though all are later additions. The **Shree Mahaboddhi Vihara** is a modern Buddhist monastery where occasional meditation courses are held. The **Mahachaitya Vihara**, at Taskar Tole in the northwest of town, was built just before the Second World War and has a number of bronze statues and other Buddhist objets d'art.

Buddhist sites

Essentials

B-C *Srinigar*, T20045, F20467. 26 rooms, restaurant, deals mostly with package groups and is expensive for individual guests, good views.

Sleeping

C *The White Lake Hotel*, T20291, F20467. 11 rooms all with bath, best rooms on north side, good restaurant for continental, Nepali and Chinese food, small conference hall, travel agent and car hire available, clean, modern. Recommended.

D-E *The Bajra*, T20443. 12 rooms all with bath, food on request, useful shop in the entrance, packaged snack foods, mineral water, etc. Recommended. **D-E** *Gauri Shankar*, T20150. 8 rooms some with bath, Nepali dining room, dark. **D-E** *Gautam Siddhartha*, T20280. 10 rooms some with bath, small Nepali dining room. **D-E** *New Siddhartha*, T20226. 12 rooms some with bath, simple Nepali restaurant, one of the better budget places near the bus park. **D-E** *White Lake Guest House*, T20291, F20467. 12 rooms some with bath, Nepali food on request, run by same people as White Lake Hotel, a good budget place.

E Around the bus park, the **E** *Dhawalagiri* (T20085), **E** *Pawan* (T20349), and **E** *Sherchan* (T20349), are all modern, though extremely basic and noisy. **E** *Lumbini Rest House*, T20455, 5 rooms all common bath.

Most of Tansen's culinary offerings are variations on dal-bhad-tarkari. The White Lake Hotel has a good restaurant with continental food. Recommended. Just north of Shitalpati, a branch of Kathmandu's *Nanglo* restaurant was due to have opened in mid-1997.

Eating

Golf: a 9-hole golf course near Srinagar Hill was established in the early 1990s, the only course outside Kathmandu. Temporary membership and equipment available, rates negotiable (T20183, Kathmandu T228506).

Shopping

Road **Buses**: leave the bus park every 30 minutes for **Butwal**, Rs 20. These are usually overflowing and the actual drive takes about 1¾ hours once you get going, but allow up to 3 hours to include any pre- and during-journey melodramas. There are connections to all destinations from Butwal.

Transport

Local buses for **Pokhara** leave the bus park at 2-hour intervals from 0600 (5 hours). The faster 'tourist' buses to Pokhara stop at the village of **Bartun** on the Siddhartha Highway without going into Tansen.

There is a daily, early afternoon bus to **Kathmandu** from the bus park (12 hours, Rs 110). There is also a daily early morning Sajha bus leaving from the crossroads near the White Lake Hotel (10 hours, Rs 110).

Directory **Banks** Tansen has two banks dealing in foreign exchange, both on the road to the east of Tansen Durbar. Allow plenty of time to complete the transaction, especially if your currency is not US$ or UK£. *Nepal Bank*, T20130, TCs only. *Rastra Banijya Bank*, T20134, TCs, currency notes, and credit card advances (Mastercard/Visa only). Both are open Sun-Thur 1000-1430, Fri 1000-1200, Sat closed. Hospitals & medical services The United Mission Hospital, 2 km northeast of town, usually has Western trained medical staff. **Communications** Area code: the area code for Tansen is 075. There are several STD/ISD places around the town centre. Post Office: the post office is southeast of Tansen Durbar. **Tourist offices** A small tourist office (T20129) on the east-west road north of the bus park was established to promote Tansen for the Visit Nepal '98 year. It has a number of handouts and can help with local information.

Excursions from Tansen

Srinagar Hill Looming some 200 metres above Tansen to the north, you can reach the top of Srinagar Hill in 45 minutes. The walk takes you through a delightful, fragrant pine forest. From the top there are panoramic views over the Kali Gandaki Valley to the Himalaya, including both peaks of Macchapuchare. On a good day you can see the entire Annapurna range and as far as Dhaulagiri. Best time to view, November-February. The way up is signposted from **Shitalpati**. Alternatively, follow the ridge up from the *Hotel Srinagar*. There is also a motorable road to the top. The **Srinagar Jatra festival** is held in August.

Rani Ghat This is probably the best walk you can make from Tansen if you are staying here for any length of time. Rani ('Queen') Ghat is the site of the magnificent skeleton of a palace built in 1896 by Khadgar Shamsher Rana (also responsible for Tansen's Shitalpati) for his wife, Tej Kumari. Khadgar was 'exiled' from Kathmandu following an unsuccessful attempt at a political coup. Although overgrown with weeds and trees, it requires little imagination to visualize the palace in its former isolated splendour, its grand colonnaded porch and terraced gardens playing host only to Khadgar's wistful thoughts of what might have been. Built on a broad spur of rock on the bank of the **Kali**

Terai & Churia Hills

Around Tansen

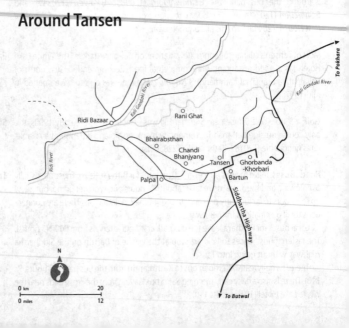

Rani Ghat

Gandaki River, work aimed at renovating the palace was started in 1996.

It is a walk of about three hours there and four hours back, so allow a full day. The path leaves Tansen at **Kailash Nagar** where there is a signboard with a map of the route. The walk is fairly straightforward, but after about one kilometre the path branches: if in doubt, ask any local for Rani Ghat. You pass through several tiny hamlets and terraced farmland before entering a narrow forested valley with a crystal clear stream. (You could probably find a discreet spot for a swim around here, modesty is appreciated.) The trail is distinct, though steep and uneven at times. You can't see the palace itself until you get to the large steel suspension bridge crossing the river. There are a couple of tea stalls and snack shops at Rani Ghat, but it is advisable to bring enough water and a substantial packed lunch with you.

Ghorabanda-Khorbari This small village lies on the Siddhartha Highway about three kilometres north of the Tansen junction. Its 'Kumal' potters are the main suppliers of pots, water vessels and other earthernware goods to the area. Because the pots have to be 'sundried', all pottery activity is confined to the dry, winter months. Little English is spoken here. The village also has good views across the valley. To get there it is best to hire a car, though there is also a cross country walking route passing close to the hospital.

Chandi Bhanjyang A hilltop viewpoint with what is locally considered to be a better Himalayan vista than from Srinagar Hill.

Ridi Bazaar Ridi is venerated by Hindus for its sacred location at the confluence of the Kali Gandaki and Ridi Khola rivers, 17 kilometres west of Tansen. The area is also rich in **saligrams**, the fossilized ammonites dating back more than 100 million years to a warmer geological age when the region was under water and before the Himalayan uplift began. Saligrams are regarded as religiously significant by Vaishnavite Hindus.

The town's **Rishikesh Mandir** is believed to have been established by the great Palpa king, Mani Mukunda Sen, though the present structure was built in the early 19th century. The temple is one of Nepal's more important pilgrimage sites. According to local legend, the temple idol ('Rishikeshab') was found in a river and has developed from youth to adulthood since it was installed. Major festivals are held in the month of Magh (January-February), including Ridi's most important festival of **Magh Sankranti** which involves fasting and bathing in the river; and in Bhadra (August-September).

Buses leave Tansen's bus park in the morning only. *En route*, nine kilometres from Tansen, is **Bhairabsthan**, with its Kala ('black') Bhairab Mandir known for having the largest *trisul* (Vishnu's trident) in Asia.

Narayanghat and Bharatpur

Phone code: 056
Colour map 1, grid B4

Narayanghat (also known as Narayanghar) is one of the most important junction towns, and one of the most unattractive, in Nepal. It links the Mahendra and Prithvi Highways and most travellers venturing into the Terai will find themselves passing through or stopping for tea, though it cannot be recommended as a destination in itself. The name comes from its position on the Narayani River. **Bharatpur** is the continuation of Narayanghat to the east. Originally two separate and distinct villages, the construction of the highway network resulted in rapid growth to the extent that they are now contiguous. While Narayanghat is the ugly bazaar town, Bharatpur is its greener, more spacious foil, where the towns' better hotels and the grass-strip airport are located. It is not a realistic alternative to staying at Chitwan, as is occasionally suggested: Tadi Bazaar is just 12 kilometres to the east, and there is an invariable surplus of accommodation at Sauraha. Curiously, Narayanghat is Nepal's only town with Ambassador taxis (a latter day, mass produced Indian version of the Morris Oxford), all appropriately 'hypothecated' (ie financed/mortgaged) to the State Bank of India (Nepal).

Narayanghat is exclusively a functional town and lacks anything of significant cultural interest. There is a small church just southwest of the *River View Hotel*, near the local bus park.

Excursions

There is a pleasant excursion to **Devghat** (Deoghat), seven kilometres to the north. It lies at the confluence of the Trisuli and Kali Gandaki rivers, seven7 kilometres north of Narayanghat. The name means 'place of the gods' after its riverside location. There are numerous temples around here which between them are dedicated to an unusually wide range of deities. Some are very old, though none stand out as architecturally exceptional. The peaceful site is surrounded by forest and hills to the west. There is not a great deal to actually do here, but if you find yourself stranded in Narayanghat for at least half a day, it is a good alternative to strolling through the bazaar. Allow two hours to walk around. There are no restaurants, only some tea stalls and street side food.

Getting there: buses leave Narayanghat at 0900 and 1500 for the 30 minutes journey, leaving Devghat at 1200 and 1500. A taxi will cost around Rs 300 for the return trip, with 30 minutes waiting time. Devghat is also within walking distance. Leave Narayanghat to the northeast, take the left hand turning after the bus park and follow the Narayani River until you reach Devghat. Allow about one and a half hours each way.

Essentials

Sleeping

Most of the towns' budget accommodation is concentrated on or near the main road through Narayanghat. The two best budget places, though, are quietly situated on the west bank of the Narayani River. To get there, walk or take a rickshaw across the bridge. Immediately after crossing, there are steps on your right down to the riverbank. The area's only quality accommodation is in Bharatpur.

Bharatpur: **B** *Safari Narayani*, T20130, F21058. 37 rooms all with a/c, TV and phone,

Narayanghat & Bharatpur

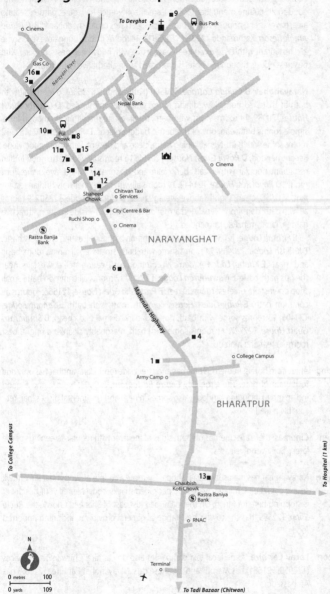

■ Sleeping

1 Chitwan Keyman	5 Kailash Lodge	9 River View	14 Sangat Lodge
2 Fishtail Lodge	6 Nawadurga Lodge	10 Royal Guest House	15 Shubaratri Guest House
3 Gainda Cottage Lodge	7 Pratiksha Guest House	11 Royal Rest House	16 Uncle's Lodge
4 Island Jungle Resort	8 Quality Guest House	12 Ruby Lodge	
	& Restaurant	13 Safari Narayani	

the best restaurant in town, beautiful and superbly maintained gardens with mango trees, bar, grass tennis court, swimming pool. Recommended. **B-C** *Chitwan Keyman*, T20200. 24 modern comfortable rooms most with a/c and TV, bright restaurant with good multi-cuisine menu, bar facilities, small conference hall, quiet garden seating area, travel agent, popular with groups, individual rates usually negotiable. **B-C** *Island Jungle Resort*, Kathmandu T220162, F223814. 14 rooms in long bungalow style some a/c, restaurant with TV, lovely garden has sal tree with huge bees' nests, popular with business guests though the hotel is promoted as an alternative to Chitwan.

Narayanghat: **D** *Gainda Cottage*, T20590 (Kathmandu T523506). 6 rooms all with bath in thatched bungalow, dining room, quiet. Recommended. **D** *Quality Guest House*, T20939. 14 rooms most with bath, small restaurant with real tandoori food, simple rooms but clean, one of the better budget places. **D** *River View*, T21151. 12 rooms some with bath, Nepali dining room, clean and decent, family run, good value. Recommended. **D** *Royal Guest House*, T20755. 16 rooms all with bath, good Indian restaurant popular with locals, bar, clean and reasonably priced, avoid the front rooms. **D** *Royal Rest House*, T21442. 14 rooms all with bath, small noisy Indian restaurant, STD/ISD, clean, slightly above average price. **D** *Uncle's Lodge*, T22502. 9 rooms all with bath, dormitory, Nepali/Indian dining room, quiet riverside location, attractive garden, family run. Recommended.

    E *Fishtail Lodge*, T20565. 12 rooms all common bath, small eating area, very basic. **E** *Kailash Lodge*, T20469. 14 rooms some with bath, small Nepali dining room, basic and cheap. **E** *Khanal Lodge*, 4 rooms all common bath, eating area downstairs, near the bus park, basic. **E** *Nawadurga Lodge*, T21815. 12 rooms all common bath, small shop downstairs, quietest rooms at rear. **E** *Pratiksha Guest House*, T21566. 6 rooms all common bath. **E** *Ruby Guest House*, 6 rooms most with bath. **E** *Sangat Lodge*, T20405. 13 rooms some with bath, no food, dark, dismal and cheap. **B** *Shubaratri Guest House*, T22727. 11 rooms some with bath, reasonably clean and bright, best rooms at rear and high up.

Eating   Apart from hotels, numerous dharbas and street side food, Narayanghat has only one restaurant of note. The large *City Centre Restaurant*, T20503, has a/c and a good Indian menu including tandoori, also some Chinese and continental dishes, bar, reasonably priced.

Entertainment   **Cinemas**: there are cinemas on both sides of the river with regular screenings of the latest 'Bollywood' releases.

Shopping   Narayanghat has the usual bazaar shops. There are a couple of shops near Pul Chowk selling cold drinks, mineral water and packaged snacks, convenient if your bus driver is stopping here for lunch. On the main road just east of Shaheed Chowk, the *Ruchi Shop*, T22589, has the town's best range of general provisions, including imported foods.

Transport   **Local Car hire**: some local taxi companies also do car hire. Chitwan Taxi Services (T22950, F21681) has Marutis and Japanese cars. Narayanghat Car Hire (T21137) has Ambassadors.

Air Everest Air, Nepal Airways and RNAC all have daily flights from Bharatpur to Kathmandu (US$50). The flight weaves its way spectacularly through the Churia Hills: it's general aviation at its most scheduled. The Bharatpur runway is a grass strip and the wailing siren before the arrival of each Dornier or Twin Otter aircraft is to warn off the grazing goats and cattle.

Terai & Churia Hills

Buses As the country's principal road junction, there are regular buses to all major Terai destinations. The Sajha booking office is a wooden hut at Pul Chowk. Buses for **Tadi Bazaar (Chitwan)** leave from the **Shaheed Chowk** stop throughout the day (30 minutes, Rs 6). Buses to all long distance destinations leave from the **Pul Chowk** stop. Buses to **Pokhara** leave from early morning (5 hours, Rs 80), 'tourist buses' at 1130 and 1230. Buses for **Kathmandu** also from early morning (5 hours, Rs 80), with 'tourist bus' departures at 1030, 1130, 1230 and 1330. Hourly departures to **Birgunj** (5 hours, Rs 50). Buses to **Janakpur** at 0400 and night bus (7 hours, Rs 120). Best bus to **Kakarbhitta** in late afternoon (12 hours, Rs 240). Late afternoon departures to **Mahendranagar** (15 hours, Rs 350). Numerous departures (best early morning and late afternoon) to **Nepalgunj** (10 hours, Rs 270). Hourly buses to **Sunauli (Belahiya)** throughout the day (5 hours, Rs 65).

Airline offices All the airline offices are located near the airport. **NB** It can be easier to book through a travel agent. *RNAC*, T20326. **Banks** Only the *Nepal Bank*, T20570, in the grid of streets northeast of Pul Chowk, deals in foreign exchange. Currency notes and TCs only, open 1000-1430 Sun-Thur, 1000-1200 Fri, closed Sat. Small amounts may be changed by the Bharatpur hotels, US$ preferred. **Communications** Area code: the area code for Narayanghat and Bharatpur is 056. There are numerous ISD/STD booths. **Hospitals & medical services** There is a small hospital 1 km east of the main roundabout in Bharatpur. Several pharmacies in Narayanghat.

Royal Chitwan National Park

Chitwan is the oldest, best known, most developed and most frequently visited of Nepal's national parks. At the heart of the Terai, it lies 120 kilometres southwest of Kathmandu and a similar distance to the southeast of Pokhara. The park itself covers 932 square kilometres and consists of swamp, tall elephant grass and dense forest, often referred to as jungle. It is a natural habitat for the tiger, great one-horned Indian rhinoceros, leopard, gaur, sloth and wild bear, sambar, hog and barking deer, civet, mongoose and otter.

Visiting

The highlight of most people's visit to Chitwan is a tour of the park. Often packaged evocatively as a *jungle safari*, there are three ways that you can do this: on the back of an elephant, by jeep or on foot. The main entrance to the park and the elephant stables are located at the southeast end of Sauraha. Here there are also a few small but interesting displays of the park's flora, fauna and conservation work. Entry fee, valid for two consecutive days, Rs 650.

Best time to visit The months between October and March when it is pleasantly warm and there is little or no rainfall have the best weather. However, elephant grass which covers significant areas of the park, grows high from the onset of the monsoon and provides cover for many of the park's animals. Beginning in late January, a fortnight is given over to local people to cut the grass inside the park – this is used for thatching and fodder. Your best chance of sighting rhinos, tigers, leopards and other animals is therefore from mid-February onwards.

Monsoon weather is hot, humid and often uncomfortable. The rising river levels make it impossible to tour the park by jeep, elephant rides being the only option, but again the tall grass reduces the chances of seeing a rhino. Many of the lodges inside the park, and some in Sauraha, remain effectively closed. But this is also the time when you can really bargain room rates down and relatively few numbers of other visitors give the place an uncongested feeling.

Soon after you enter the park you have to cross the Khaura River to get to the main area of the park. The bottom is stony and extremely uncomfortable with bare feet, so bring waterproof sandals to change. Flip-flops are available cheaply from the small shop/stall opposite the park entrance. Trainers are best for walking in the park as undergrowth can be thick.

Background The Chitwan basin embraces an area of 3,800 square kilometres and is surrounded by hills, the Siwaliks to the south and the Mahabharat range to the north, while the Narayani and Rapti rivers flow through it from west to east. The park now occupies the area between the Rapti River and its tributary, the Reu, with the centre rising to 738m. Mounts Manaslu and Himalchuli can be seen on clear days. There is an airstrip at Meghauli on the north bank of the Rapti.

The topographical boundaries of the Chitwan Valley (or *doon*) provided natural demarcation within the traditionally forested Terai belt. Following agreement with the British East India Company, Nepal's borders were extended to include the area nine years after the country's unification under King Prithvi Narayan Shah in 1768. It was populated by indigenous Tharu peoples, agricultural communities whose long established presence here suggests a remarkable resistance to malaria in what was, until the mid 20th century, a zone heavily infested by mosquitoes.

The huge programme of malaria eradication across the Terai in the 1950s led to mass immigration of people from throughout the country and the deforestation that accompanied it resulted in the reduction in the numbers of many animals and their natural habitat. Concern about the dwindling numbers led to the official establishment of the Royal Chitwan National Park in 1973 and in 1986 it was declared a World Heritage Site, events which are themselves indictments against the ecological degradation the area has witnessed during the latter half of the 20th century.

Hunting It was the attraction of Chitwan's larger wildlife – notably tigers, rhinos and bears – which elevated it to prominence in the eyes of the Nepali aristocracy and gave it informal status as a wildlife reserve. From the late 19th century, Rana Prime Ministers held Chitwan as their private hunting reserve. Groups would leave Kathmandu en masse to spend weeks stalking and shooting for leisure, and newly stuffed trophies from the expeditions would adorn Kathmandu's palace walls within weeks of their return to the capital,

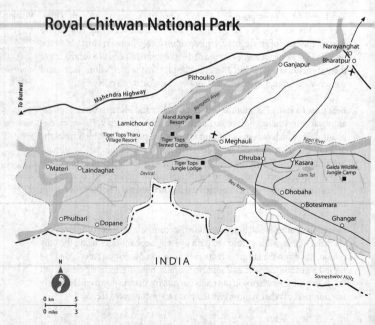

Royal Chitwan National Park

sometimes in an aggressive pose designed to underline the animal's ferocity and reflect the skill and bravery of the hunter. A huge stuffed tiger today stands at the entrance of Kathmandu's Keshar Library, immortalized by the taxonomist's skill in transforming what can only have been the fearful expression of the animal's last, uncomprehending minutes into the fearless growling poise of its natural state – those very characteristics which its hunter sought to extinguish. Although it is easy to condemn from the perspective of contemporary morality, 19th century hunters were not faced with the dilemma of endangered species and would presumably have justified the pastime as a combination of sport and social responsibility; Chitwan's villagers, moreover, would have welcomed any effort to combat the menace of large animals who regularly destroyed crops or attacked people.

In a country still suspicious of outside influence, few foreigners were permitted entry. Exceptions were made, however, usually for visiting dignitaries such as European royalty and Viceroys of India, but even then rarely beyond Chitwan. Massive hunting parties were organized, aided by a continuous line of beaters driving the game to wholesale slaughter. In his first year as monarch, King George V led a party to Chitwan in 1911, the second British royal to visit Nepal after his father who had hunted in the western Terai as an already grey bearded heir to the throne 35 years earlier. Accorded sumptuous hospitality while Queen Mary toured the more appropriately genteel attractions of western India and the Taj Mahal, the king's party is said to have shot 37 tigers and eight rhinos. During his ill fated tour of the subcontinent in 1921, Edward, Prince of Wales (later Edward VIII) escaped the hostility he faced in India with a trip to Chitwan where his group shot 18 tigers and eight rhinos. The Maharajah of Nepal and his guests, meanwhile, shot 433 tigers and 53 rhino in the period 1933-40. King Mahendra, the father of the present king, was also a keen Chitwan hunter and died in Narayanghat following a heart attack during one expedition.

The declaration of Chitwan as a national park in 1973 and the imposition of **Wildlife** strict measures against poaching and unauthorized conversion of forest to farmland saved the dwindling wildlife. Conservation measures have succeeded in increasing the numbers of some endangered species, with rhino and tiger populations rising to about 500 and 100 respectively.

Fauna The great one-horned Indian rhinoceros (*Rhinoceros palustris*) is the world's third largest land mammal and it is estimated that between one-third and a half of Asia's total population is found here. The rhino's gestation period is about 18 months and it has a life expectancy of up to 45 years. They grow up to two metres in height with an adult weighing three tonnes or more, and can run at speeds of up to 40 kilometres per hour. They feed largely on grass which is also their normal habitat and may be seen alone or in dispersed groups. During

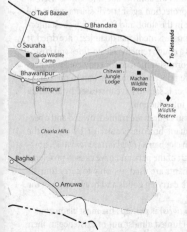

To Mugling, Kathmandu & Pokhara

Tadi Bazaar

Bhandara

Sauraha

Gaida Wildlife Camp

Bhawanipur

Chitwan Jungle Lodge

Machan Wildlife Resort

Bhimpur

To Hetauda

Parsa Wildlife Reserve

Churia Hills

Baghai

Amuwa

Terai & Churia Hills

Conserving a fragile ecology

By far the greatest hazards facing wildlife are the twin threats of environmental degradation and poaching. The destruction of vegetation cover, or its conversion into agricultural land, removes many animals' natural habitat. It also alters complex food chains of which the vegetation is a crucial component and which have been developed over thousands of years. Any assessment of an area's ecology cannot distinguish between its vegetation and the animal life it supports, so that interference in one necessarily affects the other. The rapid rate of deforestation in the Terai, as well as leaving much of its former wildlife unprotected against other predators or poachers, has placed unprecedented stress on the region's entire ecosystem and on larger mammals in particular.

Of the three official agencies with responsibility for the park, the King Mahendra Trust for Nature Conservation oversees its conservation efforts. One of the more successful programmes has been the Gharial Conservation Project. Established in 1978 as a result of growing concern over their possible extinction, it has taken gharial eggs from the Narayani River and reared the young before returning them to the wild after about three years. Numbers are estimated to have increased four-fold since the first of the project's young was released in 1981. The US Smithsonian Institute, meanwhile, has supported a Tiger Ecology Project at Chitwan since the mid-1970s which, in addition to sponsoring research into tiger ecology, has also succeeded in raising numbers to above 100. The establishment of the Parsa Wildlife Reserve to the east of Chitwan also provided an important sanctuary especially for some of Chitwan's endangered species.

the hot summer months especially, you can also see some wading or soaking in the rivers to keep cool. Rhinos can swim and are known to visit Sauraha and other nearby villages for some late night eating and stamping on of crops, an occupation that has not endeared them to local farmers. Indeed, because of the havoc and destruction they cause rhinos are an avowed enemy of agricultural communities in the area, a fact that has not helped conservation efforts, as villagers may be all too happy to conspire with or protect poachers. Although banned, poaching continues and many parts of the rhino are prized ingredients in traditional remedies, particularly in East Asia. Its blood, for example, is consumed with a herbal cocktail to cure gynaecological and menstrual problems, the powdered horn is regarded as an aphrodisiac, the skin is used to make bracelets believed to provide protection against evil spirits, while the urine is drunk when 'blood is present in the stool' and for relief of chest infections. Rhino dung, too, is believed to possess medicinal qualities: once dried, it is smoked in a pipe – astonishingly as a cough remedy. Heavy fines and custodial penalties of up to 20 years are vigorously enforced for convicted poachers and traffickers. About 40 rhinos were relocated from Chitwan to the Bardia national park in 1986 and their number is said to have increased by about 25 percent in the first decade since their introduction.

The elephants seen by most Chitwan visitors are trained, owned and operated by either the government elephant breeding centre or by one of the lodges. A small number of wild Indian elephants (*Elephantus maximus*), however, are said to exist in the eastern part of the park and have caused problems by trampling crops. The tamed elephants are used not only to carry tourists into the park, but are also put to work carrying goods and heavy cargo in the Chitwan vicinity.

The Royal Bengal Tiger (*Panthera tigris*) is perhaps the most glamorous – and elusive – of Chitwan's animals. Hunted almost out of existence in their traditional habitat in the forests of the Gangetic plain, they are now estimated to number just over 100 in Chitwan. Courtship between tigers lasts about a week, while the actual mating period lasts for two or three days. Typically, between two and six cubs are born in a litter following a gestation of between 100 and 105 days. They mark their territory by a combination of spraying urine and making distinctive scratch marks on trees. They are by nature shy creatures, not given to attack unless provoked or hunting for food. Tigers have excellent eyesight and usually feed at night, preying largely on the park's deer. They are rarely seen in large groups, favouring instead a system in which individual tigers (or family groups) control a demarcated territory. Research has demonstrated this to be an areally demanding system, that is one which is stressed by a significant reduction in the tiger to land available ratio. Depending on environment and available prey, males command an area of about 50 square kilometres and females 35 square kilometres. This would suggest limited scope for increasing tiger numbers in Chitwan very much beyond their present levels. Like another of the Royal Bengal Tiger's fabled habitats, the Sundarbans of southern Bengal, the chances of seeing one during a visit are remote.

Leeches

These unattractive little creatures are especially prevalent during the monsoon. An irritation to trekker and Chitwan visitor alike at this time, they sway on the ground or on bushes and twigs waiting for a passer by and get in boots when you are walking. When they are gorged with blood they drop off. Don't try pulling one off, as the head will get left behind and cause infection. Put some salt, or hold a lighted cigarette to it, which will make it quickly fall off. Before starting in the morning it can help to spray socks and bootlaces with insect repellent.

The likelihood of seeing a **leopard** (*Panthera pardus*) is said to be marginally greater. It hunts by day, preying also on deer as well as smaller mammals.

The **sloth bear** (*Melursus ursinus*) is probably named after its diet rather than its disposition. It can grow up to 2m in height, weigh 200 kg and feeds largely on termites and insects.

The most common sightings for most visitors to the park are **deer**, including the swamp deer (*Cervus davaucels*), spotted deer or chital (*Axis axis*), barking deer (*Muntiacus mutiak*) and hog deer. They are often found in herds of up to one hundred or more. These elegant animals are important prey species of both the tiger and leopard and usually feed around the forest margins.

Reptiles The park's rivers and swampy areas are home to various reptiles including snakes, frogs, turtles, lizards and at least two important species of crocodile, the marsh mugger (*Crocodilus palustris*) and the gharial (*Gavialis gangeticus*). The latter, which can grow up to 5m in length, is a fish eater and the destruction of its riverside habitat and of the Terai forest from the 1950s seriously threatened its eradication from Nepal. Their numbers have increased in Chitwan since the establishment of a conservation project in the late 1970s. The smaller marsh mugger, meanwhile, is aptly named as its diet and predatory instincts are not confined to fish. Growing up to 4m in length, they are likely to be seen in greater numbers in the swampy areas inside the park than along the rivers, although some are also found along the banks of the Narayani.

Birds Chitwan provides a natural habitat for over 400 species of bird. There are many seasonal migrants including waterfowl attracted by the rivers and wetlands as well as larger storks, colourful parakeets and kingfishers, various singing and laughing species, and birds of prey.

Terai & Churia Hills

Chitwan: life on the wildside

Chitwan is not a zoo, so in the interests of your own safety it is essential to maintain the utmost respect for the animals which cannot distinguish an interested visitor from a hostile intruder.

Fatalities are mercifully rare, but they do occur. In March 1994 a guide, Bhadrey Pandi, was hired by two tourists to take them on a walk through the forest. He took his normal route leading deep into the dense forest. They saw deer and some monkeys, and Pandi showed them how brightly flowering plants grow as epiphytes on many of the trees. Suddenly, the group found itself surrounded by eight rhinos. Slowly, Pandi and the tourists edged away. The guide acted as a decoy while the two in his charge ran for safety. The rhinos, though, began to get agitated. After a few seconds Pandi, too, started to run, but the undergrowth was thick and made running difficult. Chased by the rhinos, Pandi tripped, fell and was trampled to death. The following year, a tourist walking in the park was killed when a rhino spiked him with its horn, then bit and crushed him. Then, early one evening in September 1995, the same fate awaited another guide, Basu Chowdhury, this time as he hid in bushes.

Compensating for their poor eyesight, rhinos have a highly developed sense of smell. It is therefore advisable not to wear perfumes or other strong fragrances. They can swim and have been known to visit Sauraha and other villages. When feeding, they chew noisily and breathe heavily. If you find yourself surrounded by rhinos it is possible that they will simply disperse, but are especially dangerous when they are protecting their young, if they are scared by, for example, being pelted with stones or other objects, or when mating. Always take the advice of your guide. Some people believe that running in zigzags can sufficiently confuse a pursuing rhino for it to abandon the chase.

The sloth bear is among Chitwan's most dangerous animals, and is known to demonstrate far from slothful characteristics in launching defensive, but vicious and also unprovoked attacks on other animals and on humans. Local advice recommends that you make loud noises and gesticulate wildly to frighten the bear away, but if these don't succeed in repelling it you should climb as high up the nearest tall tree as possible and hold tight to resist the bear trying to shake you out of it. Alternatively, strike the bear horizontally with a strong stick.

Attacks on humans by tigers are extremely rare. They are shy animals and will normally only attack when frightened. Local advice suggests that if confronted by a tiger, you stare at it while gradually edging backwards. Don't run. There is no known local advice concerning what to do if chased by a tiger.

Flora and environment The park's vegetation is dominated by a combination of **sal** (*Shorea robusta*) forest, tall **grassland** and, in the lower wetter areas, **riverine forest** with flowering species including the sissoo (*Dalburghia sissoo*), silk cotton tree (*Bombax ceiba*) and Flame of the Forest (*Butea monosperma*). These beautiful trees bloom from January until the early spring, the large, bright red blossoms of the silk cotton tree (or simal) being especially conspicuous.

The tall growing **elephant grass** dotted with occasional tree clusters gives the park an almost savanna like appearance in parts and dominates the park's grassland. There is a total of about 60 species of grass.

The end of the dry season sees vegetation cover at a minimum, a situation that is changed dramatically by the **monsoon** rains. In the space of a few short weeks short yellow grass is transformed into a lush green cover, a startling regeneration that emphasizes the importance of the monsoon and its role in the folklore and mythology of agricultural communities throughout South Asia.

Elephant rides are the most popular and thrilling. For the views and as an experience in itself, it is awesome and is the only recommended way to visit the park during monsoon and when the elephant grass is at its highest. Sitting *gaddi*, or bareback, on top of an elephant is not as comfortable as it may look, but is bearable in a *hauda*, a box-like cushioned platform seating about four people. The *phanit*, or driver, has a number of commands which the elephant understands, but also controls and disciplines the animal by striking its head with a metal bar, a seemingly barbaric action which, so the *phanit* maintains, is more painful to the eyes of the onlooker than to the elephant. All lodges offer elephant rides. A few in Sauraha and all inside the park have their own elephants, either owned or taken on lease for one or perhaps two years. The cost is Rs 650 per person (in addition to the park entrance fee of Rs 650) for a ride of between one and one and a half hours. Rides are organized each morning and afternoon, with times varying slightly with the season. **Mid-November to mid-February**: 0900-1000, 1500-1600; **Mid-February to mid-May**: 0800-0900, 1600-1700; **Mid-May to end-September**: 0730-0830, 1630-1730; **End-September to mid-November**: 0800-0900, 1600-1700. **NB** If an elephant ride is not included in your package (it usually is) it is best to book through your lodge and well in advance in peak season. If you don't want to go through the lodge, start queueing at the office at the park entrance by 0600 the previous morning and get a slip of paper with a number written on it. If demand exceeds supply, you then wait while a lucky dip decides whether or not you have been allocated a place. Book through a lodge.

The middle of the day is too hot for the elephants in summer, while in winter they are used for carrying during these hours. One of the most spectacular sights at Chitwan is watching a long convoy of elephants wading across the river in the early dusk light. Sauraha's western riverbank makes an ideal vantage point: have your camera ready.

Most lodges run **jeep** tours of the park, but these operate only when river levels permit crossing, ie from late December until mid-June. The best months for this are from mid-February when the elephant grass has been cut allowing minimally impeded views. Most are also priced at Rs 650 per person, but usually last at least twice as long as an elephant ride.

It is also possible to **walk** inside the park and doing it this way is undoubtedly the 'closest' you can get to the forest and its life. Walkers should **always** be accompanied by at least two guides, one literally to guide and another with a rifle. Since 1995 all guides are required by law to be insured. It is important to take your guide's advice as to where to go and where not to go, especially when the vegetation is sufficiently high to hide a rhino or any other animal which may not appreciate your presence in its vicinity. Use only officially licensed guides.

Canoeing along the Rapti River as part of a walk through the park is gaining in popularity. The canoes are made from the hollowed trunk of the silk cotton tree. Most trips start from close to the park's entrance and you canoe about three kilometres to the west, or as far as the elephant breeding centre. It is not considered safe to canoe during the monsoon when river levels are high; in spring, meanwhile, when levels are at their lowest you have to push part of the way.

Kasara About three kilometres west of Sauraha along the Rapti River, Kasara has the park's headquarters as well as the **Gharial Breeding and Conservation Centre** and is the base for the Nepalese army in Chitwan. This was the site that housed George V plus entourage during their hunting expedition of 1911.

The park's headquarters contains a small and rather uninspiring display of

Viewing inside the park

It may be possible at times to extend your elephant ride, especially during the off season, by paying baksheesh to the mahout, or phanit. You'll have to bargain, but since the money will go and remain undeclared in his pocket, you can get an extra hour at a fraction of the normal rate

Terai & Churia Hills

Chitwan wildlife. The Gharial Breeding Centre is more interesting and you can see the crocodiles at all stages of life. Kasara is often included in jeep tours of the park. Alternatively, you can get there by canoe from Sauraha.

Viewing outside the park **Elephant Breeding Centre** This government run centre is situated at Khorshor, about three kilometres to the west of Sauraha. It not only breeds elephants for Chitwan but trains them to carry passengers and goods.

The breeding centre encourages the mating of elephants (the photograph adorning the walls of many Sauraha lodges and illustrating the phenomenal reproductive attribute of the male elephant was taken here) and their training. The gestation period continues for about 23 months. When they are not working, the elephants are kept chained to a central pole: plans for improving their living conditions are said to exist. ■ *0600-0900, 1600-1800 daily. Rs 100.*

Some visitors have been misled into believing the Community Forest to be Chitwan National Park, and have been charged accordingly. It is not designated a national park.

Baghmara Community Forest Successfully developed over the last few years as an area promoting environmental regeneration, the Community Forest now covers 400 hectares to the northwest of Sauraha. It is administered by the King Mahendra Trust for Nature Conservation. It shares its wildlife with Chitwan and is known to have rhino, leopards, deer, sloth bears, monkeys, wild boar, crocodiles and possibly a few tigers. Some lodges offer elephant rides in the forest, but there are no official government elephants. It has a number of pleasant walking opportunities and it takes about five hours to walk around the circumference, but again it is advisable to take a guide. Basic tourist accommodation is available.

To get there, follow the western road heading north from Sauraha, then take the second turning on the left after the Rainforest Guest House and continue along here following signs for the Alka Resort Camp to the end. It makes a pleasant half day walk from Sauraha.

Elephant rides available at Rs 200 per hour, 0600-100 and 1600-1800. ■ *0600-1800 daily, Rs 100.*

Bij Hazaar Lakes This is an option for a day out from Sauraha. The name means '20,000 lakes'. Surrounded by an ever decreasing forest dominated by sal, it is either a group of small lakes or a marshy expanse depending on when you visit. It is known for the wide variety of birdlife it attracts. The disadvantage is that it is just far enough from Sauraha to make it awkward to get there unless you cycle or have a vehicle. Take the western road from Sauraha as far as Tadi Bazaar, then follow the main road west for some three kilometres. An unmade road leads southwest from a bridge crossing a stream. Continue along here for a further three kilometres until you reach the lakes.

Parsa Wildlife Reserve This reserve, in an area covering about 500 square kilometres and bordering Chitwan National Park to the east, is designed to be an uncommercialized and protected sanctuary for the region's wildlife. It is believed to be a habitat for a number of tigers as well as a small herd of wild elephants. It is not really open to tourism, though it may be possible to make day visits by jeep if arranged by your lodge or hotel. The reserve's office and its entrance is located just off the main road (Tribhuvan Highway) at the village of Amlekganj, south of Hetauda. Apparently, a few travellers have been able to get permission from here to camp overnight in the reserve. ■ *Admission, when available, Rs 650.*

Tharu Village Tharus are the Terai's dominant ethnic group. Organized tours of a traditional Tharu village are becoming increasingly popular as a

Life of a Chitwan elephant

An elephant stays with its mother for the first two and a half years of its life, after which the two are separated. This is a highly emotional time when both the mother and child demonstrate recognizable sadness: they cry and make what have been described as 'sad noises' in ways that resemble human behaviour. They are kept separately for six months before the baby is introduced to its trainer who is supposed to stay with the animal for life. The following three years is given to full time training of the young elephant. Methods used to instil discipline are said to be harsh. At the age of six, the elephant is considered to be fully trained. Its working life begins with two years of carrying goods, then at eight years it starts to transport human passengers. The elephant can then work until the age of 65 or older, and its life expectancy is similar to that of a human.

diversion for visitors to Chitwan. These tours were first conducted by one of the larger lodges with others subsequently joining the easy money bandwagon. While the villagers may benefit financially from such tours, some people find the idea of organized gawking at people going about their daily lives in and around their houses too embarrassing to be educational.

The historical domination of the Tharus, Chitwan's indigenous ethnic group, changed following the malaria eradication programme of the 1950s when mass migration brought other ethnic groups, notably Bahuns, Chepangs, Chhetris and Tamungs, from throughout Nepal into Chitwan and the surrounding areas. The Tharus are regarded by some as commercially naive, an unfortunate reputation reinforced by the ease with which many were persuaded to sell their property in Sauraha to developers at minimal prices.

Cultural programmes Programmes of music and dance by Tharus and some of the Terai's other indigenous ethnic groups are performed most evenings in season and occasionally during off peak seasons in several of Sauraha's lodges. These are often lively and entertaining. The *Hermitage Hotel* runs a good programme. The Nepali Culture House on the main north-south road has nightly singing and dancing shows in season, Rs 150.

One story tells of how a Tharu dance group was returning home after a performance when they encountered a group of tourists and their guide in the street. Encouraged by the tourists, the dancers agreed to do an impromptu performance. They talked among themselves for a few moments, then danced and sang enthusiastically. The visitors were delighted and payed handsomely. Their embarrassed guide never told them that the words of the song translated roughly as 'Come on, tourists, give us your money ...'

■ *Admission charges can be anything from free if you eat in the restaurant to Rs 100 if you don't.*

Going as part of an organized inclusive package tour is a popular but by no means the only way to visit Chitwan. Tours are widely promoted in Kathmandu, Pokhara and other tourist centres. They are usually of 2 or 3 nights duration and can save on the hassle of finding somewhere to stay, but accommodation is abundantly available and easy to find in Sauraha. Similarly, getting tickets for elephant rides and jeep tours of the park as well as all other activities is straightforward – just ask your lodge to arrange it for you.

Some lodges, notably those inside the park, deal almost exclusively with package tours, though they will usually accommodate you at negotiable rates if you arrive without notice and demand is slack. Otherwise there is no major advantage in

Park information

Terai & Churia Hills

An armchair experience?

Chitwan tours are often promoted evocatively as jungle safaris, an image that has been hugely successful in appealing to its visitors' sense of the exotic. The theme is apparent in many of the park's tourist activities. Much of Chitwan's accommodation, for example, consists of 'lodges', 'camps' and 'resorts' rather than hotels, with their architecture, design and layout reflecting popular Western conceptions of just how a jungle lodge should be. Roofs thatched with genuine Chitwan elephant grass hide the layers of corrugated plastic beneath that keep the rain out in summer, and even mud walls sometimes form an exterior for the bricks within. This was described by one visitor as the 'Tarzan syndrome', loosely defined as an armchair experience in which thatch, mud walls and cosy elephant haudas are the cosmetics needed to stamp a mark of authenticity on to the packaged ideal. A cynical view, perhaps, but one not entirely without substance. That Chitwan continues to attract visitors in large numbers is ample testimony to its natural beauty and success as a centre for wildlife conservation. But can it build on its remarkable development of both environment and tourism whilst resisting the pressures to which Thamel and Lakeside have succumbed? Can it remain a National Park, a jewel in Nepal's nature heritage, rather than a Western inspired jungle safari theme park?

booking a package tour unless you want the security of a planned itinerary or if there is a specific place where you want to stay: indeed, budget conscious travellers often find it cheaper to make all arrangements themselves.

What to take Bring cool cottons, some in dull or 'jungle' colours, preferably with long sleeves for evenings and woollens for winter. Also take a sunhat, sunblock and insect repellant. Electricity is a recent introduction to Sauraha and power cuts are not infrequent, so take a torch. **NB** Avoid strong perfumes: rhinos compensate for their poor eyesight by a highly developed sense of smell and if one in your vicinity perceives danger it is liable to charge towards the source of the scent. A camera is a must, but film (mostly 35 mm) is available in Sauraha. If Chitwan is high on your list of touring priorities in Nepal, you might find room in your luggage for a pair of binoculars.

Sauraha

Colour map 1, grid B4   There are essentially two choices of where to stay: inside the park or at Sauraha, a village just north of the park.

Lodges inside the park are more expensive and more exclusive. Most offer 4 or 5 star comforts and rates usually include accommodation and meals (not alcohol) plus entry fees and camp activities. Apart from the luxury, these are undoubtedly the best places to stay. Some people stay up all night to watch and listen as wildlife comes foraging and feeding around their lodge, and many consider it the experience of a lifetime. The former practice of using a tethered live goat as bait for a tiger or leopard is now banned. Most lodges offer elephant rides, canoe trips on the river, jeep/Landrover rides, nature walks often accompanied by a local naturalist, fishing (in season) and birdwatching.

The great majority of visitors, however, stay at Sauraha. This was once a traditional Tharu village, but with the promotion of Chitwan as a major tourist destination it has been rapidly developed into an agglomeration of budget and mid range hotels, or lodges. Electricity was introduced to Sauraha in 1996, but supply can be erratic so a supply of candles is useful.

Terai & Churia Hills

AL *Machan Wildlife Resort*, Kathmandu T225001, F220475. 15 rooms in wooden bungalows scattered among the trees, restaurant, some cheaper tents further inside the park with meals by campfire, good for wildlife viewing including wild elephants (it has a reputation as a good place to see tigers), located at the western boundary of the park. Machan means raised platform. **AL** *Tiger Tops Jungle Lodge*, Kathmandu T222706, F414075. 30 rooms with solar heated showers in large 'tree houses' (best views upstairs), listed with the world's best 300 hotels and Nepal's most expensive, public areas have thatched roof, hardwood and ratan décor, continental and Nepali cuisine, located in the eastern part of the park close to Meghauli airport.

Lodges inside the Park

A *Chitwan Jungle Lodge*, Kathmandu T440918, F228349. 30 rooms in traditional mud and thatched huts, rustic but very clean and comfortable, good restaurant and open air bar, river for swimming, lectures, cultural shows. **A** *Island Jungle Resort*, Kathmandu T226002, F223184. 20 rooms in lodge and tents, located on Bandarijhola illand in the middle of the Narayani River, good for crocodile sightings. **A** *Temple Tiger*, Kathmandu T221585, F220178. Comfortable tents with changing rooms and hot showers, Chitwan's westernmost lodge. **A** *Tiger Tops Tented Camp*, Kathmandu T222706, F414075. 12 tents, separate bath, more modest than the Jungle Lodge but comfortable, good service and food, situated on an island in the Narayani River. **A** *Tiger Tops Tharu Village Resort*, T/F as above. Accommodation in Tharu style cottages, small pool, just outside the park to the northwest of the Rapti River.

B *Gaida Wildlife Jungle Camp*, T(Kathmandu) 220940, F227292. 13 tented rooms, inside park at the foot of the Churia Hills and south of Sauraha, good site for viewing gaur and rhino. **B** *Gaida Wildlife Camp*, T/F as above. Located north of the Rapti River and just southeast of Sauraha, but officially inside the park boundary, rooms in thatched huts.

C *Royal Park*, T(Kathmandu) 229028, F412987. 17 comfortable rooms, extensive grounds in excellent location south of the village and near the park entrance, restaurant and coffee shop overlooking the river, some facilities for the disabled. Recommended. **C-D** *Alka Resort Camp*, T29363 (Kathmandu T224771). Chalet style accommodation, restaurant, located 1½ kilometres northwest of Sauraha next to the Community Forest entrance, peaceful but rather isolated. **C-D** *Hermitage*, T/F(Kathmandu) 424390. 8 rooms with bath in brick and thatched cottages, restaurant, attractive grounds and excellent riverside location, rhinos have been known to visit at night, also has booking offices in Moscow and St Petersburg! **C-D** *Jungle World Nepal*, T29368, F(Kathmandu) 419436. 8 double rooms with bath, restaurant, resident peacock.

Sauraha

Listings are arranged approximately northwest to southeast.

D *Jungle Resort*. Accommodation in 6 thatched cottages with bath, attractive location on the western edge of Sauraha, good small restaurant. **D** *Jungle Camp*, T29366 (Kathmandu T/F222132). 16 rooms with bath in 4 bungalows each with pleasant balconies, dining room with large central chimney and bar, no electricity but candles and kerosene lamps are supplied, popular with packages. **D** *Chitwan Rest House*, 6 rooms some with bath, small restaurant uses a photocopy of the Heritage Hotel's menu. **D** *Rainforest Guest House*, T29370 (Kathmandu, T60235). 11 rooms some with bath and satellite TV, some hammocks, rooftop showers, good views of the mountains. **D** *Holiday Safari Jungle Lodge*, 10 rooms all with bath and a reasonable restaurant, popular with packages. **D** *Jungle Express Camp*, standard rooms with bath, dining room. **D** *Wildlife Camp*, T29363 (Kathmandu T228784). 15 rooms most with bath, friendly and efficient, popular with groups. **D** *Chitwan Resort Camp*, 12 rooms some with bath, good restaurant. **D** *Travellers Jungle Camp*, T29365. 16 rooms some with bath, friendly, some good value cheaper rooms. **D** *River View Jungle Camp*, T60164 (Kathmandu, T410418). 30 rooms most with bath, popular and friendly, good food.

Terai & Churia Hills

D *Rhino Lodge*, T(Kathmandu) 420316, F417146. Consists of 2 lodges, one half way along the main north-south road, the other set off the road 200 metres to the south, the second has fine views over the river, both are popular with groups but welcome individual travellers, have a private elephant – the 33-year-old Sunakali; there are 3 lodges in a peaceful woodland location near the park entrance. **D** *Jungle Safari Camp*, T20730. 17 rooms most with bath, restaurant, peaceful woodland location

Sauraha

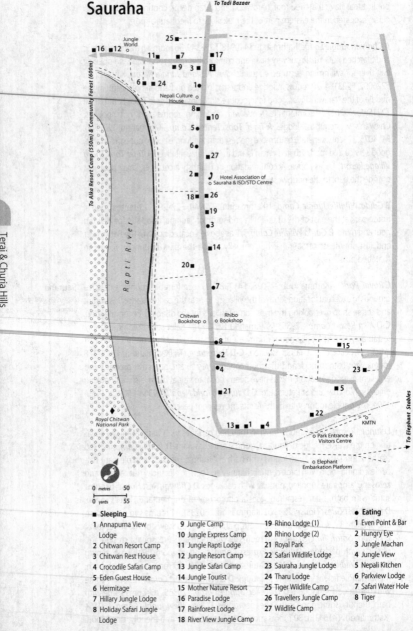

To Tadi Bazaar

Rapti River

To Alka Resort Camp (550m) & Community Forest (600m)

Jungle World

Nepali Culture House

Hotel Association of Sauraha & ISD/STD Centre

Chitwan Bookshop

Rhibo Bookshop

Royal Chitwan National Park

To Elephant Stables

KMTN

Park Entrance & Visitors Centre

Elephant Embarkation Platform

0 metres 50
0 yards 55

N

■ **Sleeping**

1 Annapurna View Lodge
2 Chitwan Resort Camp
3 Chitwan Rest House
4 Crocodile Safari Camp
5 Eden Guest House
6 Hermitage
7 Hillary Jungle Lodge
8 Holiday Safari Jungle Lodge
9 Jungle Camp
10 Jungle Express Camp
11 Jungle Rapti Lodge
12 Jungle Resort Camp
13 Jungle Safari Camp
14 Jungle Tourist
15 Mother Nature Resort
16 Paradise Lodge
17 Rainforest Lodge
18 River View Jungle Camp
19 Rhino Lodge (1)
20 Rhino Lodge (2)
21 Royal Park
22 Safari Wildlife Lodge
23 Sauraha Jungle Lodge
24 Tharu Lodge
25 Tiger Wildlife Camp
26 Travellers Jungle Camp
27 Wildlife Camp

● **Eating**

1 Even Point & Bar
2 Hungry Eye
3 Jungle Machan
4 Jungle View
5 Nepali Kitchen
6 Parkview Lodge
7 Safari Water Hole
8 Tiger

Terai & Churia Hills

near park entrance, recommended as the best of the 3. **D** *Annapurna View Lodge*, T29363. 8 rooms some with bath, restaurant. **D** *Crocodile Safari Camp*, 10 rooms some with bath, reasonable food. **D** *Safari Wildlife Lodge*, T(Kathmandu) 225897, F224466. 15 rooms most with bath, dining room. **D** *Skyline Jungle Camp*, T29363. 11 modern cottage rooms most with bath, dining area, clean and peaceful, popular with budget travellers.

E *Jungle Rapti Lodge*, 9 rooms some with bath in small mud and thatch huts, eating cabin. **E** *Hillary Jungle Lodge*, T29366. 8 rooms all common bath, small eating area, basic but clean and friendly, expert ornithologist owner, good value. Recommended. **E** *Parkview Lodge*, standard budget rooms some with bath. **E** *Jungle Tourist Camp*, T601652. 12 rooms most with bath, small restaurant serves food said to be 'absolutely unimaginative'. **E** *Eden Guest House*, 15 rooms some with bath, dining room, secluded and quiet. **E** *Mother Nature Resort*, T60180. 9 rooms some with bath, eating area, clean and basic mud and thatch cottages, remote location. **E** *Sauraha Jungle Lodge*, 8 rooms all common bath, small restaurant.

Most lodges have their own restaurant or dining area and there are relatively few restaurant-only establishments in Sauraha. Some shops sell Western tinned food brought from Kathmandu, but these are usually expensive and may be either side of their expiry date. **Eating**

Nepali Kitchen. A small dal-bhad-tarkari restaurant on the main north-south road. *Hunting Cave and Safari Water Hole*, Thamelesque menu. Also does good breads and packed lunches, bar. *Tiger Restaurant and Bar*, has a good if standard tourist menu, 1st floor thatched roof with good views over the river. *Hungry Eye*, does all types of food and a range of cocktails including regular and special bhang lassis. *Jungle View Restaurant and Bar*, delightful rooftop terrace with fine views over the river and park, standard eclectic menu, pizzas have been recommended, one of the few places where butter is discernible on 'butter toast', ideal for spending a lazy afternoon gazing across the river. Recommended.

A few Chitwan souvenirs and T-shirts are available. There are a couple of small bookshops, including the Chitwan Bookshop which also sells postcards, stationery and toilet paper. The Rhino Bookshop opposite has very few books, but does sell T-shirts, postcards and maps. The bookshop below the Hungry Eye restaurant has Sauraha's best selection of books. **Shopping**

Rafting: several rafting companies operate a package that combines rafting down the Trisuli River with a visit to Chitwan. Most trips start at Mugling and finish at Narayanghat, and are of 5 or 6 day durations. Prices can vary enormously according to what is and what is not included. Go with an established and reputable company. It is equally possible to arrange your own transport from Narayanghat and your accommodation at Chitwan/Sauraha. **Sports**

Local Cycle hire Sauraha has a couple of cycle hire places. Cycles are not permitted inside the park, but Bij Hazaar Lakes are within cycling distance or you can explore some of the Terai landscape and culture. This is a far better way to see a typical Tharu village than on an organized tour. **Transport**

Air A small private airstrip in the village of **Meghauli**, just north of the Rapti River, links Chitwan with Kathmandu. The 30-minute flight may be included in some package tours with accommodation in one of the luxury lodges inside the park. Flights are operated only in season and the airport is closed during the monsoon. Road transport

Terai & Churia Hills

is provided by your lodge itself and a vehicle will be there to meet your flight. There is also an airport at **Bharatpur**, near Narayanghat and about 20 kilometres from Sauraha, which has regular scheduled flights to and from Kathmandu.

Buses There are regular road connections between Chitwan and several major destinations in Nepal. Buses arrive and depart from the village of **Tadi Bazaar**, a small built up area stretching along the main road north of Sauraha. It is usually possible to get a lift to Sauraha in one of the many jeeps waiting around the bus stop. If you have pre-booked your Chitwan visit, a jeep from your lodge will normally be waiting to pick you up at the bus stop and will not charge for the 15 to 20-minute drive; if you have not previously made arrangements for accommodation you can still get a lift in one of these jeeps, but expect to pay around Rs 30. Touts are ever on hand to encourage you – in their own irritatingly inimitable way – to stay at a particular lodge, but they can be useful in finding you a place in a jeep even if you don't actually end up staying at 'their' lodge. Alternatively, it is possible to hire a cycle from Tadi Bazaar or hitch a lift on an ox-cart. The latter cannot be recommended for either comfort or speed. The frequencies and schedules of long distance bus connections vary with season, so check. You can make reservations through your hotel. **NB** In peak season, it is essential to book early. Fares include commission for the person you are booking through, so are negotiable.

To **Kathmandu**: mini buses depart at 1030 and take 5 hours, Rs 170; tourist buses leave at 1100 and take 5½ hours, Rs 160; public buses depart at 0800 for their 6½ hours journey, Rs 120. The Green Line bus company has the most comfortable buses to Kathmandu (Rs 480) and Pokhara (Rs 480). T60126 To **Pokhara**: tourist and mini buses have departures from 0930 and 1130, take 4½ hours and cost Rs 170; public buses leave at 0800 and 1200 and take 5½ hours, Rs 120. To **Birgunj**: regular departures throughout the morning for the 3½ hour journey, Rs 75. To **Kakarbhitta**: one public bus leaves at 1730 for the long 14-hour journey, Rs 340. To **Sunauli**: public bus services leave between 0930 and 1130, 4½ hours, Rs 115.

Directory **Banks** There are no exchange facilities in Sauraha, although there is a small bank in Tadi Bazaar. Most lodges, however, will accept payment in foreign currency including Indian Rupees. **Communications** If you can't make phone calls from your lodge, there are STD/ISD facilities in the Hotel Association of Sauraha office opposite the Parkview Lodge and Wildlife Camp. Getting a good line can be problematic. There is another STD/ISD office 100 metres along the road heading east from the Hungry Eye Restaurant. **Tourist offices** This is situated in a small hut next to the Rainforest Guest House. It is open only during the main tourist seasons, and even then it only has standard government tourist brochures.

Hetauda

Phone code: 057
Colour map 2, grid B5

Hetauda is situated to the northeast of Chitwan, at the junction of the Mahendra and Tribhuvan Highways before the latter continues its northward journey through the Churia Hills. It is also at one end of an unusual **cableline** that was constructed in the 1950s to transport cement to Kathmandu. The cement factory lies south of the town, a huge industrial unit whose gaseous emissions are visible for miles around. The Rapti Khola flows to the west of the town, with its Karra Khola tributary running to the south.

The intersection of the two highways is the focus for much of the town's activity. To the northeast is the main bazaar area, and the local hospital is 400 metres west on the Mahendra Highway. A rarely used **Royal Palace** lies 600 metres to the south and just beyond are the large premises of HMG Dept of Forestry. South of the Karra Khola is the town's burgeoning **industrial estate**, while there is a fish farm away from the built up area to the east and a '**herbal**

farm' on the west bank of the Rapti Khola. Hetauda has three temples of minor note. The **Ram Mandir** is just off the Tribhuvan Highway between the main intersection and the Royal Palace; the **Bhutan Devi Mandir** is 400 metres west of the Royal Palace; and the **Hanuman Mandir** is just east of the main intersection.

Few travellers stay in Hetauda any longer than the usual 15 minute tea stop at the main bus park.

Hetauda has a limited choice of accommodation. There are a couple of extremely **Sleeping** basic places near the bus park and around the bazaar area. **C** *Motel Avocado*, T20429 (Kathmandu, F20135). 16 rooms all with bath and some a/c, restaurant. This is by far the best place to stay and takes its name from the avocado trees in the garden, located 800 metres north of the main intersection on the Tribhuvan Highway. **D** *Rapti*, T20882. 12 rooms most with bath, restaurant, 300 metres south of the main intersection.

The main **bus park** is just to the southwest of the main intersection of the highways. **Transport** Most buses running between East Nepal and **Chitwan**, **Pokhara** and **Kathmandu** stop at Hetauda. There is a daily, early morning Sajha bus to Kathmandu (7 hours, Rs 100) via the **Tribhuvan Highway**. There is an irregular local bus service to **Daman**, but it is better to take the Kathmandu bus.

Tribhuvan Highway north to Kathmandu

Known as the original Rajpath ('Royal Way'), the Tribhuvan Highway is the oldest of Nepal's highways and links Naubise (25 kilometres west of Kathmandu) with the Indian border at Birgunj/Raxaul. It was named in memory of King Tribhuvan. Its construction was finally completed with Indian assistance in 1956, and provided the first serviceable road connection between Kathmandu and India. Before then, however, the route was already established and was that taken by the rare foreign visitor invited to Kathmandu. Like the Siddhartha Highway to the west, the best stretch is through the Terai plains, while it is an unending series of climbs and descents and twists and turns through the Churias north of Hetauda. Its total length extends some 158 kilometres from north to south. It is 32 kilometres as the crow flies from Hetauda to Naubise, but the Tribhuvan Highway makes it an astonishing 107 kilometres! It is also an amazingly picturesque ride, especially as you go through Daman from where the best mountain views south of the Kathmandu Valley are to be had. The highway has been recommended as a mountain biking route, but you would have to be both adventurous and extremely fit to do it.

Daman

Standing at 2,322 metres, Daman offers stunning (some say, Nepal's best) *Colour map 2, grid B5* views across the Himalaya. On a clear day, the panorama extends as far east as Mount Everest and as far west as Dhaulagiri. Early mornings offer the best chance of an unoccluded vista at most times of the year, however, which usually means staying overnight. This appears an attractive prospect (accommodation is available), but transport to and from Daman is problematic and deters many potential visitors.

The small village of Daman is dominated by the view tower (Rs 20), an enclosed modern structure with telescopes. From here you have superb views not only of the mountains, but also of a large section of the Kathmandu Valley and, to the south, across the Terai plains and into India. To the immediate north is the Palung Valley, while the highest point along the Tribhuvan Highway is a few kilometres to the south at Simbhanjyang (2,840 metres).

Sleeping The two more expensive options can be booked from Kathmandu as part of an inclu-
Daman is cold, sive package, including transport to/from the capital. There is a limited choice for
especially in winter, so budget travellers. **B** *Everest Panorama Resort*, Kathmandu T415372. 18 heated
bring warm clothing rooms, some in tents, restaurant/bar, short treks arranged. **C** *Mountain Resort*,
and perhaps a blanket Kathmandu T226779, F226827. Accommodation in heated tents, restaurant, expen-
or shawl as well. sive. **E** *Sherpa*, 6 rooms all common bath, Nepali food available, cold at night, basic.

Transport Buses travelling between **Kathmandu** and Hetauda pass through Daman, including
one daily morning Sajha service in each direction. There are also a couple of private
buses between Kathmandu and **Birgunj**. It can be difficult to get a seat, however, as
all may be full by the time they reach Daman. A possible, though expensive, alternative is to hire a car from Kathmandu.

Birgunj

Population: 69,005 Birgunj is one of the most used border crossings between Nepal and India. It is
(1995) a bazaar town that thrives on its border location, with shops selling all manner
Phone code: 051 of seemingly mundane goods imported from the West and especially popular
Colour map 2, grid C5 with Indian visitors. It is convenient for Chitwan National Park and has several
direct bus services to Kathmandu and Pokhara. It also has a wide catchment
area of travellers entering from India, with good road transport connections to
Patna through which it links into a nationwide rail network. Temperatures are
at their lowest in January at 5°C but can reach a stifling 41°C in May and June.

Birgunj has acquired an unfortunate reputation which is partially deserved,
but in its range of accommodation and other facilities, it emerges favourably
from comparisons with Sunauli (Belahiya) to the west, the next border crossing open to foreigners. Birgunj is by no means a town in which to linger any
longer than necessary, but if you do have to stay the night there is enough to
ensure that it is relatively comfortable and is preferable to a night in Raxaul.

The **Tribhuvan Highway** bisects the town. The older areas are on the **eastern** side, a maze of bazaar areas and busy streets lined with small shops and
local eateries, and every so often a small temple or shrine. There are also a couple of very basic guest houses here, but those on the opposite side of town are
less noisy and more used to dealing with Westerners. The **western** side consists of a planned grid of wider streets, generally less congested though not
without its share of freely honking and polluting traffic. Dominating the
northwest part of Birgunj is the imposing **town hall**, its architecture successfully combining aspects of traditional Nepali temple design with those of a
modern civic utility. Nearby is a large tank (*pokhari*) with a walkway leading to
a minor temple in the middle. An open square at the southern end of the grid of
streets marks the site of the old bus park before it was moved to its new location
in 1994. The construction of a bypass has diverted some of the traffic away
from the centre. The tall **clocktower** in the middle of a busy intersection on
the highway at the northern end of town is the most prominent landmark.
From here, the mostly unpaved and pot-holed New Road leads east to the
new bus park.

Terai & Churia Hills

Essentials

C *Diyalo*, T22370, F21570. 22 rooms all with bath, some a/c and air cooled rooms, restaurant, clean and bright, slightly expensive and reluctant to discount. **C** *Kailash*, T22384. 16 rooms some a/c and air cooled, reasonable tandoori restaurant. **C** *Makalu*, T23054, F22766. 10 rooms all with bath, most a/c and TV, excellent restaurant, bar, small conference hall, modern. The sliding scale of room charges is largely determined by the size of the TV! The best hotel in Birgunj, credit cards accepted. Recommended. **C** *Samjhana*, T22122. 40 rooms all with bath, most a/c (cheaper non a/c rooms), restaurant, bar, pleasant garden, located 1 kilometre north of the clock tower on the Tribhuvan Highway. **C-D** *Fulwari*, T23341. 8 comfortable rooms with bath and phone, some a/c, restaurant. **C-D** *Suraj*, T22859. 22 rooms all with bath, some a/c, cheaper non a/c rooms, an extraordinary ground floor: dimly lit and apocalyptic,

Birgunj

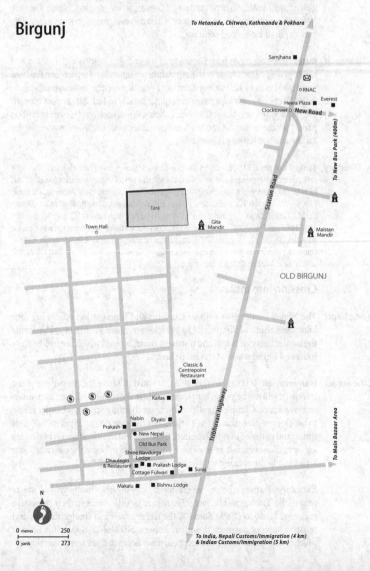

To Hetanuda, Chitwan, Kathmandu & Pokhara

Samjhana

RNAC

Heera Plaza   Everest

Clocktower   **New Road**

Station Road

To New Bus Park (400m)

Terai & Churia Hills

Town Hall   Tank   Gita Mandir   Maistan Mandir

OLD BIRGUNJ

Classic & Centrepoint Restaurant

Kailas

Tribhuvan Highway

Prakash   Nabin   Diyalo

New Nepal

Old Bus Park

Shree Navdurga Lodge

Dhaulagiri & Restaurant   Prakash Lodge

Cottage Fulwari   Suraj

Makalu   Bishnu Lodge

To Main Bazaar Area

N

0 metres 250
0 yards 273

To India, Nepali Customs/Immigration (4 km)
& Indian Customs/Immigration (5 km)

better rooms on upper floors, cavernous. On New Rd, both **C-D** *Everest* and **C-D** *Heera Plaza* are modern hotels with some a/c rooms and reasonable restaurants.

D *Hotel Prakash*, T22351. 15 rooms some with bath and air cooler, best rooms on 2nd floor, avoid ground floor cells, good Indian food.

E *Bishnu Lodge*, T22509. 6 rooms all with bath, no food, grubby and basic. **E** *Classic*, T22425. 18 rooms some with bath. **E** *Dhaulagiri Guest House*, 10 rooms, no food, dark. **E** *Nabin*, T21074, 13 rooms some with bath, no food, crude. **E** *Prakash Lodge*, T22351. A further downmarket version of *Hotel Prakash*, above. **E** *Shree Navdurga Lodge*, T22169. 12 rooms some with bath, no food, very basic.

Eating All the **C** grade hotels listed above have decent restaurants, though it is best to stick to Indian food. The *Makalu Hotel's* restaurant does especially good Indian food. The *New Nepal Restaurant*, near the old bus park, is a bit dark and gloomy, but has reasonable, budget priced Indian food and a bar.

Transport **Buses** There are buses from Birgunj to all major tourist destinations. Evening and early morning departures to both **Kathmandu** (including Sajha service) and **Pokhara** (both 8-10 hours, Rs 125/100 per night/day). Regular day buses to **Janakpur** (5 hours, Rs 70). There are many local buses throughout the day to **Tadi Bazaar** (for **Chitwan**) and one good express bus at lunchtime (3 hours, Rs 50). Booking offices are at the **bus park**, 1 kilometre west of the clock tower. Advance booking is recommended for Kathmandu and Pokhara at peak times.

Directory **Banks** *Nabil Bank*, T21476, F23156. Deals in all major foreign currencies, cash and TCs, credit card advances (Mastercard and Visa). Fast and efficient service. *Nepal Indosuez Bank*, T23327, F22932. Only buys major foreign currency notes and TCs, no credit cards. *Nepal Rastra Bank*, T22053. Will change TCs and currency notes, but slow service. *State Bank of India (Nepal)*, T21542, F23268. Deals in all major currencies, cash and American Express TCs only. All are open 1000-1430 Sun-Thur, 1000-1200 Fri, closed Sat. **Communications** **Area code:** the area code for Birgunj is 051. There are several STD/ISD booths around town, including *Hello Sir*, T21701, F23061. Opposite Hotel Diyalo which also does photocopying, lamination and car hire. **Post Office:** the post office is 300m north of the clocktower.

Crossing into India

Leaving Nepal The Nepali border post with its Customs and Immigration offices lies four kilometres south of Birgunj, Rs 10 by rickshaw. A one kilometre bridge forms the border between Nepal and northern Bihar, beyond which are Indian Customs and Immigration at Raxaul Bazaar.

At the border **Immigration** It is easy to miss these. If you don't have the proper entry/exit stamps, it will not be possible to leave/re-enter the country without maximum inconvenience. Completing all formalities and getting across the border seems to take longer here than at any of the other crossing points, especially at meal times, and patience may be required. Customs and Immigration on both sides are open 24 hours, but as elsewhere you will have to rouse the officials if you arrive late in the evening.

Exchange Birgunj's banks are clustered close together in the grid of streets west of the Tribhuvan Highway. There may be differences in their respective exchange rates, so check. Some of the larger hotels can change money, and most will accept payment in Indian Rupees. **NB** Unlike Nepal, it is normal practice in India to refuse to accept currency notes that are torn, even slightly,

Terai & Churia Hills

or defaced anywhere but in the oval space to the left of the front of the note. In order to avoid arriving in India with what is effectively a bundle of useless money, do take the time to count and carefully check each note that you have been given and don't hesitate to demand replacement of any that are damaged.

Raxaul matches Birgunj in aesthetic appeal, but is worse for accommodation. Birgunj is definitely the better place for an overnight stay. Raxaul has a railway station. The bus stop (for Patna) is another three kilometres to the south. Rickshaws cost around (IC) Rs 5. Tongas, powered by weary looking donkeys, are also available (Rs 3), but are slow with little space for baggage.

Onward into India

Several buses run daily between Raxaul and Patna's Hardinge Park bus stop (5-7 hours, IC Rs 70). The first bus from Patna leaves at around 0800. Night buses from Patna reach Birgunj early morning, and morning buses from Patna connect with the night bus to Kathmandu. Either way, at least one night bus journey is involved unless you stay at Birgunj. Buses connect Patna with Ranchi, Calcutta, Siliguri (for Darjeeling) and other regional centres. Patna has an airport with regular flights to Calcutta, Delhi, Lucknow and Ranchi (Indian Airlines city office T0612-22554, airport office T223199). There are trains from Patna Junction to Amritsar, Bombay (Mumbai), Calcutta, Delhi, Madras (Chenai) and Varanasi among others.

Eastern Terai

The Mahendra highway ends its long journey across the Terai at Kakarbhitta. Janakpur is a good place to break a journey with its almost Indian feel and myriad of temples. Here you can experience the traditional life of the Ganges plains: an endless expanse of paddies, trees and small hamlets untouched by the 20th century. Ilam, in the hills above the plain is the heart of Nepal's tea growing area and similar to the much more famous Darjeeling not far across the border in India.

Janakpur

Population: 54,710 (1991)
Phone code: 041
Colour map 1, grid B5

Arriving in Janakpur from Kathmandu is rather like leaving Nepal for India, while the town will come as a welcome change from the more dreary surroundings of Birgunj or Biratnagar if you have been travelling through the Terai. It is certainly one of the Terai's more interesting places, though some tourist literature does tend to overdo the hype. As the only major town between Birgunj (106 kilometres along the Mahendra Highway) and Biratnagar (169 kilometres) it is ideally suited for a short stay to break the numbing journey between Kathmandu and Kakarbhitta. The town is a feast of temples: there are more than 100, dominated by the spectacular **Janaki Mandir**. It also has a sizeable **Muslim** minority, mostly long term migrants from Bihar, and a small mosque (*masjid*) stands beside the Janaki Mandir. Economically it relies mainly on agriculture although there is some light industry including cigarette manufacture.

Aside from its religious role, Janakpur has the distinction of being the focus of Nepal's only extant **railway** line. This is essentially no more than a short, narrow gauge extension of a line in North Bihar and of such significance that it goes unrecorded in all but the largest of Nepal's statistical tomes. Apart from at the main hotels, little English is spoken here. There are a couple of delightful walking opportunities, though, and no other major Terai town allows you to leave the urban environment so easily and abruptly for the quiet, open and endless expanse of paddies, trees and small hamlets which, as yet largely unaffected by the baggage of the latter 20th century, so characterize traditional life in the Ganges plains.

Eastern Terai

Its contemporary significance is derived from its role as an important centre in the religious and historical geography of Nepal, and the town is often referred to as *Janakpurdham*, the suffix added in deference to its sacredness. Hindu pilgrims come from all over Nepal and from India to worship at the town's many temples, shrines and *pokharis*, and during the main Hindu festivals Janakpur is said to attract more than double its own population in visitors. It takes its

Janaki Mandir

name from King Janak, ruler of the ancient and prosperous kingdom of Mithila who, the epic *Ramayana* records, found the baby Sita lying in a field at what is now Sitamadhi village just outside Janakpur. The Vivaha Mandap, next to the marvellous Janaki Temple, today commemorates the spot of the fabled wedding.

Janaki Mandir Known locally as **Naulakha**, this temple is dedicated to Sita and houses a large image of Sita said to have been found in a river near Ayodhya and brought here by Sura Kishore. It is built of white marble and its design resembles a Mughal fort, with an arched main gate and windows and octagonal parapets set into the towers on both sides. The temple was commissioned by Brishbhana Kunwar, the Maharani of the princely state of Tikamgarh in present day Madhya Pradesh, central India. Construction was completed in 1911. The huge building contains 60 rooms and dominates the centre of Janakpur. Regular puja worship takes place at 0800 and in the late afternoon. Non-Hindu visitors are not allowed into the shrine room, but can walk around the outer courtyard where you can see the magnificent marble tracery and other artwork.

Many thousands of pilgrims visit the temple in November/December for *Vivah Panchomi* ('marriage over 5 days'), the town's major annual festival, when the marriage of Sita and Rama is celebrated with numerous re-enactments. An image of Rama is brought to the Janaki Mandir in a big procession and leaves the following day with that of Sita. This is also a popular time for modern day weddings.

Vivaha Mandap The name of his modern addition to the Janaki Mandir complex means 'marriage pavilion'. It has a pagoda roof and, uniquely, glass walls. The large images of Rama and Sita sit on a raised platform inside and commemorate their fabled wedding in full colour.

Ram Mandir This is Janakpur's oldest temple and was built in 1882 by Amar Singh Thapa, who was also responsible for Tansen's Amar Narayan Mandir. It lies at the heart of the old part of Janakpur, 200 metres southeast of the Janaki Mandir. A shrine stands in the centre of the courtyard. Non-Hindu visitors are allowed in, but shoes and leather items should be removed and left outside. Just to the east is **Danush Sagar**, one of the town's holiest pokharis where pilgrims take a ritual cleansing bath before puja.

Ganga Sagar This large *pokhari* to the southeast of the town's main chowk is considered to be the holiest of Janakpur's many ponds. On its western side is a *dharamsala* and ghat, now used mostly for washing.

Hanuman Mandir Out on the western bypass, 200 metres south of Ramanand Chowk, this small temple attracts a steady stream of visitors. They come either to worship Hanuman or simply to see his image: in this case, a live

Sights

Terai & Churia Hills

👉 *The Story of Rama and Sita*

While performing a religious rite of fertility, King Janak found Sita ('furrow') lying in a field beside a pond. Sita was acknowledged as an incarnation of the godess Lakshmi, and the king took her and raised her as his daughter. When the time came for the beautiful princess to be married, Janak set a test: only he who could bend the great bow of Shiva could marry his daughter. Many tried and failed, and it was left to the divine Rama from Ayodhya to perform the superhuman feat and claim Sita as his wife.

One day, when Rama was away, the demon Ravana came to Sita disguised as an ascetic. Once welcomed into the house, he revealed his true self and asked her to marry him. Fire burned in Sita's eyes as she pronounced her virtue and denied him. Ravana then took the shape of a giant and whisked her away to his kingdom of Lanka and there imprisoned her, but still she did not submit. After some time the offended Rama, with the help of his faithful aid Hanuman, invaded Lanka and defeated Ravana. Sita was overjoyed. But when at length she saw her husband, his words were cold. He told her that he had acted to defend his family honour and that he could no longer bear to be with her, accusing her of having been defiled and likening her presence to that of a polluting dog.

Sita felt as though she had been struck by a thunderbolt. She protested her innocence, then commanded that a funeral pyre be prepared and threw herself into the flames. But before she could commit sati the gods rescued her. Rama agreed to take her back, but only as a companion as he remained convinced of her infidelity. One day he overheard a lowly washerman refuse to take his wife back after an adulterous affair, saying that he was not as stupid as Rama. This confirmed Sita's guilt in Rama's eyes and his jealousy was so inflamed that he ordered her to be taken to the forest and put to death. By this time, however, she was pregnant and her executioner took pity and saved her. So she lived in the forest as the guest of Valmiki, a hermit, and soon gave birth to twin sons, Lava and Kusa.

Her sons became fine warriors and after many years found themselves in conflict with Rama. Rama was astonished by their resemblance to himself and asked Valmiki who they were. When he was told, he brought Sita back and publicly affirmed her innocence. But Sita had already been too wounded by Rama's past deeds. She implored Mother Earth to receive her and the ground on which she stood suddenly opened and she returned to whence she came.

monkey who is kept in a small cage and is fed with sweets, milk, bananas and other assorted fruits, all offerings to the deity, throughout the day. The continuous feeding and lack of space have resulted in an obscenely overweight primate: 55 kg and the world's largest, according to an obscurely authenticated certificate. The temple was the gift of a local high profile philanthropist in 1984. The exact age of the monkey is unknown, but it is believed to have replaced the temple's original monkey which died. It is washed daily and has its own fan to keep cool.

Walks There is no other place in the Terai region that succeeds quite as well or as naturally in combining a rich religious heritage in an urban setting with the traditional rural culture of the North Indian plains. You can leave Janakpur on foot in any direction and within minutes be surrounded by lush countryside.

One fine possibility (which is rewarding also if you can find a bike to hire for the day) is to follow the road south of the town heading towards and beyond the airport. The smooth road continues down to the **Indian border**. (**NB** Foreigners are not permitted to cross here.) Passing to the east of the airport and observing the goats whose excellent knowledge of flight schedules allows them to wander carefree along the runway, this point marks the sudden transition from town to country. From here you walk through an endless series of quiet paddy fields interspersed with the cool shade of mango groves, an occasional temple or shrine, and hamlets of thatched mud houses where women wash their clothes, pots and pans while young children in handed-down shorts and T-shirts play out their childhood before it is claimed for the fields: you won't see any pot bellies here. Be sure to take enough water with you, as none is available along the way.

Dhanukha About 20 kilometres northeast of Janakpur, Dhanukha (or Dhanukhadham) is a quiet temple site and, according to the Ramayana, is the place where Rama claimed Sita as his own by bending Shiva's bow. A peepul tree stands beside the small temple, and the spot is surrounded by forest with some delightful walking opportunities which add to its local popularity as a romantic destination for courting couples. There are only two buses a day between Janakpur and Dhanukha, leaving Janakpur for the one-hour journey at 0800 and 1000 and departing Dhanukha at 0930 and 1130, which rather restricts visiting. Alternatively, a couple of Janakpur's hotels can arrange private transport to Dhanukha, rates are normally negotiable. There is a very

Excursions

Terai & Churia Hills

Janakpur

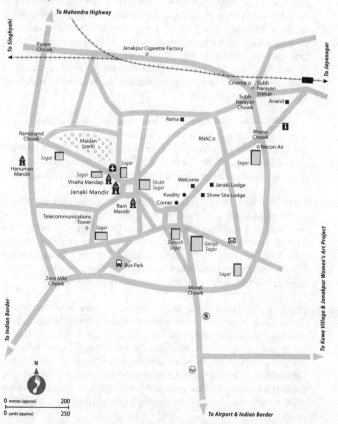

basic, but available, *dharamsala* next to the temple at Dhanukha which may be an option if you wish to stay overnight.

Jaleshwar An old temple dedicated to Shiva is the focus for a visit by many pilgrims here. Located some 15 kilometres southwest of Janakpur, the Jaleshwarnath temple contains an image of the lingam and is situated beside a deep well (Shivatri), whose waters are held as especially sacred by the devout. Many pilgrims visit Jaleshwar as part of an all day fast. There are regular bus connections from Janakpur: the first leaves at around 0600, with the last departure leaving Jaleshwar at about 1830 for the 45 minute journey.

Essentials

Sleeping Janakpur does not have a wide choice of tourist standard accommodation. Although it is usually sufficient to cater for demand, rooms are very scarce during the main festivals when it is recommended to phone and book ahead. In addition to the following, there are also some dharamsalas, temple rest houses, which may offer very basic accommodation and food.

D *Anand*, T20562, F20196. 15 rooms most with bath and some with air cooler, small restaurant does reasonable and reasonably priced Indian and Chinese food, Western breakfast, near railway station, clean. **D** *Rama*, T20059. 22 spacious rooms all with bath, some with a/c and TV, reasonable restaurant, close to RNAC office, dull concrete exterior though otherwise identical in most respects to the *Welcome* but considerably cheaper. **D** *Welcome*, T20646, F20922. 23 rooms most with bath, some a/c and TV, some good value cheaper rooms, comfortable but relatively expensive restaurant (open 0630-1000, 1030-1500, and 1730-2200) does good Indian, Chinese and Western food, excellent dal and tandoori items, large airy building in central location, no water filter so expensive mineral water available only – better to stock up with bottled water from nearby shops.

E *Janaki Lodge*, extremely basic but also cheap single rooms with bath, next to Shree Sita Lodge, no English spoken. **E** *Shree Sita Lodge*, opposite *Welcome*, 15 rooms all with bath including a couple of half decent rooms, most are very basic but clean and cheap. **E** *Shukh Sagar*, T20488. 14 rooms most with bath and some with air cooler, overlooking Janaki Mandir, very central, noisy front rooms, English speaking owner.

Eating Aside from street side food and hotel restaurants, there are only 2 other restaurants of note in central Janakpur. The *Kwality* is no relation to the Indian chain of the same name but does the standard range of Indian and Chinese food. If you are staying at the *Welcome hotel*, this is also a cheaper option for a Western style breakfast and is about 200 metres southwest of the hotel. Just around the corner, at the main intersection of roads, is the *Corner Restaurant*. This is rather more spartan but has some good Indian dishes. Both the *Rama and Welcome hotels* have decent restaurants.

Festivals Janakpur's major annual festival is *Vivah Panchomi* in November/December (see above). *Dasain*, Nepal's largest national festival, is relatively small here, but is celebrated over 10 days in October/November, with goats being sacrificed at some temples in the last 2 days. In March, meanwhile, *Ramnomi* is celebrated over 9 days and nights with music, drama, dance and other pageants taking place on the maidan. *Lakshmi Puja* is the highlight of *Diwali* in November and is marked with thousands of small candles and lights being illuminated throughout the area, music all day and all night, and firecrackers (officially banned by the local government).

Terai & Churia Hills

Mithila art

The ancient kingdom of Mithila gives its name to an art form unique to the area around Janakpur and northern Bihar, one that has been handed down over generations through three millennia and has witnessed something of a revival in recent years. Known also as **Madhubani**, it is characterized largely by painting and wickerwork and is produced mainly by women. The paintings are dominated by religious themes, typically representing scenes from the marriage of Rama and Sita who are often depicted standing face to face in the centre, with parents or respective family entourages fanning out either side. The depiction is always surrounded by a decorative border, a sort of homage to the sanctity of the portrayal. Black is used to outline the figures, the incidental decoration and border, with green, red and pastel yellow the other dominant colours.

The art is believed to have originated in the village of **Kuwa**, today located between Janakpur town centre and the airport, where the **Janakpur Women's Art Project** was established in 1979 to maintain and promote the tradition and to provide employment to some local women. Their products are on sale in some of Kathmandu's handicraft shops and Mithila paintings also adorn the walls of both Grindlays Bank and the UNDP offices in the capital as well as in Chitwan's Macchan Resort. Technically, the paintings may be described as simple, but they are not intended to be intricate masterpieces; instead it is the process of composition which is often as, if not more, important than the finished product itself. As in the Russian or Greek Orthodox Christian traditions, an iconographer may consider him or herself to pray rather than paint an icon, so in the Mithila tradition the act of painting as veneration of the subject or theme may be foremost in the artist's mind. Thus, once completed the purpose will have been fulfilled and the painting may be discarded.

Mithila art has come to be closely identified with Janakpur, and now also takes the form of the more permanent **mural** that decorates many a town wall. It has a further cultural function: before marriage a girl will often present her depiction of the wedding of Rama and Sita to her future husband.

Other Mithila handicrafts include the siki dalia, a flat basket weaved of dried siki grass. This usually has a central, symmetrical red and green star or sun type design and is popularly used as a receptacle to carry fruits and other offerings to a temple deity during puja.

There is a kiosk selling locally produced Mithila handicrafts at the airport.

Transport

Local There are no taxis in Janakpur, but most parts of the town are within easy walking distance. Rickshaws are available. From the main intersection at Ganga Sagar, the rickshaw fare to the airport is around Rs 25 and to the bus park Rs 5.

Air The airport is 2 kilometres south of the town's main intersection. There is a daily flight to/from **Kathmandu** ($55) with either Necon Air (T21900) or RNAC (T20185, airport T20088).

Buses The **bus park** is 500 metres southwest of Ganga Sagar. To **Kathmandu**: numerous day and night buses (10-12 hours, Rs 170), including 2 early morning Sajha departures. To **Pokhara**: one daily bus in the early afternoon (10-12 hours, Rs 170). To **Birgunj**: 3-4 buses from early morning (6 hours, Rs 50). To **Biratnagar**: departures at 0400, 1000, 1300 (8 hours, Rs 80). To **Kakarbhitta**: buses leave at 0500, 0600 and 1700 (10 hours, Rs 135).

Trains The railway attracts attention because it is unique in Nepal, but is not an especially comfortable or adventurous journey, and is used mainly by commuters. It runs

27 kilometres southeast to **Jayanagar** in India, and 19 kilometres northwest to **Singhyahi**. There is a further stretch of disused and now broken track to Bijalpura in the hills. Departures to Jayanagar at 0630, 1255 and 1655; from Jayanagar at 0945, 1500 and 1900 (1st Class, ie padded seats, Rs 35, 2nd Class Rs 13). Departures to Singhyahi at 0700 and 1520; from Singhyahi at 1030 and 1900 (1st Class Rs 30, 2nd Class Rs 8).

Directory **Banks** The town has several banks, but only the *Nepal Rastra Bank* on the road heading south towards the airport deals with foreign exchange. A large red building in attractive gardens, it lies about 1 km south of Dhanukh Sagar (the large pond at the central intersection of the main roads into town). It will change currency notes and TCs, but can not give credit card advances. Open 1000-1430 Sun-Thur, 1000-1200 Sat, closed Fri. **Communications** Area code: the area code for Janakpur is 041. **Tourist offices** This small office is located about 5 mins walk northeast of the Welcome hotel towards the railway station. Little English is spoken. You can normally get the standard handouts on Pokhara, Kathmandu or anywhere else that is not Janakpur (T20755). Open 1000-1700 Sun-Thur, 1000-1500 Fri, closed Sat.

Trains from Janakpur

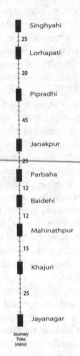

Singhyahi
25
Lorhapati
20
Pipradhi
45
Janakpur
25
Parbaha
12
Baidehi
12
Mahinathpur
15
Khajuri
25
Jayanagar

Journey Time (mins)

The Mahendra Highway between Janakpur and Biratnagar

The highway continues its eastward course from the **Janakpur** junction at **Dhalkebar** through a Terai landscape of alternate sal forest and open farm land. It passes through the occasional small village and crosses the **Kamla Khola** (18 kilometres from the Janakpur junction) and the **Balan Khola** after another 43 kilometres. The village of **Mohanpur** is the junction for the road to **Rajbiraj** (11 kilometres), the first town of any note east of Janakpur. It is a local market town and an administrative centre, and has an airport with occasional RNAC flights to/from Kathmandu. From Mohanpur, the highway heads east for another 20 kilometres before turning sharply south at **Kanchanpur** and following the wide and magnificent **Sapt Kosi** to Barda (15 kilometres) to cross the river at the impressive Kosi Barrage. East of the barrage, the road actually crosses briefly into Indian territory before reverting to a course north of the border and reaching **Itahari**, the junction for Biratnagar, Dharan and Dhankuta, after 47 kilometres.

Koshi Tappu Wildlife Reserve

Colour map 1, grid C6   *Koshi Tappu (tappu, 'island') is the easternmost and the smallest of the Terai's national parks and wildlife reserves. It covers an area of 175 square kilometres of the Sapt Koshi floodplain, immediately northeast of the Koshi Barrage, where the Sapt Koshi and Trijuga Khola rivers converge.*

It is possible to visit Koshi Tappu both independently and by package tour. **Visiting**
The entry permit costs Rs 650 from the reserve office and is valid for two consecutive days. The reserve office and headquarters is at **Kusaha**, three kilometres north of the Mahendra Highway; the turning is three kilometres west of
Laukhi village. You may also be able to hire a guide from here (ie a warden who
can take time off to show you around), but Koshi Tappu has few independent
visitors so finding a guide is very much a matter of luck.

Fauna On all but the southern side it is surrounded by forest (mostly sal) **Wildlife**
which is home to small and decreasing numbers of mammals, including a population of about 100 wild buffalo (*arna*), nilgai ('blue bull'), spotted and hog
deer, monkeys and wild boar.

Reptiles Gangetic **dolphins**, darker skinned relatives of the more familiar silver
skinned bottle nosed dolphin, are occasionally seen jumping in the rivers. The
endangered **gharial crocodile** inhabits the area in small numbers which have
been boosted by the re-introduction of more from the Chitwan breeding centre.

Birds Above all, Koshi Tappu is known for its bird life, with over 280 species
including 20 species of duck, ibises, storks, swamp partridges, herons, egrets,
Bengal floricans, and many other exotic and migratory waterfowl not found
elsewhere in Nepal.

Flora and environment The vegetation is a combination of scrub grassland
(*kharpater*) and deciduous riverine forest. The appearance of the environment
changes dramatically with the seasons. It is at its most supreme during the
monsoon when the river swells to become a wide and powerful torrent heading
south and feeding into the Ganges. Much of the floodplain is submerged to
depths of up to three metres. In the dry months leading up to the monsoon,
meanwhile, the flow is radically reduced with numerous sandy islands appearing. The plains are flat and exposed to the strong winds which are a prominent
feature of Terai weather at certain times of year. Prolonged vigorous gusts
often whip up water from the river to create oblique screens of mist to give the
area a spectacularly wild appearance.

There are a number of small villages around Koshi Tappu, notably in the
western floodplains. Many rely on fishing in the rivers for their livelihood, and
fish (eg *kaddi macha*) forms an important part of the local diet.

Vehicles are not allowed inside the reserve, but ideally you should have your **Viewing**
own vehicle to get there. There are bus services from Biratnagar and **Itahari**
that stop on the Mahendra Highway, four kilometres from the reserve headquarters. You can also visit the area and get a general impression of the environment without having to enter the reserve. Take a bus heading west from
Biratnagar/Itahari and get down at or before the village of **Bhantabari**. From
here, head up in the general direction of the wooded river embankment (there
are a couple of small rivers to cross – look out for the makeshift bridges) on top
of which there is a path running alongside the river. There are occasional spurs
leading down to the riverbank which make good locations for a peaceful picnic. **NB** Proceed with care, especially during the monsoon when the river is
high and can be dangerous.

Independent visitors: although independent visitors can camp near the park **Park**
headquarters (Rs 300 per night, bring your own equipment), the nearest practi- **information**
cal base is Biratnagar, 55 kilometres by good road from the reserve headquarters.

Terai & Churia Hills

Package tours The only package tours are offered by **B** *Aqua Birds Unlimited Camp*, Kathmandu T429515, F416516, aquabird@ccsl.com.np. In Kusaha village, next to the park head-quarters, with 10 comfortable twin-bedded 'safari tents', thatched dining room and bar. Organized tours of one to four nights, but individual non-tour visitors also welcome. **B** *Koshi Tappu Wildlife Camp*, Kathmandu T226130, F224237. Situated in the northeast corner of the reserve, the camp provides accommodation in 12 comfortable tents with attached bath. It has a restaurant and bar. Activities including boat rides and guided walks. The camp is open from October-April/May.

Transport If you are visiting Koshi Tappu on a package tour, all transport is included. Getting there from **Biratnagar** without a hire car can be problematic and time consuming. There are regular local buses to **Itahari** (45 minutes, Rs 10). From Itahari you can take any bus heading west along the Mahendra Highway and get down 3 kilometres beyond **Laukhi** (40 minutes, Rs 18) and walk the remaining 3 kilometres to the reserve headquarters and office at **Kusaha**. **Bhantabari** is the village immediately to the east of the Koshi Barrage (45 minutes, Rs 20).

Itahari

Colour map 1, grid C6 Itahari is a locally important junction town on the Mahendra Highway, with roads heading south to Biratnagar, and north to Dharan, Dhankuta, Hile and Basantpur. The main roundabout has a large statue of King Tribhuvan and is the centre for most of the town's activity. There is a bazaar area and a local branch of the Rastra Banijya Bank.

The town has a couple of basic places to stay, including the **E** *Jaya Nepal Hotel and Bar*, Saino Lodge, and Subudha Guest House, but there is little to be gained in staying here when Biratnagar is a short bus journey away. Slightly east of the main roundabout is the *Invite* restaurant which has a reasonable choice of Indian/Nepali food.

Charkosa Jhadi Forest There is an army camp road just north of the main roundabout on the Dharan road. Beyond this begins the Charkosa Jhadi Forest, part of the Terai's belt of sal forest. It was formerly inhabited by a rich variety of wildlife, including tigers, bears, elephants, deer and snakes. But today the bare scars of deforestation are apparent in much of this and the surrounding areas, although there is also encouraging evidence of attempts made to reverse the trend. Since the early 1990s in particular, reforestation has been a priority and there are several islands of newly planted trees. The forest extends either side of the road and covers most of the area between Itahari and Dharan. A small population of deer still inhabits parts of the forest. Wild elephants have also been seen here, albeit rarely, and have been known to cause traffic jams. There are a number of well trodden paths leading off from the road which would suggest some excellent walking opportunities, but locals warn of poisonous and lethal snakes in the forest, including cobra. In the months preceding the monsoon, the forest gets very dry and is especially vulnerable to fire.

Biratnagar

Population: 129,388
(1991)
Phone code: 021
Colour map 1, grid C6

Biratnagar is Nepal's second largest city and the only one with a six-figure population outside the Kathmandu Valley. It lies 23 kilometres south of Itahari on the Mahendra Highway and is the district headquarters of **Morang**. It is Nepal's foremost industrial town and the road from Itahari is lined with small factories and industrial units including timber and agricultural processing and textile production. A large proportion of its industry is owned by Marwari Indians.

Despite this, Biratnagar is not an unattractive town. Industrial units are for the most part shielded behind large walls and several attempt to mitigate their effect on the surrounding countryside with small and attractive landscaped gardens. In its layout, the town bears remarkable similarity with Nepalgunj in the western Terai, though there is a much better selection of accommodation available here. There are two long north-south running main roads between which are its main bazaar and commercial areas along with most of its hotel accommodation. The built up area has been extended to the east where the

Biratnagar

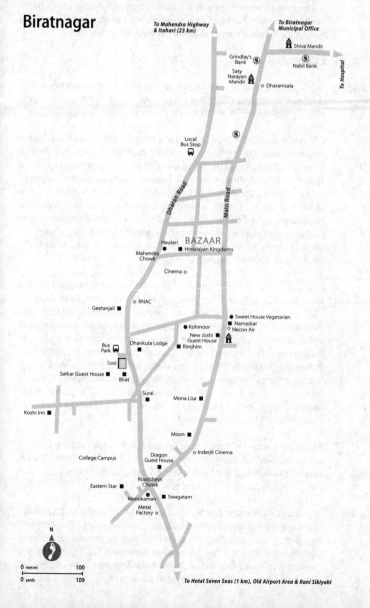

local hospital is located. The airport lies three kilometres north of the centre, while six kilometres to the south is the village of **Rani Sikiyahi** and the Indian **border**. (**NB** The border is not open to foreigners.) The Biratnagar Municipal Office, the district's administrative headquarters, is located one kilometre north of the main bazaar area.

The town is also a base for a number of NGOs working in the region. These include the third largest branch of the **Grameen Bank** (*grameen*, 'village'), a pioneering Bangladeshi NGO which provides low interest loans targeted mostly at small groups of village women – seen as traditionally dependent and marginalized – in an attempt to promote enterprise and self sufficiency.

There are a few small **temples** and shrines, but none stand out as architecturally meritorious. The town attracts few tourists, though it could be used as a base for independent visitors to **Koshi Tappu** Wildlife Reserve.

Essentials

Sleeping Biratnagar has a good selection of mid range as well as budget accommodation. Hotels near the bus park and on Dharan Rd and Main Rd can be very noisy from early morning, so take a room at the back.

C *Eastern Star*, T21588, F22874. 26 rooms all with bath and TV, some a/c, good Indian restaurant, conference hall, modern and plush. **C** *Koshi Inn*, T24408, F22874. 8 rooms all with bath, some a/c or air cooler, reasonable restaurant, resident peacock. **C** *Moon*, T22937. 11 rooms all with bath, most a/c, 2 good Indian restaurants, bar, live ghazals nightly 1830-2130. **C** *Seven Seas*, T/F24872, Kathmandu T424199, F421052. 13 rooms all with bath and TV, most a/c, reasonably priced restaurant, bar, small conference room, quietly situated 1½ kilometres south of Roadshesh Chowk, separate quarters available for your chauffeur and servants! **C** *Swagatam*, T22299, F25988. 20 rooms all with bath, some a/c and TV, some good value non a/c rooms, rather expensive Indian restaurant, just south of Roadshesh Chowk.

D *Dragon*, T27129. 8 rooms most with bath, restaurant. **D** *Geetanjali*, T27335. 8 rooms most with bath, small dormitory, Indian restaurant. **D** *Himalayan Kingdoms*, T27172, F241241. 11 rooms all with bath, some a/c and air cooler, restaurant does good Indian food though expensive continental selection, reliable associated travel agency, will meet at airport if you make advance reservation, central. Recommended. **D** *Mona Lisa*, T23319, 9 rooms most with bath, some a/c, restaurant, undistinguished. **D** *Namaskar*, T21199, F25988. 22 rooms all with bath and phone, some a/c, good Indian/continental restaurant, Mastercard/Visa accepted. **D** *Rimjhim*, T26536. 7 rooms some with bath, small Nepali/Indian restaurant, occasional ghazal programmes, popular with Indian visitors. **D** *Surai*, 8 rooms all with bath, some a/c, Indian restaurant, best rooms at the rear.

E *Birat*, 6 rooms some with bath, noisy, near bus park. **E** *Dhankuta Lodge*, T22925. 7 rooms some with bath, dining room, opposite bus park. **E** *New Joshi*, T25468. 9 rooms some with bath, Nepali/Indian eating area. **E** *Satkar*, T22793. 12 rooms some with bath, no food, near bus park, basic and noisy.

Eating Biratnagar has no shortage of decent restaurants, though in most cases it is advisable to stick to Indian/Nepali food. All the **C** grade hotels have restaurants. That at the *Koshi Inn* is popular with locals. Try dinner at the *Hotel Moon* for *ghazal* accompaniment. Occasional ghazals also at the *Manokaman Restaurant*, T23715, at Roadshesh Chowk, Indian/Chinese food and bar. The *Kohinoor Restaurant* at the southern end of the bazaar area is recommended for Indian and Nepali food.

For vegetarian food, try the nearby *Sweet House Restaurant*. Next to the *Himalayan Kingdoms Hotel* at Mahendra Chowk is the *Hautari Restaurant and Bar*, T24693, on the 1st floor.

Cinemas: there are cinemas showing Hindi movies in the bazaar area and 100 metres northeast of Roadshesh Chowk. The *Hotel Moon*, 150 metres northeast of Raodshesh Chowk, has a nightly programme of live *ghazals*, 1830-2130. Recommended.

Entertainment

Local Biratnagar has no **auto-rickshaws**, though there are plenty of **cycle rick-shaws**. A 2-hour tour of the town will cost around Rs 100. There is a **taxi** rank at Mahendra Chowk. These are meant more for longer distances than for local transport. They have no meters, so bargaining the fare in advance is necessary. You can save a lot of time and aggravation by asking your hotel for an idea of the right fare, or ask them to book it for you.

Transport

    Local **buses** every 30 minutes to **Itahari** (45 minutes, Rs 10) and on to **Dharan** (30 minutes, Rs 10), first bus at 0430, last at 1730. There are 4-5 buses from early morning to **Dhankuta**, **Hile** (6 hours) and **Basantpur**. First departure at 0430, last at 1400.

Air There are daily flights to/from **Kathmandu** (US$99), and seasonal flights to **Bhadrapur** and Northeast Nepal. The **airport** is on the Dharan Rd, 4 kilometres north of the main bazaar area. A rickshaw from the centre will cost around Rs 40, and a taxi Rs 150.

Buses The bus park is on Dharan Rd, south of Mahendra Chowk. There are regular day and night buses to **Kathmandu** (12-15 hours, Rs 250). Numerous local buses throughout the day to **Kakarbhitta** (5-6 hours, Rs 60) as well as a couple of faster buses (3 hours, check departure times). Departures to **Janakpur** from early morning (6-8 hours, Rs 90). More buses to these destinations leave from **Itahari**.

Airline offices RNAC (T25335) is on Dharan Rd, 100m south of Mahendra Chowk. Necon Air (T25987) is next to the *Hotel Namaskar*, southeast of the main bazaar area. **Banks** There are a number of banks in Biratnagar, but only *Grindlays* (T27983, F27982) and *Nabil Bank* (T26213, F26214) deal in foreign exchange. TCs, currency notes, Mastercard/Visa advances. Open 1000-1430 Sun-Thur, 1000-1230 Fri, closed Sat. Both are situated north of the main bazaar area. **Communications** Area code: the area code for Biratnagar is 021. Numerous STD/ISD booths throughout town. **Hospitals & medical services** There are several pharmacies throughout the town. The local hospital is located in the north-eastern part of town.

Directory

Terai & Churia Hills

Dharan

Dharan is a busy bazaar town on the first gradients of the Churia Hills. It serves as the principal surface gateway to the **Koshi**, **Mecchi** and **Sagarmatha** zones. The main road from the Terai to Dhankuta and beyond runs as a central artery through the town (you can see **Dhankuta** high on a hill in the distance), while steep, partly forested slopes rise to the east and west. The old part of town is known as **Chandranagar** and the new part as **Juddhanagar**. At almost double the national average, it has one of the highest literacy rates in Nepal and its schools are renowned throughout the eastern region. The town was at the centre of a powerful earthquake in 1988, several hundred casualties were suffered.

Population: 66,457 1991
Altitude: 365m
Colour map 1, grid C6

    The construction of the surfaced road all the way to Basantpur has improved communications in the area, but has also allowed goods to be more easily transported north of Dharan, thus reducing the area's longstanding reliance on Dharan.

    Dharan was one of the main traditional recruiting grounds for the British

Gurkha army and there is ample visible evidence – in numerous expensive clothes shops and the attractive modern bungalows around town, for example – of the wealth that these overseas postings have brought to the area. But the new geopolitical realities of the post cold-war world order have come to roost here too, with most of the Gurkha contingent in the British army having been demobilized since 1990. The resultant combination of wealth and high unemployment is new to Nepal, and Dharan now faces those problems of crime and drug addiction (among its youth in particular) with which the West has long been familiar. Ask around locally, and it's acknowledged in hushed, almost confessional tones. The area's limited employment opportunities suggest few immediate solutions.

Essentials

Sleeping **C** *Aangan*, T20640. 7 comfortable rooms with bath, some a/c, good multi-cuisine restaurant, ISD/STD facilities. Recommended. **C** *BAPSO Guest House*, T20978. Is meant for British aid workers, but may have rooms available to travellers.

D *Family Inn*, T20848. 8 rooms all with bath, no food, bright and friendly. **D** *Gurans*, T21309. 13 rooms most with bath, some a/c and TV, good Indian restaurant, rather dark. **D** *Lotus Guest House*, 6 rooms with bath, 1½ kilometres south of the bus park.

E *Welcome Guest House*, rooms with common bath, by the bus park, basic and noisy.

Eating Dharan's best restaurants are at the *Aangan* and *Gurans hotels*. There are numerous *dal-bhad* eateries around the bus park and in the main area of town.

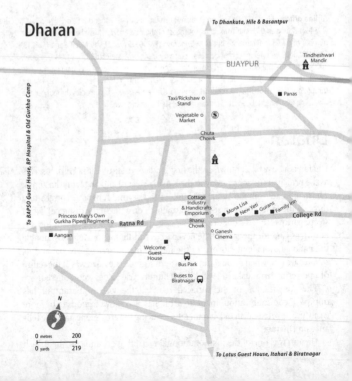

Dharan

The *Cottage Industry and Handicrafts Emporium* on the main road has a range of textiles at fixed prices. **Shopping**

Buses for **Itahari** and **Biratnagar** (1¼ hours, Rs 25) leave every 15 minutes from 0430-1730. Departures to **Dhankuta** (3 hours, Rs 60) every 30 minutes from 0430-1600. There are several buses for **Hile** (5 hours) and **Basantpur**, last at around 1500. **Transport**

Banks The *Nepal Rastra Bank* on the main road can change TCs and currency notes (US$ and UK£ preferred). It may be possible to change currency notes informally. **Communications** Area code: the area code for Dharan is 025. **Hospitals & medical services** The new BP Koirala Hospital (or just BP Hospital) is situated near the British Gurkha Camp, 2 kilometres west of the bus park. **Directory**

Dhankuta

The road from Dharan twists, turns and climbs spectacularly, crosses the Leoti and Tamur rivers and passes through several small villages on its epic 43 kilometres journey to Dhankuta. It is a small town surrounded by delightful pine and oak forest (but once again deforestation is visibly taking its toll) and there are superb Himalayan views within easy walking distance. The area around Dhankuta and along the Arun Valley is renowned for its cultivation of oranges which are considered to be the best in Nepal. The town has a large Newar population, the result of historical migration from the Kathmandu Valley, and Newari craftsmanship is evident.

Population: 17,073 (1991)
Altitude: 1,224m
Colour map 1, grid C6

The centre of town is a crescent running off the main road. The **bus park** and **bazaar** area (liveliest on Thursday) are situated along here.

With the exception of the **C** *BAPSO Guest House*, near the bus park, Dhankuta's accommodation consists of trekking standard lodges. The **E** *Hotel Parichaya* has been recommended as the best of these. Food is limited to several dal-bhad establishments. *Rangako sukuthi* (dried buffalo meat) and *thungba* (a country liquor made of distilled millet and said to be as pure as it is potent) are specialities of the area north of Dharan. **Sleeping & eating**

Transport There are buses from early morning to **Hile**, **Basantpur**, **Dharan**, **Itahari** and **Biratnagar**.

Hile and Basantpur

Some 12 kilometres north of Dhankuta, Hile is a trailhead for treks along the Arun Valley, to Solu Khumbu and Kanchenjunga. Hile is a large bazaar village stretching along the main road. In contrast to the largely Newari Dhankuta, it is populated by a wide cross-section of ethnic groups from East Nepal, including Tibetans, Rais, Magars and Bahuns. North of the bazaar is an army camp and there are superb Himalayan views if you continue up to the western ridge beyond the camp. Alternatively, walk four kilometres to the northeast towards **Jhorpati** for views of Mount Kanchenjunga.

Basantpur, 12 kilometres north of Hile, is as far north as most buses from the Terai go and is a trailhead for Kanchenjunga treks. The extension of the road from Dharan to Basantpur has led to rapid development of the village as a local centre and there is speculation that a resort hotel may be constructed here. There are some excellent short walking opportunites in most directions from the village. Snow falls in winter.

Sleeping Both Hile and Basantpur have several **E** grade, trekking standard lodges, many of which are Tibetan owned.

Transport Regular buses from early morning to Dharan, and 4-5 to Biratnagar. There is also an irregular bus service from Basantpur to Terathum ($1\frac{1}{2}$ hours).

The Mahendra Highway between Biratnagar and Kakarbhitta

From **Itahari** the highway runs relatively smoothly for almost 100 kilometres to **Kakarbhitta** before crossing the border and continuing on through **Bagdogra** to **Siliguri**. It passes open farmland and goes through forest, crossing innumerable rivers and streams along the way, including the Khadam Khola 10 kilometres east of Itahari, then the Ratuwa Khola near the village Damak 35 kilometres further on. The bazaar town of Birtamod lies 20 kilometres west of Kakarbhitta, and is the crossroads for routes to Bhadrapur and Ilam. Kakarbhitta is almost 800 kilometres from Mahendranagar in the far west of Nepal and, if you were to do it, a bus journey of no less than two full days and nights.

Damak

Colour map 1, grid C6 Damak is a small town lying on the Mahendra Highway midway between Itahari and Kakarbhitta and is at the junction of a road heading north to Ilam. There are extensive **tea gardens** owned by the Goodricke company one kilometre west of town. The centre of Damak is the roundabout which is also the focus of its busy bazaar area. There are a couple of **E** grade guest houses, including the hotels *Bhojpur* and *Dhourali*, numerous *dal-bhad* eateries and even a beauty parlour.

Birtamod

Colour map 1, grid C6 Birtamod, 25 kilometres on the Mahendra Highway from Kakarbhitta, is in many ways an enlarged mirror image of Damak. It has the same layout: a central roundabout with a statue of King Mahendra and a bazaar area around it. Just east of the roundabout is a small three-tiered concrete pagoda temple. It also has a couple of basic accommodation options, including the (**E**) *Eagle Hotel* (T40278) in a noisy roadside location west of the roundabout. There is also a local branch of the State Bank of India (Nepal). The bus stop is on the western side of the roundabout and there are stalls here selling soft drinks and mineral water. A better road heads north to Ilam, and another leads southeast to Bhadrapur.

From the Terai to Ilam

Although public buses leave from Birtamod, the best road to Ilam begins at the village of **Charali**, 10 kilometres west of Kakarbhitta on the Mahendra Highway. This excellent road heads north through attractive Terai countryside, passing **Budhabare** village after eight kilometres. After another two kilometres, the first Churia slopes begin abruptly, bringing a radical change of scenery. The wide expanses of paddy are replaced by intermittent low altitude tea gardens, terraced agriculture and agroforestry. Many of the houses here are built on stilts to withstand monsoonal downpours and many have delightful flower gardens. Nine kilometres from Budhabare, the road begins to climb steeply into the **Kuti Hills**, narrowing through a succession of tight turns with bamboo becoming increasingly dominant with height. During and after the monsoon there are numerous small waterfalls with streams flowing across the road, but the road is also affected by landslides and can be dangerous.

Tea

Probably the world's most popular drink, tea is known to have been cultivated in China as early as 2,700 BC. Its large scale introduction to the Darjeeling region began with the abolition of the East India Company's monopoly on importing tea from China after 1833. Horticulturalists at Calcutta's Botanical Gardens worked on improving varieties and produced strains that could grow at both low and high elevations. The success of Darjeeling's early tea growers, combined with virtually identical growing conditions in East Nepal, led to its introduction to Ilam from 1860.

Tea is a species of Camellia, Camellia sinensis. Left to itself, it grows into a tree up to 10 metres tall, but in the tea gardens it is pruned to waist high, flat topped bushes for the convenience of tea pluckers and to maintain a standard leaf size. There are two main types of tea bush. The **China** variety is multi-stemmed, narrow leafed and produces high quality, flavoursome tea. The larger **Assam** variety, meanwhile, is higher yielding, broad leafed and single stemmed, producing a strong liquor but less flavour. Tea is sorted into four grades: leaf, broken, fannings, and dust. Top quality, **orthodox** leaf tea is grown at elevations of between 3,000 and 4,800 ft and produces the aromatic lightly coloured liquor of the Golden Flowery Orange Pekoe in its most superior grade, commanding prices of between Rs 300-950 per kg. **CTC** ('cut, tear and crush') grades are usually lowland varieties whose strong liquor comes also from the breaking of leaf cells during the 'crushing' process, and has a market value of between Rs 120-170 per kg. Better teas are usually denser, ie heavier by volume.

Quality is further determined by the growing season ('flush'). The first flush (February/March) can produce strong and occasionally bitter teas. The second flush (April/May) is prized for its mild, top quality premium teas. The third flush, known as 'monsoon' or 'rain teas', produces the lowest quality teas, while the fourth flush (September/October) produces average, mellow tea.

In contrast to the unfermented 'green' teas, 'black' tea is produced by a process in which the leaves are first withered by being heated gently in a ventilated area for 12-14 hours, then rolled and pressed to express the juices which coat the leaves, a process which gives them the characteristic twist. They are then left to ferment on aluminium trays in a controlled humid environment. Finally, the leaves are dried by passing them through a heated chamber (220°F) and sorted.

Despite its tremendous potential, Nepal's tea industry is in trouble. There are almost 60 tea gardens in the Ilam area covering some 927 ha which, in 1995, produced a total of 0.5 million kg of tea. But in the same year Nepal imported nearly 1.4 million kg for domestic consumption. Traditionally, all tea gardens have been government owned and critics point to an underdeveloped infrastructure and financial mismanagement as the prime reasons for the tea industry's enervated condition. Since 1995 there has been an increase in the number of small scale, private holdings which some believe will push the industry out of its lassitude. Increasingly, poor farmers are also beginning to cultivate tea at home in an income generation strategy.

Terai & Churia Hills

Continuing the climb, you reach **Harkadi** after a further 17 kilometres. This marks the beginning of the main tea growing belt. Fir trees (used in the production of *agarbhati* incense) line the road, while the 'tea carpet' extends as far as the eye can see. Harkadi has a couple of dal-bhad eateries and soft drinks stalls. **Antu Danda** hill lies southeast of Fikkal and has some of the best mountain views in the area. Some hotel chains have conducted feasibility studies for possible new resort hotels here. Eight kilometres from Harkadi is the small junction town of **Fikkal** with a number of shops, some basic accommodation (including **E** *Prabhu Lodge*) and tea company offices. If you turn right (east),

Pashupatinagar is 30 minutes drive away. This small village near the Indian border has stunning mountain views (some say better than from Darjeeling), as well as a thriving trade in imported goods brought from Kathmandu and sold to Indian visitors to Darjeeling. The village is also known for its cheeses, produced largely for 'export' to Kathmandu. There is, however, no tourist accommodation or restaurants. The road continues across the border to Darjeeling.

Heading west from Fikkal, the road begins its descent into the **Mai Khola Valley**. Some 18 kilometres from Fikkal you cross a ridge and get the first sight of the Mai Khola, flowing spectacularly several hundred metres below. Beside the bridge is a wire-suspended chair crossing. Ilam lies barely 11 kilometres from here, but the road was still under construction and was unlikely to have been completed before 1999. Until then it remains an extremely rough, single lane dirt track and it can take almost one hour to reach Ilam. On the way, you pass a Women's Development Sericulture Project.

The road continues as before beyond Ilam and up to **Phidim**. A daily bus plies this route, but takes up to six hours to complete the journey from Ilam.

Ilam

Population: 13,197
(1991)
Phone code: 027
Colour map 1, grid M6

Ilam lies in the Churia Hills, some 90 kilometres by road from Kakarbhitta, and is both central to, and synonymous with, Nepal's **tea** industry. Summer temperatures rise to around 30°C in May with it dipping to about 5°C in January. The rainfall is about 1,600 mm though. It is an attractive, uncongested hill town concentrated along its main cobbled street in an almost Dickensian fashion. Long brick terraces with balconies overhanging a succession of small shops and eateries line the street as it climbs from west to east. The town square, a casual meeting place with a central statue of King Birendra atop a lotus, lies at the northeast end of town.

It is surrounded by **tea gardens** which extend like a broad belt of green carpet through the Churias of East Nepal and into India. The Ilam district is essentially an extension of the Darjeeling tea growing area and is virtually identical in climate, soil and topography. There are also pockets of **cardamom** (*Elattaria cardamomum*, aromatic seeds of the ginger family) cultivation.

Ilam

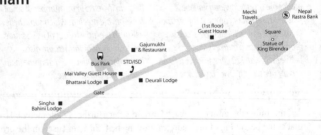

Ilam sees few Western visitors, but there is a genuine feeling of warmth (as well as an opportunity for locals to practise their English) for those that do make the trip. Although there are no Himalayan views, there are numerous opportunities for **walks**, especially through the quietly picturesque tea gardens. Theoretically, you could also embark on a trek from here. It is a two-day walk to **Sandakpur**, a small town on the Indian border (not open to foreigners) near Darjeeling, from where there are magnificent views of both Kanchenjunga and Everest. A trekking permit is not required, but it involves camping out and is not recommended without a guide (contact the *Hotel Rajat* in Kakarbhitta).

Essentials

All Ilam's accommodation is basic and close to the bus park. Food is restricted to dal-bhad-tarkari. **Sleeping**

E *Bhattarai Lodge*, T20139. 6 rooms all common bath, food available, next to the bus park. **E** *Deurali Lodge*, T20228. 6 rooms all common bath. **E** *Gajurnukhi Lodge*, T20183. 8 rooms all common bath, good little restaurant. Recommended. **E** *Mai Valley Guest House*, 12 rooms some with bath, dining room. Recommended. **E** *Singha Bahini Lodge*, 8 rooms all common bath, bamboo dining hut.

Buses leave every 30 minutes from Birtamod only from 0600-1200 (5 hours, Rs 75). **Transport** The road is old and bumpy. Many local buses from **Kakarbhitta** to Birtamod. Car/jeep hire available in Kakarbhitta.

Banks You can exchange foreign currency notes and TCs at the *Nepal Rastra Bank*, at the northern end of town. **Communications** Area code: the area code for Ilam is 027. There is an STD/ISD booth near the entrance to the bus park. **Tour companies & travel agents** Mechi Travels, T20313, in the main square can make airline bookings. Visa/Mastercard accepted. **Directory**

Kakarbhitta (Kakarvitta)

Kakarbhitta is the most easterly of Nepal's approved border crossings for foreigners. It has grown rapidly into a small thriving town by virtue of its location and because it is a focus of minor black-marketeering like all the Terai's other crossings. Foreign luxury goods transported from Kathmandu, mostly watches, electronic gadgets, cosmetics, clothing and luggage, are sold in the many small shops that line every street in and around the square. The trade caters mainly to Indians crossing the border on shopping expeditions.

Phone code: 023
Colour map 1, grid C6

The Mahendra Highway divides the Himalayan foothills rising attractively above the town's wooded northern fringe from the Terai plains to the south, and continues into India as far as Siliguri. Extending intermittently west and northwest towards Ilam, shaded tea gardens endow Kakarbhitta with pleasant surroundings. Otherwise the town can boast few tourist attractions and its *mélange* of small *dharbars*, bars, shops and travel agents is centred around the large and noisy bus stand which shares the main square with the bazaar. The new **Tashi Chhoiling Buddhist Monastery** is located to the southwest.

Essentials

With two exceptions, Kakarbhitta's accommodation is restricted to a number of small, family run lodges, most of which offer tiny rooms and limited bathroom facilities. Electricity can be more off than on. **Sleeping**

D *Koshi* has remained under construction since 1994, but has a few rooms with bath, reasonable restaurant, on the main road opposite entrance to square. **D** *Rajat*, T29026. 12 rooms all with bath, some with TV, reasonable restaurant, at the back of the main square, quiet, clean, modern, credit cards accepted, travel agency can book flights, also arranges ad hoc trips to Ilam and treks in Southeast Nepal, the best place to stay in Kakarbhitta.

E *ABC Lodge*, 8 rooms all common bath, dining room/bar, 150 metres west of square, clean and friendly when open, which is only when the owner is present. **E** *Apsara Lodge*, 6 rooms all sharing one common bath, morning bed tea, 200 metres west of square, friendly but close to a permanent congregation of noisy goats. **E** *Everest Lodge*, 10 rooms all common bath, food available, brightly coloured. **E** *Lahure*, first parallel street to the main road, west of square, small, dingy. **E** *New Kathmandu* 9 large rooms some with bath, avoid smelly ground floor rooms, restaurant/bar, ISD/STD facilities, next to Tourist Office. **E** *Helambu Lama*, and adjacent **E** *Lalupate*, 100 metres west of square, central location, but try others first.

Eating   Aside from the *Rajat* which has an extensive, reasonably priced menu and does a generous pot of coffee, and the *Koshi* which, though more comfortable, is also more expensive with a poorer selection, Kakarbhitta has only small *dal-bhad* establishments or streetside food.

Transport   **Local Car hire**: for medium and long distance vehicle hire (Marutis), eg to Ilam, try *Shree Antu Cab Ltd*, T60105.

Air The nearest airport is at **Bhadrapur**, a regional centre southwest of Kakarbhitta. Irregular seasonal flights to **Biratnagar** and on to **Kathmandu** are operated by RNAC. The airport has a grass runway which is closed during the monsoon. Since an Avro aircraft got stuck in the mud for 2 days, only small Dorniers and Twin Otters operate to Bhadrapur.

Buses There are up to 15 buses a day to **Kathmandu**, all departures between 1300 and 1715 (16-22 hours, Rs 320). Late departures may be slightly quicker, as there will be fewer unscheduled passengers to pick up and pile on along the way. **NB** This is a gruelling journey resulting in physical and mental desensitization, so it is worthwhile requesting a seat either behind the driver or behind the door at the time of booking. Stick to 2x2 buses, ie 2 seats either side of the aisle. You might think about breaking

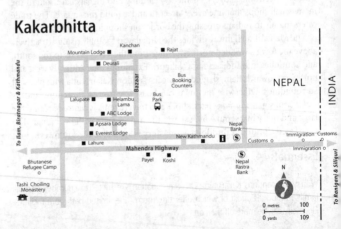

Kakarbhitta

the journey, eg at Janakpur. **Warning** During and after the monsoon, routes may be blocked by flooding or landslides, causing long delays.

Bus: Local buses depart for **Biratnagar** every 30 minutes from 0500-1700 (5-6 hours, Rs 50). Faster, 'non-stop' buses leave at 0830, 1030, 1310 and 1430 (3 hours).

There are several buses to **Janakpur** from 0630-1100, then at 30 minute intervals from 1700-1900 (10 hours, Rs 150).

Banks Only the **Nepal Rastra Bank**, a large pink building 100m from the border on the main road, can change money, but may be unwilling to change large amounts. Allow plenty of time. Open 0700-1900 daily. The **Nepal Bank**, diagonally opposite, does not deal in foreign exchange. **Communications** Area code: the area code for Kakarbhitta is 023. **Tourist offices** Located on the north side of the main road between the Nepal Bank and the square, 150m from border. Kakarbhitta's tourist officer has been stationed here for over 20 years and can help with local information, including bus times, and has all the standard tourist brochures. Open 1000-1630 Sun-Thur, 1000-1200 Fri.

Directory

Crossing into India

The border lies along a branch of the Mahananda River, which itself feeds into the Ganges 250 kilometres to the south.

Leaving Nepal

Immigration The Nepali Customs and Immigration offices are 200 metres east of the bus park, and are open from dawn to dusk. (**NB** In theory, trekking permits for the Kanchenjunga area can be issued by the immigration office here, but officials are known to be reluctant to issue them and may tell trekkers to apply in Kathmandu.) Those on the Indian side are one and a half kilometres away on the other side of the river at Raniganj, and are open 24 hours. Procedures on both sides are straightforward.

At the border

Cycle-rickshaws between Kakarbhitta and Raniganj are always available. **Local buses** (Indian Rs 8), shared taxis (ie jeeps, Rs 25) and auto-rickshaws (Rs 70) run between Raniganj, the Indian border-post, and Siliguri. The journey takes about one hour. (**NB** You are advised to arrive in Siliguri or New Jalpaiguri by daylight.) From Siliguri, buses and jeeps go as far as Raniganj, but auto-rickshaws can take you through to Kakarbhitta. If you are continuing beyond Kakarbhitta, it is best to cross early in the day to allow time to book a decent seat on the bus. (**NB** Several travel agencies in Siliguri and Darjeeling offer inclusive through-fares to Kathmandu, but it is cheaper and just as straightforward to make your own arrangements.)

Onwards to India

To Darjeeling There are regular jeeps and buses from **Siliguri** to Darjeeling (80 kilometres). The NBSTC buses are best. Jeep travel becomes decidedly cold as you climb the hill! The journey takes three to four hours. The '**toy train**' runs erratically and normally takes around eight hours, but can be disrupted by landslides caused by monsoon rains. (**NB** If you are going to Darjeeling then back down to Calcutta, make your train reservation while you are here at the Foreign Tourist Quota office at New Jalpaiguri station (see below), as this quota cannot be booked in Darjeeling.) There are also bus connections from Siliguri to **Kalimpong** (54 kilometres) and **Gangtok** (114 kilometres).

To Calcutta Trains to Calcutta (586 kilometres) leave from **New Jalpaiguri** (known as 'NJP'), a 20 minute rickshaw ride from Siliguri. The *Darjeeling Mail* departs daily at 1900, arriving at Calcutta's Sealdah station at 0900 the following morning. There is a Foreign Tourist Quota reservation office. Alternatively, there are regular **buses** from Siliguri to Calcutta. The

Terai & Churia Hills

overnight North Bengal State Transport Corporation's 'Rocket' bus is faster than the train, dep 2100, 12 hours. These are often very full and noisy (including video/audio) and are not a relaxing way to travel! Booking office on Burdwan Road.

There are **flights** on most days from Bagdogra (a military airfield) to Calcutta with Indian Airlines and Jet Air, and to Delhi with Jet Air.

Dolpa and Western Nepal

8

458

Dolpa and Western Nepal

460 Dolpa

460 Jumla

460 Khaptad National Park

8

The western region of Nepal is rarely visited. It is as densely populated and its historic and scenic grandeur approaches that of the areas north of Kathmandu and Pokhara. There is no sealed road and airstrips and flights are few. Parts have long been designated 'restricted areas' for reasons of security as well as for those of cultural and environmental conservation. But gradually many are being opened up to trekkers, although only a few companies offer treks in the region and conditions are basic. Flights to Jumla, the regional centre, are often delayed or cancelled due to bad weather.

Dolpa

Overlooked for centuries because of its bleak geography, **Dolpa** became part of Nepal 200 years ago when the Gurkhas gained control over the region. Ties of blood and religion made the district a natural refuge for Tibetans who fled the Communist Chinese 'liberation' of Tibet in 1959. Within Dolpa's ring of massive mountains live a people economically and culturally disrupted by their estrangement from Tibet.

It has much in common with Ladakh, Zanskar, Lahul and Spiti in India, and with Mustang its eastern Nepali neighbour. 1,000 year old Buddhist monasteries dot the Shey and Ban Tshang Valleys. The principal religion in Dolpa is Tibetan Buddhism. Dolpa's is a subsistence economy, based on livestock and barley cultivation wrested from the steep mountainsides at elevations as high as 4,000 metres.

Two groups of ethnic Tibetans make up Dolpa's sparse population. The **Rungba**, or 'valley farmers', whose yellow village houses belong to the monks while those painted white belong to the lay population. The **Drok** are nomadic yak herders. Interestingly, Drok girls mix grease and black root extract to use as a sunblock on their faces at high altitudes.

Jumla

Colour map 1, grid A2   Jumla is the regional centre and is an important market. It has some fine temples but very limited accommodation. It is also difficult to get flights in and out because all food has to be imported. For more details see page 98 under Trek 1.

Khaptad National Park

Colour map 1, grid A1   Khaptad is Nepal's newest national park, receiving its designation only in 1985. It consists of 225 square kilometres of forest and grassland, and lies on a plateau (c 3,000 metres) where the districts of Bajhang, Bajura, Doti and Achham meet. The **forest** comprises a mixture of tall fir, yew, rhododendron

Western Nepal

Folk dances of Western Nepal

Better, perhaps, than any other art form, folk dances are able to evoke the essence of a society, to capture its vitality and dramatize its traditions. Folk dances tend to be more spontaneous and expressive, as well as colourful and lively than the ordered form of classical dances. From the relative isolation of the ethnic groups of Northwest Nepal, there have evolved numerous distinctive folk dances which accompany religious and seasonal festivals.

*The **Sorathi** is one of the best known and most popular, performed especially in Gurung and Magar communities in the lower reaches of Northwest Nepal. Accompanied by drummers and singers, one boy dances with two girls (sometimes played by boys) at both religious and social festivals. The **Maruni** dance is an enlarged version of the Sorathi and is performed during the Tihar festival. It begins with the sacrifice of two sheep which are cooked during the festivities for*

consumption afterwards. Then, to the accompaniment of five madals, five 'couples' dance, though the female parts are played by men in full traditional women's costume. Towards the end, a single dancer joins the group and the dance continues until the feast is ready.

*The **Krishna Charitra**, a dramatization of some of Krishna's adventures as recorded in the Mahabharata, is a favourite of the Buda Magar people of Lumjung. **Sehm Daimyas** are a variety of largely free-form dances often performed during weddings and other social events by the Thakilis of Mustang. In Gurung communities, meanwhile, only virgin girls may perform the **Ghatu** which is danced on the Buddha's birthday and on Basant Panchami, the festival marking first day of spring. The form of the Ghatu is influenced by Tantrism and it is said that dancers can become so enraptured while performing that they can scarcely speak or see.*

and oak along with dense stands of bamboo and numerous shrubs, and represents one of the last remaining such areas in the lower Himalaya. The vegetation provides a natural habitat for healthy populations of **wildlife**, including the musk and barking deer, bears, leopards, monkeys, wild boar, kasturi goats, and various birds including the impeyan pheasant.

One flower, known as *bheeg* and resembling a white rose, grows in several parts of the park. It is said to be so poisonous that a single sniff from close up can be lethal!

Among Nepalis, Khaptad is best known as a holy site and is closely associated **Khaptad Swami** with a widely revered ascetic who lived here for many years and who was known simply as the '**Khaptad Swami**'. The origins and background of Khaptad Swami, who died in 1996 at the grand old alleged age of 110, are shrouded in mystery. Some speculate that he was a doctor from India who renounced his worldly life in favour of a purely spiritual existence in a remote part of the holy Himalaya. In any event, he never divulged either his name or anything of his own life to anyone – including to King Birendra who went to consult him on three occasions. He was undoubtedly a good, learned and widely read man who also had a good command of English. He lived in a cave on the eastern side of the park to where pilgrims travelled from far and wide to see him and receive his counsel and blessings. It is said that Khaptad Swami was instrumental in persuading the King to give national park status to Khaptad.

About one kilometre from the Swami's cave is the small **Bhagawan Shankar Mandir** with a dharamsala. Nearby is a small pond, or *pokhari*, whose water is said to be lethally contaminated by the *bheeg* and other toxic flowers growing around it. Symptoms of poisoning are believed to begin with joint pain, lethargy, nausea and vomiting. Some people carry lemons and chillis with them as an antidote when walking through the area, though it is interesting to remember that strings of lemons and chillis are also widely used elsewhere to ward off evil spirits. Fencing now surrounds the pond.

The **Khaptad Mela** (festival) takes place in September/October and attracts several thousand pilgrims from throughout West Nepal for whom this pilgrimage is believed to be especially meritorious. Celebrations include the pouring of milk over the linga of the Bhagawan Shankar Mandir and, reminiscent of Diwali, the lighting of ghee lamps at night.

Visiting Khaptad Very few Westerners ever visit Khaptad. The best time to visit is from **April-September**. The monsoon is relatively weak in West Nepal. At other times, snow makes travel to and through most areas impractical. The park entrance is in the tiny village of **Jhigrana** where there is also an army camp, a few shops and a couple of basic lodges. The entry fee is Rs 650. All visitors to Khaptad should be self sufficient in food and supplies, and be accompanied by a guide. It is recommended to go with an organized trekking company; book in Kathmandu.

Getting there From Mahendranagar in the far western Terai, there is one direct bus a day (15 hours) to **Silgari**. From here it is a four-hour walk along a clear trail to the park office at **Jhigrana**. From Jhigrana it is a three-hour walk to the village of **Chorpani** which has a dal-bhad-tarkari stall. **Accommodation** may be available here on request, though there is no formal accommodation in the park. The nearest **airport** is at **Dipayal** which has flights to/from Nepalgunj.

There are two other national parks. Details of the Rara National Park can be found under Trek 1, page 98 and the Shey-Phoksumdo National Park under Trek 2, page 101.

Road to Tibet

464

Road to Tibet

466 Access

466 Kathmandu to Lhasa

468 Lhasa

9

Isolated by formidable mountain barriers, the peoples of the Tibetan plateau uniquely carried a sophisticated, living, medieval culture into the 20th century. The allure of Tibet's pristine high-altitude environment and profound Buddhist traditions attracted intrepid travellers and explorers from Europe, India, and America throughout the 19th and early 20th centuries. Many faced great physical and mental hardships in their journeys to Lhasa and elsewhere; and some tragically lost their lives, without reaching their goal. The Tibetans actively discouraged such contacts and, with the exception of a few far-sighted intellectuals and lamas, no-one inside Tibet realized the implications that Tibet's self-imposed isolation would come to have in the latter half of the 20th century. Following the Chinese occupation of the plateau and the abortive Tibetan uprising of 1959, the country was plunged into the long dark night of the Cultural Revolution.

Then, suddenly, in the early 1980s, Tibet opened its doors to the outside world as a tourist destination. Delux tour operators were quick to take advantage, rekindling the allure that had motivated the early explorers. Some celebrities like Tenzing Norgay of Everest who had become a legend in his own time, were even engaged as tour leaders!

Access

Although there are still restrictions imposed on individual travel in many parts of Tibet for political reasons, ensuring that only the well-endowed traveller can afford to undertake full-scale guaranteed itineraries, bureaucracy has not deterred the adventurous hardy backpacker who can often be seen trudging through remote parts of the country, following in the footsteps of his or her illustrious predecessors. Only certain areas of Tibet are officially open. The route from Nepal to Lhasa is technically closed. Officially you can only travel as part of an organized group (minimum of five people) with a recognized tour operator. This does not imply having to take a package tour as operators are used to organizing tours for very small groups. However the road to Lhasa is somewhat of a grey area and it may well be possible to travel it independently. You will of course run the risk of being unceremoniously ejected from the country.

Kathmandu to Lhasa

Trips originating in Kathmandu typically consist of an itinerary similar to the following. Departure is invariably early in the morning, with a breakfast stop in **Dhulikhel** or elsewhere which is normally included in the price. The **Arniko Highway** is especially prone to monsoon landslides beyond **Barabise**. You may have to get out of your bus and walk for some distance before boarding another bus. There is a constant supply of willing local labour to help carry passengers' bags. All being well, you will reach **Kodari** in time to stop for lunch. The road from Kodari to the Chinese border can get extremely muddy, though you may be able to hitch a 45 minute lift on a passing truck. The bank on the Tibetan side is closed on Saturday and Sunday, though there is a thriving trade in informal (ie illegal) exchange of rupees and US dollars. For details of the Nepal part of the journey and border formalities, see pages 316-319.

Having completed the entry formalities, it is a 244 kilometre journey along a

Kathmandu to Lhasa

dirt road that runs high above the **Bhote Kosi** River to **Xegar** (4,350 metres), passing many waterfalls. On a clear day views of the high mountains (including the Langtang range, Makalu, Everest and Cho Oyu) are magnificent, but be prepared for these to be very restricted by rain or low cloud. The village of **Nyalam** (or **Tsongdu**) lies at 3,750 metres in the gorge of the **Matsang Tsangpo** just before the **Nyalam Pass** and, although a popular lunch stop, it is notable for little else. There are three simple guest houses and several basic places to eat, but ask the price before you order! Views in the area of the pass are superb, and there are many wild flowers. The scenery continues in the same vein as you continue across the Lang Pass. There are numerous prayerflags at the highest point of the pass, and there are excellent mountain views. The mountains become increasingly barren with only occasional patches of vegetation and settlements further and further apart. There are a number of police checkpoints along the route where the checking of passports and bags can be very time-consuming. The village of **Xedar** consists of little more than a hotel, a petrol station (opens at 0930: encourage the driver to fill up the night before) and some houses.

Zhigatse
Population: 79,337
Altitude: 3,900m

It's another 244 kilometres to Zhigatse. You cross two more passes – the 5,220-metre Lakpa Pass and the 4,000-metre Tsu Pass. Some groups stop at Lhatze for lunch, another undistinguished town of concrete buildings and relatively expensive restaurants. Founded in 1477, the Tashilhunpo Monastery in Zhigatse is one of the oldest and most important monasteries in Tibet, and is the historical seat of the Panchen Lamas. It was built on a sacred sky burial site, whose original stone slab you can still see. The complex includes the tall Jamkhang Chenmo building which houses the world's tallest gilded copper image (26 metres), the *Maitreya*, embodying loving kindness. There is also a three kilometre pilgrimage circuit around the complex. If you have time, it's well worth spending a whole morning (or more) here. Photography is permitted, but a 'donation' is expected. The amount varies according to what and where you are photographing.

Gyantse
Altitude: 3,950m

This town is a two-hour drive from Zhigatse. On the hilltop is the great Pelkhor Chode Temple and monastic complex whose origins date back to the early 15th century. The complex includes the *Gyantse Kumbum*, the 'Stupa of 100,000 deities', a magnificent six-storey edifice with depictions of deities and mandalas in its 75 chapels. Get there early, as many of the buildings close at around 1800.

The *Gyantse Hotel*, T08019-8172222, is a comfortable place, with a large open bar and lounge; a double room costs US$47. Slightly cheaper is the *Clothing Factory Guesthouse* and *Furniture Factory Guesthouse*, both on the west side of Dzongdun lam. The restaurant in *Gyantse Hotel* is expensive, though; a good alternative are the truck-stop restaurants opposite the *Gyantse Hotel*, the adjacent *Chinese Restaurant* or the *Mandala Tibetan Restaurant* nearer the crossroads.

The drive from Gyantse to **Lhasa** takes around eight hours, landslides permitting. The route takes you through wide valleys dotted with large sand dunes, small villages and cultivated land. Every bridge you cross is adorned with prayerflags onto which local people have attached their own handwritten invocations. From the valley, the road continues through mountains and on into **Nyemo County**. Some 65 kilometres from Lhasa, there is a junction with the main airport road and with it a distinct change in the environment. There are more trees, the fields are greener, the road is better and there are signs of greater wealth. Entering Lhasa completes the change of scenery as you drive past large, newly constructed and seemingly sterile concrete buildings.

Road to Tibet

Lhasa

Population: 160,000
Altitude: 3,490m
Phone code: (86)-891
Oxygen: 68%

The holy city is the historical capital of Tibet, situated on the north bank of the **Kyi-Chu** *River, where the valley opens out to its fullest extent. To the north of the city lies an impenetrable 5,200 metres range, extending from Mount Gephel Utse (above Drepung in the west) to Mount Dukre Tse (above Pawangka) and Mount Sera Utse (above Sera in the east). To the south, on the far bank of the river, is the Chakyak Karpo range. Smaller hills are located within the valley; the most prominent being Marpori ('Red Mountain') on which the Potala Palace is constructed, Chakpori (where Tibet's medical college and temples once stood, now dominated by a radio mast), and Bonpori (surmounted by a Chinese temple dedicated to Ling Gesar). The Kyi-Chu River at Lhasa meanders past several island sandbanks, among which Kumalingka ('Thieves' Island'), the best known and an adjacent island are now owned by a Hong Kong business consortium intent on constructing casinos and creating a Himalayan Las Vegas! The principal tributaries of the valley, ie those of Dongkar, Lhalu, Nyangdren and Dokde, have all been integrated into the Chera irrigation system.*

Most visitors will approach Lhasa from the southwest or north, whether driving the short distance from the Gongkar Airport or the longer overland routes from Nepal. These approach roads converge to the west of the city at Dongkar. Just to the west of Dongkar, the valley begins to open out into a wide plain and the Potala Palace is visible from afar. A large military HQ has recently been constructed near the intersection, where an important petrol station complex and

Lhasa

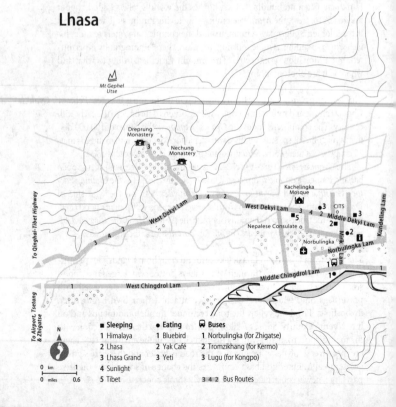

■ **Sleeping**
1 Himalaya
2 Lhasa
3 Lhasa Grand
4 Sunlight
5 Tibet

● **Eating**
1 Bluebird
2 Yak Café
3 Yeti

🚌 **Buses**
1 Norbulingka (for Zhigatse)
2 Tromzikhang (for Kermo)
3 Lugu (for Kongpo)

3 4 2 Bus Routes

the *Dongkar Restaurant* are also located. From Dongkar, two roads lead into town: the main paved route, Chingrol lam (*Chinese* Jiefang lu; also known as the Tsang-gyu lam) follows the river bank upstream all the way to the east end of the city, and a dirt road extension of Dekyi lam (*Chinese* Beijing lu) skirts the Lhasa Cement Factory (*Chinese* Sunyitrang) to enter the city through the defile between Chakpori and Marpori Hills, which formerly marked the true gateway to the city.

The Lhasa valley extends from the Dongkar intersection near the confluence of the Tolung River with the Kyi-Chu at its western extremity, as far as Ngachen and the hilltop ruins of Dechen Dzong, which overlooks the road to Yerpa and Ganden in the extreme east.

Most buildings of Lhasa may conveniently be assigned to one of three distinct phases of construction, although older sites have undergone extensive renovation in subsequent centuries. The earliest phase coincides with the construction of the **Jokhang** and **Ramoche** temples along with the first **Potala Palace** during the seventh century; the middle phase with the building of the great **Gelukpa** monasteries, the new Potala Palace and the **Norbulingka Palace** during the 15th-18th centuries; and the third phase with the recent expansion of the city under Chinese rule.

History

Sights

Aptly named after Mount Potalaka, the sacred mountain abode of the bodhisattva of compassion, Avalokiteshwar, the Potala Palace has been identified in different ages as the residence of Tibet's two illustrious and kingly emanations of Avalokiteshwar – Songtsen Gampo during the seventh century, and Dalai Lama V in the 17th century. The building which towers above the city of Lhasa rises from the slopes of Mount Marpori, for which reason it is known locally as **Tse Podrang** ('Summit Palace').

Potala Palace

The outer section, known as the **White Palace**, has functioned as the traditional seat of government and the winter residence of the Dalai Lamas, while the inner sections, known as the **Red Palace**, contains outstanding temples and the reliquary tombs of eight past Dalai Lamas. In terms of global perception, it is this relic of Tibet's past, present and future national aspirations, more than any other, which uniquely symbolizes the country, like the Great Wall in China and the Vatican in Italy. This 13-storeyed edifice was among the world's tallest buildings prior to the advent of the 20th century skyscraper, and is undoubtedly the grandest building in Tibet. It has many external vantage points – from the outer circumambulatory path

Road to Tibet

(*lingkhor*), from Kumalingka Island, from the adjacent Jokhang roofs, and elsewhere. Wherever you go in downtown Lhasa, the resplendent golden roofs of the Potala are visible on the skyline.

History Little remains of the original 11-storey Potala Palace which King Songtsen Gampo built on Mount Marpori in 637. An illustration of the earlier structure, which was destroyed by lightning in the reign of King Trisong Detsen, is found on the outer wall of the Lamrim Lhakhang within the Red Palace. It appears, however, that the foundations of the present palace do date from the earlier period, as do two of the chapels contained within the Red Palace, the **Songtsen Nyipuk** and the **Phakpa Lhakhang**.

When Lhasa was reinstated as the capital of Tibet in the 17th century after an interim period of 900 years when the seat of government had been located successively at Sakya, Tsetang, Rinpung and Zhigatse, one of the first acts to be carried out by Dalai Lama V was the reconstruction of this national symbol. Prior to its completion, he himself lived at the Ganden Palace in Drepung Monastery, and the largest building below Mount Marpori had been the palace of the Zhamarpas who had dominated the political life of Lhasa until the defeat of their powerful patrons at Zhigatse in 1641. Nonetheless, the fortress (*dzong*) of the kings of Zhigatse is said to have been taken as the prototype for the construction of the new Potala Palace.

Dalai Lama V preserved the original foundations of the 7th century edifice and had the **White Palace** built between 1645 and 1653. More than 7,000 workers and 1,500 artisans were employed on this construction, along with Manchu and **Newar** artists. The murals of the east wing and the **Kangyur Lhakhang** were completed in 1648, and the following year he moved from Drepung. The **Inner Zhol Obelisk** (*Doring Nangma*) was constructed to commemorate this event.

The central upper part, the **Red Palace**, is mostly attributed to the regent Desi Sangye Gyatso (reigned 1679-1703) and dated 1690-93. Its interior was finished in 1697. However, Dalai Lama V died in 1682 and his death was concealed by the regent until 1694, enabling him to complete the task without the distraction of political upheavals. There is also a Jesuit drawing, dated 1661, which interestingly suggests that two storeys of the Red Palace were actually constructed before his demise. Work on the funerary chapel was carried out between 1692-94 and cost 2.1 million taels of silver.

Enlargement was carried out through the 18th century. Then, in 1922, the renovation of the chapels and halls adjacent to the Phakpa Lhakhang was undertaken, along with that of the east wing of the White Palace. The Zhol printing press was also enlarged at this time. In 1959, the south face was shelled during the suppression of the Lhasa Uprising, but the damaged porch of the Red Palace and the Potala School (*Tse Lobdra*) were subsequently restored by the late Panchen Lama X. The most recent renovations have taken place since 1991, during which period the inner walls have been strengthened, the electrical supply stabilized, and the extraneous buildings in the foreground of the palace removed to create a large square.

Altogether, the interior area of the Potala is 130,000 square metres. The building is 118 metres high, 366 metres from east to west, and 335 metres from north to south. There are 1,000 rooms, housing approximately 200,000 images.

Jokhang   The Jokhang is Tibet's most sacred shrine, the focal point of pilgrims from the
Temple   entire Tibetan Plateau. Situated at the heart of the old town, it was founded by Queen Bhrikuti on a site deemed by Queen Wengcheng to be the principal geomantic power-place in Tibet.

Road to Tibet

The main gate of the temple faces west towards Nepal in recognition of Bhrikuti who bore the expense of the temple's construction. The original design appears to have had a Newar model, and only later was it said to have been modelled on Vikramashila Monastery in northwest India. The earliest phase of building, traces of which indicate distinctive Newar influence, are to be seen in the original door frames of the four ground floor inner chapels dedicated to Mahakarunika, Amitabha, Shakyamuni and Maitreya; and those of the second storey at the centre of the destroyed north wing, and the Zhalre Lhakhang of the east wing, as well as the Songtsen Chapel of the west wing. The fact that the Newar queen wished to make the third storey but never did may indicate her premature death. Later, when the third storey was added, the temple was said to represent the three buddha-bodies (Trikaya) or three world-systems (Tridhatu).

Bhrikuti installed the primary images arranged in five main chapels flanked by vihara-like cells, and with a square hall: the deity Aksobhya in the centre flanked by Amitabha and Maitreya, while those of Mahakarunika and Shakyamuni Acalavajra are on the north and south wings respectively. There were four gates, one in each of the four walls, and 37 columns represented the 37 sections of the Vinaya.

Songtsen Gampo erected the protector shrines with images of naga kings, Ravana and Kubera to safeguard the temple from the elements. He also concealed his treasures (*terma*) in important pillars of the temple, a custom perhaps linked to the age-old Tibetan tradition of concealing wealth at the foundation of buildings or pillars.

The **Inner Jokhang** in three storeys forms a square (82½ square metres), enclosing the inner hill known as Kyilkhor Thil. This structure is surrounded by the inner circumambulation pathway (*nangkhor*), beyond which is the two-storeyed Outer Jokhang or western extension which contains secondary chapels, storerooms, kitchens, bathrooms and residential quarters. The **Meru Nyingba** temple adjoins the Jokhang on the east side, while the south and west sides are adjoined by other buildings. This whole structure is surrounded by the intermediate circumambulation pathway (*barkhor*), which in turn is surrounded by the old city of Lhasa.

Founded by Princess Wengcheng at the same time as the Jokhang, Ramoche is reputed to be the princess' burial site, divined by her to be connected directly with the hells or subterranean crystal palace of the nagas. It was originally built to contain Tibet's most holy image, **Jowo Rinpoche**, which had been transported to Lhasa via Lhagang in a wooden cart. The construction of the temple was completed around the same time as the Jokhang.

Ramoche Temple

Originally, Ramoche was built in Chinese style, but after being destroyed by fires, the present three-storeyed building was constructed in Tibetan style. In 1474 it was placed under the authority of Kunga Dondrub, a second generation student of Tsongkhapa. It then became the assembly room of the **Gyuto Tratsang**, the Upper Tantric College of Lhasa, located further east, and housed 500 monks. Between 1959-1966, Ramoche housed a communist labour training committee. The temple has, however, been restored since 1985 and the central Jowo Mikyo Dorje image, which had been severed in two parts during the Cultural Revolution, was repaired when its torso was returned to Tibet, having been found in Beijing by the late Panchen Lama X in the same year. According to some, this image may not be the original, as Ramoche was also damaged by Mongol incursions in earlier centuries. Presently, the temple is once again occupied by the Upper Tantric College monks and undergoing repair.

The **Assembly Hall** has 27 lion sculptures below the skylight. The central images flank and back the throne of Dalai Lama. Behind, in a glass cabinet, are Tsongkhapa with his foremost students. Against the left wall are images of the three meditational deities, Guhyasamaja, Chakrasamvara and Bhairab.

The second floor is largely residential, but there is one main chapel containing images of Buddha as King of the Nagas, surrounded by 16 elders. An inner sanctum contains images of the eight Medicine Buddhas and a copy of the *Kangyur*. On the third floor, the front chambers are the Dalai Lama's private apartments, and the rear chamber a private chapel with a gyaphib-style roof, enclosed by a wooden balustrade.

Other sites There are of course numerous sites in and around Lhasa. In the west, there is the Norbulingka Palace, the Summer Palace of the Dalai Lamas. It is divided into three areas: the palaces, the opera grounds and the government buildings. Operatic performances are held during the Yoghurt Festival.

Further west still is Drepung Monastery built on the Gephel Utse ridge some eight kilometres northwest of Lhasa. The complex consists of the Central Assembly Hall, a series of seven colleges (Tratsang) and the Ganden Podrang, the magnificent residence of Dokhang Ngonmo.

In the north and east of Lhasa are the Sera Thekchenling Monastery, which is located at the base of Mount Purbuchok and Pawangka Monastery located to the west of Sera Thekchenling on the slopes of Mount Dukri. Both are of considerable interest.

Barkhor Square Area

Sleeping
1 Banak Zhol
2 Ganggyen
3 Kadak
4 Kyichu
5 Kyire
6 Nationalities
7 Pata
8 Pentok Guesthouse
9 Shambhala
10 Snowland
11 Tashy Dagye
12 Yak

Eating
1 Barkhor Café
2 Crazy Yak
3 Makye Ama
4 Snowland
5 Tashi
6 Upstairs Tibetan Cafe

NB Full details of these sites together with information on the whole Tibetan Plateau and extensive notes on the cultural, religious and historical background of the country can be found in Footprint's *Tibet Handbook*.

Essentials

A *Lhasa Grand Hotel (Xizang Da Sha)*, 196 Middle Dekyi lam, T6826096, F6832195. A 3-star hotel has 531 rooms, including 22 deluxe suites (US$93 per room), 184 deluxe standard rooms (US$52 per room), 52 triples (US$19 per room) and 52 economy rooms (US$15 per room), with oxygen, beauty salon, hairdresser, shops, business centre, and a dining hall with seating capacity of 1200. **A** *Lhasa Hotel (Lhasa Fandian)*, 1 Minzu Rd, T6822221, F6835796. A 3-star hotel with 450 rooms, superior category in S and C blocks with piped oxygen in rooms (US$108 per room), and the inferior category in N block without piped oxygen (US$71), all rooms have attached bath, 5 restaurants (*Himalayan* for Tibetan and Nepalese dishes, *Sichuan* for Chinese dishes, *Everest* and *Gallery* for Western buffet, and the *Hard Yak Café* for à la carte Western meals), a full meal plan costs US$54, and breakfast US$16, also has swimming pool, *Tin Tin Bar*, coffee shop, karaoke bar, business centre, tour agency, gift shop, hairdressing and massage service, beauty salon, medical consultations (including Tibetan traditional medicine), and in-house movies.

B *Tibet Hotel*, 221 West Dekyi Rd, Lhasa, T6833738/6834966, F6836787. 200 beds (US$60 per double room), with attached bathrooms, restaurant (full meal plan US$32, breakfast US$8.50), travel agency, and discotheque.

C *Himalaya Hotel*, 6 East Lingkor Rd, Lhasa, T6322293, F6334855. Located near the river and within easy walking distance of the Barkhor, it has 116 bedrooms with attached bath (US$36 per double), Chinese and Tibetan restaurants (full meal plan at US$21, breakfast US$6.50), shop, business centre facilities, and travel agency. **C** *Kadak Hotel*, East Chingdrol Rd, T6337771. Fine rooms with attached bathrooms on 4/F, (¥300 per room), dining room, disco and OK. **C** *Sunlight Hotel*, 27 Linju Rd, Lhasa, T6322227, F6335675. 133 beds (US$42 per double room), some with attached bathrooms, and restaurant (full meal plan US$32, breakfast US$8.50). **C** *Xuelian Hotel*, East Lingkor Rd, T6323824. 80 beds.

D *Yak Hotel*, 36 East Dekyi Rd, T6323496. 170 beds (range ¥200-90), some with attached bathrooms, some with shared bathing facilities, also *Crazy Yak Restaurant*. **D** *Snowlands Hotel*, Mentsikhang Rd/Tuanji lu, T6323687. 30 rooms, some of new construction with attached bathroom and most of inferior standard with basic washing facilities, but arguably one of the best restaurants in Lhasa, serving Indian and Nepalese food.

E *Kyire Hotel*, East Dekyi Rd, T6323462. 266 beds, big rooms (range ¥80-25), shared showers and a friendly restaurant. **E** *Banak Zhol Hotel*, East Dekyi Rd, T6323829. 246 beds, thin walls, and shared shower facilities. **E** *Plateau (Gaoyuan) Hotel*, North Lingkor Rd, T6324916. 180 beds, good rooms and showers.

Eating Among the major hotels, only *Lhasa Hotel* offers a wide range of Himalayan, Chinese, and continental dishes. Good Chinese cuisine is available at the *Himalaya Hotel* and the *Tibet Hotel*. Lhasa city has many restaurants of varying cuisine and standard. For Tibetan food, including *momo*, and *thukpa* try the **Sonam Dokhang**, West Dekyi lam, T6832985, where the food is excellent but expensive; *Yeti Restaurant*, West Dekyi Rd, T6833168, which is good and reasonably priced; *Friend's Corner*, Tsomoling; *Jamdrol Restaurant*, Karma Kunzang, T6336093, which caters exclusively to TTC tour groups; *Yak Café*, Mirik lam, T6834967; *Snowlands Restaurant*, near *Snowlands Hotel*, Mentsikhang lam, T6337323. *Dakini Restaurant*, West Dekyi Rd; *Crazy Yak*, near *Yak Hotel*, East Dekyi Rd, T6336845, which is good and reasonably priced, with Tibetan operatic and folk dance performances in the evenings; *Barkhor Café* overlooking Lugu lam and the Jokhang Temple, T6326892; *Yutok Restaurant*, Yutok Zampa, T6330931; *Tibetan Corner Restaurant*, T6325915; *Tashi Restaurant*, Tsomoling; *Tashi Restaurant Number Two*, Kyire Hotel, T6323462; *Tibet Unute Restaurant*, Tsomoling; and *Lost Horizons Café*, Tsomo-ling.

For Amdo food, try the *Amdo Zakhang*, Beautiful World Entertainment Centre, Tsomoling. For Sichuan food, the *Thanduohua* is excellent and cheap. For Hotpot dishes, try *Bluebird Restaurant*, (Qing Niao), West Chingdrol lam and *Yangyang Restaurant*, Tsomoling. For Cantonese dishes and seafood, in addition to Sichuan cuisine, try the *Crystal Palace (Ch Shuijing Gong)*, 180 Dekyi Rd, T6333885; and for Peking duck, try the *Gau Ya Restaurant*, on Kharngadong Rd and on Nyangdren lam, opposite CAAC.

For the best and most expensive Nepalese dishes (also Thai and continental cuisine) in sophisticated surroundings with Nepalese and Indian dance performances, try the *Snowlands Restaurant*, near the *Snowlands Hotel*, Mentsikhang Rd, T6337323; *Barkhor Café* overlooking Lugu lam and the Jokhang Temple, T6326892. The recently opened *Makye Ama*, to the rear of the Jokhang, overlooking the Barkhor. Highly recommended. *Kyichu Hotel*, Dekyi lam. *Grand Highland Palace*, 3/F Luga Market, near CAAC, T6339391; and *Mountain Restaurant*, Kyire, T6338307. For Western dishes, in addition to, try *Friend's Corner*, Tsomoling, where the food is good, clean and cheap; *Yak Café*, near *Lhasa Hotel* on Mirik Lam, T6334967, which serves clean but expensive food, and is popular with tour groups; *Tashi Restaurant*, Tsomoling, which caters mostly to individual tourists; *Snowland Restaurant*, Mentsikhang Rd, and *Lost Horizons Café*, Tsomoling.

Entertainment Lhasa has many varied forms of entertainment. The local people devote much time to picnics, parties, and board games, especially Majong. The drinking songs of Lhasa are particularly renowned. Tibetan operas are performed at the *TAR Kyormolung Operatic Company*, the *TAR Academy of Performing Arts*, the *Lhasa City Academy of Performing Arts*, and in Norbulingka Park during the Yoghurt Festival in summer. Traditional Tibetan music may also be heard at the *Himalayan* restaurant in *Lhasa Hotel*, and the *Crazy Yak Restaurant*. There are a number of nightclubs, fashion shows, discotheques, and a profusion of karaoke bars and video parlours. The *Lhasa City Cinema* is located on Yutok Rd. However, the museums such as the *Potala Museum and Exhibition Hall* on Middle Dekyi Rd, and the *Peoples' Art Museum* on the corner of East Chingdrol Rd and Do Senge Rd have little to offer in contrast to the magnificence of the city's temples, monasteries, and palaces. The *TAR historical archives*, located behind the Customs Office on West Dekyi lam, T6824184/6824823, has a fascinating collection of documents, some of which date from the era of Chogyel Phakpa.

Books, maps, cards and newspapers The *Xinhua Bookshop*, West Dekyi lam, next to *Tibet Hotel*, has a wide range of Tibetan cultural publications. Try also the *Xinhua Bookshop* on Yutok lam and the *Peoples' Publishing House Bookstore*, on North Lingkhor Rd. **Shopping**

Handicrafts The traditional market of Lhasa is located around the Jokhang temple in the Barkhor and its radial road system. Tibetan handicrafts may be found here, including textiles, carpets, jewellery, metalwork, leather goods, photographs, and religious artefacts, including paintings, incense, and books. Antiques are available, but can only be exported with discretion. Bargaining here is the norm and, as a visitor, you should strive to reduce the proposed price by as much as 50%. Handicrafts are also available from the *Friendship Store* and other antique shops on Yutok lam or at the *Kyichu Hotel*, and from more expensive shops in *Lhasa Hotel* and the *Himalaya Hotel*. For Tibetan tents and tent fabrics, contact *Tent Factory*, off East Dekyi Rd; and for new carpets, contact the *Carpet Factory*, off East Chingdrol Rd. The *Boot Factory*, on East Chingdrol Rd is also worth visiting. The Barkhor nowadays also has a number of department stores, including a new 2-storey shopping complex with escalator access, opened in 1994. Chinese textiles, clothing, household utensils, and electrical goods are available here. Most shops will accept only RMB currency, and a few will be happy to receive payment in US dollars. Unofficial currency exchange facilities are instantly available; and the Bank of China is not too far on West Lingkhor Rd. There are interesting open air markets around Tromzikhang, north of Barkhor and on Kharngadong Rd, near the Potala.

Photography Print film and processing are available at photographic shops on Middle and East Dekyi Rd, and on Kharngadong Rd; both slide and print film are available at *Lhasa Hotel*, though you are advised to carry all your film supplies from home.

Stamps These are available at GPO, on corner of East Dekyi Rd and Nyangdren Rd; and also at the reception counters or shops in the major hotels.

Textiles *Friendship Store* on Yutok Rd, and the shops around the Barkhor offer traditional fabrics including brocade silk, and traditional ready-to-wear Tibetan clothing.

Local Buses: there are seven routes around Lhasa. **1**. Lugu-Leather Factory (via Chingdrol lam); **2**. Disco Bus Station-Tolung Dechen (via Norbulingka and the Peoples' Hospital); **3**. Disco Bus Station-Cement Factory (via Lukhang, Golden Yak, and *Tibet Hotel*); **4**. Disco Bus Station-Drepung (via Lukhang and *Tibet Hotel*); **5**. Disco Bus Station-Sera (via Yutok lam and Nyangdren lam); **6**. Ramoche-Drapchi (via North Lingkhor lam and Dokde lam); **7**. *Plateau Hotel*-Ngachen Power Station (via Ngachen lam); **8**. East Lingkhor lam-Taktse (via East Zamchen lam and Pelting). **Transport**

Long distance Buses: long distance travel by public bus is uncomfortable, irregular, and slow. There are three long distance bus stations: the main Norbulingka Bus Station on West Chingdrol lam (see block), the Lugu Bus Station (for Nyemo, Lhundrub and Tsetang), and the Tromzikhang Bus Station (for Nakchu and Kermo). Hitchhiking is officially discouraged, but not impossible for the adventurous and well seasoned traveller.

Air Lhasa is connected via Gongkar Airport (96 kilometres southeast) to Chengdu (daily flights), Kathmandu (Tuesday, Thursday and Saturday), Beijing (Sunday), and Chongqing (Wednesday and Saturday), and Ziling (Monday and Friday).

For details of how to travel to Tibet from Nepal, see page 30 in Essentials.

Road to Tibet

Directory

Airline offices *CAAC*, Nyangdren lam, near Potala Palace.

Banks *Bank of China*, West Lingkhor Rd. Limited exchange facilities are also available at *Lhasa Hotel*, and *Himalaya Hotel*. Larger hotels will accept credit card payments. Money changers in Barkhor will accept and change US$ into RMB at a rate slightly above that of the banks.

Communications Fax: *Holiday Inn Business Centre, Himalaya Hotel Business Centre*. Also new communications tower on West Dekyi lam. **General Post Office** (GPO): East Dekyi Rd. Postal facilities also available in major hotels. **IDD and DDD calls**: many outlets throughout the city in addition to the above hotels and the GPO.

Embassies & consulates *Royal Nepalese Consulate*, Gyatso To Rd, near Norbulingka, T6822881, issues 15-day or 30-day tourist visas for Nepal within 24 hrs.

Hospitals & medical services *Peoples' Hospital*, North Lingkhor Rd, T6322200 (emergency department); *TAR No 2 Hospital*, Gyatso To Rd, T6322115 (emergency department). The Italian-run *CISP Emergency Medicine Centre* in TAR, 7 North Lingkhor lam, T6321059, F86891-6321049; and the *Swiss Red Cross*, 4 Nyangre Road, T6320175.

Tour companies & travel agents *Windhorse Adventure Travel (WHAT)*, Lhasa Hotel Rm 1120, 6832221 Tx 1120/6832432, F86891-6836793, Tx68012 TTB CN. *Tibet International Sports Travel (TIST)*, *Himalaya Hotel*, 6 East Lingkhor lam, T6331421/6334082, F86891-6334855. *Tibet Tourist Corporation (TTC)* also known as *China International Travel Service* – Lhasa Branch (CITS), West Dekyi lam, T6836626/6835046, F86891-6836315/6835277. *China Workers' Travel Service (CWTS)*: Tibet Branch, *Lhasa Hotel*, Lhasa, Rm 1104, T6824250, 6832221 ext 1104, F86891-6834472, Tx69025 WTBL CN. *Lhasa Hotel Tour Department*, 1 Mirik lam, T6824509, F86891-6834117. *Tibet Mountaineering Association (TMA)*, 8 East Lingkhor lam, T6322981, F(86891)6336366, Tx68029 TMA CN. *Lhasa Travel Service*, *Sunlight Hotel*, 27 Linyu lam, T6335196, 6333944, F86891-6335675, Tx68016 TRCLS CN. *China Youth Travel Service (CYTS)*, Rm 1103, *Lhasa Hotel*, 1 Mirik lam, T6824173, F86-891-6823329, Tx68017 CYTS CN. *Golden Bridge Travel Service (GBT)*, Lhasa Branch, 13 Mirik lam, T6823828/6824063, F86891-6825832, Tx68002 GBTCL CN. *China Tibet Qomolungma Travel (CTQT)*, Rm 1112, *Lhasa Hotel*, 1 Mirik lam, T6836863, F86891-6836861. *Tibet Friendship Travel Service*, North Nyangdren lam, T6334534, F86891-6334533. *Asia Dragon Tour Corporation (Yarlung Travel Service)*, 3 Mirik lam, T6835181, F86891-6835182. *Tibet Air International Travel Service*, 14 Kharngadong lam, T6333331, F86891-6333330. *Tibet Kailash Travel*, Lhasa Office, Yuanlin lam, T/F86891-6832598. *Tibet Foreign Trade International Travel Service*, 182 M Dekyi lam, T6329222, F86891-6336322. *Nyangtri Travel Service*, *Pentoc Guesthouse*, Mentsikhang lam, T/F86891-6330700/6326686. **NB** Other hotels including *Tibet*, *Ying Qiao*, and *Sernye* also have established their own travel companies.

Tourist offices *Tibet Tourism Bureau (TTB)*, Yuanlin lam, T6834315/6333635, F86891-6834632.

Useful addresses Police & public security: *Foreigners' Registration Office*, East Lingkhor lam, near *Banak Zhol Hotel*. *TAR Foreign Affairs Office*, on West Lingkhor lam, T6824992. *Lhasa City Police*, near Academy of Social Sciences.

Background

10

478

Background

History

479 Settlement and early history

479 Vedic Period

480 Licchavi Dynasty

481 Malla Era

482 Unification of Nepal

482 Shah Dynasty

484 Rana Raj

486 Since 1951

The Land

488 Geology and environment

491 Rivers

491 Climate

497 Wildlife

502 National Parks

Religion

506 Hinduism

524 Buddhism

532 Islam

532 Bon

533 Animism and Shamanism

533 Christianity

Culture

534 Peoples

536 Art and architecture

540 Music and dance

541 Literature

Modern Nepal

543 Economy

546 Nepal in South Asia

10

History

South Asia: settlement and early history

The first village communities in South Asia grew up on the arid western fringes of the Indus Plains 10,000 years ago. Over the following generations successive waves of settlers – sometimes bringing goods for trade, sometimes armies to conquer territory and sometimes nothing more than domesticated animals and families in search of land to cultivate and peace to live – moved across the mighty Indus and into India. They left an indelible mark on the landscape and culture of all the countries of modern South Asia.

The First Settlers Recent research suggests ever earlier dates for the first settlements. A site at Mehrgarh, where the **Indus Plains** met the dry Baluchistan Hills, has revealed evidence of agricultural settlement as early as 8500 BC. By 3500 BC agriculture had spread throughout the Indus Plains and in the 1,000 years following it there were independent settled villages well to the east of the Indus. By 1500 BC the entire Indus Valley Civilization had disintegrated. The causes remain uncertain: the violent arrival of new waves of **Aryan** immigrants, increasing desertification of the already semi-arid landscape, a shift in the course of the Indus and internal political decay have all been suggested as instrumental in its downfall. Whatever the causes, some features of Indus Valley culture were carried on by succeeding generations.

Vedic period

From this time, the northern region of the subcontinent entered what has been called the Vedic period. Aryan settlers from the northwest moved further and further east towards the Ganges Valley. Grouped into tribes, conflict was common. Even at this stage it is possible to see the development of classes of **rulers** – *rajas* – and **priests** – *brahmins*. In one battle of this period a confederacy of tribes known as the Bharatas defeated another grouping of 10 tribes. They gave their name to the region east of the Indus which is the official name for India today – **Bharat**. The centre of population and culture shifted east from the banks of the Indus to the land between the rivers Yamuna and Ganges. This region, known as the **doab** (pronounced *doe-ahb*, literally 'two waters'), became the heart of emerging Aryan culture which, from 1500 BC onwards, laid the literary and religious foundations of what ultimately became Hinduism.

The first fruit of this development was the **Rig Veda** from around 1300 BC. The later Vedas show that the Indo-Aryans developed a clear sense of the *doab* as 'their' territory. Modern Delhi lies just to the south of this region central both in the development of history and myth in South Asia. Later texts extended the core region from the **Himalaya** in the north to the Vindhyans in the south and to the Bay of Bengal in the east. Beyond this core region lay the land of mixed peoples and then of barbarians, beyond the pale of Aryan society. In the central valleys of **'Nepal'**, meanwhile, there ruled a series of obscure dynasties called Gopala, Mahishapala and Kirati. A fierce, war-like people possibly of middle-eastern origin, the **Kiratis** are thought to have moved towards the Kathmandu Valley from the east and established a dynasty lasting over 28 generations. The Mahabharata records one of the first Kirati kings, Yalumbar, as having been killed in the great battle. Elsewhere, small kingdoms were ruled over by clans whose society was becoming increasingly hierarchical. In around 563 BC the Buddha, Gautama Siddhartha, was born in **Lumbini**, in the northern Gangetic Plains.

Licchavi Dynasty

By the 5th century BC, there were a number of dispersed political units in the Ganges Plains region and political authority had become localized. One such unit, the **Licchavi** clan, probably originated from the area of what are now the Indian states of Uttar Pradesh and Bihar. They began to move north and by around 400 BC had succeeded in replacing the Kirantis as rulers of the Kathmandu Valley, where they remained as the first dynasty of Indian plains origin until the late 9th century AD. To the south, the Maurya dynasty established a hegemony in the Ganges Valley from 321 BC and brought the previously independent territorial states together under one administration. The greatest of its emperors, **Ashoka** who came to the throne in about 272 BC, conquered Kalinga (modern Orissa) but remorse at the destruction that this had entailed led to his religious conversion. Although it is widely said that it was Buddhism which he embraced, it was more the peaceful Buddhist philosophy of *dharma* which motivated him. Many of his edicts were inscribed on stone or on specially erected pillars and these, which include several in and around Lumbini, provide the earliest written historical records of the region.

The greatest of the Licchavi rulers was King **Manadeva I** who reigned from about 464 to 505 AD. Inscriptions from his reign constitute the earliest specifically Nepali written historical records and include one at Changu Narayan which chronicles his success in expanding and consolidating Licchavi power beyond the Kathmandu Valley. The Licchavi era was noted for its tolerance of the growth of Buddhism and other non-Hindu religions.

The next major event was the ascension of King **Amshuvarma** to the throne in 609. Though himself not a Licchavi, he had married the daughter and only child of the Licchavi king **Shivadeva** and gained the throne upon his death. By this time, the main trade route between India and China was already well established and Amshuvarman did much to strengthen cultural and political relations with Tibet and China. In 644 the first official Chinese envoy arrived in Kathmandu, a visit which was reciprocated by a Nepali envoy in 647. Amshuvarman's daughter, **Bhrikuti**, married the heir to the Tibetan throne and it was through her that Buddhism was introduced into Tibet. She has passed into Buddhist legend and its peculiarly Himalayan pantheon as one of the Tantric Taras. Amshuvarman also ushered in what is known as Nepal's **golden period**, a time in which the arts, architecture and culture flourished. He also introduced major administrative innovations, including the classification of religious and secular institutions and the first proper system of coinage. His philosophy further resulted in a number of social reforms. The king's palace, at Deopatan near the present day Pashupatinath Mandir, was renowned for its decoration and splendour. A descendant of the Licchavis, **Narendradeva**, regained the throne in 679 and further strengthened ties with Tibet.

The reign of King **Raghavadeva** began in 879 and marked the inauguration of the **Nepalese Era**. In the west, he defeated the invading army of King **Jayapida Vinayaditya** of Kashmir. The following two centuries were characterized largely by political instability, by increased conflict between rival clans and periodic warfare with Tibet, but included the reign of King **Gunakamadeva** during which the city of Kathmandu was founded. It also marked the introduction of Vajrayana Tantric Buddhism into Nepal.

Malla era 1200-1768

The post-Licchavi transitional period ended with the early hegemony of the **Malla** family in the Kathmandu Valley. The first important king was **Arideva Malla** who established his capital in Bhaktapur. Arideva was succeeded by **Abhayadeva**. Following his reign, the Valley was divided between his two sons, **Anandadeva** who ruled from Bhaktapur and **Jayadeva** who made Kathmandu his base and included Patan under his authority.

In western Nepal, meanwhile, a steady immigration of Hindu **Rajputs** (refugees from the Indian kingdom of Rajputana) and **Khasas** was taking place from the 9th century through to the 14th. It was a movement which was to shape the future course of Nepali history in ways unimaginable to those early migrants. The Rajputs were warriors and they settled and assimilated with the numerous kingdoms (*rajyas*) in the region, including the *Baishi Rajya* ('22 kingdoms') of the Karnali area and the *Chaubishi Rajya* ('24 kingdoms') in the Gandaki region.

To the south of the Valley, King **Nanyadeva** had founded the **Karnot** dynasty in 1097 which was based in Makwanpur (Simraungarh). The dynasty extended over six reigns, but disintegrated under civil unrest and later came under the control of the **Sen** dynasty. The only Muslim invasion of Nepal to have reached the Kathmandu Valley occured in 1346 when the ruler of Bengal, Sultan Shamsuddin Ilyas, launched his unsuccessful bid to wrest control from the Mallas.

Returning to events in the Kathmandu Valley, the most distinguished of the early Mallas was King **Sthithi** Malla (reigned 1372-1395) who, along with his son **Jyotir** Malla, introduced numerous social reforms including the first major codification of caste laws. The reign of King **Yaksha** Malla, from 1428 to 1482, was the last in which all 'Nepal' (the Kathmandu Valley and surrounding areas) was under a single monarch. It was marked also by the expansion of the Malla territory north into what is now Tibet, though from west to east it stretched barely 80 kilometres. While the monarch maintained his position, effective administrative power was exerted by an increasingly strong and hereditary nobility. The foundations for the eventual fall of the Mallas were laid by Yaksha who, for reasons unknown, allowed his kingdom to be divided between his three sons, with **Ratna** becoming king of Kathmandu and Patan, **Raya** of Bhaktapur and **Rana** of Banepa. The administrative nobility, however, retained all but nominal control of Kathmandu, Patan and Banepa. Petty rivalry increasingly came to characterize relations between the individual kingdoms. A result, however, was the assertion of individual identities through the blossoming of art, architecture and culture which each encouraged. Paradoxically, it was through this combination of often small-minded competition and immense pride that agricultural economies flourished, that systems for the distribution of drinking water were established and that the magnificent palaces and temple were constructed. King **Lakshmi Narasimha** Malla started the building of Kathmandu's Kasthamandap, now considered by some to be the world's oldest extant wooden building. His reign also witnessed a major increase in trade with Tibet, which was heavily promoted by one of the king's wealthiest ministers, Bhima Malla. Lakshmi Narasimha's son, **Pratapa** Malla, was noted for his vision and religious tolerance, even allowing Jesuit missionaries to settle in Kathmandu. King **Jayaprakash** Malla came to power in 1732. His was a difficult reign which faced numerous attempts to usurp his power, including one from his brother **Rajyaprakash** and another from his wife.

While the Mallas squabbled among themselves, however, something altogether more threatening to their collective security was developing beyond their borders. As the cities of Kathmandu, Patan and Bhaktapur vied for the greatest palaces and the finest temples, so the successors to the early Rajput migrants in the west sought new land for cultivation, new forests for timber and new opportunities for trade. And between the Rajput *rajya* and the Valley's Malla kingdoms lay the small state of **Gorkha**.

Unification of Nepal

Prithvi Narayan Shah was crowned king of Gorkha in 1742, aged 22. He was the 10th of the Shah Dynasty which had been founded in the 15th century by Dravya Shah. Prithvi inherited a kingdom that could not compete with its neighbours in either the fertility of its land or in its wealth. His vision of controlling the riches of the Kathmandu Valley and its fertile soils provided the initial motivation for a military campaign against the Valley and by way of incentive he promised a part of that land to all who fought with him. His first strategy, employed between 1744 and 1754, was to block the established **trade route** to Tibet which deprived Kathmandu, by then the strongest of the Valley's cities, of its Tibetan income which had until then paid for the upkeep of its mainly mercenary army. The Malla king resorted to 'plundering' the treasures of his own temples to pay the soldiers' wages, a move so unpopular that he was deposed. Somewhat optimistically, Prithvi attempted to take **Kirtipur** in 1757 but his forces' reliance on bows and arrows resulted inevitably in failure.

Maintaining his hold on the Tibetan trade route, from 1754 Prithvi turned his attention to the south, intending to cut off links with **India** and imposing an economic stranglehold on the Valley. This strategy involved taking the fortified town of **Makwanpur** in 1762, capital of the **Sen** kingdom which corresponds approximately to the modern district of Palpa.

The Sens turned to India for help and specifically to the Nawab of **Bengal**, Mir Kasim. The Nawab sent his army which was roundly defeated by the **Gorkhalis**, who had by now developed into an effective, well disciplined fighting unit. Victory also brought Prithvi prized spoils in the form of a large quantity of **muskets** which could be usefully employed in renewed attacks against the Mallas' walled defences. In 1766, he again laid siege to **Kirtipur** and, after a few weeks, succeeded in taking the town. In desperation, the Mallas turned to the **British** in India who responded to the plight of their trading partners by sending an army of 1,000 men. But the British force was unprepared. It left with minimal supplies which the Mallas were of course unable to supplement, because of the Gorkhalis' hold on all routes. It was also completely unprepared for the malarial jungle of the **Terai**, so that by the time the weary army reached the Churia Hills they were emphatically crushed by the Gorkhalis. More muskets were recovered and Prithvi went on to take **Kathmandu** with ease in September 1768. **Patan** followed in October of that year, with **Bhaktapur** the last to fall in November of the following year. With control of the Kathmandu Valley, it required little to add the rest of eastern Nepal which was completed in 1774.

Shah Dynasty 1769-1846

Prithvi Narayan Shah was a strong, even ruthless, leader who established a strong though wise system of administration. His **government** was a military meritocracy, but it depended on strong **leadership**. He even introduced appraisal schemes in which everyone was subject to an annual review. But he was aware also of the growing British presence in India and his mistrust of foreigners for fear of possible alliances which might threaten the kingdom led to the expulsion of Christian missionaries from Nepal and to the imposition of heavy restrictions of foreign trade. Recognizing the country as akin to a 'ram between two boulders', he built upon the friendship with Tibet, ensuring that no foreigners would be allowed to enter from the north. Having united Nepal politically for the first time, he now ruled over a nation as diverse in its ethnic composition as in its geography, but according to Ludwig Stiller (1993), his system 'provided a basis for union, not uniformity' – a considerable achievement by the standards of any age.

Prithvi died in 1775 and was succeeded by his son, **Pratap Singh Shah**. He, however, died in 1777 leaving his 16 month old son, **Rana Bahadur Shah**, as king of Nepal. The country was now in the hands of two competing regents: **Rajendra Lakshmi**, Rana Bahadur's mother and **Bahadur** Shah, Prithvi's second son. Ironically, within three years of Prithvi's death the seemingly brilliant system of government he introduced was held hostage by that requirement of strong leadership which he himself had so embodied.

Despite these conflicts, the Gorkhalis continued to expand their territory to the west under the command of Bahadur Shah. Conquests included the *Chaubisi* and *Baisi rajyas*. Bahadur maintained his father's policy of promising and allocating land from the newly captured territories to his men, but he soon found that the system demanded ever more land and revenue if it were not to collapse. An ill-advised war with Tibet in 1792 led to a humiliating Gorkhali defeat, then to Bahadur's imprisonment in 1797. He died in prison later that year.

In the meantime, **Rana Bahadur Shah** had begun to rule in his own name, but his reign ended when in desperation he abdicated at the request of his dying wife in 1799 and his son **Girban Juddha**, aged just 18 months, became king. This led to further factionalism and intrigue in Kathmandu and, ultimately, to Rana Bahadur's flight to India. Following discussions with the British East India Company and the signing of a *Treaty of Friendship* in 1801, Nepal agreed to accept a British **resident** in Kathmandu in exchange for assurances that the former king would be prevented from returning to Nepal. Now impoverished, however, Nepal could not keep to the financial obligations of the treaty. The British resident thus returned to India and in 1804 Rana Bahadur returned to Kathmandu to become 'adviser' to his son, the king. His own adviser, **Bhimsen Thapa**, was to play a major role in Nepali politics over the next three decades.

In 1806, Rana Bahadur unilaterally assumed the title of *Mukhtiyar* ('Chief Minister'). He was assassinated later that year by opposing factions fearing his return to the throne. An alert Bhimsen Thappa immediately charged his political opponents with the murder and had them put to death, thereby clearing the way for his own assumption of effective power. Under his control, the Nepali armies further extended their territories to the west which reached the maximum extent with the capture of **Kangra** in 1809. Meanwhile, **Rajendra Bikram Shah** was born as successor to the throne in 1816.

The Anglo-Nepali War Concerned by what was seen as Nepali land-grabbing, the British Governor General in India fired a diplomatic warning across Bhimsen's bows. He recognized, crucially, that the **Terai** lands constituted the key to Nepali wealth and were thus absolutely central to its ability to finance an army. Further discussions concerning the ownership of several Terai villages resulted in the British taking possession of these villages in 1814. Finding no resistance, the British military presence was removed that summer. Bhimsen concluded he had to act decisively and sent his troops in to retake the area. The British waited until the monsoon was over to retaliate. In the first attack, near Dehra Dun, their leader Major General Rollo Gillespie was killed, but they eventually took the village. To the east, further attacks were mounted through Butwal, along the Bagmati valley and near Janakpur. In May 1815, the Nepali forces surrendered. The resultant *Treaty of Sagauli* reduced Nepal's territory by roughly one third, depriving them of most of the previous Terai gains and re-establishing the position of the British resident in Kathmandu. The British, meanwhile, had been so impressed by the fighting qualities of their opponents that they established the so-called **Gurkha** Brigade which has continued to be an integral part of the British army until now.

There followed a period of stagnation. Bhimsen continued as *de facto* leader of the country with the support of the regent queen, **Tripura Sundari**. Following her death in 1832, King Rajendra Bikram asserted his right to power with the help of

Queen **Samrajya Lakshmi** and the influential **Pande** family. Together, they mounted a campaign against Bhimsen Thappa which succeeded in removing him in 1837. He died in prison in 1839. The intense rivalry which had become established soon after the death of Prithvi Narayan Shah, continued to influence political developments. Rajendra Bikram was a weak king and could do little to combat the increasing dominance of Queen **Rajya Lakshmi** after the death of his mother, Samrajya Lakshmi. Rajya Lakshmi desperately wanted her own son to become heir apparent in place of the legitimate heir, Surendra. But when her plan was opposed by the prime minister, General **Mathbar Singh Thappa**, she arranged for **Jung Bahadur Kanwar Rana** to have him assassinated in 1845.

The Kot Massacre The following months were imbued with political intrigue, mutual mistrust and an ineffective administration. Rajya Lakshmi was represented in government by General **Gagan Singh Bhandari**, while Jung Bahadur had been promoted to the rank of general as reward for removing Mathbar Singh Thappa. Jung Bahadur's influence grew in Kathmandu and he made sure that he was aware of every development to affect the political situation.

On 14 September 1846, as evening fell over Kathmandu and its people prepared to settle down for the night, General Gagan Singh Bhandari was murdered. Devastated, the queen arranged for a full meeting of council at the army fort – the **Kot** – that very night. The meeting took place in a heated atmosphere. While Jung Bahadur's soldiers stood guard outside, accusations and insults were exchanged. Who was responsible for the murder? Confusion and anger reigned. Then someone accused Jung Bahadur of complicity, whereupon fighting and shooting began. The prime minister, **Fatte Jung Shah**, was one of the first to die; next was one of his close aids, then others. When the guns at last stopped, over 30 of the country's most influential people lay dead. The queen almost immediately appointed Jung Bahadur prime minister, a position which was to remain Nepal's most powerful for the next century.

Rana Raj 1846-1951

At a stroke, Nepal's leading nobility and its political élite had been removed. Their families were either expelled or left the country voluntarily. The internal feuding which had so characterized the previous few decades largely disappeared and the country was once more under strong leadership. Jung Bahadur recognized the might of the British Empire in India and concluded that the most pragmatic foreign policy was one of friendship and isolation. Contact with the British, once established, was kept to a minimum. Internally Jung Bahadur maintained the monarchy, but demoted it to non-executive ceremonial status, while he had himself made **Maharaja**. The powers of Maharaja were absolute, with the king and prime minister obliged to carry out his instructions. The position was made hereditary.

In 1857, Jung Bahadur led some 8,000 Nepali troops against the Indian sepoys who were **mutineering** against British rule in India. As ever, his decision was entirely politically motivated. He saw that the sepoys were not going to overcome the greater might of the imperial forces, so it was a simple matter of backing the winner for the future interest of Nepal. In return, the British continued to respect the territorial sovereignty of Nepal.

By the time of his death in 1877, Jung Bahadur Rana had instituted several social reforms, including a revision of the penal code and the establishment of a new tax system. He also introduced a system of land ownership closely related to the *zamindari* system of India, which increased the importance of the administrative classes. But by placing members of his own wider family in positions of responsibility, he also ensured that nepotism became firmly entrenched in the social fabric. Inevitably, this led to inefficiency and corruption as established hallmarks of

Nepal during his later years and, indeed, throughout the remaining period of Rana rule. These qualities, moreover, were not entirely alien to him and by the end of his life he had amassed a considerable personal fortune.

Jung Bahadur was succeeded as prime minister by the army's Commander-in-Chief, **Ranoddip Singh**. Ranoddip persuaded the nominal monarch, King Surendra, to grant him also the title of Maharajah of **Kaski** and **Lamjung**, in which capacity he ruled – ineffectively – until his assassination by **Bir Shamsher**, Jung Bahadur's nephew, in 1885. By hook or more usually by crook, the Shamsher wing of the family remained in power for the remainder of the Rana period. Bir Shamsher introduced further tax reforms intended to increase government revenues from the Terai landowners. The government, of course, was Shamsher. It was also thoroughly corrupt, overwhelmed by often unnecessary administrative burdens and quite out of touch with the greater needs of the country.

Although Bir can claim credit for a number of public works, his preoccupation was the aggrandizement both of wealth and of self. The former was easily serviced by the system, while the British contributed to the latter by awarding him a knighthood. In turn, members of the Shamsher family increasingly invested their ill-gained wealth in the Calcutta market, but failed to invest at all in the development of Nepal's agricultural economy from which their wealth was gleaned.

Bir was succeeded by **Dev Shamsher** in 1901. Although Dev began his prime ministership with a number of social innovations which threatened to bring a degree of equity to the country, he was overthrown by his younger brother, **Chandra Shamsher**, after just three months in power. Suspicion exists that he was assisted in the coup by the British who, under Viceroy Curzon, were demonstrating an increasing and – for some – disturbing interest in Nepal. Chandra was quickly recognized by the British. At home, he soon started construction of his palace, the **Singha Durbar**. He later encouraged **trade** with India, building bridges to improve communications and laying the foundation for Nepal's first and only stretch of railway, around Janakpur. His term is also remembered for the abolition of *sati*, the introduction of electricity to Kathmandu and the revision of the civil administration including the first attempts at proper forest management. With the outbreak of war in Europe in 1914, Chandra offered military assistance to the British and more than 100,000 Nepalis served in the British army. The British in return pledged an annual payment of Rs 1mn (Indian) in perpetuity and in 1923 signed the *Treaty of Friendship* which again assured Nepal its independence.

In 1929 Chandra died and was succeeded by his brother, **Bhim Shamsher**. His term was marked by the beginnings of civil disquiet and increasing unease with Rana rule. Bhim died in 1932 and **Juddha Shamsher** became prime minister. Barely 16 months later, the great **earthquake** of 1934 rocked Nepal. Juddha, who had been on holiday in West Nepal, returned to the devastated capital and organized a remarkably successful rebuilding operation. But this could not prevent the rumours which began circulating in 1939, rumours designed to de-stabilize his position, rumours which expressed growing widespread dissatisfaction with the Ranas, rumours of a plot to overthrow the regime. In October 1940, 56 members of the *Nepal Praja Parishad* (Nepal People's Council) were arrested for plotting against the government. Many more were implicated, including the nominal king, **Tribhuvan**. Four were eventually executed, including at least one whose innocence was indisputable.

The Ranas' clock was ticking ever more loudly. The aftermath of the 1934 earthquake had placed additional burdens on the national exchequer, Nepali men were again away from the fields in their thousands fighting in the Second World War and a century of Rana rule had left the country desperately impoverished. In late 1945 Juddha resigned, handing over the reigns of power to his reluctant nephew, **Padma Shamsher**. He inherited all Juddha's unresolved problems and more. As the head of a family which had traditionally supported the British in India, Padma was faced with an India about to become independent, while on his northern borders was the newly communist China. Furthermore, the Ranas had become hopelessly divided. Padma did not have the strength to enforce his social reforms. On 15 August 1947, the day of Indian independence, Padma ordered the release from jail of **BP Koirala**, leader of the **Nepali National Congress** freedom movement. From India Jawaharlal Nehru was encouraging the Ranas towards democracy and Padma's new **Constitution of Nepal** was approved in 1948. This allowed the freedom of speech which was widely used to berate the Ranas. Padma resigned in 1948 and was succeeded by **Mohan Shamsher**.

One of Mohan's first acts was to ban the Nepali National Congress. He ordered the arrest of anyone involved in anti-Rana activities. Another plot to overthrow the regime was uncovered in 1950 and was found to implicate King Tribhuvan. Tribhuvan fled with his family to India. Following immense Indian diplomatic pressure, Tribhuvan returned to Kathmandu the following February as king and *de facto* ruler of Nepal. He initially headed a coalition government of Mohan Shamsher's Ranas and the Nepali Congress, but this had collapsed by the end of the year leaving Congress in government and MP Koirala as Prime Minister.

Since 1951

Though politically momentous, little actually changed for the common man with the restoration of the monarchy. A bicameral parliamentary system of government was adopted, but patronage remained fundamental to securing position and nepotism remained strongly entrenched. King Tribhuvan died in 1955 and his son **Mahendra** assumed the throne. Following calls for greater democracy, King Mahendra approved a new **constitution** in 1959. It embraced numerous democratic ideals, but crucially allowed the king to suspend the constitution and impose a State of Emergency. That same year, the Nepali Congress Party won the general election with a two-thirds majority. Congress used its position as the governing party to strengthen its own nationwide support, much as its namesake in India had done. In November 1959, King Mahendra used his constitutional powers to suspend the constitution, declare an **Emergency** and arrest many leading members of the Nepali Congress.

In 1962, the King established a new form of government known as the **Panchayat** system which was supposedly better fitted to Nepali conditions. A *panchayat* is a traditional village council. This model was intended to be 'partyless' and political parties were banned. Instead there was a five-tiered structure headed by the King himself and followed by the Prime Minister, a Council of Ministers and regional councils. The 'Panchayat Democracy' remained in place until 1980, though characterized by inflexibility and the continuing importance of patronage.

King Mahendra died in 1972 and was succeeded by his son, King **Birendra Bikram Bir Shah Dev**. The new king soon recognized that the country was lagging seriously in its development efforts as well as economically. The old guard was changed as Birendra brought in educated, younger people to push the country forward. This achieved considerable success in administrative reorganization, but had little effect on the country's economy. Realizing that the key to further development lay in political reform, the King called for a national **referendum** to choose between continuing with the panchayat system or reverting to a multi-party system. The result was extremely close, but resulted in the maintenance of the status quo. Officially, political parties remained banned but their existence was tolerated.

From late 1989, the major parties (including the increasingly powerful Communists), joined to campaign against the panchayat system. Strikes and frequently violent mass demonstrations followed in which several people were killed. However, the movement succeeded and on 18 April 1990 a joint-party interim government headed by KP Bhattarai was appointed to prepare for **elections** and draw up a new constitution.

Following the announcement of the new constitution on 9 November 1990 in which the king was given powers to act unilaterally only in limited exceptional circumstances, the general election was held on 12 May 1991. The Nepali Congress Party emerged as the clear winners, securing 110 of the 205 seats, with the Communist Party of Nepal (United Marxist-Leninist) [CPN-UML] forming the main opposition with 69 seats. KP Bhattarai, the former interim Prime Minister, lost his seat and **GP Koirala** became Prime Minister.

Widespread dissatisfaction since then and accusations of institutionalized corruption has resulted in a delicate political balance. Congress gained substantial absolute majorities in the local elections of 1992, but the Communists emerged victorious from the local elections of June and July 1997 in which they secured over 50 percent of the vote, with Congress managing only around 30 percent. National politics has remained unstable since no party achieved an overall majority in the November 1994 general election (CPN-UML 90 seats; Congress 87 seats; Rashtriya Prajatantra Party 19 seats; others 8 seats). After 10 months of minority rule under Prime Minister **Man Mohan Adhikari**, the CPN-UML were ousted by a coalition headed by **Sher Bahadur Deuba** of Congress in September 1995. Deuba's government lasted just 17 months, being defeated in a confidence motion in March 1997. The leader of the tiny Rashtriya Prajatantra Party, **Lokendra Bahadur Chand**, was then sworn in as Prime Minister with the support of the CPN-UML. The coalition stumbled through the next two years, surviving internal divisions and widespread accusations of corruption and inefficiency which served to further undermine public confidence in the country's political system. The coalition fell in early 1999 and elections were called in May of that year. Political commentators were expecting another hung parliament with no party able to claim an overall majority. GP Koirala remained leader of the Nepali Congress Party. In some remote areas of Northwest Nepal, insurgents of the ultra-extremist Nepal Communist (Maoist) Party began a violent campaign in early 1996 hoping to destabilize the present democracy and to abolish the monarchy. By mid-1999, the campaign had spread to the central western areas of the country, including the Gorkha region, bringing further violence and sporadic armed confrontation with police. The legal, political wing of the Maoists has benefited from the growing disillusionment with Nepal's governing parties in the late 1990s to increase its popular support in rural areas particularly and was expected to make significant gains in the May 1999 general election.

Background

The land

Nowhere else on Earth has a greater diversity of landscapes within as small an area as Nepal. In a north-south cross-section of less than 200 kilometres are the subtropical plains of the Terai, the temperate Himalayan 'foothills' of the Churia and Mahabharat ranges and the High Himalayan peaks themselves. More than half of the country is higher than 3,000 metres above sea level, around a quarter is at elevations of about 3,000 metres and less than one fifth is below 300 metres.

Geology and environment

The Terai   The Terai constitutes the northern belt of the Gangetic Plains. Sloping gently from west to east, it comprises less than 20 percent of the total land surface and is Nepal's most densely **populated** region. Dotted across its breadth are a few **towns** and cities, mostly minor commercial and light industrial centres. But more important are the thousands of **villages**, traditional farming communities cultivating the country's most **fertile** stretch of land and producing most of its agricultural output: the Terai has over a million hectares under **paddy**. The region shares much with the neighbouring Indian states of Uttar Pradesh, Bihar and West Bengal and the border is far more political in character than cultural.

The Terai was formed around 40 million years ago, during the Eocene period. Many of the rocks which form the Indian Peninsula were formed alongside their then neighbours in South Africa, Australia and Antarctica. Then, as the great plates on which the earth's southern continents stood broke up, the Indian Plate started its dramatic shift northwards, eventually colliding with the Asian plate. That collision is still reverberating and as the Indian Plate continues to get pushed under the Tibetan Plateau so the Himalaya continue to rise.

The process of **plate tectonics** is still continuing, rendering this boundary region between the two landmasses seismically unstable. Beneath its uniformly flat surface are a series of geological troughs and ridges, a sort of subterranean mountain range. The many major **rivers** flowing through the Terai deposit clay and sandy or calcareous silts which contribute to the high fertility of its **soils** and allow the cultivation of 1.4 million hectares of land (most under paddy) by over one million individual farm holdings.

Throughout all but the most recent part of its history, the Terai was almost entirely **forested** and was a zone where malaria was endemic. This belt also provided a natural barrier for the Kathmandu Valley and elsewhere against invading forces. This changed only in the second half of the 20th century, when a deliberate programme of **deforestation** was initiated with the aims of eradicating malaria and creating new lands for settlement. The result has been massive migration from the hills together with urbanization on an unprecedented scale. The forest, meanwhile, has been denuded beyond recognition: less than 50 percent now remains and gives an idea of what there once was. It is dominated by the deciduous **sal** (*Shorea robusta*), a straight and tall growing tree that reaches heights of 30m and higher. It is used as a main source of building material. There are also stands of **teak** (*Tectona grandis*), concentrated in the west, whose timber is highly sought after for building as well as in the production of furniture. Both trees have a good resistance to fire which has helped to mitigate the increasing dominance of man and his attempts to transform more land for agricultural use. Restrictions have been placed belatedly on the commercial exploitation of timber. These, however, are notoriously difficult to enforce with the appeal of additional income combined with local power structures and political allegiances often ensuring that a blind eye is turned to illegal logging operations.

Middle Zone

This region of Himalayan foothills forms a buffer zone between the Gangetic Plains to the south and the High Himalaya proper to the north. The term 'foothills' is something of a euphemism, as many of its 'hills' are higher than Ben Nevis, the highest peak in the UK! Immediately north of the Terai are the forested **Churia Hills** (known in India as the *Siwaliks* and by geologists as the *Sub-Himalaya*). The suddenness with which the flat expanse of Terai gives way to the hills and the contrast between the two can be quite dramatic. The Churias are comprised of relatively recent metamorphic rocks, including limestone and, at their northern extent, are characterized by the many *doons* (valleys). Known also as the *Inner Terai*, these are often river valleys which can be highly fertile. Elsewhere, the Churias are extensively terraced for cultivation, but soils are generally poorer which limits cropping seasons.

The Churia Hills belt have provided researchers with crucial information on the process of Himalayan **orogeny**. It is rich in the **fossils** of both fauna and flora. By boring deep into the ground and extracting a vertical sample of rock, they have been able to establish the sequence of geological, environmental and climatic changes by analysing the sediments.

To the north of the Churias is the **Mahabharat Lekh** ('Great Indian Range'), the narrow southern band of what geologists know as the *Lesser Himalaya*. Peak elevations increase to heights of up to 2,600 metres and rocks consists entirely of metamorphosed varieties, with quartzites especially evident. Slopes are also forested, sometimes heavily with evergreen oaks and firs, while in areas of higher rainfall the rhododendron tree (Nepal's national flower) flourishes. Formerly under water, much of this region has major lacustrine deposits. The broader **Pahar** zone extends from the Mahabharat Lekh to the High Himalaya. This region includes both the Kathmandu and Pokhara valleys, while elevations range from less than 1,000 metres above sea level to 4,000 metres and higher. The many river valleys in this belt allow often intensive cultivation of land, with slopes also cultivated with intricate terraces. At lower elevations (eg along the Arun Valley in East Nepal), forests are characteristically sub-tropical, while with an increase in altitude they become moist temperate, consisting largely of pine, spruce, cedars, firs and the attractive rhododendron whose white, purple or typically deep red flowers blossom from late

Nepal: geological regions

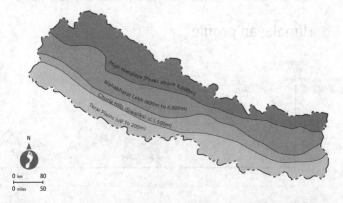

Background

March to early May. Deodars (*Cedrus deodora*) are particularly conspicuous in the west of Nepal.

High Himalaya

The High Himalaya mark the zone of maximum uplift resulting from the northward movement of the South Asian landmass into the Central Asian plate. The range stretches some 2,500 kilometres from northwest to southeast and is around 400 kilometres at its widest and is the world's highest as well as youngest mountain range. Eight of the world's 10 highest peaks are in Nepal, including, of course, Everest (8,848 metres). Its geology is complex, but consists of highly metamorphosed rocks dating from the Tertiary and all other major periods. A series of massifs are separated from one another by deep gorges: separating Dhaulagiri from the Annapurnas, the 6,000 metre deep Kali Gandaki is the deepest in the world. The mountains are still rising at up to 15 millimetres a year. The entire region is subject to intense geological activity. Satellite imagery reveals deep fault zones throughout the range and between 1870 and 1996 there have been over 50 major earthquakes (measuring over six on the Richter Scale), to have occurred here and along fault lines of the Tibetan Plateau.

Tibetan Plateau

This region covers an area as large as Western Europe, with elevations ranging from the low-lying southern gorges at 1,700 metres to the massive 8,000 metre Himalayan peaks. Most of the Tibetan Plateau is considered to have formed the bed of the Neotethys Ocean which disappeared some 210-250 million years ago with the meeting of the two landmasses. This collision, believed to have taken place some 2,012 kilometres south of the Indus-Brahmaputra watershed, finally formed the plateau around 66 million years ago following a long period of orogeny in the northern areas of Tibet between c 570-245 million years ago. The massive plateau, subject to widespread volcanicity, continues to extend upwards and outwards under its own weight, as the Indian subcontinental plate moves ever northwards at a speed of about 6.1 centimetres per year.

Origins of Uplift

Only 100 million years ago, the Indian peninsular was still attached to the great land mass in the southern hemisphere called Pangaea, or **Gondwanaland**, of which South America, South Africa, Antartica and the Indian subcontinent were part. It included some of the world's oldest rocks, such as crystalline granites and gneisses (metamorphic rocks, often layered and with high crystalline content), which today make up a large part of India south of the Ganges plains. Towards the end of the Palaeozoic Era, ie from about 160 million years ago, Gondwanaland began to separate. This process of **plate tectonics** (that is, the movement of 'plates' of the earth's crust), resulted in the northward drift through the great **Tethys Sea** of four major land masses which became South America, Africa, the Indian peninsular and

Himalayan profile

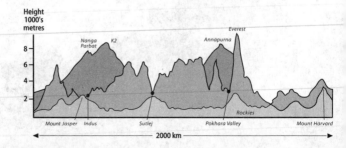

Australia. The South Asian plate was eventually subducted beneath the great Central Asian Plate around 55 million years ago creating a concertina-like folding and faulting of the area of impact – the Himalaya – and causing the uplift of the Tibetan Plateau.

The first ranges of the Himalaya to begin the mountain building process were probably the Karakoram in modern Pakistan. The central core of the Himalayan ranges did not begin to rise until about 35 million years ago, followed by further major movements between 25 and 5 million years ago. The latest mountain building period, responsible for the Siwaliks, began less than 5 million years ago and is still continuing. The rocks of the central core of the Himalaya were formed under the intense pressure and heat of the mountain building process. Before that, the present Himalayan region and what is now the Tibetan High Plateau had lain under the sea.

Rivers

Nepal's rivers descend further and faster than any other rivers in the world. As a result, many have cut sheer-sided valleys thousands of metres deep, creating enormously unstable hillsides. Any external action – an earthquake, severe rainfall, the construction of a road – can trigger catastrophic earth and rock slides which sometimes create natural dams impounding large lakes, only to burst open and flood the valleys downstream.

The country's three main river systems – the **Kosi, Gandaki** and **Karnali** – originate in glaciers and go on to form part of the Ganges river system. A few rise in Tibet, but all ultimately flow into the Ganges. In their lower courses, they are subject to severe flooding. The **Kathmandu Valley** is drained by the **Bagmati River** which rises to the north near Tare Bir (2,732 metres) and leaves the Valley through the **Chobhar Gorge**. By Nepali standards, it is not a great river.

The Himalayan region has many **glaciers**. As the west is very dry, the biggest are in the east. The Mahalangur and Khumbarkarna ranges have the largest, while the east Himalaya are also the source of the major Kanchenjunga, Yalung, Nuptse and Langtang glaciers.

Climate

The climate of Nepal reflects its topography. The **Terai** and **Churia Hills** experience a sub-tropical monsoonal climate in common with the rest of the northern Gangetic Plains. Peak temperatures in summer rise to above 40°C, while winter night temperatures drop to just above freezing. The **middle zone** of the Mahabharat and Pahar regions are temperate, with a climate similar to that of Central Europe. Summer peak temperatures can reach just below 40°C, while the winter regularly experiences temperatures below zero, with snow common in the higher areas. Neither the cities of the Kathmandu Valley nor Pokhara have snow, though the surrounding hills do. The climate of the **High Himalaya** is alpine.

The **monsoon** extends across the whole country from June to September, when over 75 percent of the annual precipitation occurs. The influence of the monsoon and the amount of rainfall decreases from east to west and from south to north. Beyond the High Himalaya and into Tibet, it is arid and cold. If you do the classic three-week Annapurna Circuit trek, you will go from the sub-tropical lushness south of the mountains to this stark arid beauty of the north.

The **post monsoon** period of October-November is characterized by settled weather, clear skies, little rain and moderate to high temperatures. As winter approaches it gets cooler, especially at night. Temperatures drop further in **winter**. At lower altitudes it is dry and often very dusty. Higher up it is extremely cold at night.

The role of the monsoon

Widely understood as a few months of heavy rainfall, the term monsoon derives from the Arabic word mausim, meaning 'season'. The Southwest monsoon, dominant from June to September, is the single most important climatic determinant of agricultural production in South Asia; it enables and supports life and plays a key role in both the economic and cultural landscape of the region. It is in many ways the culmination of the annual climatic cycle: for months weather patterns change in preparation for the rains and when the last drop has fallen the renewed land is ready to begin another year. Countless festivals are celebrated (in the Terai especially) to celebrate the rainy season, whether planting or harvesting. So influential is it that all levels of government take a keen interest in its progress, lest collective frustrations thrust the responsibility of a failed monsoon upon them. The number of tourists visiting Nepal, meanwhile (and the income they bring), drop markedly during these months. It has also been the subject of almost mystical fascination for generations, with poets and writers striving to capture its essence, be it the drama and lifted spirits of the first heavy downpour, the romance of an awesome natural power, or its pivotal role in the cycle of life.

But for many, the monsoon brings severe hardships too. Rivers burst their banks, causing heavy local flooding and landslides regularly destroy houses or even wipe away villages, leaving many homeless. This is exacerbated by deforestation in the Himalaya. Trees provide some stability for an otherwise highly unstable topography, but without them hillsides and mountain slopes are more susceptible to severe erosion and denudation, further endangering those living below. It is argued that the resultant increase in debris carried by the rivers leads to a serious increase in siltation as far downstream as Bangladesh with potentially damaging consequences for that region's agriculture. It is a season of

September-January

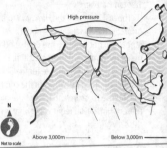

May

September-January

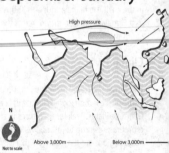

increased health risks too. The saying, 'Two Monsoons are the Age of Man', was familiar during the early period of British rule in India and reflected the high level of seasonal mortality at the time. Fortunately, things have rather improved since then, but even today low standards of environmental sanitation lead to contamination of water supplies and the ready transmission of disease, while pools of stagnant water provide ideal breeding grounds for malaria-bearing mosquitoes.

Background

The exact process leading to the onset of the southwest monsoon across most of South Asia in June is complex and is still not fully understood. The previous belief that low pressures over the surface of the Thar desert played a central role in its development have been superseded by greater emphasis placed on upper air movements.

In winter Nepal's weather is controlled by the cold high pressure system over the Tibetan Plateau. Northeasterly winds cross the Nepal Himalaya to the Indian plains, bringing dry, cold weather to Nepal. At high altitude the westerly jet stream flows to the south and north of the Himalaya. From February, as the sun warms the Indian peninsula and the Tibetan plateau, a low pressure system develops over the North Indian plains and the westerly jet streams begin to move north.

By the end of May the southern branch of the westerly jet stream shifts to the north of the Himalaya, while southwest winds push northwards across the Indian Ocean and the Bay of Bengal from the Equator. It is this system which brings the wind reversal which is the defining characteristic of monsoon climates. The cool dry northeasterlies are replaced by warm and very wet southwesterlies across much of India. However, by the time the rain bearing winds reach Nepal their direction has changed again and the winds sweep up from southeast to northwest along the Ganges plains. Rainfall thus decreases from east to west along the Himalaya and is largely concentrated between June and September. These are normally extremely wet months.

The monsoon
See box on page 492 for diagrams

Vegetation

The natural vegetation reflects altitude and climate, but has been severely modified by man in the latter 20th century.

The most significant form of vegetation in the **Terai** is its band of deciduous forest. Formerly completely forested and a malarial zone, much of the region's tree cover has been removed since the 1950s to make way for settlement and cultivation. The **sal** (*Shorea robusta*) is the Terai's dominant tree, though stands of **teak** (*Tectona grandis*) are also found. There have been efforts at reforestation which, though isolated, are portentous for the future. A few areas have also witnessed the introduction of 'community forest' schemes in which local communities have a stake in new plantations. A savanna environment of **phanta** grassland is found in the far west (Sukla Phanta Wildlife Reserve) as well as smaller areas in the mid-west and elsewhere. **Riverine** forest, including sissoo and acacia, extend along the

Backgrou

Nepal: climate

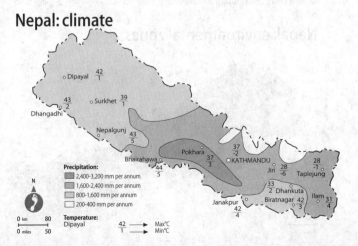

Precipitation:
- 2,400-3,200 mm per annum
- 1,600-2,400 mm per annum
- 800-1,600 mm per annum
- 200-400 mm per annum

Temperature:
Dipayal

$\frac{42}{1}$ ⟶ Max°C / Min°C

0 km 80
0 miles 50

floodplains of the main rivers. The silk cotton tree (*Bombax ceiba*) is conspicuous and grows up to 25 metres in height. The bark is light coloured, often grey and usually bears conical pines. In big trees there are noticeable buttresses at the bottom of the trunk. It has wide spreading branches and, though deciduous, keeps its leaves for most of the year. The flowers appear when the tree is leafless and have rather flashy red, curling petals up to 12 centimetres long forming a cup shape, from the middle of which the stamens all appear in a bunch. The fruit pod produces the fine silky cotton which gives it its name. The Terai's national parks have succeeded in maintaining pockets of the region's natural biodiversity as well as the habitats of endangered fauna. **Cultivation** is largely of rice, though wheat, corn, millet and vegetables also feature prominently. **Rice** (*Oryza sativa*) is a grass of which there are many hundreds of varieties with different colours, growing seasons and other characteristics.

The Terai also supports a number of **fruit** trees, the bewildering produce of which you will see in many a town market. The **mango** (*Mangifera indica*) is a fairly high tree growing up to 15 metres or higher with spreading branches forming a rounded canopy. You will often see it along roadsides (much of the Bhairahawa to Lumbini stretch is a true mango avenue). The distinctively shaped fruit is delicious. From a distance, the **jackfruit** (*Artocarpus heterophyllus*) tree looks similar to the mango. It is a large evergreen of the mulberry family with dark green leathery leaves, some of which may fall in cold weather. The bark is warty and dark brown in appearance. Its huge fruit, which can be as much as 90 centimetres long, 40 centimetres thick and can weigh more than 30 kilogrammes, grows from a short stem directly off the trunk and branches. The immature fruit is used as a vegetable. The skin is thick and rough, almost prickly. The fruit itself is an acquired taste and some find the smell of the ripe fruit unpleasant. The **banana** plant (the *Musaceae* family) is not in fact a tree but a gigantic herb arising from an underground stem. The very large leaves grow directly off the trunk and the plant can grow higher than seven metres. The leaves are often tattered and the fruiting stem bears a large purple flower (also used in cooking), which yields up to 100 fruit bunched up the stem. The **papaya** (*Carica papaya*) has a slender, palm-like trunk up to eight metres tall, though it is usually much shorter. The large hand-shaped leaves come off in one, two or three stages, with one always at the top. Only the female tree bears fruit (immature fruits are also used as vegetables) which hang down from near the base of the branches. The **leechi** tree (*Litchi chinensis*) is a native of China which has spread down through Nepal and into India. A member of the soapberry (*Sapindus*) family, it bears small round fruit containing a black stone, sweet, white, jelly-like flesh

Nepal: environmental zones

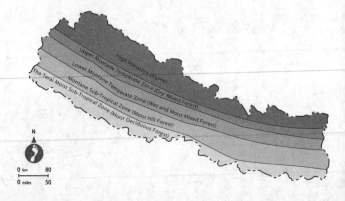

High Himalaya (Alpine)

Upper Montane Temperate Zone (Dry Mixed Forest)

Lower Montane Temperate Zone

Montane Sub-Tropical Zone (Wet and Moist Mixed Forest)

The Terai Moist Sub-Tropical Zone (Moist Hill Forest)

(Moist Deciduous Forest)

N

0 km   80
0 miles   50

and has a brittle pink or red shell. The **guava** (*Psidium guajava*) is a small tree with spherical to pear shaped fruit. The **pineapple** (*Ananas comosus*) is a bromeliaceous plant whose familiar fruit develops from a head of flowers close to the ground and has a crown of spiky leaves.

The **cashew** (*Anacardium*) tree is related to the mango and pistachio. Usually less than seven metres in height, it has bright green, shiny rounded leaves. The rather thick foliage casts a dense shadow. The nut is suspended from a fleshy fruit called a cashew apple. The **tamarind** (*Tamarindus indica*) is an evergreen with feathery leaves and small yellow and red flowers which

Cashew nut

grow in clusters. It has a short straight trunk and a spreading crown. The bark is often thickened with scar tissue which gives it an irregular appearance. The noticeable fruit pods are long, curved and swollen at intervals down their length. It has a slightly bitter pungent taste. It is widely used in south Indian cooking and is a vital ingredient in Worcester Sauce! The **coconut** palm (*Cocus nucifera*) is common throughout the Terai, with its tall (15-25 metres), slender, unbranched trunk, feathery leaves and large green fruit, so different from the brown fibre-covered inner nut which makes its way to Europe.

Several hundreds of Nepal's plants and **herbs** have been used for centuries as **ayurvedic** treatments and are increasingly exported worldwide as acceptance of their medicinal value becomes more widespread. The first definitive writings on their therapeutic uses are contained in the Hindu *Ayur Veda* (*ayur* – 'life' or 'vital power'; *veda* – 'knowledge'), written between 2500 BC and 600 BC.

The **eucalyptus** (*Eucalyptus grandis*) was introduced into the subcontinent from Australia in the 19th century. It provides both shade and firewood. There are several forms of eucalyptus, but all can be readily recognized by their characteristic thin long leaves and brown or grey bark. The leaves and fruit of the tree often have a pleasant fresh smell, especially after rain. The **banyan** tree (*Ficus benghalensis*) is featured widely in Eastern literature. Curiously, its seeds germinate in cracks in walls and in crevices in the bark of other trees. In a wall the growing roots will split the wall apart as can be seen in many old temples. As it grows more roots appear from the branches until the original host tree is surrounded by a cage-like structure which eventually strangles it. So a single banyan appears to have multiple 'trunks', which are in fact roots. Related to the banyan and growing in similar conditions is the **Peepul** tree (*Ficus religiosa*). This tree is particularly associated with holy Hindu sites and is frequently found in or by a temple or shrine. In some instances, shrines have actually been built beneath the original peepul tree. It also cracks open walls and strangles other trees with its roots. It has a smooth grey bark and can easily be distinguished from the banyan by the absence of aerial roots and by the leaves which are large, rather leathery and heart shaped, the point of the leaf tapering into a pronounced 'tail'. It bears abundant figs which are about one centimetre across.

The **Churia Hills** bring the first indications of changes in vegetation type. Population settlement is thinner here, so although there is a considerable

Peepul

Concerning the uses and Western names of some Himalayan plants

Flowers Particularly common in West Nepal but also found elsewhere, the red-flowering **geranium** is also known as stork's bill in southern Africa after the appearance of its fruit. The Greek word geranos means 'crane'. The **gentian** plant (of the genera Gentiana, Gentianella and Gentianopsis), despite its name is not related to the dye, gentian violet, used in medicine, although the root of one species (G. Lutea) is valued as a traditional herbal tonic. It is said to have been a favourite of King Gentius of the ancient kingdom of Illyria on the east coast of the Adriatic.

Buttercups belong to the genus Anemone. Its wild species often have white petals and like many other plants, its seeds are spread by the wind. The word anemone also derives from the Greek and means 'daughter of the wind'. The **orchid** can grow independently or as an epiphyte, and its delightful blue or purple flowers are seen in many mid to northern regions of Nepal. The orchid family, which includes the vanilla plant, is characterized by its small spherical roots. Curiously, it is from these roots rather than from the flowers that its botanical name derives; Orchis is the old Greek word for 'testicles'.

Trees The **spruce** is an evergreen, coniferous pine tree whose wood is occasionally used for furniture or building. It takes its name from Prussia, traditionally one of its major habitats. **Juniper** is an evergreen shrub or tree of the genus Juniperus. Its blue-black berries (or cones) are a crucial ingredient in the flavouring of gin. Medicine uses it as a diuretic, while the wood of some species is distilled to produce an oily tar applied topically in the treatment of certain skin conditions. The **laurel** (Laurus genus) may be a tree or shrub and is related to the rhododendron. It is perhaps more familiar in its form of a bay tree and takes its name from the old French word lor, meaning 'bay'.

Himalayan Hemlock is not that member of the parsley family used to silence Socrates, but a coniferous tree of the genus Tsuga. Its soft wood is sometimes used for making paper. It belongs to the **pine** family (Pinacaea), a broad term which includes several species with needle leaves. The male tree flowers with catkin-like clusters, while the female develops a scaly wooden cone. The **cedar** (genus Cedrus) is recognizable by its broad, spreading branches. The fragrant wood is often used to make incense which doubles as a potent moth repellent. The **deodar** (Cedrus deodara) is a cedar unique to the Himalaya ('the abode of the gods') and produces durable timber. The name appropriately derives from the Sanskrit devadaru – 'wood of the gods'.

amount of terraced cultivation, a reasonable proportion of the slopes remain wooded. At lower levels, sal is again prominent. In the far east, there is widespread **tea** cultivation. Tea gardens stretch from the Indian border near Darjeeling to west of Ilam, producing an attractive carpet-like landscape of deep green. **Cardamom** is also grown here in commercial quantities. With the increase in height, between 1,000 metres and 2,000 metres sal gives way to extensive stands of wet hill, coniferous forest including **pine** (notably the (*Pinus roxburghi*) along with **chestnut** (*Castanopis indica*), spruce and evergreen **oak** (*Quercus lamellosa*). Significant stands of deodars are restricted to the far west of Nepal.

Bougainvillaea is widely distributed. It is a dense bush or a climber with oval leaves and rather long spines. The flowers often cover the whole bush and can be a variety of striking colours, including pinkish-purple, orange, yellow and white. If you look carefully at one of the flowers, you will see that the brightly coloured part is not formed by the petals, which are quite small and undistinguished, but by large bracts at the base of the flower.

Continuing up into the **Mahabharat Lekh** and **Pahar** zones above 2,000 metres, **rhododendrons** are common. These trees, with their gnarled stems and twisted

Background

branches, flower profusely from late March and are Nepal's 'national flower'. They thrive in a wet climate and are found in dense tracts in East Nepal particularly along the upper stretches of the Arun and Tamur valleys. With the exception of this area, the rhododendron is rarely found in isolation. **Poplars** (eg *Populas ciliata*) which extend east into Bhutan and **larches** (*Larix* species) as well as juniper are also well represented in much of the eastern part of the country. All these species are water-demanding, so distribution diminishes with decreasing longitude. In contrast to the very low and often bone dry understorey of Terai sal forest, that of the wetter areas is full with numerous species of fungi and mosses which give the forest a characteristically fresh and heady smell. **Bamboo** (the *Bambusa*, *Phyllostachys* and *Dendrocalamus* species), is strictly speaking a grass and is another common component of forest undergrowth, though there are occasional solitary stands of enormous varieties whose stems are so strong that they are used as building materials. It is conspicuous in the lower Annapurna regions. Various **Cypress** (*Cupressus* species) trees are found in the west, including the indigenous Himalayan Cypress.

Rhododendron cover continues above 3,000 metres where **alpine** forest now becomes dominant. These elevations are characterized also by fairly extensive stands of birch, pine and juniper. The **treeline** (ie the highest altitude at which trees grow), lies at just below 5,000 metres. Again reflecting precipitation patterns, rhododendrons can flourish up to this elevation in the east, while shrubbery dominates in the west. These elevations support various grasses, with patches of grassland extending 500 metres or more above the treeline. From April, the seemingly hostile climate gives way to an array of flowering plants. These include species of **gentian**, **primroses** (some of the first to blossom), **roses** of the genus *Potentilla* and **buttercups**.

Wildlife

The widest variety of wildlife is once again found in the Terai. The steady destruction of forests and wooded areas both in the Terai and further north has removed the natural habitat of some larger mammals in particular. Nepal is also home to a huge range of birdlife. The best places for watching the wildlife are the Terai's national parks, especially Bardia and Chitwan for mammals and Sukla Phanta and Koshi Tappu for birds.

Mammals The greatest concentrations of the **Asiatic Elephant** (*Elephas maximus*) living in the wild are found in the Royal Bardia National Park which lies on a traditional elephant migratory route from the western Terai into India (including the Corbett National Park). The animals come down to water in the evening, either in family groups or in herds of individuals. Elephants are also frequently domesticated and are beasts of burden. The **Indian Rhinoceros** (*Rhinoceris unicornis*) was formerly widely distributed through the Terai, but like its African relative, it is now an endangered species (though numbers have increased since the 1980s). This thick skinned perisodactyl has a single horn (the African rhino has two), stands 1.70 metres at the shoulder with a horn of up to 60 centimetres, total body length around three metres and a tail of around 60 centimetres. Very few **buffalo** (*Bubalus bubalis*) remain in the wild, though a small herd is found in and around the Koshi Tappu Wildlife Reserve in the eastern Terai. When domesticated it is known as the **water buffalo**, a solid beast standing some 170 centimetres at the shoulder. The black coat and wide spreading, curved horns are distinctive to both sexes. It is often seen immersed in water or large, muddy puddles which it uses to keep cool.

The best known of Nepal's **felines** is, of course, the **tiger** (*Panthera tigris*). Formerly widely prevalent throughout the Terai, the tiger is a land-demanding creature and the destruction of forest has reduced numbers drastically and placed unprecedented pressures on those that remain. It has been designated an 'endangered species'. Populations have been further reduced by poachers lured by the high sums they can earn from a tiger skin or for parts of its anatomy which are prized as natural remedies or treatments especially in Southeast and East Asia. Tigers are not community animals, preferring to hunt singly or in pairs and living in small family groupings. Naturally shy, they hunt largely by night and from early evening and may be seen along or near riverbanks stalking their prey, of which deer form a major part. Another endangered species, the **leopard** or **panther** (*Panthera pardus*) is also found in Nepal, but is even more elusive than the tiger. Although it shares many of the tiger's prey species, it is generally found away from tiger habitats both in the dryer lowland areas and in the hills. The fabled **snow leopard** (*Panthera uncia*) lives in the High Himalaya. It is long-haired with a creamy-grey coat and rose-like spots. It feeds on small mammals, has a smaller head than the *pardus* and is even more elusive.

The **sloth bear** (*Melursus ursinus*) stands about 75 centimetres at the shoulder and can be seen in thinly wooded areas of scrub and rock. It is unkempt looking with a shaggy black coat and a yellowish V-shaped mark on the chest. The hairless eyelids and long dull grey snout give it a mangy look. It has a distinctively long and pendulous lower lip. One of the most common sightings are **monkeys**, which inhabit both forested and urban areas from the Terai as far north as the Pahar zone. The most widespread is the **common langur** (*Presbytis entellus*), a long-tailed monkey with a silver-grey body and black face, hands and feet. It is around 75 centimetres long with a tail of 95 centimetres, which it is often seen to use as a means of suspension. The **lesser panda** (*Ailurus fulgens*) bears little outward resemblance to the more familiar black and white giant pandas and lives in the Himalayan forests. A reddish-brown animal with a horizontally striped tail, it is related to the raccoon and is considered by some experts to be its original ancestor. It is around 60 centimetres long with a tail of 50 centimetres. The **rhesus** monkey (*Macaca mulatta*) is also widely distributed. This is the variety favoured by science for experimental use.

Nepal has five main varieties of **deer**. The attractive **chital**, or **spotted deer** (*Axis axis*) is quite small, standing only 90 centimetres at the shoulder. The bright rufous coat, spotted with white is unmistakable. The stags carry antlers with three 'spikes', or tines, on each. Chital occur in herds of 20 or so in grassy areas and are often seen near rivers. Much larger, 150 centimetres at the shoulder, is the magnificent **Sambar** (*Cervus unicolor*). It has a noticeably shaggy coat which varies in colour from brown with a yellow or grey tinge, through to dark, almost black, in older stags. The females tend to be somewhat lighter in colour. The coat of the stag is thickened around the neck to form a mane. The mature stags carry large, three-tined antlers. Immature males carry one to three tines depending on age. The sambar is a forest dwelling

deer, often also found on wooded hillsides. They do not form large herds, but live in groups of up to 10, or sometimes as solitary individuals. The **barking deer**, or **muntjac** (*Muntiacus muntjak*), 60 centimetres at the shoulder, is a small shy deer which is most often glimpsed in pairs darting for cover. It is brown with darker legs. It has white underparts, a white chest and white under the tail. The stag carries a small pair of antlers which arise from bony, hair covered protuberances and has one short tine just above the brow. The main part of the antler is only about 10-12

Chital

centimetres long and curves inwards slightly. Their startlingly staccato 'bark' is heard more often than they are seen. The **musk deer** (*Moschus moschiferus*) is found in small numbers in the middle ranges of Nepal. It is hornless and is the country's smallest deer, standing just 50 centimetres at the shoulder. Poaching has reduced numbers alarmingly. It is sought for its scent which is used in perfumery and consists of a secretion in a glandular sac beneath the skin of the abdomen of the male. Herds of **swamp deer** are found principally in the Sukla Phanta Wildlife Reserve, in the southwest corner of Nepal. The **black buck** (*Antilope cervicapra*) is found mainly in the Bardia area. It is a dark brown antelope with two single-stemmed twisting antlers up to 60 centimetres long and stands 80 centimetres high at the shoulder. The **blue bull** or **nilgai** (*Boselaphus tragocamelus*) is a large antelope standing 140 centimetres at the shoulder. The male has short horns and is a blue-grey colour, while the female is hornless and is mid-brown in colour.

There are small numbers of **canines**, including the **wild dog** (*Cuon alpinus*), a reddish-brown hunting dog with a black tipped tail and muzzle. It is present in small numbers, though may be seen individually or in pairs. The **golden jackal** (*Canis aureus*) is related to the wolf, is mainly nocturnal and rarely observed. In some areas, though, you can hear its long howl at night. The **striped hyena** (*Hyaena hyaena*) is also rarely seen. It is tawny coloured with black stripes. Much of its strength lies in its jaws and front portion. It usually scavenges and hunts in forest margins.

The **wild boar** (*Sus scrofa*) is easily identified by its sparse hair on a mainly black body and pig-like head. The hair thickens down the spine to form a sort of mane or crest. A well grown male stands 90 centimetres at the shoulder and bears tusks, which are absent in the female. The young are striped. It is commonly seen in grass and light bush especially in the Terai's two main national parks and near water where it often causes great destruction of crops.

The **common mongoose** (*Herpestes edwardsi*) is an inhabitant of scrub and open jungle, but you can also see it in gardens and fields. It is well known as a killer of snakes (including cobra and venomous varieties), but will also take rats, mice, fowl and birds' eggs. The ferret-like mongoose is tawny with a grey grizzled tinge. It is about 90 centimetres in length, of which almost half is the tail which always has a pale tip. The **marten** (*Martes flavigula*) has some physical resemblances with the mongoose, is also carnivorous and shares its habitational zones, but is shorter and arboreal. It has a long, dark brown glossy coat and a bushy tail. There are numerous **squirrels** inhabiting not just wilder places but just about every town and village in the lowlands and temperate regions. The five-striped palm squirrel (*Funambulus pennanti*) is about 30 centimetres in length, about half of which is tail. Look

Squirrel

out also for the 'flying fox' (*Pteropus giganteus*) which has a massive wing span of 120 centimetres. These are actually fruit-eating bats and are found in concentrations in the middle zones. The road between Kantipath and Lazimpath, on the western side of Kathmandu's Royal Palace, is lined with trees typically full of these hanging bats. They roost in large, sometimes huge, noisy colonies in tree tops, often in the middle of towns or villages, where they look like folded umbrellas hanging from the trees. In the evening, they can be seen leaving the roost with slow measured wing beats.

Most reptiles inhabit the warmer regions of the Terai. You will occasionally see **snakes** slithering through the undergrowth of a forest region or near water. The area of forest north of Itahari, on the road to Dhankuta, is home to a number of

Reptiles & amphibians

Background

poisonous species. These include the venomous **kraits** and the **Indian cobra** (*Naja naja*) which grows up to 180 centimetres in length and is distinguished by its ability to flatten its neck to a hood-like form when disturbed. The **common python** (*Python molorus*) is an endangered species which can be six metres or more long. It is a boa constrictor which kills its prey by coiling around it and squeezing it to death. **Vipers** (eg the *Vipera berus*), along with **coral snakes** (eg the *Micrurus fulvius*) are also common in the Terai. **Water snakes** are found around rivers and lakes, including Pokhara's Phewa Tal. There are very few venomous snakes in the middle and higher mountains.

Also represented are **turtles** and many species of **frog**, including the **hyla** and other tree frogs. You will almost certainly encounter a **lizard** of some kind. In the forested areas, **skinks** are common. The number of amphibians has declined markedly in the Terai with the indiscriminate use of anti-mosquito DDT. They generally have smooth, overlapping scales, may be striped, have long, thin tapering tails and measure between 5-10 centimetres. Most impressive, however, are the crocodiles which, previously hunted almost out of existence, have increased in number due entirely to the efforts of breeding centres, notably at Chitwan and Bardia. The **marsh mugger** (*Crocodilus palustrus*) grows up to three metres or four metres in length and is found mostly along the rivers in or near these parks. The **gharial**, or **gavial** (*Gavialis gangeticus*) is native to the Indian subcontinent and grows up to six metres in length. Its distribution is similar to that of the marsh mugger and it is listed as an endangered species.

Insects & invertebrates

These are most prevalent in the Terai, where their buzzing and warbling are particularly noticeable at night. Especially beautiful at night is the **firefly** (or **glow worm**), a nocturnal beetle of the family *Lampyridae*. Its light is produced by a special organ at the rear of the male abdomen. You will also see various species of predacious **mantis**, including the 'praying mantis' so-called because it holds its forelegs in a raised, prayerful position in preparation for its prey. **Butterflies** are found at all elevations up to the tree-line. In the mountains they are most conspicuous in late spring, in the middle regions (including Kathmandu and Pokhara) from April to September and from March to November in the Terai.

There are about 100 species of **mosquito** (the *Culicideae* family) of which around one third are vectors of malaria. These are known as **anopheline** (*Anopheles* genus) mosquitoes. They are about six millimetres long and are dipterous creatures, characterized by one pair of membranous wings towards the front. Anopheline mosquitoes are distinguished from other species by their slanting, head-down position when resting, while the non-harmful species tend to remain horizontal. The transmission of malaria is achieved by the infected female which injects thousands of microscopic sporozoites through its saliva in a single bite. The mosquito thrives in wet and moist conditions, eg swamp land. Until it was shown to be the actual cause of the disease, the term 'malaria' was coined by 18th century European colonialists to describe the fever then believed to have been caused by stale, unwholesome air (*mal* and *air*). Another unpleasant (though less harmful) invertebrate is the **leech** (eg the *Hirudo medicinalis*). It is a parasitic worm which can grow up to 15 centimetres long. It thrives in moist conditions and feeds by attaching itself to the host and sucking blood until it is full, when it drops off. It has the courtesy to inject a local anaesthetic so that the host may donate blood with minimum discomfort. It is most active between May and October.

Birds

Nepal has over 800 species of bird, including migratory species, waterfowl, parrots, songbirds, birds of prey and others. **Birds of prey** include various vultures, eagles, kites and owls. The **lammergeier** (Ger, 'lamb vulture'; *Gypaetus barbatus*) which is distributed from the mountains of southern Europe through to China is the region's largest bird of prey. It is dark brown with a distinctive 'moustache' of black feather drooping from below the beak. It has a wingspan of up to three metres which allows it to soar effortlessly through the air. It is usually found in the lower mountains at elevations of up to 4,000 metres. The **brahminy kite** (*Haliastur indus*) is a familiar scavenger and is seen around water. It has a chestnut plumage with a white head and breast. The **pariah kite** (*Milvus migrans*), also known as the **dark** or **black kite**, measures around 65 centimetres. This is a brown bird with a fairly long tail which looks either forked when the tail is closed or slightly concave at the end when spread.

The Terai once more offers the greatest diversity of bird-life, with the **Sukla Phanta** and **Koshi Tappu Wildlife Reserves** offering some of the country's finest birdwatching. Especially beautiful and numerous are **parrots**, including many species of **parakeet**, which are endemic throughout the Terai and as far north as the Pahar zone. The **rose ringed parakeet** (*Psittacula krameri*) is around 40 centimetres long. Its long tail is noticeable both in flight and when the bird is perched. Females lack the red collar. They can be very destructive to crops, but are attractive birds which are frequently kept as pets. There are also several species of **kingfisher** (*Alcedinidae* family), usually brightly coloured with long tails, a large crested head and a substantial beak. At 27 centimetres, the **white-breasted kingfisher** (*Halcyon smyrnensis*) is frequently found away from water and is readily seen as it perches on wires and posts. The rich chestnut of its body plumage contrasts with the brilliant blue of its wing feathers, particularly noticeable when it swoops down to gather its prey. The red bill and white front make it unmistakable as well as supremely beautiful. **Bee eaters** (*Meropidae* family) are often seen

White-breasted kingfisher

scavenging along the ground or putting their head down holes in search of insects. The **little green bee eater** (*Merops orientalis*) is common in open countryside and is usually seen in pairs, perching on posts and dead branches. The green of its plumage contrasts with the blue throat and chestnut top of the head. Of the many types of **flycatcher**, the **paradise flycatcher** (*Terpsiphone paradisi*) is especially conspicuous, seen flitting from its perch in pursuit of insects in woodland and open spaces. The head is a shiny metallic black with a noticeable crest which contrasts with the white of the underparts. The wings and tail can be either white or chestnut. The male has particularly long tail feathers and distinctly blue eyes. There are a few species of **hornbill** (including the *Anthrococerus malabricus*). 90 centimetres long, this is a large heavy looking bird, seen in small noisy flocks often in fruiting trees. The plumage is black and white and the long tail has white edges. The massive bill is mainly yellow and carries a black and yellow protuberance (known as a casque) along the top. It makes a spectacular sight in flight.

The **common mynah** (*Acridotheres tristis*) is about 22 centimetres long. It is mostly black, but look for the white under the tail and the bare yellow skin around the eye, the yellow bill and legs and, in flight, the large white wing patch. The **magpie robin** (*Copsychus saularis*) is 20 centimetres long. In the male, the wings, head and upper parts are mainly black, but with a noticeable white wing bar. Below, it is white. The long white and black tail is often held cocked up. The female's colour pattern is similar, but the black is greyish. It is a delightful songster and has a trim and lively appearance. The **red vented bulbul** (*Pyconotus cafer*) is another songbird (often mentioned in Persian literature and perhaps mistaken for a nightingale) and is widespread in the lower regions. A mainly brown bird, it can be identified by the slight crest and a bright red patch under the tail. The **spotted dove** (*Streptopelia chinensis*) is an attractive, 30 centimetre long bird and is found in woodland and open spaces. It can be identified by the speckled appearance of its back and by the wide half collar of white spots on a black background. The head and underparts are pink.

That most ubiquitous of birds, the **house crow** (*Corvus splendens*) is really quite smart looking with a grey body and black tail, wings, face and throat. It is common in every mid- and lowland town in South Asia, where it makes a vivacious contribution to the dawn chorus. The all black **drongo** (*Dicrurus adsimilis*) is around 30 centimetres long and is almost invariably seen perched swallow-like on telegraph wires or bare branches. Its distinctively forked tail makes it easy to identify. The related **racquet-tailed drongo** (*Dicrurus paradiseus*) is also recognized by its distinctive tail which ends in long streamers with broadened tips. The head bears a tufted crest. As well as its unique appearance in flight, it has the habit of sitting on conspicuous perches which makes it easy to identify.

Another common sight is the **egret**, of which there are several species. Two egrets are particularly common: the **little egret** (*Egretta garzetta*) which is over 60 centimetres long and the **cattle egret** (*Bubulucus ibis*) which is 50 centimetres long. In the non breeding season, both birds are white, but can be readily distinguished by their different coloured bills: yellowish in the cattle egret, but all black in the little egret. In addition, the legs of the little egret are black with yellow toes, but this is not always easy to see. The little egret is a taller more elegant looking bird, while the cattle egret often has a hunched appearance. In the breeding season the cattle egret develops golden or buffish plumes on its head and back. The **painted stork** (*Ibis leucocephalus*) stands one metre tall. It is also mainly white, but has a pinkish tinge on the back, greenish black marks on the wings and a broken black band on the lower chest. The bare yellow face and yellow down-curved bill are conspicuous.

National Parks and Wildlife Reserves

Since the 1970s there has been a welcome increase in awareness of the importance of Nepal's flora and fauna which has led to the establishment of a number of protected areas. There are now eight national parks, three wildlife reserves, one conservation area and one hunting reserve. The flora and fauna of national parks are protected and should not be removed: penalties may be enforced. All visitors are required to be self-sufficient in cooking materials; the use of firewood is prohibited and rubbish should be burned, buried or carried out. An entrance fee of Rs 650 is payable by each visitor and is valid for either two or three days. **NB** Be sure to keep the **receipt**, as you may be required to show it. Full details of exploring individual parks are included in the relevant section.

Annapurna Conservation Area (1) (See page 343) The area covers a mountainous region of over 2,600 square kilometres in central Nepal. It contains the world's deepest river gorge (of the **Kali Gandaki** River) as well as some of its highest mountains, including **Annapurna I** (8,091 metres) and the magnificent **Macchapuchare** (6,997 metres). There is a population of some 40,000 people representing numerous **ethnic groups**, including Newars and the Hindu castes of the lower regions, Gurungs, Magars, Thakalis and Manangis in addition to the Lopas and ethnic Tibetans of **Mustang**. Vegetation types range from lowland chestnut forest to oak and coniferous forest of the middle elevations and juniper and scrubland to the tree-line. There are broad tracts of rhododendron forest and more than 100 species of orchid. It is also well endowed with animal wildlife and is home to the elusive snow leopard. The Annapurna Conservation Area is Nepal's most popular trekking region, with well established routes and numerous improving facilities. It was designated a 'conservation area' in 1986 and is well managed by the King Mahendra Trust for

Nature Conservation (KMTNC) which has experienced some considerable early success in its aims of conservation, integrated development and promotion of environmentally sensitive trekking.

(See pages 386-394) Situated in Southwest Nepal, it is on the east banks of the **Karnali** River. It is the Terai's largest national park and covers an area of 968 square kilometres. It consists of almost untouched Terai forest ('jungle'), rivers and riverine forest and small areas of savanna-like *phanta* grassland. The diverse environment supports an equally diverse fauna. It is said to be the best place for tiger sightings. It has small herds of wild elephants, five species of deer, crocodiles and a few Gangetic dolphins. The rhinoceros was re-introduced from Chitwan in the 1980s and numbers have increased significantly. Accommodation is available at **Thakurdwara** village.

Royal Bardia National Park (2)

(See pages 417-426) Nepal's first and most visited national park lies within easy reach to the southwest of Kathmandu. It covers an area of 932 square kilometres of forest similar to Bardia (above) in the floodplains of the **Narayani, Rapti** and **Reu** Rivers. Its range of fauna is also similar to that of Bardia. Luxury accommodation is available inside the park and ample budget accommodation in **Sauraha**, outside the park on the northern bank of the Narayani. It has become the most commercialized of the country's parks.

Royal Chitwan National Park (3)

(See page 424) This reserve covers 499 square kilometres adjoining Chitwan to the east. The vegetation and wildlife is virtually identical to its more famous neighbour, though there is said to be a small herd of wild elephants here. Parsa is used as a nursery for protecting the tiger and other endangered species. It may be possible to camp overnight near the reserve headquarters at **Amlekhganj**.

Parsa Wildlife Reserve

The country's only hunting reserve, Dhorpatan covers 1,325 square kilometres to the south of **Dhaulagiri** (8,167 metres) in mid-west Nepal. Hunting is strictly regulated with permits issued in certain seasons by the Department of National Parks and Wildlife Conservation in Kathmandu. The hunters' principal target is the blue sheep

Dhorpatan Hunting Reserve (4)

National parks & wildlife reserves

Background

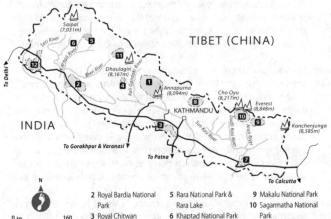

1 Annapurna Conservation Area	**5** Rara National Park & Rara Lake
2 Royal Bardia National Park	**6** Khaptad National Park
3 Royal Chitwan National Park & Parsa Wildlife Reserve	**7** Koshi Tappu Wildlife Reserve
4 Dhorpatan Hunting Reserve	**8** Langtang National Park
9 Makalu National Park	
10 Sagarmatha National Park	
11 Shey Phoksumdo National Park	
12 Royal Sukla Phanta Wildlife Reserve	

whose numbers have increased to nuisance levels for local communities. Species of goats, bears and wild game birds are also hunted. Vegetation consists largely of rhododendron, oak, pine and juniper forest.

Rara National Park (5) (See page 98) With an area of just 106 square kilometres, Rara is Nepal's smallest national park. It centres around Lake Rara (also known as *Mahendra Tal*), Nepal's largest lake and lies at altitudes of 3,000 metres plus. The **Karnali** River begins its long course to the east of the lake. The vegetation consists of thick stands of sub-alpine forest which supports a range of wildlife including the musk deer, leopard, wolf, red panda and black bear. Lake Rara is perhaps West Nepal's most popular trekking destinations with trails beginning at **Jumla**.

Khaptad National Park (6) (See page 460) This is the most recently established national park and comprises a relatively small area of 225 square kilometres in West Nepal. It contains a temple site sacred to Hindus and was the home of the 'Khaptad Babu', a Hindu sage and holy man who died in 1996. The park is situated on a 3,000-metre plateau of rhododendron, bamboo, oak and shrub forest intermingled with open grassland. There is no tourist accommodation.

Koshi Tappu Wildlife Reserve (7) (See pages 442-444) The reserve lies along 175 square kilometres of floodplains of the mighty **Sapt Koshi** River in southeast Nepal; *tappu* means 'island'. The reserve is known especially for its bird-life and is home to almost 300 species, including seasonal migrants. Itinerant mammals include deer, wild boar and blue bull, while there is also a small population of wild buffalo. Vegetation consists mainly of grassland along with riverine and deciduous forest. During the monsoon, the river changes course and floods, resulting in a dramatic change of appearance. There is one government-run lodge, but tourist facilities are otherwise virtually non-existent.

Langtang National Park (8) (See page 134) This is one of Nepal's major trekking regions. Situated north of Kathmandu, it covers 1,710 square kilometres of mountainous terrain and includes the sacred **Gosainkund Lake**. The park includes the upper catchment areas of the **Trisuli** and **Kosi** Rivers and its highest point is **Langtang Lirung** (7,234 metres). Tamangs are the dominant peoples of the southern areas, while Bhotias and ethnic Tibetans live in the north. Vegetation ranges from that of the temperate region to alpine, with rhododendron, oak and deciduous forest prominent. Common animals include various deer, monkeys and wild boar at lower elevations, with musk deer and the snow leopard inhabiting the higher reaches. The park has a reasonable selection of trekking standard accommodation. Its headquarters is in **Dhunche**.

Makalu Barun National Park (9) This has also been designated a 'Strict Nature Reserve'. It covers 2,330 square kilometres to the east of Mount Everest, bordering the **Arun** River to the east and Tibet to the north. It is best known for its wide variety of vegetation and wildlife. Sal dominates at lower levels, superseded by chestnut and firs up to 2,000 metres and some fabulous stands of rhododendron (30 species) higher up. Up to the tree-line there is juniper and scrub forest. There are also almost 50 species each of orchid and primrose. Mammals include various deer, the Himalayan Black Bear, red panda and clouded leopard. The snow leopard is thought to exist in very small numbers at high altitudes. For trekkers, there is the difficult **Tumlingtar** to **Makalu Base Camp** route.

Sagarmatha National Park (10) (See page 138) Sagarmatha is the Sherpa name for **Mount Everest** (8,848 metres) and is thus the highest park on Earth. Known also as **Khumbu**, it is a UNESCO World Heritage Site and consists of 1,148 square kilometres of mountains, including Mts Ama Dablam, Cho Oyu and Pumori. Much of its area lies above 3,000 metres, a rugged terrain of glaciers, steep ice faces and deep gorges. The region is the home of the **Sherpas**. Mammals are most conspicuous during the monsoon and include the black bear and musk deer and you are also likely to see the lammergeier vulture, Himalayan griffon and other birds of prey. Nepal's national bird, the impeyan pheasant, is found here. At lower elevations, pine forest dominates. With an increase in altitude, rhododendron is again widespread, with juniper, birch and scrub higher up. This is the second most popular trekking region in Nepal (after the Annapurnas), so lodges and trekking facilities are relatively well developed, especially in and near Lukla and Namche Bazaar.

This is Nepal's largest national park, covering an area of 3,555 square kilometres. It borders Tibet to the north and straddles the districts of **Dolpa** and **Mugu**. Shey Phoksumdo takes its name from the **Shey Monastery** and **Phoksumdo Lake**. It includes the **Kanjiroba Himal** range, with numerous peaks above 6,000 metres. Forests of willow, walnut and pine dominate in the middle elevations, with higher stands of scrub and extensive juniper. Its northeastern areas share the arid mountainous topography of Mustang.

Shey Phoksumdo National Park (11)

(See page 381) Located in the far southwest of the country, this is a unique reserve of 305 square kilometres. The name derives from the Tharu words for 'white' (*sukla*) and a particular form of savanna-like 'grassland' (*phanta*). Combined with the Terai's sal-dominated forest, it contains a diverse range of environments and wildlife. At its centre is the **Rani Tal**, a small lake which attracts a wide variety of terrestrial and aquatic bird-life, some migratory. The reserve is also renowned for a large population of swamp deer and lies on a migratory trail of tigers and wild elephants. Although it is visited by few tourists, good accommodation is available inside the reserve and Sukla Phanta remains something of an undiscovered gem in Nepal's natural heritage.

Sukla Phanta Wildlife Reserve (12)

Background

Religion

It is impossible to write briefly about religion in Nepal without greatly over-simplifying. Over 85 percent of Nepalis are Hindu and around eight percent are Buddhist. Muslims constitute a little under four percent of the population, while the remainder is made up of Animists, Christians and others. Both Hinduism and Buddhism have influenced and been influenced by the other to a high degree in their practices, with adherents of either readily accepting many of the tenets of the other. Thus, if you ask a Nepali his religion, he may reply Hindu – but Buddhist too. Both have also been influenced by forms of Animism, an ancient spiritualist religion originating in Tibet.

Hinduism

It has always been easier to define Hinduism by what it is not rather than by what it is. Indeed, the name Hinduism was given by foreigners to the peoples of the subcontinent who did not profess the other major faiths such as Islam or Christianity, but adhered to a system of beliefs and social and cultural norms indigenous to the subcontinent. The term was accepted by Hindus themselves, because there was no alternative word which could satisfactorily embrace its broad concept. The name already implies territoriality. Of those components common to all religions, which also include faith and 'escape', the element of belonging is perhaps most strongly embedded in Hinduism. In many religions, this sense is both expressed and specifically reinforced by rites of passage, such as Christian baptism and confirmation, or the assumption of the *Hajji* title by Muslims who have made the trip to Mecca. These all imply movement resulting in changes of status. There are few such processes in Hinduism; it is impossible, for example, for someone born into one caste to ascend to another. Rather, Hinduism is characterized as much by its culture, society and hierarchical social structure as by the beliefs through which they have been shaped. At the broadest level, therefore, a person is a Hindu because he is *born* into Hindu society and this becomes as much a defining characteristic as, say, his height or shoe size. Accordingly, someone born into this society but who professes no religious faith is still a Hindu.

Hinduism has no definitive creed, set of practices, canon or uniformity of worship, but embraces a wide spectrum of philosophies and approaches to a common pantheon of deities. Some Hindu scholars and philosophers talk of Hinduism as one religious and cultural tradition, in which the enormous variety of belief and practice can ultimately be interpreted as interwoven in a common view of the world. Yet, there is no Hindu organization, like a church, with the authority to define belief or to establish official practice. There are spiritual leaders and philosophers who are widely revered and there is an enormous range of literature which is treated as sacred. Despite the many thousands of gods, goddesses and lesser divinities which give it the outward appearance of a polytheistic faith, it is in essence monotheistic with these multifarious deities seen as personified attributes of a single, supreme God. On a very different scale, the Christian trinity of Father, Son and Holy Spirit as three persons in one Godhead may help in conceptualization.

Origins

There are virtually no accurate records of dates in the development of Hinduism, a 'defect' considered by the eminent Sanskrit scholar, AA Macdonell, to have 'darkened the whole course of Sanskrit literature'. Unlike the Messianic Christianity or the prophetic religions of Judaism and Islam, Hinduism does not date from a specific historical event but is characterized by continuing evolution and development of beliefs and practices. Its earliest origins probably date to pre-Dravidian **animism** (ie the belief that natural phenomena and objects have souls and the worship thereof) and **totemism** (ie tribal veneration of objects or symbols). The influence of both is still in evidence among a few (especially tribal) communities. The worship of a **mother-goddess** is noted in the region's earliest known major settlements, the **Indus Valley Civilization** (in modern Pakistan), from around 2300 BC, along with that of the **bull** and other animals. Artefacts from Harappa and Mohenjo Daro also suggest that phallus worship was common and that the peepul tree was already associated with religion, all of which feature prominently in later Hinduism. In northern India, these early practices developed into **Vedism** (or **Brahminism**) from around 1000 BC under the influence of the **Aryans**, an Indo-European people probably from the region around modern Iran, who first arrived in the subcontinent about 500 years earlier.

The following outlines the early development of Hinduism through its literature.

Vedas

The Vedic Age lasted from 1200-800 BC and was a period of immense growth and change. Aryan society was military and pastoral in character, but contained an important priestly class (the *Brahmans*) who were effectively the prototype Brahmins. The word *vedic* means 'known' and was the language in which the four **Vedas** ('books of knowledge') were composed: the Rig, Yajur, Sama and Atharva vedas. Believed to be of divine origin, these were not in fact books, but were handed down orally through generations; indeed, the first *written* records were put down about 1000 BC, although we do not have extant originals. The Vedas were largely comprised of hymns, usually chanted during rituals.

The **Rig Veda** is the earliest and most important and that from which the others take their cue. Its composition, thought to have occurred mainly in the Punjab region, began from 1500 BC and probably attained its final form in around 900 BC or later, although some sources date it much earlier on astronomical assumptions, possibly as far back as 5000 BC. It consists of over 1,000 sacrificial hymns, chants and allusions to legends, divided either into eight 'octaves' (*ashtaka*) or 10 'circles' (*mandala*). It includes the earliest references to Vishnu (here a minor divinity), Indra (previously the major Aryan god of war, but here merely the god of rain), Rudra (later to become Shiva) and to Agni, the god of fire who retains enormous contemporary relevance. Important consideration is given to the origins of the universe, though no unanimous conclusion is reached. Among its later hymns, the **Purusha shukta** ('Hymn of the Primeval Man'), is of great significance and postulates that the eponymous 'man' (or god) survived his sacrifice-by-dismemberment at the beginning of time and created the universe and the four social classes, the first reference to a caste system. For the casual reader, however, the Rig Veda is undoubtedly hard work, with an understanding of much of its content requiring wider knowledge of other texts. In purely spiritual content it is also limited, with many of its prayers considered by Bhandarkar (1940) to be 'saturated with selfish, sordid aims', while Walker (1968) maintains that it 'contains a mass of dry, stereotyped hymnology'.

The concept of **sacrifice** assumed importance from around 900 BC, its practice being seen as propitiating the gods and ensuring boons in the next life by repeating that first sacrifice of Purusha with all its associations with creation and regeneration. The **Yajur Veda** was composed between around 700 and 300 BC probably further east along the Gangetic plains, reflecting the early movement of peoples into this area of high fertility. It is based on the Rig Veda though is more concerned with instructing Brahmin priests in the performance of the sacrificial ritual (*yaja* = 'sacrifice'). It also emphasized the increasing power of the priestly class and reflected the influence which they exerted (and, to a degree, still do), on society. Somewhat fancifully, one might think, the Yajur Veda also asserts that even the gods were in some ways subservient to the will of the Brahmins.

Composed at around the same time, the **Sama Veda** is a collection of over 1,500 verses, mostly metrical and largely detailing the correct tunes, melodies and intonations to be performed in the sacrificial ritual. Specifically, many deal with sacrifices to **Soma**, god of the moon and of sacrifice. The **Atharva Veda** again deals with sacrificial practice and promotes the role of the priest. But it also contains an important magical and ayurvedic **formulary**. There are herbal prescriptions for the cure of, for example, jaundice, fevers and leprosy along with accompanying incantations, as well as charms and spells to be intoned for, inter alia, the loss of another man's virility and the recovery of one's own.

Brahmanas Strictly speaking, the Brahmanas belong to the late Vedas but are considered as a body of their own. They consist of a series of **procedures** and often highly elaborate **rituals** to be performed by **Brahmin** priests and have been alluded to as the 'Hindu Talmud'. They place particular emphasis on sacrifice and caste, thereby seeking to further underline the authority and power of the priestly class. The first dates from around 600 BC. Their spiritual relevance has been dismissed – often in delightfully sharp criticism – by scholars: in 1867 Max Muller compared them to 'the twaddle of idiots', while Ghosh (1951) considers them 'an arid desert of puerile speculations on religious ceremonies marking the lowest ebb of Vedic culture'.

Upanishads In complete contrast to the above, the Upanishads are a series of often beautiful spiritual treatises composed over a very long period: the earliest date from around 700 BC while the latest were not composed until the late medieval period. The word *upanishad* means '**sitting near**' which refers to the manner of their dissemination, ie in talks given by sages to groups of followers or interested listeners. That enlightened scholar and interpreter of Sanskrit literature, Juan Mascaro, offers the comparison of Jesus' Sermon on the Mount. By their spirituality, the Upanishads also contrast strongly with the Vedas which were more concerned with practice than devotion.

The Upanishads brought a fundamental change in the direction and form of Hindu thought and practice, a reaction against external religion. They also provided the inspiration for **Vedanta**, a range of philosophical systems which marked the conclusion of Vedic literature and systemized the teachings of the Upanishads. Whilst acknowledging the values enshrined in the Vedas, the Upanishads play down the roles of sacrifice and Brahmin ritual, instead placing greater emphasis on the unity of the individual soul (*atman*) with the 'Universal Soul' (*Brahman*). The *Svetasvatara Upanishad*, for example, asks: "Of what use is the Rig Veda to one who does not know the Spirit from whom the Rig Veda comes?" With the development of an Upanishadic tradition, **mysticism** became a cornerstone of the Hindu religion for the first time. There are over 100 Upanishads which differ in particulars and doctrine. The language of many is highly metaphysical, even rarefied, though the 19th century German philosopher, Schopenhauer, described them as '*Sie ist der Trost meines Lebens gewesen und wird der meines Sterbens sein*' ('They have been the solace of my life and will be that of my death').

The Upanishads represent some of the most important Hindu texts. The earlier

The Caste system

Socially, the most important contribution of the Vedic age was the development of the 4-stage caste system. (The word 'caste' was given by the Portuguese in the 15th century AD and means 'breed' or 'race'.) The Rig Veda records how the original single caste, the Hamsa, was divided as a result of the continuing moral decline of man through the ages. In descending hierarchical order, the **Brahmins** represent the unsullied Hamsa and were seen as coming from the mouth of Brahma, while the **Kshatriyas** are the warrior class coming from Brahma's arms, the **Vaishyas** the mercantile and professional class coming from Brahma's thighs, and the **Shudras** the working class who came from Brahma's feet. A fifth class is considered to be outside the caste system, and are known variously as **outcastes, untouchables**, **Panchama** and **Harijans**. 'Untouchable' refers to ritual pollution suffered upon contact by a caste member, while 'Panchama' means 'fifth'. The term 'Harijan' was first coined by Gandhi in the early 1930s and means 'a person of Hari (Vishnu)', or 'a child of God'. They were left with the jobs which were regarded as impure, usually associated with the dead (animal or human) or with excrement.

Those of the top three castes are considered to be dvija, or 'twice born', a reference to the additional 'spiritual birth' that takes place with the ceremony of the 'sacred thread'. The exact origins of the system are unclear. Some theories maintain that it was initially based on the obvious criterion of skin colour, or **Varna** (the Aryans were fair skinned), while others point to differences in religious practice and traditions among communities, or simply to a meritorial division of society by occupation. There are, in addition, several thousand sub-castes – including over 1,800 subdivisions of Brahmins. In theory, interaction between members of different castes is strictly regulated. There should be no intermarriage, for example, nor should those of one caste share food with lower castes lest they become polluted. In practice, a rather more pragmatic approach is often adopted: pollution may be ritually cleansed and some communities have a more liberal interpretation of marriage rules.

Even though, in modern Nepal, the strength of caste hierarchy was officially replaced by the acknowledgement of equality of all people before the law in the 1967 Constitution of Nepal, the caste system itself was not actually abolished and continues to play a central role in the structure and organization of Nepali society.

ones are much concerned with the relation of the individual with the Supreme and tend to express themselves indirectly, often through allegorical dialogue, as in this oft-quoted story from the Chandogya Upanishad (6.12-14):

"Bring me a fruit from this banyan tree." *"Here it is, father."* "Break it." *"It is broken, Sir."* "What do you see in it?" *"Very small seeds, Sir."* "Break one of them, my son." *"It is broken, Sir."* "What do you see in it?" *"Nothing at all, Sir."* Then his father spoke to him: "My son, from the very essence in the seed which you can not see comes in truth this vast banyan tree. Believe me, my son, an invisible and subtle essence is the Spirit of the whole universe. That is reality. You are that." *"Explain more to me, father."* "So be it, my son. Place this salt in water and come to me tomorrow morning." In the morning his father said to him: "Bring me the salt you put in the water last night." The boy looked into the water but could not find it, for it had dissolved. His father then said: "Taste the water from this side. How is it?" *"It is salt."* "Taste it from the middle. How is it?" *"It is salt."* "Taste it from that side. How is it?" *"It is salt."* "Look for the salt and come again to me." The son did so, saying: *"I can not see the salt. I only see water."* "In the same way, my son, you can not see the spirit. But in truth he is here.

An invisible and subtle essence is the Spirit of the whole universe. That is reality. That is truth. You are that." *The Upanishads*, trans Juan Mascaro, Penguin: 1965.

The later Upanishads, meanwhile, are often characterized by a more direct approach to a personal God: the *Svetasvatara Upanishad*, for example, includes passages directly addressing Rudra, the 'eternal seer'.

Om   The Upanishads also propagated the use of the word **Om** in contemplation. Consisting of just 12 verses, the *Mandukya Upanishad* is one of the shortest and speaks exclusively of this 'eternal word', dividing it into three distinct sounds: 'a', 'u' and 'm'. The first, it says, represents 'waking consciousness', the second 'dreaming consciousness' and the third 'sleeping consciousness'. Put together, they represent 'supreme consciousness'. The later *Maitri Upanishad* also devotes itself to contemplation and union, describing Om as the 'sound of Brahman', the intonation of which is followed by 'the silence of joy'.

The two great Hindu epics

Mahabharata   This epic poem of approximately 100,000 stanzas (including an appendix of a mere 16,375 verses), is the world's longest. It was compiled over a period probably starting around 300 BC or before and, following centuries of inflation, was completed by around 500 AD. It centres around the ancient battle between the families **Pandava** (representing incarnate deities) and **Kaurava** (incarnate demons). The historical events, originally a secular story that was transformed into a religious narrative by Brahmins, is traditionally held to have taken place at the beginning of the Kali Era (about 3000 BC), but archaeological evidence suggests a date of around 800 BC. The subject matter is seen as an expression of the gradual trend away from Brahmin domination of religion and towards one with wider relevance, in this case that of the Kshatriya (warrior) class. The process of inflation led to the inclusion of very many extraneous episodes and to the existence of no single definitive version.

The numerous renditions vary both geographically and in their often contradictory interpretations of the same incident.

The Mahabharata is especially significant for its 'introduction' of **Krishna**, a god unknown to the Vedas, who appears as an incarnation of **Vishnu**. Krishna is perhaps Hinduism's most popular god. In his youth, legend relates his particular liking for milk and butter which he obtained in the course of regular illicit forays and for the *gopis*, or cow-girls (including **Radha**), with whom he made himself especially popular. His prodigious adulthood is noted, inter alia, by 16,108 wives and 180,008 sons.

It is important to note that Krishna's narrative, recorded also in the Puranas, is considered *amoral* in relation to accepted human behavioural norms. That is, a deity is not bound by mortal morality and although Krishna is to be worshipped, his relations with the *gopis* are not meant to be followed.

Krishna

The Bhagavad Gita This, the best known of the Mahabharata's many philosophical teachings, is also one of the most influential Hindu texts. It takes the form largely of Krishna's didactic address to **Arjuna**, one of the five Pandava brothers, as they waited for the great battle of the Mahabharata to commence. Arjuna is questioning the morality of the forthcoming battle and whether it is right to pursue even a just cause if it involves destruction. Krishna replies that man should be 'concerned with the deed, not with its results' and speaks of duty and devotion to *dharma*. He says that it is better to do one's own duty imperfectly (or that of one's own caste) than to do the duty of another well. As a Kshatriya, Arjuna should therefore undertake his warrior duty without sensual attachment and with his mind cast upon the 'highest soul'. The underlying themes are concerned with 'right' and 'wrong' actions irrespective of the result (though not advocating the end as justification of the means); with adherence to the caste system; with the merit of work; with respect for one's *dharma*; and with devotion to a supreme and personal God.

The *Gita* is widely regarded as having been derived of the Upanishads, especially in respect of the stress it places on the transcendent reality of God. Though criticized by some as spiritually disappointing, excessive in its digressions and even promoting a 'cult of murder', it exerted great influence on the later development of Hindu systems of philosophy.

Ramayana

Although reciting events which predated those of the Mahabharata by around 150 years, the Ramayana was compiled later, probably between around 350 BC and 250 AD. Like the Mahabharata, the original Ramayana was secular in character and was composed in Prakrit, possibly by Buddhists. It was only later translated (and liberally augmented) by Brahmins into the Sanskrit and transformed into a religious work replete with symbolism. It consists of 24,000 stanzas which are divided into seven books. In contrast to Krishna, Rama is portrayed in a more kingly fashion. He is responsible and slightly remote, yet still loving and approachable: the ideal king and lover.

The first book deals with the boyhood of **Rama** (who many centuries later became worshipped as an incarnation of Vishnu), the second with his marriage to **Sita** (daughter of King Janak – see also the **Janakpur** section). The third describes how Sita was abducted by the demon **Ravana** (the original Prakrit version had Ravana as the non-demonic king of Ceylon, or Lanka). In the fourth book, Rama resides with the monkey king with whose help a bridge is constructed in the fifth book for Rama to cross to Lanka. The sixth book details Rama's battle with Ravana and the death of the latter, the recovery of Sita and their return to Ayodhya. The final book describes Rama's jealousy, the banishment of Sita into the forest and the birth of her sons, then the reunion of Rama and Sita followed by her return to the earth from which she came.

Ravana

Medieval Hinduism

From the early second millennium AD, Hinduism began to crystalize particularly into two main sects devoted to Shiva (*Shaivites*) and to Vishnu (*Vishnuvites*). This was part of a process which had been continuing for several centuries previously. Within both there are numerous sub-divisions.

Sexual imagery in Hinduism

Visitors to many of Nepal's Hindu temples will have seen often elaborately carved portrayals of the coital act and other 'erotic' scenes. These largely symbolize the traditionally fundamental role of creation and re-creation in Hinduism, a theme which has persisted since its early development. Evidence of linga worship has been found in seals of the Indus Valley Civilization, probably reflecting the importance these agricultural communities placed on the role of divinity in fertility and the successful cultivation of crops on which, of course, life depended. Frequently lurid details of the sexual act are recorded in the Yajur Veda, while the woman is elevated to a position of sanctity by both the Brahmanas and the Upanishads, bringing the act of copulation within the realms of the sacred.

The role of sex in Hinduism receives its fullest exposition in Tantrism. Here it is seen not so much for its procreative qualities nor necessarily for its sensual aspect, but as a means for attaining the highest spiritual experience. The act becomes a ritual, preceded by meditation and believed to lead ultimately to salvation. The distinct subject of eroticism, meanwhile, is concerned with the purely sensual and is extensively set forth in many Hindu religious texts, the best known being the Kama Sutra, written in the 5th century AD by Vatsayana (according to legend, a lifelong celibate). This and other treatises propounded etiquette and postures to be adopted during coitus. It is these, expressing the deeper religious significance, that are represented in temple art.

Siva, in the form of Kamadera at Deopatan

Background

One of the most important developments of the medieval period was the emergence of a devotional form of Hinduism known as *bhakti*. A sequence of ideas leading to this movement are found in both the *Puranas* and *Upanishads*.

Puranas The Puranas are a series of 18 principal writings (in verse) comprised of religious instructions and legends compiled between the 6th and 16th centuries AD. The word means 'ancient' and each contains interpretations on the creation of the universe, its history, destruction and recreation, on the lineage of gods and saints, on ancestral rules and traditions and on the divine legends. All are in the form of dialogue and, like the Upanishads, they stress the transcendent and personal nature of God. Historically, they are of great importance as sources of mythological chronology as well as for their reflections on regional architectural and artistic developments. They are divided equally in praise of Vishnu, Shiva and Brahma and reflect overlapping qualities of, respectively, purity (*sattva*), gloom (*tamas*) and passion (*rajas*).

The Vishnu Puranas speak of Vishnu as creator and sustainer of the world; stress the doctrine of *bhakti*; describe the youth of Krishna; explain the rites and processes of death; advocate astrology and worship of the sun; and explain the creation of the world. The Shiva Puranas contains discussions on the attributes of Shiva and on the philosophy of linga worship, as well as historical chronologies, cosmology and medicine. The first of the Brahma Puranas is dedicated to Surya, the sun-god. Others are noted for assuming the marriage of Krishna and Radha (in the *Bhagavata Purana*) in addition to advocating the cult of the mother-goddess.

Together, these 18 Puranas are referred to as the *Mahapuranas* to distinguish them from the many other *Upapuranas*, minor works often compiled much later.

Tantras

Tantrism carries popular and not altogether erroneous, notions of debauchery. Although some believe it developed from remnants of a pre-Aryan culture, its precise origins are unknown. It was an esoteric cult which held particular sway from the latter part of the first millennium AD to the medieval period. It probably originated in China and some of its philosophies are common to Hindus and Buddhists. A moderate form of Tantrism has significantly influenced approaches to both Hinduism and Buddhism in Nepal. Hindu Tantrics believe its principles, enshrined in the *Tantras*, to have been revealed by Shiva and much of Tantric scripture consists of dialogues between Shiva and his consort, Parvati. Indeed, Parvati is herself an expression of the *shakti* ('energy') aspect of Shiva. Although *shakti* is strongly identified with Tantrism (and usually specifically with Shiva), its own origins are also unclear. Evidence of devotion to a 'mother-goddess' is found in some pre-Aryan cults. The concept includes notions of unity through the dual aspect of divinity, with the incarnate form of *shakti* variously perceived as personifying fertility, motherhood, virginity, sexuality and conjugality as well as merciless terror (eg Kali and Durga). More than one of these qualities may be present in a single goddess. In temples, the *shakti* is often represented as the *yoni* in association with the *linga* of Shiva.

Though notable for its reactions against the caste system and for the equality it granted to both sexes, Tantrism is much concerned with superstitious magic or occultism and their associated rituals. The emphasis placed on the 'terrible' aspects of deities (eg Shiva in the form of Bhairab, whose name means 'terror'), is also characteristic. Taken as a whole, however, its higher principles of transcendental philosophy and meditation are considered by some to be compromised by its extremities, such as necrophilia, sexual-demonic worship and other perversions embraced in the name of mysticism. Tantric writings contain, according to Walker (1968), 'the loftiest philosophical speculation side by side with the grossest obscenities; the most rarefied metaphysics with the wildest superstition', while Chattopadhyaya (1959) described them as 'the most revolting and horrible that human depravity could think of'.

Bhakti

Although it also features in Shaivism, bhakti is a strand of Hinduism strongly associated with Vishnu, probably because Vishnu is seen as the most approachable of the Hindu trinity. The word means 'attachment' and is used to describe both ardent devotion to God and the bhakti movement that emerged in the medieval period. This stressed an intensely emotional, caring relationship between God and the individual, with God having an accessible, loving personality. In many ways, it also represents the closest that Hinduism comes to classical Christian spirituality. There are also parallels with Islamic Sufism. The 'way of bhakti' is known as *bhakti-marga*.

There are two main approaches to bhakti: *sagun-bhakti*, which emphasizes devotion to gods that have attributes and characteristics; and *nirgun-bhakti* which perceives an abstract, wholly spiritual God. Rama and Krishna feature strongly in bhakti literature. The poet **Tulsidas** (1532-1623) is perhaps the greatest of all **Rama-bhakti** writers. He is chiefly remembered for his enormously popular *Ramacharitamanasa*, a re-writing of the Ramayana characterized by themes of spiritual purity and morality which is often referred to as the 'Bible of Northern India'. He typified the Rama-bhakti beliefs of one supreme God, of the sinful unworthiness of man and that God became incarnate in the person of Rama to remove sin from the world. The story is often presented in dramatic form, making it accessible to the majority. The influence of Tulsidas has been considerable, leading Snell (1989) to assert that he 'presents not only an ideal model for Hindu society but also a devotional theology firmly based on orthodox Hinduism'. Expressions of **Krishna-bhakti**, meanwhile, take their cue from the stories of Krishna and the *gopis*. A central theme is the portrayal of Krishna as the lover, variously perceived as a friend (as with Arjuna and Krishna), as a child or parent, or with the longing of a lover (as exemplified by that of Radha and other *gopis* to Krishna).

Modern Hinduism

A number of ideas run like a thread through modern intellectual and popular Hinduism. According to the great Indian philosopher and former President of India, South Radhakrishnan, religion for the Hindu 'is not an idea but a power, not an intellectual proposition but a life conviction. Religion is consciousness of ultimate reality, not a theory about God'.

That reverence does not necessarily carry with it a belief in the doctrines enshrined in the text. Thus, the Vedas are still regarded as sacred by most Hindus, but virtually no modern Hindu either shares the beliefs of the Vedic writers or their practices, such as sacrifice, which died out 1,500 years ago. Not all Hindu groups believe in a single supreme God. In view of these characteristics, many authorities argue that it is misleading to think of Hinduism as a religion at all.

Be that as it may, the evidence of the living importance of Hinduism is visible throughout most of Nepal. Hindu philosophy and practice in Nepal has also touched and been touched by Buddhism and other minority religions particularly in terms of social institutions such as caste.

Aspects of Hindu practice

Darshana One of Hinduism's recurring themes is 'vision', 'sight' or 'view' – **darshana**. Applied to the different philosophical systems themselves, such as *yoga* or *vedanta*, 'darshana' is also used to describe the sight of the deity that worshippers hope to gain when they visit a temple or shrine. Equally it may apply to the religious insight gained through meditation or prayer.

Four human goals Many Hindus also accept that there are four major human goals: material prosperity (*artha*), the satisfaction of desires (*kama*) and performing the duties laid down according to your position in life (*dharma*). Beyond these is the goal of achieving liberation from the endless cycle of rebirths into which everyone is locked (*moksha*). It is to the search for liberation that the major schools of Indian philosophy have devoted most attention. Together with dharma, it is basic to Hindu thought.

Dharma The Mahabharata lists 10 embodiments of dharma: good name, truth, self-control, cleanliness of mind and body, simplicity, endurance, resoluteness of character, giving and sharing, austerity and continence. In Dharmic thinking these are inseparable from five patterns of behaviour: non-violence, an attitude of equality, peace and tranquillity, lack of aggression and cruelty and absence of envy. Dharma represents the order inherent in human life. It is essentially secular rather than religious, for it does not depend on any revelation or command of God.

Karma The idea of *karma*, 'the effect of former actions', is central to achieving liberation. As C Rajagopalachari, a leading Tamil philosopher, put it: 'Every act has its appointed effect, whether the act be thought, word or deed. If water is exposed to the sun, it

The four stages of life

It is widely believed that an ideal life has four stages: that of the student (brambhachari), the householder (grihast), the forest dweller (banaprasta) and the wandering dependent or beggar (sannyasi). These stages represent the phases through which an individual learns of life's goals and of the means of achieving them, in which he "carries out his duties and raises sons" and then retires to meditate alone; and then finally when he gives up all possessions and depends on the gifts of others. It is an ideal pattern which some still try to follow.

One of the most striking sights is that of the saffron clad saddhu, or wandering beggar, seeking gifts of food and money to support himself in the final stage of his life. There may have been saddhus even before the Aryans arrived. Today, most of these wanderers, who have cast off all the moral requirements of their surrounding cultures, are devotees of popular Hindu beliefs. Most give up material possessions, carrying only a strip of cloth, a staff (danda), a crutch to support the chin during meditation (achal), prayer beads, a fan to ward off evil spirits, a water pot, a drinking vessel (which may be a human skull) and a begging bowl. You may well see one, almost naked, covered only in ashes, on a Kathmandu street.

The age in which we live is seen by Hindu philosophers as a dark age, the kaliyuga. The most important behaviour enjoined by Hindus for this period was that of fulfilling the obligations of the householder. However, each of the stages is still recognized as a valid pattern for individuals.

cannot avoid being dried up. The effect automatically follows. It is the same with everything. The cause holds the effect, so to say, in its womb. If we reflect deeply and objectively, the entire world will be found to obey unalterable laws. That is the doctrine of karma'.

Rebirth

The belief in the transmigration of souls (samsara) in a never ending cycle of rebirth has been the most distinctive and important contribution to Hindu culture in South Asia. The earliest reference to the belief is found in one of the Upanishads, around the 7th century BC, at about the same time as the doctrine of karma made its first appearance. By the late Upanishads it was universally accepted and in Buddhism and Jainism there is never any questioning of the belief.

Ahimsa

AL Basham pointed out that belief in transmigration must have encouraged a further distinctive doctrine, that of non-violence or non-injury: ahimsa. Buddhism and Jainism campaigned particularly vigorously against the existing practice of animal sacrifice. The belief in rebirth meant that all living things and creatures of spirit – people, gods, devils, animals, even worms – possessed the same essential soul. One inscription which has been found in several places threatens that anyone who interferes with the rights of Brahmins to land given them by the king will 'suffer rebirth for 80,000 years as a worm in dung'. Belief in the cycle of rebirth was essential to give such a threat any weight!

It is common now to talk of six major schools of Hindu philosophy. The best known are yoga and vedanta.

Yoga

Yoga is concerned with systems of meditation that can ultimately lead to release from the cycle of rebirth. It can be traced back as a system of thought to at least the 3rd century AD. It is just one part of the wider system known as Vedanta, literally the final parts of the Vedantic literature, the Upanishads. The basic texts also include the Brahmasutra of Badarayana, written about the 1st century AD and the most important of all, the Bhagavad Gita, which is a part of the epic Mahabharata.

Background

Karma – an eye to the future

According to karma, every person, animal or god has a being or self which has existed without beginning. Every action, except those that are done without any consideration of the results, leaves an indelible mark on that self. This is carried forward into the next life and the overall character of the imprint on each person's 'self' determines three features of the next life. It controls the nature of his next birth (animal, human or god) and the kind of *family he will be born into if human. It determines the length of the next life. Finally, it controls the good or bad experiences that the self will experience. However, it does not imply a fatalistic belief that the nature of action in this life is unimportant. Rather, it suggests that the path followed by the individual in the present life is vital to the nature of its next life and, ultimately, to the chance of gaining release from this world.*

Vedanta There are many interpretations of these basic texts. Three major schools of Vedanta are particularly important:

Advaita Vedanta According to this school there is no division between the cosmic force or principle, Brahman and the individual self, *atman* (which is also sometimes referred to as soul). The fact that we appear to see different and separate individuals is simply a result of ignorance. This is termed *maya*, sometimes translated as illusion, but Vedanta philosophy does not suggest that the world in which we live is an illusion. Rather it argues that it is only our limited understanding which prevents us seeing the full and real unity of self and Brahmin.

Shankaracharya, who lived in the 7th century AD and is the best known Advaitin Hindu philosopher, argued that there was no individual self or soul separate from the creative force of the universe, or Brahman and that it was impossible to achieve liberation, or *moksha*, through any kind of action, including meditation and devotional worship. He saw these as signs of remaining on a lower level and of being unprepared for true liberation.

Vishishtadvaita Shankaracharya's beliefs were repudiated by the school of Vedanta associated with the 12th century philosopher, Ramanuja. He transformed the idea of God from an impersonal force to a personal God. His school of philosophy, known as *Vishishtadvaita*, views both the self and the world as real but only as part of the whole. In contrast to Shankaracharya's view, devotion is of central importance to achieving liberation and service to the Lord becomes the highest goal of life.

Dvaita Vedanta The 14th century philosopher, Madhva, believed that Brahman, the self and the world are completely distinct. Worship of God is a key means of achieving liberation.

Worship

The abstractions of philosophy do not mean much for the millions of Hindus living across South Asia today, nor have they in the past. South Radhakrishnan puts a common Hindu view very briefly: 'It does not matter what conception of God we adopt so long as we keep up a perpetual search after truth'.

The Sacred in Nature Some Hindus believe in one all powerful God who created all the lesser gods and the universe. The Hindu gods include many whose origins lie in the Vedic deities of the early Aryans. These were often associated with the forces

The duty of tolerance

One of the reasons why the Hindu faith is often confusing to the outsider is that as a whole it has many elements which appear mutually self-contradictory, but which are reconciled by Hindus as different facets of the ultimate truth. S Radhakrishnan suggests that for a Hindu 'tolerance is a duty, not a mere concession. In pursuance of this duty Hinduism has accepted within its fold almost all varieties of belief and doctrine and accepted them as authentic expressions of the spiritual endeavour'. Such a tolerance is particularly evident in the attitude of Hindus to the nature of God and of divinity. C Rajagopalachari writes that there is a distinction that marks Hinduism sharply from the other monotheistic faiths such as Christianity or Islam. This is that 'the philosophy of Hinduism has taught and trained the Hindu devotee to see and worship the Supreme Being in all the idols that are worshipped, with a clarity of understanding and an intensity of vision that would surprise the people of other faiths. The Divine Mind governing the Universe, be it as Mother or Father, has infinite aspects and the devotee approaches him or her, or both, in any of the many aspects as he may be led to do according to the mood and the psychological need of the hour'.

of nature and Hindus have revered many natural objects. Mountain tops, trees, rocks and above all rivers, are regarded as sites of special religious significance. The **Khaptad National Park** in West Nepal serves as one such example. They all have their own guardian spirits. You can see the signs of the continuing lively belief in these gods and demons wherever you travel in Nepal.

Reflecting the historical dynamism of Hinduism, its gods have constantly undergone changes. Rudra (the Roarer), the great Vedic god of destruction, became Shiva, one of the two most worshipped deities of Hinduism. At times, other gods disappeared, but the creative spirit of Hindus constantly led to new names being given to forces to be worshipped, because, as Basham says, 'the universe for the simple Hindu, despite its vastness, is not cold and impersonal and though it is subject to rigid laws, these laws find room for the soul of man. The world is the expression of ultimate divinity; it is eternally informed by God, who can be met face to face in all things'.

Pilgrimage

Most Hindus regard it as particularly beneficial to worship at places where God has been revealed. They will go great distances on pilgrimage, not just to the most famous sites such as Pashupatinath, but to temples, hill tops and rivers across Nepal. Many pilgrims come from throughout India, often on a whistlestop tour of Nepal's holy sites, often including a stop at the holy city of Varanasi in the Indian state of Bihar.

Puja

For most Hindus today, worship (often referred to as 'performing puja'), is an integral part of their faith. The great majority of Hindu homes will have a shrine to one of the gods of the Hindu pantheon. Individuals and families will often visit shrines or temples and on special occasions will travel long distances to particularly holy places such as Pashupatinath. Such sites may have temples dedicated to a major deity but will always have numerous other shrines in the vicinity dedicated to other favourite gods.

Acts of devotion are often aimed at the granting of favours and the meeting of urgent needs for this life – good health, finding a suitable wife or husband, the birth of a son, prosperity and good fortune. In this respect the popular devotion of simple pilgrims of all faiths in South Asia is remarkably similar when they visit shrines whether Hindu or Buddhist or those of other faiths.

Background

The story of Linga worship

"Once in the past, when all the universe had become a single ocean, Brahma, Vishnu and Rudra arose from the water. Their arrival was unwitnessed, and even wise men do not know it. The earth, which had been the domain of former beings, had been destroyed, for a piercing wind had arisen and dried up the seven oceans. A single sun appeared, rising in the east, and then a second in the south just like the first, drying up all the water with its rays and burning all that moved and was still. Then in the west a third sun arose, and in the north there arose a fourth, burning all that moved and was still; later on eight more arose, and there were twelve.

Rudra, the Fire of Doomsday, arose from the subterranean and filled all the regions out of the sky. The exalted one, as he is known everywhere, burnt all of the underworld above and sideways, without exception, and then he went to his own dwelling place which he had made before. Then clouds arose and rained in all directions, flooding the whole earth and all the regions of the sky with waters; afterwards they plunged into the single ocean which the universe had become. There was no earth, nor any regions of the

sky, no space, no heaven; everything was like a giant cask filled to the brim.

Then the three eternal gods arose from the midst of the water – Brahma, Vishnu and Rudra, whose arrivals are unwitnessed. The two – Ka and Vishnu – bowed and said to Sarva, who blazed with sharp energy and embraced the sakti of Rudra, 'You are the lord of everything, our lord. Perform creation as you wish.' 'I will perform it,' he said to them, and then he plunged into the waters and remained immersed for 1,000 celestial years. Then they said to one another, 'What will we do without him? How will creation take place?' Hari said to the creator, 'Do as I tell you, Grandfather: let no more time elapse, but make an effort to create progeny. For you are capable of creating various creatures in the worlds; I will give you your own sakti, so that you will be the creator.' Thus encouraged by the words Vishnu had spoken to him, he thought about creating, and then he created everything conducive to happiness – gods, demons, Gandharvs, Yaksas, serpents, Raksasas. When that creation had been performed, Sambhu emerged from the water, desirous of creating and thinking about it in his mind.

Background

Performing puja involves making an offering to God and darshana – having a view of the deity. Although there are devotional movements among Hindus in which singing and praying is practised in groups, Hindu worship is generally an act performed by individuals. Thus, Hindu temples may be little more than a shrine in the middle of a street, housing an image of the deity which will be tended by a priest and visited at special times when a darshan of the resident god can be obtained. When it has been consecrated, the image, if exactly made, becomes a channel for the godhead to work.

Festivals   Every temple has its special festivals. Some, like Pashupatinath in the Kathmandu Valley, have festivals that draw Hindus from all over Nepal and India. Others are village and family events. At festival times, you can see villagers walking in small groups, brightly dressed and often highly spirited.

There are two solar calendars, the Nepalese and Gregorian are in common use, but there are three lunar calendars: Nepalese, Newari and Tibetan! The latter affects the festival dates, the full moon considered especially auspicious. Eclipses are often thought to be a bad omen. Exact dates of festivals change annually and are calculated by astrologers. The Department of Tourism in Kathmandu publishes an annual brochure with dates.

Images   The image of the deity may be in one of many forms. Temples may be dedicated to

But when he saw the whole universe stretching above and below with the gods, demons, Gandharvs, Yaksas, serpents, Raksasas and men, the great god's heart was filled with anger, and he thought, 'What shall I do? Since creation had been performed by Brahma, I will therefore destroy, cutting off my own seed.' When he said this, he released from his mouth a flame which burnt everything.

When Brahma saw that everything was on fire, he bowed to the great lord with devotion and praised the lord... Sankara was pleased by Brahma's praise and told him, 'I am Sankara. I will always accomplish everything that is to be done for anyone who seeks refuge with me, devotedly. I am pleased with you; tell me what you desire in your heart.' When Brahma heard this he said, 'I created an extensive range of progeny; let that be as it was, O Lord, if you are pleased with me.' When Rudra heard this he said to Ka, 'That energy which I gathered in excess in order to destroy your creation – tell me, what shall I do with it for you?' Brahma thought carefully for the sake of the world, and then he said to Sankara, 'Cause your own energy to enter the sun, since you are lord over the sun; for you are the creator, protector and destroyer. Let us live together with all the immortals in the energy of the sun, and we will receive with devotion the sacred image of the three times (past, present and future) that was given by mankind. Then, great god, at the end of the aeon you will take the form of the sun and burn this universe, moving and still, at that moment.'

He agreed to this and laughed, for he was secretly amused, and he said to Brahma, 'There is no good use for this linga except for the creation of progeny.' And as he said this, he broke it off and threw it upon the surface of the earth. The linga broke through the earth and went to the very sky. Vishnu sought the end of it below, and Brahma flew upwards, but they did not find the end of it for all their vital effort. Then a voice arose out of the sky as the two of them sat there, and it said, 'If the linga of the god with braided hair is worshipped, it will certainly grant all desires that are longed for in the heart.' When Brahma and Vishnu heard this, they and all the divinities worshipped the linga with devotion, with their hearts set upon Rudra."

Vishnu or Shiva, for example, or to any one of their other representatives. Parvati, the wife of Shiva and Lakshmi, the wife of Vishnu, are the focus of many temple shrines. The image of the deity becomes the object of worship and the centre of the temple's rituals. These often follow through the cycle of day and night, as well as yearly lifecycles. The priests may wake the deity from sleep, bathe, clothe and feed it. Gifts of money will usually be made and in some temples there is a charge levied for taking up positions in front of the deity in order to obtain a darshan at the appropriate times.

Hindu sects

Three gods are seen as all-powerful: Brahma, Vishnu and Shiva. Their functions and character are not readily separated. While Brahma is regarded as the ultimate source of creation, Shiva also has a creative role alongside his function as destroyer. Vishnu, in contrast, is seen as the preserver or protector of the universe. There are very few images of Brahma; Vishnu and Shiva are far more widely represented and have come to be seen as the most powerful and important. Their followers are referred to as Vaishnavites and Shaivites respectively and numerically they form the two largest sects in South Asia.

Background

Deities

Brahma   Popularly, Brahma is interpreted as the creator in a trinity alongside Vishnu as preserver and Shiva as destroyer. In the literal sense, the name Brahma is the masculine and personalized form of the neuter word Brahman.

In the early Vedic writing, *Brahman* represented the universal and impersonal principle which governed the universe. Gradually as Vedic philosophy moved towards a monotheistic interpretation of the universe and its origins, this impersonal power was increasingly personalized. In the Upanishads, Brahman was seen as a universal and elemental creative spirit. Brahma, described in the early myths as having been born from a golden egg and then to have created the Earth, assumed the identity of the earlier Vedic deity Prajapati and became identified as the creator.

Some of the early Brahma myths were later taken over by the Vishnu cult. For example, in one story Brahma was believed to have rescued the earth from a flood by taking the form of a fish or a tortoise and in another he became a boar, raising the earth above the flood waters on his tusk. All these images were later associated with Vishnu.

By the 4th and 5th centuries AD, the height of the classical period of Hinduism, Brahma was seen as one of the trinity of gods – the *Trimurti* – in which Vishnu, Shiva and Brahma represented three forms of the unmanifested supreme being. It is from Brahma that Hindu cosmology takes its structure. The basic cycle through which the whole cosmos passes is described as one day in the life of Brahma – the *kalpa*. It equals 4,320 million years, with an equally long night. One year of Brahma's life – a cosmic year – lasts 360 days and nights. The universe is expected to last for 100 years of Brahma's life, who is currently believed to be 51 years old.

By the 6th century AD, Brahma worship had effectively ceased – before the great period of temple building, which accounts for the fact that there are remarkably few temples dedicated to Brahma, the most famous one being at Pushkar in the Indian state of Rajasthan. Nonetheless, images of Brahma are found in many temples. Characteristically, he is shown with four faces, a fifth having been destroyed by Shiva's third eye. In his four arms he holds a variety of objects, usually including a copy of the Vedas, a sceptre and a water jug or a bow. He is accompanied by the goose, symbolizing knowledge.

Sarasvati   The 'active power' of Brahma, popularly seen as his consort, Sarasvati has survived into the modern Hindu world as a far more important figure than Brahma himself. In popular worship, Sarasvati represents the goddess of education and learning. The development of her identity represented the rebirth of the concept of a mother goddess, which had featured strongly in the Indus Valley Civilization over 1,000 years before and which may have been continued in popular ideas through the worship of female spirits. It is possible that her origins are associated with the now dry River Sarasvati in Rajasthan, but unlike Brahma she plays an important part in modern Hindu worship. Normally shown as white coloured and riding on a swan, she usually carries a book and is often shown playing a vina. She may have many arms and heads, representing her

Vishnu

Vishnu's ten incarnations

Name	Form	Story
1 Matsya	Fish	Vishnu took the form of a fish to rescue Manu (the first man), his family and the Vedas from a flood.
2 Kurma	Tortoise	Vishnu became a tortoise to rescue all the treasures lost in the flood, including the divine nectar (Amrita) with which the gods preserved their youth. The gods put Mount Kailasa on the tortoise's back and when he reached the bottom of the ocean they twisted the divine snake round the mountain. They then churned the ocean with the mountain by pulling the snake.
3 Varaha	Boar	Vishnu appeared again to raise the earth from the ocean's floor where it had been thrown by a demon, Hiranyaksa. The story probably developed from a non-Aryan cult of a sacred pig.
4 Narasimha	Half-man, half lion	Having persuaded Brahma to promise that he could not be killed either by day or night, by god, man or beast, the demon Hiranyakasipu then terrorized everybody. When the gods pleaded for help, Vishnu appeared at sunset, when it was neither day nor night, in the form of a half man and half lion and killed the demon.
5 Vamana	A dwarf	Bali, a demon, achieved supernatural power by asceticism. To protect the world Vishnu appeared before him in the form of a dwarf and asked him a favour. Bali granted Vishnu as much land as he could cover in three strides. Vishnu then became a giant, covering the earth in three strides. He left only hell to the demon.
6 Parasurama	Rama with the axe	Vishnu was incarnated as the son of a Brahmin, Jamadagni as Parasurama and killed the wicked king for robbing his father. The king's sons then killed Jamadagni and in revenge Parasurama destroyed all male kshatriyas, 21 times in succession.
7 Rama	The Prince of Ayodhya	As told in the Ramayana, Vishnu came in the form of Rama to rescue the world from the dark demon, Ravana. His wife Sita is the model of patient faithfulness while Hanuman is the monkey-faced god and Rama's helper.
8 Krishna	Charioteer of Arjuma Many forms	Krishna meets almost every human need, from the mischievous child, the playful boy, the amorous youth to the Divine.
9 The Buddha		Probably incorporated into the Hindu pantheon in order to discredit the Buddhists, dominant in some parts of India until the 6th century AD. An early Hindu interpretation suggests that Vishnu took incarnation as Buddha to show compassion for animals and to end sacrifice.
10 Kalki	Riding on a horse	Vishnu's arrival will accompany the final destruction of this present age, Kaliyuga, judging the wicked and rewarding the good.

role as patron of all the sciences and arts. She has an honoured place in schools, colleges and universities.

Vishnu Vishnu is seen as the god with the human face. From the 2nd century AD a new and passionate devotional worship of Vishnu's incarnation as Krishna developed in south India. By 1000 AD Vaishnavism had spread across this region and it became closely associated with the devotional form of Hinduism preached by Ramanuja. Rebirth and reincarnation were already long established by the time Ramanuja's followers spread the worship of Vishnu and his 10 successive incarnations in animal and human form. For Vaishnavites, God took these different forms in order to save

Background

the world from impending disaster. In the table, AL Basham has summarized the 10 incarnations.

Rama & Krishna By far the most influential incarnations of Vishnu are those in which he was believed to take recognizable human form, especially as Rama (twice) and Krishna. As the Prince of Ayodhya, history and myth blend, for Rama was probably a chief who lived in the 8th or 7th century BC – perhaps 300 years after King David ruled in Israel and the start of the Iron Age in central Europe, or at about the same time as the Greeks began to develop city states.

In the earliest stories about Rama he was not regarded as divine. Although he is now seen as an earlier incarnation of Vishnu than Krishna, he was added to the pantheon very late, probably after the Muslim invasions of the 12th century AD. The story has also become part of the cultures of Southeast Asia.

Rama (or Ram – pronounced with a long 'a' as in arm) is a powerful figure in contemporary Hinduism, particularly in India where his supposed birthplace at Ayodhya has become a focus of fierce disputes between Hindus and Muslims. Some Hindus identified Ram's birthplace as a site occupied by a mosque. One of India's leading historians, Romila Thapar, argues that there is no historical evidence for this view, but it has taken widespread hold. The mosque was destroyed on 6 December 1992 during a huge and politically charged demonstration. The Indian government is planning to re-build it along with a temple to Rama on the same site.

Krishna is worshipped extremely widely as perhaps the most human of the gods. His advice on the battlefield of the Mahabharata is one of the major sources of guidance for the rules of daily living for many Hindus today.

Hanuman The faithful monkey assistant of Rama in his search for Sita, Hanuman is widely worshipped throughout Hindu South Asia. The Ramayana tells how he went at the head of his monkey army in search of the abducted Sita across India and finally into the demon Ravana's forest home of Lanka. He used his powers to jump the sea channel separating India from Sri Lanka and managed after a series of heroic and magical feats to find and rescue his master's wife. Whatever form he is shown in, he remains almost instantly recognizable and is often painted red.

Shiva Shiva is interpreted as both creator and destroyer, the power through whom the universe evolves. He lives on Mount Kailasa with his wife Parvati and two sons, the elephant-headed Ganesh and the six-headed Kartikkeya. Shiva is always accompanied by his 'vehicle', the bull (*Nandi*). They form a model of sorts for family life.

Shiva is often seen as rather more remote than Vishnu, but he is also widely portrayed in sculpture and art, most famously as the Natraj, or Nataranjan, dancing in a circle of cosmic fire. He is also shown as an ascetic, sitting among the mountain peaks around Mount Kailasa, accompanied by his wife Parvati and meditating on the nature of the universe.

More widely than either of these forms, Shiva is represented in Shaivite temples by the lingam, or phallic symbol, a symbol of energy, fertility and potency. This has become the most important form of the cult of Shiva. Professor Wendy O'Flaherty suggests that the worship of the linga of Shiva can be traced back to the pre-Vedic societies of the Indus Valley Civilization (c 2000 BC), but that it first appears in Hindu iconography in the 2nd century BC.

From that time, a wide variety of myths appeared to explain the origin of Linga worship. The myths surrounding the 12 jyoti linga (linga of light) found at centres like Ujjain in India go back to the 2nd century BC and were clearly developed in order to explain and justify linga worship. O'Flaherty has translated this story of competition between the gods, in which Shiva (in the form of Rudra) terrorizes the other gods into worshipping him with a devotion to the linga. Her translation of the Puranic myth is summarized above. Note that the gods appear in several forms: Shiva as Rudra, Sambha and Sankara; Vishnu as Hari; and Brahma as Ka.

Ganesh

Ganesh

Ganesh is one of Hinduism's most popular gods. He is seen as the great clearer of obstacles. Shown at gateways and on door lintels with his elephant head and pot belly, his image is revered across Nepal. Meetings, functions and special family gatherings will often start with prayers to Ganesh and any new venture from the opening of a building to the inauguration of a company will often not be deemed complete without a Ganesh puja. Successive Kings of Nepal have paid homage at a shrine to Ganesh in Kathmandu's Durbar Square as one of their first acts following the coronation.

Durga

Shakti, the Mother Goddess

One of the best known cults is that of Shakti, a female divinity also worshipped in the form of Durga. The worship of female goddesses developed into the widely practised form of devotional worship which became known as Tantrism. Goddesses such as Kali became the focus of worship which often involved practices that flew in the face of wider Hindu moral and legal codes. Animal and even human sacrifices and ritual sexual intercourse were part of Tantric belief and practice, the evidence for which may still be seen in the art and sculpture of some major temples in Nepal and India. Tantric practice affected both Hinduism and Buddhism from the 8th century AD and was further influenced by the development of Tantric Buddhism in Tibet from the 10th century.

Marriage, which is still generally arranged, continues to be dictated almost entirely by caste rules. It is usually seen as an alliance between two families. Great efforts are made to match caste, social status and economic position, although the rules which govern eligibility vary from region to region. In some groups, marriage between even first cousins is common, while among others marriage between any branch of the same clan is strictly forbidden.

Kali, Mother Goddess

Background

Buddhism

Although followed by less than 10 percent of the country's population, Buddhism is dominant in the northern, mountainous regions of Nepal and is conspicuously represented also in the middle zone. The number of Buddhists expanded greatly following the Chinese takeover of Tibet when many thousands of Tibetans sought refuge in Nepal. The area around the Bodhnath stupa, east of Kathmandu, now has a majority Tibetan population, as does that of Swayambhunath. Though notoriously difficult to define succinctly, very generally it consists of a set of existential philosophies followed on a path towards 'enlightenment'. The question of whether it is, is not or has ever been a religion is largely one of semantics, depending on the definition of 'religion'. Buddhism neither recognizes nor explicitly denies the existence of a supreme God in the traditional sense, but contains many of the hallmarks of traditional religious practice. It is characterized by, among other things, the assumption of suffering as an integral condition of human existence, systems of ethics and moral precepts and self-sufficiency in the adherent. Although India was the original home of Buddhism, today it is practised largely on the margins of the subcontinent.

There are three main schools (or 'Ways') of Buddhism: Hinayana, Mahayana and Vajrayana. Mahayana Buddhism is dominant in the northern regions of Buddhist Asia (with Tantric Vajrayana especially important in Nepal), while Hinayana predominates in the southern regions, notably in Sri Lanka.

Buddhism evolved from the teachings of Siddhartha Gautama of the Shakya clan (known as the Buddha, the 'Awakened/Enlightened One'), who lived in northern India in the 6th or 5th centuries BC. The Buddha's teachings are rooted in a compelling existential observation: that despite all persons' efforts to find happiness and avoid pain, their lives are filled with suffering and dissatisfaction. However, the Buddha did not stop there. He recognized the causes of suffering to be the dissonant mental states – delusion, attachment, aversion, pride and envy and realized that it is possible to free oneself permanently from such sufferings through a rigorous and well-structured training in ethics, meditation and insight, which leads to a profound understanding of the way things really are, that is, enlightenment.

The Buddha was born a prince (see below) and had known great opulence, but had also experienced great deprivations when he renounced his life of luxury to seek salvation through ascetic practice. He concluded that both sensual indulgence and physical deprivations are hindrances to spiritual evolution. He taught the Middle Way, a salvific path which was initially interpreted to mean isolation from the normal distractions of daily life, by living in communities devoted to the pursuit of spiritual liberation, which were disciplined but did not involve extreme deprivation. These communities, consisting of both monks and nuns, preserved and put into practice the Buddhist teachings. Initially the teachings were preserved through oral transmission, but by the 1st century BC were increasingly committed to written form. Unlike other of the world's leading religious traditions, Buddhism does not rely on a single literary source (eg the Bible, Koran or Talmud), but on a vast, rich, sophisticated literary corpus. The preservation of Buddhism brought literacy to hundreds of millions in Asia.

Buddhism's path to salvation depends largely on the individual's own efforts. Its emphasis on self-reliance and non-violence appealed to the merchant class in India and thus it spread along trade routes – north through Central Asia, into China and then into the Far East, Korea and Japan. It also spread south to Sri Lanka and Southeast Asia: Burma, Thailand, Indo-China and Indonesia. Later, Nepal and Tibet embraced Buddhism at the zenith of its development in India and it was this tradition which eventually came to permeate Mongolia, Manchuria and Kalmukya.

The sacred thread

The highest three varnas were classified as 'twice born' and could wear the sacred thread symbolizing their status. The age at which the initiation ceremony (upanaya) for the upper caste child was carried out varied according to class – 8 for a Brahmin, 11 for a Kshatriya and 12 for a Vaishya.

The boy, dressed like an ascetic and holding a staff in his hand, would have the sacred thread (yajnopavita) placed over his right shoulder and under his left arm. A cord of three threads, each of nine twisted strands, it was made of cotton for Brahmins, hemp for Kshatriyas or wool for Vaishyas. It was – and is – regarded as a great sin to remove it.

The Brahmin who officiated would whisper a verse from the Rig Veda in the boy's ear, the Gayatri mantra. Addressed to the old solar god Savitr, the holiest of holy passages, the Gayatri can only be spoken by the three higher classes. AL Basham translated it as: 'Let us think of the lovely splendour of the god Savitr, that he may inspire our minds'.

In recent years, Buddhism has also found adherents in the West.

A **Buddhist** is one who takes refuge in the **Three Precious Jewels** (*Triratna*): Buddha, Dharma (his teachings) and Sangha (the monastic community). Beyond this, Buddhism has evolved remarkably different practices to bring about liberation, its teachings having been interpreted and reinterpreted by commentators in each new generation and in each cultural milieu. For its followers, the brilliance of Buddhism lies in its universality – its compelling existential appeal and, crucially, its efficacy. Historically, it has appealed to peasants and to kings, to philosophers and to the illiterate, to prostitutes and to murderers and to those already close to sainthood. And though it was not its intention, Buddhism has transformed the cultures in its path, imbuing them with ideals of universal compassion and profound insight.

The Buddha

Siddhartha Gautama, who came to be given the title of the Buddha, was born a prince into the *Kshatriya* (warrior) caste in the gardens of Lumbini near the Sakya capital of Kapilavastu about 563 BC. Some accounts suggest that his father received an 'annunciation' prior to Siddhartha's birth, others that his mother, Maya (deified as Maya-devi) dreamt of her conception by a white elephant, representing the eternal Buddha, holding a silver lotus in its trunk. Maya died soon after giving birth. He was married to Yasodhara at the age of 16 with whom he had a son, Rahula. Following several years contemplating the nature of human existence, he left home at the age of 29. This incident, known as the *Mahabhinishkramana* ('the Great Renunciation') occurred after he awoke in the middle of the night feeling 'like a man who has been told his house is on fire'. He looked upon his sleeping wife and child, resisting the temptation to bid them a final farewell.

He exchanged his clothes with those of a beggar and wandered as an ascetic, studying with various gurus all of whom failed to satisfy his search for the truth. Neither did his life of often extreme material deprivation lead him any closer. After about six years he went to Bodh Gaya where he meditated beneath the Bo (peepul) tree, resolving not to leave until he had attained enlightenment. Here he was tempted by the demon, Mara and his daughters with all the desires of the world. Resisting these temptations, he remained in his 'trance' supposedly for one full day and night and received enlightenment (*bodhi*, or *sambodhi* – 'full enlightenment'). This, which occurred sometime between 533 and 528 BC, took the form of a vision in which he saw an endless cycle of birth and death – the destiny of all men – followed by the enlightenment.

Background

The Buddha's Four Noble Truths

The Buddha preached Four Noble Truths: that life is painful; that suffering is caused by ignorance and desire; that beyond the suffering of life there is a state which cannot be described but which he termed nirvana; and that nirvana can be reached by following an eightfold path.

The concept of nirvana is often understood in the West in an entirely negative sense – that of 'non-being'. The word has the rough meaning of 'blow out'

or 'extinguish', meaning to blow out the flames of greed, lust and desire. In a more positive sense, it has been described by one Buddhist scholar as 'the state of absolute illumination, supreme bliss, infinite love and compassion, unshakeable serenity, and unrestricted spiritual freedom'. The essential elements of the eightfold path are the perfection of wisdom, morality and meditation.

These scenes are common motifs of Buddhist art. The next landmark was the preaching of his first sermon *Dharma Chakra Pravartana* ('Setting into Motion the wheel of the Law'), to his first five disciples in the deer park at Sarnath near Benares (modern Varanasi). Other sermons followed during the course of his many travels, including the 'Fire Sermon' at Uruvela as a result of which his audience of fire-worshippers converted. The number of disciples increased as did their accounts of the Buddha's miraculous powers which he derided. Later, the Buddha returned to Kapilavastu where he met his family for the first time since he had left. His son, Rahula, joined his father. The disciple, Ananda, to whom the Buddha is recorded as speaking in scriptures ('the most intimate'), was his cousin. Another cousin named Devadutta, meanwhile, nourished a lifelong hatred of the Buddha and on three occasions tried to have him killed. The assassins sent on the first occasion confounded Devadutta by converting to Buddhism. Next, a giant rock was rolled down from Vulture Peak but broke into two pieces, both missing their target. The final attempt is perhaps the best known: a wild elephant was released to trample the Buddha to death but declined to do so, reportedly preferring to listen to the Buddha preach a sermon. Thereafter, Devadutta gave up and is believed to have converted to the Buddhist faith on his deathbed.

By the time he died, the Buddha had established a small though expanding band of monks and nuns known as the *Sangha* and had followers across North India. The all male *Sangha* was divided into *sramana* (ascetics), *bhikku* (mendicants), *upasaka* (lay disciples) and *sravaka* (laymen). The nuns were known as the *bhikkuni*, which came to include Yasodhara, the Buddha's wife. The Buddha was initially somewhat wary about the potential distractions that might result from the presence of women, wisely advising Ananda: 'Do not see them, Ananda. If you have to see them, abstain from speech, Ananda. And if you have to speak to them, keep wide awake, Ananda'. Following his death (referred to as the *parinirvana* – 'final extinction'), his body was cremated and the ashes, regarded as precious relics, were divided up among the peoples to whom he had preached. Some have been discovered as far west as Peshawar in the northwest Frontier of Pakistan and at Piprawa close to his birthplace.

After the Buddha's Death Soon after the Buddha's death, factions began to emerge among his followers. Within a year of his death, the **First Council** of the *Sangha* was convened with the aim of, if not codifying, then interpreting and systemizing his teachings to a general concensus. Another was held in around 390 BC which marked a schism between two major sects, the **Mahasanghikas** (who followed what became known as the *Mahayana* way) and the orthodox **Sthaviras**. A **Third Council** was convened at Patiliputra (modern Patna) 48 years later, where the first Buddhist canon was agreed upon. By this time the faith had seen the conversion of the great Mauryan Emperor

Background

Ashoka which had resulted from the dismay he felt at the devastation and destruction caused by his victory over the Kalingas in modern Orissa. It is said that Ceylon (Sri Lanka) was converted to Buddhism by Mahendra, Ashoka's son. This council also resulted in the expulsion of 'heretics' who were seen as having failed in their monastic duty and discipline. The final **Fourth Council** was held in Kashmir in 120 AD, the 'minutes' of which were supposedly recorded on red copper sheets, then buried. This is significant for the fact that it decreed the Buddha's divinity and published a series of Buddhist scriptures in Sanskrit. By this time there were almost 20 major Buddhist sects, though the principal branches had now crystallized into the Mahayana and Hinayana approaches. A Tantric form of Buddhism, known as *Vajrayana*, emerged from the mid-4th century AD.

The decline of Buddhism in India probably stemmed as much from the growing similarity in the practice of Hinduism and Buddhism as from direct attacks. Mahayana Buddhism, with its reverence for bodhisattvas and its devotional character, was more and more difficult to distinguish from the revivalist Hinduism characteristic of several parts of North India from the 7th to the 12th centuries AD. In south India, the Chola Empire contributed to the final extinction of Buddhism in the southern peninsula, while the Muslim conquest of northern India dealt the final death blow, being accompanied by the large scale slaughter of monks and the destruction of monasteries. Without their institutional support, Buddhism in India gradually faded away, retreating to the regions peripheral to mainland India. By this time, however, it was already well established in Tibet where it continued to grow under the influence of migrating Indian Buddhism and through indigenous cultivation. The greater part of Nepali Buddhism remains Tibetan in character.

Buddhism's decline in India

The Buddha in Dhyanmudra – meditation

India still has many sites of great significance for Buddhists around the world. Some say that the Buddha himself spoke of four places his followers should visit: **Lumbini**, the Buddha's birthplace in the central Terai near the present border with India; **Bodh Gaya**, where he attained his 'full enlightenment', is about 80 kilometres south of the modern Indian city of Patna; the deer park at **Sarnath**, where he preached his first sermon and set in motion the Wheel of the Law, is just outside Varanasi; and **Kushinagara**, where he died at the age of 80, is 50 kilometres east of Gorakhpur. In addition, there are remarkable monuments, sculptures and works of art, from Gandhara in modern Pakistan to Sanchi and Ajanta in central India.

The Buddha in Bhumisparcamudra – calling the earth goddess to witness

The three *Yana*

The *yana* are the three principal 'Ways' or 'Vehicles' of Buddhism, with their distinctive points of emphasis. The use of the word 'vehicle' derives from its conception as a vessel upon which

Reverence for life

In a description of the 'Bodhisattva Ideal', the Buddhist scholar Dr Edward Conze (1904-79) wrote of the Buddhist 'fellow feeling for all living beings' as akin to Albert Schweitzer's view of 'reverence for life'. There are, indeed, a number of interesting parallels in Schweitzer's doctrine, enshrined in his famous sermon of 1919.

Whilst concerned primarily with reason, ethics and morality, Schweitzer recognizes a 'strange duality' in the search for self-understanding. 'When reason really reaches the core of the matter,' he says, 'it ceases to be cold reason, whether it wants to or not, and begins to speak with the melody of the heart'. Vide the cherished Buddhist belief that heightened spiritual awareness results from meditation or, from a different angle, that the goings-on of an empty world appear, in the words of Seng Tsan, 'real all because of ignorance'. From this, Schweitzer continues, there develops a 'reverence for the unfathomable, infinite and living Reality ... a reverence for life in its infinite

and yet ever-fresh manifestations. How fantastic that in other existences something comes into being, passes away again, comes into being once more, and so forth from eternity to eternity!' That realization leads Schweitzer to the conclusion that 'in everything ... wherever you see life, that is yourself': in the smallest beetle struggling for existence or in the snowflake which sparkled then died.

Common to both Buddhism and Hinduism, the doctrine of ahimsa ('non-harming') expresses the sanctity of all life, and mahakaruna ('great compassion') is a cornerstone of Buddhism. Although this is personified in particular by the bodhisattvas, the Buddhist silas, or rules of conduct, also specifically prohibit the causing of pain or the destruction of life. For, as Schweitzer concludes, 'Reverence for life comprises the whole ethic of love in its deepest and highest sense; it is the source of constant renewal for the individual and for mankind'.

---

people are carried across the ocean of this world to nirvana. A primary distinction is made between the **sutra** texts which emphasize the gradual or casual approach to enlightenment and the **tantras** with their emphasis on the immediate or resultant approach.

Background

Hinayana The Hinayana ('Little Way' or 'Lesser Vehicle'), insists on a monastic way of life as the only path to achieving nirvana. Divided into many schools, the only surviving Hinayana tradition is the Theraveda Buddhism (from *thera*, meaning wise man or sage), which was that taken to Sri Lanka by Ashoka's son, Mahendra (or Mahinda). It became the state religion under King Dutthagamenu in the 1st century AD and uses the sutra, vinaya and abhidharma texts. Hinayana holds that obscurations and defilements are eliminated by renunciation.

Mahayana In contrast to the Hinayana schools, the followers of the Mahayana school ('the Great Way/Vehicle') believed in the possibility of salvation for all. They practised a far more devotional form of meditation and new figures came to play a prominent part in their beliefs and their worship – the bodhisattvas, 'saints' who were predestined to reach the state of enlightenment through thousands of rebirths. They aspired to Buddhahood not for their own sake, however, but for the sake of all living things and were believed to have returned to lead others to salvation. The Buddha is believed to have passed through numerous existences in preparation for his final mission. These additions probably represent the Hindu influence, with some considering its propositions as tending much towards hyperbole. One of the most notable Mahayana philosophers was the saint, **Nagarjuna**. Mahayana Buddhism became dominant over most of South Asia and its influence is widespread in Buddhist art.

Nagarjuna

*Widely revered by Buddhists, Nagarjuna lived in the 2nd or early 3rd century AD, the son of South Indian Brahmin parents. His name is said to derive from the Nagas with whom he lived during a part of his youth and the arjuna tree beneath which he was reputedly born. In the early part of his life, he learnt alchemy and is said to have written a treatise on it which became widely popular with future Indian alchemists. Following his conversion to Buddhism, he founded the **Madhyamika** school of Mahayana Buddhism. This was seemingly characterized by a form of nihilism which, among other things, denied the existence of material reality. Ultimately, he said, reality as we know it is an illusion; true reality is incomprehensible to the human intellect and can best be conceived of as a void, or as emptiness (sunya). It was through his use of multiple negation that Nagarjuna sought to describe the positive state leading to nirvana.*

The development of Mahayana is thought to parallel that of early Christianity and to have been influenced by it. The concept of bodhisattva, the increasing emphasis on compassion (a divergence from older Buddhism) and a preoccupation with future spiritual states all have their corollaries in the Christian ethos. Furthermore, similarities have been noted between some of the respective scriptures which seem likely to have been influenced by the existence of established trading routes which linked the areas of their composition, notably between the eastern regions of the Roman empire and southern and northwestern India. The Buddhist *Perfection of Wisdom*, for example, is referred to as 'sealed with seven seals' and is shown to a bodhisattva named 'Everweeping' who later sacrificed himself to attain the perfection of wisdom. The Bible's book of *Revelations*, meanwhile, has St John weeping bitterly as there is no one to break its seals but the sacrificial Lamb.

Vajrayana

The 'Diamond' or 'Indestructible' way is related to the Mahayana tradition, though resembles magic and yoga in some of its beliefs. The ideal of the Vajrayana Buddhist is to be 'so fully in harmony with the cosmos as to be able to manipulate the cosmic forces within and outside himself'. It had developed in the north of India by the 7th century AD, matching the parallel growth of Hindu Tantrism. Its adherents are concentrated in the northern regions, including Nepal. Its texts are the esoteric teachings of the Tantras which were transmitted by accomplished masters such as Manjushrimitra, Indrabhuti and Padmasambhava.

Lamaism and Tibetan Buddhism

Lamaism is the name sometimes used to describe Tibetan and Mongolian Buddhism. It is largely a Mahayana form which has included elements of pre-existing Bon shamanism. Much of the Buddhist Nepal, particularly in the higher Himalayan regions, is either characterized or strongly influenced by Lamaism. Among all the Buddhist countries of Asia, the highest developments of Indian Buddhism were preserved in Tibet. This was due partly to geographical proximity, partly to temporal considerations and partly to the aptitude which the Tibetans themselves displayed for the diversity of Indian Buddhist traditions. The sparse population, the slow measured pace of daily life and an almost anarchical disdain for political involvement have encouraged the spiritual cultivation of Buddhism to such an extent that it came to permeate the entire culture.

All schools of Buddhism in Tibet maintain the monastic tradition of the **vinaya**, the graduated spiritual practices and philosophical systems based on the **sutras** and their commentaries, the shastras and the esoteric meditative practices associated with the Tantras. Different schools developed in different periods of Tibetan history, each derived from distinctive lineages or transmissions of Indian Buddhism.

The oldest, the Nyingmapa, are associated with the early dissemination of Buddhism. The Sakyapa and the Kagyupa, along with the Kadampa, appeared in the 11th century on the basis of later developments in Indian Buddhism. The Gelukpa originated in Tibet during the 14th century, but can claim descent from the others, particularly the Kadumpa and the Sakyapa. Each of these schools has had its great teachers and personalities over the centuries. Each has held political power at one time or another and each continues to exert influence in different regions.

Nyingmapa The Nyingmapa school maintains the teachings introduced into Tibet by Shantaraksita, Padmasambhava, Vimalamitra and their contemporaries during the 8th century. The entire range of the Buddhist teachings are graded by the Nyingmapa according to nine hierarchical vehicles, starting from the exoteric sutras of the Lesser Vehicle and the Greater Vehicle and continuing through the classes of Outer Tantras to those of the Inner Tantras. It is the Inner Tantras, known as Mahayoga, Anuyoga and Atiyoga which are the teachings of the Nyingmapa par excellence.

Kadampa When the Bengali master Atisha (982-1054) reintroduced the teachings of the gradual path of the enlightenment into Tibet in 1042, he transmitted the doctrines of his teacher Dahrmakirti of Sumatra, which focussed on the cultivation of compassion and the propitiation of the deities Tara, Avalokiteshwar, Acala and Shakyamuni Buddha. During the early 15th century, this tradition was absorbed within the indigenous Gelukpa school.

Kagyupa The Kagyupa school maintains the lineages of the Indian masters Tilopa, Naropa and Maitripa, which emphasize the perfection stage of meditation (*sampannakrama*) and the practice of the Great Seal (*Mahamudra*). These were introduced here by Marpa Lo-tsawa (1012-96) and Zhang Tselpa (1122-93). Marpa had four main disciples including the renowned yogin Milarepa (1040-1123), who passed many years in retreat in the mountain caves of Labchi and adjacent Himalayan valleys. Milarepa is one of a select group of Tibetan masters revered for their attainment of enlightenment or Buddhahood within a single lifetime.

Atisha

Sakyapa The Sakyapa tradition represents a unique synthesis of early eigth century Buddhism and the later diffusion of the 11th century. The members of the Khon family had been adherents of Buddhism since the time of Khon Luiwangpo Sungwa, a student of Padmasambhava. Then, in 1073, his descendent, Khon Gyelpo, who had received teachings of

Tsongkhapa

the new tradition from Drokmi Lotsawa, founded the Gorum temple at **Sakya**. His tradition therefore came to emphasize the ancient teachings on Vajrakila, as well as the new teachings on Heajra, Chakrasamvara and the esoteric instruction known as the Path and its Fruit.

Other important sub-schools of Sakya also developed from the early 15th century. Among them, **Ngor** was founded in 1429 by Ngorchen Kunga Zangpo, **Nalendra** in 1435 by Rongton Sheja Kunzik and **Derge Lhundrupteng** in 1448 by Tangtong Gyelpo.

The Gelukpa school maintains the teachings and lineage of Je Tsongkhapa (1357-1419), who established a uniquely indigenous tradition on the basis of his Sakyapa and Kadampa background. He instituted the Great Prayer Festival at Lhasa and propagated his important treatises on the sutra and tantra traditions in and around the Tibetan capital. Some of his students became the prime teachers in the new Gelukpa order, including Khedrup Je who was retrospectively recognized as Panchen Lama I. Another was Dalai Lama I Gendun Drupa.

Gelukpa

The successive emanations of the Dalai and Panchen Lamas enhanced the prestige of the Gelukpa school, which swiftly gained allegiances from the Mongol forces of the northeast. Following the civil wars of the 17th century, many Kagyu monasteries were converted to the Gelukpa tradition and the regent Sangye Gyatso compiled his *Yellow Beryl* (*Vaidurya Serpo*) history of the Gelukpa tradition.

Buddhist literature

The whole corpus of Buddhist literature, including scriptures and commentaries, is to put it mildly, immense. Put together, it represents a record of the continuing Buddhist traditions which, not unlike those of the main Christian denominations, have constantly evolved, though there is no Buddhist equivalent to the Bible. In the centuries following the Buddha's death, scriptures were transmitted orally from generation to generation. They only came to be written down from around the 1st century BC, while the period from the end of the 1st century AD to around 400 AD is considered by many to be the 'golden era' of Buddhist literature, a time when the creative impulse was at its strongest.

The earliest scriptures are in **Pali** and are those used by the **Thereveda** Buddhists. These are known as the ***Tripitaka*** ('3 baskets') and were probably completed in Sri Lanka around the beginning of the 1st century BC. They comprise the *Vinaya*, a canon of monastic rules; the *Sutta*, with guidance mainly for non-monastic Buddhists, along with a miscellany of accounts of the Buddha's life, sermons, poetry and a succinct 'confession of faith' (*I put my faith in Buddha, Dharma, Sangha*); and the *Abhidhamma*, a more in-depth exposition of Buddhist philosophy. These are among the principle scriptures used today by Theraveda Buddhist of Sri Lanka and much of Southeast Asia.

Mahayana literature was largely composed in Sanskrit and is later in origin, dating from the 2nd century AD to the 6th century. Most is in *sutra* form, a combination of the Buddha's sermons along with discourses usually presented as dialogue. Principal *Sutras* include the *Saddharma pundarika* (the 'Lotus Sutra') and the 'Perfection of Wisdom' Sutra. These encouraged belief in the worship of certain divine forms, including the bodhisattvas, as well as a devotional approach akin to Hindu *bhakti*. The *Vajrachedika* ('Diamond Sutra') is largely concerned with the concept of *sunyata* ('voidness' or 'emptiness') expounded by Nagarjuna and others.

Background

Minorities

Islam

Nepal is home to almost 700,000 Muslims (known as *Mussalman* in Nepal), according to the 1991 census. The overwhelming majority live in the Terai, most first or subsequent generation migrants from the neighbouring Indian states of Uttar Pradesh and Bihar, while some Kashmiris have also moved to Nepal. Islam is little represented in the middle zone, though Kathmandu has two mosques and is virtually absent in the northern, mountainous regions. The religion made its first significant entry into the subcontinent with the victory of the Turk, Mahmud of Ghazni, over the Rajputs in 1192, establishing a 500 year period of Muslim power in India which ended with the demise of the Mughal Empire in the 18th century.

Muslim Beliefs The beliefs of Islam (which means 'submission to God') could apparently scarcely be more different from those of Hinduism. Islam has a fundamental creed: 'There is no God but God; and Mohammed was the Prophet of God' (*La Illaha illa 'illah Mohammed Rasula 'laah*). One book, the Koran, is the supreme authority on Islamic teaching and faith. Islam preaches the belief in bodily resurrection after death and in the reality of Heaven and hell. It has no priesthood. The authority of Imams derives from social custom and from their authority to interpret the scriptures, rather than from a defined status within the Islamic community. Islam also prohibits any distinction on the basis of race and colour and there is strong antipathy to the representation of the human figure. It is often thought, inaccurately, that this ban stems from the Koran itself. In fact it probably had its origins in the belief of Mohammed that images were likely to be turned into idols.

Muslim Sects During the first century of its existence, Islam split into two sects which were divided on political and religious grounds: the Shi'is and the Sunnis. The Sunnis, which are the majority in South Asia, believe that Mohammed did not appoint a successor and that abu Bak'r, Omar and Othman were the first three caliphs (or vice-regents) after Mohammed's death. Ali, whom the Sunnis count as the fourth caliph, is regarded as the first legitimate caliph by the Shi'is, who consider Abu Bak'r and Omar to be usurpers.

The Four Islamic Obligations There are four obligatory requirements imposed on Muslims. Daily prayers are prescribed at daybreak, noon, afternoon, sunset and nightfall. Muslims must give alms to the poor. They must observe a strict fast for the month of Ramadan, during which they must not eat or drink between sunrise and sunset. Lastly, they should attempt the pilgrimage to the Ka'aba in Mecca, known as the *Hajj*. Those who have done so are entitled to the prefix *Hajji* before their name.

Muslim rules differ from Hindu practice in several other aspects of daily life. Muslims are strictly forbidden to drink alcohol; (though some suggest that this prohibition is restricted to the use of fermented grape juice, that is wine, it is commonly accepted to apply to all alcohol). Eating pork, or any meat from an animal not killed by draining its blood while alive, is also prohibited. Meat prepared in the appropriate way is called *Halal*. Finally, usury (charging interest on loans) and games of chance are forbidden.

Bon

The ancient Bon religion is represented mostly in smaller Tibetan communities in some regions of the Himalaya. It is Tibetan in origin, though there are also communities in the Indian state of Himachal Pradesh. The original importance which Bon held for the Tibetan kings probably lay in its elaborate funerary rites and veneration of space. The earliest kings of Tibet are said to have been immortals who would descend from and ascend to the heavens on a sky-cord (*mu*); but following the death of Drigum Tsenpo, the mortal kings increasingly focussed on funerary rites and rituals for the averting of death through 'ransom' (*lud*). Bon was largely absorbed into Buddhism from the 7th century and this form is known as 'Translated Bon'. The Bon orders which have survived until the present are thoroughly imbued with Buddhist imagery and symbolism. They have evolved their own parallel literature to counterbalance that of the Buddhists, ranging from exoteric teachings on ethics to highly esoteric teachings on the Great Perfection (*Dzogchen*).

Animism and shamanism

The earliest form of Tibetan religion, which RA Stein has termed the 'nameless religion', was a type of animism based upon the worship of the elements and mountain deities. Incense offerings would be made to appease local mountain spirits and 'wind-horse' (*lungta*) prayer flags or cairns affixed on prominent passes to ensure good auspices. Solemn declarations of truth (*dentsik*) and oathes would be made in the presence of local deities to invoke good fortune (*gyang-khug*); and talismanic objects or places (*la-ne*) were revered as life-supporting forces. Enemies and hostile forces could then be overpowered by drawing in their life-supporting talisman in a ceremony known as *la-guk*.

The word Animism is taken from the Latin *anima*, meaning 'soul', 'breath', or 'vital force'. Its central themes are concerned with the belief that all natural phenomena in the universe, including the universe itself, possess souls which may exist independently and that the soul is the principle of health and life. It has influenced the practices of both Buddhism and Hinduism in Nepal, notably in the performance of rituals on which Animists place considerable emphasis, along with symbolism and superstition. Funeral rites, for example, can be highly elaborate. The role of the presiding *Shaman* (hence *Shamanism*) is crucial and he is seen to act as an intermediary between the material and spirit worlds. The ritualism is necessary to propitiate the powerful spirits and is thus central to Animist practice. The *Shaman* is further endowed with powers to cure illness, to control supernatural forces and foretell future events, often using traditional herbal and magic formularies.

Christianity

Around 0.2 percent of the population is Christian and many of these are Westerners working in Nepal. Outside Patan, Kathmandu and to a lesser degree Pokhara, the country has very few churches. Despite the constitutional freedom now provided to all faiths, Nepal has traditionally been wary of the influence of foreign Christian missionaries and attempts at conversion continue to be discouraged.

Background

Culture

Peoples

The distribution of **ethnic** groups reflects for the most part the geography of the country. The majority of Nepal's population (some 80 percent) are of Indo-Aryan stock, with the remainder of Tibetan origin. The latter include not only the Tibetan and Bhotia inhabitants of North Nepal (such as the Sherpas, the Dolpowas and the Lopas of Mustang), but also the related mongoloid inhabitants of the central belt: Newars, Tamangs, Rais, Limbus, Sunwars, Magars and Gurung peoples.

Names The four main divisions of caste in Hindu Nepal are known respectively as: Bahun, Chhetri, Vaishya and Shudra. The family names of some Hindu **castes** may reflect locality as well as occupation. In Newari society, for example, potters are often called *Kumar* (or *Kumali*), while the *Chippas* are masons and the *Bares*, goldsmiths or jewellers. Non-Newari Bahun (ie Brahmin) family names common in East Nepal include Gotame, **Sharma**, Regmi, Nepal, Acharya, Upadhaya, Aryal, Bhandari, Adhikari and Paudel; those from West Nepal include Pant, Joshi, Bista, Bhatta, Pandey, Lohini and Upreti. Chhetri (ie Kshatriya) family names include that of the Royal Family, Shah, in addition to Thakuri, Singh, Pal, Malla, Chand, Kalyal and Pande.

Peoples of the Terai & Churia Hills The Terai people are sometimes collectively referred to as *Madeshis*. The region is dominated by **Tharus** who number about 1.2 million (1991). Tharus are dark-skinned and slightly Mongoloid in appearance and are ethnically related to the Sakya clan into which the Buddha, Gautama Siddhartha, was born. They are the Terai's indigenous people and are mostly agricultural by occupation. Their language is also known as Tharu, though there are several dialects which have been influenced by, from west to east, Hindi, Urdu, Maithili, Bhojpuri and Bengali. Tharu religion combines elements of Hinduism, Buddhism and Animism. **Bahuns** and **Chhetris** predominate in the western and eastern Churias and **Gurungs** in the mid-western hills. Smaller populations of **Danuwars** (51,000), **Majhis** (55,000) and **Darais** (11,000) live in the eastern Churias and the central and eastern Terai. The Majhis are largely fishermen by occupation, with the Danuwars and Darais being farmers. Their language is of Sanskritic origin, but distinct from Tharu. They practice a form of Hinduism. The agricultural **Rajbanshi** communities of the eastern Terai number around 82,000 and speak a language influenced by those of northern Bihar and Assam.

Peoples of the Middle Zone The **Newars** are concentrated in the Kathmandu Valley area, though are also found in several other towns and villages of the midland belt of Nepal and total about 1.1 million. The Newari language developed out of a number of influences. Ethnically, they combine both Tibetan and Indo-Aryan aspects. There are small numbers of Newari Buddhists, but most are primarily Hindu, the practice of which has also been formed by Buddhism. **Tamangs** dominate the area around and to the east of the Kathmandu Valley, numbering over one million. Ethnically Tibetan-Mongoloid, their language is of the Tibeto-Burmese family. Tamang religion is a form of Buddhism with strands of Bon, Tantrism and Hinduism. **Rais** and **Limbus** together make up the **Kirantis**, also a Tibetan-Mongoloid people who were perhaps the first ethnic group to have settled permanently in Nepal. There are over 550,000 Rais and around 300,000 Limbus, the former concentrated in and around Dhankuta in the east Terai/Churia Hills and the latter in the far East. Both groups have contributed to the Gurkha regiments of the British and Indian armies in significant numbers. They speak a language derived from the old Kiranti, while Kiranti religion is a mixture of Animism, Buddhism and Shaivite Hinduism. In the higher parts of the central hills, the **Gurung** population is a little under 500,000. Religion again combines Lamaist Buddhism with aspects of Hinduism. The Gurung economy is both sedentary agriculture and seasonal nomadic pastoralism, though many have served in Gurkha regiments. The **Magars** are one of the largest ethnic groups of the middle zone, totalling over 1.35 million, as well as having been one the main recruiting groups for the British Gurkhas. They include the **Thakalis** who, though small in number (14,000), are conspicuous in Pokhara and in the Annapurna region as owners of tourist hotels and lodges.

Ethnically, these are almost entirely of Tibetan origin. Many **Tibetans** have moved south into Nepal since the Chinese occupation of their homeland from the 1950s. Some have assimilated with the indigenous **Bhotia** (from *Bhot* – 'Tibet') populations, while others have settled around Pokhara and Kathmandu. The **Dolpowas**, people of Dolpo, number only a couple of thousand and are concentrated to the north of Jomsom and Kagbeni. They supplement their cultivation (potatoes, barley and wheat) of the relatively infertile land of four valleys with animal husbandry, speak a dialect of Tibetan and follow Lamaist Buddhism. The **Lopas**, the people of Lo in Mustang, are similar in number, language and faith, but their economy has traditionally been characterized also by long distance trade. In the mid-eastern regions of Khumbu and around Everest, the **Sherpas** (from *shar* –

Peoples of the Higher Himalaya

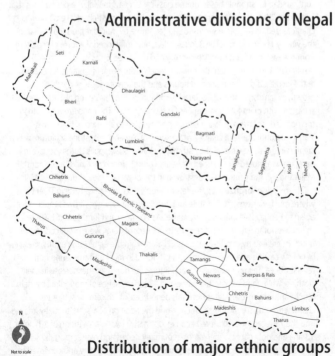

Administrative divisions of Nepal

Distribution of major ethnic groups

'east') are dominant, numbering around 110,000. Since the 1950s and 60s, they have built up a considerable reputation as mountaineering guides and porters and this has now become an important part of some communities' economy. Otherwise, they have followed a traditional agricultural lifestyle.

Art and architecture

As in many other Asian countries, there is a great deal of overlap between art and architecture in Nepal and both are, by tradition, characteristically religious. Early Nepali art and architecture is also that of northern India or southern Tibet; only with the establishment of the Licchavi dynasty in the Kathmandu Valley did it begin to demonstrate distinctive characteristics. From the 5th century AD, there emerged a tradition of **stone sculpture**, a much favoured form of artistic expression influenced by ideas and skills brought from India, notably those of the Gupta and the Pala schools. These were adopted by both Hindus and Buddhists, though differences between the two remained more iconographical than stylistic. The classic period of Licchavi sculpture lasted from the 5th to the 8th centuries and was largely dominated by Hindu representations of Vishnu in his various forms and of Umamaheshwar and by Buddhist sculptures of the Avalokiteshvaras, Vajrapani and Padmapani. The first known Vishnu sculpture from the Valley, that known as the Vishnu Vikranta Murti from the year 567, portrayed the god wearing tassles from his waist, a model which was subsequently widely reproduced both in Nepal and India. The sculpture of human and animal forms was notable for its sensitivity and naturalism and Licchavi sculpture was distinctive also for its use of a polished and lustred finish.

Its geographical separation from the heart of artistic activity to the south meant that Nepal was generally slow in adopting new techniques or forms. Sculpture continued to be strongly based on the classical Licchavi model. The period from the end of the 9th to the 14th centuries is regarded as the 'post-classical era' and was characterized, as the name seems to suggest, more by insipid reproduction than by the vitality of earlier work. The Bengali Pala school influenced the form of sculpture from the east in around the 11th century and is marked by its purity of style. This resulted in the development of some regional distinctiveness, notable, for example, in the increased ornamentation of figures and the use of a lotus pedestal. The growth of Tantrism and its associated pantheon during this period also provided sculptors with plentiful opportunities for diversification. The concurrent growth in the popularity of **bronze** as a medium, however, led to a period of innovative stagnation until the 17th century when some of Nepal's finest stone sculpture was created in the three cities of the Kathmandu Valley. Bhaktapur's Durbar Square in particular was noted for its superb statuary commissioned by King Bhupatindra Malla, though sadly much was destroyed in the devastating earthquake of 1934.

The origins of **bronze** art in Nepal are largely due to its popularity in Tibet to where much was exported. In style and development, however, it owes much once again to Bengali Pala influences from the 11th century and for the next 150 years or so images notable for their precision and fineness of detail were produced. Most is Buddhist created by Buddhist artisans in Patan. From the early 16th century, the art of hollow casting and *repoussé* (images produced in relief by hammering from the reverse), became more widespread and figures are noted for the increase in their clothing, while the 17th century witnessed a predominance of mongoloid models. Much Tantric bronze art dates from this period. Later 17th century sculpture is characterized by composite production and the addition of a 'scarf' to many images. Into the 18th century, sculpture becomes distinctive by the acquisition of a 'halo' or 'torana' and noticeably longer earlobes of many deities and higher mortals.

Nepali **painting** began in earnest from the early 11th century and consisted of

The Newari House

Many of the traditional influences that have shaped and determined the design of the Newari house, which you can see throughout the Kathmandu Valley, remain largely unchanged at the dawn of the 21st century. With trade and agriculture the predominant occupations of Newari communities in the Valley, houses were built both to complement this farming lifestyle and to accommodate the traditional extended family. Functionality is at the core of the design, with areas deliberately set aside for storage of hay and grain and for the shelter of livestock, the latter usually on the ground floor. Emphasis is also placed on security and on as economical a use of fertile land as possible. The latter resulted in vertical rather than horizontal growth. The wealthier the family, the more storeys would be added, though to a usual maximum of four. Typically, you will see three storeyed houses or, in poorer families, two storey. The kitchen and eating areas were almost always in the top storey, while the sleeping areas would be in a middle floor.

The structure would characteristically start with a rectangular edifice often with a uniform depth of around six metres. Extensions to provide further accommodation and storage space would be added at the perpendicular, with depths either similar or less than that of the original. This would eventually result in a highly symmetrical square or rectangular structure around a central courtyard, or chowk. A shrine to the family's deity was often placed at the courtyard's centre allowing this area to be used for washing, grinding or just sitting. Access to the premises was usually provided by a single doorway leading to the courtyard, with stairs typically placed at the corners. Construction was invariably of stone or sun-dried bricks and wood.

The absence of systematic water supply meant that the typical Newari house would not have a bathroom. Water would instead be collected from nearby springs or wells, while a river, or other commonly recognized area, served as the toilet.

miniature wooden-cased palm leaf illustrations of Mahayana Buddhist themes. These have been described as replicating the linear grace of the Buddhist wall paintings at Ajanta and Ellora, dating from the centuries either side of the birth of Christ. These usually accompanied Buddhist texts, though did not always correspond to the text they illustrated, fulfilling instead a 'magical, protective function'. Its development in Nepal is once again attributable to the influence of the Palas of eastern India thanks to whom the art was continued even after the destruction of most of the Indian paintings by the invading Muslim forces in the late 12th century. From the 14th century, the art of the *paubha* (or *pata* in Sanskrit; *thangka* in Tibetan), began to predominate in quality. Also representing religious (often highly metaphysical) themes, they were painted instead on cloth, either cotton or silk. Nepali *paubhas* were subject to the influences of both Tibetan and Mughal-Rajput art. There are two broad divisions of the *paubha*. The *mandala* may be thought of as painted diagrams representing the deity to whom it is dedicated, at the centre of the artist's conception of the cosmos. Often complex arrangements of circles and other geometric shapes are also typical and adhere to a prescribed rather than random formula. Rather less esoteric, meanwhile, the *pata* is usually symmetrical, with the deity at the centre of the picture surrounded by lesser divinities. Nepali painting of this and later periods was characterized by little use being made of colour and shade to produce form, with figures which were usually portrayed two dimensionally from the front and colour employed primarily to occupy otherwise empty spaces between the lines.

Background

Royal Architecture and Planning The finest examples of palace architecture are found in the three cities of the Kathmandu Valley. The peak of architectural activity here occured between the late 17th and 19th centuries, a time when Malla rule of the Valley was characterized by increasing rivalry among the family's various branches. The respective rulers of Kathmandu, Patan and Bhaktapur competed with one another for the grandest buildings as symbols of their importance. The royal **palace** was typically the city's focal point (or *layaku*) to which and from which all roads led. To reflect what was perceived as a divine legitimacy to rule, the Palace (*Durbar*) Square became a concentration of temples dedicated to numerous deities, often ornately decorated. The palace area would be surrounded by defensive walls with gateways providing access. Malla palaces characteristically comprised an original three-storeyed structure around a central **courtyard** (*chowk*) which was subsequently augmented by other buildings by later kings. The result was a complex of courtyards of varying sizes, usually containing a shrine or temple. The entrance and exterior often displayed the superb craftsmanship for which the Valley's architecture is renowned. The **Golden Gate** of Bhaktapur (1754) is one of Nepal's most astounding pieces of art, a product of the cultural blend of Newari and Tibetan styles.

For a time from the late 19th century, European styles were introduced by the aristocratic Ranas who had begun to travel overseas. The best known example is the new wing of the Hanuman Dhoka palace, at the heart of Kathmandu's Durbar Square.

Nepali pagoda

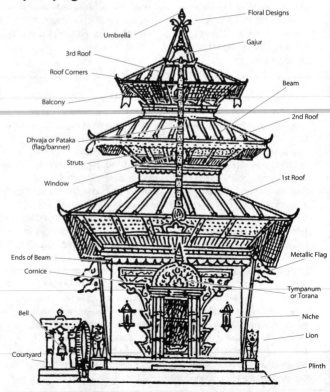

Floral Designs
Umbrella
Gajur
3rd Roof
Roof Corners
Beam
Balcony
2nd Roof
Dhvaja or Pataka (flag/banner)
Struts
Window
1st Roof
Ends of Beam
Metallic Flag
Cornice
Tympanum or Torana
Bell
Niche
Lion
Courtyard
Plinth

Principles The principles of religious building were laid down in the *Sastras*, sets of rules compiled by priests. Every aspect of Hindu and Buddhist religious building is identified with conceptions of the structure of the universe. This applies as much to the process of building – the timing of which must be undertaken at astrologically propitious times – as to the formal layout of the buildings. The cardinal directions of north, south, east and west are the basic fix on which buildings are planned. The east-west axis is nearly always a fundamental building axis. George Michell suggests that in addition to the cardinal directions, number is also critical to the design of the religious building. The key to the ultimate scale of the building is derived from the measurements of the sanctuary at its heart.

Indian-style temples were nearly always built to a clear and universal design, which had built into it philosophical understandings of the universe. This cosmology of an infinite number of universes isolated from each other in space, proceeds by imagining various possibilities as to its nature. Its centre is seen as dominated by Mount Meru, which keeps earth and Heaven apart. Continents, rivers and oceans occupy concentric rings around the mountain, while the stars encircle the mountain in another plane. By means of the **mandala** diagram, the Sastras show plans of **Jambudvipa**, the continent where humans live, organized in concentric rings and entered at the cardinal points. Such a geometric scheme could then be subdivided into almost limitless small compartments, each of which could be designated as having special properties or be devoted to a particular deity. The centre of the mandala would be the seat of the major god. The mandala thus provided the ground rules for the building of stupas and temples across the subcontinent and provided the key to the symbolic meaning attached to every aspect of religious buildings.

Nepali Architecture Nepali architects and artists travelled widely. They helped to build the great stupa at Borobodur in Java around 800 AD and went to China as court architects in the 11th century. The towering tiers of pagoda roofs, supported by elaborately carved beams and struts characteristic of the cities of the Valley, are a unique synthesis of exotic building styles. The five-storeyed **Nyatapola Mandir** in Bhaktapur is one of the country's most magnificent. In the late 13th century Kathmandu was a crossroads for Indian and Chinese architectural styles. **Arniko**, a Newar architect and craftsman after whom the highway from Kathmandu to Tibet is named, was invited to Tibet as an advisor. From here, he joined the court of the Ming Emperor of China before returning to the Valley where he introduced the multi-tiered **pagoda** style which, interestingly, had its origins in the Buddhist stupa. The word 'pagoda' actually developed from the Persian word *butkada* (*but* – 'idol'; and *kada* – 'temple' or 'dwelling'). Other Newari artists travelled abroad, many to Tibet where their skills were prized. While Bhaktapur artists tended to concentrate on wood as a building and decorative medium, Patan became the centre of metallurgy.

The other main form of Hindu temple architecture is the **Shikhara** (or *Nagara*) style which came from India. It is characterized by a tower or spire, either cone-shaped or rectangular. The idol is usually contained within the sanctum below, which may be surrounded by porticos. One of Nepal's finest examples is Patan's Krishna Mandir, built in 1636 by King Siddi Narasimha Malla. Shikhara temples are invariably built of brick or stone in contrast to the wood used mostly in the construction of pagodas. The focal point of the temple lies in the sanctuary, the home of the presiding deity known as the womb-chamber (*garbhagriha*). In large temples, a series of doorways leading through a succession of buildings allowed the worshipper to move towards the final encounter with the deity itself and to obtain *darshan* – a sight of the god. Both Buddhist and Hindu worship encourages the worshipper to walk **clockwise** around the shrine, performing *pradakshina*.

Buddhist architecture is largely characterized by its **stupas** and **viharas**. The earliest extant examples are found in and around **Lumbini** and were constructed by the Emperor and Buddhist convert Ashoka in the 3rd century BC. His supposed visit to the Kathmandu Valley and the stupas named after him in Patan are, in all probability, apocryphal. The great stupas of **Swayambhunath** and **Bodhnath** are Nepal's finest and most impressive. Swayambhunath probably formed the model for most subsequent stupa construction. In particular, the form of its finial (the ornate emblem at the top of the stupa), was widely copied and became standard from the medieval period onwards. The dome of the Bodhnath stupa is Nepal's largest. Viharas (or *baha*), Buddhist monasteries, have two distinct characteristics: a large open courtyard and an image placed opposite the main entrance.

Wood Carving   The unique **wood carvings** in the royal palaces of Kathmandu, Patan and Bhaktapur reveal a mixture of Buddhist, Hindu and early Animist influences. So profuse is the ornamentation of the temples and palaces in the Kathmandu Valley that it is said that a true Newari cannot let a piece of wood lie without first decorating it. They developed confidence in a variety of media. The magnificent wood carvings in Bhaktapur show an ability to use highly ornamented dark wood against a background of red brick.

This age of brilliance passed with the decline of the Mallas in the 18th century. The Rana regime appears to have been little interested in Newari art and even tried to suppress it. The Shah dynasty has encouraged an artistic revival since the 1950s and assistance to restore monuments has been received from Germany (especially in Bhaktapur), Japan and international agencies like UNESCO.

Music and dance

Music   Nepal has a long tradition of both classical and folk music which have been shaped by Indian as well as Tibetan influences. In common with much of that of India, Nepali classical music can trace its origins back to the metrical hymns and chants of the **Vedas**, in which the production of sound according to strict rules was understood to be vital to the continuing order of the universe. Over more than 3,000 years of development, through a range of regional schools, Nepal's musical tradition has been handed on almost entirely by ear. The chants of the Rig Veda developed into songs in the Sama Veda and music found expression in every sphere of life, closely reflecting the cycle of seasons and the rhythm of work.

Over the centuries, the original three notes, which were sung strictly in descending order, were extended to five then seven and developed to allow freedom to move up and down the scale. The scale increased to 12 with the addition of flats and sharps and finally to 22 with the further subdivision of semitones. Indian books of musical rules go back to the 3rd century AD. Most compositions have devotional texts, though they encompass a wide range of emotions and themes and many are designed to be sung for specific events or in certain seasons. Although the term *sangita* is now widely used to describe music, it originally referred to music intertwined with dance and drama.

Reflecting the close association of music and religion, many Shaivite Nepalis believe that the original five ragas were revealed by Shiva, with another added by Parvati. The development of Tantrism was also influential and helped give the otherwise very Indian tradition of classical music a distinct Nepali flavour. The essential structure of a melody is known as a **raga** which usually has five to seven notes and can have as many as nine or even 12 in mixed ragas. The music is improvised by the performer within certain governing rules and although theoretically thousands of ragas are possible, because of the need to be aesthetically pleasing only a few hundred exist of which only about 100 are commonly performed. Ragas have become associated with particular moods and specific times of the day or year. Another distinctive feature of Nepali classical music is the wider use of wind and percussion instruments, in contrast to the more commonly heard stringed instruments south of the border. These include various types of flute as well as the *madal* and *damphu*, both types of drum, although of course the saranghi and sitar are also popular.

While classical music is often localized, **folk music** exists and thrives throughout the country. It embraces a broad range of regional variations which reflect the country's enormous cultural, ethnic and environmental diversity. Many are specific to seasons, with planting or harvesting having a particularly wide stock of traditional songs and dances. Small groups of itinerant minstrels include the *Damais* and the *Gaines*.

Traditionally, music has been inseparable from dance and there is the same broad division between folk and classical forms. Classical dance is once again largely North Indian in character and the subject of much of it is based on religion and myth. Both the Mahabharata and Ramayana are widely interpreted in dance. There is an extensive grammar of movement and technique, especially in respect of hand gestures. The rules for classical Indian dance were laid down in the *Natya shastra* in the 2nd century BC and this still forms the basis for some modern dance forms. There are three essential aspects of the dance itself: *Nritta* (pure dance), *Nrittya* (emotional expression) and *Natya* (drama). The religious influence in dance was exemplified too by the tradition of temple dancers (*devadasis*), girls and women who were ostensibly dedicated to the deity of major temples to perform before them.

Dance

Literature

Although extensive, very little Nepali literature has been translated into English or any other Western language making it almost inaccessible to Western readers. With the exception of religious texts and sycophantic eulogies of royalty or aristocracy, a literary tradition does not truly begin until after the Gorkha conquest in the 18th century and the resultant unification of Nepal and spread of the Nepali language. Publication of printed books began in the early 20th century.

Probably the most important figure in Nepali literature is Bhanu Bhakta Acharya (1814-68). Often known affectionately as *Bhanu*, his statue stands in many a Nepali town. He is best known for his poetic rendering of the Ramayana. Other poets of the 19th century include Rajibalochan Joshi and Patanjali Gajured. The Rana regime did little to encourage the growth of Nepali literature. They established a system of censorship under the *Gorkha Bhasa Prakashini Samity*, which was strictly enforced. In 1918 one Krishna Lal, the author of a book enthrallingly titled *Makaiko Kheti* ('Cultivation of Maize'), was imprisoned for failing to have it approved by the censor before publication. Although several histories of Nepal were published, they invariably demonstrated both bias and inexhaustible sycophancy. Though less pronounced, this tradition has been successfully maintained by some writers into the post-Rana era.

The influence of Indian and Western literature began to assert itself in Nepal from the early 20th century. Forms of writing new to Nepal, such as modern dramas, short stories and novels, were introduced. Of the major 20th century writers, Professor T Riccardi considers Bal Krishna Sara and Lakshmi Prasad Devkota to be the most outstanding, saying of the latter that he has 'influenced the course of Nepali literature perhaps more than any other figure' since Bhanu Bhakta Acahrya.

Government and the modern country

Statistics

Official name Nepal Adhirajya
(Kingdom of Nepal).

Official Language Nepali.

Official Religion Hinduism.

National Flag Double pennant of
crimson with blue border on peaks; white
moon with rays of light in the centre of
the top peak; white quarter sun,
recumbent, in centre of bottom peak.

National Anthem *Shreeman gambhir Nepali, prachand pratapi bhupati, shree panch
sarkar Maharajadhirajako sada rahos unati, rakhun chirayu ishal, praja failiyos, pukaraun
jaya premale, hamee Nepali sarale* ('Honoured enlightened Nepali, illustrious King
glorified five times, your Majesty may you remain forever prosperous, may your
subjects increase extensively, let this be the heart-felt prayer of all Nepalis').

National Dress *Men* Labeda Suruwal; *Women* Sari.

Other National Emblems Knife (*khukuri*); Impeyan/Danfe Pheasant,
Rhododendron (*Rhododendron arboreum*).

Constitution Parliamentary monarchy.

Location Latitude, between 26°22'north and 30°north; Longitude between
80°4'east and 88°12'east.

Key Statistics *Area* 147,181 square kilometres; *Northwest to Southeast* 885
kilometres; *North to South* average 193 kilometres; *Population* 18,491,097 (1991);
Urban 7 percent; *Rural* 93 percent; *Infant mortality* 125 per 1,000; *Annual population
increase* 2.08 percent (1981-1991); *Gross Domestic Product* Rs249,896,000,000 (est
1995/96); *GDP per capita* Rs 13,514 (US$246); *Production* dominated by agriculture
(42 percent of GDP, 1995/96); *Economic Growth* 6.14 percent (1995/96); *Literacy* 32
percent (M 44 percent, F 20 percent).

Economy

The economy of Nepal is overwhelmingly **agricultural**. Around 80 percent of the population are **employed** in agriculture which accounts for about 50 percent of the country's **gross domestic product** (GDP). Since the 1970s, however, agricultural growth has been extremely poor, averaging below two percent a year. This growth, moreover, has been more attributable to expanding the area under cultivation than to an increase in production. The 1980s saw a good increase in **manufacturing**. Production, which is concentrated mainly in the Terai towns, accounts for almost 10 percent of GDP.

Trade The early 1990s have seen not only a continuation but also an increase in Nepal's trade deficit with other countries. External trade continues with India as the largest single trading partner with whom the deficit rose from Rs 9.8bn in 1991/92 to over Rs 17bn in 1994/95. An even sharper increase is noted, however, for trade with all other countries. It rose from Rs 8.4bn in 1991/92 to more than Rs 30bn in 1994/95. This is attributable more to the massive increase in imports which more than doubled over this period than to exports which have remained relatively stagnant. Exports to India are dominated by food and livestock, while those to other countries consist largely of manufactured goods.

Inflation The successive governments of the 1990s have succeeded in reducing inflation from over 20 percent to single figures.

Economic Policies In Nepal's eighth five-year Economic Plan published in 1992, economic growth was forecast at 5.1 percent per annum. With the establishment of a multi-party democracy, the government introduced new commercial and industrial policies in May 1992. These stressed the reduction of government involvement through privatization and by encouraging private domestic and foreign inward investment, while it abolished the system of government licensing of all industries but those affecting security, public health and the environment. Kathmandu now has a small stock exchange which is regulated by the separate Securities Exchange Board.

Government spending relies heavily on foreign aid. The budget of 1994/95 proposed expenditure of almost Rs 40bn (c US$360mn), of which around 40 percent came from foreign grants and concessional loans. A similar reliance on foreign assistance came in the 1995/96 budget, in which proposed spending increased by over 30 percent to Rs 51.6bn. This budget introduced value added tax. Despite the change in government, it also emphasized domestic private investment notably for public transport (air and bus), telecommunications and electronic media. Foreign investment was encouraged for the country's infrastructure, including banking, communications, water and electricity supply and transport. Longer term protection for foreign investors was proposed as was the promotion of Birgunj as an export processing centre.

At less than two percent of GDP, Nepal's defence expenditure is low.

Development Funding The World Bank has been especially active in funding hydro-electric projects, along with other international donors including the Asian Development Bank. The proposed Arun III 202 megawatt hydro-electric project has been controversial, with decisions regularly delayed because of political instability as well as problems directly related to the project. In August 1995 the World Bank decided not to continue with the project, though the Government of Nepal has since expressed its desire for the project to be re-instated. The governments of both

The South Asian Association for Regional Co-operation (SAARC)

SAARC is the first attempt made by the seven nations of South Asia (Bangladesh, Bhutan, India, the Maldives, Nepal, Pakistan and Sri Lanka), at creating a forum for regional co-operation. It is an organization whose stated objectives seek, inter alia, to 'accelerate economic growth, social progress and cultural development' through inter-governmental co-operation at various levels such as agriculture, meteorology, technology, tourism and transport. A number of features give SAARC its distinct character. The emphasis placed on 'respect for the principles of sovereign equality, territorial integrity, political independence and non-interference in the internal affairs of other states', in practice reduces political co-operation to a nominal level, but crucially also ensures that India, as the most powerful member, is able neither to dominate nor to be dominated by her six neighbours.

Origins The notion of SAARC was first mooted by the then president of Bangladesh, Zia-ur Rahman, in 1979. Preparatory ministerial meetings followed in 1981 in Colombo and again in Islamabad a year later. It was launched in 1983 at a meeting of the countries' foreign ministers and formally inaugurated with the adoption of its charter in Dhaka on 8 December 1985.

The establishment of SAARC is set in the global context both of the increasing importance of regional groupings such as the European Community and the Association of South East Asian Nations, and of the final intensification of the cold war, stimulated in part by the Soviet invasion of Afghanistan and by the hardline Reagan regime in Washington. This had implications for the countries of South Asia, both jointly and individually, for whom the raising of the global stakes for peace posed a threat. That no official mechanism for regional co-operation existed in South Asia at that time was due

India and China have made significant contributions to road construction and other infrastructure development in Nepal since the 1960s and 70s.

Resources The known deposits of coal, iron ore, pyrites, limestone and mica are too small to be mined commercially. The country's river systems offer tremendous potential for further hydro-electric development, but the Himalayan valleys present a costly and dangerous environment for large-scale development.

Education The importance attached to education in Nepal has traditionally been marginal. Occupation in rural communities is still overwhelmingly hereditary and agricultural, resulting in the widespread perception of formal education for children as luxurious and largely irrelevant. It is now recognized as a key factor in the country's development, however and increasing emphasis has been placed by successive governments on providing opportunities for education.

The majority of the population remains illiterate. While enrolment in primary education is fairly high, only one in 10 go on to higher secondary education and of that 10 percent there are twice as many boys as girls. Those figures are attributable to the early age at which children are expected to begin contributing to the family's income and to the traditional domestic role of women. In 1995 there were around 15,000 students enrolled for degree courses in the country's university and colleges.

Tourism Since the 1960s tourism has grown into one of Nepal's most important industries. It accounts for around 15 percent of the country's total foreign exchange earnings and about four percent of its gross domestic product. Official figures show that it contributed over US$88mn of foreign exchange to the exchequer in 1994 – up from around US$64mn in 1990. Curiously, there are around 50 percent more men visiting

largely to the climate of extreme mistrust between India and Pakistan and to a fear that India may have felt of being numerically outnumbered and hence outvoted by the peripheral states, all of which had India but not each other as a neighbour. The realities of the balance and structure of power in the region lay behind the caution that characterized SAARC's first years. Nevertheless, the very establishment of such a grouping was itself a considerable achievement given the existing geopolitical realities and 20th century history of the region. It was accompanied by optimism and also a sense of undefined hope which reflected the somewhat vague objectives and principles enshrined in its charter. Criticism of the organization's first decade has focussed on the failure to build substantially on positive beginnings. Probably SAARC's greatest achievement, the South Asian Preferential Trading Arrangement or SAPTA, came into effect
on 8 December 1995 and introduced a system of tariff concessions on intra-regional trade designed to promote and simplify trading within SAARC. Though still highly restricted, it represents a significant step forward and provides the springboard for its future enhancement.

SAARC Secretariat *Located on Tridevi Marg in Kathmandu, the SAARC Secretariat was established in January 1987 as the administrative heart of SAARC. It is from here that the Secretary-General together with one Director from each member state co-ordinate activities. Each Director serves a three-year tenure, renewable in exceptional circumstances for an additional three years. The Secretary-General is a rotating position, again with a three-year term. Mr Nihal Rodrigo from Sri Lanka assumed office on 1 January 1999.*

Nepal than women, while the largest proportion of visitors are in the 31-45 years old age group. About a quarter of all visitors go trekking and there is a small but consistent minority coming to Nepal specifically for pilgrimage. Approximately nine out of every 10 tourists enter the country through Kathmandu's Tribhuvan Airport. Indians form by far the largest number of visitors, while Germans lead the way of the other nationalities, followed by the British, Americans, Japanese and French. The most popular month to visit is October, while July is the least popular.

Although tourism in Nepal has come a very long way since the country first opened its doors to the outside world in 1952, there remains immense potential for it to grow still further. While there is significant government backing for the industry inside the country, little seems to have been done to promote it abroad with the government relying instead on individual and corporate entrepreneurship. The effects of tourism are widely discussed. While Nepal's economy has undoubtedly benefited, it is believed that a substantial proportion of earnings again leaves the country to pay for imports or for investment abroad. The impact of tourism is highly localized, both economically and culturally. The Kathmandu Valley is the focus for most visitors. The landscape of Kathmandu itself has changed dramatically over the last 30 years, with substantial sections now completely dominated by tourist hotels, restaurants and shops which contrast sharply with traditional architecture. Pokhara, too, is now largely geared towards tourism. Chitwan National Park has led the way in 'jungle tourism' and its consistently large numbers of visitors have probably contributed to its success in wildlife conservation. In the mountains, the Annapurna and Everest regions in particular now have many Western standard hotels and lodges.

While some people consider these places as examples of progress and development, others concentrate on the less positive impacts. They point

Background

particularly to increasing economic disparities and to the effects on the environment. Trekkers, for instance, are said to consume five times as much firewood per capita as local people, while the huge quantities of garbage they leave are devastating the natural beauty of the environment. Another major criticism is to do with the impact of increased exposure to Western culture on traditional local cultures. Although satellite TV represents a far greater challenge to traditional values than the sight of a few insensitive trekkers – even in some of the most remote areas large satellite dishes are becoming ever more conspicuous. But probably the greatest dilemma is that of Nepal's reliance on the income from tourism. It is a fragile dependence which is constantly subject to factors beyond the control of the industry. A trade dispute with a neighbouring country, for example, could again lead to closure of land border crossings. Or further adverse publicity about environmental conditions might discourage future visitors, as may have affected the drop in tourist numbers in 1993 following the serious flooding which occurred during the 1992 monsoon. Nepal has a great deal to offer the tourist, though and the development of its tourist industry since 1952 has been nothing short of spectacular.

Nepal in South Asia

Nepal has maintained a neutral position and generally friendly relations with its neighbours and other countries in the region. Relations with **India** deteriorated in 1989 when Nepal sought to replace the expiring bilateral treaties on trade and transit with a different system. India responded by asserting its regional dominance and closing 13 of the 15 border crossings, cutting off supplies to Nepal and suspending preferential trading agreements. An excellent harvest that year helped Nepal withstand the Indian pressure. The dispute was resolved first through the visit of Nepali Prime Minister Bhattarai to Delhi in 1990 and then through the reciprocal visit of his Indian counterpart Chandra Shekhar to Kathmandu early the following year during which a seven-year transit treaty and a five-year trade treaty were agreed upon. Relations between the two countries further improved with the visit of PV Narasimha Rao to Nepal in 1992 and a state visit by the King Birendra and Queen Aishwarya to India in 1993. Relations have not only survived political instability in both countries since the mid-1990s, but were again strengthened by the royal couple's third official state visit to India in January 1999.

It has become something of a tradition for all peripheral South Asian nations to engage in occasional 'India-bashing', an occupation in which some Pakistani and Bangladeshi politicians have become proficient especially in the run-up to an election. Ammunition was provided to Nepali proponents of the art when, in March 1994, a group of Delhi police arrived in Kathmandu without permission to carry out unauthorized house searches in pursuit of a suspected terrorist. Although India apologized, some left wing groups successfully arranged a general strike to protest against Indian intervention.

Relations with **Bhutan**, meanwhile, have been strained since the early 1980s. As a result of steady migration since the mid-19th century, around one-third of Bhutan's population – concentrated in the south of the country – was ethnically Nepali. Although they had integrated with the Bhutanese at all levels of society, there were persistent claims of official discrimination and maltreatment. Feeling a threat to their own ethnic identity, the Bhutanese government in 1985 passed legislation severely restricting land ownership and citizenship. In August 1990, further legislation was passed, formally prohibiting the teaching of the Nepali language in schools. Consequently, up to 100,000 ethnic Nepali Bhutanese have been pushed out of Bhutan and now live in refugee camps in Southeast Nepal (including one near Kakarbhitta). A slow process of high level diplomatic negotiations is seeking to resolve the issue.

Footnotes

11

Footnotes

549 Useful words & phrases

553 Glossary

560 Shorts

561 Index

565 Maps

566 Coloured maps

11

Useful words and phrases

There are more than 30 recognized mother tongues spoken throughout Nepal. Nepali is the offical national language and is spoken as a first language by over nine million people, with at least another five million speaking it as a second or third language, making it the most widely spoken of the country's languages. Although Nepali is widely understood in the mountainous regions of Nepal, it is quite distinct from those regions' principal languages which are of the **Tibeto-Burmese** linguistic family.

Learning Nepali

If you are staying in Nepal for any length of time, and especially if you are trekking along any of the less popular routes, some knowledge of Nepali can help you in both practical ways and in being welcomed by local people who will appreciate the effort you have made. Nepali is often considered to be one of the easier of South Asia's languages to learn. There are several short language courses on offer in Kathmandu and, to a lesser extent, in Pokhara. Keep an eye on the notice boards around Thamel; courses are also advertised by the numerous leafleteers in the city centre.

Pronunciation

The pronunciation of vowels alone is fairly straightforward, while aspirated, retroflex and dental consonants often require more practice. Remember that you don't have to have a perfect command of all of the nuances of the language to make yourself understood! All the vowel sounds also have nasal forms. (**Note** A *diphthong* is a combination of two sounds in a single syllable.)

Vowels

a　a short 'u' sound, as in *until*
aa　a long 'ar' sound, as in *cart*
ai　a diphthong, as in *bail*
au　a diphthong, as in *now*
e　a long 'eh' sound, like the first *e* in *premier*
i　a long or short 'ee' sound, as in *deem*
o　a long 'or' sound, as in *mould*
u　a long or short 'oo' sound, as in *hoot*

Consonants

Among the many different consonant sounds, there are three in particular to look out for. **Aspirated** consonants are articulated with an imaginary 'h', as if the sound is made while exhaling. In Romanized transliteration, the letter *h* after the consonant is usually used to indicate aspiration. It is most common in the following consonants: **b**; **chh** (in which the *ch* is aspirated, eg *Chhetrapati*); **d**; **g**; **k**; **p** (pronunciation varies from a very airy *p* to an *f* sound, eg *Phewa Tal*); **t** (aspiration results in a gentle dental sound between *t* and *d*, as in *Thamel*, but not as in the English word *the*).

Dental consonants are expressed with the tip of the tongue at the teeth. They comprise aspirated and non-aspirated **d** and **t**, and also **n**. These same letters are also subject to **retroflex** expression, the main difference being that the tongue is arched further back to the roof of the mouth while speaking.

Footnotes

550

Tips on speaking and grammar

Generally, the **verb** comes at the end of a phrase and sentences are usually constructed according to **subject-object verb**. Unlike most European languages, **prepositions** (eg by, for, with, from, etc) are placed *after* the noun (eg, *the preposition the noun after is placed*). The appropriate use of the familiar and honorific **forms of address** often causes difficulty. Put simply, the honorific form is used when addressing elders or superiors, whilst the familiar form is for children or friends. The **tone** in which you speak conveys far more of the meaning of what you are saying than in European languages.

Pronouns

I *Ma*
You (fam) *Timi*
You (hon) *Tapaai*
He (fam) *U*
He (hon) *Wahaa*
She (fam) *Tini*
She (hon) *Wahaa*
We *Haami*
They (fam) *Uniharu*
They (hon) *Wahaaharu*
Key: fam = familiar; hon = honorific

Verbs

A verb infinitive usually ends with the suffix *-nu*. As in any language, it gets a bit complicated when you start to conjugate verbs. Start by removing the suffix. Two of the first important verbs to learn (both meaning 'to be') are **Hunu** and **Chhanu**. The first is used to state condition, as in, '*I am* a tourist'.

Ma **hu**
Timi **hau**
Tapaai **hunuhunchha**
U/Tini **ho**
Haami **hau**
Uniharu **hun**

The other is used to state position, eg in response to 'where *are* you?'

Ma **chhu**
Timi **chhas**
Tapaai **hunuhunccha**
U/Tini **chha**

Haami **chhau**
Uniharu **chhan**

These same endings are used also for other verbs in the **simple present** tense. For example, the verb *jaanu* ('to go') is conjugated as follows: *jaanchhu, jaanchhas, jaanunchha, jaanchha, jaanchau, jaanchhan*. The **present progressive** tense is a little different and uses the stem *jaadai* to indicate process (*jaadai chhu*, 'I am going'): *jaadai chhu, jaadai chhas, jaadai hunuhuncha, jaadai chha, jaadai chhau, jaadai chhan*. The **negative** form is expressed by the additional suffix **na** (or a variation thereof) which usually also changes the verb ending. The negative form of the present progressive tense of *jaanu*, as above, is: *jaadai chaina, jaadai cchainas, jaadai hunuhuna, jaadai chhaina, jaadai chhainu, jaadai chhainan*. This, too, can get rather complicated, but if you remember to put *na* at the end of the verb, you can usually make yourself understood.

Useful phrases

Meeting and greeting

Excuse me *Hajur* (also used for 'Pardon me?', with appropriate intonation) The expressions *O, Daaju* ('O, Brother') or *O, Didi* ('O, Sister') are widely used as a less formal way of saying 'Excuse me' or for attracting someone's attention.)
Hello/Goodbye *Namaste* (said with hands together) *Namaskar* is used in very formal or respectful contexts.
How are you? *Sanchai chha?*; more familiarly *Kasto chha?*
Fine/I am well/It's going OK *Thik chha.* To follow this with an inquiry as to the questioner's health ('and you?'): *tapaailaai ni?.*
Thank you *Dhanyabad.* This is not said routinely and is usually implied and substituted by a slight sideways nod of the head. It is not considered rude not to say thank you.
I'm sorry *Maph garnus*
You're a good boy/girl *Timi raamro keta/keti ho*

What's your name? *Tapaaiko naam ke ho?*

My name is Sudeshna *Mero naam Sudeshna ho*

Speak more slowly (please) *Bistarai bolnus*

How old are you? *Tapaai kati barsha hunu bhayo?*

I'm ... years old *... barsha bhaye*

Are you married? *Tapaaiko biya bhayo?*

Yes, I'm married *Mero ta bhayo*

No, I'm not married *bhaiko chhaina*

How many sons do you have? *chhori kati chhan?*

And daughters? *chhora ni?*

See you again *Pheri betaunla*

Commands

In common with many of the languages of South Asia, the imperative is used in a quite different way than in most European languages. Once again, it is the tone of voice that is as important as the actual words and the word 'please' is implied though not spoken. In practice, this can seem somewhat abrupt at first, but it's not (necessarily), nor is it impolite.

Be quiet *chup laaga (fam); chup laagnus (hon)*

Come in *bhitra aau (fam); bhitra aaunus (hon)*

Come quickly *yahaa aau (fam); yahaa auunus (hon)*

Give (it to me) *malaai deu (fam); malaai dinus (hon)*

Go (away) *jau (fam); jaanus (hon)*

Hurry up *chhito*

Leave it *chhora (fam); chhodnus (hon)*

Put *raakha (fam); raakhnus (hon)*

Put it there *tyahaa lyau (fam); tyahaa lyaununus (hon)*

Sit down *basha (fam); bashnus (hon)*

Shopping

Bargaining is the norm when shopping. Using a few words of Nepali can increase your chances of a fair deal.

Do you have ...? *... paainchha?; ... chha?*

How much (is it)? *Kati rupiya?*

How many/much for ... rupees? *... rupiya kati?*

That's expensive (is it made of gold?) *Mahango bhayo (sonar chha?)*

Will you accept ... rupees? *... rupiya maa dine?*

No (I won't accept) *Na dine*

Then will you accept ... rupees? *... rupiya ni?*

Take it *linos*

How much in total? *jamaa kati bhayo?*

I have no change *Masanga khudra chhaina*

See you again *Ma aunechhu*

Food and lodging

Do you have a room available? *baas paainchha?*

How much is the room? *suteko kati linu hunchha?*

Do you have food? *khaana paainchha?*

Yes (there is food) *paainchha*

It will take time to prepare *samaya laagchha*

Mmm, delicious! *Mmm, mitho!*

I'm hungry *bhok laagyo*

I'm thirsty *tirkhaa laagyo*

How much is the food? *khaanako kati honi?*

When and where

what's the time? *kati bajyo?*

... o'clock *... bajyo*

quarter past one *sawaa ek bajyo*

half past one *saadhe ek bajyo*

quarter to one *paune ek baje*

about one o'clock *ek bajetira*

where are you going? *tapaai kahaa jaadai hunuhunchha?*

I'm going to ... *Ma ... jaadai chhu*

where is the ...? *... kahaa chha?*

where does this bus go to? *yo bus kahaa jaanchha?*

when does this bus leave? *yo bus kati baje jaanchha?*

how long does it take? *kati samaya laagchha?*

how far is ...? *... kati taadhaa chha?*

where is ...? *... kahaa chha?*

which direction is it ...?

to the right *daya tira*

to the left *baya tira*

straight ahead *sidaa tira*

Footnotes

Sickness

help! *guhaa!*

I have diarrhoea *Malaai dishaa paani laagyo*

I have a headache *Malaai taauko dukhchha*

I have a fever *Malaai jwaro aikochha*

what's wrong? *ke bhayo?*

where is a hospital? *haaspital kahaa chha?*

call a doctor (please) *daktar bolaidinus*

Food glossary

Snacks

aloo wo *potato fritters*

chop *fritters of spiced chopped meat or vegetables, may be covered with mashed potato and breadcrumbs*

kothe *as momo, but fried*

momo *spiced meat or vegetables covered in soft pasta and steamed*

pakora *deep fried meat or vegetables in soft batter, usually spherical or circular*

samosa *triangles of deep fried meat or vegetables in thin, crispy batter*

Meat

bangur komasu *pork*

gai komasu *beef*

hansa komasu *duck*

khasi komasu *the meat of a castrated male goat*

kukhura komasu *chicken*

machha *fish*

masu *meat*

puka masu *fried meat*

rango komasu *buffalo*

thupka *a Tibetan meat soup or stew*

tsampa *a variety of unleavened bread, popular with mountain communities*

Vegetables

aloo *potato*

bandarkobi *cabbage*

bhanta *aubergine*

chyaau *mushroom*

chukandar *beetroot*

gajar *carrot*

gholbeda *tomato*

kauli *cauliflower*

maatar *peas*

piaj *onion*

phul *egg*

saag *spinach orgreens*

simi *beans*

tarkaria *vegetable dish*

Fruits and nuts

aam *mango*

amba *guava*

angur *grape*

bhogate *grapefruit*

bhuin katahar *pineapple*

chaksi *sweet lime*

kera *banana*

kagati *lemon*

kaju *cashew nut*

mewa *papaya*

nariwal *coconut*

painyu *cherry*

rukha katahaa *jackfruit*

suntala *orange*

syau *apple*

tarbuj *water melon*

Oils, herbs and spices

aduwaa *ginger*

alaichi *black cardomom*

dalchini *cinnamon*

besar *turmeric*

garam masala *mixed spices*

jeera *cumin*

kesar *saffron*

lashun *garlic*

lwang *clove*

marich *black pepper*

noon *salt*

sukmel *green cardomom*

tejpat *bay leaf*

teel *sesame seed*

tori *mustard seed*

Flours and cereals

atta *whole wheat flour*

chamal *uncooked rice*

chamal kopitho *rice flour*

chana *gram (eg chick pea)*

chiura *beaten rice*

golphuki *puffed rice*

kodo *millet*

maida *fine wheat flour*

makai *corn*

makai kopitho *corn flour*

mas *black gram*

mung *green gram*

musur *uncooked lentils*

pitho *flour*

Glossary

(**NB** 'b' & 'v', *transliteration, spellings*)

A

acharya religious teacher

agarbathi incense

Agni Vedic fire divinity, intermediary between the gods and men

ahimsa non-harming, non-violence

ambulatory processional path

amrita ambrosia, drink of immortality

Ananda Buddha's chief disciple

Ananta huge snake on whose coil Vishnu rests

Andhaka demon killed by Shiva

Annapurna goddess of abundance; one aspect of Devi

apsara heavenly nymph figure

arak liquor fermented from potatoes, grain or fruit sap

arati Hindu worship with lamps

architrave horizontal beam across posts or gateways

Ardhanarisvara Shiva represented as half-male, half-female

Arjuna hero of the Mahabharata to whom Krishna delivered the Bhagavad Gita

Aruna charioteer of Surya

Aryans lit 'noble' (Sanskrit); prehistoric peoples who settled in Persia and N India

asana a seat or throne

ashram hermitage or retreat

Ashta Matrika the 8 mother-goddesses who attended Shiva or Skanda

astanah threshold

atman philosophical concept of universal soul or spirit

Avalokiteshwar Lord who looks down; Bodhisattva, the compassionate

avatara 'descent'; incarnation of divinity, usually Vishnu's

B

bada cubical portion of a temple up to the roof or spire

bagh garden

Bahadur title, meaning 'the brave'

baksheesh tip

bandh closed, strike

bas-relief carving of low projection

bhadra flat face of the shikhara (tower)

Bhadrakali Tantric goddess and consort of Bhairab

Bhagavad Gita 'song of the lord'; section of the Mahabharata in which Krishna preaches a sermon to Arjuna explaining the Hindu ways of knowledge, duty and devotion

Bhairab the fearful Tantric aspect of Shiva

bhang cannabis (bhang lassi)

bhatti tea house or inn, especially of the Thakalis

bhavan building or house

Bhima Pandava hero of the Mahabharata, famous for his strength

Bhimsen deity worshipped for his strength and courage

bidi tobacco leaf rolled into small cigarette

bodhisattva enlightened one; destined to become a buddha but remaining in the world to relieve suffering

Bon pre-Buddhist religion of the Tibetan Himalaya, incorporating animism and sorcery

bhumi 'earth'; refers to a horizontal moulding of a shikhara

bo-tree *Ficus religiosa*, a large spreading tree

Brahma universal self-existing power; Creator in the Hindu trinity

Brahmachari religious student, accepting rigorous discipline imposed for a short period, including absolute chastity

Brahman (Brahmin) highest Hindu caste of priests

Brahmanism ancient Indian religion, precursor of modern Hinduism and Buddhism

Buddha the enlightened

Footnotes

one; Gautama Siddhartha, the founder of Buddhism who is worshipped as a god by certain sects

C

capital upper part of a column or pilaster

caryatid sculptured human female figure used as a support for columns

cella small chamber, compartment for the image of a deity

chaam Himalayan Buddhist masked dance

chai tea (chiya)

chakra sacred Buddhist Wheel of Law; also Vishnu's discus

chamfer bevelled surface, obtained by cutting away a corner

Chamunda terrifying form of Durga

Chandra moon; a planetary deity

chatta ceremonial umbrella on stupa (Buddhist)

chauki recessed space between pillars; also entrance to a porch

chhatra honorific umbrella; a pavilion (Buddhist)

chhang strong mountain beer of fermented barley, maize, rye or millet

Chhetri Hindu warrior caste (Kshatriya), second in status to Brahmins

chiya Nepali tea, brewed together with milk, sugar and spices

chokhang Tibetan Buddhist prayer hall

chorten Himalayan Buddhist relic shrine or memorial stupa

chowk open space or courtyard

circumambulation clock wise movement around a stupa or shrine

cornice horizontal band at the top of a wall

crore 10 million

cupola small dome

curd yoghurt

curvilinear gently curving shape, generally of a tower

cusp projecting point between small sections of an arch

D

dacoit bandit

dais raised platform

dakini sorceress

darshan(a) sight of the deity

Dattatraya synchronistic deity; an incarnation of Vishnu, a teacher of Shiva, or a cousin of the Buddha

daulat khana treasury

deval memorial pavilion built to mark royal funeral pyre

devala temple or shrine (Buddhist or Hindu)

Devi goddess; later, the supreme goddess; Shiva's consort, Parvati

dharma moral and religious duty

dharmachakra wheel of 'moral' law (Buddhist)

dhobi washerman

dhyana meditation

dikpala guardian of one of the cardinal directions (N, S, E or W)

doon valley

drum circular wall on which the dome rests

durbar palace, a royal gathering

Durga principal goddess of the shakti cult; riding on a tiger and armed with the weapons of all the gods, she slays the demon Mahisha

dzong Tibetan lamasery or monastery

E

eave overhang that shelters a porch or verandah

ek the number 1, a symbol of unity

epigraph carved inscription

F

fenestration with windows or openings

filigree ornamental work or delicate tracery

finial emblem at the summit of a stupa, tower, dome or at the end of a parapet; generally in the form of a tier of umbrella-like motifs, or a pot

foliation ornamental design derived from foliage

frieze horizontal band of figures or decorative designs

G

gable end of an angled roof

gaddi throne

Ganesh popular elephant-headed son of Shiva and Parvati, the god of good fortune and remover of obstacles

gandharvas celestial musicians of Indra

ganja cannabis

gaon village

Garuda half-human, half-eagle mythical 'vehicle' of Vishnu

Gauri 'Fair One'; Parvati; Gaurishankar – Shiva with Parvati

ghat landing place; steps by a river (burning ghat, washing ghat)

ghazal Urdu lyric poetry, often sung

ghee clarified butter, used as a cooking medium

godown warehouse

gompa Tibetan Buddhist monastery

Gopala cowherd; a name of Krishna

Gopis cowherd girls, milkmaids who played with Krishna

Gorakhnath historically, an 11th century yogi who founded a Shaivite cult; an incarnation of Shiva

gram chick pea; pulse

gumpha monastery, cave temple

guru teacher or spiritual leader

H

haat market, usually weekly especially in eastern Nepal

Hanuman monkey hero of the Ramayana; devotee of Rama; bringer of success to armies

Hara (Hara Siddhi) Shiva

Hari Vishnu Harihara, Vishnu-Shiva as a single deity

harmika the finial of a stupa in the form of a pedestal where the shaft of the honorific umbrella was set

hippogryph fabulous griffin-like creature with body of a horse

hiti a water channel or spring; a bath or tank with water spouts

I

icon statue or image of worship in a temple

Impeyan a species of pheasant, Nepal's national bird

Indra king of the gods, god of rain; guardian of the East

Ishvara Lord, Shiva

J

Jagadambi lit 'mother of the world'; Parvati

Jagannath lit 'lord of the world'; Krishna

Jamuna goddess who rides a tortoise

Janaka father of Sita in the Ramayana; mythical founder of Janakpur

jangha broad band of sculpture on the outside of a temple wall

jarokha balcony

jawab 'answer'; a building which duplicates another to provide symmetry

jaya stambha victory tower

jhankri shaman, or sorcerer

-jee honorary suffix added to male names out of reverence and/or politeness

Jyotirlinga luminous energy of Shiva manifested at 12 holy places; miraculously formed lingams having special significance

K

Kailasa Shiva's heaven

kalasha pot-like finial of a tower

Kali lit 'black'; terrifying form of the goddess Durga, wearing a necklace of skulls/heads

kalyan mandapa hall with columns, used for the symbolic marriage ceremony of the temple deity

karma present consequences of past lives; impurity resulting from past misdeeds

kata ceremonial scarf presented to high Tibetan Buddhist figures

Kartik son of Shiva, god of war; also known as Skanda

khola river or stream

khukuri traditional curved knife, best known as the weapon of Gurkha soldiers

kirti-stambha 'pillar of flame'; free standing pillar in front of a temple

kot fort

kothi house

Krishna 8th incarnation of Vishnu; the mischievous child, the cowherd (Gopala) playing with the gopis; the charioteer of Arjuna in the Mahabharat epic

Kumari virgin; Durga; living goddess in the Kathmandu Valley

kumbha a vase-like motif

kumbhayog auspicious time for washing away sins

kund well, pool or small lake

kutcha raw; crude; unpaved

kwabgah bedroom; lit 'palace of dreams'

Footnotes

L

la mountain pass

lakh 100,000

Lakshmi goddess of wealth and good fortune; associated with the lotus; consort of Vishnu

lama spiritual mentor

lassi yoghurt drink

lathi bamboo stick with metal bindings, used by police

lattice screen of cross laths; perforated

linga(m) Shiva as the phallic emblem

Lokeshwar 'lord of the world'; Avalokiteshwar to Buddhists, and Shiva to Hindus

lungi wrapped-around loin cloth worn by men, often checked

M

Macchendra(nath) the guardian deity of the Kathmandu Valley, guarantor of rain and plenty; worshipped as the Rato (red) Macchendranath in Patan, and the Seto (white) Macchendranath in Bhaktapur

maha great

Mahabharata story of the great Bharatas; ancient Sanskrit epic about the battle between the Pandavas and the Kauravas

Mahabodhi great enlightenment of the Buddha

Mahadeva lit 'great lord'; Shiva

mahal palace, grand building

mahamandapam large enclosed hall in front of main shrine

maharaja 'great king'

maharani 'great queen'

Mahayana the 'greater vehicle' from Buddhism

mahseer large freshwater fish

Maitreya the future Buddha

makara crocodile-shaped mythical creature symbolizing the River Ganges

makhan butter

mandala geometric diagram symbolizing the structure of the universe, the basis of a temple plan; orders deities into pantheons

mandapa columned hall preceding the sanctuary of a temple

mandir temple

mani stones with sacred inscriptions at Buddhist sites (eg 'mani wall')

Manjushri legendary Buddhist patron of the Kathmandu Valley; god of learning; destroyer of falsehood and ignorance

mantra sacred chant for meditation by Hindus and Buddhists

Mara temptor who sent his daughters (and soldiers) to disturb the Buddha's meditation

marg wide roadway

masala spices

masjid mosque; lit 'palace of prostration'

math Hindu monastery

maya illusion

medallion circle or part-circle framing a figure or decorative motif

mela festival or fair

Meru axial mountain supporting the heavens

Mohammed 'the praised'; The Prophet, founder of Islam

moksha lit 'release'; salvation, enlightenment

momo Tibetan stuffed pasta, akin to ravioli

monolith single block of stone shaped into a pillar or monument

moonstone the semi-circular stone step before a shrine (also chandrasila)

mukha mandapa hall for shrine

N

Naga snake deity; associated with fertility and protection

nal staircase

nal mandapa porch over a staircase

Namaste traditional greeting said with joined palms

Nandi a bull, Shiva's vehicle and a symbol of fertility

nandi mandapa portico or pavilion erected over the sacred bull

Narayana Vishnu as the creator of life

nata mandapa (nat mandir; nritya sala) dancing hall in a temple

Nataraj Shiva, lord of the cosmic dance, often portrayed dancing in a circle of fire

nath suffix to indicate divinity, or place

natya the art of dance

navagraha nine planets; represented usually on the lintel or architrave of the front door of a temple

navaranga central hall of temple
nirvana enlightenment; lit 'extinguished'
niwas small palace
nritya pure dance

O

obelisk tapering and usually monolithic shaft of stone with pyramidal axis
oriel projecting window

P

pada foot or base
padam dance which tells a story
padma lotus, moulding having the curves of the lotus petal (padmasana – lotus throne)
pagoda tall structure in several stories
pahar hill
Pali ancient language derived from Sanskrit
panchayat 'council of five'; a government system of elected councils at local and regional levels; the system of national government introduced by King Mahendra in 1962
pandit teacher or wise man sometimes used as a title; a Sanskrit scholar
parapet wall extending above the roof
Parinirvana the Buddha's state prior to nirvana, shown usually as a reclining figure
Parvati daughter of the mountain; Shiva's consort, sometimes serene, sometimes fearful

pashmina a fine mountain goat's wool found mainly in NW India
Pashupati(nath) lit 'lord of the beasts'; Shiva; one of the principal deities of Nepal
paubha Newari word for thangka
pendant hanging, generally refers to a motif depicted upside down
peristyle range of columns surrounding a courtyard or temple
pilaster ornamental small column with capital and bracket
pinjra lattice work
pithasthana place of pilgrimage
pokhari pool, bathing tank
portico space enclosed between columns
pradakshina patha processional passage or ambulatory
pralaya the end of the world
prasad consecrated temple food offerings
puja ritual offerings to the gods; worship
punya merit earned through actions and religious devotion (Buddhist)
pukka solidly built, reliable; lit 'ripe' or 'finished'
Puranas Sanskrit sacred poems; lit 'the old'

R

Radha Krishna's favourite consort
raja ruler, king
rajbari palaces of a small kingdom

Rajput dynasties of W and central India
Rama 7th incarnation of Vishnu; hero of the Ramayana epic
rana warrior
ranga mandapa painted hall or theatre
rani queen
rath temple chariot; sometimes also refers to temple model
rekha curvilinear portion of a spire or shikhara
Rig Veda oldest and most sacred of the Vedas
Rimpoche blessed incarnation; abbot of a Tibetan Buddhist monastery
rishi 'seer'; inspired poet, philosopher or wise man

S

sabha columned hall (sabha madapa – assembly hall)
sadhu ascetic; religious mendicant, holy man
sal hardwood tree (*Shorea robusta*)
samadhi funerary memorial, like a temple but enshrining an image of the deceased
samsara eternal transmigration of souls
sangarama monastery
Sangha ascetic monastic order founded by the Buddha
sankha a shell, emblem of Vishnu
sanyasi wandering ascetic; final stage in the ideal life of a Hindu man
Saraswati wife of Brahma and goddess of knowledge; usually seated on a swan holding a veena
sarod Indian stringed musical instrument

Sati wife of Shiva who destroyed herself by fire; the act of self immolation on a husband's funeral pyre

satyagraha 'truth force'; passive resistance

serow a wild Himalayan antelope

Shaiva the cult of Shiva (Shaivite)

Shakti energy; female divinity often associated with Shiva; also a name of the cult

shaligram stone containing fossils worshipped as Vishnu

shaman animist priest, village doctor

Shankar Shiva

shastras ancient texts setting norms of conduct for temple architecture, use of images and worship

shikhara curved temple tower or spire

Shitala Mai a former ogress who became a protector of children; worshipped at Swayambhunath

Shiva the destroyer among Hindu gods; often worshipped as a lingam or phallic symbol

Shiva Ratri lit 'Shiva's night'; festival dedicated to Shiva

sindur vermillion powder often combined with mustard oil used in temple ritual; applied in the hair parting by some women to indicate married status

singh (sinha) lion; also Rajput caste name adopted by Sikhs

sirdar a guide, usually a Sherpa, who leads trekking groups

Sita Rama's wife, heroine of the Ramayana epic; worshipped by Hindus especially in Janakpur, her legendary birthplace

Skanda the Hindu god of war

soma sacred drink mentioned in the Vedas

soma sutra spout to carry away oblations in the shrine of a temple

sridhara pillar with an octagonal shaft and square base

stambha free-standing column or pillar, often with lamps or banners

stupa principal votive monument in a Buddhist religious complex; hemispherical funerary mound

stylobate base or sub-structure on which a colonnade is placed

Sudra the lowest of the Hindu castes

superstructure tower rising above sanctuary or gateway, roof above a hall

Surya the sun god

Swami Hindu holy man

swastika auspicious Hindu/Buddhist emblem

T

tahr wild mountain goat

tandava dance of Shiva

Tara historically the Nepali Princess Bhrikuti, now worshipped by Tantric Buddhists and Hindus in Nepal particularly

terracotta burnt clay used as a building material and for pottery

thana police jurisdiction; police station

thangka traditional Tibetan religious painting on cloth, often silk (Nep – paubha)

thukba thick Tibetan soup

tika (tilak) vermillion powder applied by Hindus to the forehead as a symbol of the divine; auspicious mark on the forehead

tole street

torana gateway with two posts linked by architraves

Trimurti the highest trinity of Hindu gods, Brahma, Vishnu and Shiva

trishul(a) trident, emblem of Shiva

tsampa Tibetan ground and roasted barley, sometimes eaten dry; often mixed with milk, tea or water

tympanum triangular space within the cornices of a pediment

U

Uma Shiva's consort in one of her many forms

Upanishads ancient Sanskrit philosophical texts

V

vahana mandapa hall in which the vahanas or temple vehicles are stored

Vaishya the 'middle class' caste of merchants and farmers

Valmiki sage, author of the Ramayana epic

Vamana dwarf incarnation of Vishnu

Varaha boar incarnation of Vishnu

varna 'colour'; possible basis for social division of Hindus by caste

Veda (Vedic) oldest
    known Hindu religious
    texts
vedi altar, also a wall or
    screen
vihara Buddhist
    monastery with cells
    opening off a central
    court
vilas house or pleasure
    palace
vimana towered
    sanctuary containing the
    cell in which the temple
    deity is enshrined
Vishnu a principal Hindu
    deity; creator and
    preserver of the universal
    order; appears in 10
    incarnations
    ('dashavatara')

wallah suffix often with
    an occupational name,
    eg rickshaw-wallah

yagasala hall where the
    sacred fire is maintained
    and worshipped; place of
    sacrifice
yajna major ceremonial
    sacrifice
Yaksha semi-divine
    being, associated with
    nature in folk religion
Yama god of death, judge
    of the living; guardian of
    the south
yantra magical diagram
    used in meditation
yashti stick, pole or shaft
    (Buddhist)
Yogini mystical goddess
yoni a hole in a stone,
    symbolizing the vagina
    or the female principle

Shorts

Short pieces on and about Nepal

426	An armchair experience?
25	Approximate Exchange Rates (November 1999)
275	Ashoka, beloved of the Gods
237	Ayurvedic medicine
209	Beggars
287	Bhaktapur Durbar Square entry fee
78	Bill Tilman: mountaineer, explorer and travelling sail's man
315	Buddha and the Hungry Tigress
526	Buddha's Four Noble Truths, the
243	Bus travel
509	Caste system, the
329	Caves of Nagarjuna Hill
422	Chitwan: life on the wildside
496	Concerning the uses and Western names of some Himalayan plants
420	Conserving a fragile ecology
119	Deforestation, degradation and conservation
265	Deities of Patan Durbar Square
318	Dust on the highway
517	Duty of tolerance, the
82	Eco-Treks
23	Embassies and consulates
107	First ascent of Annapurna, the
461	Folk dances of Western Nepal
515	Four stages of life, the
177	Goddess Kumari, the
339	Gurkhas, the
116	Gurungs, the
95	Himalayan Trust code of practice
131	Holy Waters of Gosainkund, the
227	Hot air ballooning
39	Hotel classifications
388	Jungle talk
325	Kali sacrifice
516	Karma - an eye to the future
245	Kathmandu: embassies & consulates
337	King Prithvi Narayan Shah
421	Leeches
425	Life of a Chitwan Elephant
185	Living Goddess, the
49	Missed Nomers
441	Mithila art
146	Mount Everest
126	Mustang's mountain monarch
529	Nagarjuna
537	Newari House, the
196	Parachutes and politicians
272	Patan's Sakhya Artisans: casting in

	God's image
350	Pokhara: from bazaar to bizarre
180	Pollution
345	Prayer flags
289	Quick nip to Taumadhi Square
51	Recipe: Dal-Bhad-Tarkari
528	Reverence for life
166	River Grades
492	Role of the monsoon, the
525	Sacred thread, the
512	Sexual imagery in Hinduism
266	Shakti
375	Share cropping
149	Sherpa Tenzing
190	Shiva the Destroyer
54	Shopping - Nepalese style
139	Some Park Regulations
544	South Asian Association for Regional Co-operation (SAARC)
518	Story of Linga worship, the
438	Story of Rama and Sita, the
451	Tea
111	Thakalis, the
84	The mountain people of Nepal
233	The Rug Trade
404	Through-ticketing: a traveller's woe
270	Tibetan Buddhist images in the Golden Temple of Patan
136	Tibetan Lama of Tarke Ghayang
34	Touching down
294	Tradition in clay, a
280	Traditional Tibetan carpet designs
81	Trekking agencies and services
79	Trekking for all?
521	Vishnu's ten incarnations
323	Walks around Chobhar
390	Watching out for the animals ... and also for trees
26	Wealth, charity and perceptions of tourists
194	Where the cockerel landed
142	The Yak...
143	... and the Yeti
240	Your airline ticket

Index

Note: grid references to the colour maps are shown in *italics* after place names. So 'Bhaktapur *M2B5*' can be found on Map 2, square B5.

A

acclimatization 63
accommodation 38
Ahimsa 515
AIDS 66
air 27, 41
airport tax 31
alcohol 52
alpine forest 497
altitude 63
altitude sickness 63
Anglo-Nepali War 483
Animism 533
Annapurna Base Camp Trek 5 114
Annapurna Circuit 103
Annapurna Conservation Area 502
anopheline 500
Antu Danda 451
Arniko Highway 43
art & architecture 536
Arun River 168
Ashok Vinayaka 183
Ashokan Stupas 274
Ashta Matrika 265
asiatic elephant 497
Asta Yogini Mandir 185
athlete's foot 65
auto-rickshaw 45
Avaloketeshwar 270
Ayurvedic medicine 237

B

Baghdwar 302
Baghmara Community Forest 424
Balaju Water Gardens 208
Bambasa 381
bamboo 497
banana plant 494
Banepa *M3B6* 311, 314
banyan tree 495
Baragaunle 84
bargaining 53
barking deer 498

Basantpur 449
BBC World Service 50
bee eaters 501
before you travel 21
begging 36
Begnas Tal 349
Bhai Dega Mandir 264
Bhairabnath Mandir 289
Bhairabsthan 414
Bhairahawa *M1B3* 401
Bhaktapur *M2B5* 282
Bhakti 513
Bhantabari 443
Bharatpur *M1B4* 414
Bheri River 168
Bhimsen Mandir 262
Bhimsen Tower 196
Bhote Kosi River 168
Bhotia 84
Bij Hazaar Lakes 424
bilharzia 68
Biratnagar *M1C6* 444
birds 500
birds of prey 500
Birendranagar
  See Surkhet
Birgunj *M2C5* 432
Birtamod *M1C6* 450
Bishanku Narayan *M3B3* 319
bites 67
black buck deer 499
black market 25
blue bull deer 499
Bodhnath Stupa 204
Bon 532
border crossings 29
  See also Crossing into India
bougainvillaea 496
Brahma 520
Brahmanas 508
brahminy kite 501
Buddha Shakyamuni 270
Buddha, The 525
Buddhism 524
  literature 531
  Tibetan 529
Budhanilikantha *M2B5* 302
buffalo 497
Bungamati *M3B2* 320
bus 42
buttercups 497

butterflies 500
Butwal *M1B3* 398

C

calendars 55
canines 499
car hire 45, 238
cardamom 496
cashew 495
cattle egret 502
Chabahil 204
Chandi Bhanjyang 413
Changu Narayan Mandir *M3A4* 305
Chapagaon *M3B2* 321
Charali 450
Charkosa Jhadi Forest 444
Chatradei 408
Chayasilin Mandapa 287
checklist, health 59
chestnut 496
Chisapani *M1B1* 386
chittal deer 498
Chitwan Elephant 425
Chobhar Gorge 322
Chobhar *M3A2* 322
Chorpani 462
Chowk 184
Christianity 533
cinemas 48
clay 294
climate 491
clothing 53
coconut palm 495
coconut water 52
cold 64
common langur 498
common mongoose 499
common mynah 501
common python 500
confidence tricksters 36
constipation 63
coral snakes 500
cost of living 24
credit cards 25
crime 94
Crossing into India
  Bhairahawa 403
  Birgunj 434

Kakarbhitta 455
Mahendranagar 381
Nepalgunj 396
cultivation 494
culture 534
currency 25
customs 22, 34
cycle-rickshaw 45
cycles 45
cypress 497

D

Dakshinkali Mandir *M3B1* 324
Dalai Lama 270
Dal-Bhad-Tarkari 51
Damak *M1C6* 450
Daman *M2B5* 431
Damauli *M2B2* 340
dance 541
dangerous animals 68
Danush Sagar 437
dark or black kite 501
Darshana 514
Dattaraya Square 290
Degutaleju Mandir 186
deities 265, 270, 520
  Brahma 520
  Ganesh 523
  Hanuman 522
  Rama and Krishna 522
  Sarasvati 520
  Shakti, the Mother Goddess 523
  Shiva 522
  Vishnu 521
dengue fever 68
Deoghat 414
development funding 543
Devghat 414
Devi Falls 346
Dhangadhi *M1B1* 384
Dhankuta *M1C6* 447, 449
Dhanukha 439
Dharan *M1C6* 447
Dharma 514
Dhorpatan Hunting Reserve 503
Dhulikhel *M3B6* 311

diarrhoea 62
Dipayal 462
disabled travellers 46
documentation 31
Dolpa 460
Dolpopas 84
Dram 318
drink 52
drongo 502
drugs 37
Dumre *M2B2* 339
Durga 523

E

economic policies 543
economy 543
education 544
egret 502
electricity 34
Elephant rides 423
Email 48
etiquette 34
eucalyptus 495
Everest Base Camp Trek 140
Everest, Mount 146
exchange 24
exchange rates 25

F

Fasidega Shiva Mandir 287
fax 48
festivals 56
Fikkal 451
firefly 500
flycatcher 501
food 50
food glossary 552
frog 500
fruit trees 494

G

Gaddi Baithak 184
Ganesh 265, 523
Ganga 265
Ganga Sagar 437
Garuda 265
gavial 500
Gelukpa 531
gentian 497
geography 173
geology & environment 488
getting around 40

getting in 21
getting there 27
gharial 500
Ghats 293
Ghorabanda-Khorbari 413
glow worm 500
Godavari *M3B3* 319
Goddess Kumari 177
Gokarna *M3A3* 302
Gokyo Lakes Trek 150
Golden Gate 186, 285
golden jackal 499
Golden Temple 269
Gondwanaland 490
Gorkha *M2B3* 336
Gotihawa 408
guava 495
Gurkhas 339
Gurungs 84
Gyantse 467

H

Hanuman 265, 522
Hanuman Dhoka 186
Hanuman Mandir 437
Hari Shankar Mandir 264
Harkadi 451
Health 58
heat 64
Helambu Trek 129
helicopters 42
Hepatitis 60,66
herbs 495
Hetauda *M2B5* 430
highways 43
Hile 449
Himalayan plants 496
Hinayana 528
Hindu epics 510
Hindu practice 514
Hindu worship 516
Hinduism 506
  deities 520
  festivals 518
  Four Human Goals 514
  images 518
  sects 519
history 479
holidays 55
hookworm 67
hornbill 501
hours of business 34
house crow 502
hyla frog 500

I

ice 53

Ichangu Narayan Mandir *M3A1* 328
Ilam *M1C6* 452
immunization 60
Indian cobra 500
Indian Rhinoceros 497
Indrapur Mandir 189
Indrawati River 312
inflation 543
insects 40, 64, 500
Invertebrates 500
Islam 532
Itahari 442
Itahari *M1C6* 444
Ivory Windows & Sweta Bhairava Mask 186

J

jackfruit 494
Jagannarayan Mandir 264
Jagannath Mandir 189, 263, 264
Jaleshwar 440
Jamunaha 396
Janaki Mandir 437
Janakpur *M1B5* 436
Jaundice 66
Jawalakhel 275
Jhigrana 462
Jhorpati 449
Jirels 84
Jokhang Temple 470
Jomsom to Lomanthang Trek 123
Jumla 98
Jumla *M1A2* 460
Jumla to Dunai Trek 99

K

Kabindrapur Mandir 183
Kadampa 530
Kagyupa 530
Kahnu Danda 348
Kailash Nagar 413
Kakani *M2B5* 329
Kakarbhitta *M1C6* 453
Kakarvitta
  See Kakarbhitta
Kakeshwara Mahadeva Mandir 189
Kala Bhairava 189
Kamaladi & Bagh Bazaar 192
Kanchenjunga Base Camp Trek 157
Kapilvastu 408
Karma 514
Karnali Bridge 385
Kasara 423

Kaski 348
Kasthamandap 181
Kathmandu *M2B5*
Keshar Library 209
Khaptad National Park 504
Khaptad National Park *M1A1* 460
Khokana *M3B2* 320
King Pratap Malla's Column 189
King Prithvi Narayan Shah 337
kingfisher 501
Kirantis 84
Kirtipur *M3A1* 326
Koshi Tappu Wildlife Reserve *M1C6* 442, 504
Kot massacre 484
Kot Square 190
Kotilingeshwar Mahadev Mandir 189
kraits 500
Krishna 265, 522
Krishna Mandir 188, 263, 264
Kudan 407
Kumari 185
Kumari Bahal 184
Kumha Twa (Potters' Square) 293
Kusaha 443
Kuti Hills 450
Kuwa 441

L

Lakshmi 265
Lakshmi Narayan Mandir 183
Lamaism 529
lammergeier 500
Langtang National Park 134, 504
Langtang Trek 134
language 47
larches 497
Lassi 52
leeches 77, 421, 500
leechi tree 494
Leishmaniasis 67
Lele 322
leopard 498
lesser panda 498
Lhasa 468
Licchavi Dynasty 480
Limipas 86
literature 541
little egret 502
little green bee eater 501
lizard 500
local customs 35
Lopas 86

Lukla escape Trek 152
Lumbini *M1B3* 404

M

Macchenranath 270
Madhubani 441
Magars 84
magazines 48
magpie robin 501
Mahabharata 510
Mahabuddha Stupa 207
Mahadeva Mandir 182
Mahakal Mandir 196
Mahavishnu Mandir 189
Mahayana 528
Mahendra cave 349
Mahendra Highway 44
Mahendranagar *M1B1* 378
Mahendreshwar Mandir 190
Mai Khola Valley 452
Makalu Barun National Park 504
Makalu Base Camp Trek 153
Makhan Tole 185
malaria 66
Malla era 481
mammals 497
Manakamana *M2B3* 336
Manangis 86
Manga Hiti 267
mango 494
mantis 500
marsh mugger 500
marten 499
MASTA 61
media 48
medical insurance 59
Medicines 59
meningitis 60
microlight flights 363
Mithila art 441
money 24
monkey 498
monsoon 493
mosquito 500
motorcycles 45
mountain biking 160
mountain sickness 63, 94
mountaineering 160
Mugling *M2B3* 335
Mul Chowk 188
muntjac deer 498
music 540
musk deer 499

N

Nag Pokhari 195
Nagarjun 328
Nagarjuna 529
Nagarjuna Hill 208
Nagarkot *M3A6* 307
Nagas 265
Nambai Bazaar *M1B2* 397
Namche Bazaar 145
Namobuddha 316
Nandi 265
Narasimha 187,265
Narayan Mandir 184
Narayanghat *M1B4* 414
Nasal Chowk 187
National Art Gallery 295
National Library 276
National Museum 210
National Parks and Wildlife Reserves 502
Natural History Museum 210
Naulakha 437
Nawakot 330
Nepalgunj *M1B2* 394
Nepali architecture 539
Newars 84
newspapers 48
Niglihawa 408
nilgai deer 499
Nuwakot Bhagavati Mandir 185
Nuwakot Hill 399
Nyalam 467
Nyatapola Mandir 288
Nyingmapa 530

O

oak 496
oedema, acute pulmonary 64
official time 34

P

painted stork 502
Palace of Fifty Five Windows 285
Palpa
    See Tansen
Panch Mukhi Hanuman 187
panther 498
papaya 494
paradise flycatcher 501
parakeet 501
pariah kite 501
parrots 501
Parsa Wildlife Reserve 424,503
Parvati 185
Pashupatinagar 452
Pashupatinath 197
Pashupatinath Mandir 287
Patan *M2B5* 260
Peacock Window 291
peepul tree 495
peoples 534
permit fees 81
phanta grassland 493
Pharping 323
Phewa Tal 344
Phidim 452
photography 36
Phulchowki *M3B3* 320
Pilgrimage 517
pine 496
pineapple 495
plate tectonics 490
Pokhara *M2B1* 341
police 37
Poliomyelitis 60
poplars 497
postal services 47
Potala Palace 469
prayer flags 345
prickly heat 65
primroses 497
Prithvi Highway *M2B1/5* 44, 334
private buses 42
prophylaxis 66
Puja 517
Puranas 512

R

rabies 65
racquet-tailed drongo 502
Radha 265
radio 49
rafting 161
    equipment 164
    Kali Gandaki River 166
    Karnali River 165
    Marshyangdi River 166
    safety 164
    Sun Kosi 167
    Trisuli 167
Ram Mandir 437
Rama 438, 522
Ramayana 511
Ramoche Temple 471
Rana Raj 484
Rani Bans 328
Rani Ghat 412
Rani Pokhari 195
Rani Sikiyahi 446
Rani Tal 384
Rara Lake Trek 96
Rara National Park 98,504
Ratna Park 208
Rato Macchenranath 269
reading list 69
Rebirth 515
red vented bulbul 501
religion 506
reptiles & amphibians 499
resources 544
rhesus monkey 498
rhododendrons 496
rice 494
rice paper prints 53
rickshaws 45
Ridi Bazaar 413
Riverine forest 493
rivers 491
road 42
rose ringed parakeet 501
roses 497
Royal Bardia National Park *M1B2* 386, 503
Royal Chitwan National Park *M1B4* 417, 503
Royal Palace 194, 264
Royal Sukla Phanta Wildlife Reserve *M1B1* 381
Royal Trek 118
Rudravarna Mahavihara 273
Rupa Tal 349

S

Sacred Garden, Lumbini 405
safety 36
Sagarhawa 408
Sagarmatha National Park 138,504
Sakyapa 530
sal 493
saligrams 413
sambar deer 498
Sandakpur 453
Sankhu *M3A4* 304
Sapt Kosi 442
Sarangkot 347
Sarasvati 520
Saraswati 379
Saraswati Mandir 188
Sauraha *M1B4* 426
Seti Gandaki River 168
Shah Dynasty 482
Shahid Smarak 196
Shakti 266,523

Shamanism 533
shellfish 61
Sherpa Tenzing 149
Sherpas 86
Shey Phoksumdo
   National Park 101, 505
Shiva 190, 522
shopping 53
short wave radio 50
Siddhartha Highway 44
Siddhi Lakshmi Mandir
   287
Silgari 462
Singha Durbar 193, 196
Singha Satal 183
Sipadol 294
Sita 438
skinks 500
sloth bear 498
snakes 67, 499
snow leopard 498
social behaviour 35
Special interest travel 20
special needs 46
specialist tour operators
   32
spotted deer 498
spotted dove 502
squirrel 499
Srinagar Hill 412
stomach bugs 62
Stone Vishnu Mandir
   188
striped hyena 499
student cards 33
Sukla Phanta Wildlife
   Reserve 505
Sunauli (Belahiya) M1B3
   402
sunburn 63, 65
Sundari Chowk 187,
   266, 286
Sundarijal 303
Sunwars 84
Surkhet M1B2 386
Surya Binayak Mandir
   M3B4 311
swamp deer 499
Swayambhunath 201

Tadhunchen Bahal 288
Taleju Bell 264
Taleju Mandir 190, 285
Taleju Temple 185
Tamang 84
tamarind 495
Tamur River 168
Tansen (Palpa) M2C1
   409
Tantras 513
tap water 62
Tara 185, 270

Tashi Palkhel 346
Tashiling 346
Tatopani & Baglung Trek
   120
Taulihawa 407
Taumadhi Square 288
taxis 45
tea 451, 496
teak 493
telephone 48
television 50
Temple architecture 539
Tetanus 60
Tethys Sea 490
Thakalis 84
Thakurdwara 391
thangka 53
Thankot 328
Tharu Village 424
theft 37
Thimi M3A3 310
Tibetan border 318
Tibetan carpets 54
ticks 65
tiger 497
Tilaurakot 408
tipping 36
tongas 46
tour operators 72
tourism 544
tourist buses 42
tourist offices 31
trade 543
Trailokya Mohan
   Narayan Mandir 184
travellers' cheques (TCs)
   25
travelling to Tibet 30
treeline 497
trekking
   backpacks 82
   books 87
   clothing & footwear 83
   emergencies 95
   equipment & clothing
      82
   fauna 91
   firewood 93
   flora 91
   food & cooking
      equipment 83
   health 94
   immigration office 80
   insurance 80
   maps 88
   medical kit 86
   money 87
   Mustang 123
   origins of 76
   permits 32, 80
   preparations 78
   restricted areas 82
   seasons 77
   sherpas 90
   tents & sleeping bags
      86
   wages 90

wildlife 90
women's wear 83
Tribhuvan Highway 44
Tribhuvan Museum 210
Tribhuvan University
   327
Tridevi Mandir 194
Trisuli Bazaar 330
tummy bugs 62
Tundikhel 195
turtles 500
Typhoid 60
Typhus 67

U

Upallakot 338
Upanishads 508
Upper Sun Kosi River
   168

V

vaccination 60
Vajra Jogini Mandir
   M3A4 304
Vajradhara 270
Vajrayana 529
Vatsala Durga Mandir
   287
Vatsala Mandir 287
Vedanta 516
Vedas 507
Vedic period 479
vegetation 493
vehicle hire 45
vipers 500
visas 21
Vishnu 521
Vishnu Mandir 189
Vishvanath Shiva Mandir
   262
visiting religious sites 35
Vivaha Mandap 437

W

water 53, 62
water buffalo 497
water snakes 500
what to take 22
when to go 20
where to go 19
white-breasted
   kingfisher 501
wild boar 499
wild dog 499
wildlife 497

women travellers 37
wood carving 540
working in Nepal 33
worms 67

X

Xedar 467
Xegar 467

Y

yak attacks 137
Yana 527
Yoga 515

Z

Zhigatse 467

Maps

317	Arniko Highway: the road to Tibet
401	Bhairahawa
284	Bhaktapur
291	Bhaktapur, Dattatraya Square
286	Bhaktapur, Durbar Square
288	Bhaktapur, Taumadhi Square
445	Biratnagar
433	Birgunj
205	Bodhnath
399	Butwal
305	Changu Narayan Mandir
448	Dharan
312	Dhulikhel
314	Dhulikhel, around
318	Dram
319	Godavari surroundings
303	Gokarna Mahadev Mandir
338	Gorkha
77	Himalayan Trekkng Regions
452	Ilam
439	Janakpur
454	Kakarbhitta
179	Kathmandu
212	Kathmandu, Central Thamel
215	Kathmandu, Chhetrapati
223	Kathmandu, Durbar Marg area
182	Kathmandu, Durbar Square
222	Kathmandu, Jhocchen (Freak Street)
217	Kathmandu, Jyatha & Kantipath
225	Kathmandu, Lazimpath
220	Kathmandu, Paknajol
250	Kathmandu, walks
466	Kathmandu to Lhasa
334	Kathmandu to Pokhara
174	Kathmandu Valley
327	Kirtipur
468	Lhasa
472	Lhasa Barkhor Square area
405	Lumbini master plan
408	Lumbini, around
406	Lumbini, Sacred Garden
379	Mahendranagar
308	Nagarkot
415	Narayanghat & Bharatpur
	Nepal
535	Nepal, administrative divisions
493	Nepal, climate
494	Nepal, environmental zones
489	Nepal, geological regions
490	Nepal, Himalayan profile
492	Nepal, monsoon
503	Nepal, national parks & wildlife reserves
394	Nepalgunj
43	Nepal's highways
163	Nepal's Major Rivers
199	Pashupatinath
261	Patan
263	Patan, Durbar Square
342	Pokhara
361	Pokhara, Damside
353	Pokhara, Lakeside north & west
354	Pokhara, Lakeside south & east
346	Pokhara, surrounding areas
41	Principal domestic air routes
387	Royal Bardia National Park
418	Royal Chitwan National Park
382	Royal Sukla Phanta Wildlife Reserve
348	Sarangkot
428	Sauraha
323	Southwest from Kathmandu
402	Sunauli (Belahiya)
202	Swayambhunath
410	Tansen (Palpa)
412	Tansen, around
252	Teku to Tripureshwar
372	Terai
398	Terai, Central
436	Terai, Eastern
378	Terai, Western
392	Thakurdwara
97	Trek 1: Jumla to Rara Lake
101	Trek 2: Jumla to Dunai
105	Trek 3: Annapurna Circuit North
109	Trek 4: Annapurna Circuit South
115	Trek 5: Annapurna Base Camp
121	Trek 7: Tatopani and Baglung
125	Trek 8: Jomsom to Lomanthang
130	Trek 9: Langtang-Helambu Circuit
141	Trek 11: Jiri to Namche Bazaar
145	Trek 11: Namche Bazaar to Everest Base Camp
151	Trek 12: Gokyo Lakes
155	Trek 14: Makulu Base Camp
158	Trek 15: Kachenjunga Base Camp
	Walks
259	Budhanilikanth Bodnath
251	Royal Kathmandu
257	Swayambhunath & National Museum
252	Teku to Tripureshwar
258	Thankot to Kirtipur

Nepal

Main roads

Other roads

Tracks

Hiking trail

Railway

◆ National park

International border

Altitude in metres

5000

2000

500

0

Neighbouring
Country

Map 1

A

Byasrikh Himal

Simikot

Changla Himal

Saipal
(7,031m)

Mugu Karnali River

Suadi

Baitadi

Rara
National
Park

Lake Rara

Gumgarhi

Shey Phoksundo
National Park

Mustang
Himal

Khaptad
National Park

Botan

Punga Himal

Siswe Himal

Lake
Phoksundo

Mustang
(Lomanthang)

Dhandeldhura

Seti River

Karnali River

Gopung Thela

Tangu River

Jumla

Gorthigaon

Hurikot

Chaurikot

Bheri River

Hanke

Damodar

Chulu I.
(6,419

Dillikot

Dunai

Tarakot

Jomsom

Annapurna
Conservation
Area

Manar

Mahendranagar

Ataria

Royal Sukla
Phanta Wildlife
Reserve

Dhangadhi

Chisapani

Gola

Surkhet

Musikot

Dhaulagiri Himal

Royal
Dhorpatan
Hunting
Reserve

Annapurna I
(8,091m)

Annapurna Himal

Anna
(7,9

Mahabharat Range

Royal Bardia
National
Park

Bheri River

Jelbang

Tatopani

Ghandrung

Beni

Chandrakot

Po

Baglung

Lumle

Kushma

Ru

B

Chepang

Ghorahi

Thapagaon

Thamghas

Tanse

Mahendra Highway

Pyuthan

Nepalgunj

Churia Range

Nambai
Bazaar

Koilabas

Bhagwanpur

Sagarhawa

Taulihawa

Butwal

Lumbini

Bhairahawa

Sunauli
(Belahiya)

UTTAR PRADESH

C

N

INDIA

0 km   60
0 miles   37

1   2   3

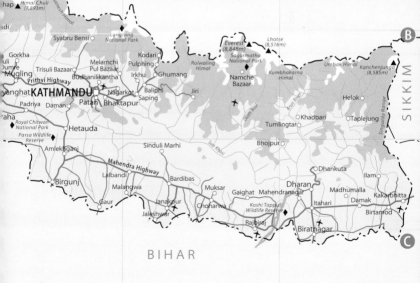

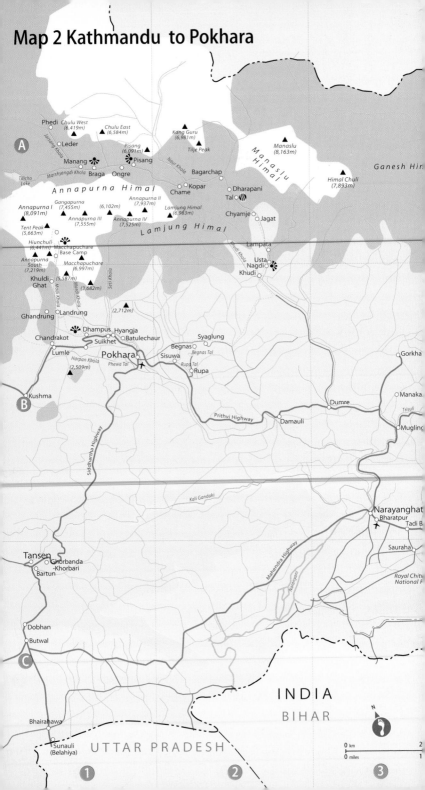

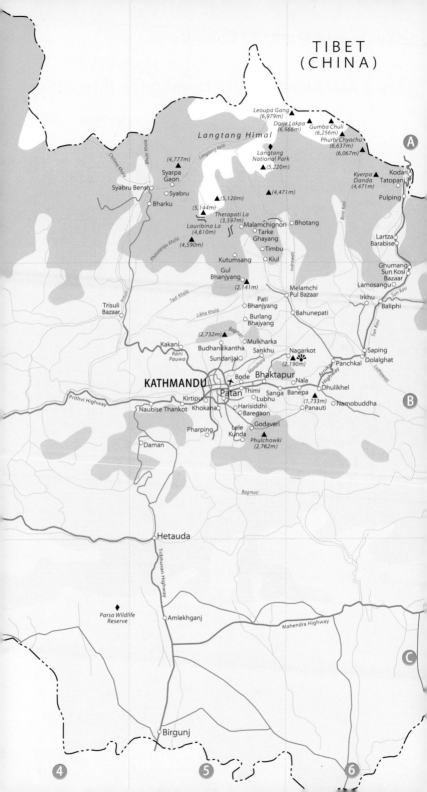

Map 3 Kathmandu Valley beyond the three cities

Ichangu
Narayan
Mandir

Nagarjun
Ban (forest)

Nagarjuna Hill
(2,096m)

To Kakani (23 km) & Trisuli

Trisuli Road

Ring Road

Lazimpath

*To Budhanilikantha (6 km
from Ring Road) & Shivapuri*

Sundarijal Road

Gokarn
Mahadeo
Mandir

Kopan

Go

Balaju

Bodhnath
Stupa

Bagmati River

Swayambhunath
Stupa

Chabahil
Stupa

A

Royal
Palace

KATHMANDU

Pashupatinath

Vishnumati River

Durbar
Square

To Pokhara (200 km)

Ring Road

Prithwi Highway

Tripureshwar

Baneshwar

Bagmati River

Manohara River

Mahalakshmi
Mandir

Bode

University

Durbar
Square

To Thankot (3 km)

Kirtipur

Patan

Ganesh
Mandir

Thimi

Balkumari
Mandir

Macchegaon

Ring Road

Adinath
Lokeshwa
Mandir

Chobhar

Jawalakhel

Jal Binayak
Mandir

Chobhar
Gorge

Path to Champa Devi (2,278m)

Dakshinkali Rd

Taudaha
Lake

Khokana

Shekali Mai
Mandir

Sunakothi

Lubhu

Godavari Road

Harisiddhi

Karya Binayak
Mandir

Bungamati

Brahmayani
Mandir

Balkumari
Mandir

Sheka
Narayan
Mandir

Rato
Macchendranath

Tibetan
Carpet Factory

Baregaon

Bishankhu
Narayan
Mandir

Vajra
Jogini
Mandir

Puikel

Theco

Vajra Varahi
Mandir

Pharping

Gorakhnath
Cave

Fishi

Bo
Ga

Dakshinkali
Mandir

Bagmati River

Chapagaon

Godavari

St Xavi
Colle

Pink Marble
Quarry

Phulchowki Mai
Mandir

Bhaga Ban
(1,774m)

Tika Bhairab
Mandir

To Lele Kunda

B

1
2
3

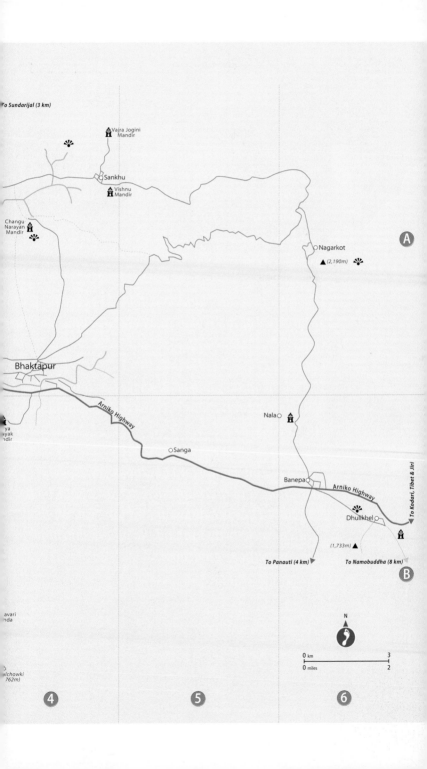

To Sundarijal (3 km)

Vajra Jogini
Mandir

Sankhu

Vishnu
Mandir

Changu
Narayan
Mandir

Nagarkot

▲ (2,190m)

A

Bhaktapur

ya
ayak
dir

Arniko Highway

Nala

Sanga

Banepa

Arniko Highway

To Kodari, Tibet & Jiri

Dhulikhel

To Panauti (4 km)

(1,733m) ▲

To Namobuddha (8 km)

B

avari
nda

lchowki
762m)

N

0 km   3
0 miles   2

4   **5**   **6**

What the papers say

"I carried the South American Handbook in my bag from Cape Horn to Cartagena and consulted it every night for two and a half months. And I wouldn't do that for anything else except my hip flask."

Michael Palin

"Footprint's India Handbook told me everything from the history of the region to where to get the best curr

Jennie Bond, BBC correspondent

"Of all the main guidebook series this is genuinely th only one we have never received a complaint about."

The Bookseller

"All in all, the Footprint Handbook series is the best thing that has happened to travel guidebooks in years. They are different and take you off the beaten track away from all the others clutching the competitors' guidebooks."

The Business Times, Singapore

Mail order
Available worldwide in good bookstores, Footprint Handbooks can also be ordered directly from us in Bath, via our website or from the address on the back cover.

Website
www.footprintbooks.com
Take a look for the latest news, to order
a book or to join our mailing list